CREATING SQL SERVER 2005 APPLICATIONS WITH *VISUAL STUDIO*®

Charles M. Morrison

University of Wisconsin—Eau Claire

Joline Morrison

University of Wisconsin—Eau Claire

PEARSON

Prentice Hall

Upper Saddle River, New Jersey 07458

Library of Congress Cataloging-in-Publication Data

Morrison, Mike
   Creating SQL Server 2005 applications with Visual Studio 2005 / Charles M. Morrison,
Joline Morrison. — 1st ed.
     p. cm.
   1. SQL server. 2. Database management. 3. Client/server computing.
I. Morrison, Joline. II. Title.
   QA76.9.D3M6585 2006
   005.75'85 — dc22   2006021771

AVP/Executive Editor: Bob Horan
VP/Editorial Director: Jeff Shelstad
Manager, Product Development:
   Pamela Hersperger
Assistant Editor: Ana Jankowski
Senior Media Project Manager: Peter Snell
AVP/Executive Marketing Manager: Debbie Clare
Marketing Assistant: Laura Cirigliano
Associate Director, Production Editorial:
   Judy Leale
Senior Managing Editor: Cynthia Zonneveld
Senior Production Editor: Anne Graydon
Permissions Coordinator: Charles Morris
Associate Director, Manufacturing: Vinnie Scelta

Manufacturing Buyer: Michelle Klein
Design/Composition Manager: Christy Mahon
Cover Design: Studio Indigo
Cover Illustration: Getty Images
Illustration (Interior): Interactive Composition
   Corporation, India
Manager, Multimedia Production:
   Richard Bretan
Composition: Interactive Composition
   Corporation, India
Full-Service Project Management:
   Interactive Composition Corporation, India
Printer/Binder: Bindright
Typface: 10/12 Times Ten Roman

Credits and acknowledgments borrowed from other sources and reproduced, with permission, in this
textbook appear on appropriate page within text.

Microsoft® and Windows® are registered trademarks of the Microsoft Corporation in the U.S.A. and other
countries. Screen shots and icons reprinted with permission from the Microsoft Corporation. This book is
not sponsored or endorsed by or affiliated with the Microsoft Corporation.

Pearson Education LTD.
Pearson Education Singapore, Pte. Ltd
Pearson Education, Canada, Ltd
Pearson Education–Japan

Pearson Education Australia PTY, Limited
Pearson Education North Asia Ltd
Pearson Educación de Mexico, S.A. de C.V.
Pearson Education Malaysia, Pte. Ltd.

10 9 8 7 6 5 4 3 2 1
ISBN: 0-13-146355-1

Dedication

This book is dedicated to the memory of our son
Kyle
who is always in our hearts (Semper Fi, Kyle)
and to our daughter
Lauren
who can do it all

Brief Contents

Contents

About the Authors

Charles M. (Mike) Morrison is an associate professor in the Computer Science Department at the University of Wisconsin-Eau Claire. He has an undergraduate degree in Geological Engineering from Colorado School of Mines, an M.S. in Geology from Oklahoma State University, an M.B.A. from Oklahoma University, and a Ph.D. in Management Information Systems from the University of Arizona. He has coauthored four textbooks on Oracle database development and two textbooks on Web/database application development. When he is not writing or teaching, you can find him riding his mountain bike or off-road motorcycles on Wisconsin trails.

Joline Morrison is an associate professor in the Computer Science Department at the University of Wisconsin-Eau Claire, where she teaches a variety of database and Web development topics. Along with her husband, she has authored books on database development and Web/database development. She has an undergraduate degree in engineering from the University of Wyoming and a Ph.D. in Management Information Systems from the University of Arizona. Her winter hobby is alpine skiing, her summertime hobby is gardening, and her year-round hobbies are quilting and walking with her dog in the woods.

Preface

TO THE STUDENT

This book describes how to use the SQL Server 2005 database management system. Aimed toward individuals interested in developing Windows- and Web-based database applications, it also provides background knowledge for students interested in pursuing careers involving database design, database application support, and database administration. It provides a foundation in database development that emphasizes practical knowledge and marketable skills.

The book is structured to support different learning styles. Each chapter presents new concepts and strives to motivate you by explaining why the information is important and how it connects with knowledge from previous chapters. Sections that address specific tasks provide step-by-step instructions on how to perform the task. Sections that describe specific programming code first provide a general syntax example, then illustrate the general syntax using a specific example. Each chapter ends with a glossary of key terms and an extensive set of review materials that include multiple choice, true/false, and short-answer questions. The end-of-chapter guided exercises allow you to apply the chapter material to different problems. Some of these exercises provide explicit instructions, while others are more free form and contain occasional hints to provide guidance in areas that the chapters do not explicitly address.

We have structured the book so that you can use different database management and application development software depending on what is available to you and/or your institution. For the database server, you can use either an enterprise-level SQL Server 2005 database, or SQL Server Express, which is a version that does not provide all of the enterprise-level management tools but still provides most of the features needed to create full-featured database applications. To complete the book exercises on Windows and Web application development, you can use the complete Visual Studio 2005 integrated development environment; alternatively, you can use VB Express to create Windows-database applications and Visual Web Developer to create Web-based applications. To complete Chapter 7, which describes how to create database reports, you must use the complete Visual Studio 2005 IDE, and it must be configured to include Crystal Reports.

At this time, VB Express and Visual Web Developer are available as free downloads from Microsoft's MSDN Web site, and they include the SQL Server Express database. Appendix A provides complete instructions for downloading and installing the SQL Server or SQL Server Express database, and Appendix B provides instructions for installing Visual Studio 2005, VB Express, and Visual Web Developer.

Chapter 1 opens by defining databases and describing the different database structures: hierarchical, relational, and object-oriented. Next it explains the steps that developers use to create database applications. Finally, it shows how to design databases using entity-relationship models and how to derive the associated database tables. The chapter approaches database design from a practical viewpoint, including tips for naming tables and fields and for structuring database tables to support applications.

Chapter 2 introduces database architectures in use today: single-tier, client/server, and N-tier. It relates these architectures to SQL Server 2005 and introduces the different SQL Server database management systems and client tools. The chapter defines a SQL Server database object and describes the files that comprise a database. Next it provides step-by-step instructions for creating databases and specifying database properties. The final section describes how to write and execute SQL commands to create database tables. It provides an in-depth discussion on SQL Server data types and describes how to create database constraints, including primary keys, foreign keys, check conditions, and not NULL constraints.

Chapter 3 provides an overview of SQL SELECT queries. The first section describes the sample databases that you use throughout the book: the Ironwood University student registration database and the Sport Motors sales and inventory management system. These databases have many inter-related tables and a wealth of sample data, providing a realistic platform for illustrating database applications. This section also provides instructions for running scripts to create the sample tables in your database. Subsequent sections show how to write SQL commands to retrieve data, perform arithmetic operations on retrieved data, use group functions to summarize retrieved data, and format query output. A section provides instructions for joining data from multiple tables and creating nested queries, and the final sections show how to create and work with views and perform set operations in queries. These topics provide a solid foundation for creating SQL queries to support database applications.

Chapter 4 begins by showing how to create SQL action queries to insert, update, and delete data. The chapter provides a detailed overview of how SQL Server manages transaction processing in multiuser systems by describing potential errors when users execute transactions that perform conflicting operations and how SQL Server uses record locking and blocking to avoid errors. It provides step-by-step instructions for configuring queries that use different levels to isolate transactions, and discusses the implications on database performance. The second half of the chapter describes T-SQL, which is the SQL Server procedural programming language. The chapter describes basic T-SQL syntax and program structures, then explains how to create T-SQL stored procedures, user-defined functions, and database triggers that execute in response to specific SQL commands.

Chapter 5 furnishes the background information you need to create Windows- and Web-based database applications. The first section describes the .NET framework and shows how it supports application development. Next you learn how to open the Visual Studio IDE and become familiar with its components. The sections that follow describe the fundamentals of the VB programming language, including decision and looping structures and classes and objects. The chapter describes how to create applications with multiple forms, and the final section shows how to use the debugging features in the IDE.

Chapter 6 integrates the material in the previous chapters by describing how to create Windows-based database applications. The first section describes how Windows applications access data in .NET, and shows how to create and work with .NET data components. The next section focuses on application design, illustrating different ways to display data in Windows-based applications. The sections that follow show how to create a variety of read-only and read-write Windows database applications using data-bound controls, which are application items that .NET provides to automatically display and update database data. You also learn how to create applications that access and interact with data using program commands, as well as how to create a database application that uses a combination of data-bound controls and program commands. The final section describes how to use asynchronous queries to retrieve and display data from large databases that may contain millions of records.

Chapter 7 describes how to create database reports, which are snapshot summaries that describe and summarize database data at a point in time. The first section focuses on design and describes commonly used database report layouts. Subsequent sections show how to create and format a simple report that displays data from a single table, create reports that display data from multiple database tables, and implement reports with master-detail layouts. Later sections show how to create reports with advanced features such as summary data and calculated values, and how to integrate reports into Windows applications by passing parameter values from form controls to reports.

Chapter 8 describes how to create Web-based database applications. It begins with an overview of the architecture of the World Wide Web, describing how Web-database applications retrieve and display data. The next section describes ASP.NET, which is the .NET approach to creating data-based Web pages, and the structure of an ASP.NET Web application. Other sections provide step-by-step instructions for creating an ASP.NET Web site containing Web pages that allow users to view and process database data using single-record, tabular, and master-detail displays. The final section describes how to enhance these pages using pick lists, validation controls, and images.

Chapter 9 describes XML (eXtensible Markup Language), which provides a way to structure data in text files, and shows how it assists database developers by providing a platform-independent way to share data. The first section describes the logical and physical structure of an XML document, with instructions for creating an XML document. The next section shows how to create a variety of SQL queries that return XML-formatted data. You learn how to write applications that use XSLTs (eXtensible Stylesheet Language Transformations), which are programs that transform XML documents into different formats, and how to use schema definitions to validate XML files. You then learn how to create Web-based database applications that create and use XML files. The final section describes how to create XML Web services and the Web service client programs to access them.

Chapter 10 focuses on database administration, describes common database administration tasks, and shows how to use some of SQL Server 2005's primary data management tools. You learn about performance issues in large databases and how to create indexes to enhance performance. Security issues and how to implement different SQL Server user authentication approaches are also covered. The next section shows how to perform backup and recovery operations, and the final section illustrates how to deploy Windows- and Web-based database applications and make them available to users.

TO THE INSTRUCTOR

Approach and Features of the Book

This book provides an overview of database design and implementation topics using Microsoft SQL Server 2005, with an emphasis on database application development using Visual Studio. You can use it in the introductory data management course, either as a stand-alone text in a course that emphasizes database system development, or as a supplement to a more conceptual text. It is aimed toward students at two- and four-year colleges and universities and career schools enrolled either in the introductory database management course, or in a more advanced database application development course. Prerequisite knowledge is a one-semester programming course in any programming language. The book presents all the required programming concepts and syntax, but the prerequisite ensures that students have an adequate level of maturity to allow the text to present elementary programming concepts quickly. This allows the text to focus on its primary objective, which is developing database applications.

After completing a course using this text, the student will:

- understand what a database is, be familiar with the different types of databases, and be able to describe the architecture of different database systems;
- understand the structure of relational database tables, and be able to create entity relationship models and derive the associated database tables;
- be able to create SQL Server databases and database tables using T-SQL scripts in the Management Studio client environment;
- be able to create and execute SQL action queries and SELECT queries in Management Studio;
- write T-SQL stored procedures and database triggers;
- understand different ways that Windows applications display database data;
- create Windows- and Web-based database applications;
- create database reports;
- understand what XML is, be able to create XML databases from retrieved database data, and be able to use XML databases in applications;
- understand database administration tasks and perform basic administration tasks in SQL Server 2005.

You can implement the course using a client/server architecture in which the database server process runs on a remote server or in a single-tier structure in which each student runs the SQL Server DBMS on his or her workstation. Alternate instructions are presented for either approach.

INSTRUCTIONAL SUPPORT: www.prenhall.com/morrison

The textbook is equally well suited for database courses in four-year institutions and in other settings, including community college courses offering product-specific instruction in SQL Server and Visual Studio VB and Web page development. No matter what type of institution you teach in, we want to make your job easier by providing a rich variety of instructional support materials for the book. It is likely that not everyone will want to use all the supplied support materials, but we believe there are subsets of the tools and supporting material that each person will like. Student and instructor materials can be found on the Web site, www.prenhall.com/morrison. Instructor materials can also be accessed through the catalog page, www.prenhall.com.

Instructor Resources

- An **Instructor's Resource Manual** provides materials describing the chapter, hints, tips, and traps. Solutions to the end-of-chapter exercises will be found in the additional files described below.
- **PowerPoint slide presentations** contain figures from the text plus selected script file text showing important SQL statements to help you organize lectures and activities.
- A **Test Item File** and **TestGen** contain a full complement of over 1,500 test questions in multiple-choice, true-false, and short-answer format. The Test Item File is available in Microsoft Word and as the computerized Prentice Hall TestGen

software, a comprehensive set of tools for testing and assessment. TestGen allows instructors to create and distribute tests for their courses, either by printing and distributing through traditional methods, or by online delivery via a local area network server. The software features Screen Wizards for assistance, and is backed with full technical support.

- The **Image Library** is a collection of the text illustrative material organized by chapter. It includes all of the figures, tables, and screenshots from the book. Images can be used to enhance lectures and slide presentations.

- **Solutions** and **Data Files** contain all the databases, the database script files to load them, other data files required to complete each step in the text, and data for the end-of-chapter guided exercises. They also contain solution files for all end-of-chapter multiple choice, true/false, short answer, and guided exercises. All of these files are available to the instructor at the book's Web site, www.prenhall.com/morrison, and are protected by usernames and passwords that are available to instructors.

ACKNOWLEDGMENTS

We want to thank the reviewers who provided suggestions and insights to help us craft the book most likely to help students succeed and instructors to teach and mentor their students. In particular, we thank the following people:

Martin Bariff, Illinois Institute of Technology

Isabelle Bichindaritz, University of Washington

Sam Chung, Washington State University

Larry M. Holt, Rollings College

Stan Kurkovsky, Central Connecticut State University

Ramon Lawrence, University of Iowa

Isaac Mitchell, TVI Community College-Alburquerque

William Shay, University of Wisconsin-Green Bay

Joe Wood, Webster University

The authors acknowledge the work of the dedicated professionals at Pearson Prentice Hall. We especially thank Bob Horan, Executive Editor; Ana Jankowski, Assistant Editor; Debbie Clare, Executive Marketing Manager; and Anne Graydon, Senior Production Editor. It has been a pleasure to work with all of you.

—**Mike Morrison**
—**Joline Morrison**

Read This Before You Begin

TO THE STUDENT

Data Files

To complete the tutorials and end-of-chapter exercises in this book, you need data files that have been created for use with the book. Your instructor will provide these files for you, or you can download them directly from `www.prenhall.com/morrison`. In the book, you are instructed to open files from the \Datafiles\DatabaseScripts folder, which contains files for creating the sample databases used in Chapters 3–10. In Chapters 5–10, you are instructed to open files from folders named \Datafiles\Chapter5, \Datafiles\Chapter6, and so forth, which contain specific data files for tutorials and exercises in these chapters. In Chapter 6, you are instructed to open the GeoData.mdf database file, which is in a folder named \Datafiles\Databases.

Solution Files

This book contains instructions for saving solution files to a folder on your computer. You should create a folder named SQLServer on your C: drive or an alternate drive on which you wish to store solutions. If you are connecting to a local SQL Server database, create a subfolder in the SQLServer folder named Databases to store your local database files. (If you are connecting to a remote SQL Server database, you do not need to create the Databases folder.) If you are connecting to either a local SQL Express database *or* to a remote SQL Server database, create a subfolder in the SQLServer folder named Solutions. In the Solutions folder, create subfolders for each chapter: Chapter1, Chapter2, Chapter3, and so forth, through Chapter10.

Using Your Own Computer

Chapters 2–10 require users to be able to connect to either a SQL Server 2005 or a SQL Express database, and Appendix A describes how to install these databases. Different chapters require users to have access to different application development tools. Appendix B summarizes the applications needed for each chapter, and describes how to install and configure these applications.

TO THE INSTRUCTOR

If you choose to have your students connect to a remote SQL Server database, you must install the database on a server, and create a login for each student, which is a unique username/password combination that allows each student to access the database. To enable students to create their own databases, you must explicitly grant to each student login the permission to create databases. We recommend that you use SQL Server authentication rather than Windows authentication to simplify grading.

The following T-SQL commands create a login named "Bob" and grant to that login the permission to create databases on the server:

```
USE master
GO
CREATE LOGIN [Bob] WITH PASSWORD=N'secret',
DEFAULT_DATABASE=[master],
CHECK_EXPIRATION=OFF, CHECK_POLICY=OFF
GO
GRANT CREATE ANY DATABASE TO Bob
GO
```

CAUTION: You can also make a login a member of the dbcreator server role; however, if you do this, your users can also alter and drop other databases on the server. SQL Server 2005 is the first version in which the dbcreator role has been broken down into its component parts, which can be granted via the GRANT statement.

Student Resources

The Companion Web site, at www.prenhall.com/morrison, contains additional materials for students. Particularly, **Student Data Files** contain all the databases, database script files other data files required to complete each step in the text, and data files for the hands-on exercises. Note that the Web site is the single source for all data files for the book.

Paths Through the Book

We designed this book to be flexible enough to satisfy several teaching approaches and styles. The book contains ten chapters that provide a comprehensive approach for a full semester, three-credit introductory database course. However, you can use the book for a course that focuses on database design and administration by presenting Chapters 1–4 and 10. A course that focuses on application development for students who have already completed an introductory database course is supported by Chapters 5–9.

CHAPTER 1

Introduction to Databases

Learning Objectives

At the conclusion of this chapter, you will be able to:

- describe a database;
- understand hierarchical, relational, and object-oriented databases;
- understand the process for developing a database system;
- create entity relationship models to describe a database design;
- derive database tables using an entity relationship model.

When you interact with a computer system such as a university registration system or a Web site for ordering books or CDs, chances are that the system uses a database to store the data you view and enter. *Databases* store and organize data that organizations need to retain, such as data about students, courses, products, or customer orders. This book describes how to create databases using Microsoft SQL Server 2005 and how to insert, update, delete, and view database data. It also describes how to create *database applications,* which are programs that enable users to interact with a database. Database applications may be programs that users install on their workstations, or Web-based programs that are displayed using Web browsers.

OVERVIEW OF DATABASES

When organizations first started using computers to process data, computer applications stored all data in data files. Each application had its own set of unique data files. For example, a university might have separate computer applications to create student schedules, student transcripts, and schedules about available courses. Figure 1-1 illustrates the *data file approach to data processing,* in which each application has a separate associated data file.

One of the problems with this approach is that the data files for different applications often contain the same data items. For example, both the student schedule and student transcript data files contain student data, such as the student's name, address, and telephone number. Similarly, the student schedule and course schedule files contain information about the day and time when specific courses meet. This data probably changes over time, and values may be updated in one file but not in others. As a result the data becomes inconsistent, and users cannot be sure which data values are correct. Also, storing duplicate data occupies valuable storage space.

FIGURE 1-1   Data file approach to data processing

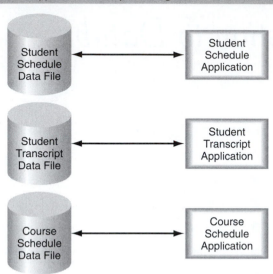

Yet another problem with the data file approach is the need to write and maintain many different programs that all perform essentially the same basic data-handling procedures. Recall that when applications use the data file approach, each application has one or more unique data files. As a result, each application must contain its own subprograms to handle the *basic data-handling procedures:*

- Inserting new data
- Viewing existing data
- Updating existing data
- Deleting existing data

From one application to another, the subprograms must all be slightly different to handle the application's specific data values, but each subprogram performs the same core functions. As a result, applications that use data files require a lot of duplicated programming effort to create and maintain their data-handling procedures. This becomes expensive, repetitious, and difficult to manage.

To address these problems, programmers developed databases to store organizational data. Based on the assumption that data is an organizational resource, a database stores all organizational data in a central location. A database has a single set of programs, called the *database management system (DBMS),* which performs among other tasks, the basic data-handling procedures of viewing, inserting, updating, and deleting data. Examples of DBMSs are SQL Server and Oracle. Programmers use programming languages, such as Visual Basic and Java, to create database applications. These database applications enable users to work with the database using attractive and easy-to-use interfaces that interact with the DBMS to perform data-handling procedures. Figure 1-2 illustrates the database approach to data processing.

In this book, you will work with the SQL Server DBMS. You will use SQL Server to create new databases and perform basic data-handling procedures. You will use the Visual Studio 2005 development environment to create database applications to allow users to interact with your databases.

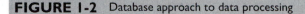

FIGURE 1-2 Database approach to data processing

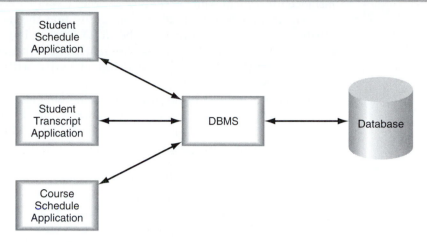

DATABASE OBJECTS AND STRUCTURES

How do databases store data? At the lowest level, all databases store data values in data files, and the DBMS manages the data files and enables users to perform basic data-handling procedures. How do you organize the data? To understand the underlying structure of a database, you must first become familiar with database objects.

Database Objects

An *entity* is an object about which a database stores data. Examples of entities are students, courses, customers, and products. An *entity instance* is a single data item of an entity, such as a particular student or a specific course. To minimize storing redundant data, the database stores the data about each entity instance only once. Figure 1-3

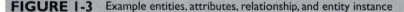

FIGURE 1-3 Example entities, attributes, relationship, and entity instance

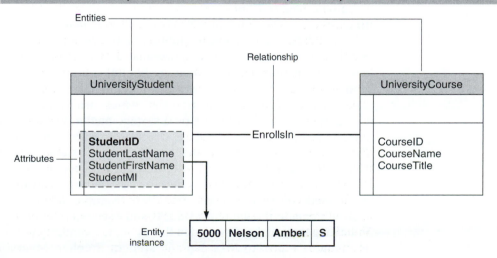

illustrates entities named UniversityStudent and UniversityCourse, and an entity instance for student Amber Nelson.

An *attribute* is a data value of an entity that the database stores. For example, attributes of a student entity might be an ID number, last name, first name, and middle initial. Figure 1-3 shows attributes StudentID, StudentLastName, StudentFirstName, and StudentMI for the UniversityStudent entity, with associated values of 5000, "Amber," "Nelson," and "S."

Databases use *relationships* to represent connections among related entities. For example, when a student enrolls in a course, the database creates a relationship between the course entity instance and the student entity instance. Figure 1-3 shows a relationship named EnrollsIn between the UniversityStudent and UniversityCourse entities.

You use entities, attributes, and relationships to define database objects. When an organization creates a new database system, it adopts and maintains naming conventions for these structures. It is a good practice to use descriptive names that are self-documenting. For example, you would name an entity that represents customer orders CustomerOrder. It is a good practice to use two words rather than one for all entities and attributes, because many database systems have *reserved words,* which are commands that define internal operations. As a result, Order is not a good choice for an entity name because some database systems might use this word to define a data-handling operation. A better choice is CustomerOrder, which combines two words that are unlikely to comprise a reserved word. In this book, we define all entities, attributes, and relationships using a descriptive two- or three-word phrase, begin each new word with a capital letter, and omit spaces between words. Examples of entity and attribute names that use this convention are CustomerOrder, OrderDate, and OrderQuantity. Entity names should be singular rather than plural: For example, you would name an entity CustomerOrder rather than CustomerOrders.

Database Structures

There are three primary database structures: hierarchical, relational, and object-oriented. These three structures store data entity instance values and represent relationships differently, thus affecting how programmers create databases and database applications. The following sections describe the three database structures.

Hierarchical Databases

In early databases, data was stored in a *hierarchical database structure,* in which all related entities have parent-to-child relationships, and one parent data item can have multiple child items. For example, in a student registration database, a student entity might be a parent data item that could have multiple related child entities, such as courses in which the student enrolls. A hierarchical database implements the parent-to-child relationships using *pointers,* which are values that specify the physical locations where data is stored on a storage media, such as a disk or tape. Figure 1-4 illustrates a hierarchical database structure in which the student entity instances are the parent data items and the course entity instances are the child data items. Databases usually store entity instance values in a tabular format as shown.

A pointer links the data values for each individual student entity instance to its associated course entity instances. For example, a pointer links student Amber Nelson's data to the data for MIS 290, and a second pointer links her data to MIS 304, indicating that she has enrolled in these courses. Similarly, pointers link student Joseph Hernandez's data to MIS 290 and student Stephen Myers' data to MIS 304 and MIS 310.

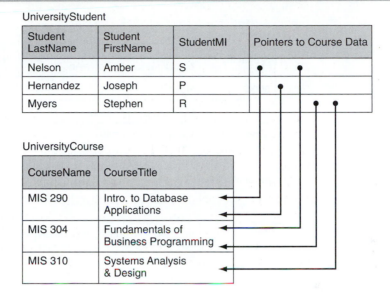

FIGURE 1-4   Hierarchical database structure

A pointer is not a physical link, but an address that uniquely defines a physical location on a storage device, such as a hard disk. Since hierarchical databases use pointers to create relationships among associated data items, the data is physically dependent on its location on the storage media. This makes it difficult to move a hierarchical database to a new storage medium when the disk becomes full or new hardware is purchased. Another problem with hierarchical databases is that all data is accessed within application programs written in languages such as COBOL that contain commands to navigate through the database pointers. Changes to the database structure require rewriting these programs, which is time-consuming and expensive. These difficulties led to the development of relational databases.

Relational Databases

Most databases developed today use a relational database structure. A *relational database structure* structures data in tables like those used in a hierarchical database. Columns, which are called *fields,* represent attributes that are associated with individual data values. Each row contains a set of related fields, which is called a *record,* that contains the data about an individual entity instance. Figure 1-5 shows an example of two relational database tables, and highlights a field and a record.

A relational database uses *key fields* to create relationships among records in different tables. There are four main types of key fields in a relational database: primary keys, surrogate keys, foreign keys, and composite keys.

Primary Keys   A *primary key* is a table field whose value uniquely identifies the record. Every table must have a primary key. The primary key field value for each record must be unique and cannot be *NULL,* or undefined. In the UniversityStudent table in Figure 1-5, the StudentID field is a good choice for the primary key field because its value is unique. The StudentLastName field is not a good primary key field choice, because multiple students might have the same last name, and the StudentLastName field contains text data that is prone to spelling errors and variations in text capitalization (such as Nelson or NELSON). Database developers use

FIGURE 1-5 Examples of relational database tables

UniversityStudent

StudentID	Student LastName	Student FirstName	StudentMI
5000	Nelson	Amber	S
5001	Hernandez	Joseph	P
5002	Myers	Stephen	R

UniversityCourse

CourseID	CourseName	CourseTitle
100	MIS 290	Intro. to Database Applications
101	MIS 304	Fundamentals of Business Programming
102	MIS 310	Systems Analysis & Design

primary keys to create relationships with other data records, so primary key values in different tables must match exactly. The best choices for primary key fields are fields that contain numerical data, such as ID numbers.

Surrogate Keys Some entities have fields that naturally serve as primary keys. For example, stock keeping units (SKUs) appear on product packages, and automobiles have vehicle identification numbers (VINs) stamped on their dashboards. However, entities such as students or customers do not naturally possess identifying numbers. For most entities, database designers create surrogate keys. A *surrogate key* is a field that the database designer creates to be a designated primary key. A surrogate key does not describe the record to which it is assigned but merely serves to uniquely identify the record. For example, StudentID is a unique number that the database creates and assigns to a student entity instance. Usually, developers configure databases to generate surrogate key values automatically for new records.

Foreign Keys Relational databases use foreign keys to create relationships among related records. A *foreign key* is a field that is a primary key in another table and creates a relationship between the two tables. A *parent table* is a table whose primary key acts as a foreign key in other tables. A *child table* is a table that contains a foreign key. Figure 1-6 shows a parent table named UniversityInstructor, which stores information about course instructors and whose primary key field is InstructorID. The figure also shows a child table named UniversityStudent, which has a foreign key field named AdvisorID that creates a relationship between each student and his or her academic advisor. Each student has an associated advisor. Amber Nelson's and Joseph Hernandez's advisor is Greg Black, and Stephen Myers' advisor is Naj Sarin.

To retrieve related records, a relational database must search the parent table to find the record that links to a child record. As a result, relational databases retrieve related data more slowly than hierarchical databases. In years past, developers avoided

FIGURE 1-6   Creating relationships using foreign keys

UniversityInstructor

InstructorID	Instructor LastName	Instructor FirstName
1	Black	Greg
2	McIntyre	Karen
3	Sarin	Naj

Primary keys

Parent table

Foreign keys

UniversityStudent

Child table

StudentID	Student LastName	Student FirstName	StudentMI	AdvisorID
5000	Nelson	Amber	S	1
5001	Hernandez	Joseph	P	1
5002	Myers	Stephen	R	3

using relational databases due to their slow retrieval rates. Recently, however, advances in hardware speed and improvements in searching techniques have made the slower response times of relational databases largely irrelevant.

An important concept in relational databases is *referential integrity,* which means that when you create a table with a foreign key, all foreign key values must exist in the parent table. For the relationship between the UniversityInstructor and UniversityStudent tables in Figure 1-6 to be valid, each value in the AdvisorID field in the UniversityStudent table must have a corresponding value in the InstructorID field in the UniversityInstructor table.

Composite Keys   When a table does not have a unique primary key field, database designers sometimes create a *composite key,* which combines multiple fields to create a unique primary key. In the CourseEnrollment table in Figure 1-7, the StudentID field is not a suitable primary key, because one student may enroll in many courses.

Similarly, the CourseID field is not a suitable primary key, because one course may enroll many students. The CourseGrade field cannot be a primary key, because many students receive the same grade in a course. Because each student enrolls in each course only once, however, the combination of the StudentID and CourseID fields creates a composite key that uniquely identifies each record.

A composite key is usually made up of foreign key fields that are primary keys in other tables. For example, the StudentID field in the CourseEnrollment table is part of the composite key, and is also a foreign key that references the StudentID field in the UniversityStudent table. Similarly, the CourseID field in the CourseEnrollment table is part of the composite key and is also a foreign key that references the CourseID field in the UniversityCourse table.

Creating composite keys is always optional. For example, in the CourseEnrollment table, you could alternatively create a surrogate key named EnrollmentID to provide a unique primary key.

FIGURE 1-7 Composite key

CourseEnrollment

CourseID	StudentID	CourseGrade
100	5000	A
100	5001	C
101	5000	B
101	5002	B
102	5002	A

Composite key

UniversityStudent

StudentID	Student LastName	Student FirstName	StudentMI
5000	Nelson	Amber	S
5001	Hernandez	Joseph	P
5002	Myers	Stephen	R

UniversityCourse

CourseID	CourseName	CourseTitle
100	MIS 290	Intro. to Database Applications
101	MIS 304	Fundamentals of Business Programming
102	MIS 310	Systems Analysis & Design

Object-Oriented Databases

Object-oriented databases structure data items as objects. An object is similar to an entity: it describes system data. There is one important difference, however. Objects are not limited to storing data. They also store *methods,* which are programs that interact with the data. In a database, an *object* stores both data and the behavior of the data. An *object instance* refers to a single unique object in the world, such as student Amber Nelson. An *object class* refers to a collection of similar objects, such as all students at a university. Therefore an object class is similar to an entity or table, and an object instance is similar to a record. However, object classes and instances can store methods for interacting with data in addition to the data, so they are not the same as tables and records.

An object class has two important characteristics: state and behavior. An object class's *state* specifies the values of its attributes and the relationships of all object instances within the class. For example, a student object class has a first name and a last name, as well as related courses in which its instances enroll. An object class's *behavior* represents the actions of its instances within the database application. For example, a student object instance can enroll in courses and request the value of its current grade point average. Methods are programs that define an object's behavior. Figure 1-8

FIGURE 1-8 Structuring data in object classes

illustrates the UniversityStudent and UniversityCourse entities structured in object classes and shows their associated relationships and methods.

An *object-oriented database management system (OODBMS)* manages data objects within an object-oriented database. The database developer first defines the object classes and their associated attributes and methods, as shown in Figure 1-8. The developer or data entry person then writes commands to create individual object instances for each data item. In an object-oriented student registration database, object instances exist for each student and each course. For example, Amber Nelson is one object, and Joseph Hernandez is another. Similarly, MIS 290 and MIS 304 are unique objects. Each object also has specific attribute values and relationships with other objects.

The advantage of object-oriented databases over hierarchical and relational databases is that they store data and associated methods together in the database, which makes database applications easier to use and maintain. Object-oriented databases are particularly useful for storing and managing data that is not readily amenable to relational databases, such as image data and sound and video clips. An object-oriented database that stores sound and video clips might define methods for viewing and listening to clips that are stored directly with each clip.

OODBMSs were initially developed during the 1990s but have not been commercially successful yet. One problem is that organizations currently have large volumes of data in hierarchical and relational formats, and it is expensive and time-consuming to migrate the data to object classes. Another problem is that object-oriented databases have not yet been able to yield the performance needed for applications that must process high transaction volumes quickly.

To address some of these problems, relational database vendors such as Oracle and IBM have developed *object-relational database management systems (ORDBMSs)*. These hybrid relational DBMSs enable developers to create data objects that they can associate with relational records. Figure 1-9 shows an example of data in an ORDBMS. In this example, the user runs the DisplayMethod for a particular student's object instance, and the ORDBMS displays the student's image.

In this book, you will learn how to create databases and database applications using SQL Server, which is a relational database management system (RDBMS), not an ORDBMS.

FIGURE 1-9   Example of an object-relational database table

UniversityStudent

StudentID	Student LastName	Student FirstName	StudentMI	StudentImage	DisplayImage
5000	Nelson	Amber	S	Binary data for image	DisplayMethod
5001	Hernandez	Joseph	P	Binary data for image	DisplayMethod
5002	Myers	Stephen	R	Binary data for image	DisplayMethod

Photo courtesy of the authors.

THE DATABASE DEVELOPMENT LIFE CYCLE

When developers create new database systems, they often follow the *database development life cycle*, which is a series of steps that define the scope of a database system, obtain system requirements, and then design, implement, and deploy the system. Figure 1-10 illustrates the database development life cycle.

The database development life cycle generally proceeds one step at a time, with developers completing each phase before moving to the next in the direction of the downward-pointing arrows. In each phase, a number of steps result in deliverables that are generally in the form of written reports, design diagrams, or program code. Sometimes developers find they must revise the deliverables from previous phases, as indicated by the upward-pointing arrows. The following sections describe each phase.

Initiation

During the *initiation phase,* system developers define the proposed database system and establish that the problem or opportunity the system addresses justifies the cost of the development effort. The initiation phase's output is the *project proposal,* which consists of the following items:

- **Organizational objectives,** which state the objectives of the organization for which the proposed database system is being built;
- **Organizational data overview,** which describes the existing organizational databases and database applications;
- **Organizational structure chart,** which describes the organization's management structure and highlights the managers and users involved in the database system development process;
- **Problem identification and strategic rationales,** which explains the problem that the database system solves or the opportunity that it exploits, as well as how the system helps the organization meet its defined objectives.

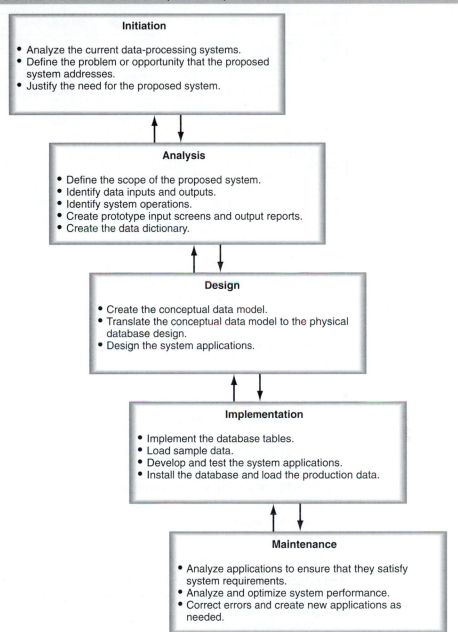

FIGURE 1-10 Database development life cycle

Initiation

- Analyze the current data-processing systems.
- Define the problem or opportunity that the proposed system addresses.
- Justify the need for the proposed system.

Analysis

- Define the scope of the proposed system.
- Identify data inputs and outputs.
- Identify system operations.
- Create prototype input screens and output reports.
- Create the data dictionary.

Design

- Create the conceptual data model.
- Translate the conceptual data model to the physical database design.
- Design the system applications.

Implementation

- Implement the database tables.
- Load sample data.
- Develop and test the system applications.
- Install the database and load the production data.

Maintenance

- Analyze applications to ensure that they satisfy system requirements.
- Analyze and optimize system performance.
- Correct errors and create new applications as needed.

Analysis

Following approval of the project proposal, system developers proceed to the *analysis phase,* in which they analyze and describe the existing or proposed system and determine how the system integrates with the other organizational systems. If the proposed system is replacing an existing one, developers should examine existing input and output screens and documents and observe the existing system in action. They should also interview current users to develop an understanding of the system's processes and the rationale for each process. If the proposed system is intended to exploit a new business

FIGURE 1-11   Example of a data dictionary

Entity	Data Item	Data Type	Description
University Student			
	StudentID	Number	Student identifier (surrogate key)
	StudentLastName	Text	Student last name
	StudentFirstName	Text	Student first name
	StudentDOB	Date/Time	Student date of birth
	StudentImage	Object	Student photograph
University Course			
	CourseID	Number	Course identifier (surrogate key)
	CourseName	Text	Course department + call number
	CourseTitle	Text	Course title, as it appears in the course catalog

opportunity, developers should interview the proposed system's users to determine system requirements. Developers should also create prototype input and output screens and report documents, and review them with users to confirm that they are correct. To help understand system processes and communicate their findings to users, they may develop analysis diagrams such as data flow diagrams or state diagrams.

The output of the analysis phase is the *initial study,* which contains the following items:

- **Description of operations,** which textually and/or graphically describes the current system or describes the proposed system if it does not yet exist, who enters data into the system and how they enter it, how the system manipulates the data, and to whom the system delivers the data outputs;
- **System inputs and outputs,** which summarizes the data items that users input into the system and items that appear on each output screen and report;
- **Sketches or prototypes of computer screens and printed output reports,** which confirm user requirements for systems that exploit new business opportunities;
- **Data dictionary,** which provides a comprehensive listing and description of each system data item.

One of the most important outputs of the analysis phase is the *data dictionary,* which defines all system data items. Figure 1-11 shows an example of a data dictionary.

Recall that in a database, an entity is an item about which the database stores data. To avoid redundancy, the database stores the data about each entity instance only once. When you create a data dictionary, it is a good practice to group data items as entities because this expedites the data-modeling process, which is done in the subsequent design phase. Each entity should have a unique identifier, which is usually a surrogate key.

Another good practice is to identify each item's *data type,* which specifies how the database internally stores the data. The basic data types in any database system are numbers, text, dates/times, and objects.

TIP: DBMSs have specific data subtypes that define data precisely by distinguishing between different types of numbers (such as integers and floating point numbers) and text data (such as fixed- and variable-length character text).

How do you select data types? In general, you store character fields such as names and addresses as text. You store numerical fields on which applications will perform calculations, such as product prices or quantities on hand, as numbers. As a general rule, if fields contain numbers that do not appear in calculations, such as postal codes and telephone numbers, store the data as text, because text data facilitates the addition of formatting characters, such as hyphens and parentheses.

Store dates, such as dates of birth or order dates, and time values, such as appointment start times, using a date/time data type. (We combine dates and times into a single data type because many DBMSs store dates and times that way.) You can store binary data, such as photographs, spreadsheets, or word processor documents, within many modern RDBMSs. However, most current RDBMSs process binary data very slowly, so developers often do not store object data, but instead store references to the underlying data filenames.

The data dictionary should be as complete as possible. It is very difficult and time-consuming to add additional data items to the system and system applications later in the development process. Therefore, it is important for developers to specify all system data items as early as possible in the development process.

Design

In the *design phase*, developers specify the relationships among the system data and define the system applications. Design involves two subphases: conceptual design and logical/physical design. *Conceptual design* transforms the data dictionary into a detailed data model that is independent of a specific database structure (hierarchical, relational, or object-oriented). The most common approach for creating a conceptual database design is entity relationship modeling, which this chapter will describe in detail. *Logical/physical design* transforms the conceptual design into a physical database design that programmers can implement using a specific DBMS.

The output of the design phase is the *project design* document, which includes the following items:

- Entity relationship model;
- Database table or object definitions;
- User interface input and output screen and printed report prototypes;
- Integrated application design and menu design;
- Implementation schedule.

Implementation

During the *implementation phase,* developers implement the database design using a specific DBMS, create the user application programs, and then deploy them to the users. Implementation involves the following steps:

- Creating the database and defining the database objects or tables;
- Loading a small set of test data;
- Creating the user applications;
- Testing and reviewing the user applications using the test data set;
- Determining the maximum number of records or objects that the system must ultimately support and then loading this amount of test data to test system scalability;
- Testing and reviewing the user applications with the large test data set and modifying the applications and/or database tuning parameters;

- Deleting the test data and loading the production data;
- Creating the user accounts;
- Placing the system in operation;
- Creating the user documentation and online help system;
- Creating and implementing a backup and recovery plan;
- Training users in system operation and procedures.

After the database developers create the database and database tables or objects, they load a small set of representative sample data. They then create the user applications, which consist of input forms and output reports, and use the test data set to test the applications. During this process, developers should periodically conduct usability reviews with users to ensure that the applications are correct and complete.

When all applications are complete, developers perform *scalability tests*, whereby they estimate the maximum number of records or objects the database might contain. Developers generate and load this data into the system and confirm that the database performs adequately under a theoretical maximum load. Developers may find they need to modify applications and/or perform *database tuning*, that is, adjust underlying DBMS parameters such as the sizes and locations of data files and memory buffers.

For database applications that replace existing systems already containing data, developers must load the existing data into the new database. This step may involve writing conversion programs to modify the format of the existing data so that it conforms to the format that the new database requires.

After testing is complete, the database developers turn database operations over to the *database administrator (DBA),* who is responsible for overseeing the day-to-day operation of the database. The DBA creates the user accounts for the new database system. For multiuser database systems, each user normally has a user name and password that restrict database access to authorized users and allow the DBA to control database access. The DBA also creates and implements security measures for applications and data, as well as a process for backing up data and recovering from system failures.

The final implementation steps are to create the user documentation and online help system and to train users in system operations and procedures. Different organizations have varying procedures and standards for these items.

Maintenance

The *maintenance phase,* the longest phase in the database development process, continues over the life of the system. Maintenance tasks include the following:

- Upgrading the DBMS software as new releases become available;
- Correcting errors in existing database applications and creating new applications as user needs evolve;
- Continually monitoring database performance and retuning the DBMS as necessary;
- Maintaining user accounts to control database access and creating new accounts as new users come on line;
- Monitoring data storage space and allocating additional storage space as necessary;
- Performing backup and recovery operations.

ENTITY RELATIONSHIP MODELING

An *entity relationship (ER) model* visually represents entities, attributes, and relationships. An ER model is often one of the outputs of the conceptual design phase of database development. Developers can use ER models to identify the structure of relational database tables and data objects and to communicate these findings to system users. The following sections describe ER model components, explain how to create an ER model, and show how to derive relational database tables from an ER model.

Entities and Attributes

In this book, we use the ER model representation shown in Figure 1-12, which depicts each entity as a rectangle labeled with the entity name and lists the entity's attributes below the entity name.

Recall that an entity is a person, thing, or concept about which you want to store data and that an entity has associated entity instances with different data values. For example, in a student registration database, UniversityStudent is an entity, because there are multiple students, and each student has a first name, last name, date of birth, and photo image. An example of an entity instance is student Amber Nelson.

Recall also that an attribute is a data item about an entity that the database stores. In an ER model, every entity must have an attribute or a combination of attributes that serve as its primary key. The primary key is a field whose value uniquely identifies each entity instance. Usually you use a surrogate key attribute for the primary key, such as StudentID or CourseID. In an ER model, you designate the primary key attribute by underlining and labeling it, as shown in Figure 1-12.

There are three types of attributes: atomic, composite, and derived. An *atomic attribute* represents a single data item that the database stores. In a relational database, this type of value appears as a single data item in a field; an object-oriented database represents it as a discrete object. In Figure 1-12, StudentID and StudentDOB represent atomic attributes.

A *composite attribute* is an attribute that is made up of one or more atomic attributes. Common composite attributes include names (which have components of first name, last name, and middle initial) and addresses (which have components such as street address, city, state, and postal code).

In general, you should break composite attributes down into their component parts so that they store atomic data values. This facilitates sorting data by individual components, such as sorting students by their last names. It also allows users to search for specific values, such as all students who live in a given postal code, or to format data in documents such as form letters. In Figure 1-12, you would decompose the StudentName attribute into the atomic attributes of StudentFirstName, StudentMiddleInitial, and StudentLastName.

FIGURE 1-12   ER model entity and attributes

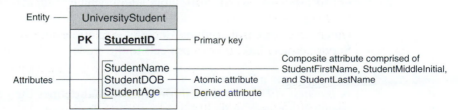

FIGURE 1-13   ER model relationships

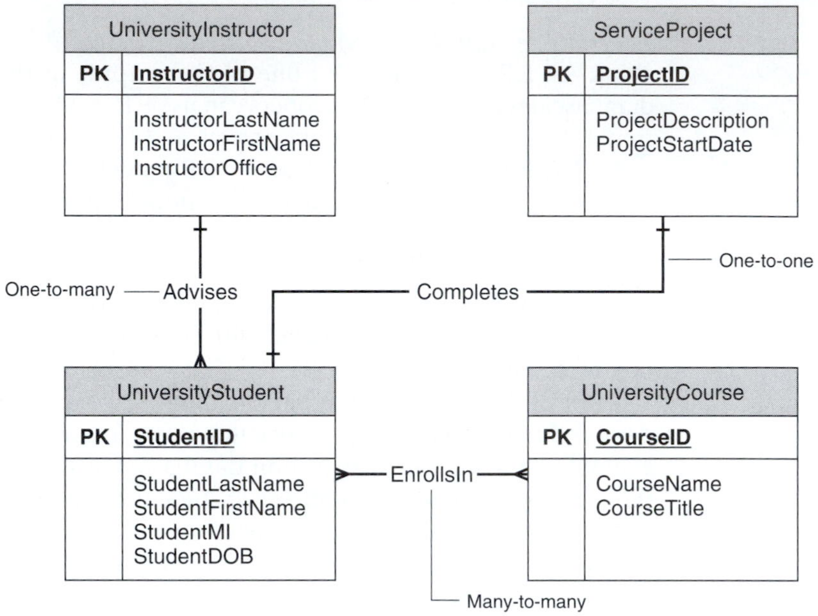

A *derived attribute* is an attribute whose value can be derived from other atomic attribute values. For example, you can derive a person's age based on his or her date of birth, and you can derive the value of a product's inventory by multiplying the item cost by the quantity on hand.

If a derived attribute's underlying values never change, then you should not store the derived attribute value in the database. For example, you always determine a person's age by subtracting his or her date of birth from the current date. Therefore, you should not store ages as attributes. However, if the underlying values can change, you should store the actual value of the derived attribute. For example, the cost of an inventory item may increase or decrease over time, so you cannot reliably calculate the value of all inventory items at a given point in time based on current costs times quantity on hand. In this case, you should store the derived value as a derived attribute.

Relationships

Relationships represent associations between entities. In this book, we represent relationships as a line between the two entities with a label that describes the relationship. For example, the relationship between the UniversityStudent and UniversityCourse entities might be labeled EnrollsIn. Figure 1-13 illustrates relationships among four entities on an ER model for a student registration database.

The Advises relationship between the UniversityInstructor and UniversityStudent entities specifies which instructors advise which students. The EnrollsIn relationship between the UniversityStudent and UniversityCourse entities describes courses in which students enroll, and the Completes relationship between UniversityStudent and ServiceProject links service projects to the students who complete them.

Relationship Cardinality

A *business rule* is a statement or practice that defines the policies and procedures an organization uses in its business processes. For example, a business rule in a student registration database might state that every student has one and only one advisor.

Another business rule might state that a student cannot enroll in a course unless he or she has completed its prerequisites.

An ER model describes relationships in terms of *cardinality,* which specifies the minimum and maximum number of entity instances with which you can associate a related entity instance. Relationship cardinalities enforce the business rules of an organization. The *maximum cardinality* specifies the maximum number of entity instances with which a related entity instance can be associated. The *minimum cardinality* specifies the minimum number and usually has a value of zero or one.

Usually you describe the relationship between two entities in terms of its maximum cardinalities. The three possible maximum cardinality combinations are the following:

- In a *one-to-one* combination, one instance of the first entity is associated with one and only one instance of the second entity. In Figure 1-13, the Completes relationship shows that each student completes a single service project, and each service project entity instance is associated with only one student. Note that the diagram shows a horizontal crossbar on the line that connects each entity to the relationship. This indicates that each entity instance of the UniversityStudent entity is related to a maximum of one entity instance of the ServiceProject entity and vice versa.
- In a *one-to-many* combination, one instance of the first entity can be associated with multiple instances of the second entity, but each instance of the second entity is associated with only one instance of the first. (In the context of an ER model, *many* specifies a value that is greater than one and has an unknown upper limit.) In Figure 1-13, the Advises relationship is one-to-many, because each instructor may advise multiple students, but each student has only one advisor. The UniversityInstructor entity is connected to the relationship with a single line having a horizontal crossbar, and the UniversityStudent entity is connected with a multiple-line "crow's foot." These symbols indicate that a single entity instance of the UniversityInstructor entity can be associated with multiple entity instances of the UniversityStudent entity, but each entity instance of the UniversityStudent entity is associated with only one UniversityInstructor instance.
- In a *many-to-many* combination, multiple instances of the first entity can be associated with multiple instances of the second entity, and multiple instances of the second entity can be associated with multiple instances of the first entity. In Figure 1-13, the EnrollsIn relationship shows that multiple instances of the UniversityStudent entity can be associated with multiple instances of the UniversityCourse entity and vice versa. In other words, each student can enroll in many courses, and each course can enroll many students.

ER model relationships also show minimum cardinalities. Consider the UniversityStudent entity within the Advises relationship in Figure 1-13. Suppose that the university has a policy whereby each student must have exactly one advisor, no more or no less. The maximum cardinality is one and specifies that a student cannot have more than one advisor. Figure 1-14 adds notation for minimum cardinalities to the ER model for the student registration database.

The symbol next to the entity rectangle specifies the maximum cardinality, and the symbol farthest from the entity specifies the minimum cardinality. You can conceptualize the relationship as a sentence by stating the name of the first entity as a noun, the relationship as the verb, and the cardinality as an adjective; you can then state the second entity as the final noun. For example, for the Advises relationship, you would state, "A UniversityInstructor advises zero or many UniversityStudent instances," and "A UniversityStudent instance is advised by one and only one UniversityInstructor instance."

FIGURE 1-14   ER model relationship showing minimum cardinalities

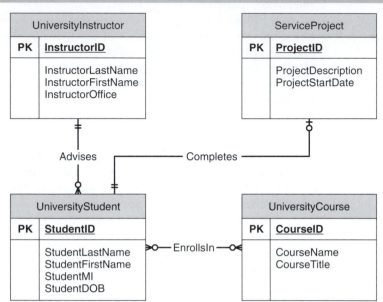

When the minimum cardinality is zero, the relationship is an *optional relationship;* for example, a specific instructor does not necessarily advise any students. In the Advises relationship, the UniversityInstructor entity's participation in the relationship is optional because an instructor does not have to advise any students. When the minimum cardinality is one, the entity's participation in the relationship is *mandatory*. In the Advises relationship, the UniversityStudent entity's participation is mandatory because each student entity instance must have an associated instructor entity instance as an advisor.

In the EnrollsIn relationship, a UniversityStudent entity instance can enroll in zero or many courses. Similarly, a UniversityCourse entity instance can have zero or many enrolled students. (In this example, a course is allowed to enroll no students initially and a student is allowed not to enroll in any courses initially.) For the EnrollsIn relationship, participation by both the UniversityStudent and UniversityCourse entities is optional. For the Completes relationship, a specific student can complete zero or one service project. Each service project instance is completed by one and only one student entity instance. The UniversityStudent entity instance's participation in this relationship is optional; a UniversityStudent entity instance can exist in the database and not have an associated ServiceProject entity instance. However, the ServiceProject entity instance's participation in the relationship is mandatory: if a ServiceProject entity instance exists in the database, it must have one and only one associated UniversityStudent entity instance.

Relationship Attributes

Sometimes as you create an ER model you discover that a many-to-many relationship has one or more associated attributes of its own. For example, consider the CourseGrade attribute in a student registration database, which represents the grade value (such as A, B, C, D, or F) that a specific student receives for a specific course. This value is not an attribute of the UniversityStudent entity, because during an academic career a specific student receives many different grades. Similarly, this grade value is not an attribute of the UniversityCourse entity, because an instructor assigns multiple grades for each student who enrolls in a course. Rather, CourseGrade is an attribute of the EnrollsIn

FIGURE 1-15   Relationship with an attribute

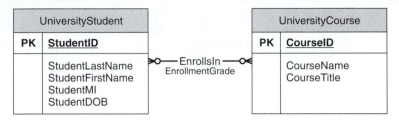

relationship between the UniversityStudent and UniversityCourse entities. When a relationship has one or more attributes, you place the attribute below the relationship name, as shown in Figure 1-15. Only many-to-many relationships have attributes.

Some database developers prefer not to show relationships with attributes on ER models. An equivalent way to represent a relationship with an attribute is to replace the relationship with a new entity and then create two new relationships to connect the new entity with the two existing ones. These two new relationships are always one-to-many. In the new one-to-many relationships, the maximum cardinality on the side of the existing entities is always one, and the maximum cardinality on the side of the new entity is always many. Figure 1-16 illustrates how you replace a relationship that has one or more attributes with an entity and two one-to-many relationships.

In Figure 1-16, a new entity named CourseEnrollment replaces the "EnrollsIn" relationship. Two new one-to-many relationships connect the CourseEnrollment entity to the UniversityStudent and UniversityCourse entities. Note that in the cardinalities, one UniversityStudent entity instance can have zero or many associated CourseEnrollment entity instances, but each CourseEnrollment entity instance has one and only one related UniversityStudent instance. Similarly, each UniversityCourse entity instance can have zero or many CourseEnrollment entity instances, but each CourseEnrollment entity instance has one and only one associated UniversityCourse instance.

FIGURE 1-16   Creating a new entity in place of a relationship with an attribute

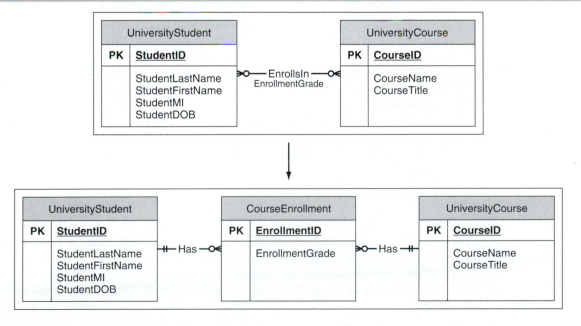

FIGURE 1-17   Unary relationships

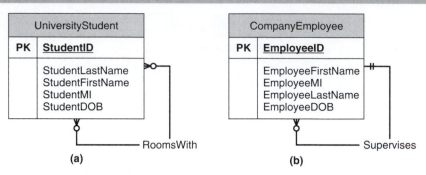

(a)   (b)

Degree of a Relationship

The *degree of a relationship* specifies the number of entities that participate in the relationship. All of the relationships presented thus far involve two entities, so the degree of these relationships is two. A relationship with a degree of two is a *binary relationship* and is the most common relationship type. Relationships, however, can involve different numbers of entities.

A relationship that involves one entity has a degree of one and is called a *unary relationship*. In effect, the entity has a relationship with itself. Figure 1-17 shows examples of unary relationships.

In Figure 1-17(a), the ER model notation shows that each UniversityStudent entity instance can room with zero or many other UniversityStudent instances and vice versa. Figure 1-17(b) shows how instances of a CompanyEmployee entity supervise other entity instances. From the supervisor's point of view, a CompanyEmployee entity instance can optionally supervise zero or many other CompanyEmployee instances. From the supervised employee's point of view, each employee instance has one and only one supervising employee.

Occasionally relationships involve three or more entities. A relationship that involves three entities is called a *ternary relationship*. For example, a university offers a tutoring service and creates a database to track tutoring session dates, times, and outcomes. Figure 1-18 shows the three entities making up this relationship: UniversityStudent, UniversityTutor, and UniversityCourse.

The ternary relationship in the figure represents a single tutoring session and shows that a specific student is tutored by a specific tutor for a specific course. The relationship has attributes of SessionDate, SessionTime, and SessionOutcome. You cannot represent these relationships using three separate binary relationships among the three entities because all three entities describe a single tutoring session. Often, ternary relationships have additional attributes. The cardinalities for all three entities in a ternary relationship are zero-to-many, and they specify that many instances of each entity can participate in the relationship but that each entity optionally participates in the relationship.

Creating ER Models

Creating an ER model is a three-step process:

1. Use the data dictionary output from the database analysis phase to identify all data entities and their associated attributes.
2. Define a primary key for each entity.
3. Create relationships and define cardinalities based on the organization's business rules.

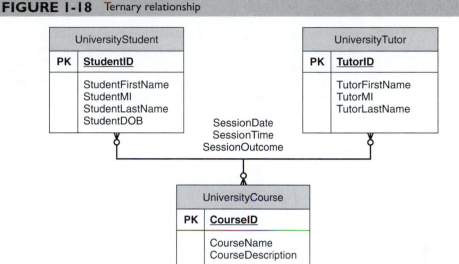

FIGURE 1-18   Ternary relationship

Creating a correct and complete ER model requires practice and experience, and it often involves multiple iterations. The following sections describe best-practice strategies.

Identifying Entities and Attributes

One of the first challenges that novice database developers encounter when creating ER models is deciding whether an item is an entity or an attribute. An item is an entity if multiple entity instances exist in the database and the developer is not sure exactly how many instances will exist. For example, there are multiple students at a university, and this number varies over time. Therefore, UniversityStudent is an entity. If a data item has a single value for each entity instance, then it is an attribute. For example, suppose student Amber Nelson is an entity instance of the UniversityStudent entity. Since she has one and only one first name, last name, date of birth, and photo image, all of these items are attributes.

If an item has one and only one entity instance in the database, you do not include it as an entity on the ER model. For example, UniversityRegistrar is not an entity because a student registration system most likely has only one entity instance of this entity.

Sometimes an item that a database developer originally identifies as an attribute turns out to be an entity. For example, suppose the database developer decides to store multiple photo images of each student. To store exactly two images for each student, the developer can represent these images as attributes named StudentImageOne and StudentImageTwo. However, to allow students to store an unspecified number of images, the developer needs to create an entity named StudentImage and connect this entity to the UniversityStudent entity by means of a relationship.

Another issue that sometimes confuses novice database developers is determining with which entity to associate an attribute. For example, in the student registration database, each UniversityStudent entity instance has one and only one academic advisor. Should the advisor's name be an attribute of the UniversityStudent entity? The answer is no because each advisor advises multiple students, and duplicating the advisor name for each student entity would be redundant and could lead to inconsistent data values if the advisor's name changes and the change is not made for every student instance.

At the end of the design phase, it is essential that the ER model be complete and contain all data attributes that the system will display in output screens and reports. Suppose that a database development team creates an incomplete ER model and then creates the database tables or objects based on the incomplete model. The team then starts coding database applications based on the incomplete tables or objects and later determines that the database is missing entities or attributes. They add the entities and/or attributes, but this usually forces them to recode large parts of all of the applications they have made so far, which is a lot of work!

Even highly experienced database developers find small errors in their database design during application development. However, these errors should be avoided as much as possible by spending adequate time and effort when creating the ER model.

Defining Entity Primary Key Attributes

Recall that a primary key attribute is an attribute whose value is unique and serves to identify the instance. A primary key should be a value that never changes. Some entities have natural primary keys, such as inventory item SKUs and automobile VINs. Most entities do not have natural primary keys, so you should create surrogate keys (database-generated unique identifiers), such as student IDs or employee IDs. Do not use telephone numbers for primary keys, because multiple people can share a telephone number, and the numbers often change. Do not use United States social security numbers as primary keys, because social security numbers provide access to sensitive information, and should be stored in as few tables as possible. (Using a social security number as a primary key includes the value throughout the database as a foreign key in tables linked to the person.) To represent a primary key on an ER model, you usually show the primary key attribute as the first attribute of an entity, and you underline the attribute name and/or label it with the code PK.

Entity and Attribute Naming Conventions

You should use descriptive names to define entities and attributes. Combine two words (such as UniversityStudent or CourseGrade) to avoid reserved word conflicts, and use singular nouns (such as UniversityStudent rather than UniversityStudents). It is a good practice to make the first word of an attribute a derivative of its associated entity so that developers can easily associate the attribute with its entity. For example, for the UniversityStudent entity, create attributes that start with the word Student, such as StudentID and StudentFirstName. This practice assigns a unique name to every database attribute, which minimizes confusion and ultimately reduces errors.

USING AN ER MODEL TO DEFINE RELATIONAL DATABASE TABLES

You use an ER model to design the normalized relational database tables for a database system. *Normalization* describes the transformation of the logical data design specified by the ER model into the tables that will be created within the database. Recall that a database stores all organizational data in a central location and avoids storing duplicate data, which can become inconsistent over time. Normalization is the process that makes this happen. This section describes how to transform an ER model into a normalized relational database table design by identifying the required database tables and their associated primary and foreign keys. (Recall that a foreign key is a table field that is a primary key in a related table and creates a relationship between the two tables.)

NOTE: This section provides guidelines for creating a database table design in third normal form, which is adequate for most business database applications. A complete discussion of relational database normal forms and their implications is not included in this book but can be found in many other database textbooks.

The following steps transform an ER model into a normalized database table design:

1. Create a database table to represent each entity, and designate the entity's primary key as the table's primary key.
2. Represent relationships using foreign keys and linking tables, and identify whether foreign key values can be NULL (undefined).

The partially-completed ER model in Figure 1-19 will be used to illustrate the process of transforming an ER model into a relational database table design. This ER model contains most of the relationship cardinality combinations that you generally

FIGURE 1-19   ER model for a student registration database

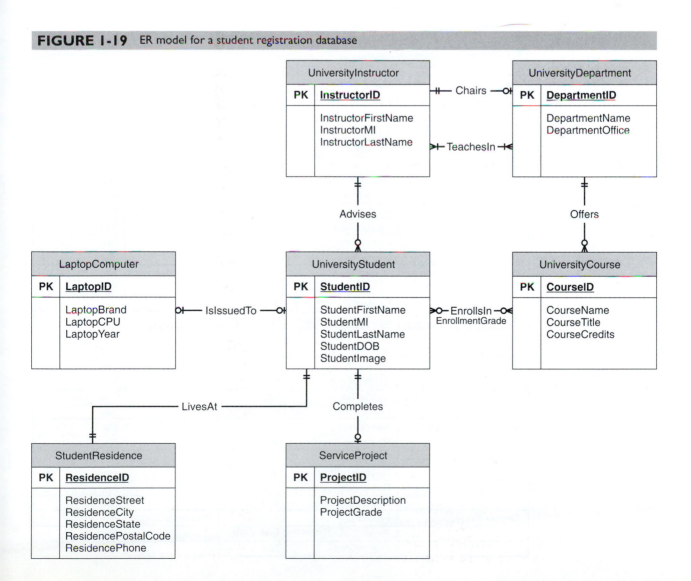

encounter in database systems. (A comprehensive registration system would have additional entities and relationships, but we omit them here to keep the diagram manageable.) The following paragraphs discuss the process in detail.

Creating Database Tables to Represent Each Entity

The first step in the transformation process is to create a database table to represent each entity. You specify a field to represent each attribute and designate the entity's primary key attribute as the table's primary key. (At this point, you do not create the table to represent the EnrollsIn relationship. You will do that later.) You also specify the field's data type (number, text, date/time, or binary) and whether the value can be NULL within an entity instance's record. Primary key values cannot be NULL. For other fields, you must determine if they should have not-NULL constraints to ensure the integrity of the database and database applications. For example, it is logical to specify that the UniversityStudent entity's StudentFirstName and StudentLastName fields cannot be NULL. However, you would not specify that the StudentMI (student middle initial) field cannot be NULL, because some people do not have middle initials.

FIGURE 1-20   Preliminary table design showing tables to represent entities

Table	Field	Data Type	Key	NULL Allowed
UniversityInstructor	InstructorID	Number	Primary surrogate	No
	InstructorFirstName	Text		No
	InstructorMI	Text		Yes
	InstructorLastName	Text		No
UniversityDepartment	DepartmenttID	Number	Primary surrogate	No
	DepartmentName	Text		No
	DepartmentOffice	Text		Yes
LaptopComputer	LaptopID	Number	Primary surrogate	No
	LaptopBrand	Text		Yes
	LaptopCPU	Text		No
	LaptopYear	Date		Yes
UniversityStudent	StudentID	Number	Primary surrogate	No
	StudentFirstName	Text		No
	StudentMI	Text		Yes
	StudentLastName	Text		No
	StudentDOB	Date		No
	StudentImage	Binary		Yes
UniversityCourse	CourseID	Number	Primary surrogate	No
	CourseName	Text		No
	CourseTitle	Text		Yes
	CourseCredits	Number		Yes
StudentResidence	ResidenceID	Number	Primary surrogate	No
	ResidenceStreet	Text		No
	ResidenceCity	Text		No
	ResidenceState	Text		No
	ResidencePostalCode	Text		No
	ResidencePhone	Text		Yes
ServiceProject	ProjectID	Number	Primary surrogate	No
	ProjectDescription	Text		No
	ProjectGrade	Text		Yes

TABLE 1-1 Rules for representing relationships in database tables

Relationship Type	Rule	Foreign Key NULL Constraints
One-to-many	Place the primary key of the entity on the "one" side of the relationship into the table that represents the entity on the "many" side of the relationship.	If the minimum cardinality on the "many" side of the relationship is zero, the foreign key value *can* be NULL; if the minimum cardinality on the "many" side is one, the foreign key value *cannot* be NULL.
Many-to-many	Create a linking table that has a primary key made up of the primary keys of both of the entities in the relationship, and contains other attributes of the relationship if they exist. The composite key values are also foreign keys.	Foreign keys *cannot* be NULL because they are part of the primary key.
One-to-one (both entities with minimum cardinality of zero)	If the relationship exists for most of the entity instances, place the primary key from one of the tables into the other table.	The foreign key *can* be NULL.
	If the relationship does not exist for most of the entity instances, create a linking table made up of the primary keys of both of the entities in the relationship.	Foreign keys *cannot* be NULL because they are part of the primary key.
One-to-one (one entity with minimum cardinality of zero, one entity with minimum cardinality of one)	Place the primary key of the entity with minimum cardinality of zero into the table representing the entity with minimum cardinality of one.	The foreign key *cannot* be NULL.
Mandatory one-to-one	Drop the individual tables for each entity and merge the attributes for each entity into a single table. Designate the primary key of one of the entities as the primary key of the new table and delete the other.	No foreign keys are created.

In general, you should make your database as flexible as possible by making database tables as unrestrictive as possible and keeping not-NULL constraints to a minimum.

Figure 1-20 shows the preliminary table design for the ER model in Figure 1-19. It defines seven tables, one for each entity. Each entity's primary key attribute represents the associated table's primary key and is created using a surrogate key.

Specifying Relationships

The next step of the transformation process is to represent each ER model relationship within the database tables. To correctly represent relationships in database tables, you follow a set of rules based on the each relationship's cardinality. Table 1-1 summarizes the rules for representing each relationship type, and the following subsections discuss each relationship type in detail.

One-to-Many

To represent a one-to-many relationship in a database table, place the primary key of the entity on the "one" side of the relationship as a foreign key in the table that represents the entity on the "many" side of the relationship. For example, in Figure 1-19, Advises is a one-to-many relationship between UniversityInstructor and UniversityStudent. It specifies that one instructor can advise zero or many students and that each student must have one and only one instructor as an advisor. The UniversityInstructor entity is on the one side of the relationship, and the UniversityStudent entity is on the many side of the relationship, so you place the primary key of the UniversityInstructor table, which is InstructorID, into the UniversityStudent table as a foreign key.

Similarly, the Offers relationship is a one-to-many relationship between UniversityDepartment and UniversityCourse, and it specifies that a department can offer zero or many courses and that each course is offered by one and only one department. UniversityDepartment is on the one side of the relationship, so place the primary key of the UniversityDepartment table, which is DepartmentID, into the UniversityCourse table as a foreign key.

How do you determine whether a foreign key value can be NULL? It depends on the minimum cardinality of the entity on the many side of the relationship. If the minimum cardinality is zero, the foreign key value can be NULL. If the minimum cardinality is one, the foreign key value cannot be NULL. A business rule states that every student must have one and only one advisor, so the UniversityStudent entity's participation in this relationship is mandatory and the minimum cardinality of the UniversityStudent entity is one. Therefore, the value of the InstructorID foreign key in the UniversityStudent table cannot be NULL. Similarly, the minimum cardinality of the UniversityCourse entity in the Offers relationship states that a course can have one and only one department, so the DepartmentID foreign key value in the UniversityCourse table cannot be NULL. Figure 1-21 shows how to represent these two foreign keys in the database table design and how to specify that the foreign key values cannot be NULL.

How do you name foreign key fields in tables? Usually they retain the field names they have in their original (parent) tables, except when a new name describes the relationship more clearly. For example, in the UniversityCourse table, the DepartmentID

FIGURE 1-21   Representing one-to-many relationships as foreign keys

Table	Field	Data Type	Key	NULL Allowed
University Student	StudentID	Number	Primary surrogate	No
	StudentFirstName	Text		No
	StudentMI	Text		Yes
	StudentLastName	Text		No
	StudentDOB	Date		No
	StudentImage	Binary		Yes
	StudentAdvisorID	Number	Foreign, references UniversityInstructor	No
University Course	CourseID	Number	Primary surrogate	No
	CourseName	Text		No
	CourseTitle	Text		Yes
	CourseCredits	Number		Yes
	DepartmentID	Number	Foreign, references UniversityDepartment	No

Foreign keys

FIGURE 1-22 Relational tables representing a one-to-many relationship using foreign key values

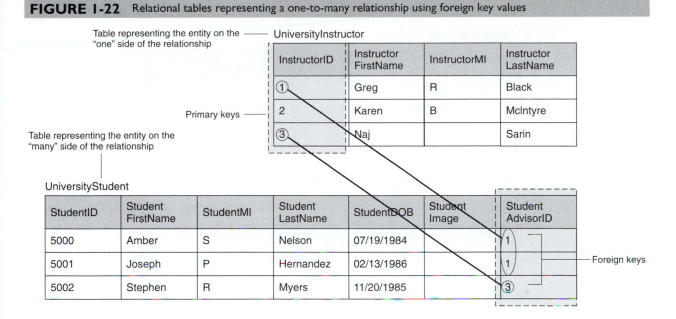

foreign key retains its original name. In the UniversityStudent table, we change the InstructorID field name to StudentAdvisorID to describe the role of the InstructorID in the UniversityStudent record. Leaving the field name as InstructorID might be confusing: someone unfamiliar with the database might wonder how a student could have a single associated instructor.

Figure 1-22 illustrates the UniversityStudent and UniversityInstructor tables populated with data. Note how the foreign key field values represent the table relationships.

Recall that relational database tables must support referential integrity; that is, when a table contains a foreign key, the foreign key value must exist in the parent table. In Figure 1-22, the StudentAdvisorID foreign key values 1 and 3 exist as primary keys in the UniversityInstructor parent table. If these values did not exist in the UniversityInstructor table, the database would be inconsistent.

What happens if you make a mistake and place the foreign key in the table that represents the entity on the "one" side of the relationship? Figure 1-23 illustrates scenarios that can occur when a novice database developer incorrectly represents the Advises relationship by placing the primary key of the many side of the relationship (StudentID) into the table that represents the entity on the one side of the relationship (UniversityInstructor).

Recall from Figure 1-22 that instructor Greg Black advises students with StudentID values 5000 (Amber Nelson) and 5001 (Joseph Hernandez). Figure 1-23(a) represents this relationship in the UniversityInstructor table by delimiting the multiple StudentID values with commas. This is incorrect, however, because it creates a nonrelational database table: in a relational database table, each field must contain a single atomic data value. Figure 1-23(b) creates the relationship by repeating the UniversityInstructor data for each advisee, but this also creates a nonrelational database table because in a relational database table, each record must have a unique identifier, and Figure 1-23(b) repeats the InstructorID value of 1 for each of Greg Black's advisees. In addition, this approach repeats Greg Black's name numerous times, which unnecessarily consumes storage space and opens the possibility for inconsistent data.

FIGURE 1-23   Representing a one-to-many relationship incorrectly

UniversityInstructor

InstructorID	Instructor FirstName	InstructorMI	Instructor LastName	StudentID
1	Greg	R	Black	5000, 5001
2	Karen	B	McIntyre	
3	Naj		Sarin	5002

← Attribute has multiple values (nonrelational)

(a)

UniversityInstructor

InstructorID	Instructor FirstName	InstructorMI	Instructor LastName	StudentID
1	Greg	R	Black	5000
1	Greg	R	Black	5001
2	Karen	B	McIntyre	
3	Naj		Sarin	5002

← Record repeats for each foreign key value (nonrelational)

(b)

Many-to-Many

To represent a many-to-many relationship, create a new database table called a *linking table* or *bridge table,* which represents a unique combination of instances of the two relationship entities. Usually, developers name linking tables with a variation of the name of the many-to-many relationship (such as "CourseEnrollment") or join the names of the two contributing entities to create the table name (such as "StudentCourse").

The primary key of a linking table is usually a composite key made up of the primary keys of both of the relationship entities. You can alternatively create a new surrogate key, such as EnrollmentID, to represent the unique combination. Because each field that makes up the primary key is a primary key in another table, these fields are also foreign keys. Because these fields are part of the primary key, their values cannot be NULL. If the many-to-many relationship has attributes, place the attributes in the linking table.

Figure 1-24 illustrates the design for the CourseEnrollment linking table that represents the EnrollsIn relationship in Figure 1-19. Note that the table design designates

FIGURE 1-24   Design for the CourseEnrollment linking table

Table	Field	Data Type	Key	NULL Allowed
CourseEnrollment	StudentID	Number	Primary, composite with CourseID; foreign, references UniversityStudent	No
	CourseID	Number	Primary, composite with StudentID; foreign, references UniversityCourse	No
	EnrollmentGrade	Text		Yes

FIGURE 1-25   CourseEnrollment linking table and associated parent tables

UniversityStudent

StudentID	Student FirstName	StudentMI	Student LastName	StudentDOB	StudentImage	Student AdvisorID
5000	Amber	S	Nelson	07/19/1984		1
5001	Joseph	P	Hernandez	02/13/1986		1
5002	Stephen	R	Myers	11/20/1985		3

Composite primary key

CourseEnrollment

StudentID	CourseID	CourseGrade
5000	100	A
5000	102	B
5001	100	B
5002	100	
5002	101	
5002	102	

Foreign key references

UniversityCourse

CourseID	CourseName	CourseTitle
100	MIS 290	Intro. to Database Applications
101	MIS 304	Fundamentals of Business Programming
102	MIS 310	Systems Analysis & Design

StudentID and CourseID as a composite primary key and as foreign keys. Because these fields are part of the primary key, their values cannot be NULL. Note that the CourseGrade attribute of the relationship also appears in the CourseEnrollment linking table.

Figure 1-25 illustrates the CourseEnrollment linking table populated with data, along with its corresponding parent tables (UniversityStudent and UniversityCourse). To preserve referential integrity, each StudentID and CourseID value must also appear in its associated parent table.

One-to-One

Representing a one-to-one relationship in a relational database depends on the relationship's minimum cardinalities. Three cases exist:

1. Both entities have a minimum cardinality value of zero.
2. One entity has a minimum cardinality of zero, and the other entity has a minimum cardinality of one.
3. Both entities have a minimum cardinality of one.

The following subsections describe how to represent each case in relational database tables.

One-to-One with Both Entities Having a Minimum Cardinality of Zero Figure 1-19 shows that in the student registration database, the university can optionally issue a laptop computer to a student. Each laptop computer can be issued to only one student at a time. If a laptop computer is not currently in use, then it does not have an associated student. This is a one-to-one relationship in which the minimum cardinality of both entities is zero.

The way you represent this relationship in database tables depends on whether the relationship exists for most of the relationship entities. If it does, place the primary key of one entity in the other entity's table as a foreign key. In Figure 1-26, we place the primary key of the UniversityStudent table as a foreign key in the LaptopComputer table. Our rationale is that it is unlikely there will be as many laptops in inventory or checked out to students as there are total students. The database saves storage space by placing the StudentID as a foreign key in the LaptopComputer table, as opposed to placing the LaptopID as a foreign key in the UniversityStudent table.

What if the relationship exists for only a small number of the entity instances? Suppose that most students do not check out laptops and that most laptops are not checked out to students but are used for other purposes. In such a case, create a linking table containing a composite key made up of the primary keys of both of the entities in the relationship. Because each field that comprises the primary key is a primary key in another table, these fields are also foreign keys. Figure 1-27 shows the resulting linking table for two entities with a one-to-one relationship in which only a small number of entity instances participate in the relationship.

One-to-One with a Minimum Cardinality of Zero for One Entity and a Minimum Cardinality of One for the Other. In the student registration database in Figure 1-19, the Completes relationship has maximum cardinalities of one-to-one. The UniversityStudent entity has a minimum cardinality of zero (a student can optionally complete a service project), and the ServiceProject entity has a minimum cardinality of one (a ServiceProject entity instance must have an associated student). To represent this relationship in a relational database, place the primary key of the entity with the minimum

FIGURE 1-26 Representing a one-to-one relationship with a minimum cardinality of zero for both entities and most entity instances participating in the relationship

Table	Field	Data Type	Key	NULL Allowed
UniversityStudent	StudentID	Number	Primary surrogate	No
	StudentFirstName	Text		No
	StudentMI	Text		Yes
	StudentLastName	Text		No
	StudentDOB	Date		No
	StudentImage	Binary		Yes
	StudentAdvisorID	Number	Foreign, references UniversityInstructor	No
LaptopComputer	LaptopID	Number	Primary surrogate	No
	LaptopBrand	Text		Yes
	LaptopCPU	Text		No
	LaptopYear	Date		Yes
	StudentID	Number	Foreign, references UniversityStudent	Yes

Foreign key ⎯

FIGURE 1-27	Database representing a one-to-one relationship with a minimum cardinality of zero for both entities and most entity instances not participating in the relationship

Table	Field	Data Type	Key	NULL Allowed
UniversityStudent	StudentID	Number	Primary surrogate	No
	StudentFirstName	Text		No
	StudentMI	Text		Yes
	StudentLastName	Text		No
	StudentDOB	Date		No
	StudentImage	Binary		Yes
	StudentAdvisorID	Number	Foreign, references UniversityInstructor	No
LaptopComputer	LaptopID	Number	Primary surrogate	No
	LaptopBrand	Text		Yes
	LaptopCPU	Text		No
	LaptopYear	Date		Yes
StudentLaptop	StudentID	Number	Primary, composite with LaptopID; foreign, references UniversityStudent	No
	LaptopID	Number	Primary, composite with StudentID; foreign, references LaptopComputer	No

cardinality of one as a foreign key into the table that represents the entity that has a minimum cardinality of zero. The foreign key value cannot be NULL.

To represent the Completes relationship, designate StudentID as a foreign key in the ServiceProject table. Since the ServiceProject entity has a minimum cardinality of one (every project must have an associated student), the StudentID foreign key value cannot be NULL. Figure 1-28 illustrates the design of this table.

Figure 1-29 shows tables populated with example data values. Note that all records in the ServiceProject table contain values for the StudentID field because the ServiceProject table's StudentID foreign key values cannot be NULL.

FIGURE 1-28	Representing a one-to-one relationship with a minimum cardinality of one for one entity and zero for the other

Table	Field	Data Type	Key	NULL Allowed
ServiceProject	ProjectID	Number	Primary	No
	ProjectDescription	Text		Yes
	ProjectGrade	Text		Yes
	StudentID	Number	Foreign, references UniversityStudent	No
UniversityStudent	StudentID	Text		No
	StudentFirstName	Text		No
	StudentMI	Text		Yes
	StudentLastName	Text		No
	StudentDOB	Text		Yes
	StudentImage	Text		Yes
	StudentAdvisorID	Number	Foreign, references UniversityInstructor	No

Foreign key

FIGURE 1-29 Database tables with a one-to-one relationship with a minimum cardinality of one for one entity and zero for the other entity

UniversityStudent

StudentID	Student FirstName	StudentMI	Student LastName	StudentDOB	StudentImage	Student AdvisorID
5000	Amber	S	Nelson	07/19/1984		1
5001	Joseph	P	Hernandez	02/13/1986		1
5002	Stephen	R	Myers	11/20/1985		3

ServiceProject

ProjectID	ProjectDescription	ProjectGrade	StudentID
1	Create a database for the Red Cross	A	5000
2	Teach computer literacy class at the Senior Citizen Center	B	5002

Mandatory One-to-One Relationships. The LivesAt relationship in the student registration database in Figure 1-19 links the UniversityStudent entity to the StudentResidence entity. The StudentResidence entity contains attributes representing the student's on-campus street address, city, state, and postal code. Participation in this relationship is mandatory for both entities: each StudentResidence entity instance must have a single associated UniversityStudent instance and vice versa. In this situation, you create a single table that combines the attributes of both entities. Either primary key can serve as the entity's primary key. Figure 1-30 illustrates the design of the table that represents this relationship.

You could name the resulting table either UniversityStudent or StudentResidence. UniversityStudent is the preferred name because it participates in several other relationships and is more descriptive of the combined table. We dropped the ResidenceID surrogate primary key from the StudentResidence entity because it provides no data about the entity and serves only as a unique primary key.

FIGURE 1-30 Combining a mandatory one-to-one relationship into a single table

Table	Field	Data Type	Key	NULL Allowed
UniversityStudent	StudentID	Number	Primary surrogate	No
	StudentFirstName	Text		No
	StudentMI	Text		Yes
	StudentLastName	Number		No
	StudentDOB	Text		No
	StudentImage	Text		Yes
	StudentResidenceStreet	Text		No
	StudentResidenceCity	Text		No
	StudentResidenceState	Text		No
	StudentResidencePostalCode	Text		No
	StudentAdvisorID	Number	Foreign, references UniversityInstructor	

Fields from StudentResidence entity

Representing Nonbinary Relationships

So far, you have learned to represent all of the different connectivity and cardinality configurations for binary relationships. How do you represent nonbinary relationships in database tables? The following subsections explain how to represent unary and ternary relationships.

Unary Relationships   When an ER model contains a unary relationship, use the same rules as you use for binary relationships. Consider the RoomsWith unary relationship in Figure 1-17(a). Recall that this relationship specifies that each student can room with multiple other students. This is a many-to-many relationship; so you create a linking table to represent the relationship, as shown in Figure 1-31(a).

In Figure 1-31(a), the RoomsWith linking table's primary key is a composite key made up of the primary keys of both entities in the relationship. Because two fields in a relational database table cannot have the same name, you must modify the field names so that each is unique. In this example, we change the StudentID field names to StudentIDOne and StudentIDTwo.

The Supervises relationship in Figure 1-17(b) is a unary relationship with one-to-many cardinality and shows that one employee supervises multiple other employees. Recall that for a one-to-many relationship, you place the primary key of the entity on the "one" side of the relationship in the table that represents the entity on the "many" side of the relationship. Since the same table represents both the one and the many sides of the relationship, you must create a foreign key that references the table's primary key. The CompanyEmployee table design in Figure 1-31(b) creates this relationship using a field named SupervisorID that references the EmployeeID field in the same table. This field will contain the EmployeeID value of the employee's supervisor.

FIGURE 1-31   Database tables for unary relationships

Table	Field	Data Type	Key	NULL Allowed
RoomsWith	StudentIDOne	Number	Primary, composite with StudentIDTwo; foreign, references StudentID in UniversityStudent	No
	StudentIDTwo	Number	Primary, composite with StudentIDOne; foreign, references StudentID in UniversityStudent	No

(a)

Table	Field	Data Type	Key	NULL Allowed
Company Employee	EmployeeID	Number	Primary surrogate	No
	EmployeeName	Text		No
	EmployeeDOB	Date		Yes
	SupervisorID	Number	Foreign, references EmployeeID in CompanyEmployee	No

(b)

FIGURE 1-32   Representing a ternary relationship in a database table

Table	Field	Data Type	Key	NULL Allowed
TutoringSession	StudentID	Number	Primary, composite with CourseID and TutorID; foreign, references StudentID in the UniversityStudent table	No
	CourseID	Number	Primary, composite with StudentID and TutorID; foreign, references CourseID in the UniversityCourse table	No
	TutorID	Number	Primary, composite with StudentID and CourseID; foreign, references TutorID in the UniversityTutor table	No
	SessionDate	Date		No
	SessionTime	Time		No
	SessionOutcome	Text		Yes

Composite primary key

Ternary Relationships   Recall that a ternary relationship involves three entities with many-to-many cardinalities. You represent a ternary relationship in a relational database table by creating a linking table with a primary key made up of the primary keys of the three tables that the relationship connects. Consider the TutoringSession ternary relationship in Figure 1-18, which connects the UniversityStudent, UniversityCourse, and UniversityTutor entities and records the dates, times, and outcomes of tutoring sessions. Figure 1-32 shows the table design for the TutoringSession linking table that represents this relationship.

Note that in Figure 1-32, the table's primary key is comprised of the StudentID, CourseID, and TutorID fields and that these fields are also foreign keys. Also, the table contains the relationship attributes of SessionDate, SessionTime, and SessionOutcome.

IN CONCLUSION . . .

In this chapter, you have learned about databases and database terminology, and you have seen relational, hierarchical, and object-oriented database structures. You have also explored the process for designing a database system by creating an entity relationship model and deriving its associated database tables. The next step is to implement the table designs using a relational database. In Chapter 2, you will learn how to create database tables using the SQL Server DBMS.

SUMMARY

- Databases store and organize data that organizations need to retain over time.
- Database applications are programs that enable users to interact with a database. They may be programs that users install on their workstations, or Web-based programs that Web browsers display.
- Early database applications used the data file approach to data processing, in which each application has a separate associated data file. Problems with this approach are that data files tend to contain redundant data which can become inconsistent over time and occupy valuable storage space; also, each application contains redundant programs that handle the basic data-handling procedures of inserting, updating, deleting, and viewing data.
- A database stores all data in a single location and has a single set of programs, called the database management system (DBMS), which performs basic data-handling procedures.
- In a database, an entity is an object about which a database stores data. An entity instance is a single data item of an instance, such as a particular student or a specific course. To minimize storing redundant data, the database stores the data about each entity only once. An attribute is a characteristic of an entity that the database stores. The database contains relationships to show how different records are related.
- In a database, columns are called fields, and represent attributes that refer to individual data values. Each row contains a set of related fields, called a record, for an individual entity instance.
- Early databases used a hierarchical structure, in which related entities have parent-to-child relationships created using pointers. Problems with this approach are that it depends on the characteristics of the physical media on which the data is stored and that custom programs must be written to access the data.
- A relational database creates relationships among records in different tables through key fields.
- A primary key is a relational database table field whose value is unique for each record and serves to identify the record.
- A surrogate key is a field that the database designer creates to be the record's primary key identifier.
- A foreign key is a field that is a primary key in a parent table and that creates a relationship between a parent table and a child table.

- A composite key is a primary key that database designers create by combining two or more fields.
- In object-oriented databases, data items and their behaviors are structured as objects, which are entities in the data application's domain. An object instance is a single unique object, and an object class refers to a collection of similar objects. An object class's state specifies the attributes, relationships, and behavior of all object instances within the class. An object class's behavior contains all the methods (programs) defining the actions that are available to instances within the database application.
- An object-oriented database management system (OODBMS) stores all data and associated operations (methods) together in the database, thus facilitating database application use and maintenance. Some vendors have developed object-relational database management systems (ORDBMSs), which are hybrid relational DBMSs that enable developers to create data objects that they can associate with relational records.
- When developers create new database systems, they usually follow the database development life cycle, which involves the phases of initiation, analysis, design, implementation, and maintenance.
- An entity relationship (ER) model visually expresses data items in terms of entities, attributes, and relationships, and it is often one of the outputs of the database development design phase.
- An ER model describes relationships in terms of cardinality, which specifies the minimum and maximum number of entity instances with which you can associate an entity instance in a relationship, and enforces the business rules of an organization.
- The degree of an ER model relationship describes how many entities participate in the relationship. Most relationships involve two entities, have a degree of two, and are called binary relationships. Other relationship types are unary relationships, which involve one entity, and ternary relationships, which involve three entities.
- To transform an ER model into a set of normalized database tables, you follow a series of rules that specify how to represent each entity and each relationship. You use the ER model cardinality definitions to determine whether foreign key values can be NULL.

KEY TERMS

Analysis phase   Database development phase that analyzes and describes the existing or proposed system and that determines where the system fits in with the other organizational systems

Atomic attribute   Attribute that represents a single data item

Attribute   Characteristic of an entity that a database stores

Basic data-handling procedures   Inserting, updating, deleting, and retrieving data

Behavior   Action and object instances

Binary relationship   Relationship that involves two entities

Bridge table (also called linking table)   Table that represents a unique combination of entity instances from two related entities.

Business rule   Statement or practice that defines the policies and procedures an organization uses in its business processes

Cardinality   Specifies the minimum and maximum number of entity instances with which you can associate an entity instance in a relationship

Child table   Table that contains a foreign key

Composite attribute   Attribute that is made of multiple atomic attributes

Composite key   Primary key made by combining multiple fields

Conceptual design   Database design process that transforms the data dictionary into a data model

Database   Structures that store and organize data that organizations need to retain

Database administrator (DBA)   Person responsible for the day-to-day operation of the database

Database application   Program that enables users to interact with a database

Database development life cycle   Series of steps that define the process for defining the scope of a database system, obtaining system requirements, and then designing, implementing, and deploying the system

Database management system (DBMS)   Program that, among other functions, performs the basic data-handling procedures for a database

Database tuning   Process of adjusting DBMS parameters so a database system performs adequately under transaction loads

Data dictionary   Document that defines all of the data items in a system

Data file approach to data processing   Nondatabase data-processing approach whereby each application maintains a separate data file

Data type   Specification of how a database stores data internally

Degree of a relationship   Specifies the number of entities that participate in the relationship

Derived attribute   Attribute whose value can be derived from another attribute

Design phase   Phase of database development that specifies the relationships among the system data and defines the system applications

Entity   Object about which a database stores data

Entity instance   Single data item of an entity

Entity relationship (ER) model   Data model that visually expresses data in terms of entities, attributes, and relationships

Field   Column of data

Foreign key   Field that is a primary key in another table and creates a relationship between the tables

Hierarchical database structure   Database structure in which all related entities have one-way, parent-to-child relationships

Implementation phase   Phase of database development that implements the database design using a specific DBMS and that deploys applications to users

Initial study   Output of the database development analysis phase

Initiation phase   Database development phase in which developers define the proposed database system and justify the problem or opportunity that the system addresses

Linking table (also called bridge table)   Table that represents a unique combination of entity instances from two related entities

Logical/physical design   Database design process that transforms a data model into a physical database design that developers can implement

Maintenance phase   Database development phase that extends over the life of the system and that involves tasks such as upgrading software, correcting errors, and creating new applications

Mandatory relationship   Relationship in which an entity has a minimum cardinality of one

Many-to-many relationship   Relationship in which multiple instances of the first entity can be associated with multiple instances of the second entity, and multiple instances of the second entity can be associated with multiple instances of the first

Maximum cardinality   The maximum number of entity instances with which a related entity instance can be associated

Method   Program that defines an object's behavior

Minimum cardinality   The minimum number of entity instances with which a related entity instance can be associated, usually a value of zero or one

Normalization   Transformation of the logical data design specified by the ER model into the tables that will be created within the database so the database tables do not have inconsistencies and do not store redundant data

NULL   Undefined data field value

Object   Item in a database that stores both data and information about the data's behavior

Object class   A collection of similar objects

Object instance   A single instance of an object

Object-relational database management system (ORDBMS)   Hybrid relational DBMS that allows developers to create objects associated with relational records

Object-oriented database management system (OODBMS)   Database system that manages data stored as objects

One-to-many relationship   Relationship in which one instance of the first entity can be associated with multiple instances of the second entity, but each instance of the second entity is associated with only one instance of the first entity

One-to-one relationship   Relationship in which one instance of the first entity is associated with one and only one instance of the second

Optional relationship   Relationship in which an entity has a minimum cardinality of zero

Parent table   Table whose primary key is a foreign key in other tables

Pointer   Value that specifies where data is stored physically on a storage medium

Primary key   Relational database table field whose value serves to uniquely identify its record

Project design   Output of the database design process

Project proposal   Output of the database development initiation phase

Record   Individual row in a table

Referential integrity   Premise that when you create a table with a foreign key, all foreign key values must exist in the parent table

Relational database structure   Database structure that stores data in tables and columns

Relationship   Connection between related entity instances

Reserved words   Commands that define database operations

Scalability test   Implementation process in which developers test the database under realistic data and transaction loads

State   Values of an object's attributes and relationships

Surrogate key   Field that a database designer creates to be the record's primary key

Table   Grid with columns and rows that stores data

Ternary relationship   Relationship that involves three entities

Unary relationship   Relationship that involves one entity having a relationship with itself

---

STUDY QUESTIONS

Multiple-Choice

1. _____ are programs that enable users to interact with a database.
   - a. Database management systems
   - b. Database applications
   - c. Web browsers
   - d. Basic data-handling procedures

2. A(n) _____ is an object about which a database stores data, and a(n) _____ is a single data item of an instance.
   - a. Entity, relationship
   - b. Attribute, entity
   - c. Entity, entity instance
   - d. Object instance, method

3. A _____ key must be a _____ key in another table.
   - a. Foreign, primary
   - b. Primary, foreign
   - c. Primary, composite
   - d. Surrogate, primary

4. The _____ phase of database development specifies the characteristics of the database applications.
   - a. Initiation
   - b. Design
   - c. Implementation
   - d. Analysis

5. The value of a(n) _____ attribute is based on the values of other existing attributes.
   - a. Composite
   - b. Object
   - c. Entity
   - d. Derived

6. One-to-many is an example of relationship _____.
   - a. Normalization
   - b. Cardinality
   - c. Degree
   - d. Associations

7. When an entity's minimum cardinality is zero, the entity's participation in the relationship is:
   a. Mandatory
   b. Optional
   c. Represented using a foreign key in the other entity's table
   d. Represented using a linking table
8. You can replace a _____ relationship with a new entity and two one-to-many relationships.
   a. One-to-one   c. Many-to-many
   b. One-to-many   d. Unary
9. To represent a one-to-many relationship in a relational database, you:
   a. Place the primary key of the "one" side of the relationship in the table representing the entity on the "many" side of the relationship
   b. Place the primary key of the "many" side of the relationship in the table representing the entity on the "one" side of the relationship
   c. Create a linking table
   d. Place the primary key of either entity in the table representing the opposite entity

True/False

1. Object-oriented databases are suitable for storing binary data such as sound and video clips.
2. The initiation phase of database development identifies the data items that the data dictionary stores.
3. Referential integrity specifies that when a value exists as a foreign key in a child table, the corresponding value must exist in a parent table.
4. A surrogate key is a value that the DBMS automatically generates to uniquely identify database records.
5. A ternary relationship can equivalently be represented by two one-to-many relationships.

Short Answer

1. What is an object-relational database management system, and what advantage does it provide over a standard relational DBMS?
2. List and briefly describe the five steps of the database development life cycle.
3. List two characteristics of a database entity.
4. When should you use a surrogate key to identify a database entity?
5. How do you represent a ternary relationship in relational database tables?

Guided Exercises

1. **Identifying Relational Database Table Key Fields**
   Figure 1-33 shows the relational database tables for a wholesale bakery. Identify all primary, foreign, composite, and surrogate keys in each database table.
2. **Deriving Database Tables from an ER Model**
   Figure 1-34 shows an ER model for a database for a youth basketball league.
   a. Derive the associated database tables for the ER model.
   b. Label all keys, specify the data type for each attribute, and indicate whether field values can be NULL, using the format shown in Figure 1-32.
3. **Creating an ER Model and Relational Database Table Design: Automotive Repair Shop System**
   Sam's Garage is an automotive repair shop that has asked you to help track their data needs. When a customer brings a car in to be repaired, the system records the customer's name, address, phone number, car make, car model, car year, and VIN. A customer can own multiple cars, and each car is owned by a single customer. After recording the customer information, the service manager completes a work order that contains the date the work is performed, the name of each service performed, a description of each service, and the charge per hour for each service. As the mechanics complete the requested services, they record how many hours each service takes to perform for the given work order. Each work

FIGURE 1-33   Sample database tables for a wholesale bakery

BakeryCustomers

CustomerID	CustomerName	CustomerAddress	CustomerPhone
1	The Candy Man	1234 Main St.	577-1231
2	Sweet Success	231 Harris Blvd.	577-7664
3	Sue's Bakery	1889 20th N.E.	577-9090
4	Ron's Foods	194 Bay View	577-8909

BakeryProducts

ProductID	ProductDescription	ProductPrice
100	Death By Chocolate Cheesecake	15.95
101	Carrot Cake Supreme	12.95
102	Monster Cinnamon Rolls	10.95
103	White Fudge Macademia Bars	5.95
104	Nutty Coconut Pie	8.95

CustomerOrders

OrderID	ProductID	CustomerID	OrderPlacedDate	OrderDeliveryDate	OrderQuantity
1000	100	1	28-Oct-07	28-Oct-07	10
1000	102	1	28-Oct-07	30-Oct-07	5
1002	103	2	28-Oct-07	28-Oct-07	2
1003	100	3	28-Oct-07	28-Oct-07	6
1003	101	3	28-Oct-07	2-Nov-07	8
1003	102	3	29-Oct-07	29-Oct-07	10
1004	102	2	29-Oct-07	29-Oct-07	12
1005	105	3	29-Oct-07	29-Oct-07	15
1006	101	4	29-Oct-07	30-Oct-07	10
1006	102	4	29-Oct-07	29-Oct-07	5
1006	105	4	29-Oct-07	2-Nov-07	10

FIGURE 1-34   ER model for a youth basketball league database

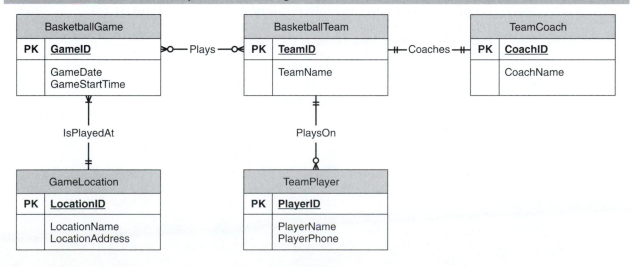

order must list at least one service. Some available services have not yet appeared on a work order.

 a. Draw the ER model for this database. Apply the naming convention specified in Chapter 1 to describe each entity and attribute. Specify maximum and minimum cardinalities on the diagram. Create surrogate keys as needed for each entity.

 b. Derive the associated relational database tables for your ER model. Label key fields, specify attribute data types, and indicate whether field values can be NULL, using the format shown in Figure 1-32.

4. **Creating an ER Model and Relational Database Table Design: Pharmacy System**

Fred's Meds is a chain of pharmacies that has offered to give you a lifetime supply of prescription medicines if you design a database for them. Given the rising cost of health care, you agree. Here is the information that you gather:

- Patient information includes names, addresses, and birth dates. A patient must have an associated prescription before he or she is placed in the database.
- Doctor information includes name and address. Each doctor has a primary specialty (such as pediatrics or orthopedics).
- For each drug, the trade name and formula are recorded. A drug can have one or more generic equivalents, which must be tracked. Some drugs have never been dispensed in prescriptions.
- Each pharmacy branch store has a name, address, and phone number.
- Each pharmacy sells several drugs, and each sells each drug at a different price. For example, the Eau Claire store could sell Prozac for $30, and the Chippewa Falls store could sell the same drug for $25.
- Doctors prescribe prescriptions for patients. Each prescription has a unique number, date, quantity, refill date, and prescribing doctor. Each prescription is for a single drug.

 a. Draw the ER model for this database. Apply the naming convention of using at least two words to describe each entity and attribute. Specify maximum and minimum cardinalities on the diagram. Show the attributes of each entity on the ER model. Create surrogate keys for each entity as needed.

 b. Derive the associated database tables for your ER model. Label all keys, specify the data type for each attribute, and indicate whether or not field values can be NULL, using the format shown in Figure 1-32.

CHAPTER 2

Creating SQL Server Databases and Tables

Learning Objectives

At the conclusion of this chapter, you will be able to:

- describe different database architectures;

- recognize the server and client components of a SQL Server database;

- understand SQL Server database objects;

- use SQL commands to create databases and to create and modify database tables;

- recognize common errors in SQL commands that create database tables.

In Chapter 1, you learned about databases and became familiar with the steps for developing a database application. In the remaining chapters, you will learn how to create databases using the Microsoft SQL Server 2005 DBMS and how to develop database applications using Visual Studio .NET. This chapter describes database architectures and the structure of a SQL Server database. It shows how to use SQL commands to create a SQL Server database and define database tables.

DATABASE SYSTEM ARCHITECTURES

Recall from Chapter 1 that databases store and organize data and that applications are programs that enable users to interact with the database. The database management system (DBMS) is the program that performs the basic data-handling procedures of retrieving, inserting, updating, and deleting data. Before you can begin using the SQL Server DBMS, you must understand its different configuration options. The following sections describe the most common database system architectures in use today: single-tier, two-tier, and N-tier.

Single-Tier Database Systems

In a *single-tier database system*, the DBMS and the database applications run on the same host computer. In the early days of databases, both the DBMS and the applications ran on hosts that were mainframe computers, and remote users connected to them using terminals. (*Terminals* are devices that connect over a network to a host computer, provide keyboard input and video output to users, but do not perform any processing.) Figure 2-1 illustrates a single-tier database system running on a host computer.

Single-tier host systems allow users at separate locations to share data. They also make it easy to deploy new database applications to users: Information system (IS)

FIGURE 2-1 Single-tier database system on a host computer

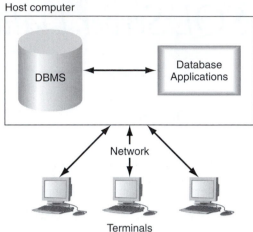

professionals simply install the new applications on the host computer. The host computer provides a single point for maintaining security, and administrators can easily back up and recover data in the event of a system failure.

A primary disadvantage of the single-tier host computer architecture is that the hardware may be expensive and the software is usually proprietary. Applications are usually written by information system professionals, and due to the time needed to write these custom applications, users often do not have the necessary data in a timely fashion. The terminal-based interface also presents a problem: Because the terminals are simple input/output devices, interfaces are usually text-based and command line-driven.

As distributed computing and microcomputers became popular during the 1980s, personal databases such as DBase and Access emerged. With these systems, the DBMS and the database applications run on the same computer. This is usually a single user's personal computer (PC). Figure 2-2 illustrates a single-tier database system running on a PC.

PC databases enable users to control and manage their own data and create applications using graphical user interfaces (GUIs). PC databases usually do not provide strong backup and recovery features, and security is often lax or nonexistent. PC databases can be used in networked environments to share data among multiple users, but these databases do not adequately handle concurrency issues among multiple users. For example, suppose two users simultaneously access an airline reservation database,

FIGURE 2-2 Single-tier database system on a personal computer

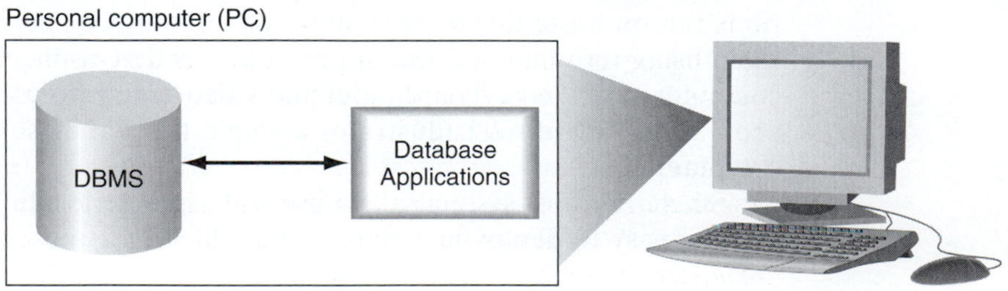

Personal computer (PC)

DBMS ⟷ Database Applications

FIGURE 2-3 Two-tier (client-server) database system

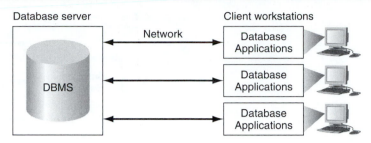

see that a specific seat is available on a flight, and try to reserve it simultaneously. Both users will think they booked the seat, but only the last seat reservation will be stored.

Two-Tier Database Systems

As networked computing became popular in the late 1980s and early 1990s, two-tier systems emerged. With a *two-tier database system,* which is also called a *client-server database system,* the DBMS runs on a server, and the database applications run on client workstations that are connected to the server through a network. A *server* is a computer that shares resources, such as files, printers, and programs, with other computers. A *client* is a program that requests and uses server resources. The DBMS is a program that runs on the server and accepts requests from client applications to view and modify database data. Figure 2-3 illustrates a two-tier database system.

The two-tier architecture distributes processing between the DBMS and the database application to share the processing workload effectively. Users can display and interact with data using the graphical user interface provided by the client workstation. The database server provides a central location to enforce system security and to perform backup and recovery operations.

A problem of the two-tier database architecture is that database applications often become large and complex and must be individually installed on every client workstation. This becomes a formidable task in an organization that has thousands of users. Furthermore, the database applications must be upgraded every time an application changes as a result of changing a business rule encoded in the application. (Recall that a business rule is a statement or practice that defines policies and procedures within an organization's business processes, such as validating customer credit card numbers or determining that a student has taken required course prerequisites.)

N-Tier Database Systems

To help handle the challenge of installing and upgrading applications on client computers, organizations are moving toward *N-tier database systems,* which distribute database application processing among multiple computers. N-tier database applications perform two basic types of services: (1) *user services,* which run on the user's client workstation and include basic display tasks such as displaying and formatting data; (2) *business services,* which run on servers and enforce business rules. Figure 2-4 illustrates an N-tier database system.

Many modern database systems have Web-based interfaces that enable users to view and modify data using a Web browser. This version of an N-tier database system eliminates installation issues on individual users' client computers. All a user needs is a network connection and a browser.

FIGURE 2-4 N-tier database system

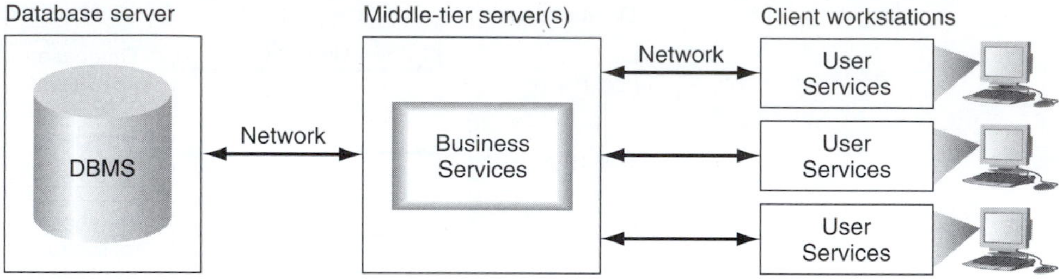

N-tier systems distribute processing across multiple servers, allowing the use of less powerful client workstations. These systems are easier to upgrade than two-tier systems, because most or all of the database application resides on middle-tier servers. A primary disadvantage of this approach is the complexity of managing multiple servers and networks. Additionally, the architecture's complexity introduces several points for potential failures and security breaches.

In this book, you have the option of using the SQL Server DBMS either with a one-tier database architecture in which the DBMS and the client applications run on the same PC or with a two-tier database architecture in which the DBMS runs on a physically separate database server to which your client workstation connects using a network. Aside from minor differences in how you connect to the database, the database and the database applications work the same in either configuration.

SQL SERVER 2005 DBMSs AND CLIENT APPLICATIONS

> **NOTE:** Specific instructions for installing and configuring the DBMS and client applications are provided in the appendixes in the back of this book ("Installing the SQL Server Database" and "Installing Application Development Tools").

Recall that a two-tier or N-tier database system consists of a DBMS and a set of client applications that interact with the server. When installing a database system, a DBA must install the DBMS and then the client applications that allow users to work with the DBMS. The following subsections describe the different versions of the SQL Server 2005 DBMSs and their related client database administration applications.

DBMSs

The SQL Server 2005 DBMS is available at four levels, depending on your installation's needs and your budget:

1. The **Enterprise Edition,** the most advanced and powerful edition, is appropriate for large database installations with a large number of clients and database transactions. This version has no limits on server memory, number of CPUs, and database file size for a server. In addition, it provides the full range of additional features, such as partitioning, parallel index operations, and text mining, that are available with SQL Server.

2. The **Standard Edition,** which is appropriate for many database installations, limits the number of server CPUs to four and supports a maximum of two nodes for

failover database clustering. (Database *clustering* involves using two or more separate servers to share database server duties. A cluster of servers appears on the network as if it were a single server. Failover clustering allows transferring processing from one server in the cluster to another should one become unavailable.) It does not allow partitioning or parallel index operations, and it lacks a few other features provided in the Enterprise Edition.

3. The **Workgroup Edition** is similar in most respects to Standard Edition, except that it limits the number of server CPUs to two and limits the server's main memory to three gigabytes. It has a fewer additional features than the Standard Edition.

4. The **Express Edition** is distributed by Microsoft with application development tools such as Visual Studio 2005 and VB Express. (Recall that Visual Studio is an application development environment. VB Express is a slimmed-down version of Visual Studio that Microsoft distributes at a reduced price.) The Express Edition limits the number of server CPUs to one, the server main memory to one gigabyte, and the maximum database size to four gigabytes (this is the only version that limits the database size). This edition omits functions to support reporting, notification, integration, and a few other features included with the higher editions.

TIP: Microsoft prices all SQL Server 2005 DBMSs except Express Edition per server CPU, with additional costs for client access licenses.

TIP: Microsoft is positioning Express Edition as a replacement for Microsoft Access for single-user database applications and small multiuser databases.

Client Database Administration Applications

When you install a SQL Server 2005 Enterprise, Standard, or Workgroup Edition DBMS, you have the option of installing a set of client database administration tools called SQL Server Management Studio. Another option is to use SQL Server Management Studio Express to perform database administration tasks. The Express version is a free application that has fewer functions than Management Studio but contains a Query Editor feature that enables you to work with and administer a SQL Server 2005 DBMS using SQL queries. You can install either Management Studio version on a client workstation and use it to administer any SQL Server 2005 DBMS running on a networked database server.

This book provides instructions for performing database administration tasks using both Management Studio and Management Studio Express. Chapter 10 specifically addresses database administration and provides additional instructions for performing advanced database administration tasks that can be done only with the full version of Management Studio.

SQL SERVER DATABASE OBJECTS

Within a SQL Server DBMS, a *database object* is a set of logically related tables and programs that belong to a specific database application. From this point forward, we refer to a database object as a database. In general, you place all the tables for a database system in a single database. A DBMS can manage multiple databases. The total number of databases that a DBMS manages depends on the server's hardware configuration and the size of the databases.

A DBA might divide a large database system, such as an airline reservation system or a large e-commerce Web site such as Amazon.com, into multiple databases. Dividing a large system into smaller databases simplifies file backup and management and facilitates specifying user security permissions. For this book, you will store all the database tables that you create in a single database.

When a DBA installs one of the SQL Server DBMSs, the system automatically creates multiple system databases. A *system database* is a database that the DBMS uses to manage internal functions. A new SQL Server DBMS installation contains the following four system databases:

1. **Master** contains system tables. *System tables* contain all the information about the database system, such as the names of all the other databases and their associated tables. You can query the system tables and view useful information, such as system user names or the names of all the foreign key constraints in a database. The DBMS automatically updates the system tables as DBAs and other users create and modify databases. You should not attempt to manually change or delete any objects in the master database.
2. **Model** is a database that serves as a template on which the system creates new databases. As with the master database, you should not attempt to manually change or delete any objects in the model database.
3. **Msdb** contains programs for scheduled tasks that the database performs, such as backups.
4. **Tempdb** is a database that the DBMS uses as a temporary storage space for operations that users perform on other system databases.

Connecting to a Database Instance

When installing the SQL Server DBMS, you create a *database instance,* which is a specific database server process running on a specific server. A single server can theoretically run multiple database instances. During the database server installation process, you can explicitly name the database instance. Alternatively, you can specify that the DBMS is the *default instance,* that is, the DBMS to which users connect when they specify the server name but do not specify an instance name. When explicitly naming a database instance, a DBA must provide the instance name to users to enable them to connect to the DBMS.

TIP: When you install one of the higher-level (non-Express) DBMS editions, the installation process creates an unnamed default instance unless you explicitly name the instance something else. You only need to know the server's name to connect to a default database instance (a database instance name isn't used). When you install Express Edition, the installation process creates a database instance named SQLExpress unless you explicitly name it something else.

When you use any client application with a SQL Server database, you must first create a *connection* to the database instance, which is a communication link between the client tool and the instance. To create a connection, you must specify the server name and, if not connecting to a default database instance, the database instance name.

You can use Management Studio or Management Studio Express to connect to a database instance. Now you will learn how to connect to your database instance.

NOTE: To perform the following steps, you must have access to a SQL Server database and either the Management Studio or Management Studio Express client tools.

Connection Steps

Step 1: *If you are using Management Studio,* click Start on the taskbar, point to All Programs, point to Microsoft SQL Server 2005, and click SQL Server Management Studio.

If you are using Management Studio Express, click Start on the taskbar, point to All Programs, point to Microsoft SQL Server 2005, and click SQL Server Management Studio Express CTP. The SQL Server Express Manager window opens and prompts you to enter a Server Instance.

Step 2: *If you are using Management Studio and connecting to a database instance on your local workstation,* accept the default values for Server Type (which should be Database Engine), for Server Name (which should be the name of the local workstation), and for Authentication (which should be Windows Authentication). Click Connect.

If you are using Management Studio Express and connecting to a SQL Server Express database instance on your local workstation, type "localhost\sqlexpress" in the Server Instance field, and click Connect. (Note that this entry is not case sensitive.)

If you are using either Management Studio version and connecting to a remote database, your instructor must provide you with the correct Server Instance value, which is the name of a remote database server, and with the name of the database instance if it is not the default instance. For example, for a server named CSDEV running a default SQL Server instance, the entry would be csdev. For a server named CSDEV running a SQL Server instance named SQLServerProduction, the entry would be csdev\sqlserverproduction. Open the Authentication list, select SQL Server Authentication, type the Login and Password values that your instructor provides, and then click Connect.

NOTE: Chapter 10 discusses database instance authentication and security options.

Management Studio provides an environment for managing database objects. It has two main windows, as shown in Figure 2-5. The Object Explorer window allows you to select and work with different database objects and other objects. Other windows open depending on the object you select in the Object Explorer. The default Summary window summarizes information about the current object selection, shows details about the selected object, and allows you to view and work with objects. The Express version of Management Studio has similar windows to the full version but supports fewer database administration features.

Recall that a new SQL Server DBMS contains system databases that the system uses to manage its internal functions. Next you will open the Databases node in the Object Explorer and view the default system databases.

Viewing the System Databases

In the Object Explorer, open the **Databases** node, then the **System Databases** node. The system databases appear.

FIGURE 2-5   Management studio windows

Each database managed within a database instance must have a unique name. A database name contains between one and 128 characters and can include any combination of alphanumeric characters, symbols, underscores, and blank spaces. Database names are not case sensitive. It is a good practice to use descriptive names made up of two or more words delimited using upper- and lowercase letters, such as UniversityRegistration or SportMotors. Avoid using blank spaces in database names because they can cause problems in some application development environments.

When you create a new SQL Server database, the DBMS creates files in the database server's file system that the DBMS uses to store and manage the database. The first file created is the *primary data file,* which is a binary file containing all the information about the database, including database data and information about other database objects, such as stored programs. The primary data file also contains links to all the other files in the database. The default name of the primary data file is *DatabaseName*.mdf. For example, a database named UniversityRegistration has a primary data file named UniversityRegistration.mdf. The file does not have to have an .mdf extension, but it makes the primary data file easy to identify.

The second file that the DBMS creates is the *transaction log file.* As users insert, update, and delete database data, the SQL Server DBMS writes these changes to the transaction log file. Periodically, the DBMS issues a *checkpoint,* which is a signal to write the changes from the transaction log file to the data files. Every database must have at least one transaction log file, and a database can have multiple transaction log files. The default transaction log file extension is *.ldf,* and the default name is *DatabaseName*_log.*ldf.* For example, a database named UniversityRegistration has an initial transaction log file named UniversityRegistration_log.ldf. The file does not have to have an .ldf extension, but, again, the extension makes the file easier to identify.

Optionally, a database can use additional files, called *secondary data files,* to assist with storing data. You create secondary files to keep the primary database file from becoming overly large and difficult to manage and to make it easier to create backups and perform recovery operations. The default file extension for secondary database files is *.ndf.* For example, a secondary data file named UniversityRegistration1 would appear in Windows Explorer as UniversityStudent1.ndf. As with other files, a secondary data file does not have to have an .ndf extension, but using it makes the file easier to identify and manage.

Each database data file also has an associated *logical file name,* which is the name that the system uses to reference the file internally. Usually the logical file name is the same as the associated file name, omitting the extension. For example, for the UniversityRegistration database, the logical names of the primary data and transaction log files would be UniversityRegistration and UniversityRegistration_log, respectively.

TIP: By default, SQL Server stores all the database files in the C:\Program Files\Microsoft SQL Server\MSSQL.1\MSSQL\DATA folder on the database server.

CREATING AND MANAGING DATABASES

NOTE: If you are connecting to a remote SQL Server database instance, your user account must have the dbcreator server role to create a new database.

You can use SQL queries to create databases and tables. Management Studio also provides visual tools for creating and modifying databases and database tables. This section describes both approaches.

Creating and Managing Databases Using SQL Queries

It is important to understand how to use SQL commands to create and manage databases because many DBMSs do not have visual tools like those provided with SQL Server 2005, and it is important to understand alternate ways for performing these tasks. An advantage of using SQL commands is that you can store the commands as a text file and then easily create the same or similar databases on alternate servers.

A *query* is a text command that DBAs and database developers use to interact with a database. (In this book, we use the terms *query* and *command* interchangeably.) *SQL* (*Structured Query Language*) is the standard query language of relational databases. The American National Standards Institute (ANSI) oversees standards for SQL. The latest published SQL standard is SQL-2003, to which the SQL queries in this book comply. You can store a series of SQL queries as a text file, then connect to a database server, and run the commands to create a database and its related database tables.

SQL queries fall into two basic categories:

1. *Data definition language (DDL)* creates and modifies new database objects, such as databases, tables, and stored procedures.
2. *Data manipulation language (DML)* performs the basic data-handling operations of inserting, updating, deleting, and viewing data.

In this section, you will learn how to use DDL queries to create and modify databases and database tables. In Chapters 3 and 4, you will learn how to use DML queries to interact with existing database tables.

Every relational DBMS supports a slightly different SQL dialect for DDL and DML operations. Microsoft's extended SQL dialect for the SQL Server DBMS is called *Transact-SQL,* sometimes shortened to *T-SQL.* The following sections describe the SQL and T-SQL commands to create and delete databases and to create, modify, and delete database tables.

SQL queries are text-based and use a combination of reserved command words and user-supplied values for naming objects such as databases, tables, and fields. SQL queries are not case sensitive, but it is a good practice to use upper and lowercase letters as shown in this book to make your commands easier to read. SQL queries ignore line breaks, so you can format commands on multiple lines to make them easier to read.

In this book, we present the general syntax for SQL queries and then provide specific examples. In the general syntax, we present SQL reserved words in all capital letters. We denote placeholders that represent user-supplied values in lowercase italics. We place optional commands or parameters in square brackets. For parameters that can have more than one value, we separate the possible values with the bar (|) symbol.

Creating, Executing, and Saving SQL Queries

You will create, execute, and save SQL queries using the Management Studio Query Editor window shown in Figure 2-6.

To create a query in Management Studio, select the database on which you want to run the query in the Object Navigator and click New Query on the toolbar. A Query Editor window opens that has a tab indicating the name of the database on which the query will run. You then type the query text in the Query Editor window.

To execute a query, click Execute on the toolbar. When you do this, a program called the *T-SQL interpreter* checks the command for syntax errors. If it finds errors, it displays an error message in the Messages window. If it does not find errors, it forwards the query to the DBMS. If the DBMS successfully executes the query, it displays a confirmation message in the Messages pane and the retrieved data in the Results pane. If the query is not successful, the DBMS returns an error message in the Messages pane.

FIGURE 2-6   Management Studio Query Editor window

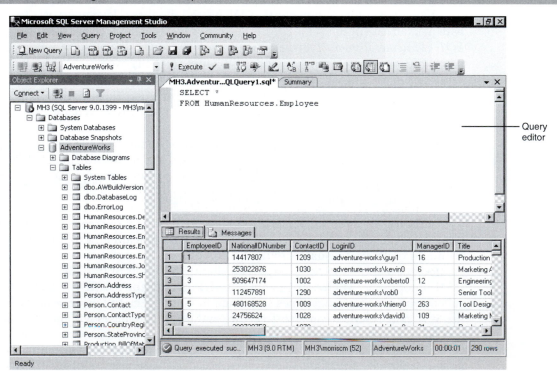

Note that when you click Execute, the Query Editor processes all the text in the Query Editor window. If you write a series of queries and want to execute only one of them, you can highlight the target query and click Execute, and the Query Editor will execute only the highlighted query text.

You can save all the text in the Query Editor window in a text file with an .sql extension. You can then open the file later and continue working with the same queries. To save the query text to a file, click File on the menu bar. A file dialog box opens and prompts you to select a folder path and enter a file name. The file name then appears on the selected tab at the top of the Query Editor window. You can create and work with multiple query files simultaneously.

Creating a Database

To create a new SQL Server database, use the following general syntax: CREATE DATABASE *DatabaseName*. When you execute the **CREATE DATABASE** command with no additional parameters, the DBMS creates a database with default properties: It has a primary database file named *DatabaseName*.mdf, which it stores in the default C:\Program Files\Microsoft SQL Server\MSSQL.1\MSSQL\DATA folder. The initial file size is two megabytes, and it grows in one-megabyte increments as needed. The DBMS creates a transaction log file named *DatabaseName*_log.ldf, which it also stores in the default folder. The initial size of the transaction log file is one megabyte, and it grows in increments that are 10% of its current size as needed.

To specify database parameters with values other than the defaults, use the following general command:

```
CREATE DATABASE DatabaseName
[ON [PRIMARY]]
([NAME = 'LogicalPrimaryFileName',]
FILENAME = 'PathToPrimaryDataFile'
[, SIZE = InitialFileSizeInMBOrKB]
[, MAXSIZE = MaxFileSizeInMBOrKB]
[, FILEGROWTH = MBOrKB|Percentage])]
[LOG ON
([NAME = 'LogicalLogFileName',]
FILENAME = 'PathToLogFile'
[, SIZE = InitialFileSizeInMBOrKB]
[, MAXSIZE = MaxFileSizeInMBOrKB]
[, FILEGROWTH = MBOrKB|Percentage])]
```

As before, *DatabaseName* specifies the database name and is the only required parameter. All the other parameters are optional; if you omit them, the DBMS assigns default values to the database. The ON [PRIMARY] clause specifies the values for the primary data file, including the logical file name, file location, and initial size. The initial file size must be at least two megabytes. If [PRIMARY] is omitted, the first file listed in the CREATE DATABASE statement becomes the primary file. You can optionally include an ON [SECONDARY] clause, which has the same format as the ON [PRIMARY] clause, to create a secondary filegroup. The LOG ON clause optionally specifies the parameters of the transaction log file.

The following steps describe how to create and execute a SQL query that creates a new database named Ch2*yourDatabaseName*. Preface the database name with Ch2 so that it does not conflict with the database that you will create and use in later chapters. You should replace *yourDatabaseName* with a unique identifier, such as your system user name, so that your database name is unique. The steps also describe how to save the query file.

NOTE: If you are connecting to a SQL Express database running on your local computer, this books assumes you will store all database files in a folder named C:\SQLServer\Databases and all solution files in a folder named C:\SQLServer\Solutions\Chapter2. If you have not yet set up these folder structures, do so now. If you are saving your databases or solutions to a different drive letter or folder path, you need to modify the commands in the exercises that specify these folder paths.

NOTE: If you are connecting to a remote database server, do not specify the location or properties of the database files; instead, accept the default locations and values.

Using a SQL Command to Create a New Database

1. *If you are connecting to a SQL Server database on your local computer,* click New Query on the toolbar, then type the following query in the Query Editor. Change *yourDatabaseName* to your unique user name. (The folder paths and filenames should all appear on a single line with no line breaks.)

```
CREATE DATABASE Ch2yourDatabaseName
ON PRIMARY
(NAME = 'Ch2yourDatabaseName ',
FILENAME =
'c:\SQLServer\Databases\
Ch2yourDatabaseName.mdf',
SIZE = 3MB,
MAXSIZE = 50MB,
FILEGROWTH = 2MB)
LOG ON
(NAME = ' yourDatabaseName_log',
FILENAME =
'c:\SQLServer\Databases\
Ch2yourDatabaseName_log.ldf',
SIZE = 1MB,
MAXSIZE = 10MB,
FILEGROWTH = 10%)
```

If you are connecting to a remote SQL Server database, click New Query on the toolbar and type the following query in the Query Editor. This query creates a database that accepts the default database properties. You must change *yourDatabaseName* to your unique user name or an error will occur because a remote server instance cannot create multiple databases with the same name.

```
CREATE DATABASE yourDatabaseName
```

2. To execute the query, click the Execute button on the toolbar. The confirmation message "Command(s) completed successfully" appears in the Messages window.

CAUTION: If the Editor window contains multiple queries when you click Execute, all queries in the Query Editor execute, and an error may occur. If you have multiple queries, select the query you wish to execute, and click Execute.

Another way to execute the query is to right-click anywhere in the Query Editor window, and then click Execute.

HELP: An error will occur if the folders that you specify in the command do not exist or if the folder path is typed incorrectly.

HELP: If you successfully create the database but want to change its properties, you must first delete it. To delete a database, execute the following SQL command: `DROP DATABASE Ch2YourDatabaseName`.

HELP: If you are connecting to a remote SQL Server database instance, your user account must have the dbcreator server role to create a new database.

3. To view your database in the Object Navigator, right-click on the Databases node in the Object Explorer, then click on Refresh. Your new database should appear in the database list.
4. To save the query:
   If you are using Management Studio Express, click File on the menu bar, click Save SQLQuery1.Sql As, navigate to the SQLServer\Solutions\Chapter2 folder, type CreateDatabase.sql as the file name, and click Save.
   If you are using Management Studio, click File on the menu bar, click Save SQLQuery1.sql As, navigate to the SQLServer\Solutions\Chapter2 folder, type CreateDatabase.sql as the file name, and click Save.
5. Click the Close button on the Query Editor window to close the query. (Do not close Management Studio.)

Deleting a Database

The SQL command to delete a database is `DROP DATABASE DatabaseName`. This command drops the database and deletes the database's data files and transaction log files. You cannot drop a database while users are connected to it. However, an administrator can forcibly disconnect users from a database, then drop it.

Creating and Managing Databases Using Management Studio Visual Tools

As an alternative to SQL commands, you can use the Databases node in the Object Explorer window to create new databases and work with existing databases. To create a new database, right-click the Databases node, then click New Database. This action opens the New Database window (Figure 2-7).

The New Database window has the following pages:

- **General,** which allows you to specify the database name, as well as add, delete, or modify data and log files
- **Options,** which allows you to specify a variety of database properties
- **Filegroups,** which allows you to create a SQL Server *filegroup,* a collection of data files for which you can specify common properties to simplify database administration tasks such as backups.

To modify the properties of an existing database, right-click the database node in the Object Explorer and then click Properties. This action opens the Database Properties window shown in Figure 2-8, which has pages that enable you to modify the selected database's properties.

FIGURE 2-7   Management Studio New Database window

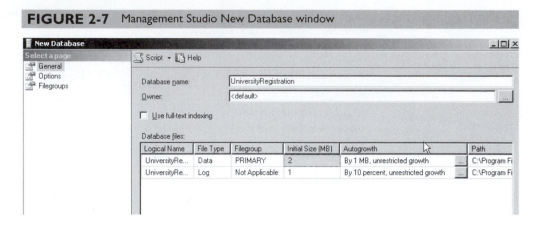

FIGURE 2-8   Management Studio Database Properties window

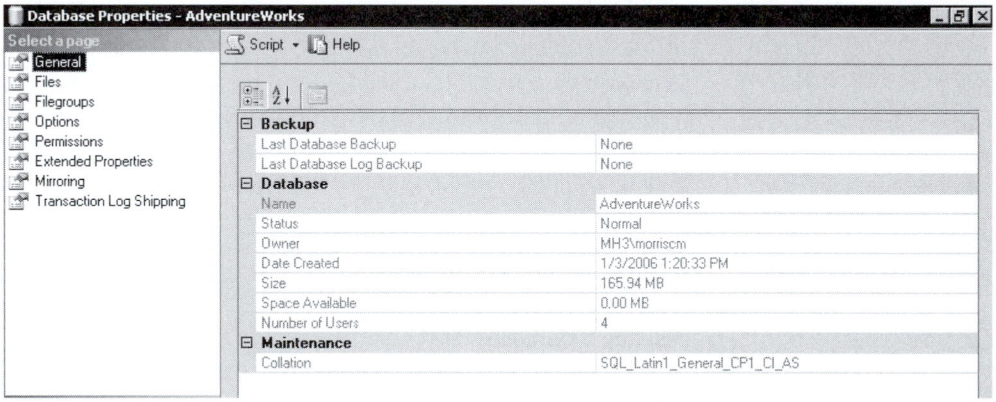

To remove a database, right-click the database node in the Object Explorer and click Delete. This action removes the database and deletes the database's files from the server file system.

CREATING AND MANAGING DATABASE TABLES

In this section, you will learn how to use SQL commands to create database tables. To illustrate these commands, we use part of the table design for the university registration database that you learned about in Chapter 1, as shown in Table 2-1. You will use this table design throughout the rest of the chapter to create database tables. (The next section describes the specific data types that the figure shows.)

Use the following general SQL syntax to create a database table and specify the column names and data types:

```
CREATE TABLE TableName (
Column1Name DataType [(Length)] NULL|NOT NULL [ConstraintSpecification],
Column2Name DataType [(Length)] NULL|NOT NULL [ConstraintSpecification],
. . .
)
```

TABLE 2-1   University registration database partial table design

Table	Field	Data Type	Max. Length	Key	NULL Allowed
UniversityInstructor	InstructorID	Bigint		Primary surrogate	No
	InstructorFirstName	Varchar	50		No
	InstructorMI	Char	1		Yes
	InstructorLastName	Varchar	50		No
	InstructorPhoneNumber	Varchar	15		Yes
UniversityCourse	CourseID	Bigint		Primary surrogate	No
	CourseName	Varchar	50		No
	CourseTitle	Varchar	50		No
	CourseCredits	Tinyint			No
UniversitySection	SectionID	Bigint		Primary surrogate	No
	SectionNumber	Varchar	2		No
	SectionTerm	Varchar	50		No
	SectionDay	Varchar	50		No
	SectionTime	Datetime			No
	SectionMaxEnrollment	Smallint			No
	SectionCurrentEnrollment	Smallint			Yes
	CourseID	Bigint		Foreign – references UniversityCourse	No
UniversityStudent	StudentID	Bigint		Primary surrogate	No
	StudentFirstName	Varchar	50		No
	StudentMI	Char	1		Yes
	StudentLastName	Varchar	50		No
	StudentDOB	Datetime			No
	AdvisorID	Bigint		Foreign – references UniversityInstructor	No
UniversityEnrollment	StudentID	Bigint		Primary - Composite Foreign – references UniversityStudent	No
	SectionID	Bigint		Primary – Composite Foreign – references CourseSection	No
	EnrollmentGrade	Char	1		Yes

In this syntax, *TableName* and *ColumnName* can be between one and 128 characters, can include any combination of alphanumeric characters and the symbols @, #, $, and _, and must begin with a letter. If a table or column name begins with a character other than a letter, or if it contains a symbol other than @, #, $, or _, or if it is a reserved word, you must place the table or field name in square brackets.

TIP: To make your database compatible with the majority of user applications that may access its data, avoid names requiring square brackets to delimit table and field names.

DataType specifies one of the SQL Server data types. You specify the optional *Length* parameter for text data types and for number data types that have a specific width and number of decimal places. The NULL|NOT NULL parameter options specify whether the column allows NULL values, and the optional *ConstraintSpecification* specifies constraints on column values. Note that the command encloses all column name specifications (everything after the *TableName*) in parentheses and separates each column definition from the next by a comma. The following subsections describe the SQL Server data types, show how to use them in column definitions, and how to create constraint specifications.

SQL Server Data Type Definitions

In addition to specifying how the database stores data values internally, column data types provide a means for error checking: When you specify a data type for a column, inserted data values must conform to the data type or an error occurs. For example, you cannot insert the text "Amber" in a field that has a number data type.

In Chapter 1, you learned that the basic database data categories are numbers, text, dates/times, and binary values. The following paragraphs describe the specific SQL Server data types that correspond to these categories, as well as data types for special situations.

Number Data Types

Recall that you use a number data type to store data values that an application uses in calculations, such as prices and quantities. Different SQL Server number data types specify the maximum size of the numbers that each data type can store, whether they can store positive and/or negative numbers, the amount of memory space that the database uses to store each value, and whether they can store numbers that contain decimal fractions. *Integers* are whole numbers that do not contain decimal fractions, and *decimal numbers* are numbers that contain decimal fractions. Table 2-2 summarizes the SQL Server number data types.

Decimal and Numeric   These data types are identical and store numeric values that have a specific maximum width and maximum number of decimal places. When you create a column with the Decimal or Numeric data type, you must specify the *precision*, which is the maximum number of digits that the number can contain, including

TABLE 2-2   SQL Server number data types

Data Description	Data Type	Memory Used (bytes)	Value Range	Sample Column Definition
Decimal numbers of a specific total width (precision) and rounded up to a specific number of decimal places (scale) using the format *DataType* (*Precision, Scale*)	Decimal or Numeric	Varies	-10^{38} to $10^{38} - 1$	`ProductWeight DECIMAL (5,2)`
Decimal numbers that contain as many decimal places as required to express the value	Float	8	$-179E^{308}$ to $179E^{301}$	`StudentGPA FLOAT`
	Real	Varies	$-3.40E^{38}$ to $3.40E^{38}$	`StudentGPA REAL`
Integer with a value of either 0 or 1	Bit	1	0 or 1	`PaidOrderFlag BIT`
Integer numbers	Tinyint	1	0 to 255	`StudentAge TINYINT`
	Smallint	2	$-32,768$ to $32,767$	`CourseID SMALLINT`
	Int	4	-2^{31} to $2^{31} - 1$	`CourseID INT`
	Bigint	8	-2^{63} to $2^{63} - 1$	`CourseID BIGINT`
Money values, rounded to 4 decimal places.	Smallmoney	4	$-214,748.3648$ to $214,748.3647$	`ProductPrice SMALLMONEY`
	Money	8	-2^{63} to 2^{63}	`ProductPrice MONEY`

all digits to the left and to the right of the decimal point. The precision value does not count the decimal point or separator commas as digits. You must also specify the *scale,* which is the maximum number of digits that the number can contain to the right of the decimal point. You specify the precision and scale using the following general format: *DataType*(*Precision, Scale*).

For example, to store data that has a maximum value of 10,000 to an accuracy of four decimal places, the precision is 9, the total number of digits. The scale value is 4, the total number of digits to the right of the decimal point. Use the following data declaration to create this column using the decimal data type: `SampleNumber(9, 4)`.

Float and Real   These data types store numeric data values for which you cannot predict the precision or scale. You typically use these data types to create columns that store calculated values for which a great deal of numeric precision is required, such as financial values.

Bit   This data type stores data values that can have values of either zero or one. Since SQL Server does not support a Boolean data type, you can use the Bit data type to store data that has one of two values, such as True/ False or On/Off.

Tinyint, Smallint, Int, and Bigint   These types store integer data values of varying sizes. To optimize how the database uses data storage space, select the integer data type that is sufficient to store the largest data value that you anticipate storing in the database, but do not use a larger type than needed.

Smallmoney, Money   The money data types store data values that represent monetary units. These values can contain any monetary unit, not just dollars. Using the money data types allows you to perform specific monetary calculations on data values and to format data values using currency symbols.

Text Data Types

Recall that you store character fields, such as names and addresses, and numeric fields, such as telephone numbers and postal codes, as text data. The SQL Server text data types distinguish whether a text data field is fixed- or variable-length and specify the data's coding scheme. A *fixed-length* text field contains a specific number of characters. If the actual data value in the field contains fewer characters, the DBMS pads the text value with blank spaces so that it takes up the total number of required characters. A *variable-length* text field has a specified maximum number of characters, but if the actual data value does not contain the specified number of characters, the DBMS does not pad the value.

Computers encode all data values using the binary digits zero and one, and they use different encoding schemes to represent character values as binary numbers. SQL Server supports *eight-bit character coding,* which represents characters as eight-bit binary values. This coding scheme represents the 26-character Roman alphabet used in the United States, United Kingdom, and Western Europe, as well as most of the special symbols found on computer keyboards. SQL Server also supports *Unicode,* which represents characters as 16-bit binary values. Unicode encodes a much more extensive character set that includes characters from many other alphabets (such as Cyrillic and Arabic) and a large array of special symbols. Data types encoded in eight-bit encoding occupy one byte of memory space for each character. Data types that use Unicode (16-bit) encoding occupy two bytes of memory for each character. Table 2-3 summarizes the SQL Server text data types and their associated data coding schemes.

Char and Nchar   These data types store fixed-width character data encoded in the eight-bit and Unicode coding schemes, respectively. Use these data types to store text data with a specific number of characters, such as two-character state abbreviations. If

TABLE 2-3   SQL Server text data types

Data Description	Data Type	Coding Scheme	Maximum Number of Characters	Definition Example Column
Fixed-width text	Char	8-bit	8,000	`InstructorMI CHAR(1)`
	Nchar	Unicode	4,000	`InstructorMI NCHAR(1)`
Variable-width text	Varchar	8-bit	8,000	`StudentLastName VARCHAR(30)`
	Nvarchar	Unicode	4,000	`StudentLastName NVARCHAR(30)`
	Text	8-bit	$2^{31} - 1$	`StudentEssayText TEXT`
	Ntext	Unicode	$2^{30} - 1$	`StudentEssayText NTEXT`

there is any question as to whether a data value might not have the exact number of characters, avoid the fixed-width character data types, and use the variable-length text data types.

Varchar, Nvarchar, Text, and Ntext   The Varchar and Text data types store variable-width character data encoded in an eight-bit coding scheme, and the Nvarchar and Ntext data types store character data in Unicode. Select the appropriate data type based on the maximum number of characters that the column can store. Specify the maximum number of characters by enclosing the integer value in parentheses. For example, to declare a variable-length text field with a maximum width of 30 characters, use the following column declaration: `StudentLast Name VARCHAR(30)`.

Date/Time Data Types

Recall that you store date values, such as dates of birth or order dates, and time values, such as appointment start times, as Date/Time data types. Table 2-4 summarizes the SQL Server Date/Time data types.

Datetime   This data type stores a combined date and time value as two four-byte integers. The first four bytes contain the date portion of the value, represented as the number of days before or after the DBMS's base date of January 1, 1900. The second four-byte integer contains the time portion of the value, represented as the number of milliseconds after midnight. The time portion of the value displays minutes and seconds as integers from zero to 59 and displays fractional seconds rounded to three decimal places.

Smalldatetime   If your database contains a date/time column that does not require this degree of time precision, you can use the Smalldatetime data type, which stores a combined date and time value as two two-byte integers. The first two-byte integer stores the date portion of the value as the number of days after January 1, 1900, and the second two-byte integer stores the number of minutes since midnight.

TABLE 2-4   Server Date/Time data types

Date/Time Range	Data Type	Memory Used (bytes)	Accuracy	Example Value	Example Column Definition
January 1, 1753, to December 31, 9999	Datetime	8	3.33 milliseconds, rounds values to increments of .000, 0.003, or 0.007 milliseconds	1998-01-01 22:59:59.993	`SectionTime DATETIME`
January 1, 1900, to June 6, 2079	Smalldatetime	4	Rounds values either up or down to the nearest minute	1998-01-01 23:00	`StudentDOB SMALLDATETIME`

TABLE 2-5 Server binary data types

Description	Data Type	Maximum Size (bytes)	Example Column Definition
Fixed-length binary data	Binary	8,000	`StudentEssay BINARY`
Variable-length binary data	Image	$2^{31} - 1$	`StudentImage IMAGE`
	Varbinary	8,000	`StudentEssay VARBINARY`

Binary Data Types

Databases use binary data types to store binary data representing images, sound clips, or data for application files such as word processor documents or spreadsheets. Table 2-5 summarizes the SQL Server binary data types.

Binary   The SQL Server Binary data types can store any type of data encoded as hexadecimal (base 16) numbers, such as text, images, application files, and compressed files. The Binary data type is fixed length and stores binary data values that occupy exactly 8,000 bytes, which is the space occupied by exactly 1,000 hexadecimal characters.

Varbinary and Image   If your binary data may occupy less than 8,000 bytes, use the Varbinary data type, which can store 8,000 bytes or less. If your binary data values may occupy more than 8,000 bytes, use the Image data type, which can store larger quantities of any type of binary data.

Special Data Types

SQL Server provides data types in support of special data values that do not fit into any of the previously described data categories. Table 2-6 summarizes the SQL Server special data types.

Sql_variant   When a user inserts a data value into a column with the Sql_variant data type, the column automatically assumes the correct data type for the given data value. An Sql_variant column cannot assume the Text, Ntext, Timestamp, and Image data types. Use this data type when a column may contain values for which the data type is unknown before you insert the data value. You can then use other built-in functions to determine the data type of the value and process it in the application.

Timestamp   This data type automatically records a binary number that indicates the sequence in which a user inserts or updates a database record. The value is primarily used in DBMS recovery operations for reconstructing the database after a failure. Users cannot explicitly insert or update values in Timestamp columns. If you want to record the actual time at which a record is inserted or updated, create a Datetime column and write a program to record the system time when the record is changed.

TABLE 2-6 SQL Server special data types

Description	Data Type	Maximum Size (bytes)
Stores any type of data	Sql_variant	Varies
Records a sequential value that indicates the order in which the corresponding record is inserted or updated	Timestamp	8
Automatically generates a globally unique number	Uniqueidentifier	16

Uniqueidentifier This data type automatically generates a 16-byte binary value that is guaranteed to be globally unique: No other computer in the world will generate a duplicate value. Use this data type to generate a unique identifier in a networked environment. An example of a Uniqueidentifier value is `0xff19966f868b11d0b42d00c04fc964ff`.

TIP: You should not use a Uniqueidentifier column to create surrogate key values because the values are long and obscure, and they do not follow any patterns that make them meaningful to users. Instead, use one of the larger integer data types such as Int or Bigint, and specify that the column is an identity column, which causes the DBMS to automatically assign a sequenced number to every new record that a user inserts. The section on creating primary key constraints describes identity columns in detail.

Constraints

A *constraint* is a rule restricting the data values that a column contains. There are two general types of constraints: integrity constraints and value constraints. An *integrity constraint* defines a primary or foreign key.

A *value constraint* specifies that a column must contain a specific data value. In SQL Server, value constraints may be (1) *check constraints,* which specify that a column must contain a specific value or range of values; (2) *NOT NULL constraints,* which specify that a column must contain a not-NULL data value; (3) *default constraints,* which specify a default data value that a column contains if the user does not explicitly assign a value; or (4) *unique constraints,* which specify that every value within a table column must have a unique value.

Every table and column constraint has a unique constraint name that the SQL Server DBMS uses to manage the constraints. When you create a constraint, you can supply the name, or you can allow the SQL Server DBMS to supply it. It is a good idea to supply constraint names because SQL Server names are not particularly descriptive or helpful. After you create a table, you might forget which constraints you placed on it, and you would like to be able to review them. Naming conventions enable you to assign descriptive names to constraints to describe the constraint type and the column or columns that the constraint involves. Table 2-7 summarizes the constraint types and associated naming conventions.

Each constraint type has a two-character prefix that describes the constraint type: PK for primary key, FK for foreign key, and so forth. *TableName* specifies the table in which you create the constraint, and *ColumnName* specifies the column. For composite primary keys, the constraint name contains all column names making up the constraint. For foreign keys, the constraint name includes both the table and column of the foreign key, and the table and column that the foreign key references.

Generally avoid creating value constraints (check, NOT NULL, default, and unique) because they enforce business rules. Recall from the discussion of database system architectures that it is a good practice to enforce business rules in a middle tier of an N-tier database system because placing the rules in the database slows down data processing. Additionally, once you populate the database with data, it is very difficult to change value constraint rules in the database.

Creating Primary Key Constraints

Recall from Chapter 1 that a primary key is a field whose value uniquely identifies a table record, and it should use a number data type to avoid spelling errors and capitalization variations. Also, it is a good practice to create surrogate keys, which are numeric fields with no real relationship to the data in a record, to serve as unique primary key identifiers. To create a surrogate key, create a column using one of the larger integer data types (Int or Bigint), and specify that the column is an identity column. With a SQL Server *identity column,* the DBMS automatically assigns a sequenced number to every new record that a user inserts. When you create an identity column in a database table, you specify the *seed value,* which is the starting value, and the *increment,* which is the amount the value increases for every record.

For example, suppose you create a column named InstructorID as a surrogate key in the UniversityInstructor table, and you specify that this column is an identity column with a seed value of one and an increment value of one. When you insert the first record, you do not specify the value for the InstructorID column, and the DBMS automatically inserts the value one. When you insert the second record, you again omit the value for the InstructorID column, and the DBMS automatically inserts the value two.

To designate a column as a primary key directly within the column name definition, use the following general syntax:

```
ColumnName DataType [(Length)]
[IDENTITY[(seed, increment)]]
ConstraintName PRIMARY KEY CLUSTERED
```

In this syntax, IDENTITY creates an identity column for a surrogate key, and optionally specifies the seed and increment values. If you omit the seed and increment values, they default to 1 and 1 respectively. The CLUSTERED keyword specifies that the DBMS creates an index on the primary key column, which improves database performance. *ConstraintName* specifies the name of the constraint using the conventions that Table 2-7 describes. Since this column is designated as a primary key, the DBMS automatically applies to it a NOT NULL constraint, so you do not have to explicitly include it.

TIP: If you do not explicitly name a primary key constraint, the DBMS automatically assigns a descriptive name. The name will begin with the PK__ prefix, followed by the table name, two underscores, and a randomly generated number. For example, for the UniversityInstructor table, the DBMS generates a constraint name that might look like this: PK__UniversityInstructor__71D1E811.

TABLE 2-7 Server constraint types and naming conventions

Constraint Type	Naming Convention	Example Constraint Name
Primary key (PK)	PK_TableName_ColumnName	PK_UniversityInstructor_ InstructorID
Composite primary key (PK)	PK_TableName_Column1Name_ Column2Name	PK_UniversityEnrollment_ StudentID_SectionID
Foreign key (FK)	FK_ CurrentTableNameColumnName_ ParentTableNameColumnName	FK_UniversityStudentAdvisorID_ UniversityInstructorInstructorID
Check (CK)	CK_TableName_ColumnName	CK_UniversityStudent_ StudentGender
NOT NULL (NN)	NN_TableName_ColumnName	NN_UniversityStudent_ StudentFirstName
Default (DF)	DF_TableName_ColumnName	DF_UniversitySection_SectionTerm
Unique (UK)	UK_TableName_ColumnName	UK_UniversityStudent_StudentUserID

FIGURE 2-9   SQL commands to create a primary key

```
CREATE TABLE UniversityInstructor (
      InstructorID BIGINT IDENTITY
            CONSTRAINT PK_UniversityInstructor_InstructorID
            PRIMARY KEY CLUSTERED (InstructorID),
      InstructorFirstName VARCHAR(50) NOT NULL,
      InstructorMI CHAR(1) NULL,
      InstructorLastName VARCHAR(50) NOT NULL,
      InstructorPhoneNumber VARCHAR(15) NULL,
)
```
Primary key

a) placing the constraint definition within the initial column definition

```
CREATE TABLE UniversityInstructor (
      InstructorID BIGINT IDENTITY,
      InstructorFirstName VARCHAR(50) NOT NULL,
      InstructorMI CHAR(1) NULL,
      InstructorLastName VARCHAR(50) NOT NULL,
      InstructorPhoneNumber VARCHAR(15) NULL,
      CONSTRAINT PK_UniversityInstructor_InstructorID
            PRIMARY KEY CLUSTERED (InstructorID)
)
```
Primary key

b) placing the constraint definition at the end of all of the column definitions

Alternatively, you can define a primary key by creating a separate constraint definition at the end of the CREATE TABLE command, after all the column definitions. In this approach, you must still specify the primary key column as an IDENTITY column in the column definition. Figure 2-9 shows examples of SQL commands that create the UniversityInstructor table and designate the InstructorID column as the primary key. The first command does this in the initial column definition, and the second command places the constraint definition at the end of all the column definitions.

Creating Foreign Key Constraints

A foreign key is a column referencing a primary key column in another table. When you create a database table containing a foreign key, you must first create the parent table, which is the table containing the column as a primary key. When you create the table in which the column is a foreign key (the child table), specify the foreign key link. Figure 2-10 illustrates these dependencies in the University registration database design in Table 2-1.

Note that the UniversityInstructor and UniversityCourse tables do not contain any foreign keys; so you create these tables first. The UniversityStudent table contains the AdvisorID foreign key column, which references InstructorID in the UniversityInstructor table. You can create the UniversityStudent table only after you create the UniversityInstructor parent table.

Similarly, the UniversitySection table contains the CourseID foreign key column, which references CourseID in the UniversityCourse table. You can create the UniversitySection table only after you create the UniversityCourse parent table.

Finally, the UniversityEnrollment table contains two foreign keys (StudentID and SectionID), which reference the primary keys in the UniversityStudent and University-Section tables, respectively. Therefore, you can create the UniversityEnrollment table only after creating the UniversityStudent and CourseSection parent tables. A possible order for creating the tables in Table 2-1 is UniversityInstructor, UniversityCourse, UniversityStudent, UniversitySection, UniversityEnrollment.

FIGURE 2-10   University registration database primary key-foreign key dependencies

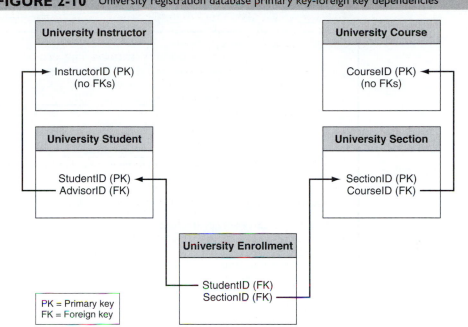

A foreign key column *must* have the same data type as the primary key column in the parent table. You do not specify a foreign key column as an identity column because the DBMS does not generate the foreign key values but instead references the values in the parent table. The following general syntax designates a column as a foreign key within the column definition:

```
ColumnName DataType [(Length)] NOT NULL|NULL
CONSTRAINT ConstraintName
FOREIGN KEY
REFERENCES ParentTable(ParentColumnName)
```

In this syntax, *ParentTable* is the name of the table in which the column is a primary key, and *ParentColumnName* is the name of the referenced column within the parent table. The first SQL command in Figure 2-11 creates the UniversityStudent table and creates a foreign key reference to the InstructorID column in the UniversityInstructor table directly in the AdvisorID column definition. You can also specify a foreign key constraint after the column definitions. The second command in Figure 2-11 creates the UniversityStudent table and defines the AdvisorID foreign key by placing the foreign key constraint definition at the end of the column definitions.

CAUTION: The commands in Figure 2-11 would fail if you tried to execute them before creating the UniversityInstructor table because they reference the UniversityInstructor table in their foreign key constraint.

TIP: When you create a foreign key constraint, the data type in the column in which the value is a foreign key must exactly match the data type in the column in which the value is a primary key.

FIGURE 2-11 SQL command to create a foreign key constraint outside the column definitions

```
CREATE TABLE UniversityStudent (
        StudentID BIGINT IDENTITY PRIMARY KEY CLUSTERED,
        StudentFirstName VARCHAR (50) NOT NULL,
        StudentMI CHAR (1) NULL,
        StudentLastName VARCHAR (50) NOT NULL,
        StudentDOB DATETIME,
        AdvisorID BIGINT NOT NULL
                CONSTRAINT
                        FK_UniversityStudentAdvisorID_UniversityInstructorInstructorID
                REFERENCES UniversityInstructor(InstructorID)
)
```
Foreign key

(a) Specifying a foreign key constraint within a column definition

```
CREATE TABLE UniversityStudent (
        StudentID BIGINT IDENTITY PRIMARY KEY CLUSTERED,
        StudentFirstName VARCHAR (50) NOT NULL,
        StudentMI CHAR (1) NULL,
        StudentLastName VARCHAR (50) NOT NULL,
        StudentDOB DATETIME,
        AdvisorID BIGINT NOT NULL,
        CONSTRAINT
                FK_UniversityStudentAdvisorID_UniversityInstructorInstructorID
                FOREIGN KEY(AdvisorID)
        REFERENCES UniversityInstructor(InstructorID)
)
```
Foreign key

(b) Specifying a foreign key constraint outside of a column definition

Creating a Composite Key

A composite key is a primary key consisting of two or more columns to create a unique identifier and that usually the fields defining a composite key are also foreign keys that reference other tables. Because a composite key is made up of multiple columns, you cannot define it in a single column definition; rather, you must define it after you define the columns that it includes. Use the following general syntax to designate multiple columns as a composite key:

```
CONSTRAINT ConstraintName
PRIMARY KEY CLUSTERED
(Column1Name, Column2Name, ... )
```

In this syntax, you list the columns constituting the primary key in parentheses and separate each column name with a comma. The command in Figure 2-12 creates the UniversityEnrollment table and defines the composite key made up of the StudentID and SectionID columns. (Notice that these columns also contain foreign key references; so you would have to create the UniversityStudent and UniversitySection tables before successfully executing this command.)

Creating Check Constraints

Check constraints specify that a numeric column's data value falls within a specific numeric range (such as between zero and 100) or that a text column's data value is from a set of allowable values (such as M or F). A check constraint can serve to confirm that a text column that requires numeric characters, such as a telephone number, actually contains numeric characters.

FIGURE 2-12   SQL command to create a composite primary key

```
CREATE TABLE UniversityEnrollment (
      StudentID BIGINT NOT NULL,
      SectionID BIGINT NOT NULL,
      CourseGrade CHAR(1) NULL,
      CONSTRAINT PK_UniversityEnrollment
            PRIMARY KEY CLUSTERED(StudentID, SectionID),
      CONSTRAINT
            FK_UniversityEnrollmentStudentID_UniversityStudentStudentID
            FOREIGN KEY (StudentID) REFERENCES
            UniversityStudent(StudentID),
      CONSTRAINT
            FK_UniversityEnrollmentSectionID_UniversitySectionSectionID
            FOREIGN KEY (SectionID)
            REFERENCES CourseSection(SectionID)
)
```

Composite key

To create a check constraint, create an expression that the DBMS can evaluate as either true or false. The expression has the following format:

```
ColumnName Operator Value
```

In this expression, *ColumnName* specifies the column on which you place the check constraint. *Operator* specifies the nature of the constraint, and *Value* specifies the constraint value or values.

Table 2-8 summarizes the SQL Server check constraint operators and provides example check constraints. Use the basic arithmetic operators of greater than (>), less than (<), greater than or equal to (>=), and less than or equal to (<=) to place a constraint on a number value. Use the BETWEEN operator to specify that a number value must fall within a specific range and the IN operator to specify that a text value must be within a certain set of choices. Use the LIKE operator to confirm that each character within a text field contains numeric characters and/or embedded formatting characters. When you create a check constraint using LIKE, always place the expression within single quotation marks on the same editor line, or an error will occur.

You can use the AND and OR logical operators to combine check constraint expressions. Place each expression in parentheses. If you join the expressions with the AND operator, both expressions must be true for the check condition to be true. If you

TABLE 2-8   SQL Server check condition operators

Description	*Operator(s)*	*Example*
Restricts numeric data values to a specific range	>, <, >=, <= BETWEEN	CourseCredits > 0 CourseCredits BETWEEN 0 and 10
Limits text values to a specific set of choices	IN	StudentGender IN ('M', 'F')
Specifies that a text field contains numeric characters with embedded formatting characters, such as (555) 555-5555	LIKE	StudentPhoneNumber LIKE '([0-9][0-9][0-9]) [0-9][0-9][0-9] – [0-9][0-9][0-9][0-9]'

FIGURE 2-13 SQL commands to create check constraints

```
CREATE TABLE UniversityCourse (
        CourseID BIGINT IDENTITY PRIMARY KEY CLUSTERED,
        CourseName VARCHAR (50) NOT NULL,
        CourseTitle VARCHAR (50) NOT NULL,
        CourseCredits TINYINT NOT NULL
                CONSTRAINT CK_UniversityCourse_CourseCredits
                CHECK (CourseCredits > 0 AND CourseCredits < 10)
)
```
Check constraint

(a) Check constraint within a column definition

```
CREATE TABLE UniversityCourse (
        CourseID BIGINT IDENTITY PRIMARY KEY CLUSTERED,
        CourseName VARCHAR (50) NOT NULL,
        CourseTitle VARCHAR (50) NOT NULL,
        CourseCredits TINYINT NOT NULL,
        CONSTRAINT CK_UniversityCourse_CourseCredits
                CHECK (CourseCredits > 0 AND CourseCredits < 10)
)
```
Check constraint

(b) Check constraint outside of a column definition

join the expressions with the OR operator, either expression may be true for the check condition to be true. For example, the following check condition evaluates whether the CourseCredit column value is greater than zero and less than 10 by combining two expressions:

```
(CourseCredits > 0) AND (CourseCredits < 10).
```

To define a check constraint directly within a column definition, use the following general syntax:

```
ColumnName DataType [(Length)]
CONSTRAINT ConstraintName CHECK (expression)
```

The first command in Figure 2-13 creates the UniversityCourse table. It contains a check constraint specifying that the CourseCredits column must contain an integer greater than zero and less than 10 using a constraint definition in the column definition. The second command creates the same check condition constraint but defines the constraint after all the table column definitions.

Creating Unique Constraints

Unique constraints ensure that the data value for every row in a table column is unique. You might create a unique constraint on a column that contains student database system user names for logging on to a database system. When you create a unique constraint for a new table, the DBMS ensures that all data values entered by users are unique. If a user attempts to insert a duplicate name, an error occurs. If you create a unique constraint on a column in an existing table, the DBMS checks the existing data to confirm that it complies with the constraint. If it does not comply, you must modify the data before you can add the constraint. Primary key fields automatically have unique constraints; so you do not need to create them explicitly.

Usually you define unique constraints directly within the column definition using the following general syntax:

```
ColumnName DataType [(Length)]
CONSTRAINT ConstraintName UNIQUE
```

Figure 2-14 shows the SQL command to create the UniversityInstructor table. It contains a unique constraint to specify that every instructor must have a unique value in the InstructorPhoneNumber column.

Creating Not-NULL and Default Constraints

If a user does not specify a data value for a specific column when inserting a new table record, SQL Server automatically inserts a NULL value (indicating that the value is unknown or undefined). If a table specification indicates that a column value cannot be NULL, the DBMS displays an error message that prompts the user to specify a value for the column when trying to save the record.

To avoid this scenario, you can specify that a column has a *default value,* which is the most likely value that the column will contain. For example, you might assign a default value of zero to numeric columns or the text string "Not Available" to text columns. When the user inserts a record with a NULL value, the DBMS automatically inserts the default value. You should not specify default values for fields in which it is imperative that the user enter an actual value. Figure 2-15 illustrates how to define that the default value for the CurrentEnrollment field in the UniversityEnrollment table is zero.

FIGURE 2-14 SQL commands creating a unique constraint

```
CREATE TABLE UniversityInstructor (
InstructorID BIGINT IDENTITY
CONSTRAINT PK_UniversityInstructorInstructorID
PRIMARY KEY CLUSTERED,
InstructorFirstName VARCHAR(50) NOT NULL,
InstructorMI CHAR(1) NULL,
InstructorLastName VARCHAR(50) NOT NULL,
InstructorPhoneNumber VARCHAR(15) NOT NULL
CONSTRAINT UK_UniversityInstructor_InstructorPhoneNumber
UNIQUE
)
```
Unique constraint

(a) Specifying a unique constraint within a column definition

```
CREATE TABLE UniversityInstructor (
InstructorID BIGINT IDENTITY
CONSTRAINT PK_UniversityInstructorInstructorID
PRIMARY KEY CLUSTERED,
InstructorFirstName VARCHAR (50) NOT NULL,
InstructorMI CHAR(1) NULL,
InstructorLastName VARCHAR(50) NOT NULL,
InstructorPhoneNumber VARCHAR(15) NOT NULL,
CONSTRAINT UK_UniversityInstructor_InstructorPhoneNumber
UNIQUE (InstructorPhoneNumber)
)
```
Unique constraint

(b) Specifying a unique constraint outside of a column definition

FIGURE 2-15 SQL command creating a column default value

```
CREATE TABLE UniversitySection (
    SectionID BIGINT IDENTITY PRIMARY KEY CLUSTERED,
    SectionNumber VARCHAR (2) NOT NULL,
    SectionTerm VARCHAR (50) NOT NULL,
    SectionDay VARCHAR (50) NOT NULL,
    SectionTime DATETIME NOT NULL,
    SectionMaxEnrollment SMALLINT NOT NULL,
    SectionCurrentEnrollment SMALLINT NOT NULL DEFAULT 0,    ──── Default
                                                                  constraint
    CourseID BIGINT NOT NULL
    CONSTRAINT
            FK_UniversityCourseCourseID_UniversitySectionCourseID
            REFERENCES UniversityCourse(CourseID)
)
```

Creating Database Tables

As with creating new databases, it is useful to understand the SQL commands for creating database tables because you can use them (with slight variations for data types) with any DBMS and because you may be working with a database that does not provide visual tools for creating tables. In SQL Server, before you can execute a SQL query to create or work with tables in a database, you must specify the target database. There are three ways to do this:

1. Select the target database in the Object Explorer.
2. Select the target database in the database list on the Management Studio toolbar.
3. Execute the T-SQL USE command.

The USE command has the following general syntax:

```
USE DatabaseName
```

The following steps show how to use SQL commands to create the UniversityStudent and UniversityInstructor tables in Table 2-1. (The other tables will be created in the Guided Exercises at the end of the chapter.) The steps consist of creating a new query file, typing the commands to use the Ch2*yourDatabaseName* database that you created earlier, creating the tables, and executing the queries.

1. Click the New Query button on the toolbar. A new tab appears in the Query Editor window.
2. Type the following commands to instruct Query Editor to use your database and then create the UniversityInstructor table. Be sure to substitute the name of the database you created earlier for Ch2*yourDatabaseName*.

```
USE Ch2yourDatabaseName
CREATE TABLE UniversityInstructor (
  InstructorID BIGINT IDENTITY
  CONSTRAINT PK_UniversityInstructor_InstructorID
  PRIMARY KEY CLUSTERED (InstructorID),
  InstructorFirstName VARCHAR(50) NOT NULL,
  InstructorMI CHAR(1) NULL,
  InstructorLastName VARCHAR(50) NOT NULL,
  InstructorPhoneNumber VARCHAR(15) NULL
)
```

3. Execute the query. The confirmation message "Command(s) completed successfully" should appear in the Messages pane.

HELP: If the confirmation message does not appear, read "Troubleshooting SQL Queries" later in this chapter.

---

4. Save the query file as CreateTables.sql in your SQLServer\Solutions\Chapter2 folder.

5. Insert two blank lines below your current CREATE TABLE command, then type the following command to create the UniversityStudent table:

```
CREATE TABLE UniversityStudent (
  StudentID BIGINT IDENTITY
    CONSTRAINT PK_UniversityStudent_StudentID
    PRIMARY KEY CLUSTERED,
  StudentFirstName VARCHAR (50) NOT NULL,
  StudentMI CHAR (1) NULL,
  StudentLastName VARCHAR (50) NOT NULL,
  StudentDOB DATETIME,
  AdvisorID BIGINT NOT NULL
    CONSTRAINT FK_UStudentAdvisorID_UInstructorInstructorID
    REFERENCES UniversityInstructor(InstructorID)
)
```

CAUTION: Constraint names must all appear on a single line, with no hard returns or spaces anywhere in the name. You may abbreviate constraint names to make them shorter, as shown above, as long as their table and field names are clearly defined.

---

6. Select the command you just entered, and then click Execute on the toolbar to execute the selection. The confirmation message "Command(s) completed successfully" should appear in the Messages pane.

TIP: You can also run a query or a selection by pressing F5 or by right-clicking anywhere in the Query Editor window and then clicking Execute.

---

7. Save your file and close it in the Query Editor window.

Deleting Database Tables

Compared with creating database tables, deleting them is a piece of cake. The basic syntax to delete a database table is:

```
DROP TABLE TableName
```

When you delete a table, the system automatically removes the table and all its associated data. The only tricky part is that you cannot delete a parent table in a foreign key relationship unless you delete the child table first. For example, recall that a foreign key relationship exists between the UniversityInstructor and UniversityStudent table, in which UniversityInstructor is the parent table and UniversityStudent is the child table. You cannot delete the UniversityInstructor table unless you delete the UniversityStudent table first.

Modifying Existing Database Tables

In Chapter 1 you learned that it is very important to create a correct and complete database design so that you do not need to alter the structure of your database after you or your project team members create database applications. Sometimes, however, you find that you omitted a data item or that you need to change the properties of an existing column. SQL Server supports the `ALTER TABLE` SQL command, which enables you to modify existing database tables by adding new columns, deleting columns, and altering the properties of existing columns. SQL Server also supports special commands that allow you to rename database tables and table columns. The following subsections describe these commands.

Adding New Database Columns to an Existing Table

The general syntax to add new columns to an existing database table is:

```
ALTER TABLE TableName
ADD Column1Name DataType [(Length)]
ConstraintDefinition(s) ,
Column2Name DataType [(Length)]
ConstraintDefinition(s),
. . .
```

When you add a new column to an existing table, you must specify either that the column allows NULL values or that it has a default value. If the table already contains records, the existing records will have NULL values for the new column, which violates a NOT NULL constraint. If applications have already been written to retrieve, insert, delete, or update data in the database, you probably have to make some code revisions to keep the applications working after making this type of database modification. The following command adds columns named InstructorUserName and InstructorPassword to the UniversityInstructor table:

```
ALTER TABLE UniversityInstructor
ADD InstructorUserName varchar(30) NULL,
InstructorPassword varchar(30) NULL
```

Modifying Properties of Existing Database Columns

You can modify the data type and length properties of existing columns using the following general syntax:

```
ALTER TABLE TableName
ALTER COLUMN ColumnName
    NewDataType [(Length)][NULL|NOT NULL]
```

The following command changes the data type of the CourseCredits column in the UniversityCourse table to Smallint:

```
ALTER TABLE UniversityCourse
ALTER COLUMN CourseCredits SMALLINT NOT NULL
```

If you need to modify the data type or length of a column that is either the parent column or child column in a foreign key relationship, you must first drop the foreign key constraint. Then you modify the column properties and add the foreign key constraint back to the table. (You will learn how to do this in a later section.)

Deleting Table Columns

The following command deletes columns from a database table:

```
ALTER TABLE TableName
DROP Column1Name, Column2Name, . . .
```

Use this command with caution: As soon as it executes, the column and all its data disappear, and you get no second chances. If a column you wish to drop has an associated foreign key constraint, you must first delete the constraint before dropping the column. As with adding columns, if applications exist that retrieve, insert, delete, or update data in the database, you probably have to make code revisions to keep the applications working after dropping columns from a table.

Adding and Deleting Constraints

To add a new constraint to a table, use the following command:

```
ALTER TABLE TableName [WITH NOCHECK]
ADD CONSTRAINT
ConstraintName ConstraintDefinition
```

In this syntax, the WITH NOCHECK option allows you to add a constraint that the DBMS ignores for existing table data but enforces for all records that users insert in the future. *ConstraintName* is the name of the new constraint, based on the constraint naming conventions in Table 2-7. *ConstraintDefinition* defines the constraint, using the syntax you learned earlier for creating constraints outside of column definitions. For example, the following command adds a check constraint to the InstructorPhoneNumber column in the UniversityInstructor table specifying that all data values inserted from this point must be formatted as phone numbers using the format (999)999-9999:

```
ALTER TABLE UniversityInstructor WITH NOCHECK
ADD CONSTRAINT CK_UInstructorPhoneNumber
CHECK (InstructorPhoneNumber LIKE
'([0-9][0-9][0-9]) [0-9][0-9][0-9] - [0-9][0-9][0-9][0-9]')
```

CAUTION: When you create a check constraint using the LIKE operator always place the values within single quotation marks on the same editor line, or an error will occur.

To modify a table constraint, delete the existing constraint and then add a new one with the desired properties. To delete a constraint, use the following syntax:

```
ALTER TABLE TableName
DROP CONSTRAINT ConstraintName
```

In this syntax, *ConstraintName* is the name of the constraint, as specified when you created the table. Use the following command to drop the check constraint on the InstructorPhoneNumber column:

```
ALTER TABLE UniversityInstructor
DROP CONSTRAINT CK_UInstructorPhoneNumber
```

FIGURE 2-16   Retrieving primary and foreign key constraint names

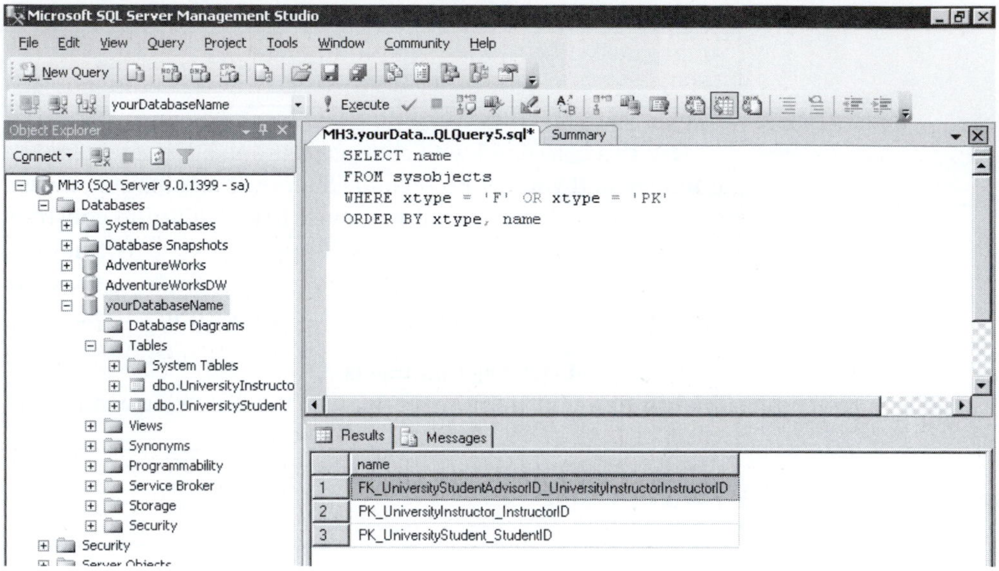

You can find the names of the constraints in your database using the following SQL query:

```
SELECT name
FROM sysobjects
WHERE xtype = 'F' OR xtype = 'PK'
ORDER BY xtype, name
```

This command retrieves data from a system table named sysobjects that manages the internal workings of your database. (You will learn more about retrieving data using SQL queries in Chapter 3.) Figure 2-16 shows how the command retrieves the name of all the current database's foreign and primary key constraints.

Renaming Database Tables and Columns

SQL Server has over 1,200 *system stored procedures (SPs)* to retrieve information about the database and perform administrative tasks. The SP_RENAME stored procedure allows you to rename database objects, including table and column names. Changing existing table and column names is a risky business that you should avoid because these operations almost surely break existing database applications (e.g., it causes them to crash or fail in a variety of ways). The following sections present the syntax to perform these operations; however, we hope you do not have to use them after applications have been written that use the affected database. If you do use them, expect to spend a good amount of time rewriting the applications.

TIP: You can view all the SQL Server SPs by opening the following nodes in the Object Explorer: System Databases, master, Programmability, Stored Procedures, System Stored Procedures.

The basic syntax for the command to rename a database table is:

```
SP_RENAME 'FormerTableName', 'NewTableName'
```

Use the following command to change the name of the UniversityInstructor table to IronwoodFaculty:

```
SP_RENAME 'UniversityInstructor', 'UniversityFaculty'
```

The basic syntax for the command to rename a table column is:

```
SP_RENAME 'TableName.FormerColumnName', 'NewColumnName'
```

In this command, you must preface the existing column name with the table name so that the DBMS recognizes the table in which the column resides. Use the following command to change the name of the PostalCode column in the UniversityStudent database to StudentPostalCode:

```
SP_RENAME 'UniversityStudent.PostalCode', 'StudentPostalCode'
```

You cannot rename a parent table in a foreign key constraint, and you cannot rename a table column if it contains any constraints. If you want to perform these operations, you must first drop the constraint(s).

TROUBLESHOOTING SQL COMMANDS

Despite your best intentions, your SQL commands sometime contain errors. The following subsections describe common errors that database developers encounter when running SQL commands to create and delete databases and database tables.

Syntax Errors

A *syntax error* is an error that occurs when a command's syntax does not follow a programming language's syntax rules. Examples of common SQL syntax rules include misspelling reserved words (e.g., CREATE as CRAETE) or making an error in the structure of a command (e.g., omitting the comma between field names in the CREATE TABLE command). Figure 2-17 shows an example of an error message that appears when a command contains a syntax error.

In Figure 2-17, the command defining the InstructorFirstName column does not end with a comma to separate it from the next column definition. The error message in the Output window ("Incorrect syntax near 'InstructorMI'") indicates that the T-SQL interpreter encounters the error in the command defining the next column. Often, syntax errors do not occur exactly on the command that the interpreter reports but rather on a previous line.

Sometimes a command contains an error that you just cannot locate. When this happens, simplify the command to get something working and then add on to it. For example, if the command in Figure 2-17 contains an error that you cannot locate, attempt to create the table with only the first column (InstructorID). If this works, you know the InstructorID column definition is not causing the problem. Then drop the table, and create it again, using the definitions for the first two columns. If this works, you know the definitions for the first two columns are all right. Drop the table again, and repeat the process until you find the column definition causing the error.

FIGURE 2-17   Message describing a SQL syntax error

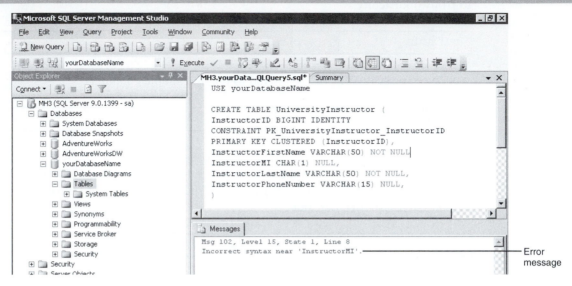

Attempting to Drop the Parent Table in a Foreign Key Relationship

Recall that you cannot drop a parent table unless you first drop the child table containing the foreign key column or disable the foreign key constraint. (A table is the parent table in a foreign key relationship when its primary key occurs as a foreign key in a child table.) Figure 2-18 shows the error message that appears when a user attempts to drop the parent table in a foreign key relationship.

In Figure 2-18, the user attempts to drop the UniversityInstructor table. Recall that the UniversityStudent table references the InstructorID column in the UniversityInstructor table as a foreign key. Therefore, an error occurs. To avoid the

FIGURE 2-18   Error that occurs when trying to drop the parent table in a foreign key relationship

FIGURE 2-19   Error that occurs when attempting to create a table that already exists

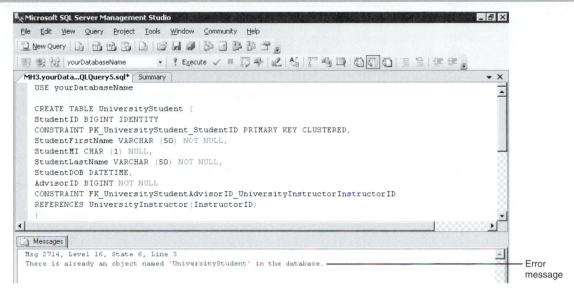

error, drop the UniversityStudent table and then drop the UniversityInstructor table. Alternatively, disable the foreign key constraint in the UniversityStudent table, and then drop the UniversityInstructor table.

Attempting to Create a Table That Already Exists

In a specific database, every table must have a unique name. Sometimes users attempt to create the same table twice. When they do, the error shown in Figure 2-19 occurs.

This error may occur when you forget to execute the USE *DatabaseName* command before attempting to create a new table, and the DBMS attempts to create the table in a different database than you intended. It may also happen if you create a table and then attempt to create it again. You can view the tables in a database by selecting the database's Tables node in the Object Explorer, but remember to refresh the display by right-clicking on the database's Tables node, then clicking on Refresh.

A similar error occurs when a user attempts to drop a table that does not exist. Again, use the Object Explorer to check the existing tables in your database before you attempt to drop the table, and always execute the USE command to specify the database containing the table.

IN CONCLUSION . . .

In this chapter, you learned that databases can use single-tier, two-tier, or N-tier architectures to distribute processing across client and server workstations. You became familiar with the different SQL Server database servers and client tools, and you learned how a SQL Server 2005 DBMS uses multiple databases to manage data. You also learned how to use SQL commands to create SQL Server databases and how to create and modify database tables. In Chapter 3, you will learn how to use SQL commands to retrieve data from SQL Server databases.

SUMMARY

- In a single-tier database system, the DBMS and the database applications all run on the same computer. This architecture can run either on a host computer, to which users connect using terminals, or on a personal computer.
- In a two-tier (client-server) database system, the DBMS runs on a database server, and the database applications run on client workstations that are connected to the server through a network.
- In an N-tier database system, the DBMS runs on a server, the business services aspects of the database applications run on one or more separate servers, and the user services aspects of the database applications run on one or more separate servers.
- When you create a SQL Server database installation, you install the DBMS and then install client applications that allow you to work with the DBMS.
- In SQL Server, a database object, or database, is a set of logically related tables and programs.
- When you install a SQL Server DBMS, you create a database instance. A single database instance can support multiple databases.
- To work with a database instance, you must create a connection by specifying the server name and database instance name.
- SQL (Structured Query Language) is the standard command language of relational databases. SQL has data definition language (DDL) commands, which create and modify new database objects, and data manipulation language (DML) commands, which perform the basic data-handling operations of inserting, updating, deleting, and viewing data.
- Use SQL queries to create and manage relational databases. SQL queries are text-based and relatively standard for most DBMSs. Management Studio provides a Query Editor for creating, executing, and saving SQL queries.
- To create a new SQL Server database, write a SQL query that specifies the database name and information about the files that store and manage the database.
- To create a new database table, specify the table and column names, column data types and maximum widths, and data and value constraints.
- Use SQL Server number data types to store numeric data that might be used in calculations. Some of the number data types specify whether the value stores a specific number of digits to the right and left of the decimal point.

- Text data types store character data and numeric data that is not used in calculations. Text data types can be fixed-length, which store a specific number of characters, no more or no less. Text data types can also be variable-length, with a maximum number of characters, but can store text strings of different lengths without adding trailing blank spaces.
- Use date/time data types to store date and time data, and binary data types to store binary data such as images or sound clips.
- Constraints restrict the data that a column contains. Integrity constraints define primary and foreign keys. Value constraints include check constraints, which restrict values to specific data values or ranges of values; unique constraints, which specify that a field value must be unique with respect to every other table row; NOT NULL constraints, which specify that a field value cannot be NULL; and default constraints, which specify a default value that the DBMS assigns to the field if the user does not supply an alternate value.
- Always assign to constraints explicit names that identify the constraint's table, column, and type.
- To create a surrogate key, specify the column as a primary key, and designate the column as an identity column to which the DBMS automatically assigns unique sequential values.
- When you create a database table that contains a foreign key, you must first create the parent table that the foreign key references. A foreign key column must have the same data type as its parent column.
- When you delete a database table, the system removes the table and its associated data. You cannot delete a parent table that a foreign key constraint references without first dropping the foreign key constraint.
- You can execute SQL commands to add and delete table columns, modify column data types, and add and drop constraints. You can use system stored procedures (SPs) to rename existing tables and table columns.
- Common errors in SQL DDL commands include basic typographical errors in the SQL command, trying to drop a table that contains a column that is referenced as a foreign key by another table, and trying to create a table that already exists.

KEY TERMS

Binary data type   Data type that stores binary data representing images, sound clips, or application files

Business services   Database application components that validate the business rules the system enforces

Check constraint   Constraint specifying that a field must contain a specific value or range of values

Checkpoint   Signal that instructs a SQL Server database to write changes from the transaction log file to the data files

Child table   In a foreign key relationship, the table containing the column as a foreign key

Client   Program that requests and uses server resources

Clustering   Combination of two or more separate servers that share database server duties, appear on the network as a single server, and provide fault tolerance

Connection   Communication link between a client tool and a database instance

Constraint   Rule that restricts the data values that a column contains

Database instance   Specific database server process running on a specific server

Database object   Group of logically related tables and programs

Database server   Program that runs on a server and accepts requests from client programs to view and modify database data

Data definition language (DDL)   SQL commands that create and modify new database objects, such as databases

Data manipulation language (DML)   SQL commands that perform basic data-handling operations of inserting, updating, deleting, and viewing data

Decimal number   Number that includes digits on both the right and left sides of the decimal point

Default constraint   Constraint specifying the default data value that a column will contain if the user does not explicitly assign a value

Default value   Value that a data column most likely will contain.

Eight-bit character coding   Coding that represents characters as eight-bit binary values

Filegroup   Collection of SQL server data files that have common properties for the purpose of simplifying database administration tasks

Fixed-length text field   Text field containing a specific number of characters, no more or no less

Identity column   Column specification that instructs the DBMS to automatically assign a sequenced number to every new record

Increment   Amount an identity column value increases for every record

Integer   Whole numbers that do not contain digits to the right of the decimal point

Integrity constraint   Constraint that defines a primary or foreign key

Logical file name   File name that uniquely identifies a primary or secondary data file and that specifies how the file is referenced in programs that interact with the database

NOT NULL constraint   Constraint specifying that a column must contain a data value

N-tier database system   Database system that runs the user services and business services components of database applications on multiple servers

Parent table   In a foreign key relationship, the table containing the column as a primary key

Precision   Maximum number of digits that a number can contain, including all digits to the left and right of the decimal point

Primary data file   Binary file that contains links to all the other files in a SQL Server database

Query   Text command used to interact with a database

Scale   Specifies the maximum number of digits that the number can contain on the right side of the decimal point

Secondary data files   Binary files that a SQL Server database can optionally use in addition to the primary data file to store database data

Seed value   Identity column starting value

Server   Networked computer that shares resources such as files, printers, and programs with other computers

Single-tier database system   Database system in which the DBMS and the database applications all run on the same computer

SQL (Structured Query Language)   Standard command language of relational databases, consisting of about 30 basic commands

Stored procedure   Sequential program written in T-SQL that manipulates data using programming constructs such as if/then conditional statements and loops

Syntax error   Error that occurs when a command's syntax does not follow a programming language's syntax rules

System database   Database that the SQL Server DBMS uses to manage its internal functions

System tables   Database tables that contain all the information about the database, such as the names of all the other databases and their associated tables

Terminal   Device that provides keyboard input and video output to users, but does not perform processing

Transaction log file   Binary file in which a SQL Server database periodically records database changes as a result of user inserts, updates, or deletes

T-SQL   Microsoft's extended SQL dialect for the SQL Server DBMS

T-SQL interpreter   Program that parses a SQL query and checks it for syntax errors

Two-tier (client-server) database system   Database system in which the DBMS runs on a database server and the database applications run on client workstations connected to the server through a network

Unicode   Coding representing characters as 16-bit binary values and encoding an extensive character set that includes characters from many other alphabets

Unique constraint   Constraint specifying that every value within a table column must have a unique value

User services   Database application components that perform basic tasks of displaying and formatting data

Value constraint   Constraint specifying that a field must contain a specific data value

Variable-length text field   Text field that has a variable number of characters depending on the data value

STUDY QUESTIONS

Multiple-Choice Questions

1. In a(n) _____ database system, the DBMS runs on a database server, and the database applications run on client workstations.
   a. Two-tier
   b. N-tier
   c. Client-server
   d. Both a and c

2. On a SQL Server database server, the _____ contain(s) all the information about the database system, such as the names of the databases and their associated tables.
   a. Model database
   b. System tables
   c. DBMS
   d. Primary data files

3. In a SQL Server database, the _____ file records all changes to the database since the last checkpoint.
   a. Primary data
   b. Secondary data
   c. Transaction log
   d. Project solution

4. A database _____ is identified by a server name and a database name.
   a. User
   b. Instance
   c. Table
   d. Object

5. You use SQL _____ commands to work with database objects and _____ commands to work with database data.
   a. CREATE, UPDATE
   b. Server, Client
   c. DML, DDL
   d. DDL, DML

6. A _____ text field contains a specific number of characters, and if the actual data value that the field stores contains fewer characters, the DBMS pads the text value with blank spaces so that it occupies the total number of required characters.
   a. Unicode
   b. Fixed-length
   c. Variable-length
   d. Char

7. To define a column that contains numeric data not used in calculations, you use an _____ data type.
   a. Text
   b. Integer
   c. Numeric
   d. Fixed-width

8. To create a column that is a surrogate key, you use a(n) _____ data type.
   a. Identity
   b. Integer
   c. Text
   d. Uniqueidentifier

9. A column that contains numeric data with a maximum value of 99,999.99 (rounded to two decimal places) has a precision value of _____ and a scale value of _____.
   a. 7, 2
   b. 7, 8
   c. 8, 2
   d. 2, 8

10. Which of the following is *not* a legal SQL Server table name?
   a. My$teryTable
   b. [Joline's Table]
   c. a#TimeSheet_1
   d. @Employees

True/False Questions

1. Every SQL Server database must have at least one primary data file and one secondary data file.

2. You must execute the USE command before you can create a new database.
3. To modify an existing table constraint, you must delete the current constraint and then create a new one.
4. A single database server can support multiple database instances.
5. To define a foreign key, you must create the table in which the column is a foreign key before creating the table in which the column is a primary key.

Short Answer Questions

1. Recommend a SQL Server data type for the following data columns:
   a. An employee's social security number
   b. The time at which an employee punches his or her time card in the morning, accurate to the second
   c. A digitized image of a product, stored in a file that occupies 1.25 megabytes of file space
   d. An employee's date of birth, accurate to the month, day, and year
   e. The text value describing an employee's annual job performance review, which could be up to 10,000 characters long
   f. The extended total (price times quantity) on a sales invoice for which the values never exceed $10,000
2. What happens when you omit the constraint name in a constraint definition?
3. When should you use an N-tier database system architecture?
4. Briefly describe the SQL Server primary data files, secondary data files, and transaction log files.
5. When should you use a data type that uses Unicode data encoding?

Guided Exercises

1. **Creating and Modifying Relational Database Tables for a Wholesale Bakery Database**
   Figure 2-20 shows the relational database tables of a database for a wholesale bakery. In this exercise, you create the tables using SQL Server.
   a. Create a database table design for each table that specifies the table name, column names, and whether a column is a primary or foreign key. Specify an appropriate SQL Server data type for each column, and use your best judgment to specify whether NULL values should be allowed.
   b. List the table names in the order in which you will create them, based on foreign key dependencies.
   c. Create a query file named 2Exercise1Create.sql that contains the SQL commands to create all the tables. Be sure to write the commands so that they create the tables in the correct order. Execute the queries using the Ch2*yourDatabaseName* database that you have already created.
   d. Create a second query file named 2Exercise1Modify.sql that adds a check condition constraint on the CustomerPhone column in the BakeryCustomer table, which specifies that the column must be formatted as three digits followed by a hyphen, followed by four more digits ("999-9999").
2. **Creating and Modifying Relational Database Tables for a Video Rental Store Database**
   Figure 2-21 shows the relational database tables for a video rental store.
   a. Create a database table design for each table that specifies the table name, column names, and whether a column is a primary or foreign key. Specify an appropriate SQL Server data type for each column, and use your best judgment to specify whether NULL values should be allowed.
   b. List the table names in the order in which you will create them, based on foreign key dependencies.
   c. Create a query file named 2Exercise2Create.sql that contains the SQL commands to create all the tables. Be sure to write the commands so that they create the tables in the correct order. Execute the queries using the Ch2*yourDatabaseName* database that you have already created.

FIGURE 2-20 Sample database tables for a wholesale bakery

BakeryCustomer

CustomerID	CustomerName	CustomerAddress	CustomerPhone
1	The Candy Man	1234 Main St.	577-1231
2	Sweet Success	231 Harris Blvd.	577-7664
3	Sue's Bakery	1889 20th N.E.	577-9090
4	Ron's Foods	194 Bay View	577-8909

BakeryProduct

ProductID	ProductDescription	ProductPrice
100	Death By Chocolate Cheesecake	15.95
101	Carrot Cake Supreme	12.95
102	Monster Cinnamon Rolls	10.95
103	White Fudge Macadamia Bars	5.95
104	Nutty Coconut Pie	8.95

BakeryOrder

OrderID	ProductID	CustomerID	OrderDate	OrderDeliveryDate	OrderQuantity
1000	100	1	28-Oct-08	28-Oct-08	10
1000	102	1	28-Oct-08	30-Oct-08	5
1002	103	2	28-Oct-08	28-Oct-08	2
1003	100	3	28-Oct-08	28-Oct-08	6
1003	101	3	28-Oct-08	2-Nov-08	8
1003	102	3	29-Oct-08	29-Oct-08	10
1004	102	2	29-Oct-08	29-Oct-08	12
1005	105	3	29-Oct-08	29-Oct-08	15
1006	101	4	29-Oct-08	30-Oct-08	10
1006	102	4	29-Oct-08	29-Oct-08	5
1006	105	4	29-Oct-08	2-Nov-08	10

  d. Create a second query file named 2Exercise2Modify.sql that contains the SQL command to add a field named TitleReleaseYear to the VideoTitle table. Use a Smalldatetime data type, and specify that NULL values are allowed.

3. **Creating Relational Database Tables for an Employee Database**
   Figure 2-22 shows the relational database tables for an employee database.
    a. Create a database table design for each table that specifies the table name, column names, and whether a column is a primary or foreign key. Specify an appropriate SQL Server data type for each column, and use your best judgment to specify whether NULL values should be allowed.
    b. List the table names in the order in which you will create them, based on foreign key dependencies.
    c. Create a query file named 2Exercise3Create.sql that contains the SQL commands to create all the tables. Be sure to write the commands so that they create the tables in the correct order.
    d. Create a second query file named 2Exercise3Modify.sql that adds a check condition constraint on the DependentRelationship column in the CompanyDependent table, which specifies that the value must be either 'Daughter,' 'Son,' or 'Spouse.'

FIGURE 2-21   Sample database tables for a video rental store

VideoCategory

CategoryID	Category Description
1	New Release
2	Action
3	Horror
4	Comedy
5	Children's

VideoFormat

FormatID	FormatDescription
1	VCR
2	DVD
3	Playstation
4	Nintendo 64
5	Sega

VideoCustomer

CustomerID	Customer LastName	Customer FirstName	CustomerAddress	CustomerCity	Customer State	CustomerZip Code
1	Johnson	Edward	222 Main Street	Cheyenne	WY	82001
2	Bailey	Bill	4233 Oxford Drive	Cheyenne	WY	82001
3	Freeman	Mary	9822 Boston Road	Cheyenne	WY	82001
4	Harrison	Susan	822 Water Street	Cheyenne	WY	82001
5	Clemons	Arlo	9833 Guthrie Street	Cheyenne	WY	82001

VideoRental

RentalID	RentalDateOut	RentalDateDue	RentalDateIn	RentalDeliveryStatus	RentalLate Fee	CustomerID	TitleID
1	22-Sep-08	24-Sep-08	24-Sep-08	pickup	$0.00	1	3
2	23-Sep-08	25-Sep-08		delivery	$1.00	2	4
3	25-Sep-08	27-Sep-08	26-Sep-08	pickup	$0.00	2	2
4	25-Sep-08	27-Feb-08	26-Sep-08	pickup	$0.00	2	5
5	27-Sep-08	28-Sep-08		delivery	$0.00	4	6

VideoTitle

TitleID	TitleDescription	FormatID	TitleRentalCost	CategoryID
2	The Matrix	1	$2.00	2
3	The Evil	1	$2.00	3
4	Super Mario World	4	$1.00	5
5	The Princess Bride	1	$2.00	5
6	Men In Tights	2	$2.00	4

FIGURE 2-22 Sample database tables for an employee database

CompanyEmployee

Employee ID	Employee SSN	Employee FirstName	Employee MI	Employee LastName	Employee Gender	Employee Salary	Department ID
1	123456789	John	B	Smith	M	30000	3
2	333445555	Franklin	T	Wong	M	40000	3
3	453453453	Joyce	A	English	F	25000	3
4	666884444	Ramesh	K	Narayan	M	38000	3
5	888665555	James	E	Borg	M	55000	1
6	987654321	Jennifer	S	Wallace	F	43000	2
7	987987987	Ahmad		Jabbar	M	25000	2
8	999887777	Alicia	P	Zelaya	F	25000	2

CompanyProject

ProjectID	Project Name	Project Location	Department ID
1	Contact Manager	Bellaire	3
2	Ignition	Sugarland	3
3	Development	Stafford	2
4	Reengineer	Houston	2
5	IT	Houston	2
6	Administration	Houston	1

CompanyDepartment

Department ID	Department Name
1	Headquarters
2	Production
3	Research

CompanyEmployeeProject

EmployeeID	ProjectID	Employee Project Hours Worked
1	1	32.5
2	2	10
3	1	20
7	4	35
8	5	10

CompanyDependent

Dependent ID	EmployeeID	Dependent LastName	Dependent FirstName	Dependent MI	Dependent Gender	Dependent BirthDate	Dependent Relationship
1	1	Smith	Alice	T	F	12/31/2000	Daughter
2	1	Smith	Elizabeth	R	F	5/5/1973	Spouse
3	1	Smith	Michael	J	M	1/1/1996	Son
4	2	Bakhtiyarova	Alice	C	F	4/5/1995	Daughter
5	2	Wong	Joy	D	F	5/3/1967	Spouse
6	2	Wong	Theodore	S	M	10/25/1992	Son
7	8	Bauer	Abner		M	2/1/1978	Spouse

CHAPTER 3

Creating SQL Queries to View Database Data

Learning Objectives

At the conclusion of this chapter, you will be able to:

■ describe the sample databases and run scripts to create them;

■ write SQL commands to retrieve database data;

■ perform arithmetic operations on retrieved data;

■ use group functions to summarize retrieved data;

■ format query output;

■ join data from multiple tables;

■ create nested queries;

■ create and work with views;

■ perform set operations in queries.

Recall from the first two chapters that database applications allow users to enter, modify, and view database data using forms and reports. A *form,* like a paper form, presents an interface that allows users to enter, modify, delete, and retrieve data values. A *report* summarizes data values at a specific point in time. Users can view report data on a computer screen or as hard copy printouts. Forms and reports retrieve data using queries, which are commands that the DBMS processes to retrieve data.

Recall from Chapter 2 that SQL is the standard query language of relational databases, that SQL includes Data Description Language (DDL) commands to create and modify database objects, and that it includes Data Manipulation Language (DML) commands to insert, modify, and view data values. In Chapter 2, you learned how to create and execute DDL commands that create and modify databases and database tables. This chapter describes how to create and execute SQL DML queries to retrieve and manipulate database data.

SAMPLE DATABASES

Throughout this book, two sample databases provide the data for example queries and database applications. The following sections describe these sample databases in detail and provide instructions for executing the files that contain the SQL commands to create and populate the databases.

Ironwood University Student Registration Database

Ironwood University is a fictitious university that uses a database to track students, courses, and enrollments. (This database is similar to the university registration database you worked with in the first two chapters.) Figure 3-1 shows the Ironwood University database tables and displays the primary key-foreign key links visually. Note that each table's primary key displays a key icon on the left edge of the field name. The foreign key links display an infinity symbol on the "many" side of the relationship, and the referenced primary key appears beside the key icon on the "one" side of the relationship.

In this database, students enroll in course sections. A single course, such as MIS 101, has multiple course sections, which are offered in different terms and on different days and times and which are taught by different instructors. Students can receive tutoring help for specific course sections; each tutoring session occurs on a specific date, has a start and end time, and is taught by a specific tutor. Each student has a single instructor who serves as his or her academic advisor. Students can also check out

FIGURE 3-1   Ironwood University database diagram

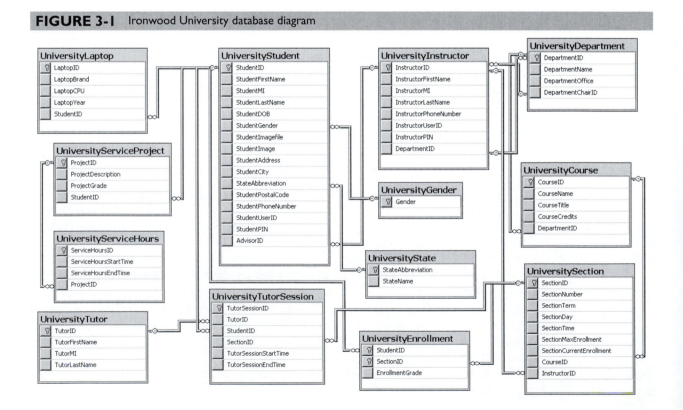

laptop computers. Students complete service projects, and the database tracks each project by the start and end times on the days on which the student works.

University instructors work for different departments, and a single department chair oversees each department. The department chair is also an instructor. Each department offers one or many courses, and each course can have multiple sections that meet on different days and at different times.

The database contains two *lookup tables,* which are general tables containing data values that populate other tables. The UniversityGender lookup table contains a Gender field that contains the possible values of "M" (for male) and "F" (for female). The UniversityState table contains state abbreviations and associated state names.

Figure 3-2 shows the database tables and fields in tabular form with sample data records. Note that in the UniversityStudent table, the StudentDOB column values contain both a date and a time element. This is because the column uses the Date/Time data type, which represents both date and time values within a single data value. Because the dates of birth do not store a time component, the time appears as 12:00:00 a.m. for all records. Similarly, the SectionTime column in the UniversitySection table uses a Date/Time data type but does not store a date component, so the SQL Server DBMS displays the default date value, which is 1/1/1900.

Sport Motors Sales and Product Inventory Database

Sport Motors is a fictitious retail establishment that sells motorized vehicles and accessories. Because many accessories involve special orders, Sport Motors requires a database to track customers and customer orders as well as inventory and inventory suppliers. Figure 3-3 presents a database diagram of the Sport Motors database.

Sport Motors has multiple departments, and each employee works for a specific department. Employees create customer orders. Each order can have multiple detail lines that describe the inventory item, order quantity, and price of the order item. Because the store awards commissions to employees for the items they sell, the database tracks the employee's sales commission rate.

Sport Motors classifies its inventory using categories such as "Apparel" or "Motorcycles" and associated subcategories, such as "Off Road" or "Street." Each inventory item has a specific supplier.

The Sport Motors database has three lookup tables: SportPaymentType, which lists possible payment options for orders, such as "Cash" or "Loan"; SportState, which stores state abbreviations and associated state names (and is identical to the UniversityState table in the Ironwood University database); and SportColor, which lists possible color choices (such as "Black" or "Metallic Blue") for inventory items.

Figure 3-4 shows the database tables and fields, with sample data records.

Running Scripts to Create and Populate the Sample Database Tables

A *script* is a text file with an .sql extension containing a series of SQL commands that perform a series of related tasks, such as creating all the tables in a database or inserting all the data in a lookup table. Scripts are the same as the query files you created in Chapter 2 to store commands to create databases and database tables. In this section, you will run scripts that we provide with this book that contain commands to create a database containing the tables in the Ironwood University and Sport Motors databases.

FIGURE 3-2 Ironwood University sample database data

UniversityStudent

StudentID	StudentFirstName	StudentMI	StudentLastName	StudentDOB	StudentGender	StudentImagefile	StudentImage
1	Clifford	NULL	Wall	5/29/1988 12:00:00 AM	M	wallc.jpg	NULL
2	Dawna	H	Voss	11/1/1981 12:00:00 AM	F	vossd.jpg	NULL
3	Patricia	E	Owen	1/23/1987 12:00:00 AM	F	owenp.jpg	NULL
4	Raymond	P	Miller	8/9/1988 12:00:00 AM	M	millerr.jpg	NULL
5	Ann	NULL	Bochman	4/12/1988 12:00:00 AM	F	bochmana.jpg	NULL
6	Brenda	S	Johansen	3/27/1989 12:00:00 AM	F	johansenb.jpg	NULL
7	David	R	Ashcraft	10/15/1989 12:00:00 AM	M	ashcraftd.jpg	NULL

UniversityStudent (continued)

StudentAddress	StudentCity	StateAbbreviation	StudentPostalCode	StudentPhoneNumber	StudentUserID	StudentPIN	AdvisorID
3403 Level St	Ironwood	MI	49938	7158362331	wallc	1234	1
524 Lakeview Dr Apt 12	Ashland	WI	54806	7158382413	vossdh	4321	8
513254 County Rd 71	Ironwood	MI	49938	7158360982	owenpe	1122	8
231 Edgewood Ct Apt 23	Ashland	MI	54806	7158382319	millerrp	2211	9
112 Rainetta Blvd	Ashland	WI	54806	7158382231	bochmana	2233	4
520 Congress Rd	Ironwood	MI	49938	7158368891	johansenb	3322	10
331 1st Ave Apt 11	Ashland	WI	54806	7158384437	ashcraftdr	3344	9

UniversityDepartment

DepartmentID	DepartmentName	DepartmentOffice	DepartmentChairID
1	Management Information Systems	Schneider 418	1
2	Accounting	Schneider 419	2
3	Physics	Phillips 007	3
4	Computer Science	Phillips 112	4
5	Chemistry	Phillips 201	5
6	Geology	Phillips 123	6
7	Foreign Languages	Hibbard 211	7

UniversityState (not all records are shown)

StateAbbreviation	StateName
AK	ALASKA
AL	ALABAMA
AR	ARKANSAS
AZ	ARIZONA
CA	CALIFORNIA
CO	COLORADO
CT	CONNECTICUT
DC	DISTRICT OF C…
DE	DELAWARE
FL	FLORIDA
GA	GEORGIA
HI	HAWAII
IA	IOWA
ID	IDAHO

UniversityCourse

CourseID	CourseName	CourseTitle	CourseCredits	DepartmentID
1	MIS 240	Information Systems in Bu…	3	1
2	MIS 310	Systems Analysis and Design	3	1
3	MIS 344	Database Management Sy…	3	1
4	MIS 345	Introduction to Networks	3	1
5	ACCT 201	Principles of Accounting	3	2
6	ACCT 312	Managerial Accounting	3	2
7	PHYS 211	General Physics	4	3
8	CS 245	Fundamentals of Object-…	4	4
9	CHEM 205	Applied Physical Chemistry	3	5
10	GEOL 212	Mineralogy and Petrology	5	6
11	CHIN 110	Intensive Beginning Chine…	5	7

UniversityGender

Gender
F
M

FIGURE 3-2   Ironwood University sample database data (*continued*)

UniversityInstructor

InstructorID	InstructorFirstName	InstructorMI	InstructorLastName	InstructorPhoneNumber	InstructorUserID	InstructorPIN	DepartmentID
1	Lauren	J	Morrison	5558362243	morrislj	1122	1
2	Adam	K	Dutton	5558364522	duttonak	2222	2
3	Eagan	T	Ruppelt	5558366487	ruppeltet	3333	3
4	Charles	H	Murphy	5558362113	murphych	3211	4
5	Richard	P	Harrison	5558364901	harrisrp	1233	5
6	Judith	D	Bakke	5558360089	bakkejd	4455	6
7	Diane	O	Adler	5558365960	adlerdo	5566	7
8	Ted	NULL	Buck	5558362531	buckt	6655	1
9	Roberta	V	Sanchez	5558363628	sanchezrv	6677	1
10	Lillian	S	Hogstad	5558366946	hogstadls	7766	1
11	Brian	L	Luedke	5558362419	luedkebl	5544	2
12	Anthony	K	Downs	5558362988	downsak	4466	2
13	Nancy	NULL	Gardner	5558364345	gardnern	6699	2

UniversitySection (not all records are shown)

SectionID	SectionNumber	SectionTerm	SectionDay	SectionTime	SectionMaxEnrollment	SectionCurrentEnrollment	CourseID	InstructorID
1	001	SUMM08	MTWTHF	1/1/1900 8:00:00 AM	30	25	1	1
2	001	SUMM08	MTWTHF	1/1/1900 10:00:00 AM	30	19	5	1
3	001	FALL08	MWF	1/1/1900 8:00:00 AM	65	65	1	1
4	002	FALL08	TTH	1/1/1900 2:00:00 PM	80	71	1	8
5	001	FALL08	TTH	1/1/1900 8:00:00 AM	65	61	2	9
6	001	FALL08	TTH	1/1/1900 8:00:00 AM	40	39	3	10
7	001	FALL08	MWF	1/1/1900 9:00:00 AM	40	40	4	8
8	001	FALL08	MWF	1/1/1900 9:00:00 AM	40	36	5	11
9	001	FALL08	TTH	1/1/1900 11:00:00 AM	40	38	6	12
10	001	FALL08	TTH	1/1/1900 9:00:00 AM	35	35	7	3
11	001	FALL08	MWF	1/1/1900 1:00:00 PM	60	51	8	4
12	001	FALL08	MWF	1/1/1900 10:00:00 AM	60	34	9	5
13	001	FALL08	TTH	1/1/1900 10:00:00 AM	35	26	10	6
14	001	FALL08	TTH	1/1/1900 11:00:00 AM	50	23	11	7
15	001	SPR09	MWF	1/1/1900 8:00:00 AM	65	0	1	1
16	002	SPR09	TTH	1/1/1900 2:00:00 PM	80	0	1	8
17	001	SPR09	TTH	1/1/1900 10:00:00 AM	65	5	2	9
18	001	SPR09	TTH	1/1/1900 9:00:00 AM	40	3	3	10
19	001	SPR09	MWF	1/1/1900 11:00:00 AM	40	21	4	8
20	001	SPR09	MWF	1/1/1900 3:00:00 PM	40	17	5	11

(*continued*)

FIGURE 3-2   Ironwood University sample database data (*continued*)

UniversityEnrollment (not all records are shown)

StudentID	SectionID	EnrollmentGrade
1	1	C
1	10	B
1	11	C
1	13	B
1	14	A
2	1	A
2	8	B
2	10	B+
2	12	B
2	13	A
2	17	NULL
2	18	NULL
2	21	NULL
2	26	NULL
3	2	B-
3	3	A-
3	8	B
3	10	C
3	13	C+

UniversityLaptop

LaptopID	LaptopBrand	LaptopCPU	LaptopYear	StudentID
1	DELL	Latitude D788	5/21/2008 12:00:00 AM	1
2	DELL	Latitude D788	5/21/2008 12:00:00 AM	NULL
3	DELL	Inspiron 7109	5/21/2008 12:00:00 AM	NULL
4	IBM	Thinkpad T3501	12/1/2008 12:00:00 AM	3
5	IBM	Thinkpad T3501	12/1/2008 12:00:00 AM	NULL

UniversityServiceProject

ProjectID	ProjectDescription	ProjectGrade	StudentID
1	Help Desk Assistant at Elder Care Center	NULL	2
2	Create Database for Elder Care Center	NULL	4

UniversityServiceHours

ServiceHoursID	ServiceHoursStartTime	ServiceHoursEndTime	ProjectID
1	10/11/2008 8:00:00 AM	10/11/2008 11:00:00 AM	1
2	10/13/2008 8:00:00 AM	10/13/2008 11:00:00 AM	1
3	10/16/2008 8:00:00 AM	10/16/2008 1:00:00 PM	1
4	11/3/2008 10:00:00 AM	11/3/2008 5:00:00 PM	2

UniversityTutor

TutorID	TutorFirstName	TutorMI	TutorLastName
1	Cheryl	D	Glastner
2	Andrew	H	Beagle
3	Michael	NULL	Hannity

UniversityTutorSession

TutorSessionID	TutorID	StudentID	SectionID	TutorSessionStartTime	TutorSessionEndTime
1	1	4	13	9/21/2008 7:00:00 PM	9/21/2008 8:00:00 PM
2	1	4	12	9/22/2008 6:30:00 PM	9/22/2008 7:30:00 PM
3	1	4	13	10/26/2008 6:00:00 PM	10/26/2008 7:30:00 PM
4	1	4	12	10/27/2008 4:00:00 PM	10/27/2008 5:00:00 PM
5	3	1	11	10/3/2008 4:30:00 PM	10/3/2008 5:30:00 PM
6	3	1	11	10/4/2008 6:30:00 PM	10/4/2008 7:30:00 PM
7	3	1	11	10/31/2008 7:00:00 PM	10/31/2008 8:00:00 PM

NOTE: In a production environment, you would probably create a unique SQL Server database for Ironwood University, and a second unique database for Sport Motors. To simplify classroom administration, you will create the tables for both databases in the same SQL Server database.

Starting the Tool and Opening the Script

To run a SQL Server script, start Management Studio, open the script file in the Query Editor, and execute the script. The following steps explain how to do this.

FIGURE 3-3 Database diagram for the Sport Motors database

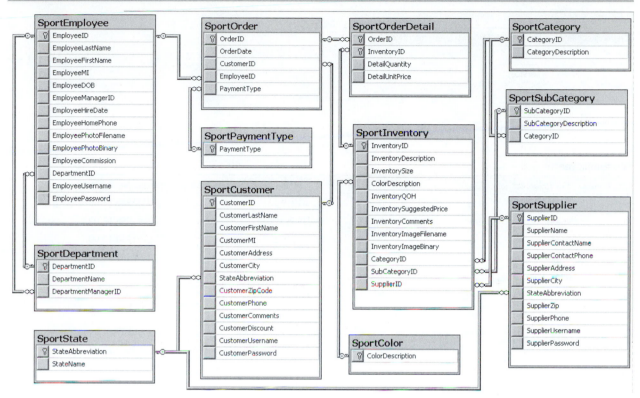

1. Start Management Studio and connect to your database server instance. (Chapter 2 provides detailed instructions for completing this step.)
2. Click the Open File button on the toolbar and navigate to the \Datafiles\ DatabaseScripts folder, where you are storing the data files for this book.
    If you are connecting to a local SQL Server database, select CreateIronwoodLocal.sql and click Open.
    If you are connecting to a remote SQL Server database, select CreateIronwoodRemote.sql and click Open.
3. If necessary, connect to the database instance. The script appears in the Query Editor window.

The first section of the script contains commands to create a new database called *yourUserName.* These commands have been commented out. When you *comment out* a command in a script or program, the T-SQL interpreter does not execute the command but rather treats it as an internal documentation comment. To comment out a T-SQL command, preface the command with two hyphens (--).

If you have not yet created a database, or if you want to create a new database, remove the two hyphens from the commands to create the database. If you are using a local SQL Server database, remove the hyphens from the commands that instruct the DBMS to store your database data and log files in a folder named C:\SQLServer\Databases, which you have already created on your computer. If you are using a remote database server, removing the hyphens from the commands instructs the

FIGURE 3-4 Sport Motors database sample data

SportDepartment

DepartmentID	DepartmentName	DepartmentMan...
1	Parts	2
2	Service	3
3	Sales	1
4	Apparel	5
5	Accounting	4

SportEmployee

EmployeeID	EmployeeLastName	EmployeeFirstName	EmployeeMI	EmployeeDOB	EmployeeManagerID	EmployeeHireDate
1	Mathews	Roy	D	2/28/1949 1...	NULL	3/15/1986 12:00...
2	Kaiser	Greg	M	5/4/1955 12...	1	3/30/1995 12:00...
3	Jones	Mark	J	3/21/1965 1...	1	11/3/1990 12:00...
4	Ward	Dennis	NULL	11/4/1960 1...	1	3/15/1986 12:00...
5	Rumell	Alicia	B	7/9/1951 12...	1	3/15/1986 12:00...
6	Haugen	Sarah	R	3/21/1992 1...	1	5/1/1992 12:00:...
7	Smith	Jerry	K	12/11/1982 ...	3	11/3/2001 12:00...
8	Milner	Chris	P	8/25/1969 1...	4	10/13/1991 12:0...
9	Balmer	Janet	T	11/19/1972 ...	4	9/24/2003 12:00...
10	Akey	Corey	R	4/9/1949 12...	4	2/11/1993 12:00...
11	Crain	Craig	K	2/22/1973 1...	2	4/1/2002 12:00:...
12	Heyde	Jennifer	E	8/16/1975 1...	2	6/1/2003 12:00:...

SportEmployee (continued)

EmployeeHomePhone	EmployeePhotoFilename	EmployeePhotoBinary	EmployeeCommission	DepartmentID	EmployeeUsername	EmployeePassw...
7155552923	mathews.jpg	NULL	0	3	mathewsr	plant
7155554498	kaiserg.jpg	NULL	0	3	kaiserg	theone
7155559998	jonesm.jpg	NULL	0	1	jonesm	indiana
7155550089	wardd.jpg	NULL	0	2	wardd	redhot
7155554936	rumella.jpg	NULL	0	4	rumella	rapunzel
7155552031	haugens.jpg	NULL	0	5	haugens	daze
7155559933	smithj.jpg	NULL	0	1	smithj	credenza
7155551188	milnerc.jpg	NULL	0	2	milnerc	yoohoo
7155550437	balmerj.jpg	NULL	0	2	balmerj	ceo
7155559290	akeyc.jpg	NULL	0	2	akeyc	bones
7155553989	crainc.jpg	NULL	0	3	crainc	hiddenvalley
7155555459	heydej.jpg	NULL	0	3	heydej	redgreen

FIGURE 3-4 Sport Motors database sample data *(continued)*

SportCustomer

CustomerID	CustomerLastName	CustomerFirstName	CustomerMI	CustomerAddress	CustomerCity	StateAbbreviation	CustomerZipCode
1	Scholten	Allison	G	1605 Broad Blvd	Eau Claire	WI	54701
2	Potter	Anthony	R	1304 W Back St	Eau Claire	WI	54702
3	Knutson	Stacey	T	2402 131st St	Chippewa Falls	WI	54729
4	Endres	Bernard	A	993 Beverly Dr	Altoona	WI	54720
5	Askland	Sandra	NULL	3215 E Fillmore St	Hallie	WI	54728
6	O'Conner	Robin	J	6775 Lamont Rd	Eau Claire	WI	54703
7	Wendt	Daniel	B	642 River Rd	Chippewa Falls	WI	54729
8	Zimmerman	Leland	S	N8194 Highway 93	Hallie	WI	54728
9	Sessions	Gene	NULL	1219 Lawrence	Chippewa Falls	WI	54729
10	McGinnis	Paul	N	157 Bartig Rd	Eau Claire	WI	54701

SportCustomer (continued)

CustomerPhone	CustomerComments	CustomerDiscount	CustomerUsername	CustomerPassword
7155553929	NULL	0.05	scholtena	asdfjk
7155551411	Frequent Customer	0.15	pottera	qwerty
7155550032	NULL	0.1	knutsons	clever
7155551352	NULL	0.1	endresb	fluffy
7155554493	NULL	0.05	asklands	f92eruy4r
7155553399	NULL	0.05	oconnerr	secret
7155555489	NULL	0.15	wendtd	shadow
7155552190	NULL	0.1	zimmermanl	submarine
7155553376	NULL	0.15	sessionsg	gene
7155553329	NULL	0.1	mcginnisp	bartig

SportPaymentType

PaymentType
Cash
Check
Credit Card
Loan

SportOrder

OrderID	OrderDate	CustomerID	EmployeeID	PaymentType
1	3/11/2007 12:00...	1	2	Loan
2	3/11/2007 12:00...	6	3	Check
3	3/11/2007 12:00...	10	4	Cash
4	3/12/2007 12:00...	8	4	Credit Card

SportOrderDetail

OrderID	InventoryID	DetailQuantity	DetailUnitPrice
1	3	1	8595.0000
1	18	1	45.9500
2	27	1	95.9900
2	29	1	15.3900
2	32	4	8.9900
3	25	1	25.9500
4	28	1	299.9500
4	31	2	89.9900

(continued)

FIGURE 3-4   Sport Motors database sample data (*continued*)

SportInventory (all records are not shown)

InventoryID	InventoryDescription	InventorySize	ColorDescription	InventoryQOH	InventorySuggestedPrice
1	RC 99	NULL	Red	1	12000.0000
2	CR 250	NULL	Red	2	5499.0000
3	NightFlyer	NULL	Metallic Blue	1	8995.0000
4	Tour Master 1500	NULL	Pearlescent Silver	1	14950.0000
5	KLX 450	NULL	Green	1	5799.0000
6	FLHR Custom	NULL	Black	1	21000.0000
7	FXLX Tour Master	NULL	Black	1	19950.0000
8	Sahara 600	NULL	Grey	2	7000.0000
9	Mojave 400	NULL	Green	1	5199.0000
10	Leather Gloves	XS	Black	2	34.9500
11	Leather Gloves	S	Black	3	34.9500
12	Leather Gloves	M	Black	3	34.9500
13	Leather Gloves	L	Black	2	34.9500
14	Leather Riding Pants	S	Black	1	149.9900
15	Leather Riding Pants	M	Black	1	149.9900
16	Leather Riding Pants	L	Black	1	149.9900
17	Riding Gloves	S	Black	3	45.9500
18	Riding Gloves	M	Black	3	45.9500
19	Riding Gloves	L	Black	2	45.9500
20	Riding Gloves	XL	Black	2	45.9500

SportInventory (Continued – all records are not shown)

InventoryComments	InventoryImageFilename	InventoryImageBinary	CategoryID	SubCategoryID	SupplierID
991 CC Sport Motorcycle	rc55.jpg	NULL	2	5	1
250 CC Motocross Motorcycle	cr250.jpg	NULL	2	4	1
800 CC Cruiser Motorcycle	nightflyer.jpg	NULL	2	5	1
1500 CC Touring Motorcycle	tourmaster.jpg	NULL	2	5	2
450 CC Dual Purpose Motorcycle	klx450.jpg	NULL	2	5	2
1500 CC Factory Customized Cruising Motorcycle	flhrcustom.jpg	NULL	2	5	3
1500 CC Touring Motorcycle	tourmaster.jpg	NULL	2	5	3
600 CC Sport ATV	sahara600.jpg	NULL	3	7	1
400 CC Sport/Utility ATV	mojave400.jpg	NULL	3	6	2
NULL	w_gloves.jpg	NULL	1	1	6
NULL	w_gloves.jpg	NULL	1	1	6
NULL	w_gloves.jpg	NULL	1	1	6
NULL	w_gloves.jpg	NULL	1	1	6
NULL	lr_pants.jpg	NULL	1	1	6
NULL	lr_pants.jpg	NULL	1	1	6
NULL	lr_pants.jpg	NULL	1	1	6
NULL	m_gloves.jpg	NULL	1	2	6
NULL	m_gloves.jpg	NULL	1	2	6
NULL	m_gloves.jpg	NULL	1	2	6
NULL	m_gloves.jpg	NULL	1	2	6

FIGURE 3-4   Sport Motors database sample data (*continued*)

SportSupplier

SupplierID	SupplierName	SupplierContactName	SupplierContactPhone	SupplierAddress	SupplierCity	StateAbbreviation
1	Red Cycle Supply	Rhonda Hanover	3335551928	110 Industrial Blvd	Indianapolis	IN
2	Green Cycle Imports	Reed Hoke	4445552290	2371 910 St	Detroit	MI
3	Thunder Cycles	Harley Westover	1115554989	2001 Thunder Rd	Milwaukee	WI
4	No Limit Parts	John Swallow	2225553325	23 Diesel Dr	Dallas	TX
5	Fast Gear	Malcom Smith	1235559948	1090 Rodeo Dr	Los Angeles	CA
6	Cycle Riding Attire	Mike O'Brien	3215553948	835 E Fifth St	Minneapolis	MN

SportSupplier (continued)

SupplierZip	SupplierPhone	SupplierUsername	SupplierPassword
29388	3335552292	redcycle	rhan3
22333	4445550939	greencycle	zxcvj
54777	1115552321	thunder	gjfkdl
73400	2225559829	nolimit	parts
22022	1235552939	fastgear	smoking
44555	3215552291	cycleridin	password

SportCategory

CategoryID	CategoryDescription
1	Apparel
2	Motorcycles
3	All Terrain Vehicles
4	Snowmobiles
5	Parts

SportState (all records are not shown)

StateAbbreviation	StateName
AK	ALASKA
AL	ALABAMA
AR	ARKANSAS
AZ	ARIZONA
CA	CALIFORNIA
CO	COLORADO
CT	CONNECTICUT
DC	DISTRICT OF C...
DE	DELAWARE
FL	FLORIDA
GA	GEORGIA
HI	HAWAII
IA	IOWA
ID	IDAHO

SportColor

ColorDescription
Black
Blue
Green
Grey
Metallic Blue
Metallic Red
Orange
Pearlescent Silver
Red
Tan
Tangerine
White
Yellow

SportSubcategory

SubCategoryID	SubCategoryDescription	CategoryID
1	Women's	1
2	Men's	1
3	Children's	1
4	Off Road	2
5	Street	2
6	Utility	3
7	Sport	3
8	Motorcycle	5
9	ATV	5
10	Snowmobile	5
11	Miscellaneous	5

DBMS to store your data and log files in the default location for the database, and the command that creates the database does not specify the database file location.

Recall that every database in a SQL Server database instance must have a unique name, so if you are connecting to a remote database instance, you must change *yourDatabaseName* to a unique user name before you execute the script.

The script also contains commands to drop all the foreign key constraints and tables in the database, and then recreate the tables and insert the data values into the tables. The script first drops the constraints and tables so that, if necessary, you can run the script multiple times to remake the tables or refresh the data values. (You cannot create a table if it already exists, so you need to drop the table first then recreate it.) If you run the script multiple times, you need to comment out the command that creates the database.

The script also contains PRINT commands that print the current script operation to the screen so that you can monitor what is happening while the script runs. Also, the script contains GO commands that T-SQL uses to make the changes permanent within the database. The following instructions show how to execute the script.

Executing the Script

1. *If you are using an existing database,* replace *yourDatabaseName* with your unique user name. To do this, click Edit on the menu bar, point to Find and Replace, click Quick Replace, type *yourDatabaseName* in the Find what field, type your unique username (such as "morrisjp") in the Replace with field, and click Replace All. A dialog box with the message "8 occurrence(s) replaced" should appear. Click OK, and close the Find and Replace window.
2. *If you want to create a new database,* remove the hyphens from the commands that create the new database.
3. *If you are connecting to a local SQL Server database,* save the file.
4. If necessary, click the Query Editor window to make it active, then click Execute on the toolbar to run the file. A series of confirmation messages appear in the Messages window, confirming that the script successfully created the tables and inserted the data records.

FIGURE 3-5   Error messages when the script attempts to drop tables that do not yet exist

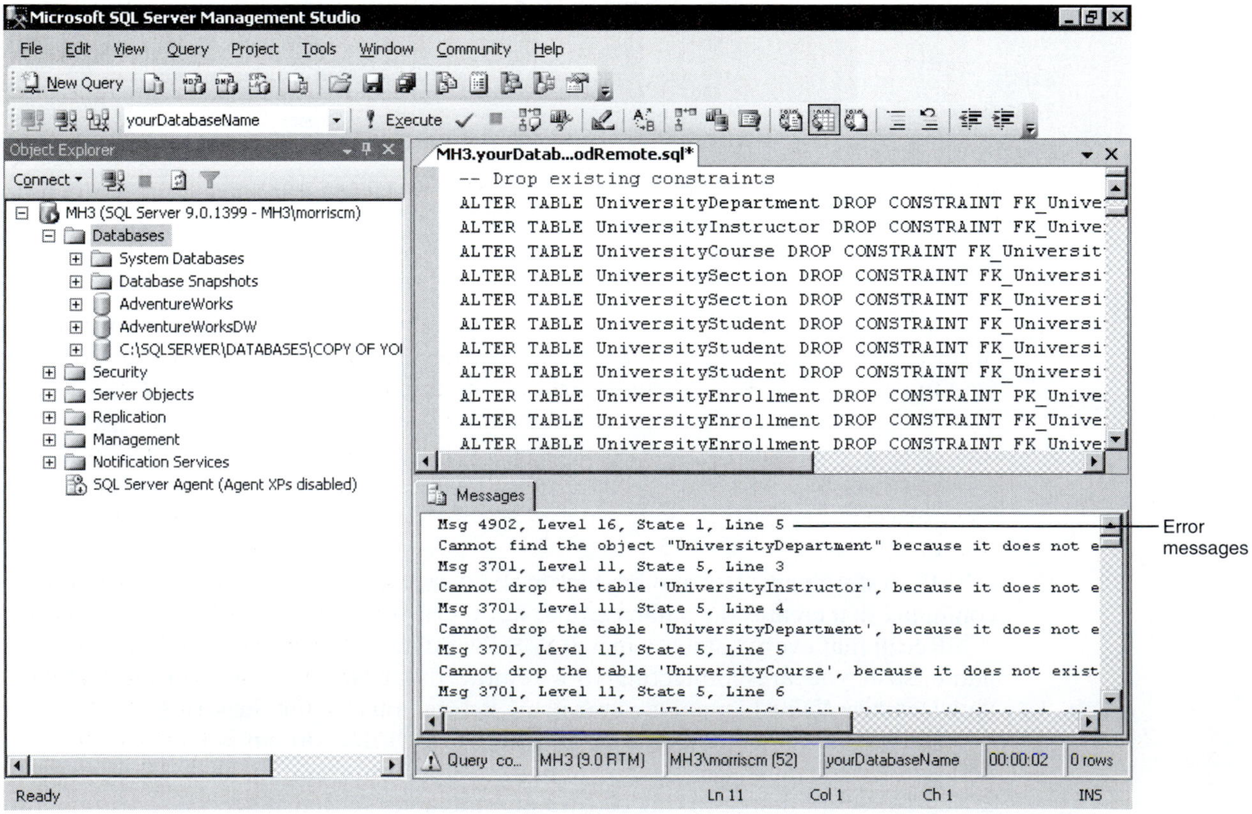

HELP: The first time you run the script, a series of error messages appears at the top of the Messages window stating "Cannot drop the table '*TableName*' (see Figure 3-5). This is not an error because the script always first tries to drop all the database tables, and the first time you run the script, the tables do not yet exist.

---

5. Open the *yourDatabaseName* node, then open the Tables node to confirm that the new tables appear. The 13 Ironwood University database tables should appear in your table listing.
6. Repeat the previous steps to open and execute the Sport Motors database script file. (If you are connecting to a local database, use the CreateSportMotorsLocal.sql file; if you are connecting to a remote database, use the CreateSportMotorsRemote .sql file. Be sure to change *yourDatabaseName* to your unique user name in the file.) After you run the script, the 12 Sport Motors database tables should appear in your table listing.
7. Close both script files in the Query Editor.

USING SQL QUERIES TO RETRIEVE DATABASE DATA

NOTE: All the query examples in this chapter refer to the Ironwood University database tables in Figures 3-1 and 3-2.

Given that SQL is the universal command language of relational databases, you can write SQL queries that retrieve data from existing database tables and that manipulate the data using arithmetic calculations, group summary operations, and set operations. You can include parameters within SQL queries to format the output data.

The general syntax for a SQL query that retrieves data from a single database table is:

```
SELECT Column1, Column2, . . .
FROM TableName
WHERE SearchCondition(s)
```

In this syntax, the SELECT clause lists the names of the columns from which you want to display data. The FROM clause specifies the table that contains the columns, and the optional WHERE clause contains one or more search conditions that seek to match specific records. You will learn how to create search conditions later in this section. If you omit the search condition(s), the query retrieves all the table records.

In this chapter, you will type SQL queries in the Query Editor, and then execute the queries. The retrieved data values appear on the Results tab in the lower output window, as shown in Figure 3-6.

The following steps show how to create a new query file in Management Studio, enter and execute the query in Figure 3-6, and then save the query file. Note that the USE command appears as the first line in the query file. After you start Management Studio but before you execute your first SELECT query, you must tell Management Studio which database to use. The Query Editor will use this database for all subsequent queries. If you want to use a different database in the same Query Editor session, you must execute the USE command again to instruct Query Editor to use the alternate database.

FIGURE 3-6   Running a SQL query using the Query Editor

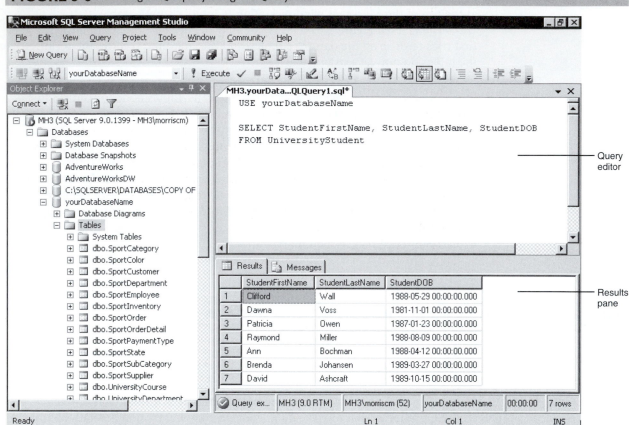

Recall from Chapter 2 that when you click the Execute button on the Query Editor toolbar, all queries in the Query Editor window execute. If you want to execute a single query, highlight the query and click Execute.

Creating a Query File and Entering and Executing the Query

1. Click New Query on the toolbar. A new query file appears in the Query Editor window. Save the file as 3Tutorial.sql in your C:\SQLServer\Solutions\Chapter3 folder. (The drive letter or folder path where you save your solution files may be different.)
2. Type the USE command and SELECT query shown in Figure 3-6 in the Query Editor, and then click Execute on the toolbar. The retrieved data values appear in the Results pane, as shown in Figure 3-6. (You may need to resize the columns in the Results pane to display all the data values.)
3. Save the query file.

NOTES: You can use this query file to enter and execute the rest of the sample queries that appear throughout the chapter if your instructor tells you to do so; however, the chapter does not provide explicit instructions for testing each query.

From this point on, the chapter displays query commands and retrieved data as text rather than in Management Studio.

To retrieve all the column values in a table, replace the individual column names in the SELECT clause with the asterisk (*) wildcard character. For example, the following query retrieves all the column values for every record in the UniversityStudent table:

```
SELECT *
FROM UniversityStudent
```

CAUTION: We present the wildcard (*) syntax because many developers use it, and you may see it in existing queries and applications. However, we do not use this syntax anywhere else in this book, and we strongly discourage you from using it. It can introduce errors into database applications if the structure of the query's database table changes. Note that this query always retrieves all table columns in the order in which they were created. If a DBA removes a column or adds a new column, the query retrieves different data than it did originally, which may break other code within the database application containing the query.

SQL queries are not case sensitive. To make queries easier to read and understand, we always place reserved words in uppercase letters. Also recall that in the Query Editor, SQL queries do not require line breaks to appear in any particular place, and you could place an entire SQL query on the same editor line. However, to facilitate reading queries, it is a good practice to place the SELECT, FROM, and WHERE clauses on different lines. When a clause becomes very long, you can wrap the text to a new line so that all the query text appears in a single editor window without your having to scroll horizontally.

Search Conditions

Note that the query in Figure 3-6 retrieves all the student records from the UniversityStudent table. You can add a search condition to a query to specify that it retrieves specific records. A *search condition* is an expression that seeks to match one or more table records. The general syntax of a search condition is:

```
ColumnName ComparisonOperator SearchValue
```

In this syntax, *ColumnName* is the name of the table column whose value you seek to match. *ComparisonOperator* is an operator that specifies the type of search, such as equal to (=), greater than (>), or less than (<). *SearchValue* is a data value to which you are comparing the column value. Table 3-1 summarizes commonly used SQL comparison operators, and the sections that follow describe how to use the operators to create search conditions.

Searching for Text Values

When you search for a value in a text column, you enclose the *SearchValue* in single quotation marks, and the *SearchValue* is not case sensitive. For example, the StudentGender column in the UniversityStudent database table represents gender values as 'M' or 'F', so that the following query retrieves the records for all females in the UniversityStudent database table:

```
SELECT StudentFirstName, StudentLastName
FROM UniversityStudent
WHERE StudentGender = 'F'
```

TABLE 3-1 SQL search condition comparison operators

Operator	Description	Example
=	Equal to	StudentID = 1 StudentGender = 'F'
>	Greater than	SectionCurrentEnrollment > 20
<	Less than	SectionMaxEnrollment < 50
>=	Greater than or equal to	SectionCurrentEnrollment >= 30
<=	Less than or equal to	SectionMaxEnrollment <= 40
<>, !=	Not equal to	LaptopBrand <> 'DELL' LaptopBrand != 'IBM'
!>	Not greater than	SectionCurrentEnrollment !> 50
!<	Not less than	SectionMaxEnrollment !< 10
BETWEEN	Determines if the data value is between 2 specified value (inclusive).	SectionCurrentEnrollment BETWEEN 5 AND 20
LIKE	Uses pattern matching in text strings; uses the percent sign (%) and underscore (_) wildcard characters. % represents any number of characters, and _ represents exactly one character.	DeptOffice LIKE 'Phillips%' CourseTitle LIKE '%Chinese%' SectionTerm LIKE 'FALL__'
IS NULL	Determines if the data value is NULL.	StudentMI IS NULL
IS NOT NULL	Determines if the data value is not NULL.	StudentMI IS NOT NULL
IN	Determines if the data value is a member of a search set.	EnrollmentGrade IN ('A', 'B') DepartmentID IN (1, 5, 6)
NOT IN	Determines if the data value is not a member of a search set.	EnrollmentGrade NOT IN ('C', 'D')

TIP: Because the search condition is not case sensitive, you can alternatively write the search condition as WHERE StudentGender = 'f'.

Suppose you need to search for a text value that contains an embedded single quotation mark, such as the text string "Women's." To do this, type the embedded quotation mark two times, so that your search condition appears as follows:

```
WHERE SubCategoryDescription = 'Women''s'
```

The LIKE operator allows you to search for text values by matching part of a character string, using the following general syntax:

```
WHERE ColumnName LIKE 'search_string'
```

To facilitate partial matches, `'search_string'` should contain either the percent sign (%) or underscore (_) wildcard character. The percent sign (%) represents multiple characters. If you place % on the left edge of the search string, the DBMS searches for an exact match on the rightmost characters and allows an inexact match for the characters represented by %. For example, the following query retrieves data from the UniversityCourse table in which the rightmost characters of the CourseTitle column are "Accounting":

```
SELECT CourseID, CourseName, CourseTitle
FROM UniversityCourse
WHERE CourseTitle LIKE '%Accounting'
```

Similarly, if you place the % wildcard character on the right edge of the search string, the DBMS searches for an exact match on the leftmost characters and allows an inexact match for the characters represented by %. The following query retrieves data from the UniversityCourseSection table in which the leftmost characters are "SUMM":

```
SELECT SectionID, SectionNumber, SectionTerm
FROM UniversitySection
WHERE SectionTerm LIKE 'SUMM%'
```

You can place the % wildcard character on both the right and left edges of the search string to retrieve text values in which the search string appears anywhere within the text value. For example, the following search condition retrieves all records within the UniversityCourse table in which the search string "Management" appears anywhere within the value:

```
SELECT CourseID, CourseName, CourseTitle
FROM UniversityCourse
WHERE CourseTitle LIKE '%Management%'
```

The underscore (_) wildcard character represents a single character within the search string. For example, the following query retrieves values from the UniversityStudent table in which the first character in the StudentState column is the letter *W*, followed by exactly one character:

```
SELECT StudentLastName, StateAbbreviation
FROM UniversityStudent
WHERE StateAbbreviation LIKE 'W_'
```

You can combine the % and _ wildcard characters in a single search string. For example, the following query retrieves records from the UniversityCourse table for 200-level courses. The CourseName column values for these courses are course numbers for which there can be a variable number of characters from the left edge of the name to the numeral *2* and the third from the last character is always the number *2*. Note that in this syntax, the number *2* is followed by two underscores.

```
SELECT CourseID, CourseName
FROM UniversityCourse
WHERE CourseName LIKE '%2__'
```

Searching for Number Values

To search for number values, specify *SearchValue* as the number to match. Do not place the number value in quotation marks. Use the equal to operator (=) to create an *exact search condition* that returns records that exactly match the *SearchValue*. For example, the following query contains an exact search condition that returns the records in the UniversitySection table for which the MaxEnrollment column value is exactly 40:

```
SELECT SectionID, SectionNumber
FROM UniversitySection
WHERE SectionMaxEnrollment = 40
```

Use the inequality operators (>, <, >=, <=, !>, !<) to create *inexact search conditions* that return records falling within a range of values. For example, the following query contains an inexact search condition that returns all records in the UniversitySection table for which the MaxEnrollment column value is greater than or equal to 40:

```
SELECT SectionID, SectionNumber
FROM UniversitySection
WHERE SectionMaxEnrollment >= 40
```

Searching for Date Values

Recall that in a SQL Server database, the Date/Time data types represent both date and time values. You can create either exact search conditions to retrieve records that contain values exactly matching a given date and/or time, or inexact search conditions that match a range of dates/times. To do this, specify the *SearchValue* as a text string. SQL Server automatically converts this text string to a Date/Time data type, provided the text string is in a Date/Time format that SQL Server recognizes. Which Date/Time formats does SQL Server recognize? SQL Server applications use the following sources to determine if a text string is a date:

- **Locale-specific** is the date format that the Windows Regional Settings Properties dialog box specifies. (To view this format, click Start on the Taskbar, click Control Panel, and double-click Regional and Language Options.)
- **Database-specific** includes a variety of common formats that the database understands. These values depend on where the DBMS was purchased and whether the DBA changed the location after installing the database.

Figure 3-7 illustrates queries that retrieve data using text strings representing date and time values in their search conditions. Note that in the output, the retrieved records show their Date/Time data values using the locale-specific date and time formats, which in this example is English (United States).

You can create inexact search conditions to search for dates that occur before or after a given date. For example, the following query contains a search condition that returns all records from the UniversityStudent table for students who were born on or before January 1, 1985:

```
SELECT StudentFirstName, StudentLastName
FROM UniversityStudent
WHERE StudentDOB <= '01/01/1985'
```

Similarly, the next query contains a search condition to return data for all records from the UniversitySection table for course sections that start after 1 p.m.

FIGURE 3-7   Search conditions for date and time values

```
SELECT StudentFirstName, StudentLastName, StudentDOB
FROM UniversityStudent
WHERE StudentDOB = '5/29/1988'————————— Date search condition

StudentFirstName   StudentLastName   StudentDOB
----------------   ---------------   ----------
Clifford           Wall              5/29/1988

SELECT SectionNumber, SectionTerm, SectionDay, SectionTime
FROM UniversityCourseSection
WHERE SectionTime = '10:00:00 AM'————————— Time search condition

SectionNumber SectionTerm SectionDay SectionTime
------------- ----------- ---------- ----------------------
001           SUMM06      MTWTHF     1/1/1900  10:00:00 AM
001           FALL06      MWF        1/1/1900  10:00:00 AM
001           FALL06      TTH        1/1/1900  10:00:00 AM
001           SPR07       TTH        1/1/1900  10:00:00 AM
001           SPR07       TTH        1/1/1900  10:00:00 AM
```

```
SELECT SectionID, SectionNumber
FROM UniversitySection
WHERE SectionTime > '01:00:00 PM'
```

Searching for NULL and NOT NULL Values

Sometimes you need to create a query that retrieves records for which a particular column value is NULL. To do this, use the following search condition syntax:

```
WHERE ColumnName IS NULL
```

In the UniversityLaptopComputer table, laptop computers that are currently not assigned to students have a NULL value for the StudentID foreign key column. The first query in Figure 3-8 retrieves the laptop IDs, brands, and CPU specifications for all laptop computers that are not currently assigned to a student.

Similarly, sometimes you need to create a query that retrieves records for which a column value is not NULL. The second query in Figure 3-8 retrieves the laptop IDs, brands, and CPU specifications for all laptops that have been assigned to students so that their StudentID column values are not NULL.

Combining Search Conditions Using the AND and OR Operators

Sometimes you need to create queries that use multiple search conditions. For example, suppose you want to determine which course sections offered during the SUMM08 (Summer 2008) term have current enrollments of over 20 students. This query needs to specify that the SectionTerm column value is 'SUMM08' and that the SectionMaxEnrollment column value is greater than 20.

You can specify multiple search conditions in the same query using the AND and OR logical operators. When you combine two search conditions using the AND operator, both search conditions must be true for the overall search expression to be true. When you combine two search conditions using the OR operator, either search condition must be true for the overall search expression to be true. Figure 3-9 shows examples of queries that combine search conditions using the AND and OR operators.

FIGURE 3-8   Search conditions for retrieving records with NULL and NOT-NULL column values

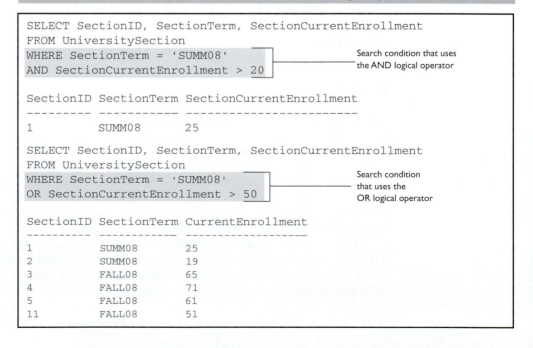

```
SELECT LaptopID, LaptopBrand, LaptopCPU
FROM UniversityLaptop
WHERE StudentID IS NULL


LaptopID LaptopBrand LaptopCPU
-------- ----------- -------------
2        DELL        Latitude D788        Computers that have not been checked out to
3        DELL        Inspiron 7109        students (StudentID is NULL.)
5        IBM         Thinkpad T3501


SELECT LaptopID, LaptopBrand, LaptopCPU
FROM UniversityLaptop
WHERE StudentID IS NOT NULL


LaptopID LaptopBrand LaptopCPU
-------- ----------- -------------
1        DELL        Latitude D788        Computers that have been checked out to students
4        IBM         Thinkpad T3501       (StudentID is not NULL.)
```

The first query in Figure 3-9 uses the AND logical operator, and retrieves all UniversitySection records for which both the SectionTerm value is 'SUMM08' and the enrollment is greater than 20 students. If you examine the records in the UniversitySection table, you will see that two records exist for the 'SUMM08' term: The first section has a current enrollment value of 25, and the second has a current enrollment value of 19. Because this search expression requires both search conditions to be true, the query retrieves only the record for which the current enrollment value is 25.

FIGURE 3-9   Search conditions that use the AND and OR logical operators

```
SELECT SectionID, SectionTerm, SectionCurrentEnrollment
FROM UniversitySection
WHERE SectionTerm = 'SUMM08'                          Search condition that uses
AND SectionCurrentEnrollment > 20                     the AND logical operator


SectionID SectionTerm SectionCurrentEnrollment
--------- ----------- ------------------------
1         SUMM08      25

SELECT SectionID, SectionTerm, SectionCurrentEnrollment
FROM UniversitySection
WHERE SectionTerm = 'SUMM08'                          Search condition
OR SectionCurrentEnrollment > 50                      that uses the
                                                      OR logical operator


SectionID SectionTerm CurrentEnrollment
--------- ----------- -------------------
1         SUMM08      25
2         SUMM08      19
3         FALL08      65
4         FALL08      71
5         FALL08      61
11        FALL08      51
```

The second query in Figure 3-9 uses the OR logical operator to retrieve all UniversitySection records for which either the SectionTerm value is 'SUMM08' or the current enrollment value is greater than 50. The query retrieves both records for which the SectionTerm value is 'SUMM08'. The query also retrieves all records for which the current enrollment is greater than 50, regardless of their SectionTerm Value.

Using the NOT Logical Operator

If you preface any search condition with the NOT logical operator, the query retrieves all records that do *not* match a search condition. The NOT operator has the following general syntax in a search condition:

```
WHERE NOT (search_condition)
```

For example, the following query retrieves the brands and CPU descriptions for all laptop computers for which the LaptopBrand value is not 'IBM':

```
SELECT LaptopBrand, LaptopCPU
FROM UniversityLaptop
WHERE NOT (LaptopBrand = 'IBM')
```

Using the DISTINCT Qualifier to Suppress Duplicate Output Rows

An SQL SELECT query retrieves data for every record that matches the criteria the query specifies. Sometimes this results in duplicate outputs. For example, suppose a user wants to retrieve a listing of the different types of laptop CPUs available for student checkout. The first query in Figure 3-10 retrieves the CPU descriptions for all laptops in the UniversityLaptopComputer table. Note that the output displays duplicate values.

The duplicates occur because multiple records in the UniversityLaptopComputer table have the same CPU description value. To suppress the duplicate rows, use the

FIGURE 3-10   Using the DISTINCT modifier to suppress duplicate output values

```
SELECT LaptopCPU
FROM UniversityLaptop

LaptopCPU
---------
Latitude D788
Latitude D788
Inspiron 7109     ——— Output with duplicate values
Thinkpad T3501
Thinkpad T3501

SELECT DISTINCT LaptopCPU
FROM UniversityLaptop

LaptopCPU
---------
Inspiron 7109
Latitude D788     ——— Output with duplicate values suppressed
Thinkpad T3501
```

DISTINCT modifier in the SELECT clause. The DISTINCT modifier has the following syntax:

```
SELECT DISTINCT Column1, Column2, . . .
FROM TableName
WHERE SearchCondition(s)
```

The second query in Figure 3-10 shows the query using the DISTINCT modifier. Note that in the query output, the DBMS suppresses the duplicate rows.

Sorting Query Output

In the SELECT queries that you have seen so far, the retrieved records do not appear in any particular order. Actually, the DBMS returns the data in the order that is the easiest and most efficient to use when processing the query. This may be the order in which the data values were inserted into the database, the order in which they are stored in the data files, or some other order. To specify a sort order for retrieved data, use the ORDER BY clause, which has the following syntax:

```
SELECT Column1, Column2, . . .
FROM TableName
WHERE SearchCondition(s)
ORDER BY SortKey [DESC]
```

The ORDER BY clause always appears as the last line in the query, after the search conditions. *SortKey* specifies the *sort key,* which is the name of the column by which you want to sort the data. By default, the DBMS sorts the records in ascending order: number values appear from the smallest to the largest, text values appear alphabetically, and date values appear from least recent to most recent. To reverse the default ascending sort order, append the optional [DESC] modifier to the ORDER BY clause. Figure 3-11 shows examples of queries that use the ORDER BY clause to sort data values.

FIGURE 3-11   Using the ORDER BY clause to sort query output

```
SELECT CourseName, CourseTitle
FROM UniversityCourse
WHERE CourseName LIKE 'MIS%'
ORDER BY CourseTitle

CourseName CourseTitle
---------- -----------
MIS 344    Database Management Systems          ┐ Query output sorted by
MIS 240    Information Systems in Business      │ CourseTitle values
MIS 345    Introduction to Networks             │
MIS 310    Systems Analysis and Design          ┘

SELECT StudentLastName, StudentFirstName, StudentDOB
FROM UniversityStudent
WHERE StudentGender = 'F'
ORDER BY StudentDOB DESC

StudentLastName StudentFirstName StudentDOB
--------------- ---------------- ----------------------
Johansen        Brenda           1989-03-27 00:00:00.000   ┐ Query output sorted by
Bochman         Ann              1988-04-01 00:00:00.000   │ StudentDOB values in
Owen            Patricia         1987-01-23 00:00:00.000   ┘ reverse (descending) order
```

FIGURE 3-12   Using the ORDER BY clause with multiple sort keys

```
SELECT SectionID, SectionMaxEnrollment, SectionCurrentEnrollment
FROM UniversitySection
WHERE SectionTerm = 'SPR09'
ORDER BY SectionMaxEnrollment, SectionCurrentEnrollment

SectionID SectionMaxEnrollment SectionCurrentEnrollment
--------- -------------------- ------------------------
  22          35                      23           Query output sorted by the first sort key
  25          35                      29           (SectionMaxEnrollment)
  21          40                       0
  18          40                       3           Then, within records with the same
  20          40                      17           values for the first sort key, query
  19          40                      21           output sorted by the second sort key
  26          50                      31           (SectionCurrentEnrollment)
  24          60                      12
  23          60                      38
  15          65                       0
  17          65                       5
  16          80                       0
```

Sometimes you need to sort retrieved records based on values in multiple columns. To do this, use multiple sort keys and configure the ORDER BY clause as follows:

```
ORDER BY SortKey1, SortKey2, ...
```

The DBMS first sorts the output by the *SortKey1* values. For records that have the same value for *SortKey1,* the DBMS then sorts the output by *SortKey2*. You can specify any number of sort keys within the ORDER BY clause. Figure 3-12 shows an example of a query that retrieves the Section ID, maximum enrollment, and current enrollment values for classes offered during the SPR09 term at Ironwood University. In the query output, the DBMS sorts the output first by the maximum enrollment values. For records that have the same maximum enrollment value, the DBMS then sorts the records by the current enrollment values.

USING ARITHMETIC OPERATIONS IN QUERIES

You can create queries that perform arithmetic operations on retrieved column values. For example, you can retrieve the number of available seats in each course section in the UniversitySection table by subtracting the SectionCurrentEnrollment column value from the SectionMaxEnrollment value. You could alternatively retrieve the SectionCurrentEnrollment and SectionMaxEnrollment values and then write a program within a client application to perform this calculation, but it is more efficient to have the DBMS perform these types of operations. Why? One reason is that this approach reduces network traffic: the network needs to transmit only the final result to the client, rather than all the values needed in the calculation. Also, there is no need to spend the time and effort to write a special program to perform these simple

TABLE 3-2   SQL Server query arithmetic operators

Operator	Description	Example Expression
+	Addition	`SELECT CourseCredits + 1`
–	Subtraction	`SELECT SectionMaxEnrollment – SectionCurrentEnrollment`
*	Multiplication	`SELECT CourseCredits * 2`
/	Division	`SELECT SectionCurrentEnrollment/SectionMaxEnrollment`
%	Modulo (division operation that returns only the remainder)	`SELECT SectionMaxEnrollment%SectionCurrentEnrollment`

calculations when the DBMS can easily do it. The following paragraphs describe how to perform simple arithmetic calculations in queries and how to perform more complex calculations using built-in functions.

Creating Arithmetic Expressions

To create a query expression that performs a simple arithmetic operation, form expressions within the SELECT clause using the following syntax:

```
Value Operator Value
```

In this syntax, *Value* can represent either a table column name (such as CurrentEnrollment) or a numeric constant (such as the number 3). *Operator* represents one of the arithmetic operators that SQL Server supports. Table 3-2 summarizes the SQL Server query arithmetic operators.

You can perform arithmetic operations on columns that use either number or date data types. The following sections describe how to do this.

Creating Arithmetic Operations on Number Columns

You can perform addition, subtraction, multiplication, and division operations on columns that use any of the number data types (Int, Smallint, Tinyint, Decimal, Number, Float, Real, Money, or Smallmoney). You can perform modulo operations only on columns that use the integer data types (Int, Smallint, or Tinyint).

Figure 3-13 illustrates a query containing an arithmetic expression that retrieves the difference between the SectionMaxEnrollment and SectionCurrentEnrollment

FIGURE 3-13   Performing arithmetic operations on number columns

```
SELECT SectionID, SectionMaxEnrollment - SectionCurrentEnrollment
FROM UniversitySection
WHERE SectionTerm = 'SUMM08'

SectionID           (No column name)
------------------  -----------------
1                   5
2                   11      Calculated values
```

column values in the UniversitySection table for the course sections offered in the SUMM08 term.

Difficulties can arise when performing division operations within the SELECT clause, because when the SQL Server DBMS evaluates an arithmetic expression, it always returns the result as the same data type as the inputs. In other words, when you create an expression using two decimal numbers, the result appears as a decimal number value. When you create an expression using two integer values, the result appears as an integer. This is not a problem for addition, subtraction, multiplication, and modulo expressions, because whenever you add, subtract, multiply, or derive the modulus of two integers, the result is always an integer. However, when you divide two integers, the result often returns a decimal value rather than an integer. When this happens, the DBMS *truncates,* or rounds the output down, to the nearest integer.

To avoid this problem, use the CONVERT function to convert the integer inputs to number data types that include decimal values, such as real or float. This causes the DBMS to return the output as a decimal number value. The CONVERT function uses the following general syntax:

```
CONVERT (TargetDataType, SearchValue)
```

The first query in Figure 3-14 illustrates a query that divides the SectionCurrentEnrollment value by the SectionMaxEnrollment value for the two courses offered during the SUMM08 term to determine the percentage by which the course's enrollments have reached their maximum values.

In the first query, the output for both courses appears as zero, because the DBMS truncates the output to the nearest integer (zero). The second query converts the SectionCurrentEnrollment and SectionMaxEnrollment input values to the Real number data type before performing the division operation; so the outputs appear as decimal values.

Creating Arithmetic Operations on Date/Time Columns

Sometimes you need to perform arithmetic operations on columns that store dates and times. For example, you might need to determine a date that is a specific number of

FIGURE 3-14   Division operations on columns that use the Integer data type

```
SELECT SectionCurrentEnrollment/SectionMaxEnrollment
FROM UniversitySection
WHERE SectionTerm = 'SUMM08'

(No column name)
----------------

0            ── Division operation output truncated to the nearest integer
0

SELECT CONVERT(Real, SectionCurrentEnrollment)/
CONVERT(Real, SectionMaxEnrollment)
FROM UniversitySection
WHERE SectionTerm = 'SUMM08'

(No column name)
----------------

0.8333333    ── Output appearing as real numbers with decimal values
0.6333333
```

FIGURE 3-15   Performing arithmetic operations on Date/Time columns

```
SELECT LaptopID, LaptopYear, LaptopYear + 730
FROM UniversityLaptop

LaptopID LaptopYear              (No column name)
-------- -----------------------  ----------------
1        2008-05-21 00:00:00.000  2010-05-20 00:00:00.000
2        2008-05-21 00:00:00.000  2010-05-20 00:00:00.000
3        2008-05-21 00:00:00.000  2010-05-20 00:00:00.000
4        2008-12-01 00:00:00.000  2010-11-30 00:00:00.000
5        2008-12-01 00:00:00.000  2010-11-30 00:00:00.000
```

Calculated dates that are
2 years (730 days) after
retrieved dates

```
SELECT TutorSessionID, TutorSessionStartTime,
TutorSessionStartTime - .041667
FROM UniversityTutorSession
WHERE StudentID = 1

TutorSessionID TutorSessionStartTime    (No column name)
-------------- -----------------------  -------------------
5              2008-10-03 16:30:00.000  2008-10-03 15:30:00.000
6              2008-10-04 18:30:00.000  2008-10-04 17:30:00.000
7              2008-10-31 19:00:00.000  2008-10-31 18:00:00.000
```

Calculated times that are
1 hour (0.041667 days)
before retrieved times

days before or after a known date, or you might want to determine the number of days or years between two known dates. You can also create arithmetic expressions for columns that use the Date/Time data types.

To determine a date that is a specific number of days and/or fractions of days before or after a retrieved Date/Time value, subtract or add a decimal value representing the number of days or fractional number of days. For example, to find a date that is 30 days beyond a given date, add 30 to the given date. To find a time that is 12 hours before a retrieved time, subtract 0.5 (which represents half of a day, or 12 hours) from the known time. Figure 3-15 shows examples of queries that perform arithmetic operations on date columns.

The first query in Figure 3-15 retrieves the Laptop ID and LaptopYear values of all records in the UniversityLaptop table, along with a calculated value representing a date that is two years (730 days) after the LaptopYear value. The second query retrieves tutor session ID values, along with the session start time, and a time that is one hour (1/24, or 0.041667) before the scheduled start time.

You can also perform a variety of calculations on Date/Time fields using the SQL Server built-in scalar functions. The next section describes these functions.

USING IN-LINE FUNCTIONS IN QUERIES

You can use the SQL Server built-in in-line scalar functions to retrieve calculated values based on stored data values. An *in-line scalar function* is a function that you apply within the SELECT clause of a SQL query to operate on a single data value. For example, you might use an in-line function to convert a retrieved text value to all uppercase letters or to find the absolute value of a number value. (This is in contrast to an aggregate function, which operates on data from multiple records, such as creating a summary total for a group of records. You will learn about aggregate functions in a later section.)

In general, in-line scalar functions use the following general syntax within the SELECT clause:

```
SELECT FunctionName(Expression), ...
```

In this syntax, *Expression* can be a column name, a constant value (such as the text string "Joline" or the number 0.031415) or an arithmetic expression (such as SectionMaxEnrollment - SectionCurrentEnrollment). SQL Server supports scalar functions that operate on text, number, and date data columns. The following sections describe these functions.

Text Functions

The text functions operate on columns that use the char or varchar data types. Table 3-3 summarizes commonly used text in-line functions.

Figure 3-16 shows examples of queries that use in-line scalar text functions. The first query uses the UPPER function to retrieve the last name of student ID 1 (Clifford Wall) and display the result in all uppercase letters. The second query uses the concatenation operator (+) to retrieve a student's first and last names and concatenate the column values into a single text string with a blank space between them. The third query uses the SUBSTRING function to first retrieve the course names of all courses offered by department 1 and then extract a three-character substring beginning at character number 5.

TABLE 3-3   Commonly used text scalar functions

Function	Description	General Syntax	Example
Concatenation (+)	Concatenates (joins) two text strings to form a single text string.	`TextString1 + TextString2`	`StudentFirstName + 'is great!'`
LEN	Returns the number of characters in a text string.	`LEN(TextString)`	`LEN(CourseName)`
LOWER	Converts a text string to all lower-case characters.	`LOWER(TextString)`	`LOWER (StudentFirstName)`
LTRIM	Trims leading blank spaces from a text string.	`LTRIM(TextString)`	`LTRIM(CourseName)`
RTRIM	Trims trailing blank spaces from a text string.	`RTRIM(TextString)`	`RTRIM(CourseName)`
SUBSTRING	Returns a substring within a text string.	`SUBSTRING (TextString, StartPosition, Length)`	`SUBSTRING (CourseName, 4, 3)`
UPPER	Converts a text string to all upper-case characters.	`UPPER(TextString)`	`UPPER (StudentLastName)`

FIGURE 3-16   Queries that use in-line scalar text functions

```
SELECT UPPER(StudentFirstName)
FROM UniversityStudent
WHERE StudentID = 1

(No column name)
----------------
CLIFFORD

SELECT StudentFirstName + ' ' + StudentLastName
FROM UniversityStudent
WHERE StudentID = 1

(No column name)
----------------
Clifford Wall

SELECT SUBSTRING(CourseName, 5, 3)
FROM UniversityCourse
WHERE DepartmentID = 1

(No column name)
----------------
240
310
344
345
```

Date/Time Functions

The date/time in-line scalar functions operate on columns that have the Datetime or Smalldatetime data types. Table 3-4 summarizes commonly used date/time functions.

Many of the date/time functions in Table 3-4 use a *DatePart* parameter, which represents a component of a date expression. Table 3-5 summarizes the allowable *DatePart* parameter values for different date expression components.

Figure 3-17 illustrates queries that use the date/time functions to calculate values for the first record in the UniversityServiceHours table. The first query in Figure 3-17 uses the DATEADD function to add an interval of one hour to the ServiceHoursStartTime value, which is 8 a.m., and returns a time of 9 a.m. The second query uses the DATEDIFF function to determine the time interval between the ServiceHoursStartTime and ServiceHoursEndTime values for the record and returns an interval of three hours. The third query illustrates how to nest scalar functions: It repeats the DATEADD function from the first query but nests the outcome in the DATENAME function, which extracts a text string representing the hour value, which is nine.

Number Functions

The number in-line functions perform mathematical operations on columns that use the number data types. Table 3-6 summarizes commonly used number functions.

Figure 3-18 illustrates two queries that use in-line scalar number functions within the SELECT clause. The first query uses the RAND function with the seed value 13 to generate a random number. The second query repeats the first query and includes the ROUND function to round the output to three decimal places.

TABLE 3-4   Commonly used date/time functions

Function	Description	General Syntax	Example
DATEADD	Returns a new date/time value by adding an interval (expressed in days or fractions of days) to a known value.	DATEADD(*DatePart, Interval, DateValue*)	DATEADD(hh, 1, ServiceHoursStartTime)
DATEDIFF	Returns an integer representing the difference between two date values.	DATEDIFF(*DatePart, StartDate, EndDate*)	DATEDIFF(hh, ServiceHoursStartTime, ServiceHoursEndTime)
DATENAME	Returns a text string representing a specific part of a date value, such as the month or hours.	DATENAME(*DatePart, DateValue*)	DATENAME(hh, SectionTime)
GETDATE	Returns the current date and time from the database server.	GETDATE()	
MONTH	Returns an integer representing the month of a date value.	MONTH(*DateValue*)	MONTH(StudentDOB)
YEAR	Returns an integer representing the year of a date value.	YEAR(*DateValue*)	YEAR(StudentDOB)

TABLE 3-5   *DatePart* parameter values

Date Component	DatePart Value
Year	yy, yyyy
Quarter	qq, q
Month	mm, m
Day of year	dy, y
Day of month	dd, d
Week of year	ww, wk
Hour	hh
Minute	mi
Second	ss

FIGURE 3-17   Queries that use in-line scalar date/time functions

```
SELECT DATEADD(hh, 1, ServiceHoursStartTime)
FROM UniversityServiceHours
WHERE ServiceHoursID = 1

(No column name)
----------------
2006-10-11 09:00:00.000
SELECT DATEDIFF(hh, ServiceHoursStartTime, ServiceHoursEndTime)
FROM UniversityServiceHours
WHERE ServiceHoursID = 1

(No column name)
----------------
3
SELECT DATENAME(hh, DATEADD(hh, 1, ServiceHoursStartTime))
FROM UniversityServiceHours
WHERE ServiceHoursID = 1

(No column name)
----------------
9
```

Date/time functions

Nested functions

USING AGGREGATE FUNCTIONS IN QUERIES

In the previous section you learned how to perform arithmetic calculations on column values in a single record. Sometimes you need to perform calculations on groups of retrieved records. For example, you might want to calculate the total current enrollment in all courses or the average enrollment in all course sections during a specific term. To do this, use one of the SQL aggregate functions. An *aggregate function* performs a summary operation on a group of values and returns a single value. The following subsections describe the aggregate functions and show how to use them with the GROUP BY and HAVING clauses.

SQL Aggregate Functions

Table 3-7 summarizes commonly used SQL aggregate functions. All the aggregate functions except COUNT operate exclusively on columns that have number data types, and they return a value that is the same data type as the column to which you apply the function. If you apply the function to an integer column, the result appears truncated to the nearest integer; if you apply the function to one of the decimal data types, the result appears as a decimal data type. All the functions except COUNT omit NULL values from their calculations.

The COUNT function reports the number of rows that a query retrieves, regardless of the data type of the selected column name. This function has two versions: COUNT(*) and COUNT(*ColumnName*). The COUNT(*) version counts all records, including ones that have NULL values in any of the table columns. The COUNT(*ColumnName*) version counts only records for which the value of *ColumnName* is not NULL.

Figure 3-19 shows examples of queries that use aggregate functions. The first query calculates the sum, maximum, minimum, and average current enrollments for all course sections during the FALL08 term. The second and third queries illustrate the two versions of the COUNT function. The second query reports the total number of laptop computers in the UniversityLaptop table. The third query reports the number of laptop computers that are currently available and not checked out to students; so their StudentID values are NULL.

Using the GROUP BY Clause with Aggregate Functions

Suppose that a query retrieves multiple records and the values in one column have duplicate values by which you can group the output and apply an aggregate function to the grouped values. For example, you can retrieve the term descriptions and current enrollments for all course sections in the UniversitySection table and calculate the

TABLE 3-6   Commonly used in-line scalar number functions

Function	Description	General Syntax	Example
ABS	Returns the absolute value of a numerical expression.	`ABS(Expression)`	`ABS(MaxEnrollment - CurrentEnrollment)`
CEILING	Returns the smallest integer greater than or equal to the given numeric expression.	`CEILING(Expression)`	`CEILING (CurrentEnrollment/ MaxEnrollment)`
FLOOR	Returns the largest integer less than or equal to the given numeric expression.	`FLOOR(Expression)`	`FLOOR (CurrentEnrollment/ MaxEnrollment)`
PI( )	Returns the constant value pi.	`PI()`	
POWER	Returns the value of an expression raised to a given power.	`POWER(Expression, Power)`	`POWER(8,2)`
RAND	Returns a random number between 0 and 1.	`RAND([Seed])` Seed optionally provides a start value	`RAND(32)`
ROUND	Returns a numeric expression, rounded to a specified length or precision.	`ROUND(Expression, Length, [Function])` Length is a positive integer specifying the number of rounded decimal places; Function specifies if the expression is rounded or truncated; if Function is 0 or omitted, the expression is truncated; otherwise, it is rounded.	`ROUND (CurrentEnrollment/ MaxEnrollment, 2, 1)`
SQUARE	Returns the square of the given expression.	`SQUARE(Expression)`	`SQUARE(8)`
SQRT	Returns the square root of a the given expression.	`SQRT(Expression)`	`SQRT(8)`

FIGURE 3-18   Queries that use in-line scalar number functions

```
SELECT RAND(13)

(No column name)
----------------
0.713815588868022

SELECT ROUND(RAND(13), 3)

(No column name)
----------------
0.714
```

TABLE 3-7 Commonly used SQL aggregate functions

Function	Description	Example
AVG	Returns the average value of a group of values.	`SELECT AVG(SectionCurrentEnrollment)`
COUNT	Returns the number of records that a query returns.	`SELECT COUNT(*)` or `SELECT COUNT(StudentID)`
MAX	Returns the maximum value of a group of values	`SELECT MAX(SectionCurrentEnrollment)`
MIN	Returns the minimum value of a group of values.	`SELECT MIN(SectionCurrentEnrollment)`
SUM	Returns the sum of a group of values.	`SELECT SUM(SectionCurrentEnrollment)`
STDEV	Returns the standard deviation of a group of values.	`SELECT STDEV(SectionCurrentEnrollment)`
VAR	Returns the statistical variance of a group of values.	`SELECT VAR(SectionCurrentEnrollment)`

total current enrollment for each term. To do this, you must use the GROUP BY clause to group the duplicate values, then apply the SUM aggregate function. The GROUP BY clause has the following general syntax:

```
GROUP BY ColumnName
```

The GROUP BY clause appears as the last line in the query, after all the search conditions. Figure 3-20 illustrates queries that use the GROUP BY clause. The first

FIGURE 3-19 Queries that use aggregate functions

```
SELECT SUM(SectionCurrentEnrollment), MAX(SectionCurrentEnrollment),
MIN(SectionCurrentEnrollment), AVG(SectionCurrentEnrollment)
FROM UniversitySection
WHERE SectionTerm = 'FALL08'


--- ---- ---- ----
519   71   23   43


SELECT COUNT(*) ————————————  Reports the total number of all
FROM UniversityLaptop                 retrieved records, including those
                                      with columns with NULL values

----
5


SELECT COUNT(StudentID) ————————  Reports the total number of records,
FROM UniversityLaptop                 omitting records for which the
                                      specified column's value is NULL

----
2
```

FIGURE 3-20   Using the GROUP BY clause in aggregate function queries

```
SELECT SectionTerm, SUM(SectionCurrentEnrollment)
FROM UniversitySection
GROUP BY SectionTerm

SectionTerm  (No column name)
-----------  ----------------
FALL08       519
SPR09        179
SUMM08        44

SELECT AdvisorID, COUNT(*)
FROM UniversityStudent
GROUP BY AdvisorID

AdvisorID (No column name)
---------  ---------------
1          1
4          1
8          2
9          2
10         1
```

query reports the sum of the current enrollment values for each term, and the second query reports the number of students each university instructor advises by counting the number of times that each advisor's ID appears in the UniversityStudent table.

You can use the GROUP BY clause to group data that uses any data type except Ntext, Text, Image, or Bit. Whenever you use an aggregate function, the query returns a single value for the column, to which you apply the aggregate function. If the SELECT clause lists any other columns, these columns *must* appear in a GROUP BY clause, or an error will occur. Figure 3-21 illustrates this error.

This query attempts to retrieve the section term descriptions and associated sums of current enrollments but does not include the SectionTerm column in a GROUP BY clause. The DBMS tries to retrieve all of the SectionTerm values in the table, and also tries to calculate a single value for the sum of the term enrollments. It cannot reconcile retrieving a single value for each SectionTerm as well as the aggregate function result, so an error occurs. Always remember that when you use an aggregate function in a query, all other columns that appear in the SELECT clause must also appear in a GROUP BY clause.

Using the HAVING Clause with Aggregate Functions

Sometimes you need to create a query that uses the result of an aggregate function as a search condition. For example, suppose you want to know which terms have total enrollments exceeding 100 students. To do this, use the HAVING clause. The HAVING clause is like a search condition, except that it uses the result of an aggregate function as the search value. Always use the HAVING clause in conjunction with and following the GROUP BY clause. The DBMS applies the HAVING search condition after it performs the grouping operation and displays only the records that meet the search criteria.

FIGURE 3-21   Error that occurs when you omit the GROUP BY clause

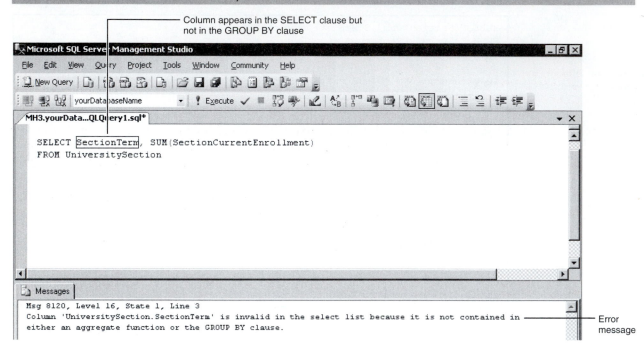

Figure 3-22 shows examples of queries that use the HAVING clause. The first query in Figure 3-22 retrieves the term description for every term in which the total enrollment exceeds 100 students. The second query illustrates how the aggregate function expression that appears in the HAVING clause does not have to appear in the SELECT clause. This query displays the Advisor ID values for all advisors who have more than one advisee, but it does not display exactly how many advisees the advisors

FIGURE 3-22   Using the HAVING clause in aggregate function queries

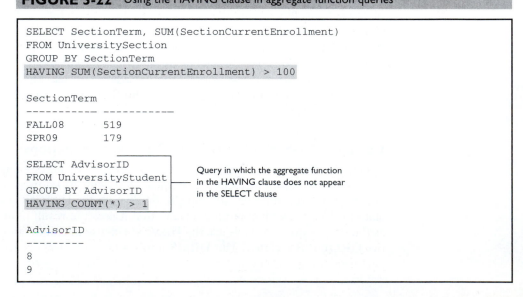

have. Note that because this query uses an aggregate function in the HAVING clause, it must use the GROUP BY clause to group the output by the column appearing in the SELECT clause.

FORMATTING QUERY OUTPUT

So far we have accepted the default output formats for retrieved data: dates appear using the default date for the database server, and noninteger numbers appear in the default format for the number. Column headings for data columns appear as the database column names. In Management Studio, column headings stating "(No column name)" appear for results of arithmetic calculations and functions. The following subsections describe how to format query outputs using the CONVERT and STR functions and how to display columns using alternate column headings.

Modifying Output Formats Using CONVERT

To change the output format of data that uses the one of the Date/Time or money (Money, Smallmoney) data types, use the CONVERT function. (Recall that you used the CONVERT function earlier to convert Integer columns to Real columns when you used them in a division calculation.) This section shows how to use the CONVERT function to convert a Date/Time or number data value to a text string that appears in a specific output style.

To do this, use the following general syntax for the CONVERT function:

```
CONVERT (TargetDataType, InputValue, [Style])
```

In this syntax, *TargetDataType* is the data type to which you wish to convert the *InputValue*. When you format query output data, this value will be Char or Varchar. *InputValue* can be a column name, an expression that contains an arithmetic calculation, or an in-line or aggregate function. *Style* is an integer that represents specific data formats. If you omit the *Style* parameter, the CONVERT function returns the data in the standard format for the target data type. If you include the *Style* parameter, the CONVERT function converts the *InputValue* to a character string that has a specific format. Table 3-8 summarizes commonly used date output formats and their associated *Style* values.

TABLE 3-8 Date output formats and associated style values

Output Format	Description	Example	Style Value
mm/dd/yy	USA – 2-digit year	11/20/06	1
mm/dd/yyyy	USA – 4-digit year	11/20/2006	101
yy.mm.dd	ANSI – 2-digit year	06.11.20	2
yyyy.mm.dd	ANSI – 4-digit year	2006.11.20	102
dd/mm/yy	British/French – 2-digit year	20/11/06	3
dd/mm/yyyy	British/French – 4-digit year	20/11/2006	103
hh:mi:ss	Time	11:59:59	108

TABLE 3-9   Money output formats and associated style values

Output Format Description	Example Value	Style Value
2 digits to the right of the decimal point; no commas	12345.67	0 (default)
2 digits to the right of the decimal point; commas every 3 digits to the left of the decimal point	12,345.67	1
4 digits to the right of the decimal point; no commas	12345.6789	2

NOTE: You can retrieve a complete listing of all date formats and style values in the SQL Server online help system.

By default, SQL Server interprets two-digit years based on a cutoff year of 2049. It interprets the two-digit year 49 as 2049 and the two-digit year 50 as 1950. Some client applications use different cutoff years; so, to be safe, always specify years using a four-digit format.

Table 3-9 summarizes commonly used money output formats and their associated *Style* values. Figure 3-23 illustrates queries that use the CONVERT function to format date and time output values using alternate formats.

Modifying Output Formats Using STR

To convert a numeric data value to a text string that displays a specific number of decimal places, use the STR function. (You could alternatively use the CONVERT function, but the STR function gives you more control over the output format.) The STR function requires that the input number value has the float data type. The function uses the following general syntax:

```
STR(FloatExpression, [Length,] [Decimal])
```

FIGURE 3-23   Using the CONVERT function to format query output

```
SELECT CONVERT(varchar, StudentDOB, 1)
FROM UniversityStudent

(No column name)
----------------
05/29/88
11/01/81
01/23/87
08/09/88
04/12/88
03/27/89
10/15/89

SELECT CONVERT(char, SectionTime, 108)
FROM UniversitySection
WHERE SectionTerm = 'SUMM08'

(No column name)
----------------
08:00:00
10:00:00
```

FIGURE 3-24   Using the STR function to format query output

```
SELECT STR(AVG(CONVERT(float, SectionCurrentEnrollment)), 10, 2)
FROM UniversitySection
WHERE SectionTerm = 'FALL08'

(No column name)
----------------
           43.33
```

In this syntax, *FloatExpression* can be a column name, arithmetic expression, or other expression that has the Float data type. *Length* optionally specifies the total length of the output character string, including the sign, digits, and decimal point. The default value of *Length* is 10. *Decimal* optionally specifies the number of digits that appear on the right side of the decimal point. If you omit *Decimal,* SQL Server truncates the decimal places so that the string conforms to the *Length* value. Figure 3-24 shows a query that uses the STR function to format the average enrollment for the SUMM08 term so that the value is rounded to two decimal places. Note that this query first uses the CONVERT function to convert the data type of the SectionCurrentEnrollment column to the Float data type. It then uses the AVG function to calculate the average enrollment, and it finally uses the STR function to format the query output.

Modifying Column Headings

By default, output data column headings appear as the database column names. When you create an output column that uses an arithmetic or function calculation, the column heading appears in Express Manager and Management Studio as the text "(No column heading)". You can modify column headings by specifying an alias, which is an alternate column heading, as a text string.

To create an alias, use the following syntax:

```
SELECT ColumnName [AS] Alias,...
```

An alias must follow the SQL Server rules for naming columns: it must start with a character, contain between 1 and 128 alphanumeric characters, and can contain the at (@), pound (#), dollar ($), and underscore (_) symbols. Note that *Alias* does not appear in quotation marks. If you want the alias to contain blank spaces you must place it within either double quotes or square brackets. You can also optionally include the keyword AS.

A column alias can be used in a query's ORDER BY clause. In the WHERE, GROUP BY, or HAVING clauses, however, you must use the actual column name or arithmetic operation.

FIGURE 3-25   Creating a column alias

```
SELECT SectionID,
SectionMaxEnrollment-SectionCurrentEnrollment AvailableSeats
FROM UniversitySection
WHERE SectionTerm = 'SUMM08'
ORDER BY AvailableSeats DESC              ── Column alias


SectionID AvailableSeats
--------- --------------
2         11
1         5
```

RETRIEVING DATA FROM MULTIPLE TABLES

All the SQL queries that you have created so far retrieve data from a single table. SQL allows you to create *join queries,* which are queries that combine data from multiple tables that have foreign key relationships. There are two main types of join queries: inner joins and outer joins. The following subsections describe these query types.

Inner Joins

An *inner join* occurs when you join two tables by matching the value of a column in one table to the value of a column in a second table. An inner join returns one or more column values for all records that have matching values. An inner join is sometimes called an *equality join, equijoin,* or *natural join.* Figure 3-26 shows how you can join the UniversityDepartment and UniversityCourse tables based on the values in the DepartmentID primary key and foreign key columns.

Inner join queries contain *join conditions* to specify the table and column names on which the DBMS joins the tables. The following subsections describe the SQL syntax for creating inner joins of two tables and three or more tables, as well as how to create query design diagrams to identify join conditions.

Inner Joins of Two Tables

There are two formats for SQL inner join queries. The first approach, which adheres to the SQL ANSI standards established since 1992, specifies the join condition(s) in the FROM clause and uses the following general syntax to join two tables:

```
SELECT Column1, Column2, ...
FROM Table1
INNER JOIN Table2
ON Table1.JoinColumn = Table2.JoinColumn
AND SearchCondition(s)
```

In this syntax, the SELECT clause lists the names of the columns whose values the query retrieves. These columns can be in either table. Both table names appear in the

FIGURE 3-26   Inner join based on shared key values

UniversityDepartment

DepartmentID	DepartmentName	DepartmentOffice	DepartmentChairID
1	Management Information Systems	Schneider 418	1
2	Accounting	Schneider 419	2

Shared key values

UniversityCourse

CourseID	CourseName	CourseTitle	CourseCredits	DepartmentID
1	MIS 240	Information Systems in Bu...	3	1
2	MIS 310	Systems Analysis and Design	3	1
3	MIS 344	Database Management Sy...	3	1
4	MIS 345	Introduction to Networks	3	1
5	ACCT 201	Principles of Accounting	3	2
6	ACCT 312	Managerial Accounting	3	2

FROM clause and are separated by the keywords INNER JOIN. The ON clause contains the join condition, which specifies the table names and the *JoinColumn,* which is the name of the column joining the tables. The *JoinColumn* is not required to have the same column name in both tables, but recall from Chapter 1 that in most cases it is a good design practice to name foreign key columns using the same name as their parent primary key column. The *SearchCondition(s)* specify search criteria to determine the records you want the query to retrieve and can contain column names from either table.

Note the query formatting: The FROM, INNER JOIN, and ON clauses all appear on separate lines. This formatting makes the query easier to understand and debug. This becomes especially important when you create queries that join more than two tables, which you will learn how to do in the next section.

A second approach for creating inner joins, which many programmers still use, follows the older 1986 SQL ANSI standard. This query format specifies the join condition(s) as search conditions in the WHERE clause, using the following general syntax:

```
SELECT Column1, Column2, ...
FROM Table1, Table2
WHERE Table1.JoinColumn = Table2.JoinColumn
AND SearchCondition(s)
```

The SELECT clause lists the names of the columns from which the query retrieves values. Both table names appear in the FROM clause and are separated by commas. The WHERE clause specifies the join condition. The join condition can appear anywhere in the WHERE clause: before the search conditions, within two search conditions, or after the search conditions.

Figure 3-27 shows queries that use both inner join syntaxes. The first query illustrates an inner join query that displays the department name and the course name of all courses that provide exactly four course credits, and it places the join condition in the FROM clause. Note that this query displays columns from both tables (UniversityDepartment and UniversityCourse) and joins the tables on the DepartmentID column. The second query lists both tables in the FROM clause and places the join condition in the WHERE clause, just before the search condition.

FIGURE 3-27   Alternate syntaxes for creating an inner join query

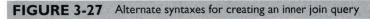

```
SELECT CourseName, DepartmentName                    Join condition in the
FROM UniversityDepartment                            FROM clause
INNER JOIN UniversityCourse
ON UniversityDepartment.DepartmentID = UniversityCourse.DepartmentID
WHERE CourseCredits = 4


SELECT CourseName, DepartmentName
FROM UniversityDepartment, UniversityCourse
WHERE UniversityDepartment.DepartmentID = UniversityCourse.DepartmentID
AND CourseCredits = 4

                                                     Join condition in the
                                                     WHERE clause
```

FIGURE 3-28   Query with omitted join condition

```
SELECT StudentFirstName, StudentLastName, ProjectDescription
FROM UniversityStudent, UniversityServiceProject
WHERE ProjectID = 1

StudentFirstName  StudentLastName ProjectDescription
----------------  --------------- -----------------------------
Clifford          Wall            Help Desk Assistant at Elder Care Center
Dawna             Voss            Help Desk Assistant at Elder Care Center
Patricia          Owen            Help Desk Assistant at Elder Care Center
Raymond           Miller          Help Desk Assistant at Elder Care Center    Cartesian
Ann               Bochman         Help Desk Assistant at Elder Care Center    product
Brenda            Johansen        Help Desk Assistant at Elder Care Center
David             Ashcraft        Help Desk Assistant at Elder Care Center
```

Most database developers believe that queries using the syntax in which the join condition appears in the FROM clause are easier to understand and interpret: if an inner join query contains many search conditions, the join condition can become lost in the search conditions. Also, placing the join condition in the FROM clause makes it nearly impossible to omit the join condition. From this point forward, all join queries in this book will use the syntax that places join conditions in the FROM clause.

Qualifying a Column

What happens if you create a query that uses the second syntax approach, lists two tables in the FROM clause, but does not contain a join condition? Figure 3-28 illustrates a query that retrieves data from two tables but does not contain a join condition.

This query attempts to retrieve the student's first and last names and the project description of project ID 1 by joining the records in the UniversityStudent and UniversityServiceProject tables on the StudentID foreign key column. If the query is written correctly, it retrieves one record that displays the first and last names of student ID 2 (Dawna Voss), along with her project description (Help Desk Assistant at Elder Care Center). Because the query omits the join condition, the DBMS creates a *Cartesian product,* which joins every row in the UniversityStudent table to the row matching the search condition in the UniversityServiceProject table. As a result, seven rows appear and display each student's name along with the retrieved project description.

What happens if you list a column in the SELECT clause that is in both tables? The DBMS is unable to determine which table to use for the specified column, so it returns an error message. The query in Figure 3-29 shows the error message that appears when the query attempts to display the DepartmentID column in the query that joins the UniversityDepartment and UniversityCourse tables. Because DepartmentID is in both tables, the error message reports that the column name is ambiguously defined.

To correct this error, you must *qualify* the column in the SELECT clause by specifying the name of its associated table, followed by a period and the column name. Because the column appears in both tables, you can qualify it using either table name. Figure 3-30 shows how to qualify the DepartmentID column in the SELECT clause using the UniversityDepartment table.

FIGURE 3-29 Query containing a column that exists in multiple tables

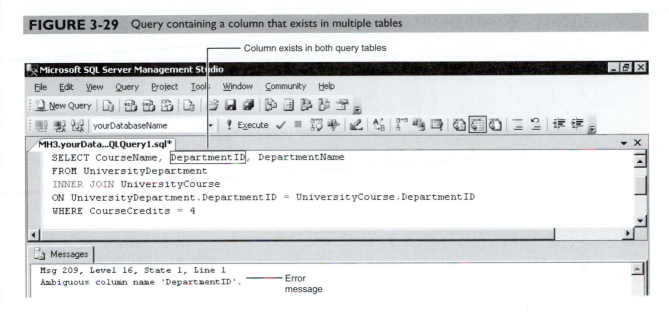

Column exists in both query tables

```
SELECT CourseName, DepartmentID, DepartmentName
FROM UniversityDepartment
INNER JOIN UniversityCourse
ON UniversityDepartment.DepartmentID = UniversityCourse.DepartmentID
WHERE CourseCredits = 4
```

```
Msg 209, Level 16, State 1, Line 1
Ambiguous column name 'DepartmentID'.
```

Error message

FIGURE 3-30 Qualifying a column that exists in multiple tables

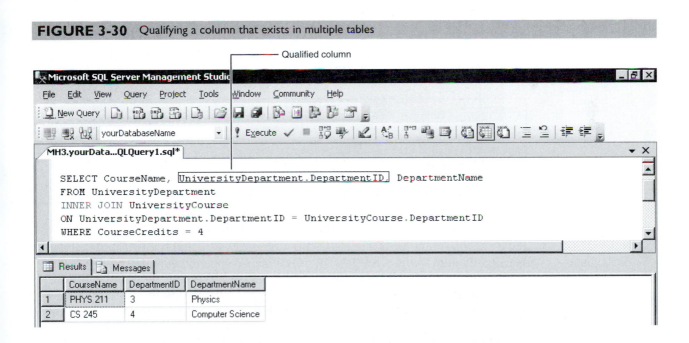

Qualified column

```
SELECT CourseName, UniversityDepartment.DepartmentID, DepartmentName
FROM UniversityDepartment
INNER JOIN UniversityCourse
ON UniversityDepartment.DepartmentID = UniversityCourse.DepartmentID
WHERE CourseCredits = 4
```

	CourseName	DepartmentID	DepartmentName
1	PHYS 211	3	Physics
2	CS 245	4	Computer Science

Inner Joins of Three or More Tables

You can create SQL queries that retrieve data from any number of tables, provided the tables are related by key columns. For example, suppose you want to display the first and last names of the tutor and of the student being tutored for the tutoring session with ID number 1. Figure 3-31 shows that this query joins three tables: UniversityTutor, UniversityTutorSession, and UniversityStudent.

FIGURE 3-31   Query joining three tables

UniversityTutor

TutorID	TutorFirstName	TutorMI	TutorLastName
1	Cheryl	D	Glastner
2	Andrew	H	Beagle
3	Michael	*NULL*	Hannity

UniversityTutorSession

TutorSessionID	TutorID	StudentID	SectionID	TutorSessionStartTime	TutorSessionEndTime
1	1	4	13	9/21/2008 7:00:00 PM	9/21/2008 8:00:00 PM
2	1	4	12	9/22/2008 6:30:00 PM	9/22/2008 7:30:00 PM

UniversityStudent

StudentID	StudentFirstName	StudentMI	StudentLastName	StudentDOB	StudentGender
1	Clifford	*NULL*	Wall	5/29/1988 12:00:00 AM	M
2	Dawna	H	Voss	11/1/1981 12:00:00 AM	F
3	Patricia	E	Owen	1/23/1987 12:00:00 AM	F
4	Raymond	P	Miller	8/9/1988 12:00:00 AM	M

You perform this operation in a single query by first joining two of the tables, then joining the result to the third table. To do this, use the following general syntax:

```
SELECT Column1, Column2, ...
FROM Table1
INNER JOIN Table2
ON Table1.JoinColumn1 = Table2.JoinColumn1
INNER JOIN Table3
ON Table2.JoinColumn2 = Table3.JoinColumn2
WHERE SearchCondition(s)
```

In this syntax, the first three lines specify the join operation between the first two tables (*Table1* and *Table2*) and use the same syntax for joining two tables that you learned earlier. The second INNER JOIN clause specifies joining the result of this operation with *Table3,* and its associated ON clause specifies the join condition. As before, the WHERE clause contains the query's search conditions.

Figure 3-32 shows the SQL syntax for the query that joins the UniversityTutor, UniversityTutorSession, and UniversityStudent tables. In this query, the first join operation joins the UniversityTutor and UniversityTutorSession tables. The second join is between this result and the UniversityStudent table.

You can expand this syntax to join any number of tables in a single query. For example, to join four tables, join the first two and then join the result to the third table. Then join the result of this operation to the fourth table. Figure 3-33 shows the syntax for a query that joins the UniversityTutor, UniversityTutorSession, UniversityStudent, and UniversitySection tables and retrieves the last names of tutors and their associated students for every tutor session that involves a course section offered during the FALL08 term.

FIGURE 3-32   SQL syntax for a query joining three tables

```
SELECT TutorFirstName, TutorLastName, StudentFirstName, StudentLastName
FROM   UniversityTutor
INNER JOIN UniversityTutorSession
ON     UniversityTutor.TutorID = UniversityTutorSession.TutorID
INNER JOIN UniversityStudent
ON     UniversityTutorSession.StudentID = UniversityStudent.StudentID
WHERE TutorSessionID = 1


TutorFirstName   TutorLastName   StudentFirstName   StudentLastName
--------------   -------------   ----------------   -----
Cheryl           Glastner        Raymond            Miller
```

FIGURE 3-33   SQL syntax for a query joining four tables

```
SELECT TutorLastName, StudentLastName, TutorSessionStartTime
FROM   UniversityTutor
INNER JOIN UniversityTutorSession
ON     UniversityTutor.TutorID = UniversityTutorSession.TutorID
INNER JOIN UniversityStudent
ON     UniversityTutorSession.StudentID = UniversityStudent.StudentID
INNER JOIN UniversitySection
ON UniversitySection.SectionID = UniversityTutorSession.SectionID
WHERE SectionTerm = 'FALL08'


TutorLastName   StudentLastName   SessionStartTime
-------------   ---------------   -----------------------
Glastner        Miller            2008-09-21 19:00:00.000
Glastner        Miller            2008-09-22 18:30:00.000
Glastner        Miller            2008-10-26 18:00:00.000
Glastner        Miller            2008-10-27 16:00:00.000
Hannity         Wall              2008-10-03 16:30:00.000
Hannity         Wall              2008-10-04 18:30:00.000
Hannity         Wall              2008-10-31 19:00:00.000
```

Outer Joins

Recall that an inner join query returns one or more column values for all records with matching values in the join columns. If no matching values exist for a join column record, the query does not return any values for the record. For example, consider a query that joins the UniversityStudent and UniversityLaptop tables, as shown in Figure 3-34.

Suppose you wish to retrieve the LaptopID and LaptopCPU values for each laptop, along with the last name of the student to whom the laptop is assigned. If you create this query as an inner join, it retrieves only the records for laptops currently assigned to students, as shown in Figure 3-35.

Note that the query retrieves records only for laptops in which the StudentID value in the LaptopComputer table is not NULL. The query omits the other laptop records (Laptop IDs 2, 3, and 5) from the join operation because their join column values in the StudentID column are NULL. To avoid this omission, you must create an outer join.

FIGURE 3-34   Joining the UniversityLaptopComputer and UniversityStudent tables

UniversityLaptop

LaptopID	LaptopBrand	LaptopCPU	LaptopYear	StudentID
1	DELL	Latitude D788	5/21/2008 12:00:00 AM	1
2	DELL	Latitude D788	5/21/2008 12:00:00 AM	NULL
3	DELL	Inspiron 7109	5/21/2008 12:00:00 AM	NULL
4	IBM	Thinkpad T3501	12/1/2008 12:00:00 AM	3
5	IBM	Thinkpad T3501	12/1/2008 12:00:00 AM	NULL

UniversityStudent

StudentID	StudentFirstName
1	Clifford
2	Dawna
3	Patricia
4	Raymond
5	Ann
6	Brenda
7	David

An *outer join* retrieves all the records from one table and the matching columns from a second table, even if the records in the first table do not have matching records in the second. SQL syntax supports three types of outer joins: left, right, and full.

A *left outer join* displays all the rows in the *left table,* which is the first table in the join operation, along with the matching rows in the right table, which is the second table in the join operation. A left outer join uses the following general syntax:

```
SELECT Column1, Column2, . . .
FROM Table1 LEFT OUTER JOIN Table2
ON Table1.JoinColumn = Table2.JoinColumn
AND SearchCondition(s)
```

Figure 3-36 illustrates a left outer join query that displays all the records in the left table (UniversityLaptop) and the matching records (if they exist) in the right table. UniversityLaptop is the left table because it appears first in the join operation. This

FIGURE 3-35   Inner join query that omits records for which the join column value is NULL

```
SELECT UniversityLaptop.LaptopID, LaptopCPU, StudentLastName
FROM UniversityLaptop
INNER JOIN UniversityStudent
ON UniversityLaptop.StudentID = UniversityStudent.StudentID

LaptopID LaptopCPU       StudentLastName
-------- --------------  ---------------
1        Latitude D788   Wall
4        Thinkpad T3501  Owen
```

FIGURE 3-36   Left outer join query

```
SELECT UniversityLaptop.LaptopID, LaptopCPU, StudentLastName
FROM UniversityLaptop
LEFT OUTER JOIN UniversityStudent
ON UniversityLaptop.StudentID = UniversityStudent.StudentID

LaptopID LaptopCPU         StudentLastName
-------- -------------     ---------------
1        Latitude D788     Wall
2        Latitude D788     NULL
3        Inspiron 7109     NULL
4        Thinkpad T3501    Owen
5        Thinkpad T3501    NULL
```

query retrieves all the UniversityLaptop records and displays student last names in the StudentLastName column for the records in which the StudentID join column value is not NULL. Note that if the record's StudentID join column value is NULL, the query output displays a NULL value.

A *right outer join* displays all the rows in the *right table,* which is the second table appearing in the join operation, along with the matching columns from the left table. (Recall that the left table is the first table in the join operation.) A right outer join query uses the same syntax as a left outer join, except that you replace the keyword LEFT with RIGHT.

Figure 3-37 repeats the query in Figure 3-36, but performs a right outer join. This query retrieves all the records in the right table (UniversityStudent, which appears second in the FROM clause) and displays NULL values for the LaptopID and LaptopCPU column values for the records in which the StudentID join column value is NULL.

A *full outer join* displays all the records in both tables, as well as NULL values for which the join column value is NULL. Figure 3-38 illustrates a full outer join on the UniversityLaptop and UniversityStudent tables.

Note that this query retrieves all the UniversityStudent records and the corresponding UniversityLaptopComputer records, as well as all the UniversityLaptopComputer

FIGURE 3-37   Right outer join query

```
SELECT UniversityLaptop.LaptopID, LaptopCPU, StudentLastName
FROM UniversityLaptop
RIGHT OUTER JOIN UniversityStudent
ON UniversityLaptop.StudentID = UniversityStudent.StudentID

LaptopID LaptopCPU         StudentLastName
-------- -------------     ---------------
1        Latitude D788     Wall
NULL     NULL              Voss
4        Thinkpad T3501    Owen
NULL     NULL              Miller
NULL     NULL              Bochman
NULL     NULL              Johansen
NULL     NULL              Ashcraft
```

FIGURE 3-38   Full outer join query

```
SELECT UniversityLaptop.LaptopID, LaptopCPU, StudentLastName
FROM UniversityLaptop
FULL OUTER JOIN UniversityStudent
ON UniversityLaptop.StudentID = UniversityStudent.StudentID
ORDER BY LaptopID

LaptopID LaptopCPU          StudentLastName
-------- ---------------- ----------------
NULL     NULL             Voss
NULL     NULL             Miller
NULL     NULL             Bochman
NULL     NULL             Johansen
NULL     NULL             Ashcraft
1        Latitude D788    Wall
2        Latitude D788    NULL
3        Inspiron 7109    NULL
4        Thinkpad T3501   Owen
5        Thinkpad T3501   NULL
```

records and the corresponding UniversityStudent records. It essentially combines the result of the left and right outer join queries.

CREATING NESTED QUERIES

Sometimes you need to create queries that retrieve records based on the results of another query. For example, suppose you want to retrieve the first and last names of every student who lives in the same postal code as student Dawna Voss. One solution is first to execute a query that retrieves Dawna's postal code, then to write a second query that contains this value as a search condition. A simpler approach is to create a *nested query,* which is a single query made up of multiple queries that retrieve intermediate values appearing in search conditions.

A nested query consists of a main query and one or more subqueries. The *main query* is the first query. The *subquery* appears in a search condition and retrieves values that the main query seeks to match. You can create nested queries with subqueries that return either a single value or multiple values. You can also create nested queries with multiple subqueries or with subqueries that are also nested. The following sections explore these variations.

Nested Queries With Subqueries That Return a Single Value

When a subquery returns one and only one value (such as Dawna Voss's postal code), use the equal to (=) operator to create a nested query with a subquery to retrieve a single value that the main query's search condition seeks to match. Figure 3-39 shows the general syntax for this type of nested query.

In this syntax, the main query's search condition specifies a *SearchColumn,* and the subquery's SELECT clause retrieves a value for it. Note that you enclose the subquery in parentheses to specify that the result of the subquery provides the *SearchColumn* value. It is a good practice to indent the subquery to make the query easier to read and debug. Figure 3-40 shows an example of a nested query with a subquery that retrieves a single value.

FIGURE 3-39   General syntax for creating a nested query in which the subquery returns a single value

```
SELECT Column1, Column2, . . .  ── Main query
FROM Table1
WHERE SearchColumn       = (SELECT SearchColumn
                            FROM Table2
                 Subquery ── WHERE SearchCondition(s))
```

FIGURE 3-40   Nested query with a subquery that retrieves a single value

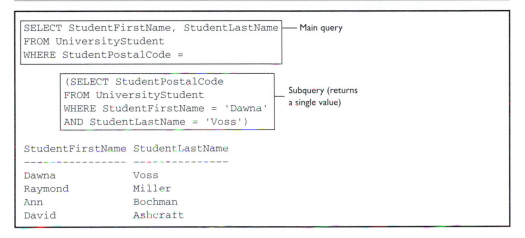

```
SELECT StudentFirstName, StudentLastName ── Main query
FROM UniversityStudent
WHERE StudentPostalCode =

      (SELECT StudentPostalCode
       FROM UniversityStudent        ── Subquery (returns
       WHERE StudentFirstName = 'Dawna'     a single value)
       AND StudentLastName = 'Voss')


StudentFirstName  StudentLastName
----------------  ---------------
Dawna             Voss
Raymond           Miller
Ann               Bochman
David             Ashcraft
```

In this query, the subquery retrieves Dawna Voss's postal code, and the main query then retrieves the first and last names of all students with this postal code. Because the subquery returns a single value (Dawna Voss's postal code), the main query uses the equal to (=) operator in its search condition and returns the names of the students whose postal codes exactly match Dawna's postal code. You can use this syntax only when the subquery retrieves a unique value on which the main query can match its search column value.

You can use a nested query in any query search condition. For example, you can create a nested query in a query in which the main query and/or the subquery join multiple tables using either inner or outer joins. You can also create multiple subqueries in a single query to specify values for multiple search conditions.

Nested Queries with Subqueries That Return Multiple Values

What if a nested query's subquery might retrieve multiple values, any of which would satisfy the search condition? In this case, you can use either the IN or EXISTS operator in the main query's search condition to determine the search values.

Using the IN Operator

The IN operator uses the following syntax to determine if a search condition data value is a member of a search set:

```
WHERE SearchColumn IN (DataSet)
```

Figure 3-41 shows examples of nested queries in which the main query uses the IN operator in a search condition containing a subquery that retrieves multiple values.

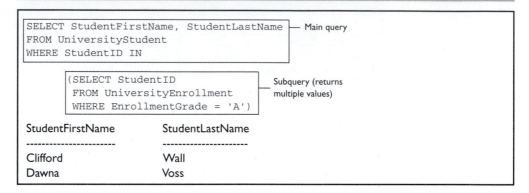

FIGURE 3-41   Nested queries that use the IN operator

```
SELECT StudentFirstName, StudentLastName    — Main query
FROM UniversityStudent
WHERE StudentID IN

    (SELECT StudentID                        Subquery (returns
     FROM UniversityEnrollment               multiple values)
     WHERE EnrollmentGrade = 'A')

StudentFirstName          StudentLastName
----------------------    ----------------------
Clifford                  Wall
Dawna                     Voss
```

The first query's subquery retrieves the student ID values of all students who have received a grade of A. The main query then retrieves the students' names.

NOTE: You could retrieve the same values by joining the UniversityStudent and UniversityEnrollment tables using an inner join. However, some people find it more straightforward to create nested queries rather than join queries. Also, sometimes the only way you can retrieve the data you need is by using a nested query.

Using the EXISTS Operator

Use the EXISTS operator in nested queries to determine whether a record exists in a subquery. If the record exists, the EXISTS operator returns the value TRUE, and the main query retrieves a related record. If the record does not exist, the EXISTS operator returns FALSE, and the main query does not retrieve a related record. The subquery must contain a search condition that relates a column in the main query to a column in the subquery.

The first query in Figure 3-42 retrieves the names of students who have participated in tutoring sessions. Note that the subquery retrieves all the columns in the UniversityTutorSession table and contains a search condition that relates the StudentID column in the UniversityTutorSession table to the StudentID column in the UniversityStudent table. If a StudentID exists in the UniversityTutorSession table, the main query retrieves the associated UniversityStudent record.

You can combine the NOT logical operator with the EXISTS operator to retrieve all the records that do not exist in the subquery's search condition. The second query in Figure 3-42 uses the NOT EXISTS operator to retrieve the names of students who have *not* participated in tutoring sessions. The subquery retrieves the records of students who have participated in tutor sessions, and the NOT EXISTS operator retrieves the logical opposite, which are the names of the students who have not participated in tutoring sessions.

Queries with Nested Subqueries

A *nested subquery* is a subquery containing a second subquery that specifies a search condition value. Figure 3-43 shows an example of a query with a nested subquery.

This query retrieves the names of all students who received a grade of either A or B in courses with the text string "Accounting" anywhere in the course title. Note that the inner subquery (Subquery 2) retrieves the Section ID values of all courses whose titles contain the course string "Accounting," and the outer subquery (Subquery 1)

FIGURE 3-42   Nested queries that use the EXISTS operator

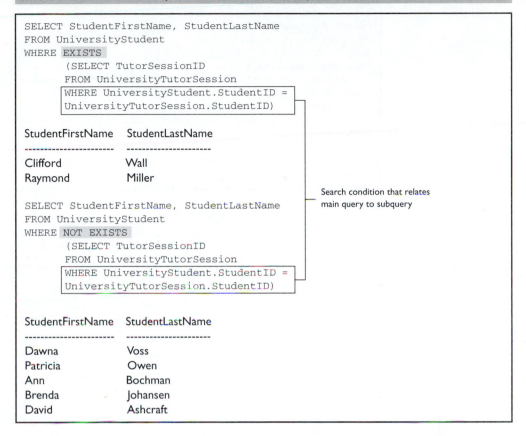

```
SELECT StudentFirstName, StudentLastName
FROM UniversityStudent
WHERE EXISTS
      (SELECT TutorSessionID
      FROM UniversityTutorSession
      WHERE UniversityStudent.StudentID =
      UniversityTutorSession.StudentID)
```

StudentFirstName	StudentLastName
Clifford	Wall
Raymond	Miller

Search condition that relates main query to subquery

```
SELECT StudentFirstName, StudentLastName
FROM UniversityStudent
WHERE NOT EXISTS
      (SELECT TutorSessionID
      FROM UniversityTutorSession
      WHERE UniversityStudent.StudentID =
      UniversityTutorSession.StudentID)
```

StudentFirstName	StudentLastName
Dawna	Voss
Patricia	Owen
Ann	Bochman
Brenda	Johansen
David	Ashcraft

FIGURE 3-43   Query that contains a nested subquery

```
SELECT StudentFirstName, StudentLastName        — Main query
FROM UniversityStudent
WHERE StudentID IN

      (SELECT StudentID
      FROM UniversityEnrollment                  — Subquery 1
      WHERE EnrollmentGrade IN ('A', 'B')
      AND SectionID IN

          (SELECT SectionID
          FROM UniversitySection
          INNER JOIN
          UniversityCourse                       — Subquery 2
          ON UniversitySection.CourseID =
          UniversityCourse.CourseID
          WHERE CourseTitle LIKE '%Accounting%'))

StudentFirstName StudentLastName
---------------- ----------------
Dawna            Voss
Patricia         Owen
```

FIGURE 3-44   Join query that retrieves the same data as the nested query in Figure 3-43

```
SELECT StudentFirstName, StudentLastName
FROM UniversityStudent
INNER JOIN
UniversityEnrollment
ON UniversityStudent.StudentID = UniversityEnrollment.StudentID
INNER JOIN
UniversitySection
ON UniversityEnrollment.SectionID = UniversitySection.SectionID
INNER JOIN
UniversityCourse
ON UniversitySection.CourseID = UniversityCourse.CourseID
WHERE CourseGrade IN ('A', 'B')
AND CourseTitle LIKE '%Accounting%'

StudentFirstName StudentLastName
---------------- ----------------
Dawna            Voss
Patricia         Owen
```

retrieves the Student ID values of students who received a grade of either A or B in those courses. The main query then retrieves the associated student names.

When you create nested subqueries, it is vitally important to indent them as shown in Figure 3-43. Otherwise, the commands become unwieldly and hard to understand.

Subquery Usage Issues

Often you can retrieve identical data using either nested queries with subqueries or queries that join database tables. For example, the query in Figure 3-44 uses a join query to retrieve the same data that the query in Figure 3-43 retrieves using nested subqueries.

Nested queries with subqueries are usually easier to understand and create. However, a nested query tends to retrieve records more slowly than an equivalent inner join query. For the query in Figure 3-43, the DBMS must first retrieve the SectionID values associated with the text string "Accounting." It then must scan every record in the UniversityEnrollment table and determine which records match the retrieved SectionID values. Finally, it must scan every record in the UniversityStudent table to determine which records match the retrieved StudentID values. This can be a slow process for tables that contain hundreds of thousands of records. Conversely, for inner join queries, the DBMS automatically creates an optimized execution plan for retrieving the records that optimizes performance. As a general rule, avoid using nested queries for applications that retrieve records from database tables containing large numbers of records.

Another drawback of nested queries is that they limit the final output that the query can display. The subqueries can retrieve data from different tables, but a nested query's final output can only come from the fields specified in the initial, highest level query.

DATABASE VIEWS

A database *view* is a virtual table based on a query. It represents data in a tabular format and enables you to perform database operations on the view just as if it were a table. A view does not actually store data; rather, it provides a way to work with data that is different from how it is stored in the underlying database tables.

FIGURE 3-45   View that contains a subset of columns from a single table

UniversityInstructor (not all records are shown)

InstructorID	InstructorFirstName	InstructorMI	InstructorLastName	InstructorPhoneNumber	InstructorUserID	InstructorPIN	Dep
1	Lauren	J	Morrison	5558362243	morrislj	1122	1
2	Adam	K	Dutton	5558364522	duttonak	2222	2
3	Eagan	T	Ruppelt	5558366487	ruppeltet	3333	3
4	Charles	H	Murphy	5558362113	murphych	3211	4
5	Richard	P	Harrison	5558364901	harrisrp	1233	5

UniversityInstructorView

InstructorID	InstructorFirstName	InstructorMI	InstructorLastName	InstructorPhoneNumber	DepartmentID
1	Lauren	J	Morrison	5558362243	1
2	Adam	K	Dutton	5558364522	2
3	Eagan	T	Ruppelt	5558366487	3
4	Charles	H	Murphy	5558362113	4
5	Richard	P	Harrison	5558364901	5

A view can represent a subset of the columns or rows in a single table. A view can also combine columns from multiple tables. Database developers create views to restrict access to sensitive data and to store data from multiple tables in a format that is easier to access and use. Figure 3-45 shows the UniversityInstructor table and a view named UniversityInstructorView that contains a subset of the UniversityInstructor table columns. The view omits the InstructorUserID and InstructorPIN columns because some users should not be able to view or change these columns.

Figure 3-46 shows the UniversityDepartment and UniversityCourse tables, along with an associated view named UniversityDepartmentCourseView. This view contains columns from both tables, and provides a way for users to easily associate department names with courses without having to create an inner join query.

After you create a view, you can use it in SELECT commands just like a database table: you can retrieve data, perform function and arithmetic operations on the data, and so forth. However, you cannot use a view to change the contents of the underlying tables if the view contains columns from multiple tables. The following paragraphs describe how to create, use, and delete views.

Creating Views

Use the following general syntax to create a view:

```
CREATE VIEW ViewName
AS
SourceQuery
```

In this syntax, *ViewName* is any legal table name. Every view in a database must have a unique name. *SourceQuery* can be any SELECT query, including join and nested queries. The following SQL commands create the views in Figures 3-45 and 3-46:

FIGURE 3-46 View that contains a subset of columns from multiple tables

UniversityCourse

CourseID	CourseName	CourseTitle	CourseCredits	DepartmentID
1	MIS 240	Information Systems in Bu...	3	1
2	MIS 310	Systems Analysis and Design	3	1
3	MIS 344	Database Management Sy...	3	1
4	MIS 345	Introduction to Networks	3	1
5	ACCT 201	Principles of Accounting	3	2
6	ACCT 312	Managerial Accounting	3	2
7	PHYS 211	General Physics	4	3
8	CS 245	Fundamentals of Object-...	4	4
9	CHEM 205	Applied Physical Chemistry	3	5
10	GEOL 212	Mineralogy and Petrology	5	6
11	CHIN 110	Intensive Beginning Chine...	5	7

UniversityDepartment

DepartmentID	DepartmentName	DepartmentOffice	DepartmentChairID
1	Management Information Systems	Schneider 418	1
2	Accounting	Schneider 419	2
3	Physics	Phillips 007	3
4	Computer Science	Phillips 112	4
5	Chemistry	Phillips 201	5
6	Geology	Phillips 123	6
7	Foreign Languages	Hibbard 211	7

UniversityDepartmentCourseView

DepartmentName	CourseName	CourseTitle	CourseCredits
Management Information Systems	MIS 240	Information Systems in Business	3
Management Information Systems	MIS 310	Systems Analysis and Design	3
Management Information Systems	MIS 344	Database Management Systems	3
Management Information Systems	MIS 345	Introduction to Networks	3
Accounting	ACCT 201	Principles of Accounting	3
Accounting	ACCT 312	Managerial Accounting	3
Physics	PHYS 211	General Physics	4
Computer Science	CS 245	Fundamentals of Object-Oriented Programming	4
Chemistry	CHEM 205	Applied Physical Chemistry	3
Geology	GEOL 212	Mineralogy and Petrology	5
Foreign Languages	CHIN 110	Intensive Beginning Chinese (Mandarin)	5

```
CREATE VIEW UniversityInstructorView
AS
SELECT InstructorFirstName,
InstructorMI, InstructorLastName,
InstructorPhoneNumber, DepartmentID
FROM UniversityInstructor

CREATE VIEW DepartmentCourseView
AS
SELECT DepartmentName, CourseName,
CourseTitle, CourseCredits
FROM UniversityDepartment
INNER JOIN UniversityCourse
ON UniversityDepartment.DepartmentID =
UniversityCourse.DepartmentID
```

You can use arithmetic expressions and in-line and group functions in the *SourceQuery's* SELECT clause, but you must always create column aliases to specify column names containing expressions or functions. You cannot use the ORDER BY clause to specify the order of the records. A view can contain a maximum of 1,024 columns, so the SELECT clause cannot specify more than 1,024 columns. If you create a view and subsequently drop one of the source tables in the *SourceQuery,* the view becomes invalid. If you remake the source table, the view becomes valid again, provided the source table has the same name structure as when you originally created the view.

Retrieving Records From Views

You can retrieve records from a view using a SELECT query just as if the view were a database table. You can use a view in join queries and nested queries. Figure 3-47 shows queries that retrieve records from the UniversityInstructorView and UniversityDepartmentCourseView views.

FIGURE 3-47   Queries that retrieve records from views

```
SELECT InstructorLastName, InstructorPhoneNumber
FROM UniversityInstructorView
WHERE DepartmentID = 1

InstructorLastName  InstructorPhoneNumber
------------------  ---------------------
Morrison            5558362243
Buck                5558362531
Sanchez             5558363628
Hogstad             5558366946

SELECT DepartmentName, CourseName
FROM DepartmentCourseView
WHERE CourseName LIKE '%MIS%'

DepartmentName                  CourseName
------------------------------  ----------
Management Information Systems  MIS 240
Management Information Systems  MIS 310
Management Information Systems  MIS 344
Management Information Systems  MIS 345
```

Dropping Views

To remove a view from a database, use the DROP command, which has the following syntax:

```
DROP VIEW ViewName
```

Dropping a database view does not affect the underlying source tables in the view's source query.

PERFORMING SET OPERATIONS IN QUERIES

Sometimes you need to create queries to combine records in ways that foreign key relationships do not represent. For example, suppose you need to create a directory that lists the last and first names of all students and instructors, along with their telephone numbers. This requires a query that combines the results of two separate and unrelated queries. Alternatively, suppose you want to retrieve the names of all students who have taken courses offered by the Management Information Systems department and who have also taken courses offered by the Computer Science department. This requires a query that finds the common set of records retrieved by two separate queries. To create these queries, you use query set operators.

A *query set operator* combines the results of two independent queries. The primary database set operations are as follows:

- UNION, which retrieves all records from both queries and suppresses duplicate records
- UNION ALL, which retrieves all records from both queries and includes duplicate records
- INTERSECT, which retrieves the matching records returned by both queries
- MINUS, which retrieves the difference of the records returned by the queries

The following subsections describe how to implement these set operations in SQL Server.

UNION and UNION ALL

The UNION and UNION ALL set operations combine the output of two independent queries into a single output. The SQL Server *UNION* operator returns all records and does not display duplicates, while the *UNION ALL* operator returns all records, including duplicates.

The general syntax for a UNION query is:

```
Query1 UNION [ALL] Query2
```

In this syntax, *Query1* specifies the first query, and *Query2* specifies the second. The only constraints are that *Query1* must have the same number of display columns in its SELECT clause as *Query2*, the columns must have the same data types, and the columns with the matching data types must appear in the same order in the SELECT clause. For example, suppose *Query1* retrieves two columns, and the first column has a number data type and the second column has a text data type. *Query2* must also retrieve two columns, and the first column must have a number data type and the second column must have a text data type.

FIGURE 3-48   Query using the UNION set operator

```
SELECT StudentFirstName, StudentLastName
FROM UniversityStudent
INNER JOIN UniversityTutorSession
ON UniversityStudent.StudentID = UniversityTutorSession.StudentID
UNION
SELECT StudentFirstName, StudentLastName
FROM UniversityStudent
INNER JOIN UniversityServiceProject
ON UniversityStudent.StudentID = UniversityServiceProject.StudentID


StudentFirstName StudentLastName
---------------- ----------------
Clifford         Wall
Dawna            Voss            —— Duplicates are suppressed
Raymond          Miller
```

Figure 3-48 illustrates a query that uses the UNION set operator to determine the names of students who have been involved in tutoring sessions and who have also worked on service projects. In this query, the UNION operator joins the results of a query that retrieves the first and last names of all students who have been involved in a tutoring session with the first and last names of the all students who have been involved in a service project. Note that the output displays three unique records.

Figure 3-49 illustrates a query that retrieves the same records, but instead uses the UNION ALL set operator. In this query, the output retrieves four records, and student Raymond Miller's record appears twice. This is because both queries return Raymond's record, and the UNION ALL operator does not suppress the duplicate record.

TIP: When you create a UNION or UNION ALL query, the query output column names in the Results pane correspond to the column names in the first SELECT command in the query.

FIGURE 3-49   Query using the UNION ALL set operator

```
SELECT StudentFirstName, StudentLastName
FROM UniversityStudent
INNER JOIN UniversityTutorSession
ON UniversityStudent.StudentID = UniversityTutorSession.StudentID
UNION ALL
SELECT StudentFirstName, StudentLastName
FROM UniversityStudent
INNER JOIN UniversityServiceProject
ON UniversityStudent.StudentID = UniversityServiceProject.StudentID


StudentFirstName              StudentLastName
----------------              ----------------
Clifford                      Wall
Raymond                       Miller          —— Duplicates are displayed
Dawna                         Voss
Raymond                       Miller
```

```
SELECT DISTINCT StudentID
FROM UniversityTutorSession
WHERE EXISTS
     (SELECT StudentID
     FROM UniversityServiceProject
     WHERE UniversityTutorSession.StudentID =
     UniversityServiceProject.StudentID)
StudentID
---------
4
```

INTERSECT

An *INTERSECT set operation* returns the intersection, or matching rows, in two unrelated queries. For example, suppose you want to retrieve the StudentID values for students who have attended a tutoring session and have also completed a service project. If you scan the records in the UniversityTutorSession table, you will see that the set of StudentID values is (4, 1). If you scan the UniversityServiceProject table, you will see that the resulting StudentID set values are (2,4). The intersection of these two sets is (4).

SQL Server does not directly support the INTERSECT operator. To perform an INTERSECT set operation on a SQL Server database, you can use the EXISTS operator in a subquery. The subquery retrieves one set of records, and the main query retrieves the other set. Figure 3-50 illustrates a query that uses the EXISTS operator in a subquery to perform an INTERSECT set operation that retrieves the Student ID values for all students who have attended a tutoring session and who have also worked on a university service project.

In this query, the subquery retrieves column values for all records in the UniversityServiceProject table; it also contains a search condition that associates the StudentID of each record in the UniversityTutorSession table with the StudentID of records in the UniversityServiceProject table. The main query retrieves distinct StudentID values for records in the UniversityTutorSession table that also exist in the UniversityServiceProject table.

MINUS

The *MINUS set operation* returns the difference of the results of two unrelated queries. In other words, it retrieves a set of records based on the first query, then removes the matching records retrieved by a second query. For example, suppose you want to retrieve the StudentID values for all students who have completed a service project (2, 4), then remove the records for students who have attended a tutoring session (4, 1). The MINUS operation removes the common record, which is (4), and shows that the difference between the two sets is StudentID 2.

SQL Server does not directly support the MINUS set operation but allows you to perform an equivalent operation using the NOT EXISTS operator in a nested query. The main query retrieves the main set of records, and the subquery retrieves the records you wish to subtract from the main set of records. Figure 3-51 illustrates this query.

In this query, the subquery retrieves column values for all records in the UniversityTutorSession table; it also contains a search condition that associates the StudentID of each record in the UniversityTutorSession table with the StudentID of records in the UniversityServiceProject table. The main query retrieves distinct

FIGURE 3-51   Using the NOT EXISTS operator to perform a MINUS set operation

```
SELECT DISTINCT StudentID
FROM UniversityServiceProject
WHERE NOT EXISTS
      (SELECT *
      FROM UniversityTutorSession
      WHERE UniversityServiceProject.StudentID =
      UniversityTutorSession.StudentID)
StudentID
---------
2
```

StudentID values for records in the UniversityServiceProject table that do <u>not</u> exist in the UniversityTutorSession table.

IN CONCLUSION . . .

In this chapter, you learned to retrieve data from SQL Server databases using basic SELECT queries, join queries, and nested queries. You learned how to use arithmetic operations and group and in-line functions to manipulate retrieved data. You also learned how to form queries that use set operations. You will use these queries in the database applications you create in future chapters. In the next chapter, you will learn how to insert, update, and delete data, as well as how to create T-SQL scripts that perform sequential processing operations on data.

SUMMARY

- A script is a text file with an .sql extension containing a series of SQL commands that perform a series of related tasks, such as creating all the tables in a database or inserting all the data in a lookup table. You can run a script file in Management Studio to execute a series of related SQL commands.

- In a SQL query, the SELECT clause lists the names of the columns for which you want to display data, the FROM clause specifies the table that contains the columns, and the optional WHERE clause contains one or more search conditions that seek to match specific records.

- To retrieve all table columns in a SQL query, replace the column names in the SELECT clause with the asterisk (*) wildcard character. If you omit the WHERE clause, the query retrieves all table records.

- A search condition is an expression that seeks to match one or more table records. You can create search conditions on number, text, and date data values.

- When you combine two search conditions using the AND operator, both conditions must be true for the search expression to be true. When you combine two search conditions using the OR operator, either condition may be true to validate the expression.

- If you use the NOT logical operator in a search condition, the query retrieves all records that do not match the search condition.

- The DISTINCT qualifier in the SELECT clause suppresses duplicate output rows in a query.

- The ORDER BY clause specifies the order in which query output appears. The ORDER BY clause always appears as the last clause in the query, and specifies one or more sort keys, which are the columns by which the DBMS sorts the query output.

- You can create arithmetic operations in the SELECT clause to add, subtract, multiply, divide, or return the modulus of number data values. For division operations that involve integer values, you must convert the output to a real number; otherwise, the

DBMS converts the result to an integer and truncates decimal remainder values.

- You can perform arithmetic operations on date data values to retrieve a date that is a specific number of days before or after a given date.

- SQL Server in-line scalar functions perform operations such as concatenating text values, rounding number values, or finding the number of days between two retrieved dates.

- SQL aggregate functions perform calculations on groups of data values, such as finding the sum or average of a set of retrieved values. You can use the GROUP BY clause to group aggregate output by duplicate data values and the HAVING clause to search for an aggregate value.

- To format retrieved data, you use the CONVERT function to convert output to a text string in a specific output style. You use the STR function to convert number data to a text string that has a specific number of decimal places.

- To format output column headings, you can create a column alias. A column alias creates an alternate column name that you can reference in the ORDER BY clause.

- An inner join combines columns in two tables by matching values in the first table to values in the second table. Inner join queries contain join conditions to specify the table and field names on which the DBMS joins the tables.

- An inner join query must contain a separate join condition for every link between two tables.

- If you create a query that lists two or more tables in the SELECT clause but does not specify a join condition, the DBMS creates a Cartesian product, which joins every record in the first table to every row in the second table.

- If you create a query that joins two tables and if one of the columns in the SELECT clause appears in both tables, you must qualify the column name by prefacing it with the name of one of the tables in which it appears.

- An outer join retrieves all the records from one table and the matching columns from a second table. If the records in the first table do not have matching records in the second table, the outer join query still retrieves them.

- A left outer join retrieves all the rows in the left table, which is the first table appearing in the FROM clause, along with the matching rows in the right table, which is the second table listed in the FROM clause. A right outer join displays all the rows in the right table, which is the second table appearing in the FROM clause. A full outer join displays all the tables in both tables, with NULL values for the table column values for which the join column value is NULL.

- A nested query contains a main query and a subquery that retrieves intermediate values in search conditions.

- In a nested query, if the subquery retrieves one and only one value, use the equal to (=) operator to join the queries. If the subquery might retrieve multiple values, use the IN operator to join the queries.

- In a nested query, you can retrieve records in the main query based on whether a record exists in the subquery using the EXISTS operator.

- A query can contain a nested subquery, which is a subquery containing a second subquery that specifies a search condition value.

- Nested queries with subqueries are usually easier to understand and create than inner join queries, but a nested query tends to retrieve records more slowly than an equivalent inner join query.

- A view is a virtual table that is based on a query. It represents data in a tabular format, and enables you to perform database operations on a view just as if it were a table. It does not actually store data but represents a way of working with data that is different from how it is stored in the underlying database tables.

- You can combine the results of unrelated queries using the UNION, INTERSECT, and MINUS set operations.

- The SQL Server UNION set operator combines the results of two unrelated queries and suppresses duplicates, while the UNION ALL set operator combines the results and returns all values, including duplicates. SQL Server does not provide INTERSECT and MINUS set operators, but you can perform these functions using nested queries joined by the EXISTS operator.

KEY TERMS

Aggregate function Function that performs a summary operation on a group of values and returns a single value, such as SUM or MAX

Cartesian product Product created when an inner join query omits the join condition and causes the DBMS to join every row in the first table to every row in the second table

Column alias An alternate name for a query column that you can use in the ORDER BY and GROUP BY clauses

DISTINCT qualifier Qualifier specifying that a query suppresses duplicate data values

Exact search condition Condition that returns records exactly matching a search value

Form Application that presents a database interface allowing users to enter, modify, delete, and retrieve data values

FROM clause Clause specifying the database table(s) from which a query retrieves data values

Full outer join Outer join query that displays all the records in both tables and displays NULL values for the column values for which the join column value is NULL

GROUP BY clause Clause specifying the grouping of query output by duplicate values and then the application of an aggregate function to the grouped values to summarize the data

HAVING clause Clause specifying the use of the result of an aggregate function as the search value in a search condition

Inexact search condition Condition returning records that fall within a range of values

In-line scalar function Function applied in the SELECT clause of a SQL query to operate on and return a single data value

Inner join Join of two tables by matching the value of a column in one table to the value of a column in a second table; also called equality join, equijoin, or natural join

INTERSECT set operation Operation that combines the results of two independent queries and returns the matching rows

Join columns In a join query, the key columns linking related tables through primary and foreign key values

Join condition Condition specifying the table and column names on which the DBMS joins tables in an inner join

Join query Query that retrieves values from multiple related tables

Left outer join Outer join query that displays all the records in the left table and the matching records in the right table

Left table In an outer join query, the table that appears first in the FROM clause

Main query In a nested query, the query that appears first in the SELECT clause

MINUS set operation Operation that returns the difference of the results of two unrelated queries

Nested query Query that uses other queries to retrieve intermediate values in search conditions

Nested subquery Subquery in a nested query that contains a second subquery

ORDER BY clause Clause that specifies the order in which a query displays retrieved data

Outer join Join query that retrieves all the records from one table and the matching columns from a second table, even if the records in the first table do not have matching records in the second table

Query Command that the DBMS processes to retrieve data.

Query set operator Query that combines the results of two independent queries using the UNION, UNION ALL, INTERSECT, or MINUS set operation

Report Summary of database data values at a specific point in time; allows users to view data on a computer screen or as hard copy printouts

Right outer join Outer join query that displays all the records in the right table and the matching records in the left table

Right table In an outer join query, the table that appears second in the FROM clause

Script Text file with an .sql extension containing a series of SQL commands that perform a series of related tasks, such as creating all the tables in a database or inserting all the data in a lookup table

Search condition Expression that seeks to match one or more table records

SELECT clause Specifies the column names whose values a query retrieves

Sort key The column by which you want to sort data within an ORDER BY clause

Subquery A query that retrieves intermediate search values in a nested query

Truncate In an arithmetic operation, rounding a number down to the nearest whole number

UNION ALL operator Operator that combines the results of two independent queries and includes duplicates

UNION operator Operator that combines the results of two independent queries and does not display duplicates

View Virtual table that is based on a query and that provides a way of working with data that is different from how it is stored in the underlying table or tables

STUDY QUESTIONS

Multiple-Choice Questions

1. The _____ search operator allows you to search for text values by matching part of a character string.
   a. IN
   b. LIKE
   c. HAVING
   d. *

2. To search for a date value in a SQL Server database, you specify the search value as:
   a. A text string that is in a Date/Time format that the database recognizes
   b. A date value enclosed in pound (#) signs
   c. A text string that you convert to a date using the CONVERT function
   d. A text string that you convert to a date using the TO_DATE function

3. A(n) _____ function returns a single value that it calculates based on values retrieved from multiple records.
   a. In-line
   b. Aggregate
   c. Date/time
   d. RAND

4. You use the _____ clause to create a search condition in a query that contains an aggregate function.
   a. WHERE
   b. GROUP BY
   c. HAVING
   d. IN

5. When you join two search expressions using the AND logical operator, _____ expression(s) must be true for the overall expression to be true.
   a. Both
   b. Either
   c. Neither

6. You use the _____ function to change a date or number data value to a text string that appears in a specific output style.
   a. DATENAME
   b. STR
   c. CONVERT
   d. Both b and c

7. If you create a join query but omit the join condition, a(n) _____ results.
   a. Cartesian product
   b. Outer join
   c. Error
   d. Inequality join

8. An inner join query that joins six tables must contain _____ INNER JOIN clauses.
   a. Four
   b. Five
   c. Six
   d. You cannot determine this from the given information

9. A _____ displays all the rows in the left table, along with the matching rows in the right table.
   a. Left outer join
   b. Right outer join
   c. Left inner join
   d. Full outer join

10. The _____ set operation returns all the records in two unrelated queries, including duplicate records.
    a. UNION
    b. UNION ALL
    c. INTERSECT
    d. MINUS

True/False Questions

1. If you omit the WHERE clause in a SQL query, the query returns all the table columns.
2. You can specify multiple sort keys in the ORDER BY clause.
3. You cannot use an alias as a sort key.
4. You can create inner join queries to join any number of tables, provided the tables contain foreign key links.
5. In an outer join, the right table is the first table that appears in the FROM clause.
6. A database view is a physical table that you create based on a SQL query.
7. To perform the MINUS set operation in SQL Server, you use the NOT EXISTS operator in the query's search condition.

Short Answer Questions

1. When do you use the DISTINCT operator in a SQL query?
2. List two reasons why it is more efficient to have the DBMS instead of client-side programs perform arithmetic operations.
3. Why might you need to use the CONVERT function when performing division arithmetic operations?
4. When do you need to use the GROUP BY clause in a query?
5. When should you use the STR function to format output data?
6. When do you need to qualify a column name in an inner join query's SELECT clause?
7. When should you create a column alias, and when should you create an alternate column heading?
8. Describe the differences between an inner join and an outer join.
9. In a nested query, when do you use the IN operator, and when do you use the EXISTS operator?
10. List two reasons for creating a database view.
11. What are the restrictions on the queries whose output you join using the UNION or UNION ALL set operations?

Guided Exercises

NOTE: All guided exercises refer to the Sport Motors database in Figures 3-3 and 3-4. Before you can perform the guided exercise queries, you must run the SportMotors.sql script. Instructions for doing this are provided in the section titled "Sample Databases" in this chapter.

1. **Creating Queries That Retrieve Data from a Single Database Table**
   Create a new query file named 3Exercise1.sql, then write SQL queries to retrieve the following records:
   a. All the columns from all the records from the SportEmployees table
   b. The InventoryQOH and InventoryComments values for all SportInventory items for which the InventorySuggestedPrice value is greater than $1,000
   c. The last and first names of all customers who live in Chippewa Falls, Wisconsin
   d. The first and last names of all employees born between January 1, 1970 and December 31, 1979, inclusive
   e. Colors in the SportColor table that contain all or part of the text string "Blue"
   f. InventoryDescription values from the SportInventory table for items for which either the InventorySize or the ColorDescription values are NULL
   g. InventoryImageFilename values, with duplicate filenames suppressed and with the output sorted so that it appears alphabetically
2. **Creating Queries with Arithmetic Calculations, In-Line and Aggregate Functions, and Formatted Outputs**
   Create a new query file named 3Exercise2.sql, then write SQL queries to retrieve the following records:
   a. The Order ID, Inventory ID, detail quantity, and detail unit prices from the SportOrderDetail table, along with a column that calculates the extended total (DetailQuantity times DetailUnitPrice). Create a column alias named "ExtendedTotal" for the calculated column, and format the column so that it displays only two decimal places. (Hint: Use both the STR and CONVERT functions.)
   b. The first and last names of all Sport Motors customers, concatenated to form a single text string output with a blank space between the first and last names. For example, the first record would appear as a single field with the value Allison Scholten. Create an alternate column heading titled Customer Name for the retrieved values.
   c. The last and first names and associated ages of all Sport Motors employees: Calculate the age as the difference between the current system date and the employee's birth

date. Create a column alias named EmployeeAge for the calculated column, and sort the output by descending age values.

d. The Order ID and total cost of each order, calculated as the sum of the DetailQuantity times the DetailUnitPrice, for each order. Display totals only for orders in which the total order cost is over $100.

e. Employee ID values and a count of the total number of orders sold by each employee. Create a column alias named TotalOrders for the calculated column, and sort the output by descending total number of orders.

3. **Creating Inner Join Queries**

Create a new query file named 3Exercise3.sql, then write SQL queries to retrieve the following records:

a. The DepartmentID, DepartmentName, and the first and last names of each department's manager

b. The OrderIDs, OrderDates, customer first and last names, and employee first and last names for all SportOrder records

c. The customer first and last names, order dates, inventory descriptions, order quantities, and item unit prices for all detail items in order ID 2

d. The inventory IDs, inventory description, color descriptions, inventory sizes, supplier names, category descriptions, and subcategory descriptions for all inventory items that contain the text string "Gloves" anywhere in the InventoryDescription column value

4. **Creating Outer Join Queries**

Create a new query file named 3Exercise4.sql, then write SQL queries to retrieve the following records:

a. The first and last names of all customers. as well as the OrderID, OrderDate, and PaymentType values for their corresponding orders. If a customer has not yet placed an order, structure the query so that it displays NULL values for the order-related columns. Use a left outer join query.

b. The name of each supplier, along with the inventory description of each item the supplier supplies. If a supplier does not currently supply any items, display NULL values for the inventory-related columns. Use a right outer join query, and suppress duplicate outputs.

c. The InventoryID and InventoryDescription of each inventory item, along with every OrderID and OrderDate corresponding to the item. If the item has never been ordered, display NULL values for the order-related columns. (Hint: Use either a left or right outer join along with an inner join.)

5. **Creating Nested Queries**

Create a new query file named 3Exercise5.sql, then write SQL queries to retrieve the following records:

a. The first and last names of all employees who work in the Parts department, using a nested query in which the subquery retrieves the DepartmentID using "Parts" in a search condition

b. The InventoryDescription of all inventory items that are in either the Motorcycles or All Terrain Vehicles categories. Use a nested query in which the subquery retrieves the CategoryID using the IN operator.

c. The order IDs and order dates of all orders sold by employee Dennis Ward. Create a nested query that uses the EXISTS operator, and use Dennis and Ward as search conditions in the subquery.

d. The order IDs, order dates, and customer first and last names of all orders that contained items from CategoryID 2. Use a nested subquery to identify inventory items for CategoryID 2, and create an inner join in the main query.

6. **Creating Database Views**

Create a new query file named 3Exercise6.sql, then write SQL queries to create the following views and retrieve the associated records:

a. Create a view named SportEmployeeView that contains the employee ID, department name, employee first and last names, and employee date of birth. Then write a SQL query that retrieves the department name and employee last and first name of all view records. Sort the output alphabetically first by department name and then by employee last name.

b. Create a view named SportInventoryCategoryView that contains the inventory ID, category description, and subcategory description for each item in the SportInventory table. Then write a SQL query that uses the view to list each category description and count the number of items in each category. Assign the alias TotalItems to the column that displays the number of items.

c. Create a view named SportOrderView that lists the order ID, order date, employee first and last name, inventory description, detail quantity, and detail unit price for every customer order. Then write a SQL query that lists each employee's last name and the corresponding total sales revenue generated by the employee's orders. Create a column alias named TotalSales for the calculated column, and order the output by descending total sales. (Hint: To calculate revenue, multiply detail quantity times detail price.)

7. **Creating Queries That Use Set Operations**

Create a new query file named 3Exercise7.sql, then write SQL queries to retrieve the following records:

a. The last and first name of all customers and employees, along with their associated telephone numbers. Use the UNION set operator to join the output of two independent queries. Change the output column names to Last Name, First Name," and "Telephone Number."

b. The first and last names of customers who have either purchased over $400 of merchandise from Sport Motors or who have purchased an item in the Motorcycles, All Terrain Vehicles, or "Snowmobiles" categories. Use the UNION ALL set operator to combine the output of the two independent queries and not to suppress duplicate outputs. You can use either inner join or nested queries.

CHAPTER 4

Introduction to Action Queries and T-SQL Programming

Learning Objectives

At the conclusion of this chapter, you will be able to:

■ create SQL action queries to insert, update, and delete data;

■ understand action query transactions and record locking and blocking;

■ understand basic T-SQL programming concepts;

■ create T-SQL stored procedures;

■ create T-SQL user-defined functions;

■ create database triggers that execute in response to DDL and DML commands.

Database applications allow users to enter, modify, and view database data using forms and reports. In Chapter 3, you learned how to create SQL queries to retrieve database data. In this chapter, you will learn how to write SQL data manipulation language (DML) commands to insert, modify, and delete data values. In later chapters, you will learn how to incorporate the DML commands into applications to allow users to easily enter and modify data values.

T-SQL is the SQL command dialect for SQL Server database queries. T-SQL includes programming commands that allow database developers to write programs that automate data processing through assigning variables, creating IF/THEN decision structures, and performing looping operations. For example, you could write a T-SQL program to calculate the number of hours that an Ironwood University tutor has worked during a specific time period and then to calculate the tutor's gross and net pay based on his or her pay rate. Or you could write a T-SQL program that retrieves the course grades a student has received and then calculates the student's grade point average. In this chapter, you will learn how to write different types of T-SQL programs to automate data processing tasks.

INSERTING, UPDATING, AND DELETING DATABASE DATA

NOTE: The query examples in this chapter reference the Ironwood University database in Figures 3-1 and 3-2 in Chapter 3.

When database developers create applications to allow users to interact with databases, they often must write SQL commands to allow them to insert, update, and delete database data. The SQL INSERT, UPDATE, and DELETE commands are called

FIGURE 4-1   Executing an INSERT action query in Management Studio

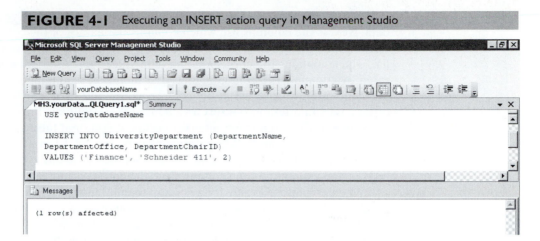

data manipulation language (DML) commands. These commands create *action queries,* which are queries that change the data values in database tables. This section describes how to create and execute INSERT, UPDATE, and DELETE action queries.

Executing Action Queries

You can execute action queries in Management Studio using the same steps as in Chapters 2 and 3 to execute SELECT queries. You connect to the database instance as before, type the query into the Query Editor window, and then execute the query. As with SELECT queries, you must first execute the USE command to specify the database you want to use before you execute any queries. Figure 4-1 shows an example of executing an INSERT action query in Management Studio. (You will learn about INSERT action queries in the next section.) Note the confirmation message "(1 row(s) affected)" appears on the Messages tab and confirms that the action query modified one record.

> **NOTE:** If your instructor tells you to enter and execute the sample action queries that appear in this section, start Management Studio, connect to your database, and create a query file named 4ActionQueries.sql using the instructions in Chapter 3. The chapter text does not provide explicit instructions for testing each query.

> **NOTE:** To execute the queries, you must first create the Ironwood University database tables by executing either the CreateIronwoodLocal.sql or CreateIronwoodRemote.sql script using the instructions in Chapter 3.

INSERT Action Queries

There are two formats for SQL INSERT action queries. The first format, which we call the *columns-list format,* lists column names and corresponding values explicitly. The second format, which we call the *no-columns-list format,* does not list column names and requires the user to supply a value for every table column.

The general syntax for an INSERT action query that uses the columns-list format is:

```
INSERT INTO TableName (Column1, Column2, ...)
VALUES(Column1Value, Column2Value, ...)
```

In this syntax, *TableName* is the name of the table into which you want to insert the data. Next is the columns list, which contains the names of the columns for which you want to insert data values. Next comes the VALUES keyword, followed by the values list, which contains the corresponding data values, enclosed in parentheses and separated by commas. The column names and their corresponding values must appear in the same order in each list. If the column names and their values are not in the same order, and you attempt to insert a value that does not have the same data type as the corresponding column name, an error occurs. If you omit table columns and their corresponding values, the DBMS automatically inserts NULL for these columns. If a column has a NOT NULL constraint that specifies that the column value cannot be NULL, you cannot omit the column from the columns and values lists.

When you insert a value for a column that has a number data type, you specify the number value, such as 3 or 2.2577. When you insert a value for a column that has a text data type, you enclose the value in single quotation marks, such as 'Finance'. To insert a value with an embedded single quotation mark, type the quotation mark two times, such as 'Lauren''s'. When you insert a value for a column that has a date/time data type, insert the value as a text string using one of the common date output formats shown in Table 3-8.

In Chapter 2 you learned how to create a surrogate key by designating a primary key column as an identity column to enable the DBMS to automatically generate unique sequential values. (Recall that a surrogate primary key is a primary key value that the DBMS creates to uniquely identify a record.) When you insert a new record in a table that contains an identity column, you omit the identity column name in the INSERT action query. This causes the DBMS to automatically generate the next sequential value and insert it into the table. You cannot explicitly insert a value for a column that is designated as an identity column. If you try, an error occurs.

Recall from Figure 3-1 that the UniversityDepartment table contains four columns: DepartmentID, DepartmentName, DepartmentOffice, and DepartmentChairID. The following INSERT action query uses the columns-list format to insert a new record into the UniversityDepartment table:

```
INSERT INTO UniversityDepartment (DepartmentName,
        DepartmentOffice, DepartmentChairID)
VALUES ('Finance', 'Schneider 411', 2)
```

Note that this query omits the DepartmentID value from the columns and values lists, because DepartmentID is an identity column. The DBMS automatically inserts the next DepartmentID value, along with the given values for DepartmentName, DepartmentOffice, and and DepartmentChairID. Also note that the values appear in the values list in the same order as the column names appear in the columns list.

When you insert a record that contains a foreign key value, the foreign key value must already exist in the parent table before you can insert the value in the child table. (Recall that in a foreign key relationship, the parent table is the table in which the column is the primary key, and the child table is the table in which the column is the foreign key.) In the INSERT command example, DepartmentChairID is a foreign key column that references the InstructorID column in the UniversityInstructor table. The value that the INSERT action query inserts in the foreign key column, which is InstructorID 2, must already exist in the UniversityInstructor table, or an error occurs.

The no-columns-list format of the INSERT action query omits the columns list and requires you to supply a value for every table column. The general syntax for this format of an INSERT action query is:

```
INSERT INTO TableName
VALUES(Column1Value, Column2Value, ...)
```

In this syntax, *TableName* is the name of the table in which you want to insert the data. You omit the columns list; therefore, the VALUES keyword comes next, followed by the values list. The values list must contain a value for every table column, and the column values must appear in the order in which the columns were listed when you created the table. You cannot use the no-columns-list format of the INSERT query if a table contains an identity column for the primary key value.

If you need to insert a NULL value into a column, place the word NULL in the values list in place of the column value. Usually you place the NULL marker in all capital letters, although it can appear in mixed- or lowercase letters. Note that the NULL marker does not appear in quotation marks.

Here are two action queries that use the no-columns-list format to insert records into the UniversityEnrollment table:

```
INSERT INTO UniversityEnrollment VALUES
(5, 15, 'B-')
INSERT INTO UniversityEnrollment VALUES
(5, 16, NULL)
```

The first query inserts a value for all three table columns, and the second query inserts a NULL value for the CourseGrade column.

In this book, we always use the columns-list format of the INSERT action query, which specifies the columns list along with the values list, and we urge you always to use this format as well. You must use this format with identity columns, and it creates queries that are easier to maintain over the life of a database because its syntax does not change if a DBA adds additional columns to the table.

You use the INSERT action query to insert data values that have number, text, or date data types. How do you insert other types of data? The best way to insert data into a column containing one of the binary data types is to write an application that allows the user to select the file, and then the application inserts the data using program code. To insert data into a column that has a Timestamp or Uniqueidentifier data type, use the format of the INSERT action query that lists the table columns and values and omit the column name from the column list. The DBMS automatically inserts the correct value.

UPDATE Action Queries

You use UPDATE action queries to update data values in existing records. The UPDATE action query has the following general syntax:

```
UPDATE TableName
SET Column1 = Column1Value,
    Column2 = Column2Value, ...
WHERE SearchCondition(s)
```

In this syntax, *TableName* is the name of the table in which you want to update data. A single UPDATE action query can update data in only one table. *Column1, Column2,* and so forth represent the names of the columns for which you want to update the data values, and *Column1Value, Column2Value,* and so forth represent the corresponding new data values. These data values can contain arithmetic expressions. You represent number values as numerals, place text values as characters in single quotation marks, and represent dates as text strings in date formats that SQL Server

FIGURE 4-2   Examples of UPDATE action queries

```
UPDATE UniversityStudent
SET StudentAddress = '5453 Water Street',
    AdvisorID = 2                              ——Updates a single record
WHERE StudentID = 1
```

(1 row(s) affected)

```
UPDATE UniversityCourse
SET CourseCredits = 4      ——Updates multiple records
WHERE DepartmentID = 2
```

(2 row(s) affected)

```
UPDATE UniversityServiceProject     ┐ Updates every table record by
SET ProjectGrade = 'A'              ┘ omitting search condition
```

(2 row(s) affected)

recognizes. If you update a column that contains a foreign key constraint, the new value must already exist in the parent table.

The *SearchCondition(s)* specify the records that the command updates. If the *SearchCondition(s)* match a single record, then the action query updates only one record. If the *SearchCondition(s)* match multiple records, then the action query updates all matching records. If you omit the search condition, then the UPDATE action query updates all table records.

Figure 4-2 shows examples of UPDATE queries and their associated confirmation messages. The first UPDATE query updates multiple column values (StudentAddress and AdvisorID) for a single record in the UniversityStudent table because the search condition matches exactly one table record. Note that AdvisorID is a foreign key, so the new value (AdvisorID 2) must already exist in the parent table, which is the UniversityInstructor table. The second query updates two records in the UniversityCourse table, because the search condition matches two table records. The third query omits the search condition and updates the ProjectGrade column in all records in the UniversityServiceProject table.

DELETE Action Queries

You use DELETE action queries to delete existing table records. The DELETE action query has the following general syntax:

```
DELETE FROM TableName
WHERE SearchCondition(s)
```

In this syntax, *TableName* is the name of the table from which you want to delete the data. A single DELETE action query can remove data from one table only. The *SearchCondition(s)* specifies which record or records the command deletes. If the *SearchCondition(s)* matches a single record, then the action query deletes only one record; if it matches multiple records, the action query deletes all matching records. If you omit the search condition, the DELETE action query deletes all table records.

Figure 4-3 shows examples of DELETE action queries. The first query deletes the record for StudentID 7 (David Ashcraft) in the UniversityStudent table. The second query deletes five records from the UniversityTutorSession table, which are the records for in which the SessionStartTime value is on or after 10/1/2008.

FIGURE 4-3 Examples of DELETE action queries

```
DELETE FROM UniversityStudent
WHERE StudentID = 7

(1 row(s) affected)

DELETE FROM UniversityTutorSession
WHERE TutorSessionStartTime >= '10/1/2008'

(5 row(s) affected)
```

You cannot delete a record that is the parent record in a foreign key relationship. For example, consider the first record in the UniversityStudent table (StudentID 1, Clifford Wall). You cannot delete this record because it is referenced as a foreign key in the first five records in the UniversityEnrollment table and in the final three records in the UniversityTutorSession table.

DATABASE TRANSACTIONS AND LOCKING/BLOCKING

When database users execute action queries, the DBMS has to provide safeguards to ensure that the action queries execute correctly. For example, suppose that two people try to reserve the same seat on an airplane simultaneously. Will both be successful? Suppose a customer tries to transfer money from a savings account to a checking account and the system crashes after withdrawing from the savings account but before adding the amount to the checking account. Is the money lost to the customer and gained by the bank? To deal with such issues, databases provide functions for creating transactions, locking records, and blocking action queries.

Database Transactions

In database processing, a *transaction* represents a logical unit of work made up of one or more action and/or SELECT queries. All queries in a transaction must succeed, or none of them should succeed. Otherwise, the database is left in an inconsistent state and contains data with errors. After entering all the queries in a transaction, a user *commits* the transaction, which makes the query changes permanent in the database and visible to other users. If an error occurs partway through the transaction, the user can *roll back,* or discard, all the action queries executed to that point.

Consider an application that allows students to enroll in courses at Ironwood University. The application inserts a record into the UniversityEnrollment table that contains the student's ID number and the section ID number. At the same time, the application must increment the section's SectionCurrentEnrollment field value in the UniversitySection table to reflect that the course's current enrollment has increased by one. Both action queries must succeed to complete the transaction, or neither should succeed. Figure 4-4 illustrates these two action queries comprising a transaction.

Recall from Chapter 2 that a SQL Server database stores database data in a data file and a record of database changes in a transaction log file. As users execute action queries, the DBMS immediately notes changes in the transaction log file and updates the data files later. If a user rolls back a transaction, the DBMS modifies the transaction log file and reverses the changes. When a user commits a transaction, the DBMS notes

FIGURE 4-4 Action queries that comprise a transaction

```
INSERT INTO UniversityEnrollment
VALUES(6, 14, NULL)

UPDATE UniversitySection
SET SectionCurrentEnrollment = SectionCurrentEnrollment + 1
WHERE SectionID = 14
```

in the transaction log file that the data has been committed, and the change cannot be rolled back. This process of writing actions to a transaction log file and noting when action queries have been committed to the data file creates database transactions.

After a database failure such as a power failure or a hardware malfunction, the database automatically performs a recovery operation when it restarts. In a *database recovery* operation, the database instance restores all database data back to a consistent state. One of the tasks is to use the transaction log to roll back all uncommitted transactions.

SQL Server 2005 supports three types of transactions:

- **Autocommit:** These transactions commit each action query as soon as it executes. This is the default transaction mode and does not require any specific transaction control commands.

- **Explicit:** Each transaction starts with a BEGIN TRANSACTION statement that signals the beginning of a transaction. All SQL commands that follow are part of the transaction. The transaction ends with a COMMIT TRANSACTION statement, which signals the end of the transaction and commits the transaction.

- **Implicit:** Each transaction starts as soon a user connects to a database instance. The user can enter one or more queries, and all the queries become part of the current transaction. The user can execute a COMMIT TRANSACTION command to commit the transaction, or execute a ROLLBACK TRANSACTION command to roll back the transaction. These commands end the current transaction and mark the start of the next transaction.

With implicit and explicit transactions, the changes made by user action queries are not visible to other users until the user explicitly commits the transaction. The following subsections describe in detail how to create transactions.

Creating SQL Server Transactions

Autocommit Transactions To create an autocommit transaction, you do not need to include special commands. Write and execute a series of action queries, and the SQL Server database instance attempts to commit each action query as soon as it executes. For example, when you run the script that creates the Ironwood University database, the database instance commits each action query as soon as it executes. If an action query fails and cannot be committed, the database instance displays an error message in the Messages pane but continues to execute the rest of the script commands. (This can cause cascading errors because many times subsequent action queries depend on the success of prior ones!)

To illustrate an autocommit transaction, we use a series of action queries similar to the ones in Figure 4-4 that involve the UniversityEnrollment and UniversitySection tables. Recall that whenever a student enrolls in a course section, a database application inserts a record in UniversityEnrollment that contains the student's ID number and the course section ID number. This value is a composite primary key and must be unique; therefore, a student can enroll in a specific course section only once. Moreover, when a student enrolls in a course section, the course section's current enrollment value increases by one.

NOTE: If you perform the following steps, you must first run the CreateIronwoodLocal.sql or CreateIronwoodRemote.sql script to refresh your Ironwood University database tables. Otherwise, the script commands may not execute as shown. To run the Ironwood University script and create the transaction script:

1. If necessary, start Management Studio and connect to the database.
2. *If you are connecting to a local database,* open CreateIronwoodLocal.sql and then execute the file. (Do *not* close the file, because you will use it later.)

   If you are connecting to a remote database, open CreateIronwoodRemote.sql and then execute the file. (Do *not* close the file, because you will use it later.)
3. Create a new query file named 4Transactions.sql, and save it in your \SQLServer\Solutions\Chapter4 folder.

The following steps show how to create an autocommit transaction that executes a series of action queries, some of which succeed and some of which fail. To help identify errors, the transaction includes PRINT commands that print output to the Results pane during query execution.

The first autocommit transaction inserts a UniversityEnrollment record to specify that student ID 6 (Judith Bakke) enrolls in course section ID 10. It also executes an associated UPDATE query that updates the current enrollment in the course by one. An error occurs in the UPDATE query for section ID 10 because the current enrollment for the section is 35, which happens to be the maximum allowable enrollment. A check condition exists on the UniversitySection table that does not allow the maximum enrollment to exceed the current enrollment, so this course is closed and cannot enroll any more students. The second autocommit transaction repeats this process to allow Judith to enroll in course section 11. These action queries should succeed.

To create autocommit transactions in which some action queries fail:

1. Type the following commands in the Query Editor to create the autocommit transactions:

```
USE yourDatabaseName
--autocommit transaction that fails
INSERT INTO UniversityEnrollment
(StudentID, SectionID, EnrollmentGrade)
VALUES(6, 10, NULL)
PRINT 'Inserted into UniversityEnrollment'
UPDATE UniversitySection
SET SectionCurrentEnrollment = SectionCurrentEnrollment + 1
WHERE SectionID = 10
PRINT 'UniversitySection Updated'
--autocommit transaction that succeeds
INSERT INTO UniversityEnrollment
(StudentID, SectionID, EnrollmentGrade)
VALUES(6, 11, NULL)
PRINT 'Inserted into UniversityEnrollment'
UPDATE UniversitySection
SET SectionCurrentEnrollment = SectionCurrentEnrollment + 1
WHERE SectionID = 11
PRINT 'UniversitySection Updated'
```

2. Execute the queries. Figure 4-5 shows the messages that appear in the Results pane.

FIGURE 4-5 Executing action queries using autocommit transactions

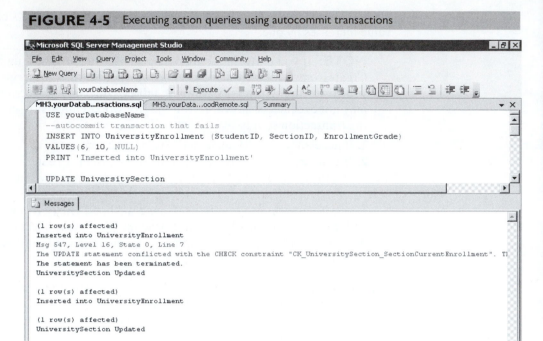

The first message indicates that the transaction successfully inserted the first record into the UniversityEnrollment table. The second message is an error message, indicating that the first UPDATE action query failed due to the check constraint on the SectionCurrentEnrollment column. The third and fourth messages indicate that the second INSERT and UPDATE action queries succeeded. This exercise illustrates that, for autocommit transactions, even when one transaction fails, subsequent transactions execute.

Explicit Transactions   With explicit transactions, you include commands to explicitly begin and end each transaction. To create an explicit transaction, use the following general syntax:

```
SET XACT_ABORT ON
BEGIN TRANSACTION [TransactionName]
  Action Query(ies)
  [ROLLBACK TRANSACTION [TransactionName]]
COMMIT TRANSACTION [TransactionName]
```

In this syntax, SET_XACT_ABORT ON instructs the SQL Server database instance not to use the default autocommit mode.

TIPS: 1. If you omit the SET_XACT_ABORT ON command, the database instance attempts to commit every action query immediately, regardless of the other transaction control commands that you execute.
2. If you want to reset your database connection so that it autocommits transactions, execute the command SET XACT_ABORT OFF.

The BEGIN TRANSACTION command marks the beginning of the transaction and can have an optional *TransactionName*. (The database ignores the *TransactionName*, but you can use it to document your SQL commands internally.) The queries that comprise the transaction follow.

If you execute the ROLLBACK TRANSACTION command anywhere in a transaction, the DBMS rolls back all the action queries executed since the last BEGIN TRANSACTION command. The COMMIT TRANSACTION command explicitly commits the transaction, which makes the transaction's action query changes permanent and visible to other users.

The following steps show how to execute the script that creates the Ironwood University database tables again to refresh the tables and undo the changes made by the previous transactions. They also describe how to create an explicit transaction allowing student Judith Bakke to enroll in course section ID 10 by inserting a record into the UniversityEnrollment table and updating the current enrollment value in the UniversitySection table. This transaction should fail because course section ID 10 is full. Finally, they execute a SELECT query to confirm that the transaction did not insert the record into the UniversityEnrollment table.

To create an explicit transaction:

1. Select the Query Editor tab for the Create Ironwood script, and then click Execute to execute the script and refresh the database tables.

CAUTION: If you do not refresh your database tables, the next transaction will not execute correctly because you have already inserted the StudentEnrollment records that it attempts to insert.

---

2. Click the 4Transactions.sql tab, place the insertion point at the end of the existing text, add some blank lines, and then type the following commands to create an explicit transaction:

```
SET XACT_ABORT ON
BEGIN TRANSACTION UpdateEnrollment
  INSERT INTO UniversityEnrollment
    (StudentID, SectionID, EnrollmentGrade)
  VALUES(6, 10, NULL)
  UPDATE UniversitySection
    SET SectionCurrentEnrollment = SectionCurrentEnrollment + 1
    WHERE SectionID = 10
  PRINT 'Transaction Succeeded'
COMMIT TRANSACTION UpdateEnrollment
```

3. Execute the transaction. An error message appears in the Messages pane, indicating that the transaction failed as a result of the check condition constraint error.

4. Type the following SELECT query as the last line in the Query Editor:

```
SELECT StudentID, SectionID, EnrollmentGrade
FROM UniversityEnrollment
WHERE StudentID = 6
```

5. Highlight the query and then execute it. The Results pane shows that the query retrieves no records, confirming that no UniversityEnrollment records exist for StudentID 6 and that the INSERT command did not execute.

As expected, the transaction did not insert the record into the UniversityEnrollment table. Because the UPDATE action query failed, the INSERT action query also failed.

Another way to structure an explicit transaction is to place it in a TRY/CATCH block. A *TRY/CATCH block* is a program structure that contains a series of program commands in the TRY block and a series of error-handling commands in the CATCH block. It has the following general syntax:

```
BEGIN TRY
     Program Command(s)
END TRY
BEGIN CATCH
     Error Handling Command(s)
END CATCH
```

If an error occurs in any of the commands in the TRY block, execution immediately switches to the CATCH block, which contains commands to handle the error. You can place a transaction's queries in the TRY block and a ROLLBACK TRANSACTION command in the CATCH block.

The following steps show how to create and execute the transaction that attempts to insert the record to enroll Judith Bakke in Section ID 10 within a TRY/CATCH block. They also show how to run the SQL SELECT command to confirm that, because the UPDATE command fails, the INSERT command fails also.

To create and execute an explicit transaction within a TRY/CATCH block:

1. Place the insertion point at the end of the existing text in 4Transactions.sql, add some blank lines, and then type the following commands to create an explicit transaction:

```
BEGIN TRY
  BEGIN TRANSACTION UpdateEnrollment
    INSERT INTO UniversityEnrollment
      (StudentID, SectionID, EnrollmentGrade)
      VALUES(6, 10, NULL)
    UPDATE UniversitySection
      SET SectionCurrentEnrollment = SectionCurrentEnrollment + 1
      WHERE SectionID = 10
    PRINT 'Transaction Succeeded'
    COMMIT TRANSACTION UpdateEnrollment
END TRY
BEGIN CATCH
    ROLLBACK TRANSACTION UpdateEnrollment
    PRINT 'Transaction Failed'
END CATCH
```

2. Highlight the transaction and then execute it. The messages "1 row(s) affected" and "Transaction Failed" appear in the Messages pane. The first message indicates that the INSERT command succeeded, and the second message indicates that the transaction failed as a result of the check condition constraint error.

3. To confirm that the INSERT action query was rolled back, highlight and execute the SELECT query that you created in the previous set of steps to retrieve the data for StudentID 6 in the UniversityEnrollment table. Note that the query retrieves no records, confirming that no UniversityEnrollment records exist for StudentID 6 and that the INSERT command was rolled back.

Implicit Transactions   With implicit transactions, the first transaction begins when the user first connects to the database and ends when the user executes a COMMIT or ROLLBACK command. This action also signals the beginning of the next transaction.

To create an implicit transaction, use the following general syntax:

```
SET IMPLICIT_TRANSACTIONS ON
--begin Transaction 1
Action Query(ies)
[ROLLBACK TRANSACTION]|[COMMIT TRANSACTION]
--begin Transaction 2
Action Query(ies)
[ROLLBACK TRANSACTION]|[COMMIT TRANSACTION]
...
```

You begin an implicit transaction with the SET IMPLICIT_TRANSACTIONS ON command, which instructs the DBMS instance to use implicit transactions. (To discontinue executing implicit transactions, execute the command SET IMPLICIT_TRANS-ACTIONS OFF.) The action queries comprising the first transaction follow. (Note that you omit the BEGIN TRANSACTION command.) You can execute the ROLLBACK TRANSACTION command in the action queries to discard the changes made to the database since the transaction began. When the transaction's action queries are complete, execute the COMMIT TRANSACTION command to commit the changes and to mark the beginning of the next transaction. Note that, with implicit transactions, you cannot explicitly name transactions using the *TransactionName* parameter.

The following steps show how to create an implicit transaction to allow student Judith Bakke to enroll in course section ID 10. This is similar to the explicit transaction in the previous set of steps, except that it omits the BEGIN TRANSACTION command.

To create an implicit transaction:

1. Place the insertion point at the end of the existing text in the 4Transactions.sql script, add some blank lines, then type the following commands to create an implicit transaction:

```
SET IMPLICIT_TRANSACTIONS ON
    INSERT INTO UniversityEnrollment
     (StudentID, SectionID, EnrollmentGrade)
     VALUES(6, 10, '')
    UPDATE UniversitySection
        SET SectionCurrentEnrollment = SectionCurrentEnrollment + 1
        WHERE SectionID = 10
    PRINT 'Transaction Succeeded'
COMMIT TRANSACTION
```

2. Highlight and execute the transaction. The "1 row(s) affected" and error message appear in the Messages pane, indicating that the INSERT command executed but that ultimately the transaction failed as a result of the check condition constraint error.
3. Highlight the SELECT query that retrieves the data for Student ID 6, and then execute it. Again note in the Results pane that the query retrieves no records, again confirming that no UniversityEnrollment records exist for StudentID 6 and that the INSERT command was rolled back.
4. Type and execute the following command to switch implicit transactions off:

```
SET IMPLICIT_TRANSACTIONS OFF
```

Locking and Blocking

When logging on to a SQL Server database, the user creates a database connection. All the transactions the user executes belong to that user's database connection. Problems can arise when different users create *competing transactions,* which are transactions that attempt to view, update, and delete the same records simultaneously. These problems fall into the following categories:

- **Lost updates** occur when two or more transactions attempt to update a record at the same time. Each transaction is unaware of any others, and the last update overwrites the updates made by the previous transactions and they are lost.

- **Dirty reads** occur when the READUNCOMMITTED isolation level is used (this is discussed shortly in the Isolation Levels section in this chapter) and when a transaction reads a record that has been inserted or updated by another transaction but has not yet been committed. For example, suppose one user executes the transaction in Figure 4-4 that inserts a record into the UniversityEnrollment table and updates a record in the UniversitySection table. At the same time, a second user executes a query that retrieves the SectionCurrentEnrollment value for the course section, which represents the updated value. The first user then rolls back his or her transaction and resets SectionCurrentEnrollment to its original value. The data that the second user retrieves is incorrect.

- **Nonrepeatable reads** occur when a transaction retrieves the same record multiple times but retrieves a different data value each time. This is caused by a dirty read: the first time the user reads an updated but uncommitted value; the second time the user reads the original value because the uncommitted value was rolled back.

- **Phantom reads** occur when a transaction reads a record that has been inserted by another transaction but has not yet been committed. If the inserted record is subsequently rolled back and no longer exists, it is a "phantom record."

A DBMS prevents these problems through locking and blocking. *Locking* prevents a transaction from accessing data currently in use by another transaction by placing a lock on it. The DBMS releases the lock when the user commits the transaction. Locking allows a transaction to run in isolation, that is, as if it is the only transaction running on the database instance. Transactions can have different *isolation levels,* which specify whether they behave as if they are executing by themselves or whether they can safely run at the same time as other transactions.

Blocking occurs when a transaction tries to access data locked by another transaction. The transaction cannot access the locked data and therefore cannot continue until the lock is released. Usually, a transaction has a *timeout interval,* which is a specific time period that the transaction waits for a lock to be released. If the timeout interval expires before the locked record becomes available, the transaction fails.

To understand locks, you need to know about the different types of locks and the levels at which they lock database data. Locks have modes, which specify how they block other transactions. The following subsections explore lock types, levels, and modes. It also discusses how SQL Server manages locks in SELECT queries, and explores transaction isolation levels.

Lock Types, Levels, and Modes

There are two basic types of locks: read locks and write locks. A *read lock* prevents a transaction from accessing a value using a SELECT query, which reads the data but does not change it. A *write lock* prevents a transaction from accessing a value using an action query that attempts to modify the data.

Locking can occur at different levels in a database. SQL Server 2005 always tries to create *record locks,* which lock an entire record of data and are the lowest level at which the DBMS can lock data. As a result, this level blocks the fewest transactions. A SQL Server DBMS has limits as to how many locks it can manage at one time, however. When it reaches this limit, the DBMS starts to lock data in larger increments of pages, extents, tables, and even the entire database. It can create *page locks,* which lock storage units of 8,060 bytes in a database. A page lock can contain a variable number of rows, depending on the volume of data in each row. A DBMS can also create *extent locks,* which lock a fixed allocation unit of eight contiguous pages. Finally, a DBMS can create a *database lock,* which locks an entire database.

Lock modes specify how locks block competing transactions. SQL Server has multiple locking modes, but the three most common modes are shared, exclusive, and update. SQL Server uses shared locks for data that a transaction is currently reading but not changing. A *shared lock* is a read lock that multiple transactions can share. The DBMS releases shared locks as soon as a SELECT command finishes processing. Shared locks let other locks know that a transaction is currently reading this data but do not block other transactions from reading the data. Other transactions cannot place other types of locks on a record until the shared lock is released, preventing dirty reads.

An *exclusive lock* prevents other transactions from either reading or updating the locked record. A transaction can acquire an exclusive lock only when all other locks on the record are released.

An *update lock* is a combination of a shared lock and exclusive lock. It allows a transaction to read a data value and then update it. During the reading portion of the transaction, the lock behaves as a shared lock, and other transactions can read the data. During the update portion of the transaction, the lock changes to an exclusive lock, and other transactions cannot read or update the record. Other transactions cannot acquire update locks on the data until the current transaction releases its update lock.

Managing Locks in SQL Server SELECT Queries

When a transaction contains an action query, the SQL Server DBMS acquires exclusive locks on the query records. When a transaction contains a SELECT query, the SQL Server DBMS acquires a shared lock. These are the default SQL Server lock types. Sometimes these default locks block too many transactions, however, and transaction processing becomes too slow. To improve performance, database developers can specify lock types other than shared locks for SELECT queries.

To specify alternate lock types on SELECT queries, use *table hints,* which are parameters that you include in the FROM clause. The general syntax to include a table hint in a SELECT query is:

```
SELECT Column1, Column2, ...
FROM TableName WITH (Hint1, Hint2, ... )
WHERE SearchCondition(s)
```

Table 4-1 lists and describes SQL Server table hints, and the following section on isolation levels describes how to use them.

Isolation Levels

Recall that a transaction's isolation level specifies whether the transaction runs as if it is the only transaction running on the database instance or whether it can safely run at the same time as other transactions. To be totally safe and always avoid lost updates, dirty reads, nonrepeatable reads, and phantom reads, all transactions should run in isolation. However, this makes database transactions execute very slowly, and it can even lock up the database if developers forget to commit their transactions!

To improve transaction processing performance, SQL Server supports five different isolation levels to control how transactions acquire locks and how they behave when they encounter locks held by other transactions. The following subsections describe these levels, starting with the lowest.

TABLE 4-1   Table hints for transaction locking

Hint	Description
HOLDLOCK	Forces a shared lock for the duration of the transaction; same as SERIALIZABLE.
NOLOCK	Instructs to use no lock for the transaction, which permits dirty reads; same as READUNCOMMITTED.
PAGELOCK	Forces the use of a page-level lock.
READCOMMITTED (default hint)	Releases the lock as soon as the command completes; data can change prior to completion of the transaction, so phantom reads are possible.
READPAST	Instructs to skip locked rows during a read; can be used only with the READCOMMITTED isolation level hint and works only with row-level locks.
READUNCOMMITTED	Instructs to use no-lock for the transaction, which permits dirty reads; same as NOLOCK.
REPEATABLEREAD	Instructs to hold the lock until the transaction completes; data can change prior to completion of transaction; so phantom reads are possible.
ROWLOCK	Forces a row-level lock if possible; if the DBMS's maximum lock limit has been reached, the lock level still escalates to page, extent, table, and database.
SERIALIZABLE	Forces a shared lock for the duration of transaction; same as HOLDLOCK.
TABLOCK	Forces a shared lock on the entire table.
TABLOCKX	Forces an exclusive lock on the entire table.
UPDLOCK	Forces an update lock and holds it for the entire transaction.
XLOCK	Forces an exclusive lock and holds it for the entire transaction.

1. Read Uncommitted   This isolation level does not acquire any locks for SELECT or action queries. However, database developers can use table hints to acquire locks manually. It ignores locks set by other transactions and reads all data, including uncommitted data. The only data it does not read is physically corrupt data. As a result, it does not avoid any of the transaction control problems. When should you use it? Use it if you are interested in generating reports quickly, your transactions rarely modify data, and you can accept reports that have errors caused by uncommitted reads, phantom reads, and so forth.

The command to set a transaction's isolation level to Read Uncommitted is:

```
SET TRANSACTION ISOLATION LEVEL READ UNCOMMITTED
```

2. Read Committed   This is the default isolation level for SQL Server transactions. It honors locks created by all other transactions and reads only committed data. Transactions in this level acquire shared locks for SELECT queries and immediately release them after the SELECT query completes and before remaining commands in the transaction execute. Transactions in this isolation level acquire exclusive locks for action queries and hold them for the duration of the transaction in case they need to be rolled back. This level prevents dirty reads but does not avoid lost updates, unrepeatable reads, or phantom reads. Although this is the default isolation level, you can set it explicitly using the following command:

```
SET TRANSACTION ISOLATION LEVEL READ COMMITTED
```

3. Repeatable Read   Transactions created in this level honor locks created by all other transactions and read only committed data. When a transaction in this level acquires shared locks for a SELECT query, it keeps the locks until all remaining commands in the transaction execute. This prevents lost updates, dirty reads, and unrepeatable reads but does not prevent phantom reads. The command to set this isolation level is:

```
SET TRANSACTION ISOLATION LEVEL REPEATABLE READ
```

4. Snapshot   This isolation level, introduced in SQL Server 2005, creates transactions that do not block other transactions. Instead, when a transaction acquires a lock on data, a second transaction views a copy, or snapshot, of the original data. The second transaction operates on the snapshot data to the point of committing any changes. At that point, the second transaction tests to see if the original data is different from the snapshot in a way that affects its operations. If the original data has been changed, the second transaction rolls back and tries again. This isolation level works best in a system with applications that primarily read data and rarely insert, update, or delete it. To use snapshot isolation, a DBA must first execute the following command to enable it in the database instance:

```
ALTER DATABASE yourDatabaseName
SET READ_COMMITTED_SNAPSHOT ON
```

Altering the database for READ_COMMITTED_SNAPSHOT changes the behavior of the default READ COMMITTED isolation level for the entire database. After making this database alteration, setting the isolation level to READ COMMITTED will use snapshot isolation.

5. Serializable   This isolation level isolates transactions from one another by never allowing a transaction to see uncommitted data. It guarantees that none of the transaction processing problems ever occur but also usually affects performance adversely, so it should be used with extreme caution in busy databases. The command to set this isolation level is:

```
SET TRANSACTION ISOLATION LEVEL SERIALIZABLE
```

Recall that when logging on to a database instance, the user creates a database connection, and all the transactions the user executes are associated with that database connection. Other database connections may create competing transactions that attempt to simultaneously view and update the same database records. The following steps illustrate transaction locking and blocking by working with two independent database connections that simultaneously execute competing transactions. The first connection's transaction uses the default Read Committed isolation level and contains an UPDATE action query that updates the CourseCredits value from 4 to 3 for Course ID 7 in the UniversityCourse table. Recall that transactions in this isolation level acquire exclusive locks for action queries and hold them until the transaction commits.

The second database connection's transaction attempts to retrieve the data about Course ID 7 in a SELECT query. The transaction uses different isolation levels to demonstrate how the SQL Server DBMS blocks locked data.

To illustrate transaction locking and blocking:

1. Start a second Management Studio session and create a new database connection. We will call this Session 2. (You will have two copies Management Studio running at the same time.)

NOTE: You need to use two different Management Studio sessions because SQL Server determines the owner of a lock based on the database connection that creates the transaction acquiring the lock.

---

2. Switch back to the first Management Studio session, which we will call Session 1. Place the insertion point at the end of the 4Transactons.sql script, enter a few blank lines, then type and execute the following query, which uses the default Read Committed isolation level and obtains an exclusive lock on the updated record:

```
SET TRANSACTION ISOLATION LEVEL READ COMMITTED
BEGIN TRANSACTION UpdateCourseCredits
UPDATE UniversityCourse
SET CourseCredits = 3
WHERE CourseID = 7
```

NOTE: Do *not* commit the transaction yet because you want to see how its lock blocks another transaction.

---

3. Switch to Session 2 and type the following transaction to read the data that the first transaction just updated. Be sure to change *yourDatabaseName* to the name of the database you are using in Session 1. Note that this transaction uses the Repeatable Read isolation level, which honors all locks created by other transactions.

```
USE yourDatabaseName
SET XACT_ABORT ON
SET TRANSACTION ISOLATION LEVEL REPEATABLE READ
BEGIN TRANSACTION SelectCourseData
SELECT CourseID, CourseCredits
FROM UniversityCourse
WHERE CourseID = 7
COMMIT TRANSACTION SelectCourseData
```

4. Execute the transaction. The query "hangs," indicating that the desired record is locked and cannot be retrieved.
5. Switch back to Session 1, and type and execute the following command to roll back the current transaction.

```
ROLLBACK TRANSACTION UpdateCourseCredits
```

6. Switch back to Session 2, and note that the transaction has now successfully executed.
7. Switch back to Session 1, and execute the transaction again. Do *not* commit the transaction yet.
8. Switch back to Session 2, and modify the current (SelectCourseData) transaction's isolation level so that it reads the uncommitted record by changing the third line, which sets the isolation level. It appears as follows:

```
SET TRANSACTION ISOLATION LEVEL READ UNCOMMITTED
```

9. Execute the transaction. This time, the SELECT query retrieves the data for the uncommitted transaction, which shows the Course Credits value to be 3. This is a

dirty read because the transaction in the first database connection might be rolled back.

10. Switch to Session 1, which contains the uncommitted UPDATE action query, and execute the command to roll back the current transaction.

11. Switch to Session 2, which contains the SELECT query, and execute the transaction again. This time, the Results pane displays the Course Credits value to be 4. You have just performed a nonrepeatable read, which is an error!

12. Save the query file in Session 2 as 4SelectTransactions.sql in your \SQLServer\ Solutions\Chapter4 folder. Do not exit Session 2 yet.

Locking Records in SELECT Queries

A common locking/blocking scenario occurs when an application retrieves data using a SELECT query and then performs an action query based on the retrieved data. Consider the example of reserving a seat in a specific course section: first the transaction executes a SELECT query to determine whether seats are still available. After reviewing the course sections with available seats, the user chooses one and attempts to enroll in it. This is when locking comes in. What if another user enrolls and gets the last available seat while the first user is making a decision? The SELECT command that retrieves the available seat list must also acquire an exclusive lock on the record(s) containing the available seats to prevent a second user from simultaneously viewing and reserving the same seat.

To create a SELECT query that acquires an exclusive lock on the records it retrieves, use the following general syntax:

```
SELECT Column1, Column2, ...
FROM TableName WITH (xlock)
WHERE SearchCondition(s)
```

This syntax adds the `WITH (xlock)` modifier to the FROM clause. This instructs the DBMS to lock the selected row(s) until the transaction commits. The following commands illustrate transactions that lock a record in a SELECT command and then update the record.

To lock a record within a SELECT command:

1. In Session 1, type the following transaction to view and lock the records for all course sections in the SUMM08 term with open seats. Do *not* commit the transaction yet.

```
SET XACT_ABORT ON
BEGIN TRANSACTION ViewAvailableSeats
SELECT SectionID, SectionDay, SectionTime
FROM UniversitySection WITH (xlock)
WHERE SectionTerm = 'SUMM08'
AND SectionCurrentEnrollment < SectionMaxEnrollment
```

2. Execute the transaction. The Results pane displays the data for Section IDs 1 and 2. Recall that because you executed this query using the `WITH (xlock)` option, it acquires exclusive locks on the selected records.

3. Copy all the commands just entered in step 1, switch to Session 2, and paste the copied commands at the bottom of the Query Editor, below the existing commands.

4. Execute the pasted commands. The transaction "hangs," indicating that the target records are indeed locked and not available to other transactions.

5. Switch back to Session 1, and type the following command to commit the transaction and release the locks:

```
COMMIT TRANSACTION ViewAvailableSeats
```

6. Switch back to Session 2, and note that the transaction has successfully executed.
7. In Session 2, type and execute `COMMIT TRANSACTION ViewAvailableSeats` to commit the transaction in this session also.
8. Exit Session 2 and save the query file.

In an actual registration system, the initial query to retrieve all sections with available seats would not lock any sections. However, when a user selected a section in which to enroll, a transaction would first run a SELECT query to determine if the section still had available seats. If this query succeeded, then the transaction would run other action queries to allow the student to enroll.

T-SQL PROGRAMMING

Sometimes database applications require developers to write scripts to automate database-related tasks. You ran the script to create the Ironwood University database, create the tables, and insert the data values. Scripts can contain SQL commands as well as commands to perform common programming tasks, such as assigning variables, manipulating numbers and text, and displaying outputs. You use scripts to automate tasks that you perform repeatedly, such as creating a database or a series of database tables. You can also use scripts to perform data processing tasks that are too complicated for a single query, such as retrieving data about a specific student's courses and then using it to calculate the student's grade point average. In this section, you will learn how to write scripts that use T-SQL commands to perform basic programming tasks.

> **NOTE:** This book assumes that readers already understand basic programming concepts, so it focuses on specific T-SQL applications of these concepts rather than on concept definitions.

T-SQL Batches

You can write a T-SQL script in the Query Editor and then execute it just as you would any SQL query. Recall that each time you execute a query, the T-SQL interpreter parses the query to confirm that it does not contain syntax errors. During the parsing process, the interpreter translates the query into machine-readable format and creates an *execution plan,* which contains instructions for running the query so that it executes in the fastest way possible. When you execute multiple T-SQL and SQL commands in a single script, the T-SQL interpreter creates a single execution plan. Many times in a script, you need to create a *batch,* which is group of commands that the T-SQL interpreter treats as a unit. Each batch has a single execution plan and is executed by the DBMS as a unit.

You need to create batches because sometimes a script must complete one task before it can perform the next. For example, you have to create a database before you can create its tables, and you must create a table before you can insert its records. To create a batch within a script, use the GO command. The GO command instructs the Query Editor to send to the T-SQL interpreter all the preceding commands from the beginning of the script or the last GO command. The GO command must be on its own command line in the script. Figure 4-6 shows how you use the GO command to create batches in a T-SQL script.

Batches can generate two types of errors: compile errors and run-time errors. A *compile error* is the same as a syntax error and results when the program statements do not obey the rules of the language. A *run-time error* occurs when the command syntax is correct, but an error occurs and is detected by the DBMS. Examples of run-time errors are

FIGURE 4-6   Creating batches in a T-SQL script

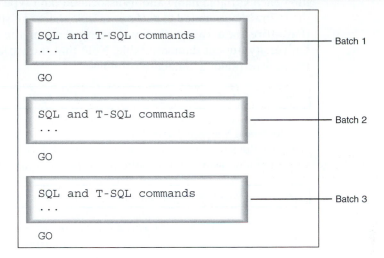

constraint violations, such as trying to insert a record with a nonunique primary key value or trying to insert a record with a value that does not follow an existing check condition.

If a batch has a compile error, the T-SQL interpreter reports the compile error in the Messages pane and does not execute the batch. If the batch has a run-time error, execution usually stops, and the remaining script commands do not execute. However, if a constraint violation occurs in an autocommit transaction, then the rest of the commands execute. But if the error causes the transaction to fail, then the DBMS rolls back the previously executed commands.

Variables

A *variable* references a memory location that stores a data value. When you write T-SQL programs, you use variables to reference data values that program commands manipulate. The following subsections describe how to declare and assign values to variables.

Declaring Variables

When you declare a variable, the T-SQL interpreter sets up a location in the server's main memory to store the variable's data value. You use the following general syntax to declare a T-SQL variable:

```
DECLARE @variableName DataType
```

In this syntax, *variableName* is the name that identifies the variable and references its value. Note that you always prefix the variable name with the at sign (@). A variable name must conform to the naming rules for database tables and fields: it must begin with a letter and can contain the special characters of @, $, #, and _. Variable names cannot contain embedded blank spaces. To avoid reserved words, create descriptive variable names made up of two joined words. Use mixed-case letters, start the first word with a lowercase letter, and start subsequent words with an uppercase letter. Example variable names are @currentMonth and @extendedTotal. For variables referencing data values that you retrieve from a database, it is a good practice to make the variable name the same as the table field name, such as @studentID or @enrollmentGrade. The *DataType* can be any of the SQL Server data types you learned about in Chapter 2 except text, ntext, or image.

You can use a single DECLARE command to declare multiple variables by delimiting each variable name and its associated data type with a comma. For example, use the following command to declare variables named @studentID and @studentLastName that store data values that you retrieve from the corresponding columns in the UniversityStudent database table. Note that the variables use the same data types as their corresponding database columns.

```
DECLARE @studentID BIGINT, @studentLastName VARCHAR(50)
```

Assigning Values to Variables

Assign values to variables using either the SET or the SELECT command. To assign a variable value using SET, use the following general syntax:

```
SET @variableName = ScalarExpression
```

In this syntax, *ScalarExpression* is an expression that represents a single data value, such as the text string "Mike" or the arithmetic expression @loopCounter + 1. For example, use the following command to set a variable named @studentID to the value 1:

```
SET @studentID = 1
```

You also can use SET to assign a variable value to a data value that a SQL query retrieves, provided the query retrieves a single data value. For example, use the following command to retrieve the last name of the student whose ID value is assigned to the @studentID variable and to assign the retrieved value to the @studentLastName variable:

```
SET @studentLastName =
(SELECT StudentLastName
FROM UniversityStudent
WHERE StudentID = @studentID)
```

Alternatively, you can use the SELECT command to assign values to variables. The SELECT command uses the following general syntax:

```
SELECT @variableName = ScalarExpression
```

An advantage of SELECT is that you can use it to assign values to several variables at once, using the following syntax:

```
SELECT @variable1Name = ScalarExpression,
variable2Name = ScalarExpression, ...
```

For example, use the following SELECT command to assign values for two variables:

```
SELECT @studentID1 = 100, @studentID2 = 202
```

You can also use SELECT to assign a value that a query retrieves, using the following syntax:

```
SELECT @variableName = ColumnName
FROM TableName
WHERE SearchCondition(s)
```

For example, the following command retrieves the last name of the student whose ID value is @studentID and assigns the retrieved value to the @studentLastName variable:

```
SELECT @studentLastName = StudentLastName
FROM UniversityStudent
WHERE StudentID = @studentID
```

When should you use SET and when should you use SELECT? Generally, use SET to assign a constant value to a single variable, and use SELECT to assign values to several variables at once or to assign a retrieved data value to a variable.

After you declare a variable, its initial value is NULL. You must always assign an initial value to a variable before performing an operation on it, or else its value remains NULL. In T-SQL, if you add a value to a number variable whose value is NULL, its value remains NULL. If you concatenate a text string to a text variable whose value is NULL, its value remains NULL.

Arithmetic and Text String–Handling Operations

T-SQL supports arithmetic and string-handling operations that are common to most programming languages. The following subsections describe these operations.

Arithmetic Operations

Table 4-2 summarizes the T-SQL arithmetic operators. You can perform these arithmetic operations on any of the number data types. You can perform addition and subtraction operations on the date data types to add or subtract days or fractions of days from a known date.

As with most programming languages, the precedence of operations is multiplication, division, modulo, then addition and subtraction. To force a different order, place the operation to be evaluated first in parentheses. When you perform arithmetic operations in program commands, you have to be careful to assign the result to a variable whose data type is appropriate for the result. For example, if you divide two integer values, the result may have a decimal value, so the variable needs to use one of the number data types with a decimal portion.

String-Handling Operations

When you work with text strings in programs, you might need to *concatenate,* or join, two separate text strings. You might also need to *parse,* or separate, a single text string into its component parts. To concatenate multiple text strings into a single string, use the plus sign (+) operator. For example, the following code example concatenates two variables that reference the @studentFirstName and @studentLastName variable values into a single text string, and assigns the result to a variable named @studentFullName. Note that the operation also concantenates a string that contains a blank space between the first and last name.

TABLE 4-2   T-SQL arithmetic operators

Operator	Description	Example	Result
+	Addition	5 + 2	7
–	Subtraction	5 – 2	3
*	Multiplication	5 * 2	10
/	Division	5 / 2	2.5
%	Modulo (remainder of a division operation)	5 % 2	1

TABLE 4-3   Commonly used T-SQL string functions

Function	Description	General Syntax	Example	Result
CHARINDEX	Returns the starting position of a substring within a string.	CHARINDEX (*String, Substring*)	SET @myString = CHARINDEX('abcd', 'c')	3
LEFT, RIGHT	Returns a specific number of characters from the left or right edge of a string.	LEFT(*String, Length*)	SET @myString = LEFT('abcdef', 2)	'ab'
		RIGHT(*String, Length*)	SET @myString = RIGHT('abcdef', 2)	'ef'
LTRIM, RTRIM	Trims all blank spaces from the left or right edge of a string.	LTRIM(*String*)	SET @myString = LTRIM('abcdef')	'abcdef'
		RTRIM(*String*)	SET @myString = RTRIM('abcdef')	'abcdef'
SUBSTRING	Returns a substring from within a string.	SUBSTRING (*String, StartPosition, Length*)	SET @myString = SUBSTRING('abcdef', 3, 2)	'cd'

```
@studentFullName = @studentFirstName + ' ' + @studentLastName
```

T-SQL provides several functions to support string handling. Table 4-3 summarizes commonly used string functions and shows the general syntax for the input values these functions receive.

Data Type Conversions

Sometimes you need to convert a value to a different data type. Consider the following T-SQL batch, which declares and assigns a value to an integer variable and then attempts to display the result using the PRINT command. The resulting error message is also shown.

```
DECLARE @myNumber SMALLINT
SET @myNumber = 2
PRINT 'My number is ' + @myNumber
GO
Conversion failed when converting a value
of type varchar to type smallint. Ensure
that all values of the expression being
converted can be converted to the target
type, or modify query to avoid this type
conversion.
```

What happened? The problem occurs in the PRINT command: T-SQL attempted to convert the text string 'My number is' to a number, so that it could then add the value to the value of @myNumber. Unfortunately, the code intended for this to be a concatenation operation, not an addition operation. The solution? Convert

@myNumber to a text string in the PRINT command. To convert a value to a different data type, you can use either the CAST or CONVERT function.

CAST

The CAST function converts a scalar expression to a different data type using the following general syntax:

```
CAST(ScalarExpression AS NewDataType)
```

To correct the data type error in the previous program, modify it as follows:

```
DECLARE @myNumber SMALLINT
SET @myNumber = 2
PRINT 'My number is ' + CAST(@myNumber AS VARCHAR)
GO
My number is 2
```

CONVERT

As with the CAST function, the CONVERT function converts a scalar expression to a different data type. It has additional functionality, however: when you convert a date/time or number data value to a character data type, CONVERT allows you to specify the output format using an optional *Style* parameter. The CONVERT function has the following general syntax:

```
CONVERT (NewDataType, ScalarExpression, Style)
```

Table 4-4 summarizes commonly used style values. The following commands retrieve the current system date using the GetDate() function and then displays the date in the default format and in a format specified using the CONVERT function.

```
DECLARE @todaysDate SMALLDATETIME
SET @todaysDate = GetDate()
--print in default format
PRINT @todaysDate
--print in different format
PRINT 'Today is ' +
CONVERT(VARCHAR, @todaysDate, 101)
GO
Jun 29 2009 6:37PM
Today is 06/29/2009
```

System Functions

T-SQL supports a variety of *system functions*, which are functions that return information about the DBMS, objects in the DBMS, or the current database connection. T-SQL prefixes system functions with two at signs (@@). You call T-SQL system functions using the following syntax:

```
variableName = @@SystemFunctionName
```

In this syntax, *variableName* represents a previously declared variable that must be of the same data type as the value that the system function returns. The following subsections describe some important system functions.

TABLE 4-4   CONVERT function style values

Input Data Type	Style Value	Format	Example
Float Real	0	Maximum of 6 digits; uses scientific notation when appropriate.	123456
	1	Exactly 8 digits; always uses scientific notation.	12345678E2
	2	Exactly 16 digits; always uses scientific notation.	1234567891234567E-3
Smallmoney Money	0	No commas every 3 digits to the left of the decimal point; exactly 2 digits to the right of the decimal point.	1234.56
	1	Commas every 3 digits to the left of the decimal point; exactly 2 digits to the right of the decimal point.	1,234.56
	2	No commas every 3 digits to the left of the decimal point; exactly 4 digits to the right of the decimal point.	1234.5678
Smalldatetime Datetime	100	mon dd yyyy hh:miAM (or PM)	JUN 29 2009 12:39 PM
	101	mm/dd/yyyy	11/29/2009
	108	hh:mm:ss	12:39:00

IDENTITY

The IDENTITY system function returns the identity column value that was last inserted into a table. (Recall that an identity column automatically generates values for surrogate primary keys.) Many times when you use an identity column to generate a record's primary key, you need to know the value of the primary key value so that you can use it as a foreign key value in a subsequent operation. For example, suppose you insert a record for a new course in the UniversityCourse table and then immediately need to insert a record for an associated course section in the UniversitySection table. Figure 4-7 shows the T-SQL commands to do this.

This code first declares a variable named @courseID to reference the result of the IDENTITY function. Note that this variable uses the BIGINT data type, which is the same data type as the identity column in the UniversityCourse table. Next, the code inserts the record into UniversityCourse and then retrieves the just used identity column value and assigns the result to @courseID. Finally, it uses the retrieved identity column value within the next INSERT command, which inserts a record into UniversitySection. Always remember that @@IDENTITY returns the identity column value for the most recently executed INSERT command for the current database connection. If the current database connection has not executed an INSERT command that retrieved a new value from an identity column, the IDENTITY function returns NULL.

ROWCOUNT

The ROWCOUNT system function returns an integer that represents the number of rows affected by the last SQL command. For an INSERT command, this is always one. For UPDATE, DELETE, or SELECT commands, this is the number of rows that match the search condition. This function is useful for determining whether an error

FIGURE 4-7   Using the IDENTITY function

```
--declare the variable to represent the primary key
DECLARE @courseID BIGINT


--insert the parent key record
INSERT INTO UniversityCourse(CourseName, CourseTitle, CourseCredits,
DepartmentID)
VALUES('ACCT 315', 'Accounting Systems', 3, 2)


--find the identity column value of the previous record
SET @courseID = @@IDENTITY                               Finding the value of the identity column


--insert the child key record
INSERT INTO UniversitySection
(SectionNumber, SectionTerm, SectionDay, SectionTime, SectionMaxEnrollment,
SectionCurrentEnrollment, CourseID, InstructorID)
VALUES                                    Using the value in another INSERT command
(1, 'SPRING 09', 'MWF', '9:00 AM', 30, 0, @courseID,  2)
```

exists in a search condition that updates or deletes a specific record, as well as for warning users before they execute queries that could potentially retrieve a lot of records and take a long time to execute. The following code shows the T-SQL commands to retrieve all the records from the UnivesitySection table and then use @@ROWCOUNT to display the number of retrieved rows in the Messages pane.

```
DECLARE @sectionRows SMALLINT
--retrieve all table records
SELECT SectionID, SectionNumber
FROM UniversitySection
--determine how many records were retrieved
SET @sectionRows = @@ROWCOUNT
PRINT @sectionRows
GO
 (30 row(s) affected)
30
```

TIP: Although the Query Editor Messages pane automatically displays the @@ROWCOUNT value, many applications do not.

Decision Control Structures

Decision control structures are program structures that allow program execution to take different paths depending on the values of specific variables. T-SQL provides an IF . . . ELSE decision control structure that has the following general format:

```
IF (BooleanExpression)
BEGIN
   Statements that execute if
   BooleanExpresssion is true
END
[ELSE
BEGIN
   Statements that execute if
   BooleanExpression is false
END]
```

TABLE 4-5   T-SQL comparison operators

Comparison Operator	Description	*Example* **BooleanExpression**
=	Equal	@myNumber = 5
<>	Not equal	@myNumber <> 5
!=		@myNumber != 5
>	Greater than	@myNumber > 5
<	Less than	@myNumber < 5
>=	Greater than or equal to	@myNumber >= 5
<=	Less than or equal to	@myNumber <= 5
!>	Not greater than	@myNumber !> 5
!<	Not less than	@myNumber !<5

In this syntax, *BooleanExpression* is an expression that T-SQL can evaluate as either true or false. It usually compares two values, such as a variable and a constant. Table 4-5 shows the T-SQL comparison operators and usage examples.

If *BooleanExpression* evaluates as true, the first block of program statements executes. If it evaluates as false, the second block executes. Each block starts with the keyword BEGIN and ends with the keyword END. The ELSE portion of the structure is optional: if you omit the ELSE block and *BooleanExpression* is not true, then no program statements execute.

The following commands illustrate an IF . . . ELSE decision structure. The code first retrieves the maximum and current enrollment values for Section ID 7. The *BooleanExpression* compares the maximum enrollment to the current enrollment. If the maximum enrollment equals the current enrollment, then the program displays a message stating the section is closed. Otherwise, the program displays a message stating the section is open.

```
DECLARE @sectionMaxEnrollment SMALLINT,
@sectionCurrentEnrollment SMALLINT
SELECT @sectionMaxEnrollment = SectionMaxEnrollment,
       @sectionCurrentEnrollment = SectionCurrentEnrollment
FROM UniversitySection
WHERE SectionID = 7
IF (@sectionMaxEnrollment = @sectionCurrentEnrollment)
  BEGIN
    PRINT 'The section is closed'
  END
ELSE
  BEGIN
    PRINT 'The section is open'
  END
GO
```

You can combine multiple *BooleanExpressions* using the AND and OR operators. For example, the following *BooleanExpression* determines whether the section's maximum enrollment is equal to the current enrollment and if the section is also offered during the Fall 2008 term:

```
IF ((@sectionMaxEnrollment = @sectionCurrentEnrollment) AND
    (@sectionTerm = 'FALL08'))
```

Note that when you combine multiple *BooleanExpressions* using the AND and OR operators, you must enclose each expression in parentheses, and the overall expression must appear in parentheses.

You have to be careful if *BooleanExpression* evaluates as NULL rather than as true or false. This can happen if any variables used in the *BooleanExpression* currently have a NULL value. If *BooleanExpression* evaluates as NULL, then the IF . . . ELSE structure executes as if the expression evaluates as false.

Loops

A *loop* is a program structure that executes a series of program statements multiple times. The loop periodically evaluates an *exit condition,* which is a Boolean expression that determines whether the loop continues to repeat or terminates. T-SQL provides a WHILE loop, which has the following general syntax:

```
WHILE BooleanExpression
BEGIN
  Statements that execute while
  BooleanExpression is true
  CONTINUE
END
```

In this syntax, *BooleanExpression* is an expression that the loop evaluates as either true or false. If *BooleanExpression* is true, the statements that follow execute. Then the loop evaluates *BooleanExpresion* again. If it is still true, the cycle repeats, and the loop continues to repeat until *BooleanExpression* becomes false. Therefore, the statements must also modify the *BooleanExpression* variable(s) so that the expression eventually becomes false and the loop exits. If *BooleanExpression* is false initially, none of the loop statements execute.

To illustrate a WHILE loop, we use the NumberTable in Table 4-6, which contains a single column named NumberID that contains integer values starting with one and ending with five. We will use a script that contains a WHILE loop to insert the values.

TABLE 4-6   NumberTable with values inserted using a WHILE loop

NumberID
1
2
3
4
5

The following batch creates the table, uses a WHILE loop to insert the data values, and then contains a SELECT command to view the table contents:

```
--create the table
CREATE TABLE NumberTable
(NumberID SMALLINT)
GO
--declare and initialize variable
--to represent NumberID
DECLARE @currentNumber SMALLINT
SET @currentNumber = 1
WHILE (@currentNumber <= 5)
BEGIN
  --insert the record
  INSERT INTO NumberTable(NumberID)
    VALUES(@currentNumber)
  --increment the number
  SET @currentNumber = @currentNumber + 1
  CONTINUE
END
--view table contents
SELECT NumberID
FROM NumberTable
GO
```

STORED PROCEDURES

The scripts you have seen so far have been stand-alone programs stored as text files in your workstation's file system. SQL Server allows you to expand the power of scripts by creating *stored procedures,* which are T-SQL scripts that the database stores and that you can make available to other users. A stored procedure can call another stored procedure, as well as pass and accept input parameters.

Why create stored procedures? In a multiuser environment, you can easily make them available to other users because you store them in the database. They enable you to create more modular and reusable code because you can call procedures from other procedures as well as from regular scripts. Stored procedures also make it easier to enforce database security because you can set security levels on your stored procedures to prevent unauthorized access. Finally, because stored procedures accept input parameters, you can use them to perform complex tasks without modifying the underlying code.

When should you create a stored procedure? Create a stored procedure if you want to make a script available to other database users; when a script becomes long and complex and would benefit from being broken down into smaller modules; or when your code performs tasks that could compromise the security of the database, so that you can set explicit security levels for its use. The following subsections describe how to create, call, and drop stored procedures, and also show how to use input and output parameters.

Creating a Stored Procedure

To create a stored procedure, use the following general syntax:

```
CREATE PROCEDURE
  [SchemaName.]ProcedureName [ParameterList]
AS
    Procedure program statements
```

In this syntax, *SchemaName* optionally specifies the name of the database that creates and stores the procedure. When you work in a multiuser environment, all users must either work in the same database or have specific permissions to manipulate the objects in another database. (You will learn more about database object permissions in Chapter 10.) For now we will omit the *SchemaName* and store procedures in the default database.

ProcedureName specifies the name of the stored procedure. All stored procedures in a database must have a unique name and must follow the naming conventions for other SQL Server database objects. Many T-SQL developers preface procedure names with the prefix usp_, which identifies the procedure as a user-defined stored procedure. The optional *ParameterList* specifies the procedure's input and output parameters, which the next section describes. Next comes the keyword AS, followed by the procedure's program statements.

A stored procedure can contain most types of T-SQL program statements. You can declare and assign *local variables,* which are variables that are declared, assigned, referenced, and visible only to the current stored procedure. Stored procedures can contain most SQL DDL and DML statements, with a few exceptions: for example, stored procedures cannot create views or other stored procedures. Stored procedures cannot contain the USE command because they are stored in a specific database and can execute only in that database.

The following commands create a stored procedure named `usp_PrintCurrentDate` that has no parameters. This stored procedure retrieves the current system date, formats it using the CONVERT function, and then prints it to the screen.

```
CREATE PROCEDURE usp_PrintCurrentDate
AS
PRINT 'Today is ' + CONVERT(VARCHAR, GetDate(), 100)
GO
Command(s) completed successfully.
```

When you create a stored procedure, "Command(s) completed successfully" appears in the Messages pane, indicating that the DBMS successfully created the stored procedure.

Calling a Stored Procedure

To call the stored procedure, use the EXECUTE command, which has the following general syntax:

```
EXEC[UTE] [SchemaName.]ProcedureName
ParameterValueList
```

Use either EXEC or EXECUTE to execute the procedure. If the procedure is stored in the current database schema, you can omit the *SchemaName*. The *ParameterValueList* must contain an entry for every parameter in the stored procedure's parameter list. For input parameters, it contains a data value that you pass to the procedure; for output parameters, it contains a variable name referencing the value that the procedure returns. The parameters in the *ParameterValueList* must appear in the same order as they appear in the CREATE PROCEDURE command. (You will learn more about parameters in the next section.)

Use the following command to execute the `usp_PrintCurrentDate` stored procedure. (Recall that this procedure has no parameters; so the command omits the *ParameterValueList.*) The procedure's output appears in the Messages pane.

```
EXECUTE usp_PrintCurrentDate
GO
Today is Jul 5 2009 11:19AM
```

Altering and Deleting Stored Procedures

If you create a stored procedure and subsequently want to change it, replace CREATE in the CREATE PROCEDURE command with ALTER, using the following syntax:

```
ALTER PROCEDURE [SchemaName.]ProcedureName
   [ParameterList]
AS
 Modified procedure program statements
```

To delete a stored procedure, use the following syntax:

```
DROP PROCEDURE ProcedureName
```

You can alter or drop a procedure only if it is in a database that you created or if you have explicit privileges to drop it. If you attempt to alter or delete a procedure that does not exist, an error occurs.

Using Parameters in Stored Procedures

Stored procedures receive inputs and deliver outputs using *parameters,* which are variables that pass data values from one program to another. When you create a stored procedure, you declare parameters within the *ParameterList,* which follows the *ProcedureName* in the CREATE PROCEDURE command. The *ParameterList* has the following general syntax:

```
@parameter1Name DataType [ParameterType],
@parameter2Name DataType [ParameterType],
...
```

In this syntax, each parameter has a *parameterName,* which you specify using the naming rules for T-SQL variables, and a corresponding *DataType.* As with other variables, parameters can be any data type except text, ntext, and image. *ParameterType* specifies whether the parameter is an *input parameter,* which is a data value that the procedure receives from the program calling it, or an *output parameter,* which is a data value the procedure passes to a program that it calls. If a parameter is an input parameter, omit *ParameterType.* If the parameter is an output parameter, the *ParameterType* value is OUT or OUTPUT.

You reference input parameter values in T-SQL or SQL commands like any variable values. You set output parameter values using SET or SELECT commands.

The following commands create a stored procedure named usp_FindStudentName that accepts a StudentID value as an input parameter, retrieves the student's first and last name from the database using the input parameter value within a query search condition, and then returns the student's first and last names as output parameters.

```
CREATE PROCEDURE usp_FindStudentName
@studentID BIGINT,
@studentFirstName VARCHAR(50) OUTPUT,
@studentLastName VARCHAR(50) OUTPUT
AS
SELECT @studentFirstName = StudentFirstName,
       @studentLastName = StudentLastName
FROM UniversityStudent
WHERE StudentID = @studentID
GO
```

Note that in this procedure, the output parameters appear on the left side of the SELECT command assignment statements, and the input parameter appears on the right side of the query search condition.

How do you call a stored procedure with input and output parameters? Include the input parameter values and the output parameter variables in the EXECUTE command's *ParameterValueList*. To bind the parameters from the EXECUTE command to the stored procedure, list the parameters in exactly the same order as they appear in the CREATE PROCEDURE command. For example, for the `usp_FindStudentName` stored procedure, you must list the parameters in the following order: @studentID, @studentFirstName, @studentLastName.

For input parameters, you pass a constant or variable that represents the input parameter value. For output parameters, pass the parameter as an assignment statement using the following syntax:

```
@OutputParameterName = @LocalVariableName OUTPUT
```

In this syntax, *OutputParameterName* is the name of the parameter as it appears in the CREATE PROCEDURE command. *LocalVariableName* is the name of a variable in the program that calls the stored procedure. For example, use the following commands to call the `use_FindStudentName` stored procedure:

```
--Declare the variables to store
--the output parameter values
DECLARE @localStudentFirstName VARCHAR (50),
        @localStudentLastName VARCHAR (50)
--Execute the stored procedure
EXECUTE usp_FindStudentName 1,
        @studentFirstName = @localStudentFirstName OUTPUT,
        @studentLastName = @localStudentLastName OUTPUT
--Print the outputs
PRINT @localStudentFirstName + ' ' + @localStudentLastName
GO
Clifford Wall
```

These commands declare the variables that store the output variables, and then execute the stored procedure by listing the procedure name, the input parameter value (StudentID 1), and the assignment statements for the output parameters. Finally, the program displays the output variable values in the Messages pane.

USER-DEFINED FUNCTIONS

In most programming languages, a *function* is a program that can accept multiple input values and that returns a single output value you assign to a variable in the calling program. For example, the T-SQL CAST function accepts an input data value and data type specification, converts the value to the specified data type, and then returns the converted value. SQL Server allows you to create user-defined functions, which are similar to stored procedures except that they return a single value. You create a stored procedure to modify multiple output values, and you create a user-defined function to return a single value. For example, you might create a function to calculate a person's age based on his or her date of birth. You might also create a user-defined function that returns a text string representing the name of a person's city and state based on his or her ZIP code.

T-SQL allows you to create different types of user-defined functions. The following subsections describe the two main types: scalar functions and table functions.

Scalar Functions

A *scalar function* returns a single scalar value, such as the number "300" or the text string "John Smith." To create a scalar function, you use the following general syntax:

```
CREATE FUNCTION FunctionName
(@parameter1Name DataType,
@parameter2Name DataType,
...)
RETURNS DataType
AS
BEGIN
  Program statements
  RETURN ReturnValue
END
```

The *FunctionName* must be unique in the database and must follow the rules for naming database objects. You enclose the parameter list in parentheses, and separate each parameter name and its associated data type with a comma. Functions use input parameters only and cannot return output parameters.

The RETURNS clause specifies the data type that the function returns. A scalar function can return any of the SQL Server data types except text, ntext, image, or timestamp. The RETURN command specifies the function's *ReturnValue,* which is a scalar expression with the data type that the RETURNS clause specifies. Usually, you declare a local variable within the function's program statements, perform the required program manipulations using the variable, and then specify the variable's value as the *ReturnValue.*

The following commands create a function named `CalculateAge` that receives a date representing a person's date of birth, the current date, and returns an integer value representing the person's age in years.

```
CREATE FUNCTION CalculateAge
  (@inputDOB DATETIME, @currentDate DATETIME)
RETURNS SMALLINT
AS
BEGIN
  DECLARE @ageInYears SMALLINT
  SET @ageInYears = 0
  SET @ageInYears =
    CAST(@currentDate - @inputDOB AS SMALLINT)
```

```
   SET @ageInYears = @ageInYears/365.25
   RETURN @ageInYears
END
GO
```

Note that this function receives two input parameters: @inputDOB represents the input date of birth, and @currentDate represents the current date. The function returns a SMALLINT value that represents the difference between the current date and the input date of birth value in years. The subtraction operation calculates this value in days; to represent the age in years, the function contains a command that divides the difference by 365.25, which is the average number of days in a year.

TIP: You cannot use the GetDate() function in a user-defined function.

You can execute a scalar function in a SET or SELECT command that assigns a T-SQL variable value. You can also execute a scalar function in a SQL command's SELECT clause. To execute a function in a SET command, use the following syntax:

```
SET @localReturnVariable = SchemaName.FunctionName(ParameterList)
```

The *localReturnVariable* must be the same data type that the function returns. When you call a function, you must always specify the *SchemaName;* otherwise, the T-SQL interpreter assumes that the function is a system function. To reference the functions you create in your own schema, preface the function with dbo, which stands for "database owner." As with stored procedures, the *ParameterList* values must be passed in the same order that they appear in the CREATE FUNCTION command.

The following commands use a SET command to execute the CalculateAge function in a T-SQL script and then print the output to the Messages pane. (If you execute this command, your result will depend on your current system date.)

```
DECLARE @localAgeInYears SMALLINT
SET @localAgeInYears = dbo.CalculateAge('7/14/1988', GetDate())
PRINT @localAgeInYears
GO
20
```

The following command executes the CalculateAge function directly in a SQL command. It retrieves the date of birth of student ID 1 (Clifford Walls) and the current system date within the function parameter list, and it passes these values to the function. The output displays his age in years in the Results pane. (If you execute this command, your result will depend on your current system date.)

```
SELECT dbo.CalculateAge(StudentDOB, GetDate())
FROM UniversityStudent
WHERE StudentID = 1
GO
20
```

Table Functions

A *table function* is similar to a scalar function except that it returns a variable that has the TABLE data type, which is a special T-SQL data type that stores a set of rows.

A table function is very similar to a view: it does not create a new database table but provides a way to view existing data from one or more tables. The advantage of a table function over a view is that you can pass to it parameter values that can serve as search condition values.

To create a table function, use the following general syntax:

```
CREATE FUNCTION FunctionName
(@parameter1Name DataType,
@parameter2Name DataType,
...)
RETURNS TABLE
AS
RETURN
  SELECT command to define table
```

Use the following commands to create a table function that receives parameters of values for a studentID and section term and that returns a table listing the student's schedule information for the given term:

```
CREATE FUNCTION PrintSchedule
(@studentID BIGINT,
@sectionTerm VARCHAR(8))
RETURNS TABLE
AS
RETURN
  SELECT CourseName, SectionNumber, SectionDay, SectionTime
  FROM UniversitySection
  INNER JOIN UniversityEnrollment
  ON UniversitySection.SectionID = UniversityEnrollment.SectionID
  INNER JOIN UniversityCourse
  ON UniversityCourse.CourseID = UniversitySection.CourseID
  WHERE StudentID = @studentID
  AND SectionTerm = @sectionTerm
GO
```

Call a table function within a SELECT command using the following general syntax:

```
SELECT Column1, Column2, ...
FROM FunctionName
  (parameter1Value, parameter2Value, ...)
[WHERE SearchCondition]
```

In this command, *Column1, Column2,* and so forth must be column names in the TABLE variable that the function creates. Pass the parameter values in the list just as with a call to a scalar function. Use the following command to call the PrintSchedule function and pass to it the values 1 (for @studentID) and 'FALL08' (for @sectionTerm). (This command uses the CONVERT function to format the SectionTime value so that it displays only the hour and minutes portion of the DateTime variable.)

```
SELECT CourseName, SectionNumber, SectionDay,
       CONVERT(VARCHAR, SectionTime, 108) "Section Time"
FROM PrintSchedule(1, 'FALL08')
```

FIGURE 4-8   Command to call a user-defined table function

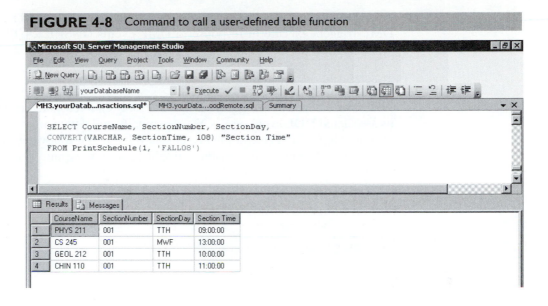

Figure 4-8 shows the output that appears in the Results pane as a result of executing this command in the Query Editor.

TRIGGERS

A *trigger* is a stored procedure that automatically executes in response to a database DDL event, such as creating, altering, or dropping an object, or a database DML event, such as inserting, updating, or deleting a record. You use DDL triggers primarily to capture auditing information, such as recording when a user creates a new table or alters an existing table. DML triggers can automatically maintain database integrity constraints. For example, when a student enrolls in a course, a trigger could automatically update the SectionCurrentEnrollment value in the UniversitySection table. Alternatively, if a user deletes a course section record in the UniversitySection table, a trigger might automatically delete all the associated enrollment records in the UniversityEnrollment table (after warning the user, of course!). You can also use DML triggers to capture auditing information. For example, a trigger could record the username of every user who modifies the EnrollmentGrade column in the UniversityEnrollment table.

Triggers are different from stored procedures in two important ways: first, they cannot accept input parameters or deliver output parameters. Second, they execute only in response to DDL or DML commands. You cannot explicitly execute a trigger using an EXECUTE command or any other command.

When should you create a trigger? The answer is, only when absolutely necessary. Triggers slow down database performance, and, because they execute automatically, they might cause unwanted actions to occur. You should avoid using triggers to enforce referential integrity. For example, if a user tries to delete a UniversityStudent record, you should not create a trigger that automatically deletes all the student's enrollment records because this could be a disaster.

DDL triggers execute in response to DDL events (CREATE, ALTER, DROP); DML triggers execute in response to DML events (INSERT, UPDATE, DELETE). The following subsections describe both types of triggers.

DDL Triggers

When you create a new trigger, it is automatically enabled, and it executes the next time its associated DDL event occurs. You can modify and delete an existing trigger; you can also disable the trigger and then re-enable it later. The following subsections describe the commands for creating, enabling, disabling, modifying, and deleting DDL triggers.

Creating DDL Triggers

Use the following syntax to create a DDL trigger:

```
CREATE TRIGGER [SchemaName.]TriggerName
ON {ALL SERVER | DATABASE}
{FOR | AFTER} EventTypeList
AS
    TriggerProgramStatements
```

TriggerName must be unique in the database and must follow the rules for naming SQL Server database objects. As with other database objects, you can optionally preface the *TriggerName* with the *SchemaName*. The ON clause specifies the scope of the trigger. ALL SERVER specifies that the trigger fires when the event occurs in any database on the server, while DATABASE confines the trigger to the current database.

The next clause defines the trigger's timing and event type. The trigger timing defines whether the trigger executes at the same time as the SQL statement executes or after it executes. The FOR option specifies that the trigger executes at the same time and is useful for reporting errors. The AFTER option specifies that the trigger executes only after the statement successfully completes and is useful for recording auditing information. *EventTypeList* values can be CREATE_TABLE, ALTER_TABLE, and/or DROP_TABLE. If a DDL trigger fires for multiple events, separate each event with a comma. For example, a FOR trigger that fires whenever you create or alter a database table would appear as `FOR CREATE_TABLE, ALTER_TABLE`.

TriggerProgramStatements can include most T-SQL and SQL commands. In DDL triggers, the program statements usually insert values in tables that record auditing information. For example, Table 4-7 illustrates the DatabaseDDLLog table, which records whenever any user performs a DDL action in a specific database.

The following commands create a trigger named LogCreateEvent that inserts the current date/time, along with the text string "Table created," into this table whenever any user in the current database creates a table.

```
--create trigger for CREATE TABLE event
CREATE TRIGGER LogCreateEvent
ON DATABASE
AFTER CREATE_TABLE
AS
INSERT INTO DatabaseDDLLog (LogDateTime, LogAction)
VALUES(GetDate(), 'Table created')
GO
```

TABLE 4-7	DatabaseDDLLog table
LogDateTime	*LogAction*
7/22/2008 12:03:00	Table created
7/22/2008 13:15.00	Table created
7/22/2008 16.42.00	Table dropped
7/22/2008 16.44.00	Table created
7/22/2008 16.42.00	Table altered

Modifying DDL Triggers

To modify an existing DDL trigger, use the following syntax:

```
ALTER TRIGGER [SchemaName.]TriggerName
ON {ALL SERVER | DATABASE}
{FOR | AFTER} EventTypeList
AS
   TriggerProgramStatements
```

If you try to alter a trigger that does not exist, an error occurs.

Deleting DDL Triggers

To delete an existing DDL trigger, use the following command:

```
DROP TRIGGER [SchemaName.]TriggerName
ON {ALL SERVER | DATABASE}
```

Note that you must include the ON clause when you drop a trigger, or the command fails. If you try to delete a trigger that does not exist, an error occurs.

Enabling and Disabling DDL Triggers

Recall that when you create a new trigger, it is automatically enabled and executes the next time its event occurs. Sometimes you may want to retain a trigger in the database but temporarily disable it. To disable a trigger, use the following command:

```
DISABLE TRIGGER TriggerName
ON {ALL SERVER | DATABASE}
```

To enable a disabled trigger, use the following command:

```
ENABLE TRIGGER TriggerName
ON {ALL SERVER | DATABASE}
```

Creating the DatabaseDDLLog Table and LogCreateEvent

The following steps describe how to create the DatabaseDDLLog table shown in Table 4-7 to record audit information whenever a database user performs a DDL operation, and how to create a trigger named LogCreateEvent that inserts a record into the audit table. They test the trigger by creating a new table named TestTable, which has a single column named TestID. Creating this table should execute the trigger.

To create the audit table and trigger and test the trigger:

1. In the Query Editor, type and execute the following command to create the audit table:

```
--create table to log database DDL actions
CREATE TABLE DatabaseDDLLog
(LogDateTime DATETIME,
LogAction VARCHAR(50))
GO
```

2. Type and execute the following commands to create the LogCreateEvent trigger:

```
CREATE TRIGGER LogCreateEvent
ON DATABASE
AFTER CREATE_TABLE
AS
INSERT INTO DatabaseDDLLog (LogDateTime, LogAction)
VALUES (GetDate(), 'Table created')
GO
```

3. To test the trigger, type and execute the following command to create the TestTable. After you execute this command, the message "1 row(s) affected" should appear in the Messages pane, indicating that the trigger executed and inserted the auditing information.

```
CREATE TABLE TestTable (TestID BIGINT)
```

4. To confirm that the trigger correctly inserted the auditing information, type and execute the following command to query the DatabaseDDLLog audit table. The Results pane should display the table with one record showing the current date and time, along with the message "Table created."

```
SELECT *
FROM DatabaseDDLLog
```

5. To clean up your database, type and execute the following command to delete the TestTable:

```
DROP TABLE TestTable
```

6. Type and execute the following command to disable the LogCreateEvent trigger:

```
DISABLE TRIGGER LogCreateEvent
ON DATABASE
```

DML Triggers

Recall that DML triggers execute in response to the DML INSERT, UPDATE, and DELETE events. The general syntax to create a DML trigger is:

```
CREATE TRIGGER [SchemaName.]TriggerName
ON {TableName | ViewName}
{FOR|AFTER|INSTEAD OF} EventTypeList
AS
  TriggerProgramStatements
```

As with DDL triggers, the *TriggerName* must be unique in its database, must follow the rules for naming SQL Server database objects, and can be optionally prefaced with the *SchemaName*. In a DML trigger, the ON clause specifies the name of the table or view with which you associate the trigger.

The next clause defines the trigger's timing and event type. As with DDL triggers, the FOR option specifies that the trigger executes at the same time as the triggering event and is useful for reporting errors. The AFTER option specifies that the trigger executes only after the statement is successfully completed and records auditing information. The INSTEAD OF option specifies that the trigger program statements execute in place of the DML command that fires the trigger. INSTEAD OF triggers are useful for allowing users to insert data values into a view that joins multiple tables by providing alternate SQL commands that insert the user-supplied values into the underlying tables.

The *EventTypeList* values can be INSERT, UPDATE, and/or DELETE. If a DDL trigger fires for multiple events, separate each event with a comma. For example, a FOR trigger that fires whenever a table record is inserted or deleted would appear as FOR INSERT, DELETE. The *TriggerProgramStatements* can include most T-SQL and SQL commands.

Often DML triggers need to reference data values that the triggering event uses. For example, if you write a trigger that increments the UniversitySection's current enrollment value whenever a student enrolls in a section, you need to know the SectionID value. If you write a trigger that creates an audit trail whenever a user updates the EnrollmentGrade column in the UniversityEnrollment table, it would be useful to record the StudentID value whose grade was updated.

To reference values in the SQL command that executes a trigger, use the INSERTED and DELETED tables. These are temporary system tables that contain a copy of the values that the last SQL command inserted or deleted. The column names are the same as the column names in the original table. Suppose you insert a new record into the UniversityEnrollment table specifying that StudentID 1 (Clifford Wall) enrolls in SectionID 2. The INSERTED table would look like Table 4-8.

To retrieve values from the INSERTED or DELETED tables, create one or more local variables to reference the values, then use a SELECT command to retrieve the values and assign them to the local variables. For example, the following commands create a DML trigger named UpdateCurrentEnrollment, which executes whenever a user inserts a record into UniversityEnrollment. The trigger's program commands retrieve the SectionID value from the INSERTED table and then update the CurrentSectionEnrollment value for the course section.

```
CREATE TRIGGER UpdateCurrentEnrollment
ON UniversityEnrollment
AFTER INSERT
AS
--declare and assign value of section ID
DECLARE @localSectionID BIGINT
SELECT @localSectionID = SectionID
FROM INSERTED
--update current enrollment
UPDATE UniversitySection
SET SectionCurrentEnrollment = SectionCurrentEnrollment + 1
WHERE SectionID = @localSectionID
GO
```

TABLE 4-8 INSERTED table values after inserting a UniversityEnrollment record

StudentID	SectionID	EnrollmentGrade
1	2	NULL

The following steps show how to create and test this DML trigger by inserting a new UniversityEnrollment record, confirming that the trigger updated the section's current enrollment value.

To create and test the DML trigger:

1. In the Query Editor, type and execute the commands shown above to create the UpdateCurrentEnrollment trigger. The message "Command(s) completed successfully" appears in the Messages pane when the trigger is successfully created.

2. Type and execute the following command to insert a new UniversityEnrollment record to enroll StudentID 1 (Clifford Wall) into course section ID 2. The message "1 row(s) affected" should appear two times in the Messages pane, once for when the DBMS inserts the UniversityEnrollment record and once for when it updates the UniversitySection record.

```
INSERT INTO UniversityEnrollment (StudentID, SectionID)
VALUES (1, 2)
```

3. Type and execute the following command to confirm that the trigger correctly updated the SectionCurrentEnrollment value. Currently, the enrollment value for SectionID 2 is 19, and the updated value should appear as 20.

```
SELECT SectionCurrentEnrollment
FROM UniversitySection
WHERE SectionID = 2
```

Modifying, Deleting, and Disabling DML Triggers

To modify a DML trigger, use the same syntax as the CREATE TRIGGER command, but replace the CREATE keyword with ALTER. To enable or disable a DML trigger, use the following syntax:

```
{ENABLE|DISABLE} TRIGGER TriggerName
ON TableName
```

To delete a DML trigger, use the following syntax:

```
DROP TRIGGER TriggerName
```

IN CONCLUSION . . .

In this chapter, you learned how to write SQL DML commands to insert, update, and delete database data. You learned how SQL Server processes database transactions and how to modify the default transaction processing and locking/blocking modes. The chapter also described the T-SQL language and showed how to write T-SQL stored procedures, user-defined functions, and triggers. Database application developers need to understand how to execute DML commands and execute transactions in user applications. Developers can use T-SQL programs to enhance their applications and help manage the database system.

SUMMARY

- The SQL data manipulation language (DML) commands are INSERT, UPDATE, and DELETE. These commands create action queries, which change the contents of database tables.
- You can create INSERT commands using either the columns-list format, which lists the names of the columns in which you want to insert data, or the no-columns-list format, which requires you to insert a value for every table column. It is a good practice to always use the columns-list format because you must use it for tables that contain identity columns and because it is not affected if you subsequently add or remove a table column.
- When you insert a number value, insert the numeral. When you insert a text value, enclose it in single quotation marks. When you insert a date value, insert it as a text string using one of the SQL Server date formats.
- When you insert a record that contains a foreign key, the foreign key value must already exist in the parent table, or an error occurs.
- Use the UPDATE command to update values in records that already exist in the database. An UPDATE command updates records in a single table.
- Use the DELETE command to delete table records. You cannot delete a record if it is a parent value in a foreign key relationship.
- In database processing, a transaction is a series of queries that represent a logical unit of work. All of a transaction's queries must succeed, or none of them should succeed; otherwise, the database is left in an inconsistent state.
- When a user commits a transaction, the changes become permanent and visible to other users. When a user rolls back a transaction, the changes are discarded.
- SQL Server supports three types of transactions: (1) autocommit transactions, which commit immediately after each action query executes; (2) explicit transactions, which start with the BEGIN TRANSACTION command and end with the END TRANSACTION command; and (3) implicit transactions, which start as soon as the user connects to the database and end with the END TRANSACTION command, and which also starts the next transaction.
- In a multiuser database system, competing transactions occur when different database connections attempt to view, insert, update, and delete the same records. This can result in lost updates, dirty reads, nonrepeatable reads, and phantom reads. The DBMS prevents these problems through locking, which prevents a transaction from accessing data in use by another transaction, and through blocking, which occurs when a transaction tries to access data in use by another transaction.
- Lock types include read locks, which prevent a transaction from reading a data value, and write locks, which prevent a transaction from changing a data value. SQL Server locks data at the record, page, extent, table, and database level.
- Locks can be shared (multiple transactions may acquire read locks on the data), exclusive (only one transaction may acquire a write lock on the data), and update (a combination of a shared and an exclusive lock).
- A transaction's isolation level specifies either that the transaction runs as if it is the only transaction running on the database instance or that it can safely run at the same time as other transactions. SQL Server supports different isolation levels to control how transactions acquire locks.
- A T-SQL batch is a group of commands that the T-SQL interpreter treats as a unit. Use the GO command to signal the end of a batch. You create batches when you need to complete one task before you can perform the next one.
- A variable references a memory location that stores a data value. When you declare a variable, the T-SQL interpreter sets up its memory location. You use the DECLARE command to declare variables and either the SET or SELECT command to assign values to variables.
- Use the T-SQL CAST or CONVERT function to convert a value to a different data type.
- T-SQL provides an IF . . . ELSE decision control structure and a WHILE loop for performing iterative operations.
- A stored procedure is a T-SQL script that the database stores and that you can make available to other users. A stored procedure can call another stored procedure, and pass and accept input parameters.
- A user-defined function is a stored procedure that can accept multiple input values and that returns a single output value. A scalar function returns a value that is one of the common SQL Server data types, and a table function returns data in a tabular format.
- A database trigger is a stored procedure that automatically executes in response to a database DDL event (creating, altering, or dropping an object) or a DML event (inserting, updating, or deleting a record). Use triggers to capture auditing information or enforce database integrity constraints.

KEY TERMS

Action query   INSERT, UPDATE or DELETE query that changes data values in database tables

Autocommit transaction   Type of transaction that commits each action query as soon as it executes; the SQL Server default mode, not requiring any specific transaction control commands

Batch   Group of commands that the T-SQL interpreter executes as a unit

Blocking   Action that occurs when a transaction tries to access data locked by another transaction

Columns-list format   INSERT command format that explicitly lists column names and corresponding values

Commit   In transaction processing, making a transaction's changes permanent and visible to other users

Compile error   Syntax error when program statements do not obey the rules of the language

Concatenate   Joining of two or more separate text strings to create a single string

Database lock   Action that locks an entire database

Database recovery   After a failure or malfunction, the actions that the database takes to restore all the database data to a consistent state

Decision control structure   Program structure that allows execution to take different paths depending on the values of specific variables

Dirty read   Result when a transaction reads a record that has been inserted or updated by another transaction but has not yet been committed

Exclusive lock   Write lock that prevents other transactions from either reading or updating the locked record

Execution plan   Instructions created by the T-SQL interpreter for running a query or batch so that it executes in the fastest way possible

Exit condition   Boolean expression that determines whether a loop continues to repeat or exits

Explicit transaction   Transaction that starts with a BEGIN TRANSACTION statement, which signals the beginning of a transaction, and ends with a COMMIT TRANSACTION statement, which signals the end of the transaction and commits the transaction

Extent lock   Lock on a fixed allocation unit of eight contiguous pages

Function   Program that can accept multiple input parameters and returns a single value

Implicit transaction   Transaction that starts a new transaction as soon a user connects to a database instance and ends when the user executes a COMMIT TRANSACTION or ROLLBACK command

Input parameter   Data value that a program receives from its calling program

Isolation level   Level specifying either that a transaction behaves as if it is executing by itself or that it can safely run at the same time as other transactions

Local variable   Variable that is declared, assigned, referenced, and visible only in the current program

Locking   Action preventing a transaction from accessing data currently in use by another transaction by placing a lock on it

Loop   Program structure that executes a series of program statements multiple times until an exit condition is reached

Lost update   Result when two or more transactions attempt to update a record at the same time. (With each transaction unaware of the others, the last update overwrites the updates made by the others, and the updates are lost.)

No-columns-list format   INSERT command format that does not list column names and requires the user to supply a value for every table column

Nonrepeatable read   Result when a transaction retrieves the same record multiple times but retrieves different data values each time because of reading uncommitted data

Output parameter   Data value that a program passes back to its calling program

Page lock   Locks an 8,060-byte storage unit in a database

Parameter   Variable that passes data from one program to another

Phantom read   Occurs when a transaction reads a record that has been inserted by another transaction, but has not yet committed and is subsequently rolled back

Read Committed   Default isolation level that honors locks created by all other transactions and reads only committed data, releases shared locks immediately after reading, and acquires exclusive locks for action queries and holds them for the duration of the transaction

Read lock   Lock preventing a transaction from accessing a record using a SELECT command

Read Uncommitted   Isolation level that does not acquire any locks for SELECT or action queries and that ignores locks set by other transactions

Record lock   Locks an entire record

Repeatable Read   Isolation level that honors locks created by all other transactions and reads only committed data, and acquires and holds shared and exclusive locks for the duration of the transaction

Roll back   In transaction processing, discarding a transaction's changes

Run-time error   Result when the command syntax is correct but an error occurs and is detected by the DBMS

Scalar function   User-defined function that returns a scalar value

Serializable   Isolation level that completely isolates a transaction by never allowing it to view uncommitted data

Shared lock   Read lock that multiple transactions can share

Snapshot   Isolation level that forces competing trans-actions to view a copy of locked data

Stored procedure   T-SQL script that the database stores and that you can make available to other users A stored procedure can call another stored proce-dure and can pass and accept input parameters.

System function   Function that returns values about the DBMS, objects within the DBMS, or information about the current database connection

Table function   User-defined function that returns a set of rows

Table hints   Parameters in the FROM clause that specify alternate lock types in SELECT queries

Timeout interval   Specific time period that a transac-tion waits for a lock to be released

Transaction   Series of queries that represent a logical unit of work

Trigger   Stored procedure that automatically executes in response to database DDL or DML event

TRY/CATCH block   Program structure that contains a series of program commands in the TRY block and a series of error-handling commands in the CATCH block

Update lock   Combination of a shared lock and exclu-sive lock that allows a transaction to read a data value and then update it. During the reading portion, it behaves as a shared lock, and during the update por-tion it changes to an exclusive lock.

Variable   Program object referencing a memory loca-tion that stores a data value

Write lock   Lock preventing a transaction from accessing a record using an action query that would change the data

STUDY QUESTIONS

Multiple-Choice Questions

1. In SQL Server 2005, a(n) _____ transaction starts with the BEGIN TRANSACTION command and ends with the COMMIT TRANSACTION command.
   - a. Autocommit
   - b. Explicit
   - c. Implicit
   - d. Snapshot

2. A _____ is stored in the database, receives one or more input parameters, and returns a single output value.
   - a. User-defined function
   - b. Batch
   - c. Stored procedure
   - d. Trigger

3. A _____ occurs when a transaction reads a record that has been inserted or updated by another transaction but has not yet been committed.
   - a. Lost update
   - b. Dirty read
   - c. Nonrepeatable read
   - d. Phantom read

4. The _____ function allows you to convert a value to a different data type and specify its output format.
   - a. TO_CHAR
   - b. CAST
   - c. FORMAT
   - d. CONVERT

5. In SQL Server 2005, the SET_XACT_ABORTON command instructs the database instance to:
   - a. Use autocommit transaction processing
   - b. Not use autocommit transaction processing
   - c. Use explicit transaction processing
   - d. Use implicit transaction processing

6. The _____ isolation level supports the fastest possible transaction processing.
   - a. Read Uncommitted
   - b. Read Committed
   - c. Repeatable Read
   - d. Snapshot
   - e. Serializable

7. When you create an INSERT command that uses the no-columns-list format and you need to insert a NULL value, you specify it in the values list as:
   a. "NULL"   c. NULL
   b. <NULL>   d. None of the above
8. In SQL Server 2005's default isolation mode, a(n) _____ lock prevents a competing transaction from accessing a record during an UPDATE action query.
   a. Read   c. Update
   b. Write   d. Serializable
9. In a CREATE TRIGGER command, the FOR option specifies that the trigger executes:
   a. Just before the triggering event
   b. At the same time as the triggering event
   c. Just after the triggering event
   d. None of the above
10. A _____ lock blocks more transactions than a _____ lock.
   a. Record, page   c. Page, Extent
   b. Extent, database   d. Page, record

True/False Questions

1. When you pass a parameter list to a stored procedure, you pass values for the input parameters and you omit the output parameters.
2. You cannot execute a trigger using the EXECUTE command.
3. A scalar function returns a single value, while a table function returns multiple values in a table.
4. Triggers speed up database performance.
5. You can associate a DML trigger with one and only one database table.
6. If you omit the search condition in an UPDATE command, the command does not update any records.
7. A transaction can contain only action queries.
8. You must use the columns-list format of the INSERT command to insert records into tables that contain an identity column.
9. You cannot roll back an autocommit transaction.
10. You can configure a DDL trigger so that it executes whenever its triggering event occurs in any database on a server.

Short Answer Questions

1. List and describe the default SQL Server 2005 transaction isolation levels.
2. What happens if a T-SQL IF . . . ELSE structure's *BooleanExpression* evaluates as NULL?
3. Why is it important always to assign initial values to variables that you use in arithmetic calculations?
4. Describe the differences between an explicit and an implicit transaction.
5. List three situations when you should create a stored procedure rather than a script.
6. What is a table hint, and when should you use one?
7. What is the purpose of the IDENTITY system function?
8. Name and describe an application of a DDL trigger and an application of a DML trigger.
9. What is a T-SQL batch, and when do you need to create one?
10. What is the difference between a stored procedure and a user-defined function?

Guided Exercises

NOTE: Some of the guided exercises refer to the Sport Motors database illustrated in Figures 3-3 and 3-4. Before you can perform these exercises, you must run the SportMotors.sql script. Instructions for doing this are provided in the section titled "Sample Databases" in Chapter 3.

1. **Creating INSERT Action Queries**
   Create a new query file named 4Exercise1.sql, and then write SQL and T-SQL commands to perform the following actions:
   a. Insert a new SportEmployee record for employee Jim R. Lee, date of birth 7/15/1977, hire date 6/30/2008, home phone number 7158889999, photo name lee.jpg, commission 0.05, username leej, password 1j2k3k. Jim works in the Parts Department and is managed by Greg Kaiser.
   b. Insert a new SportOrder record for customer Anthony Potter, dated 4/19/2008. The order was sold by employee Craig Crain, and the payment type is Cash.
   c. Declare a variable and then write an assignment statement that calls the IDENTITY function to retrieve the OrderID in the previous step. Then insert a new SportOrderDetail record for the order. Specify that the order was for 2 pairs of leather gloves, size L, color black. Assume the sales price was $30 for each pair of gloves.

2. **Creating UPDATE Action Queries**
   Create a new query file named 4Exercise2.sql , and then write SQL commands to perform the following actions:
   a. Update the DepartmentManagerID of the Sales department to EmployeeID 5.
   b. Update the DetailQuantity to 2 for the SportOrderDetail record for OrderID 2 and InventoryID 27.
   c. Add 5 units to the existing InventoryQOH value for InventoryID 13.
   d. Increase the InventorySuggestedPrice by 10% for all SportInventory items in which the current InventorySuggestedPrice is greater than or equal to $5,000.

3. **Creating DELETE Action Queries**
   Create a new query file named 4Exercise3.sql , and then write SQL commands to perform the following actions:
   a. Delete all the records for OrderID 4 in the SportOrder table. (You first need to delete the OrderDetail records and then delete the SportOrder record.)
   b. Delete all the SportInventory records for items supplied by SupplierID 2, then delete the record for SupplierID 2 in the SportSupplier table.

4. **Creating Transactions**
   Create a new query file named 4Exercise4.sql , and then write SQL and T-SQL commands to perform the following actions:
   a. Create a transaction named CreateNewOrder that uses explicit transaction processing and that creates a new order, dated today, for CustomerID 2, sold by EmployeeID 2, paid by a Loan. Use the GetDate() function to specify the current date. Next declare a local variable, and set the variable to the just inserted OrderID value using the IDENTITY function. Finally, insert two records in the SportOrderDetail table to purchase two items of your choice. Select whatever quantity and DetailUnitPrice you wish. Use the value returned by the IDENTITY function for the OrderID value.
   b. Create a transaction named CreateNewCategory that uses implicit transaction processing and that inserts a new record into SportCategory with CategoryDescription value 'Boats.' Next, declare a local variable and set the variable to the just inserted CategoryID value using the IDENTITY function. Finally, insert two new records into the SportSubCategory table with SubCategoryDescription values of 'Fishing' and 'Runabout.'

5. **Creating and Executing a Stored Procedure Using an IF ... ELSE Decision Control Structure**
   Create a new query file named 4Exercise5.sql, and then write SQL and T-SQL commands to perform the following actions:
   a. Create a stored procedure named usp_RetrieveInventoryData that receives an input parameter of an InventoryID value and that returns output parameters of the InventoryDescription, InventoryQOH, and InventorySuggestedPrice values.
   b. Write T-SQL commands that call the stored procedure and evaluate the output values. If the item's InventoryQOH value is equal to one and the item's InventorySuggestedPrice is less than or equal to $1,000, print a message stating, "*InventoryDescription* QOH value is *InventoryQOH,* and needs to be reordered"

(without the quotation marks). (Insert actual data values for *InventoryDescription* and *InventoryQOH*.) If either of these conditions is not true, print a message stating, "*InventoryDescription* QOH value is *InventoryQOH*"(without the quotation marks). For example, for InventoryID 1, print, "RC 99 QOH is 1, and needs to be reordered" or "RC 99 QOH value is 1" (without the quotation marks). Write one batch that tests the program for InventoryID 7 and a second batch that tests the procedure for InventoryID 14.

6. **Creating and Executing a Stored Procedure That Uses a Loop**
   Create a new query file named 4Exercise6.sql , and then write SQL and T-SQL commands to perform the following actions:
   a. Create a stored procedure named usp_CreateDateLookupTable that receives an input parameter of the current date and that creates a table named DateLookup containing a DateID identity column and a DateDescription column with the DateTime data type. Then use a loop to insert values into the table so that the first DateDescription value is today's date, the second value is tomorrow's date, and so forth. Populate the table so that it contains date records for exactly one year.
   b. Write a T-SQL command to call the usp_CreateDateLookupTable stored procedure, and then write a SQL command to view the first 10 records in the DateLookup table.

7. **Creating and Executing a User-Defined Scalar Function**
   Create a new query file named 4Exercise7.sql , and then write SQL and T-SQL commands to perform the following actions:
   a. Create a user-defined function named CategoryInventoryValue that receives an input parameter of a SportCategoryID value and that returns the sum of the value of the inventory for all items in that category. (The inventory value for a single item is the InventoryQOH times the InventorySuggestedPrice. For example, the total value for all items in the Motorcycles category is $80,237.30.)
   b. Create a batch that calls the CategoryInventoryValue function, passes to it the CategoryID value for the Motorcycles category, and then prints the output in the Messages pane.

8. **Creating and Executing a User-Defined Table Function**
   Create a new query file named 4Exercise8.sql , and then write SQL and T-SQL commands to perform the following actions:
   a. Create a user-defined function named RetrieveCustomerSales that receives an input parameter of a SportCustomerID value and that returns a table listing the OrderID, OrderDate, EmployeeFirstName, EmployeeLastName, InventoryDescription, DetailQuantity, and DetailUnitPrice for all purchases the customer has ever made.
   b. Write a SELECT command that displays all the columns that the RetrieveCustomerSales table function retrieves. Format the OrderDate output so that it shows only the date component of the data and omits the time component.

9. **Creating and Executing DDL Triggers**
   Create a new query file named 4Exercise9.sql , and then write SQL and T-SQL commands to perform the following actions:
   a. If necessary, create a new database table named MyDatabaseLog that has the same columns as Table 4-7. The LogDateTime column uses a DateTime data type, and the LogAction column uses a VARCHAR data type.
   b. Create a DDL trigger named CreateTableLog that executes whenever a user creates a new table in the database. The trigger inserts a record in MyDatabaseLog that shows the time of the action and the text "Table created."
   c. Create a second DDL trigger named AlterTableLog that executes whenever a user alters an existing database table. The trigger inserts a record in MyDatabaseLog that shows the time of the action and the text "Table altered."
   d. Create a third DDL trigger named DropTableLog that executes whenever a user drops a database table. The trigger inserts a record in MyDatabaseLog that shows the time of the action and the text "Table dropped."
   e. To test the triggers, write and execute DDL commands to create a table, alter the table, and then drop the table. (You can configure the test table any way you choose.)

f. Write a SELECT command to view all the records in MyDatabaseLog.

g. Write commands to disable all the triggers that you created.

10. **Creating and Executing a DML Trigger**

Create a new query file named 4Exercise10.sql , and then write SQL and T-SQL commands to perform the following actions:

a. Create a DML trigger on the SportOrderDetail table named UpdateInventoryQOH that executes after a user inserts a new table record. The trigger action subtracts the DetailQuantity of the inventory item from the InventoryQOH value in the SportInventory table.

b. To test the trigger, insert a record into the SportOrderDetail table using values of your choice.

c. Write a SELECT command to confirm that the InventoryQOH quantity for the selected inventory item was updated correctly.

d. Write a command to disable the UpdateInventoryQOH trigger.

CHAPTER 5

Introduction to Visual Basic and the VB Integrated Development Environment

Learning Objectives

At the conclusion of this chapter, you will be able to:

■ describe the .NET framework;

■ use the VB IDE to create Windows applications;

■ understand the fundamentals of the VB programming language;

■ use VB's decision and looping structures;

■ understand VB classes and objects;

■ create applications that have multiple forms;

■ work with the IDE debugging features.

You have used SQL Server Management Studio to create and work with database tables and write T-SQL scripts. The next step is to make Windows-based applications that enable users to interact with databases. In this chapter, you will become familiar with the programming environment used to create these applications. (You learn how to use this environment to make database applications in Chapter 6.)

You can use either the Visual Studio 2005 (VS 2005) or Visual Basic 2005 Express Edition (VB Express) integrated development environment to create this chapter's applications. An *integrated development environment (IDE)* is an environment for developing a program that has several components and displays multiple windows for performing different programming tasks. Often an IDE supports different programming languages. For example, the VS 2005 IDE supports multiple languages, including C# (C-Sharp), J# (J-Sharp), C++, and Visual Basic (VB). In this book, we use the VB programming language.

NOTE: Microsoft has significantly changed VS 2005 from the earlier Visual Studio 2002 and 2003 versions. VS 2005 allows you to open Windows applications written using previous VS versions, work with them, and run them, and in the process converts them to the latest VS format. The applications you create using VS 2005, however, are not backward compatible with earlier VS versions because they use new objects and features that the older versions do not support.

This chapter introduces the .NET framework, which provides the foundation for applications you will develop. It also introduces the VB IDE, explores VB programming concepts, and describes the integrated debugging environment.

NOTE: To perform the tutorials and exercises in this chapter, you can use either VS 2005 or VB Express. VB Express contains a subset of VS 2005's features and functions and provides all you need to create VB database applications connecting to SQL Server Express. Projects that you create in VS 2005 can be opened, edited, and executed in VB Express and vice versa. From this point forward, we refer to the integrated development environment as the VB IDE, rather than as the VS 2005 or VB Express IDE. Our examples use VB Express, but we describe differences between VS 2005 and the Express Edition as they occur.

.NET FRAMEWORK

The .NET framework provides the foundation for .NET applications, including Windows-based database applications written using VB. When you install VS 2005, VB Express, SQL Server Express, or SQL Server 2005, the installation program determines if the .NET framework is present. If not, the installation program installs it prior to installing its program-specific components.

What is the .NET framework? Its primary components are the *Common Language Runtime (CLR),* which is an environment that provides services to manage application execution, regardless of the development programming language, and the *Framework Class Libraries (FCL),* which are libraries that contain code assisting with common programming tasks. The following sections describe the CLR and FCL in more detail.

The Common Language Runtime (CLR)

The CLR provides the execution engine for .NET framework applications. Some of the services provided by the CLR are:

- loading and executing an application's code;
- isolating application memory to prevent one application from harming another;
- converting Microsoft Intermediate Language (MSIL, a CPU-independent instruction set generated by .NET compilers from .NET languages such as J#, C# or Visual Basic) code to native code;
- enforcing code access security;
- handling *exceptions,* which are run-time errors thrown by the system or by program code written to catch user logic errors;
- supporting debugging.

The main focus of the CLR is to ensure that programs are reliable and do not harm other applications. Code that runs through the CLR is referred to as *managed code.*

TIP: Within .NET, you can write programs that bypass the CLR using older languages such as C++, but you cannot do this with newer .NET languages, such as VB or C#.

When you write a program in any language, the commands you type are called *source code*. When you compile a .NET program, the compiler first translates your source code into Microsoft Intermediate Language (MSIL) code. (A *compiler* is a program that decodes instructions written in a higher-level language and produces instructions in a lower-level language such as assembly language.) MSIL code is a hardware-independent set of instructions that can be efficiently converted to native binary code to run on a specific hardware platform. Think of MSIL as a generic assembly language. An MSIL code file has an .exe or .dll file extension. (A file with an .exe extension is called an *executable file* and can directly run on a computer. A file with a .dll extension is a *dynamic link library (DLL)*, which is a code library that executable programs call, or link to, at the time the executable program runs. A DLL can be linked to many different executing programs at the same time.)

Once your .NET source code is compiled into an .exe or .dll MSIL file, it is called an *assembly*. An assembly contains MSIL code, as well as program configuration information about content, versioning, and dependencies on other programs. Every workstation that runs the Microsoft Windows operating system contains a registry. The *registry* is a hierarchical database that stores system and program configuration information. A problem with the registry is that it can be difficult to configure and repair. Because .NET applications store program configuration information directly in the assembly, they do not have to rely on registry values to function properly. As a result, assemblies make applications more reliable and easier to deploy. In many cases, you can install a .NET-based application by simply copying its assemblies to a target computer, as long as the target computer has the .NET framework installed on it.

Before an assembly can execute, a compiler must convert it to binary code that runs on a specific hardware platform. This compiler is called a *just-in-time (JIT)* compiler, which is a compiler that compiles and then immediately runs the target program. The CLR supplies a JIT compiler for a variety of computer hardware architectures; so the same MSIL code can be compiled and run on a variety of different types of hardware.

The JIT compiler compiles an assembly the first time a user runs the assembly. After the assembly is compiled, the executable code is cached, or stored, on the target computer in either the native assembly cache or the Global Assembly Cache. The *native assembly cache* stores stand-alone executable programs, and the *Global Assembly Cache (GAC)* stores programs that multiple applications share. For example, the code for the CLR itself is stored in the GAC.

TIP: You can use Windows Explorer to show a logical view of the assemblies (both native and GAC) that have been compiled to executable code when you open the C:\WINDOWS\assembly folder. This provides a logical view of the assemblies. To see the actual files in the Windows Explorer, you first have to modify the HKLM\Software\Microsoft\Fusion registry key by adding to it a binary value named "DisableCacheViewer" and assigning to it any nonzero value.

Framework Class Libraries

Recall that Framework Class Libraries (FCLs) are libraries that contain code for creating common programming objects. Table 5-1 shows examples of FCL namespaces and the tasks they support. (A *namespace* is a naming scheme that uses a hierarchical dotted naming convention to provide a hierarchical, folder-like organization for FCL classes.)

TABLE 5-1 FCL namespaces	
Namespace(s)	*Task(s)*
System.Windows.Forms	Create graphical user interfaces
System.Data System.XML	Work with data from different databases
System.IO	Work with files
System.Net System.Net.Sockets	Create network applications
System.Web	Create Web-based applications

TIP: Because VB uses the same .NET code libraries as C# and other .NET languages, translating between VB and C# is easy if you have prior experience with any C-oriented programming language. Points to remember are that C# is case sensitive, while VB is not; C# uses semicolons to terminate lines of code, while VB uses new line characters; and C# uses curly braces to delimit blocks of code, while VB blocks exist within logical and looping structures and within subroutines and functions.

USING THE VB INTEGRATED DEVELOPMENT ENVIRONMENT (IDE)

An IDE is an environment for developing programs that has multiple components and that displays multiple windows for performing different programming tasks. The following steps describe how to start the VB IDE. You can configure the IDE for Visual Basic development as well as for development in a number of other languages and environments. The steps also describe how to change to the VB configuration.

To start and configure the VB IDE:

1. *If you are using VB Express,* click Start on the taskbar, point to All Programs, and then click Microsoft Visual Basic 2005 Express Edition.

   If you are using Visual Studio 2005, click Start on the taskbar, point to All Programs, point to Microsoft Visual Studio 2005, and then click Microsoft Visual Studio 2005. If necessary, select Visual Basic Development Settings for the Default Environment Settings.

2. The VB IDE appears, as shown in Figure 5-1.

HELP: If your IDE window looks different than Figure 5-1, reset it to the Visual Basic Development Settings by clicking Tools on the menu bar, clicking Import and Export Settings, selecting the *Reset all settings* option button, and then clicking Next. On the Save Current Settings page, select the *No, just reset settings, overwriting my current settings* option button. If you are using Visual Studio 2005, select Visual Basic Development settings. Click Finish; then click Close.

NOTE: VS 2005 has two additional buttons on the top button bar that do not appear on VB Express. One is for creating a Web site, and the other enables you to open a command window. Neither is needed to complete the exercises and assignments in this chapter.

FIGURE 5-1   VB IDE components

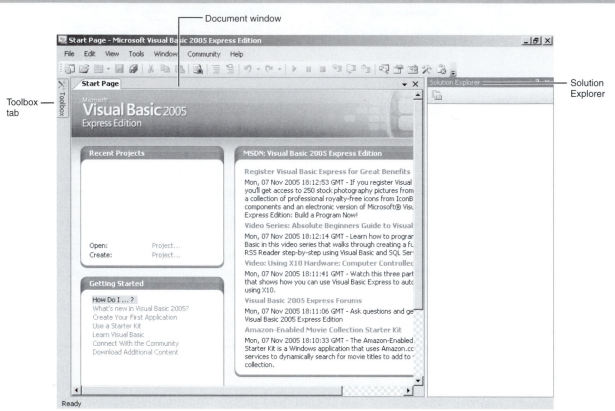

When you first open the VB IDE, the main window is the Document window, which displays the Start Page. From the Start Page, you can retrieve your current projects, receive help about common tasks, read the latest developer news, and interact with the online developer community. The Toolbox tab allows you to access tools to create application items such as command buttons and lists. The IDE also displays the Solution Explorer window, which displays your solutions and their components hierarchically.

In the VB IDE, you can create a *project,* which is a collection of files that comprise an application. A project contains one or more *forms,* which are objects containing the application items with which a user interacts, such as text boxes, buttons, and labels, along with the code to make these items functional. A *solution* is made up of one or more projects. Figure 5-2 shows the folder and file hierarchy of VB solutions, projects, files, and project subfolders.

NOTE: All solutions that you create in this chapter will be made up of a single project.

The IDE stores forms in three separate files. In Figure 5-2, the HelloWorld project contains a form named Form1 that is stored in three files whose names begin with Form1. The *designer file,* which is named Form1.Designer.vb, contains the code that the IDE automatically generates to represent the visual components of a form, such as text boxes, buttons, and other objects. The *resource file,* which is named Form1.resx, stores application resources, which are nonexecutable items that are logically deployed with an application, such as binary images. The *code file,* which is named Form1.vb, stores the additional code that the developer adds to the form.

FIGURE 5-2   VB project structure

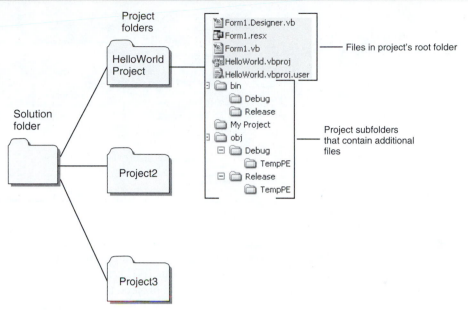

The *project file,* which is named HelloWorld.vbproj in Figure 5-2, keeps track of the files and framework libraries that the project uses. You select this file in the IDE to open the project. A *solution file* is a file with an .sln file extension that keeps track of the projects that a solution contains. If a solution contains a single project, it makes no difference whether you choose to open a project from its .vbproj file or from its .sln file. If a solution contains multiple projects, you must open the solution file to access its underlying projects.

The following subsections describe how to create a new VB project, add objects to the project, and write code to make the project functional.

Creating a Project

To create a new project that will be a Windows application, base the project on the Windows Application template and specify the project name. When you save the project, specify the folder location, and the VB IDE creates a new folder for the project and writes to the folder a series of files and folders that comprise the underlying project structure. When you first save a project, you have the option of placing the project in an existing solution or creating a new solution. In this chapter, the project folder and solution folder will always be the same.

When you create a new Windows project, the IDE creates a single form in the project. You can create additional forms as needed. The following steps show how to create the Hello World project, which has the form shown in Figure 5-3.

This project contains a single form that displays a label, text box, and button. The user can type his or her name in the text box and click OK, and the message box showing the greeting appears.

To create the project:

1. In the VB IDE, click File on the menu bar, then click New Project. The New Project dialog box opens. (If you are using VS 2005, your New Project dialog box should look like Figure 5-4. If you are using VB Express, your New Project dialog box will not display the Project types pane on the left side of the dialog box.)

FIGURE 5-3 Hello World project form

HELP: If you are using VS 2005 and your New Project dialog box does not look like Figure 5-4, then your IDE is not configured for Visual Basic. Click Cancel to cancel creating the project, then configure your IDE for Visual Basic using the instructions given in the section on starting and configuring the IDE. Then repeat Step 1 to create the project again.

2. *If you are using VB Express,* select Windows Application from the Templates window, change the Name field to HelloWorld, and then click OK.

If you are using VS 2005, select Visual Basic in the Project Types pane, select Windows Application in the Templates pane, change the Name field to HelloWorld, and then click OK.

FIGURE 5-4 New Project dialog box (VS 2005)

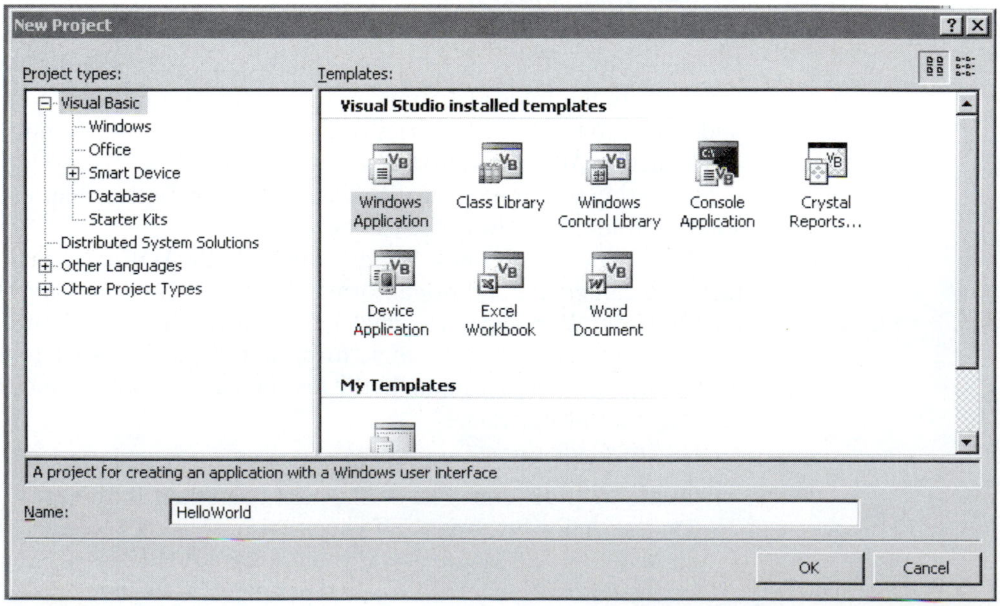

FIGURE 5-5   VB project development environment

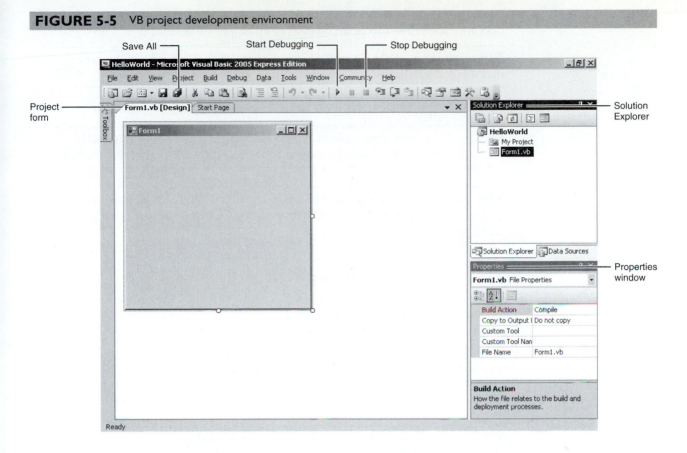

3. The IDE displays the project form and the VB project development environment components, as shown in Figure 5-5.

When you first create a project, the VB development environment components include the Form tab, which is labeled with the form name and the word "Design" and which displays a visual representation of the form. If you change the form, an asterisk (*) appears on the form tab, indicating it has been changed but the changes have not yet been saved. After you save the form, the asterisk disappears.

The Solution Explorer window displays different project components and allows you to access and open them. The Properties window allows you to modify properties of the selected object on the Form tab. Currently, the form itself is selected; so its properties appear in the Properties window.

When you save a project, the IDE automatically creates a folder that has the same name as the project and places the project file, which has a .vbproj extension, in the project folder. It also places additional project files in the folder and its subfolders. You can optionally choose to have the IDE automatically create a parent solution folder for a project; however, you will not do this in this chapter. The following steps show how to save and run the project.

To save and run the project:

1. To save the project, click the Save All button on the toolbar. Make sure that the Name field's value is HelloWorld, click Browse, navigate to your SQLServer\ Solutions\Chapter5 folder, and click Open.
2. To instruct the IDE not to create a solution folder, make sure that the Create directory for solution checkbox is cleared, then click Save.

3. To run the project, click the Start Debugging button on the toolbar. The application appears and at this point consists of an empty project form.

> **TIP:** Other ways to run a project are to press F5 or to click Debug on the menu bar, then click Start Debugging.

4. To close the application, click the Close button on the form window.

> **HELP:** If an error appears in the Error List pane at the bottom of the IDE, proceed to the section titled Debugging VB Projects at the end of the chapter.

> **TIP:** Other ways to close an application are to click the Stop Debugging button on the toolbar, or to click Debug on the menu bar and then click Stop Debugging.

Closing and Reopening a Project

After you have saved a project, you can close the project or the entire IDE and then reopen it again later. The following steps describe how to close and reopen the project.

To close and then reopen the project:

1. To close the project, click File on the menu bar, then click Close Project. The project no longer appears in the Document window or Solution Explorer, and the Start Page reappears.
2. To reopen the project, click HelloWorld in the Recent Projects pane.

> **TIP:** Another way to reopen the project is to click File on the menu bar, click Open Project, navigate to the SQLServer\Solutions\Chapter5\HelloWorld folder, select HelloWorld.sln, then click Open.

Using the Solution Explorer

The Solution Explorer allows you to access and view project components in different views. Figure 5-6 shows the Solution Explorer window.

FIGURE 5-6 Solution Explorer components

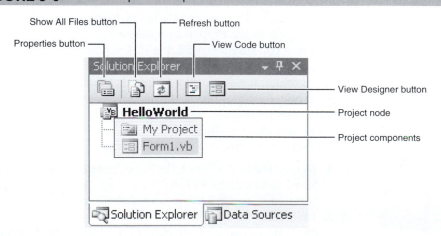

TIP: If the Solution Explorer is currently not visible in the IDE, click View on the menu bar, then click Solution Explorer.

On the Solution Explorer toolbar, the Properties button allows you to view a component's properties. The Show All Files button allows you to alternately view or hide all the project's folders and files. The Refresh button refreshes the Solution Explorer display to reflect recent changes made to the project's files or folders. The View Code button displays the current form in *Code view,* which displays an editor that allows you to enter the program code that you write to add functionality to the form. The View Designer button displays the form currently selected in *Designer view,* which provides a graphical view of the form and allows you to add and position items such as text boxes and buttons.

In the Solution Explorer, the project appears as the top node, and the project components appear as subnodes in an alphabetical list. The My Project node allows you to view and change properties for the overall project. When you create a new project, the IDE creates a form named Form1, which it displays in Designer view. The IDE saves Form1 in the project folder in a file named Form1.vb.

Renaming Form Files

It is a good practice to give your forms descriptive filenames. You should preface form filenames with the prefix frm, followed by a descriptive name. This way, all the project forms appear together in the Solution Explorer display. Example form code filenames are frmLogin.vb or frmStudentData.vb. Remember that a form is defined by three separate files: the code file (which has a.vb extension), the Designer file (which has a .Designer.vb extension), and the resource file (which has a .resx extension). Renaming the .vb file in the IDE renames all three files. The following steps show how to rename the form files.

To rename the project form files:

1. Select Form1.vb in the Solution Explorer.
2. Click File on the menu bar, click Save Form1.vb As, make sure that the HelloWorld project folder appears in the Save in list, change the File name field value to frmHelloWorld.vb, then click Save. The modified filename appears in the Solution Explorer.

TIP: Another way to rename a form's files is to select the form in the Solution Explorer, right-click, then click Rename. Type the new name, then press Enter.

Adding Controls to a Form

Windows applications use *controls,* which are objects in visual applications that display information and allow users to interact with the application. Examples of controls are text boxes, buttons, and labels. In the VB development IDE, the Toolbox displays the controls available for Windows forms, as shown in Figure 5-7.

TIP: If the Toolbox is not currently visible in the IDE, click View on the menu bar, then click Toolbox. You can also click the Toolbox button on the toolbar to display the Toolbox.

The Toolbox contains nodes that represent categories of controls, such as Common Controls and Containers. Within these nodes are subnodes that represent individual

FIGURE 5-7 Form Toolbox components

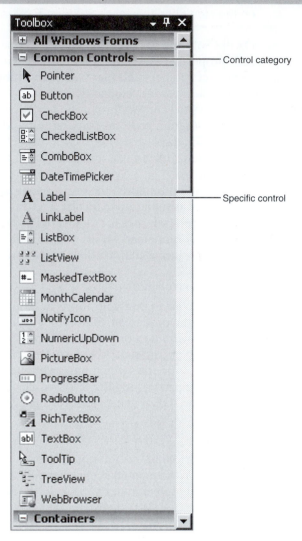

Control category

Specific control

controls, such as lists and labels. The Toolbox content varies depending on the current project type and on whether the form Designer window or Code window is currently displayed.

To add controls to a form, open the Toolbox, select the desired control, then draw it on the form. By default, the Toolbox is in Auto Hide mode, which displays the Toolbox tab on the left edge of the IDE. When you place the mouse pointer on the tab, the Toolbox opens; when you move the pointer off the Toolbox, it closes. You can right-click the title bar of the Toolbox window and clear Auto Hide to make the Toolbox always appear or click Hide to close the Toolbox. The following steps show how to open the Toolbox and add a label, text box, and button control to a form.

To use the Toolbox to add controls to a form:

1. Move the mouse pointer onto the Toolbox tab on the left edge of the IDE and, if necessary, open the All Windows Forms node. The Toolbox opens, as shown in Figure 5-7.

HELP: If the Toolbox tab is not visible, click the Toolbox button on the toolbar, or click View on the menu bar and click Toolbox. To place the Toolbox in Auto Hide mode and display the Toolbox tab, right-click the title bar of the Toolbox window, then click Auto Hide. Experiment with using the Toolbox in different ways to see what works best for you.

HELP: A form must be open in Designer view for the Toolbox to display the All Windows Forms node.

2. Scroll down in the Toolbox, click Label, move the mouse pointer onto Form1, and draw a rectangle anywhere on Form 1. A label with the text "Label1" appears on the form. Drag the label to the upper left corner of the form, where "Please Enter Your Name:" is shown in Figure 5-3.
3. Open the Toolbox again, click Textbox, and then draw a rectangle anywhere on Form1. Reposition the text box so that it appears on the right edge of the label, as shown in Figure 5-3.
4. Open the Toolbox again, click Button, draw a rectangle anywhere on Form1, then reposition the button so it appears under the label and text box, as shown in Figure 5-3.
5. Click the Save All button on the toolbar to save the project.

Modifying Project, Form, and Control Properties

All form objects, including the form itself, have *properties* that control the object's appearance and behavior. You set the values for object properties in the Properties window. You can also set property values in program code to change control properties while the form is running. Figure 5-8 shows the components of the Properties window.

TIP: If the Properties window is currently not visible in the IDE, click View on the menu bar, then click Properties Window.

The Properties window contains an Object list, which lists all the form objects. When you select an object, the Object list displays the name of the selected object. The Properties window also displays property names and their associated values. The Property hint describes the property that is currently selected.

The Properties window toolbar allows you to configure the window's appearance. The Categorized button configures the Properties window to display property names sorted by categories, such Appearance and Behavior. The Alphabetical button configures the window to display all the property names in an alphabetized list. The Properties button, which is enabled by default, configures the Properties window to display properties for the currently selected object. The Events button configures the Properties window to display events that are associated with the currently selected object. (You will learn about events a little later.) The Property Pages button, which is enabled when the project is selected in the Solution Explorer, displays properties about the overall project.

Every object has a Name property, which specifies how the project references the object internally. When you show properties in Categorized view, the Name property appears under the Design category; when you show properties in Alphabetical view, the Name property appears at the top of the window. Different object types have different properties. For example, objects that display text on the form, such as labels and text boxes, have a Text property, which specifies the text that appears in the object.

FIGURE 5-8   Properties window components

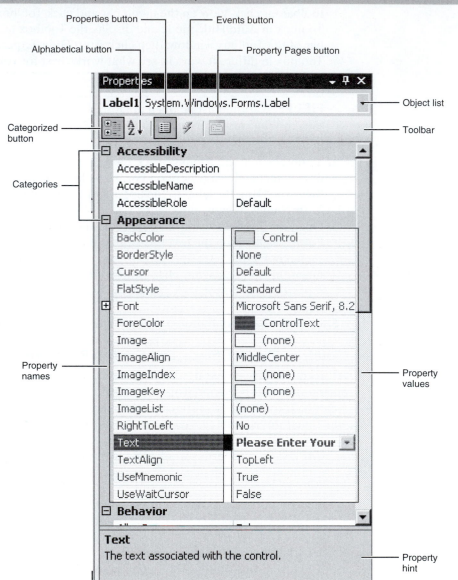

When you create an object, it has default property values. For example, the default Name value for a text box is TextBox1. You should change the Name property of any form control whose properties you might reference or change in your program code to a meaningful name. This makes the code easier to understand and work with. In this book, we specify control names using our adaptation of *Hungarian notation,* which is a standard object notation that many Microsoft developers use to specify object names using a two- or three-letter prefix that specifies the object type, followed by a descriptive name made up of one or more words. You start the first word with a lowercase letter and the second and subsequent words with uppercase letters. Table 5-2 shows object name prefixes for common form controls.

The following steps show how to use the Properties window to modify the initial properties of the Hello World form and controls. They rename the form controls using

TABLE 5-2   Object name prefixes

Control Type	Description	Prefix	Example
Check box	Control that gives the user the choice between two options, such as True or False	chk	`chkPaid`
Combo box	Drop-down list combined with an editing field	cbo	`cboState`
Command button	Button that a user can click to select an option or initiate an action	btn	`btnSubmit`
Connection	Object to connect to a data source	cn	`cnUniversity`
Data adapter	Object to connect to a data source	da	`daStudent`
Data set	Structure for storing retrieved data	ds	`dsStudent`
Form	Object that contains controls and related code	frm	`frmLogin`
Label	Descriptive text that users cannot edit	lbl	`lblTime`
List box	Scrollable or drop-down list that allows users to select from predefined items	lst	`lstState`
Menu	Pull-down menu bar	mnu	`mnuMain`
Option button	Item within a group of related items, of which only one can be selected at a time	opt	`optGender`
SQL command	Object that stores the text of a SQL command	sql	`sqlInsertName`
Text box	Editable text field	txt	`txtName`

Hungarian notation, and change the text that appears on the form, label, text box, and button. (The steps do not rename Label1 using Hungarian notation because the label is not referenced when the program is running.)

To modify the form and control properties:

1. Select Label1 on the form. Confirm that Label1 appears in the Object list at the top of the Properties window, which indicates that it is the selected object.
2. If necessary, click the Categorized button on the Properties window toolbar to display object properties according to categories.
3. Scroll to the Appearance category in the Properties window, change the Text property value to Please Enter Your Name:, then select another property to apply the change. Note that the new label text appears on the form.
4. Select the text box, and confirm that TextBox1 appears in the Object list. Scroll to the Design category, and change the Name property value to txtUserName.
5. Select the button, and change its Name property value to btnSubmit and its Text property value to Submit.
6. Select the form so that selection handles appear on its borders, and confirm that Form1 appears in the Object list. Click the Alphabetical button on the toolbar to

sort the properties by name, then change the form's properties as follows:

Property Name	New Value
FormBorderStyle	FixedSingle
MaximizeBox	False
Name	frmHelloWorld
StartPosition	CenterScreen
Size	298, 192
Text	Hello World!

HELP: At this point you may not be able to run the project because you have changed the form name, and you need to modify the project's Startup form property to the new form name. The following sections describe how to do this.

7. Save the project.

Modifying Project Properties

You can also modify properties of the overall project, such as the name of the project assembly, the security model that the project uses, or the project startup form. To modify project properties, use the project Property pages, as shown in Figure 5-9.

The left pane of the project Property Pages displays a series of tabs that allows you to access different property pages. The right pane allows you to access and modify current project property values. If you modify a property value, the IDE saves the change when you close the Property pages window. Most of the time, you use the default project property values.

FIGURE 5-9 Project Property pages

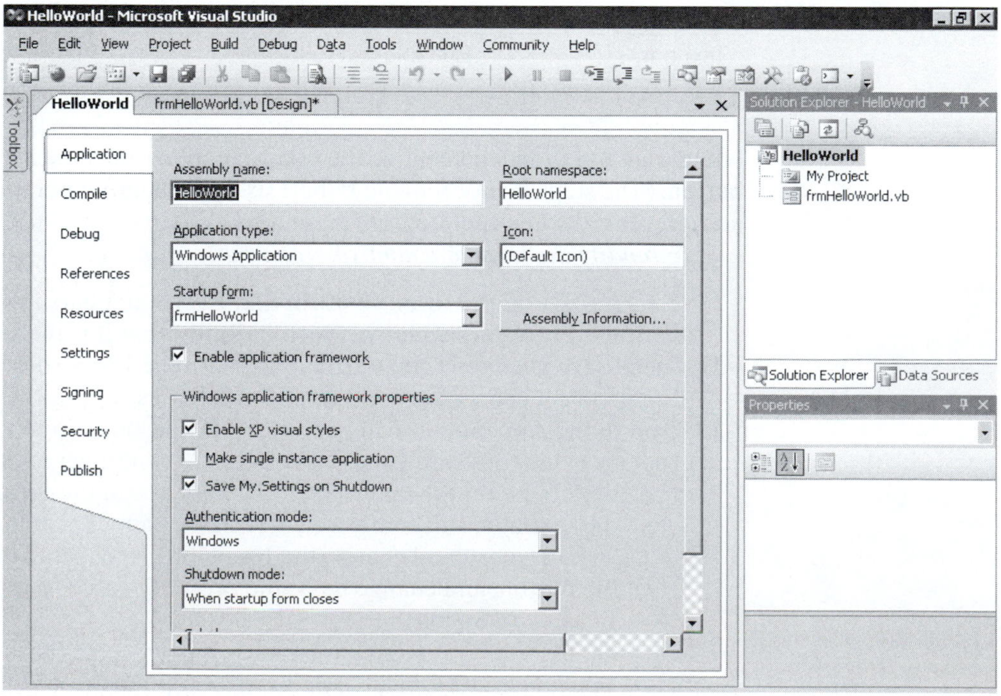

To open the project Property pages, click Project on the menu bar, then click *ProjectName* Properties. You can also either right-click the top project node in the Solution Explorer and then click Properties, or select the project node in the Solution Explorer and click the Properties button on the Solution Explorer toolbar.

Specifying the Project Startup Form

A project has a *Startup form,* which is the first form that appears when you run the project. When you first create a project, this is the default Form1. If you change Form1's name property, or if you delete it and create a new form that you intend to use as the project's Startup form, you must modify the project's Startup form property on the project Property Pages to reflect this change. The following steps describe how to change the project's Startup form and then run the project.

To modify the project Startup form and run the project:

1. To modify the project Startup form, double-click My Project in the Solution Explorer to display the project's Property pages.

TIP: Other ways to display a project's Property pages are to right-click the project node in the Solution Explorer and click Properties or to select Project from the menu bar and click *ProjectName* Properties, where *ProjectName* is the name of the current project.

---

2. If necessary, select the Application tab in the left window pane, then select frmHelloWorld in the Startup form list.
3. Close the project Property Pages window, then save the project.
4. Click the Start Debugging button to run the revised form. Your application should look like Figure 5-3.
5. Close the application or click the Stop Debugging button. (Do not close the form in the IDE.)

Adding Code to a Form

At this point you can type text in the text box and click Submit, but nothing happens. To display the message box in Figure 5-3, you need to add code to the form. In Windows applications, program commands execute in response to an *event,* which is a user action, such as clicking a button or typing text into a text box, or in response to a system action, such as loading a form. Project components have *event handlers,* which are programs that execute in response to specific events. For example, when the user clicks Submit, an event handler runs, displaying the greeting message. The following subsections describe how to create an event handler and how to add code to the event handler.

Creating an Event Handler

Actions that users perform in applications, such as mouse clicks and keyboard key presses, raise events that might have associated event handlers. In addition, the system raises events when the .NET framework delivers a message to the program, such as when a database query encounters an error. Events are not required to have associated event handlers, however. If you want your program to ignore user events such as mouse clicks or key presses, do not write event handlers for them.

To work with a form's event handlers, open the form in Code view, as shown in Figure 5-10. To open a form in Code view, select the form in the Solution Explorer, and then click the View Code button on the Solution Explorer toolbar. You can also right-click the form in either the Solution Explorer or Designer view, then click View Code.

FIGURE 5-10 Form in Code view

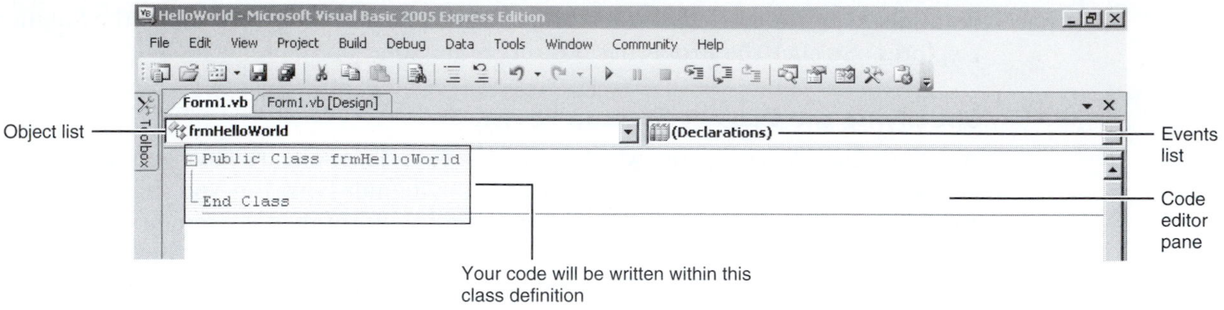

Your code will be written within this class definition

When you display a form in Code view, a tab appears that shows the form name and that displays all the form code in the Code editor pane. (The tab that shows the form in Designer view is still visible, and you can click it to return to the graphical view of the form.) In Code view, the Object list appears on the left side of the Code view window and shows the form object (frmHelloWorld), along with all the form controls. The Event list appears on the right side of the Code view window and displays all the events for the selected object.

A class defines similar objects. In a VB project, classes define forms, controls, and variables. When you create a new form, the IDE creates a form class definition, which contains the commands that define the form object. When you run the form, the .NET framework *instantiates,* or creates an object instance, of the form class (you can instantiate more than one object from the same class; for example, with a few lines of code, you can display multiple copies of the same form).

Although the Code view window for frmHelloWorld.vb appears to have an empty class definition, remember that a form is defined by three files: the Code (.vb) file, the Designer (.Designer.vb) file, and the Resource (.resx) file. When you add controls to your form, the IDE automatically generates additional code that it stores in the Designer file. This code is not visible in the Code file. If you want to view the code in the Designer file, click the Show All Files button on the Solution Explorer toolbar, open the form node, then double-click the file with the .Designer.vb extension to display its contents.

CAUTION: It is usually a bad idea to modify the code in the Designer file directly. This can cause the application to crash or possibly run but with errors.

The code for form event handlers appears in the form's Public Class and End Class commands. To create a new event handler for an object such as a form or control, select the object in the Object list, then select the associated event from the Event list. The event handler declaration appears in the Code editor, in the form's class declaration.

If you double-click an object in Designer view, the IDE creates an event handler for the object's *default event,* which is the event for which developers most commonly write event handlers. For example, the default event for a button is the Click event, and the default event for a form is the Load event.

There are three ways to create an event handler declaration:

1. Open the form in Code view, and select the control in the Object List and the desired event in the Event list.

FIGURE 5-11 Event handler declaration

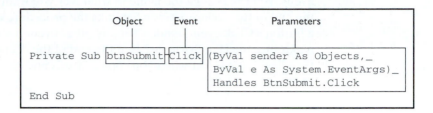

2. Open the form in the form Designer window, and double-click the desired control on the form, which creates an event handler for the control's default event.

3. Select the control in Designer view, click the Events button at the top of the Properties window, and double-click the desired event.

NOTE: If you really want to, you can directly type the code to declare an event handler. This probably is not a good idea, however. Event handlers have two parameters passed to them that are not always the same. If you type in the event handler declaration, you are likely to make a mistake in how you declare these parameters. You will find using any of the previous three methods faster and more reliable.

When you create a new event handler, the IDE creates the event handler declaration, which specifies the event handler's object, event, and parameters. Figure 5-11 shows the event handler declaration for the Submit button's Click event.

In this syntax, the `Private` keyword means this procedure is visible only to other procedures in the form. `Sub` means this is a VB subprocedure, which is a code block that does not return a value. Next comes the object name (`btnSubmit`), followed by an underscore and then the event name (`Click`). This is followed by the parameter list, which has the following general syntax:

```
(PassingMethod Parameter1 DataType,
  PassingMethod Parameter2 DataType,... )
```

In the parameter list, the *PassingMethod* specifies how the procedure passes the parameter values. Legal values are `ByVal`, which indicates that the procedure passes a copy of the actual data value of the parameter, and `ByRef`, which indicates that the procedure passes the original parameter (a reference to the memory location storing the parameter).

The first parameter is `sender`, which is of data type Object. This references the object that triggers this event, which is the `btnSubmit`. The second parameter is `e`, of data type `System.EventArgs`. The parameter `e` references the event, and its data type varies depending on the type of object and the type of event being handled. The things you can do with `e` differ widely. For example, in a button Click event, you do not use `e` at all. In an event that validates data that a user types into a text box, you might reference `e` to cancel the validation event. Next comes the keyword `Handles`, followed by the object and event name. This is what connects the event handler to the event.

> **TIP:** The name of the event handler does not link the procedure to the event. You can change the name to whatever you want. The Handles clause at the end of the declaration is what links the procedure to the desired event. If a button's Click event handler (or any other event handler) fails to be called, make sure the Handles clause is at the end of the declaration. Sometimes the Handles clause is lost when you copy controls and code from one form to another.

In VB, you delimit, or mark the end of, each program command by placing each command on separate line. If a command scrolls past the right edge of the Code editor, it is a good practice to break the line so that you can see the entire command without scrolling horizontally. To inform the VB compiler that the current command continues to the next line, type the *line continuation character,* which is a space followed by an underscore (_).

> **TIP:** Other languages use different ways to delimit commands; for example, Java uses a semicolon (;) to mark the end of each command, which might continue across multiple text editor lines.

Figure 5-12 uses the line continuation character to display the event handler's parameter list on multiple lines. If you make an error, the IDE underscores the error with a blue wavy line, as also shown in Figure 5-12.

The error in Figure 5-12 is caused by trying to use a line continuation in a string literal. If a line continuation is really needed after "Hello," you must split the string into multiple strings, as follows:

```
MessageBox.Show("Hello " & _
                userName.Text, "Greetings", _
                MessageBoxButtons.OK, _
                MessageBoxIcon.Information)
```

The following steps show how to create a Click event handler for the form's Submit button. The example formats the event handler's parameter list so that it appears on multiple Code editor lines.

FIGURE 5-12   Command with line continuation error

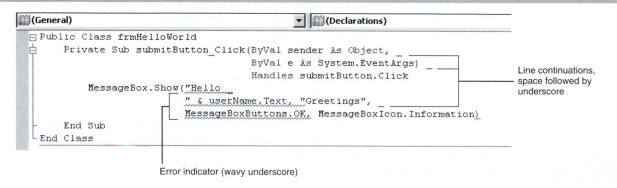

To create an event handler for the Submit button:

1. Select the form in the Solution Explorer, and then click the View Code button on the Solution Explorer toolbar. The form opens in Code view, as shown in Figure 5-10.

HELP: If the Code editor contains code other than that shown in Figure 5-10, you may have created other event handler declarations when testing the methods we presented for creating event handlers. Delete these declarations or any other code except the form's class definition that appears in Figure 5-10.

---

2. To create an event handler for the Submit button, open the Object list on the left side of the Code view window, and select btnSubmit. Then open the Event list on the right side of the window and select Click. VB adds the event handler declaration for the button's Click event.
3. To display the event parameter list on multiple lines, place the insertion point just before `ByVal  e`, type an underscore (_), then press Return. Press Tab several times to align the parameters directly under one another.
4. Add another line continuation character before `Handles` to place the Handles clause on a separate line so that your event declaration format looks like Figure 5-11.

HELP: If a blue wavy line appears anywhere under your event declaration, you probably made a mistake with the line continuation characters. Make sure you included a space before the underscores and placed them at the correct places in the code.

---

5. Save the project.

Adding Program Commands

The next step is to enter the event handler's program commands. As you type VB commands in the Code editor, the IDE automatically includes *code completion support,* which provides explanations of parameters in commands. It also displays *Intellisense lists,* which are code completion lists that provide legal values for argument values.

This event handler creates a *message box,* which is a dialog box that displays a short message and one or more buttons allowing the user to take different actions. This event handler uses a simple message box that displays the message "Hello World" and that has only an OK button. To create this message box, use the MessageBox object, which is defined in the .NET framework class libraries. The MessageBox object has a `Show()` method that uses the following parameters:

```
MessageBox.Show(Prompt[, Title][, Style])
```

In this syntax, *Prompt* is a character string that represents the text that the message box displays, such as "Hello World!" The optional *Title* represents the character string that appears in the message box window's title bar. The optional *Style* represents either character strings or numbers that define the buttons and icon that appear on the message box. The following steps describe how to add the code to create the message box.

To add the code to create the message box:

1. Place the insertion point on the blank line before End Sub, and press Tab so that the code is indented in the event handler declaration.
2. Type MessageBox, followed by a period (.). An Intellisense list opens, showing the object methods. Select Show, then press Tab to enter your selection in the Code editor.
3. Type ("Hello World!," "Greetings",. Note that after you type the opening parenthesis and after each comma, a hint appears describing the current parameter value. After you type the final comma (,), a list opens to show possible Style values.
4. Select MessageBoxButtons.OK from the list, press Tab to display the selection in the Code editor, then type) to end the command.
5. Save the project, and then click the Start Debugging button on the IDE toolbar to run the application.
6. Click Submit. The message box appears, as shown in Figure 5-3. (The position of your message box will be different.)
7. Click OK, then close the application.

HELP: If an error appears when you try to run the program, click No, then look at the error message(s) reported in the Errors list. (If you click Yes, you lose all your recent changes since the last time you ran the project.) Double-click the first error, and the IDE places the insertion point at the location of the first error. Double-check your code for errors, then fix the error.

---

8. To close the project, click File on the menu bar, then click Close Project.

Project Folders and Files

A VB Windows application project contains several interrelated files and folders. For example, the project that you just created involves nine folders and a total of 26 files. You explicitly created and named some of the files, such as the form and project files, and the IDE automatically created other files and folders to support the project. Figure 5-13 shows the project folder and its underlying folders and files.

The *project folder* stores all the project's files and subfolders. In Figure 5-13, HelloWorld is the project folder. If you create a separate *solution folder,* it is a parent folder of the project folder and contains multiple project folders. The project folder contains the following subfolders:

- The **Bin** folder contains the project assemblies (an assembly is a file that contains MSIL code compiled into executable code using a processor-specific JIT compiler). The Bin folder contains subfolders named *Debug* and *Release.* The IDE stores the assemblies in the Debug folder until the developer is ready to release

FIGURE 5-13   Project folders and files

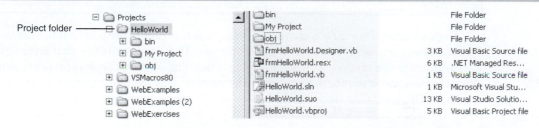

the project for deployment to users. When the developer configures the project for release, the IDE stores the finished assemblies in the Release folder.

- The **Obj** folder contains intermediate files that the IDE uses to create the assemblies. As with Bin, Obj contains subfolders named Debug and Release.
- **TempPE** is a subfolder of the Obj\Debug folder and stores temporary assemblies created by *IDE designers,* which are objects that assist the IDE with tasks such as adding objects into windows forms, connecting to databases, and creating queries.

The project files are as follows:

- **SolutionName.sln** is a text file that specifies the names of all the projects in a solution.
- **SolutionName.suo** is a binary file that stores the current configuration for the solution.
- **ProjectName.vbproj** is an XML file that stores data about the configuration, build settings, and list of project files for a specific project.
- **ProjectName.vbproj.user** is an XML file that stores data about the current configuration for a specific project.
- **ProjectName.pdb** is a binary database file that stores project debugging and state information.
- **ProjectName.vshost.exe** is a binary file that the IDE uses to support execution and debugging tasks.
- **ProjectName.exe** is the binary assembly that stores the project's MSIL code.
- **FormName.vb** is a text file that stores the program code for a form.
- **FormName.resx** is an XML data file that stores form resources such as binary images.
- **FormName.Designer.vb** is a text file that stores designer-generated code for a form.

As a novice developer, you need to concern yourself mainly with the *SolutionName*.sln and *FormName*.vb files. To open a project in the IDE, open the *SolutionName*.sln file or the *ProjectName*.vbproj file. To open a solution containing several projects, use the *SolutionName*.sln file, not the *ProjectName*.vbproj file. To simultaneously start the VB IDE and open a project, you can double-click the *SolutionName*.sln or *ProjectgName*.vbproj file in the Windows Explorer.

TIP: When you create new project forms, make sure to save the files in the project folder. Otherwise the forms may be lost (not copied along with the rest) if you move your files to an alternate location.

VB PROGRAMMING FUNDAMENTALS

Now that you are familiar with the VB IDE and how to create a project, you are ready to learn more about the VB programming language. VB commands appear in both upper- and lowercase letters. To create comments to document your VB programs internally, start the comment line with a single quotation mark, as follows:

```
'This is a VB program comment
```

The following subsections describe VB program structures, elementary data types, variables, object properties and methods, and arithmetic and string operations. The final subsections show how to enforce strong data typing and convert values to different data types.

VB Program Structures

VB code is organized into classes, procedures, and blocks. VB program classes are code templates that define the objects in an application. A project contains class definitions that are instantiated into objects when the project runs. You can create as many objects as you like from a single class definition. Classes are the fundamental building blocks of a VB application. For example, the Code view window of a form (see Figure 5-10) shows the form's class definition.

A *procedure* is a named set of commands that can receive parameters and that other procedures can call. In VB programs, you declare procedures as either functions or subroutines. A *function* returns a value to the calling procedure, while a *subroutine* manipulates data values but does not return a specific value. (You will learn how to create functions and subroutines later in the chapter.)

> **TIP:** C++, Java, or C# functions are equivalent to VB procedures. When a C++, Java, or C# function returns a value, it is equivalent to a VB function. Otherwise, it is equivalent to a VB subroutine.

A *block* is a set of related program commands that execute as a group. In a VB procedure, everything between the declaration and the `End Sub` or `End Function` command is in a block. This block can contain smaller blocks; for example, commands in a decision control structure or a loop also constitute a block. Figure 5-14 shows the blocks in a subroutine that contains a decision control structure. (You will learn the syntax for VB decision control structures like If/Then in a later section in this chapter.)

Elementary Data Types

VB supplies a set of *elementary data types*, which are data types that reference a scalar (single) data value of a specific size and format. Table 5-3 lists common elementary data types, how much memory the system allocates for them, and values they can store. It also lists the prefixes you use to create variable names and provides example variable names.

Variables

Recall that a variable references a memory location that can store data values that a program accesses while it is running. A *literal* is a data value that you hard code, or directly write, in a program command. For example, in the expression `X + 3`, `X` is variable and `3` is a numeric literal. Literals can also be strings, such as `"Hello."` Variables have data types, which specify the type of data they reference.

FIGURE 5-14   Examples of blocks

```
Private Sub DoSomething()
    Dim intUserResponse As Integer
    intUserResponse = MessageBox.Show("Do you want to quit?", _
                    "Quit", MessageBoxButtons.YesNo)
    If intUserResponse = MsgBoxResult.Yes Then
        MessageBox.Show("Quitting")
    End If
End Sub
```

TABLE 5-3   VB elementary data types

Data Type	Memory Used	Description	Value Range	Variable Name Prefix	Example Variable Name
Boolean	2 bytes	Boolean true or false	True or False	bln	blnCheckFlag
Date	8 bytes	Date and time	Midnight on January 1, 0001 through 11:59:59 PM on December 31, 9999	dat	dtStart
String	4 bytes	Text string	0 to approximately 2 billion Unicode characters	str	strName
Object	4 bytes	Pointer to other data	Any data type, data structure, or class can be referenced by an object	obj	objStudent
Single	4 bytes	Signed floating point number	−3.4028235E+38 through −1.401298E−45 1.401298E−45 through 3.4028235E+38	sng	sngAge
Double	8 bytes	Signed floating point number	−1.79769313486231570E+308 through −4.94065645841246544E−324 4.94065645841246544E−324 through 1.79769313486231570E+308	dbl	dblGPA
Byte	1 byte	Unsigned integer number	−32,768 through 32,767 (signed)	byt	bytStudentID
Short	2 bytes	Signed integer number	−32,768 through 32,767 (signed)	sht	shtCourseID
Integer	4 bytes	Signed integer number	−2,147,483,648 through 2,147,483,647 (signed)	int	intCourseID
Long	8 bytes	Signed integer number	−9,223,372,036,854,775,808 through 9,223,372,036,854,775,807	lng	lngEnrollmentID

Most programming languages define variables in terms of scope and persistence. *Scope* specifies the procedures and classes in which the variable is visible and can be used. *Persistence* specifies when the program allocates memory for the variable and when the program clears the memory for other uses.

In VB, the keyword you use to declare the variable and the location from which you declare the variable determine the variable's scope and persistence. VB has three main types of variables:

- **Public variables** are defined in a class declaration. (A public variable cannot be defined in a procedure.) A public variable persists from the time the object in which you declare it is instantiated until the time its object is destroyed. For example, if you declare a variable in the class declaration of a form, the variable is available as long as the form is loaded. A public variable can be read and modified by code in any other class in the application.

- **Private variables** are defined in a class declaration. (Private variables cannot be defined in a procedure.) A private variable persists from the time its object is instantiated until the time it is destroyed. A private variable can be read and modified only by procedures written in its class.

- **Dim variables** are local variables defined in a procedure or block. When you declare a Dim variable in a procedure, it is local to the procedure. It persists from the time the procedure begins to execute until the time the execution ends, and it is visible only within the procedure. If you declare a Dim variable in a block in a procedure, it persists only during execution of that block and is visible only in that block.

TIP: If you declare a Dim variable in a class, it is equivalent to a private variable. Avoid this practice (use Private for private variables) to avoid confusing local with private variables.

The following subsections describe how to declare and assign values to variables.

Declaring Variables

Use the following general syntax to declare a variable:

```
{Public [| Private | Dim} VariableName As DataType
```

The keywords Public, Private, or Dim define the variable type. Next is the *VariableName,* which can be from one to 255 characters in length and can contain letters, numbers, or underscores. Variable names must begin with a letter. It is a good practice to use short, descriptive names for variables. In this book, we use Hungarian notation for variable names, which prefaces the variable's name with an abbreviation that indicates its data type. The following examples show how to declare variables of the three different types:

```
Public strImportantMessage As String
Private intCurrentCount As Integer
Dim dtTodaysDate As Date
```

NOTE: This book does not explain how to enable implicit variable declarations because we strongly advise against using them. With an implicit variable declaration, VB treats any sequence of letters in a command that is not a keyword or known variable as a declared variable of the generic *object* type. This practice allows mistyped words to be inadvertently used as variables, which causes errors that are difficult to find and correct.

Assigning Values to Variables

In VB, assign values to variables using the following general syntax:

```
VariableName = ScalarExpression
```

In this syntax, *VariableName* represents the name of the variable, and *ScalarExpression* is an expression that represents a single value, such as the number 2, the text string "Hello," or the arithmetic expression intCounter + 1. For example, use the following command to assign the text string "Hello" to a variable named strGreeting:

```
strGreeting = "Hello"
```

TABLE 5-4	Example assignment statements and default initial values	
Data type	**Example Assignment Statement(s)**	**Default Initial Value**
Boolean	`blnOrderPaidStatus = True` `blnOrderPaidStatus = False`	False
Date	`datOrderDate = #7/15/2008#`	12:00 a.m. January 1, 0001 AD
String	`strGreeting = "Hello"`	Empty string (" ")
Object	`objMyObject.Property =` `Value`	No initial value
All number data types	`sngOrderTotal = 323.11` `intCurrentAge = 33`	0

Table 5-4 provides examples of assignment statements for variables of different data types. To assign a value to a Boolean variable, use the keyword True or False, and do not enclose the word in quotation marks. To assign a value to a Date variable, enclose a string representing any of the common date/time formats shown in Table 3-8 in pound signs (#12/31/2008#). To assign a value to a String variable, enclose the text in double quotes ("text"). To assign a value to a number variable, simply type the number.

VB assigns default initial values to variables. Table 5-4 shows the default initial values of variables that have the common VB data types.

You can declare a variable and assign its initial value in a single command. For example, the following command declares a Dim variable named strGreeting, and assigns its initial value as "Hello":

```
Dim strGreeting String = "Hello"
```

Object Properties and Methods

Recall that everything in a VB project is an object: forms, controls, and variables. These VB objects have properties and methods that allow you to manipulate them. Object properties allow you to specify or retrieve information about an object's value. For example, a text box has a Text property that specifies the text currently in the text box. Similarly, a variable that has the String data type has a Length property, which represents the number of characters that the current value of the variable contains. To reference an object property, use the following general syntax:

```
ObjectName.PropertyName
```

For example, to assign the value "Hello" to a TextBox control named txtUserName, use the following command:

```
txtUserName.Text = "Hello"
```

The following commands (1) store the text that appears in the txtUserName control in a variable that has the String data type, (2) determine the length of the string, and (3) assign the string length to an Integer variable named intUserNameLength:

```
Dim strUserName As String, intUserNameLength As Integer
strUserName = txtUserName.Text
intUserNameLength = strUserName.Length
```

Methods provide a way to act on or modify a control or a variable. For example, a TextBox control has a method named Clear that clears the contents of the text box; a variable that has the Date data type has a method named AddDays that adds a specific number of days to the variable's current value.

To call a method, use the following syntax:

```
ObjectName.MethodName[(ParameterList)]
```

For example, the following commands create and set an initial value for a Date variable, then use the AddDays method to add 30 days to the initial date:

```
Dim datMyDate As Date = #7/14/2008#
datMyDate = datMyDate.AddDays(30)
```

Note that in this example, you pass the number of days that the AddDate method adds to the Date variable as a parameter.

The best way to use object properties and methods is to use the Intellisense code completion lists that the VB IDE provides. To display the code completion list, type the variable name, followed by a period (.). The list opens, as shown in Figure 5-15.

Code completion lists display *glyphs,* which are the icons on the left side of the list, to differentiate between methods and properties. The Flying Box glyph denotes methods such as AddMinute and AddMonths, which are programs that modify the data

FIGURE 5-15 Object properties and methods

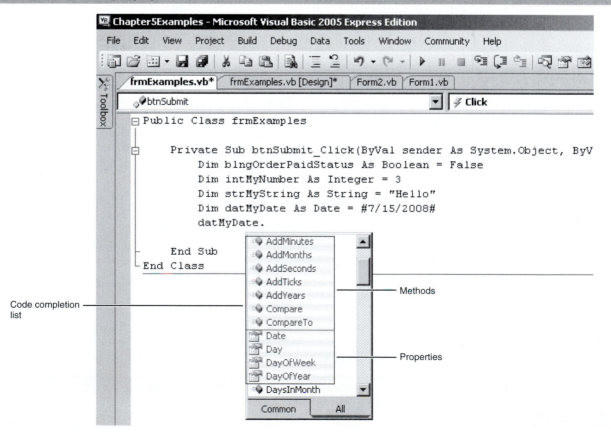

value that the Date variable stores. The Notecard glyph denotes properties, such as Date and Day. These properties assign a value to all or part of a variable's contents, or they retrieve and transform all or part of the data value. The Common tab displays the most commonly used properties and methods, and the All tab displays all available properties and methods.

To select a property or method, double-click it. You can also use the arrow keys to scroll up or down the list until you select the desired property or method, press Tab to select the item, and close the list. Then you type an opening parenthesis (( ), and a hint appears describing the property or method and its parameters.

Arithmetic and String-Handling Operations

In VB, you can create expressions using common arithmetic and string-handling operations. Table 5-5 summarizes VB's arithmetic and string-handling operators.

As with most programming languages, VB's order of precedence of arithmetic operations is as follows: exponentiation, multiplication/division/integer division, then addition and subtraction. To force a different order, place the operation to be evaluated first in parentheses. The following command assigns the result of a complex arithmetic expression to a variable:

```
sngCircleArea = 3.14157 * sngCircleRadius ^ 2
```

You can use either the ampersand (&) or plus sign (+) operators to concatenate multiple strings into a single string. You should avoid using the plus sign, however, because it is an overloaded operator that also serves as an addition operator, and its use can lead to errors. The following command concatenates three text strings into a single string:

```
strMessage = "Found" & intOverdueTotal & _
             "overdue balances"
```

TABLE 5-5 Arithmetic and string-handling operators

Operator	Symbol	Example	Result
Addition	+	5 + 2	7
Subtraction	–	5 - 2	3
Multiplication	*	5 * 2	10
Division	/	5 / 2	2.5
Integer division (performs a division operation and returns the integer portion of the result)	\	5 \ 2	2
Exponentiation	^	5 ^ 2	25
String concatenation	&, +	"Hello" & "Joline" "Hello" + "Joline"	"Hello Joline"
Adds an expression to the current variable value	+=	Dim intCount As Integer = 3 intCount += 1	4

ENFORCING STRONG DATA TYPING

Recall that VB requires you to declare variables explicitly before you use them in program commands. When you write a command that uses an incompatible data type in an operation such as an arithmetic or string-handling expression, VB attempts to convert the value to the correct data type. For example, if you attempt to concatenate a number variable to a text string, VB converts the number to a string, then performs the concatenation. Similarly, if you attempt to add an integer to a floating-point number, VB converts the floating-point number to an integer, then performs the operation.

> **TIP:** In an arithmetic expression that requires data type conversions, the VB compiler assigns the data type of the leftmost value to the expression, then converts the other values.

This process of converting values to compatible data types is called *weak typing*. Weak typing is the lazy programmer's friend. Programmers do not have to think through the types of data that users might enter or that a program might read from a file or other data source. They do not need to worry about specifying appropriate data type conversions. In most situations, VB's automatic data type conversions work correctly. The problem with weak typing, however, is that automatic type conversions do not always make the correct conversion.

Consider the following code block:

```
'Update bank account balance
Dim sngCheckingWithdrawal As Single = 10.56
Dim intAccountBalance As Integer = 100
'Subtract withdrawal from account balance
intAccountBalance = intAccountBalance - sngCheckingWithdrawal
```

In this example, an automatic data type conversion occurs in the last command, which subtracts the checking withdrawal amount, a Single floating-point data type, from the account balance, an Integer data type. VB assigns the Integer data type to the expression, and automatically converts the Single data type value (10.56) to an Integer data type. When it performs this conversion, it rounds the value up to 11 before it performs the subtraction operation. It then subtracts 11 from the integer value of 100, which leaves the customer with a checking account balance of $89 rather than $90.44.

In contrast, *strong typing* requires programmers to explicitly specify the data type of each expression in an operation and explicitly convert values into compatible types as needed. If the programmer does not do this, an error occurs. This means more work for the programmer. However, strong typing is recognized universally as the preferred way to write code that has fewer errors and is easier to maintain.

Many programming languages require strong typing. By default, the VB IDE is configured to allow weak typing, but you should not use it. To configure the IDE to enforce strong typing, open the VB IDE Options dialog box in Figure 5-16 and enable Option Strict by setting its value to On.

When you enable the Option Strict option in the VB IDE Options dialog box, all future VB projects that you create in the IDE enable Option Strict. To enable Option Strict, click Tools on the menu bar, then click Options. In the Options dialog box, open the Projects and Solutions node, and select VB Defaults. To enable or disable Option strict in an individual project, select the Compile tab on the project Property pages and modify the project's Option Strict setting.

FIGURE 5-16 VB IDE Options dialog box

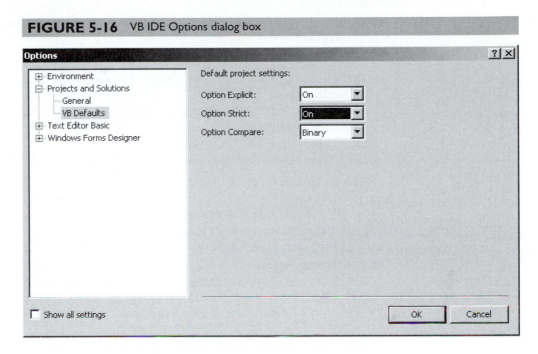

When you enable Option Strict, the VB compiler does not compile commands that contain incompatible data types. Figure 5-17 shows how the code that updates the bank account balance appears in the Code editor when Option Strict is enabled.

Note that the Code editor places a wavy blue line under the subtraction operation to indicate that it is not a legal conversion. When you place the mouse pointer on the error, a hint describes the problem.

Even with strong typing, VB performs certain types of automatic data type conversions. For example, VB performs automatic conversions that widen the data type with no loss of data. When you make a data type wider, the data type stores more information than the original data type. For example, a variable with the Single data type (which includes values to the right of the decimal point) can store anything that a variable with the Integer data type (which does not include decimal values) stores. When Option Strict is enabled, VB automatically converts an Integer value to a Single value. However, it does not convert a Single value to an Integer value, as is attempted in Figure 5-17.

From this point forward, we configure all projects to require strong typing. When you change the VB IDE's default setting to require strong typing, the current project

FIGURE 5-17 Code with incompatible type conversion (Option Strict enabled)

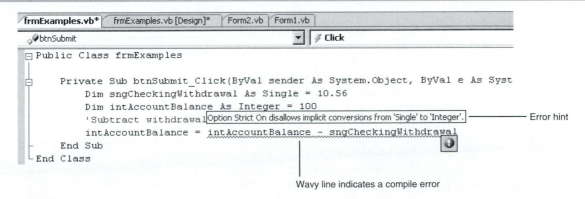

and all future projects will require strong typing. This change does not affect projects that you created before you changed the setting.

To configure the VB IDE to require strong typing:

1. In the VB IDE, click Tools on the menu bar, then click Options. The Options dialog box opens.
2. If necessary, open the Projects and Solutions node in the left-hand pane, then select VB Defaults, as shown in Figure 5-16.
3. Open the Option Strict list, and select On.
4. Click OK to close the Options dialog box and apply the change.

You can alternatively set Option Strict setting to On for individual projects. You might do this to convert a project you created prior to setting the IDE's default setting to On or if you work in a computer lab that does not allow you to change the IDE's default settings. To change the Option Strict setting for an individual project, open the project's Property pages, select the Compile tab, open the Option Strict list, and select On, as shown in Figure 5-18.

TIP: Recall that to open a project's Property Pages, right-click the project in the Solution Explorer, then click Properties.

After you enable Option Strict for a project, the setting is saved with the project. If you open the project on a different computer in which the IDE is configured with Option Strict disabled, the project still uses Option Strict as enabled.

FIGURE 5-18 Setting Option Strict to On for a project

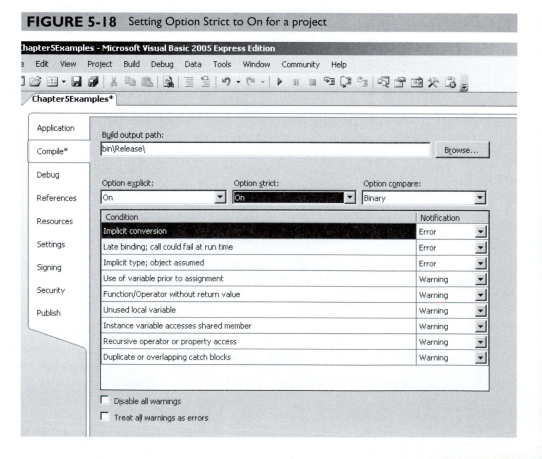

TABLE 5-6   Data type conversion functions

Function	ReturnType	Example Expression
CBool(*Expression*)	Boolean	blnFlag = CBool(strStatus)
CDate(*Expression*)	Date	datMyDate = CDate(strMyDate)
CStr(*Expression*)	String	strNumber = CStr(intNumber)
CObj(*Expression*)	Object	objStudent = CObj(strStudent)
CSng(*Expression*)	Single	sngTotal = CSng(intTotal)
CDbl(*Expression*)	Double	dblTotal = CDbl(intTotal)
CByte(*Expression*)	Byte	bytAge = CByte(intAge)
CShort(*Expression*)	Short	shtAge = CShort(intAge)
CInt(*Expression*)	Integer	intAge = CInt(dblTotal)
CLng(*Expression*)	Long	lngTotal = CLng(intTotal)
CType(*Expression,Type*)	Specified type	intAge = CType(dblTotal, Integer)

Data Type Conversions

When you enforce strong data typing in your projects, you must use commands to convert values from one data type to another explicitly. Table 5-6 summarizes commonly used VB conversion functions.

Many VB objects have data type conversion methods that you can use instead of these conversion functions. For example, numeric and date variables have a ToString method that converts the current value of a variable or control to a String data type. (You can find these data type conversion functions in the object's code completion list.) The conversion function or the object method works equally well, and you should use whatever seems easiest in the situation.

The following code block uses both the CStr conversion function and the ToString conversion method to modify the data type of a value with a Single data type to a String data type:

```
Dim sngAccountBalance As Single = 1024.30
Dim strAccountBalance As String

'convert the data type using the CStr function
strAccountBalance = CStr(sngAccountBalance)

'convert the data type using the ToString method
strAccountBalance = sngAccountBalance.ToString
```

Composite Data Types

Earlier you learned about the VB elementary data types, which are data types that store scalar values such as the integer value 3 or the string value "Hello." VB also provides *composite data types,* which are data types that store multiple scalar values. Composite data types are useful for storing and manipulating database records, which contain columns that have different data types. The following subsections describe the array, array list, and structure data types.

Arrays

An *array* is a list of similar data items. Arrays are useful for storing and processing values that a program reads from a file or database. An array has an *index,* which

TABLE 5-7	One-dimensional array
Index	*Value*
0	SUMM08
1	FALL08
2	SPR09

represents the item's position in the array and one or more associated data values. A *one-dimensional array* has one data value. Table 5-7 illustrates a one-dimensional array of term descriptions at Ironwood University.

TIP: In a one-dimensional array, the first item has an index value of zero, the second item has an index value of one, and so forth.

To create a one-dimensional array in VB, use the following general syntax:

```
{Dim|Private|Public} ArrayName(MaxRows) As DataType
```

In this syntax, *ArrayName* represents the name of the array. You preface the array name with the data type prefix of the data that the array stores. *MaxRows* is an integer that represents the maximum number of rows that the array can store. Because the first row has the index value zero, *MaxRows* represents the maximum number of rows you want to store minus one. For example, if you want to store a total of 50 rows, the *MaxRows* value is 49. *DataType* represents the type of data that the array values store. When you declare an array, the program allocates memory to store values for all array rows.

To assign a value to a one-dimensional array, use the following general syntax:

```
ArrayName(Index) = DataValue
```

To retrieve an array value and assign it to a variable, use the following syntax:

```
VariableName = ArrayName(Index)
```

The following commands create a one-dimensional array named strCourseTerms and assign to it the elements shown in Table 5-7. (For this array, we specify the *MaxRows* value as 9, so the array will store a total of 10 rows.) The final command retrieves one of the array values and assigns it to a previously declared variable.

```
'Declare the array
Dim strCourseTerms(9) As String
'Declare a variable to store an array value
Dim strCurrentTerm As String

'Add data values to the array
strCourseTerms(0) = "SUMM08"
strCourseTerms(1) = "FALL08"
strCourseTerms(2) = "SPR09"

'Reference an array value
strCurrentTerm = strCourseTerms(1)
```

TABLE 5-8	Two-dimensional array	
	Term Abbreviation	*Term Description*
Index	0	1
0	SUMM08	Summer 2008
1	FALL08	Fall 2008
2	SPR09	Spring 2009

A *two-dimensional array* contains two data values. Both data values must have the same data type. In a two-dimensional array, both the columns and the rows have indexes. Table 5-8 illustrates a two-dimensional array that stores term abbreviations and associated descriptions.

In a two-dimensional array, the first dimension represents the column index value, and the second dimension represents the row index value. For example, the index coordinate (0,0) represents the value "SUMM08," (1,0) represents "Summer 2008," and (0,1) represents "FALL08."

Use the following general syntax to declare a two-dimensional array and assign its data values:

```
{Dim|Private|Public} ArrayName (MaxColumns, MaxRows) As DataType
ArrayName(ColumnIndex, RowIndex) = DataValue
```

The following commands create the two-dimensional array in Table 5-8, assign its data values, and reference two of its values:

```
'Declare the array
Dim strCourseTerms(10) As String

'Declare variables to reference array values
Dim strCurrentTermAbbreviation As String
Dim strCurrentTermDescription As String

'Add data values to the array
strCourseTerms(0,0) = "SUMM08"
strCourseTerms(1,0) = "Summer 2008"
strCourseTerms(0,1) = "FALL08"
strCourseTerms(1,1) = "Fall 2008"
strCourseTerms(2,0) = "SPR09"
strCourseTerms(2,1) = "Spring 2009"

'Reference array values
strCurrentTermAbbreviation = strCourseTerms(0,1)
strCurrentTermDescription = strCourseTerms(1,1)
```

You can create *multidimensional arrays*, which are arrays with three or more dimensions. These are usually avoided, however, because the different dimensions are hard to visualize and manage.

Array Lists

Recall that when you create a multidimensional array, all the column values must have the same data type. What if you want to create an array that stores values with different data types? To do this, you create an *array list*, which is a composite data type that stores a set of values that can be of any data type.

TABLE 5-9 Structure of an array list

Index	Value	Type
0	SUMM08	String
1	Summer 2008	String
2	1/21/2008	Date
3	FALL08	String
4	Fall 2008	String
5	3/25/2008	Date

An array list is similar to a one-dimensional array, except that it can store values of any data type. Table 5-9 shows the structure of an array list.

Note that the array list has an index indicating the row position and a value that you associate with the index value. Also note that the values are of different data types: "SUMM08" and "Summer 2008" are text strings, while 1/21/2008, which represents the first day that students can enroll in the term, is a date.

An array list's value can be another composite data type, such as an array or another array list. An array list has methods for performing data operations such as sorting values and inserting, updating, and deleting values in specific array locations. These methods are not available with standard arrays. This makes an array list a better choice than an array if you do not know how many items will eventually be stored in it and need array list methods like count, sort, etc. To create an array list, you use the following general syntax:

```
{Dim|Private|Public} ArrayListName As New ArrayList
```

This declaration creates a new object that is of the type ArrayList. After you create the array list, you can work with it using its properties and methods. Figure 5-19 illustrates commonly used array list properties and methods.

FIGURE 5-19 Commonly used array list properties and methods

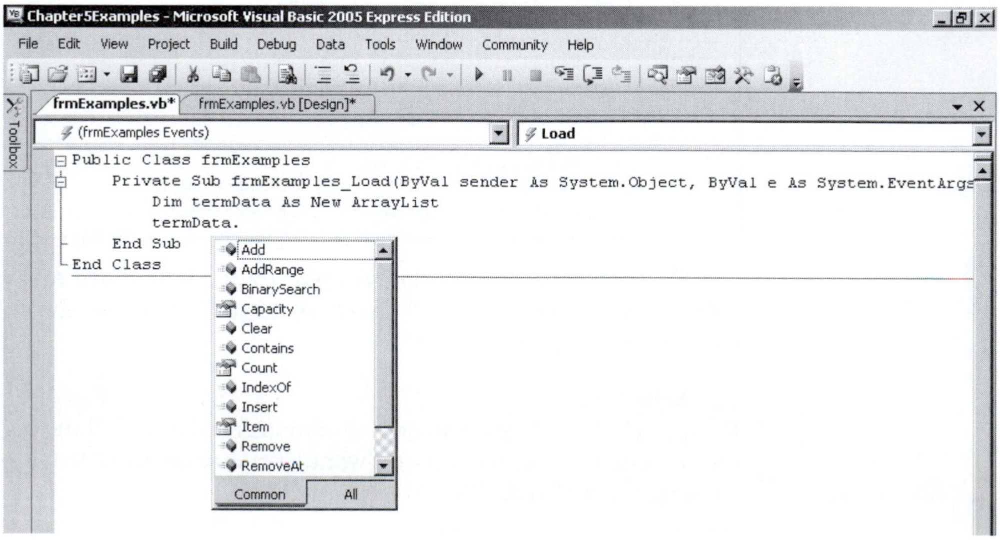

To reference a value in an array list, use the following general syntax:

```
ArrayListName(Index)
```

An important feature of an array list is that it stores the data items as objects rather than as elementary data type values. When retrieving an item from an array list with Option Strict On, consider storing the retrieved value in a variable of the Object data type. This provides flexibility in working with the list items, especially if you do not know the item data type at design time.

The following commands illustrate how to create an array list, use the Add method to add the first three items in Table 5-9 to the list, and then display the value of a specific data item:

```
'Declare the array list
Dim TermData As New ArrayList

'Declare an object variable
'to reference a list item
Dim CurrentObject As Object

'Add objects to the list
TermData.Add("SUMM08")
TermData.Add("Summer 2008")
TermData.Add(#1/21/2008#)

'Retrieve and display a specific list object
CurrentObject = TermData(2)
MessageBox.Show(CurrentObject.ToString, "Data", MessageBoxButtons.OK)
```

Structures

A *structure* is a composite data type that allows you to store and manipulate multiple related data items, such as individual fields in a record. A structure can also store procedures that you use to manipulate data items that the structure stores. Each individual data item or procedure is called a *member* of the structure. Table 5-10 illustrates a structure with four members that stores data values about course terms and with a procedure that retrieves the total enrollment for a term.

You can declare a structure within a class declaration, such as the class declaration of a form. The general syntax to declare a structure is:

```
{Public|Private} Structure StructureName
   Public MemberName1 As {DateType|Procedure}
   Public MemberName2 As {DateType|Procedure}
   [. . .]
End Structure
```

This syntax shows that you declare a structure as either a public or private variable. (You do not usually declare a structure as a Dim variable, because the only time you create a Dim variable is in a procedure.) In the structure declaration, you define each member either as an object, with an elementary or composite data type, or as a

TABLE 5-10	Structure that stores term information		
Term Abbreviation	*Term Description*	*TermEnrollmentDate*	*RetrieveCurrentEnrollment (Procedure)*
SUMM08	Summer 2008	1/21/2008	

subroutine or function. Structure members can be public or private variables or procedures; private members are visible only to procedures created in the structure.

You could use the following commands to declare a structure named CourseTerms that represents the data in Table 5-10. This structure declaration appears in the class declaration of a form named frmExamples:

```
Public Class frmExamples
  Private Structure TermStructure
    'declare structure members
    Public TermAbbreviation As String, _
           TermDescription As String, _
           TermEnrollmentDate As Date
    'declare function that is in structure
    Public Function RetrieveTermEnrollment _
                  (ByVal CurrentTermAbbreviation As String) _
                  As Integer
           'commands to retrieve term enrollment
    End Function
  End Structure
End Class
```

To use a structure, first instantiate an instance (row) of the structure, using the following syntax:

```
{Public|Private|Dim} InstanceName As StructureName
```

To assign a value to a structure member, use the following general syntax:

```
InstanceName.MemberName = DataValue
```

The following commands create an instance of the TermStructure and assign values to its members. You can place these commands in any procedure of the class in which you define the structure.

```
Dim CurrentTermData As TermStructure
CurrentTermData.TermAbbreviation = "SUMM08"
CurrentTermData.TermDescription = "Summer 2008"
CurrentTermData.TermEnrollmentDate = #1/21/2008#
```

CONTROLLING PROGRAM FLOW

So far, all the VB program commands that you have seen execute sequentially, beginning with the first command in the code block and ending with the last command. VB supports decision structures to control the program execution path and loops to support iterative operations.

Decision Structures

In VB, decision structures control the program execution path based on whether a Boolean expression is true or false, whether a variable has a specific value, or whether an error condition occurs. VB's most commonly used decision structures are If...Then...Else, Select...Case, and Try...Catch...Finally. The following subsections describe these decision structures.

TABLE 5-11   VB comparison operators

Operator	Description	Example Condition
=	Equals	`txtUserName.Text = "morrislm"`
>	Greater than	`intCurrentAge < 30`
<	Less than	`intCurrentAge > 18`
>=	Greater than or equal to	`intCurrentAge >= 18`
<=	Less than or equal to	`intCurrentAge <= 30`
<>	Not equal	`txtStudentPin.Text <> "1234"`
Is	Compares two objects to determine if they are equivalent	`objStudent1 Is objCurrentStudent`
IsNot	Compares two objects to determine if they are not equivalent	`objStudent1 Is Not objCurrentStudent`
TypeOf ... Is *ObjectType*	Determines if an object is a specified data type	`TypeOf objCurrent Is TextBox`
TypeOf ... IsNot *ObjectType*	Determines if an object is not a specified data type	`TypeOf objCurrent IsNot TextBox`

If...Then...Else

The `If...Then...Else` decision structure contains one or more *Conditions*, which are Boolean expressions that evaluate as either true or false. Program execution proceeds based on the evaluation outcomes. A condition usually compares two values, such as a variable and a constant. Table 5-11 summarizes VB's comparison operators and provides example conditions.

Expressions in conditions can be of any of the elementary data types. A condition must compare similar data types, however. For example, you cannot compare strings with numbers or dates with strings, unless you include commands to make the appropriate data type conversions prior to the comparison operation.

You can create complex conditions by joining individual conditions using the VB logical operators. Table 5-12 summarizes the VB logical operators and describes their outcomes.

TABLE 5-12   VB logical operators

Operator	Syntax	True If	False If
And	`Expression1 And Expression2`	Both are true.	Either is false.
Or	`Expression1 Or Expression2`	Either is true.	Both are false.
Xor	`Expression1 And Expression2`	Only one is true.	Both are true. Both are false.
Not	`Not Expression`	Expression is false.	Expression is true.
AndAlso	`Expression1 AndAlso Expression2`	Both are true.	Either is false.
OrElse	`Expression1 OrElse Expression2`	Either is true.	Both are false.

Using the new `AndAlso` and `OrElse` operators can improve program performance. With the `AndAlso` logical operator, VB evaluates the first expression. If its value is false, VB does not evaluate the second expression because the overall expression's value will always be false. Similarly, with the `OrElse` logical operator, VB evaluates the first expression; if it returns true, VB does not evaluate the second expression, because the result of the overall expression will always be true.

The simplest format of the `If...Then...Else` decision structure is the `If` structure, which has the following general syntax:

```
If Condition Then
    Program statements
End If
```

In this decision structure, if *Condition* evaluates as true, then the *Program statements* execute. Otherwise, nothing executes. The following commands illustrate a simple `If` decision structure:

```
Dim strColor As String = "Red"
If strColor = "Red" Then
  MessageBox.Show("Color is Red", _
                  "Color Message", MessageBoxButtons.OK)
End If
```

The `If...Else` variation allows you to specify alternate program statements that execute if the condition is false. It has the following general syntax:

```
If Condition Then
    Program statements
Else
    Alternate Program statements
End If
```

The following commands illustrate an `If...Else` decision structure:

```
Dim strColor As String = "Red"
If strColor = "Red" Then
  MessageBox.Show("Color is Red", _
                  "Color Message", MessageBoxButtons.OK)
Else
  MessageBox.Show("Color is not Red", _
                  "Color Message", MessageBoxButtons.OK)
End If
```

The most complex and powerful version is `If...ElseIf...Else`, which allows you to test for several different, unrelated conditions and to execute alternate program statements based on the outcome. The `If...ElseIf...Else` decision structure has the following general syntax:

```
If Condition1 Then
    Program statements
ElseIf Condition2 Then
    Alternate Program statements
ElseIf ...
Else
    Alternate Program statements
End If
```

When you use this decision structure, the program first evaluates *Condition1*. If *Condition1* is false, then the program moves on and evaluates *Condition2*. If *Condiition2* is false, then the program continues to evaluate conditions until it finds one that evaluates as true. It then executes the associated program statements and exits the structure. If none of the `ElseIf` conditions are true, the program executes the program statements under `Else`. An `If...ElseIf...Else` structure can contain as many `ElseIf` clauses as you need.

The following commands illustrate an `If...ElseIf...Else` structure:

```
Dim strColor As String = "Red"
If strColor = "Red" Then
  MessageBox.Show("Color is Red", _
                  "Color Message", MessageBoxButtons.OK)
ElseIf strColor = "Green" Then
  MessageBox.Show("Color is Green", _
                  "Color Message", MessageBoxButtons.OK)
ElseIf strColor = "Yellow" Then
  MessageBox.Show("Color is Yellow", _
                  "Color Message", MessageBoxButtons.OK)
Else
  MessageBox.Show("Color is not known", _
                  "Color Message", MessageBoxButtons.OK)
End If
```

Currently, the block displays a message box stating "Color is Red." If the initial value of strColor had been assigned as the text string "Blue," then the message box displays "Color is not known."

Select...Case

The `Select...Case` decision structure evaluates the value of a specific object and executes different program statements depending on the object's value. It uses the following general syntax:

```
Select TestExpression
    Case Value1
        Program statements
    Case Value2
        Program statements
    ...
    Case Else
        Program statements
End Select
```

TestExpression must evaluate to one of the elementary data types, such as a String or Integer value. *Value1, Value2,* and so forth represent possible values of the *TestExpression*. You can include as many `Case` statements as you need in the decision structure. If *TestExpression* does not evaluate to any of the values, the `Case Else` program statements execute.

The following commands illustrate a `Select...Case` decision structure:

```
Dim strColor as String = "Red"
Select Case strColor
  Case "Red"
    MessageBox.Show("Color is Red", _
                    "Color Message", MessageBoxButtons.OK)
```

```
          Case "Green"
            MessageBox.Show("Color is Green", _
                            "Color Message", MessageBoxButtons.OK)
          Case "Yellow"
            MessageBox.Show("Color is Yellow", _
                            "Color Message", MessageBoxButtons.OK)
          Case Else
            MessageBox.Show("Color is unknown", _
                            "Color Message", MessageBoxButtons.OK)
    End Select
```

A `Select...Case` decision structure always compares the *TestExpression* value to the values in the individual `Case` statements until it finds a match. Although our `If...ElseIf...Else` program example had the same functionality as the `Select...Case` example, the two decision structures are different in an important way: The `Select...Case` structure uses the same comparison expression for all cases, while the `If...ElseIf...Else` structure can use different comparison expressions.

The following program illustrates an `If...ElseIf...Else` decision structure that uses more complex conditions:

```
Dim Color As String = "Red"
Dim Size as String = "Large"
If Color = "Red" And Size = "Large" Then
  MessageBox.Show _
    ("Color is Red and Size is Large", _
     "Color Message", MessageBoxButtons.OK)
ElseIf Color = "Green" And Size = "Large" Then
  MessageBox.Show _
    ("Color is Green and Size is Large", _
     "Color Message", MessageBoxButtons.OK)
Else
  MessageBox.Show _
    ("Color and Size are unknown", _
     "Color Message", MessageBoxButtons.OK)
End If
```

`Try...Catch...Finally`

In general, a TRY/CATCH block is a program structure that contains a series of program commands in the TRY block and a series of error-handling commands in the CATCH block. If an exception, or run-time error, occurs in any of the TRY block's program commands, execution immediately switches to the CATCH block, which contains exception handlers, that is, commands to handle exceptions. In VB, a `Try...Catch...Finally` block has the following general syntax:

```
Try
  Program statements being monitored for errors
Catch
  Exception handlers
[Finally
  Program statements that always execute]
End Try
```

In this syntax, the `Try` block contains a series of program statements that can potentially "throw" an error, that is, cause an error to occur. (In database application development, these are usually program statements that make database connections or retrieve database data.) The `Catch` block contains one or more exception handlers, which are code blocks either displaying information about the error or programmatically correcting it. The optional `Finally` block contains program statements that always execute. These are typically "clean-up" statements, such as commands to close a database connection or file that the `Try` block commands open.

The following program commands illustrate a typical VB `Try...Catch...Finally` structure:

```
Try
  ' try to open a file
  FileOpen(1, "TESTFILE", OpenMode.Input)
Catch ex As Exception
  MessageBox.Show(ex.Message)
Finally
  'close the file
  FileClose(1)
End Try
```

In these commands, the `Try` block contains a command that attempts to open a file named "TESTFILE." (You do not need to understand how the FileOpen command works because we do not use it elsewhere in this book; we only use it here to illustrate an exception.) The `Catch` block contains the clause `ex As Exception`, which creates an instance of the VB *Exception class,* which is a class with properties and methods for handling errors. The `Catch` block then executes an exception handler that displays a message box containing the current exception's error message. The `ex.Message` command displays the exception's error message. In this example, it displays the system error message. The `Finally` block "cleans up" by closing the file. Figure 5-20 illustrates the message box that the Catch block's exception handler displays when the system cannot find the file.

Loops

A loop is a program structure that executes a series of program statements multiple times until it reaches an exit condition. A loop can be a *pretest loop,* which first evaluates the exit condition and then executes the program statements, or a *posttest loop,* which executes the program statements first and then evaluates the exit condition. A loop can also execute a specific number of iterations. In this book, you use the VB `Do`, `Do While`, `Do...Loop Until`, `For...Next`, and `For Each...Next` loops.

FIGURE 5-20   Message box that exception handler displays

Could not find file 'C:\sqlserver\Solutions\Chapter5\TutorialExamples\bin\Debug\TESTFILE'.

OK

Do Loops

A Do loop can be either a pretest or a posttest loop. It has the following general syntax:

```
Do
  [Program statements]
  If Condition = True Then Exit Do
  [Program statements]
Loop
```

You can structure a Do loop as a posttest loop if the program statements execute before the command that tests the *Condition*. You structure it as a pretest loop if the program statements execute after the command that tests the *Condition*.

TIP: Recall that *Condition* is a Boolean expression to evaluate as either true or false. *Condition* can be a value comparison or a test to see if all the records in a file or database query have been processed.

The following example illustrates both types of the Do loop:

```
'Do loop structured as posttest loop
Dim intCounter As Integer = 0
Do
  intCounter = intCounter + 1
  If intCounter = 10 Then Exit Do
Loop
MessageBox.Show(intCounter.ToString)

'Do loop structured as pretest loop
intCounter = 0
Do
  If intCounter = 10 Then Exit Do
  intCounter = intCounter + 1
Loop
MessageBox.Show(intCounter.ToString)
```

Do While Loop

The VB Do While loop is a pretest loop that first evaluates a *Condition*. If the *Condition* is true, the program statements execute and the loop evaluates the *Condition* again. When the *Condition* becomes false, the loop exits. The Do While loop has the following general syntax:

```
Do While Condition
  Program statements
Loop
```

The following commands illustrate the Do While loop:

```
Dim intCounter As Integer = 0
Do While intCounter < 10
  intCounter = intCounter + 1
Loop
MessageBox.Show(intCounter.ToString)
```

Do...Loop Until Loop

The VB `Do...Loop Until` loop is a posttest loop that executes some program statements, then evaluates a *Condition*. If the *Condition* is false, the program statements execute again and the loop evaluates the *Condition* again. When the *Condition* becomes true, the loop exits. The `Do...Loop Until` loop has the following general syntax:

```
Do
    Program statements
Loop Until Condition
```

The following commands illustrate the `Do...Loop Until` loop:

```
Dim intCounter As Integer = 0
Do
  intCounter = intCounter + 1
Loop Until i = 10
MessageBox.Show(intCounter.ToString)
```

For...Next Loop

The `For...Next` loop is a loop that you set to iterate a specific number of times. It has a built-in *CounterVariable* that acts as the counter controlling the number of times the loop executes. The loop automatically increments the counter by a *StepValue* that you specify.

The `For...Next` loop has the following general syntax:

```
For CounterVariable = StartValue To EndValue [StepValue]
     [Program statements]
     [If Condition Then Exit For]
     [Program statements]
Next [CounterVariable]
```

In this syntax, *CounterVariable* specifies the variable that controls the number of times the loop executes. (*CounterVariable* is declared outside the loop.) *StartValue* specifies the *CounterVariable's* start value, and *EndValue* specifies its end value. *StepValue* specifies the value by which the *CounterVariable* increments with each loop iteration. If you omit *StepValue*, it defaults to a step value of one. The loop increments the *CounterVariable* automatically. The `If Condition` clause allows you to specify a *Condition* that, when true, causes the loop to exit before it performs the specified number of iterations (however this is optional—the loop will terminate when the counter variable reaches its end value).

The following commands illustrate `For...Next` loops. The first loop increments by the default value of one. The second loop increments by a specified value of two, and uses the `If Condition` clause to exit the loop early.

```
'For...Next loop that iterates all 10 times
Dim intCounter As Integer
For intCounter = 0 To 10
  MessageBox.Show(intCounter.ToString)
Next intCounter

'For...Next loop that steps by 2
'and exits early
For intCounter = 0 To 1000 Step 2
  If intCounter > 10 Then Exit For
  MessageBox.Show(intCounter.ToString)
Next intCounter
```

For Each...Next Loop

You use the For Each...Next loop with VB collections. A *collection* is any data structure that represents a group of related items, called *elements*. For example, an array list is a collection. You use the For Each...Next loop to process every object in a collection, starting with the first object and continuing to the last. You can optionally include an If *Condition* clause to exit the loop early.

The For Each...Next loop uses the following general syntax:

```
For Each ElementName In CollectionName
   [Program Statements]
   [If Condition Then Exit For]
   [Program statements]
Next
```

The following commands create the array list in Table 5-9 and then use a For Each...Next loop to display the contents of each array list object in a message box:

```
'Declare the array list
Dim TermData As New ArrayList

'Declare an object variable
'to reference a list item
Dim CurrentObject As Object

'Add objects to the list
TermData.Add("SUMM08")
TermData.Add("Summer 2008")
TermData.Add(#1/21/2008#)

'Use a For Each...Next loop
'to display each element
For Each CurrentObject In TermData
  MessageBox.Show(CurrentObject.ToString)
Next
```

USER-DEFINED PROCEDURES

VB procedures are subroutines or functions that other procedures can call. You have already seen subroutines that serve as event handlers, such as the one in Figure 5-11. The following subsections describe how to create user-defined subroutines and functions.

Subroutines

A subroutine is a named procedure that can receive input parameters and manipulate variable values. You create a subroutine using the following general syntax:

```
{Public|Private} Sub SubroutineName ([ParameterList])
    Program statements
End Sub
```

You create a subroutine in a class declaration. You use the Public or Private keyword to specify the scope of the subroutine: a public subroutine is visible outside its class, while a private subroutine is visible only in its class.

TIP: In older VB versions (6.0 and earlier), programmers often created procedures in *modules,* which were code files containing commands that could be used anywhere in a project. All versions of VB .NET continue to support modules; however, we recommend placing this code in classes, which are easier to maintain.

The optional *ParameterList* specifies the values that the procedure receives. In the discussion of event handlers earlier in the chapter, we showed that a VB *ParameterList* has the following general syntax:

```
(PassingMethod Parameter1 DataType,
 PassingMethod Parameter2 DataType, ...)
```

The *PassingMethod* specifies how the calling program passes the parameter to the procedure. A program can use the `ByValue` keyword and pass a parameter *by value,* which means that the procedure is passed a copy of the data value as the parameter. Alternatively, a program can use the `ByRef` keyword and pass a parameter *by reference,* which means that the procedure passes a reference to the memory location that stores the parameter and the original parameter value is accessed (not a copy). By default, VB passes all parameters by value. If you omit the *PassingMethod* specification in a procedure declaration, VB automatically inserts `ByVal`.

To clarify this, when a calling program passes a parameter to a procedure by value, VB makes a temporary copy of the variable for use by the procedure. If the procedure changes the variable's value, this change is made to the copy of the variable, not to the original. When execution returns to the calling program, the variable value that it passed to the procedure remains unchanged. When a calling program passes a parameter by reference, VB passes a pointer to the memory location where the original data value is stored. If the procedure changes the variable's value, this change is made to the original variable value. When execution returns to the calling program, the value is changed.

The following commands create a subroutine named ComputeArea that calculates the areas of different types of shapes. (You would place this code in the class definition of a form.) The subroutine receives a String parameter that specifies the shape type (either "Rectangle" or "Triangle"), and two Double parameters that represent the shape's length and width. The subroutine displays a message box that shows the calculated area.

```
Private Sub ComputeArea_
              (ByVal strShapeType As String, _
               ByVal dblLength As Double, _
               ByVal dblWidth As Double)
  Dim dblArea As Double
  Select Case strShapeType
    Case "Rectangle"
      dblArea = dblLength * dblWidth
    Case "Triangle"
      dblArea = 0.5 * dblLength * dblWidth
  End Select
  'display area in message box
  MessageBox.Show(dblArea.ToString)
End Sub
```

To call a subroutine, use the following general command:

```
SubroutineName(Parameter1Value, Parameter2Value, ...)
```

In this command, the parameters must appear in the same order as in the command that creates the subroutine, and they must have the correct data types. For the ComputeArea subroutine, pass the value that specifies the shape type first and then the number values that represent the length and width. To call the subroutine and have it display the area of a rectangle with length 25 and width 4, use the following command, which you could place in an event handler:

```
ComputeArea("Rectangle", 25, 4)
```

Functions

A function is a procedure that can receive one or more input parameters and returns a single value. The general syntax to create a function is:

```
{Public|Private} Function ProcedureName _
                            ([ParameterList]) _
                            As DataType
      Program statements
      Return ValueOfFunctionType
End Sub
```

As with a subroutine, you create a function in a class declaration and use the `Public` or `Private` keyword to specify the function's scope. The `As DataType` clause, which appears after the *ParameterList*, specifies the data type of the value that the function returns.

The following commands create a function named CalculateAge, which receives an input parameter of a date of birth and returns a value that represents the person's age in years.

```
Private Function CalculateAge (ByVal datInputDOB As Date) As Long
   'determine the current system date
   Dim datCurrentDate As Date = Now.Date
   'return the difference between the input date
   'and the current system date
   Return DateDiff(DateInterval.Year, datInputDOB, datCurrentDate)
End Function
```

TIP: In these commands, `Now.Date` returns the current system date. `DateDiff` is a system function that returns the difference between two dates.

To call a function, use the following general command:

```
VariableName = FunctionName (Parameter1Value, Parameter2Value, ...)
```

In this syntax, *VariableName* represents a previously declared variable that has the same data type as the function. As with a subroutine, the parameter values must be passed in the same order as you listed them when you created the function, and they must be of the correct data type. Use the following commands to declare a variable to store the function return variable, call the function, pass to it a date of birth of 7/14/1988, then display the output in a message box:

```
Dim lngCurrentAge As Long
lngCurrentAge = CalculateAge(#7/14/1958#)
MessageBox.Show(lngCurrentAge.ToString)
```

CUSTOM CLASSES

VB is an object-oriented language that represents all program elements as objects. So far, we have used built-in classes to create objects, such as forms and controls. VB enables programmers to create custom classes and then instantiate class objects.

Recall that a class defines object properties and methods. Properties store the current state of an object, and methods are procedures in the class. You might create a custom class named BankCustomers that defines the properties and methods of customers of a bank. Properties could include name, address, account number, and account balance. Methods might include procedures for opening an account, making a deposit, or requesting an account balance.

You can create custom classes in VB projects to perform application tasks. Why create custom classes? The advantage is that the code for an object class is a self-contained module. You can use it in different applications or use it several times within a single application, and multiple programmers can use it. When you create complex applications with many forms and controls and thousands of lines of code, classes speed up development time and make the application easier to maintain and debug.

TIP: The controls you drag from the Toolbox to your forms are classes that instantiate objects of themselves when you drop them on a form. Although the classes you make in this chapter do not appear in the Toolbox, you can use them as often as you need to instantiate objects of themselves.

The following subsections describe how to create a custom class in a VB project and how to create and reference a class object. The final subsections describe class property elements and show how you can incorporate exception handling into classes.

Creating a Custom Class

To create a custom class in a VB project, click Project on the menu bar, then click Add Class. A dialog box opens that allows you to specify the class name and create the class. After you create the class, a new tab appears in the Document window that contains the class declaration, which has the following syntax:

```
Public Class ClassName
   Commands to define class properties and methods
End Class
```

NOTE: VB allows you to declare other types of classes than Public, but we will focus on Public classes.

After you create the class, you can add commands to define class properties and methods. In a class declaration, it is useful to create code *regions,* which are areas containing code that creates similar items. For example, you might create a region that contains all the class's public variables, and another region that contains all the class's methods. The Code editor represents each region as a node that you can either expand to view its underlying code or collapse to view only the region description. By creating code regions, you can view the class's code on a single display window and expand the region in which you are currently working. To create a region, use the following command:

```
#Region "RegionDescription"
  'Region commands
#End Region
```

The #Region keyword defines the beginning of a region; after you enter "*RegionDescription*" and press Enter, the IDE automatically inserts #End Region and creates the nodes you use to collapse or expand the region.

To illustrate a custom class, you will work with a project that contains the form in Figure 5-21. This project contains a form named frmExcitementLevel, which displays a text box that allows the user to enter a type of car and click the Show Level button. A message box then displays the "Excitement Level" for the car type: For car type "Sedan" the excitement level is "Low" and for car type "Convertible" the excitement level is "High." For all other car types, the excitement level is "Unknown."

The form contains a custom class named CarExcitement. Figure 5-22 uses a class diagram to illustrate this class.

This diagram shows that the frmExcitementLevel form instantiates an object named objCarExcitementObject, which is an object of the CarExcitement class. CarExcitement has a public variable named strCarType, which represents the car type, and a public method named DetermineExcitement, which determines the excitement level for different types of cars.

FIGURE 5-21 Project to illustrate a custom class

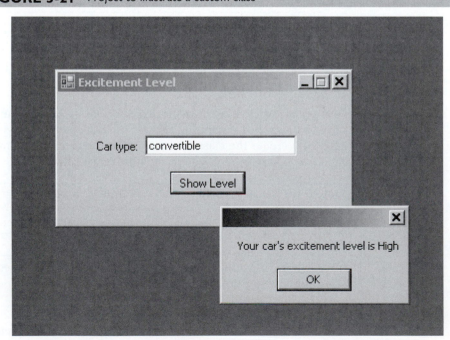

FIGURE 5-22   Class definition of CarExcitement class

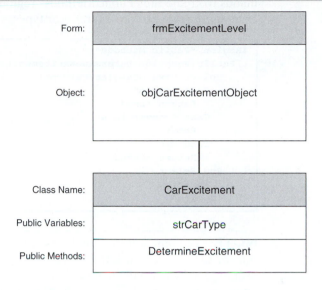

The following steps describe how to open a VB project named OOExample that contains a partially completed project. The form's controls and properties have already been created and configured. The steps show how to create the CarExcitement class and its strCarType public variable and DetermineExcitementLevel public method.

To open the OOExample project and create a custom class:

1. In Windows Explorer, copy the OOExample folder and all its contents from the SQLServer\Chapter5\Datafiles folder to your SQLServer\Chapter5\Solutions folder.
2. In the IDE, click File on the menu bar, click Open Project, navigate to your SQLServer\Chapter5\Solutions\OOExample folder, select OOExample.sln, then click Open. The project appears in the IDE.
3. To create the custom class, click Project on the menu bar, then click Add Class. The Add New Item—OOExample dialog box opens, which allows you to add different types of items to the project.

TIP: Another way to add a custom class to a project is to right-click the project in the Solution Explorer, point to Add, then click Class.

---

4. Confirm that the Class template is selected, change the Name field to CarExcitement.vb, then click Add. A new tab appears with the title "CarExcitement.vb," and displays the class declaration in the Code editor.
5. Place the insertion point on the blank line in the class declaration, then add the following commands to define a code region named "Public Variables" and the class's public variable. (Note that after you type the first line and press Enter, the IDE automatically inserts the third line.)

```
#Region "Public Variables"
  Public strCarType As String
#End Region
```

6. Close the "Public Variables" code region.

7. Create a new blank line under "Public Variables," then enter the following commands to create the "Public Methods" region and a function that returns the excitement level for the different car types:

```
#Region "Public Methods"
  Public Function DetermineExcitementLevel() As String
    Select Case LCase(strCarType)
      Case "sedan"
        Return "Low"
      Case "convertible"
        Return "High"
      Case Else
        Return "Unknown"
    End Select
  End Function
#End Region
```

NOTE: The function uses the LCase function, which converts the text that follows to all lowercase letters. As a result, it does not matter whether the user enters the car type in uppercase, lowercase, or mixed-case letters. An alternate approach would be to use the string variable's ToLower method. For example: Select Case strCarType.ToLower()

---

8. Save the project.

Creating and Using Custom Class Objects

To use the custom class, you must create a new object instance of the class. To create an object instance, use the following general syntax:

```
{Public|Private} ObjectName As New ClassName
```

In this syntax, `Public` specifies that the object is visible outside the form, and `Private` specifies that the object is visible only in the form. The `New` keyword creates the object and allocates the memory space that stores the object's property values. The *ObjectName* points to the memory location that stores the object. If you omit `New`, the program creates a variable capable of referring to a preexisting object, but it does not allocate memory for a new object's methods and properties. The variable does not reference an actual object unless you assign its value to a preexisting object.

When you create a form control or variable, you can type the item's name followed by a period in the Code editor, and a code completion list appears that shows the item's properties and events. This also happens when you create a new object that you instantiate from a custom class. Figure 5-23 shows the code completion list that appears when you create a new object named objCarExcitementObject.

Note that the code completion list displays default object methods (Equals, GetHashCode, GetType, and ToString) that exist for every object. The list also shows the object's user-defined property (strCarType) and user-defined method (DetermineExcitementLevel).

The following steps show how to create the objCarExcitementObject instance of the CarExcitement custom class. They create an event handler for the form's Submit button that sets the object's strCarType property to the value in the form's text box and that displays a message box calling the object's DetermineExcitementLevel method and showing the car's excitement value.

FIGURE 5-23 Code completion list for a custom class object

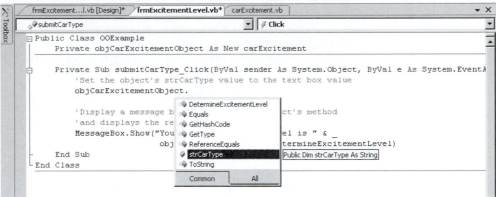

To create and use the new object:

1. Display the frmExcitementLevel form in Code view. To create the new object, place the insertion point on the blank line in the form's class declaration, and add the following command:

```
Private objCarExcitementObject As New CarExcitement
```

2. To create an event handler for the Submit button, open the Object list in Code view, and select btnSubmitCarType. Then open the Event list, and select Click. The declaration for the Click event handler appears in the Code editor.
3. Type the following commands in the event handler declaration:

```
'Set the object's strCarType value
'to the text box value
objCarExcitementObject.strCarType = txtCarType.Text

'Display a message box that calls the
'object's method and displays the result
MessageBox.Show ("Your car's excitement level is " & _
                 objCarExcitementObject.DetermineExcitementLevel)
```

4. Save the project, then run the application. When the form appears, type "Convertible" in the Car type field, then click Show Level. The message box proclaiming "Your car's excitement level is High" should appear.
5. Click OK, then close the application.

Property Elements

A class property stores a data value about an object instance, such as a bank customer name. In the previous example, you defined the car object's type using a public variable. Another way to define a class property is to use a property element. A *property element* has an associated value, and it also has *property procedures,* which are procedures controlling how a property element's value is set or returned.

A property element has a *Set procedure,* which executes when a program command sets the property value, and a *Get procedure,* which executes when a command retrieves the property value. For example, a property that stores the balance of a bank account might use code in a Get property procedure to add accrued interest and subtract service charges before returning the available balance. The Set procedure might provide code that sends an exception notice to the customer when his or her balance falls below a certain level.

To create a property element in a class definition, use the following general syntax:

```
{Public|Private} Property PropertyName() As PropertyDataType
  Get
    Commands that execute when value is retrieved
    Return ClassVariableName
  End Get
  Set (ByVal value As PropertyDataType)
    Commands that execute when value is set
    ClassPrivateVariableName = value
  End Set
End Property
```

In this syntax, you declare the property element as either public or private. The *PropertyDataType* is the data type that the property gets and sets. The Set procedure has a parameter list that declares a variable named `value` that the procedure uses to manipulate the property value before it is set. This value must have the same data type as the property.

Commands in the Set procedure are often used to validate the property value or to modify the value's format. The final command in the Set procedure assigns the property element's `value` to a previously declared private class variable. The Get procedure contains commands that execute when a command retrieves the property value and then returns the current value, represented as the previously declared private class variable.

The following steps demonstrate how to modify the OOExample project so that it stores the text representing Car Type as a property. First, they change the scope of the previously declared strCarType variable to Private. Next they create a property element named TypeOfCar. The element's Set procedure verifies that the car type is either "Sedan" or "Convertible." If it is not, the Set procedure displays a message box describing the available car type values. The Get procedure does not perform additional processing but simply returns the text string representing the type of car.

To add a property element to the custom class:

1. Click the CarExcitement.vb tab to display the class definition.
2. Open the "Public Variables" node, and change the code so that it appears as follows:

```
#Region "Private Variables"
    Private strCarType As String
#End Region
```

3. Type the following commands to create a new region named "Public Properties," then create the property. (This definition references the Private class variable you created in Step 2.)

```
#Region "Public Properties"
   Public Property TypeOfCar() As String
     Get
       Return strCarType
     End Get
     Set(ByVal value As String)
       If value.ToLower <> "sedan" _
       And value.ToLower <> "convertible" Then
         MessageBox.Show("Allowed car types are " & _
                         "Sedan and Convertible")
       End If
       strCarType = value
     End Set
   End Property
#End Region
```

4. Save the project.

To reference a property element, use the following syntax:

```
ObjectName.PropertyName
```

When you enter the *ObjectName* in the Code editor and type a period, the code completion list automatically displays a list of the object's properties and methods. When you create a property element, it appears in this list, and you use it to reference the property value in assignment operations. The following steps modify the OOExample project's Submit button event handler so that it retrieves the object property using the property element rather than the text property of the form's text box. Then the steps test the form to confirm that the new error message appears.

To modify the event handler to use the property element:

1. In the IDE, select the frmExcitementLevel.vb tab to display the form in Code view, then modify the first three lines of the Submit button's event handler so that they appear as follows:

```
'Set the object's TypeOfCar property
'value to the text box value
objCarExcitementObject.TypeOfCar = txtCarType.Text
```

2. Save the project, then run the application.
3. Type Coupe in the Car type field, then click Show Level. Because this is not one of the defined car types, the error message appears.
4. Click OK two times to dismiss the message boxes, then close the application.

Exception Handling in Classes

One of the primary reasons for using property elements in class definitions is to incorporate data validation and error handling. Currently, the TypeOfCar property element monitors the value of the car type and displays a message box if the value is not correct. This performs error handling but demonstrates a poor programming practice because it incorporates interface elements in the object. Suppose a developer who uses the object wants to use a different error message or not show an error message at all? He or she would have to modify the object. These modifications would probably break other applications that use the object.

When a property element detects an error condition, it should create, or "throw," an exception. Each developer who uses the object can then write a custom exception handler to display (or not display) his or her custom message in a `Try...Catch` block. Now you will learn how to create an exception in a property element definition and how to create a custom exception handler.

To create an exception in a property element definition, use the following general syntax:

```
Throw New Exception ("ExceptionMessage")
```

This command creates a new object of the Exception class and sets its default error message text to *ExceptionMessage*. You can include this command in any code in which you want to throw exceptions that are later caught in a `Try...Catch` block.

NOTE: The `Throw New Exception ("ExceptionMessage")` command also causes code execution in a procedure to end and return to the calling procedure. There is no need for a `Return` or `Exit Sub` or `Exit Function` command following `Throw New Exception`.

The following steps modify the OOExample project so that if the CarOfType property's Set procedure encounters an error, it throws an exception rather than displaying a message box. They also modify the form's event handler so that it uses a `Try...Catch` block to catch the error. This places the error-handling actions in the form's event handler rather than in the class definition.

To add exception handling to the class definition:

1. If necessary, select the CarExcitement.vb tab to display the class declaration.
2. Change the eighth and ninth lines of the Public Properties region, which is the command that displays the message box showing the allowed car types, so that it appears as follows:

```
Throw New Exception _
("Allowed car types are sedan and convertible")
```

3. Click the frmExcitementLevel.vb tab to display the form in Code View, then change all the code in the Submit button's event handler so that it appears as follows. (The bolded text shows the new code that you need to insert.)

```
Try
   'Set the object's TypeOfCar property value
   'to the text box value
   objCarExcitementObject.TypeOfCar = txtCarType.Text
   'Display a message box that
   'calls the object's method
   'and displays the car's excitement level
   MessageBox.Show("Your car's excitement level is " & _
                 objCarExcitementObject.DetermineExcitementLevel)
Catch ex As Exception
   MessageBox.Show(ex.Message)
End Try
```

4. Save the project, then run the application.
5. Type Coupe in the Car type field, then click Show Level. This time the message box shows the message that the exception handler defines.

6. Click OK to dismiss the message box, then close the application.

7. Close the project in the IDE.

PROJECTS WITH MULTIPLE FORMS

So far, all the example projects in this chapter have had a single form. Many Windows applications have multiple forms that work together. This section describes how to create a project with several forms. To illustrate this, we use the MultipleForms project, which contains the forms in Figure 5-24.

In this project, the first form, which is named frmFirstForm, contains a text box and button as shown. When you type an entry in the form text box and click Display Second Form, the second form, which is named frmSecondForm, appears and has the application's *focus,* which means that it is the active object. The second form's text box displays the text you typed in the first form. When you click View First Form, the first form reappears. The following steps describe how to open the MultipleForms project, specify the project's startup form, and run the application.

To open the project, specify the startup form, and run the application:

1. In Windows Explorer, copy the \SQLServer\Datafiles\Chapter5\MultipleForms folder and all its contents to your \SQLServer\SolutionFiles\Chapter5 folder.

2. Open the project in the IDE.

3. If necessary, select MultipleForms in the Solution Explorer, then click the Properties button on the Solution Explorer toolbar to display the project's Property Pages.

4. Make sure that the Application tab is selected, open the Startup form list, make sure that frmFirstForm is selected as the project startup form, then close the Property Pages to apply the change.

5. Save the project, then run the application. The first form appears. (If you click the form buttons, nothing happens because you have not written their event handlers yet.)

6. Close the application.

FIGURE 5-24   Forms in the MultipleForms project

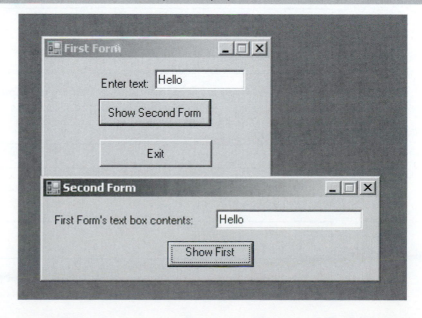

The following subsections describe how to display a second form, reference items on different forms, redisplay and reference the startup form, and create modal forms.

Displaying a Second Form

When you create a new VB Windows application, the IDE automatically creates a class declaration for a default form. When you run the application, VB instantiates the form object and displays the startup form. You can display a second form using the following approaches:

1. By creating a new object of the second form's class

> **NOTE:** This is the only way to display a second form from VB if using Visual Studio .NET 2002 or 2003, and is still required when using other VS 2005 .NET languages such as C#.

2. By displaying the second form using the `Show()` method

The following subsections describe how to implement these approaches.

Creating a New Object of the Second Form's Class

To use this approach, write commands in the first form's class declaration that declare and instantiate an object of the second form using the following general syntax:

```
{Dim|Private|Public} FormObjectName As New FormClassName
FormObjectName.Show()
```

In this syntax, *FormObjectName* is a name you select for the new form instance. *FormClassName* is the name of the form class, as it appears in the form in Code view. The `Show()` method displays the specified form.

What do you use for *FormObjectName?* You could create a form object name that is the same as the form class name; however, this can lead to confusion between form objects and form classes. We suggest specifying form object names by prefacing them with the letter *f*. For example, for the form class frmFirstForm, name the form object fFirstForm. This is how the code would look in the first form's button Click event handler if we used this approach in our MultipleForms example:

```
'Create the second form object
Dim fSecondForm As New frmSecondForm
'Show the second form
fSecondForm.Show()
```

Displaying Using the Second Form Class Definition's `Show()` Method

To display the second form using the second form class definition's `Show()` method, use the following general syntax:

```
FormClassName.Show()
```

For example, the following command displays the second form, whose class is named frmSecondForm:

```
'Show the second form
frmSecondForm.Show()
```

Using this approach, there is no need to create an object of the second form prior to displaying it, because you use the second form's class definition to display the form.

(This syntax reverts to how Visual Basic versions prior to VB .NET displayed subsequent forms.) One minor drawback to the approach is that it does not allow you to display multiple copies of the same form. For example, you might want to show three copies of the second form on the screen at the same time. This is not a common occurrence, however; so in our examples we will use the second, simpler way to display forms. If you want to display several copies of the same form on the screen at the same time, you need to use the first approach and declare object variables for each instance of the form you want to display, then show the multiple copies using each object's `Show()` method.

The following steps describe how to create the event handler for the Display Second Form button in frmFirstForm. This event handler uses the `Show()` method to show frmSecondForm.

To create the event handler that displays the second form:

1. In the Solution Explorer, select frmFirstForm.vb, then click View Designer on the Solution Explorer toolbar to view the form in Designer view.
2. To create the event handler, double-click the Display Second Form button on the form. The form opens in Code view and displays the declaration for the Click event handler.
3. Type the following commands in the event handler to create and display the second form:

```
'Show the second form
frmSecondForm.Show()
```

4. Save the project, then run the application. The first form appears.
5. Click Display Second Form. The second form appears.
6. Close the second form window, then close the first form window.

Referencing Items on Different Forms

To reference a form item on a different form, preface the item name with the form's name, using the following general syntax:

```
FormName.ItemName.{Property|Method}
```

In the MultipleForms project, the second form's name is frmSecondForm, and the Name property value of its text box is txtSecondText. You reference this text box's Text property as follows:

```
frmSecondForm.txtSecondTextbox.Text = txtFirstTextbox.Text
```

The following steps describe how to add commands to the first form's Show Second Form button event handler so that the text the user types in the first form appears in the text box on the second form. To do this, the first form must reference the text box on the second form.

To set the text in the second form's text box so it displays the text in the first form's text box:

1. Make sure that the frmFirstForm.vb tab is selected, then add the following command as the first command in the btnDisplaySecondForm_Click event handler, just before the comment describing the frmSecondForm.Show() command:

```
frmSecondForm.txtSecondTextbox.Text = txtFirstTextbox.Text
```

2. Save the project, then run the application.

3. Type any text in the text box, then click Display Second Form. The second form appears, and its message box displays the text you typed in the first form's message box.

4. Close both form windows to exit the application.

Referencing the Startup Form on Subsequent Forms

So far you have learned how to display forms subsequent to the Startup form and how to reference items on subsequent forms. How do you reference items on the Startup form? Preface the item name and property with the form name. For example, the following command references the first form's text box in the second form's Code file:

```
frmFirstForm.txtFirstText.Text = txtSecondText.Text
```

In the MultipleForms project, when you click the second form's Change First Form's Text button, the first form should display the text the user types in the second form's text box. To make this happen, create an event handler for the second form's Show First Form button that changes the text in the first form. The following steps show how to do this.

To reference the startup form in the second form:

1. Select frmSecondForm.vb in the Solution Explorer, then click View Design to open the second form in Designer view.

2. Double-click the Change First Form's Text button to create a Click event handler declaration.

3. Type the following commands in the event handler to assign the second form's text box text to the first form's text box:

```
'Alter the text in the first form
'from the second form
frmFirstForm.txtFirstTextbox.Text = txtSecondTextbox.Text
```

4. Save the project, then run the application.

5. Type any text in the text box, then click Display Second Form. The second form appears, and its text box displays the text you typed in the first form's message box.

6. Delete the text in the second form's text box, type something different, then click Change First Form's Text. View the second form, and note that the text in the first form has changed.

7. Close both forms.

Displaying, Hiding, and Exiting Modal Forms

In this project, both forms are visible and active, and you can multitask between them. In practice, most applications allow only one form to be active at a time, and usually the first form is not visible when the second form appears. To make an application allow only one active form at a time, you must create modal forms. A *modal form* commands all the application's attention. A user cannot interact with any other forms in the application until he or she closes or hides the modal form.

To open a form so that it is modal, use the `ShowDialog()` method instead of the `Show()` method. The `ShowDialog()` method has the following syntax:

```
FormName.ShowDialog()
```

When you execute this command in a form, code execution pauses and the second form opens. When the user closes the second form, execution resumes in the first form with the command following the command that calls the `ShowDialog()` method.

You usually hide the calling form when you display a second modal form. To do this, use the `Hide()` method, which has the following syntax:

```
FormName.Hide()
```

When you hide a form, it is still in memory, and its objects are still available to other forms in the application. It is just not visible on the display screen. Usually, you execute the `Hide()` method just before you execute the `Show()` or `ShowDialog()` method.

To close a form and unload its contents from memory, use the `Dispose()` method, which has the following syntax:

```
FormName.Dispose()
```

Alternately, you can use the following command to close the form containing this code:

```
Me.Dispose()
```

The following steps show how to modify the command showing the second form so that it first hides the first form and then shows the second form as a modal form using the `ShowDialog()` method.

To modify the project to use modal forms:

1. Click the frmFirstForm.vb tab to display the first form in Code view. Modify its `btnDisplaySecondForm_Click` event code to match the following code:

```
frmSecondForm.txtSecondTextbox.Text = txtFirstTextbox.Text
'Hide the first form
Me.Hide()
'Show the second form
frmSecondForm.ShowDialog()
'Redisplay the first form when
'the second form is closed
Me.Show()
```

2. Select the frmSecondForm.vb [Design] tab to view the second form in Designer view, then double-click the Return to First Form button to create its Click event handler.
3. Add the following command to the event handler to close the second form:

```
Me.Dispose()
```

4. Save the project, then run the application. The first form window appears.
5. Type any text in the text box, then click Show Second Form. The second form appears, and the first form is hidden.
6. Click Return to First Form. The second form closes, and the first form appears again.
7. Close the application.
8. Close the project.

USING THE IDE DEBUGGING FEATURES

As you develop VB applications, you can use the IDE's debugging features to help locate and correct errors. You can step through programs one command at a time to view how execution proceeds, to monitor form property values, and even to reset values during execution. This can help you understand the program's logic and allow you to experiment with changing the commands while the program is running.

To gain experience with the VB debugging features, we will demonstrate how to debug a project named Debug. The Debug project contains a form that allows you to generate a Fibonacci series. A Fibonacci series starts with zero and one as the first two numbers. To determine the third number, you add these numbers, and the result is one. You then add the values that are the last two numbers in the series (one and one) to determine the next value, which is two. You again add the last two numbers in the series (one and two) to determine the next value in the series, which is three. A list of the first eight Fibonacci numbers is (0, 1, 1, 2, 3, 5, 8, 13).

To use the Debug project, type the number of Fibonacci numbers you want to generate, then click Generate. The Fibonacci series appears in a message box. Currently, however, the program has a bug. The following steps show how to open the project, run the application, and confirm that it is not working correctly.

To open and run the Debug project:

1. Copy the \SQLServer\DataFiles\Chapter5\Debug folder and all its contents to your \SQLServer\Solutions\Chapter5 folder.
2. Open the project in the IDE, then run the application.
3. Type 8 in the *How many do you want* field, then click Generate Fibonacci Numbers. A message box displays a series of zeros and ones, which is not the correct Fibonacci series.
4. Click OK to close the message box, then close the application.

The following subsections describe how to use the IDE debugging features. You will become familiar with the basic environment, learn how to use the Immediate and Locals windows in a debugging session, and learn how to create a watch to view how a value changes during execution.

The Debugging Environment

Figure 5-25 shows the IDE components that you use for debugging. In the Code editor, you can set a *breakpoint,* which pauses execution on a specific command. A red dot appears at the left edge of a command that contains a breakpoint, and the IDE reverse-highlights the command in red. Then you run the application. After execution begins, the *execution arrow* marks the command that executes next. When you place the mouse pointer over code during a debugging session, a Tooltip appears that shows the item's current value.

The IDE execution buttons control application execution and debugging. The buttons, from left to right, are:

- **Start Debugging/Continue,** which allows you to run an application or to continue running an application when execution pauses for a breakpoint;
- **Break All,** which is enabled only when the application is running and allows you to dynamically pause execution and view the program in the Debugger;
- **Stop Debugging,** which ends execution;
- **Step Into,** which executes the next command while debugging;

FIGURE 5-25   Debugging components

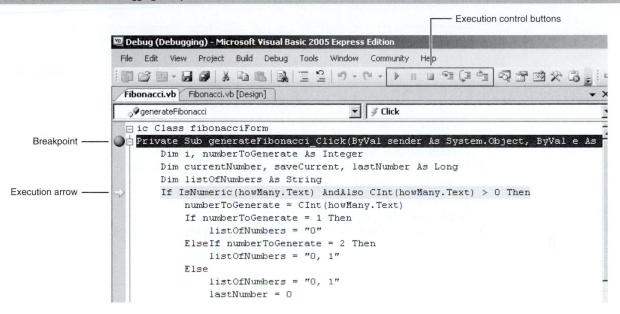

- **Step Over,** which executes the next command, unless the command calls a procedure; if it calls a procedure, then Step Over executes the procedures and pauses on the command after the procedure call;
- **Step Out,** which executes all the commands and then exits the current procedure.

To set a breakpoint, click in the gray area on the left side of the Code editor. To step through the program commands, click Step Into on the toolbar. To view the value of a form item, place the mouse pointer on a reference to the item in the Code editor. The following steps show how to set a breakpoint on the command that declares the Generate button's Click event handler and how to step through the program commands and examine the program values.

To set a breakpoint and examine program values:

1. Select Fibonacci.vb in the Solution Explorer, then click View Code to view the form in Code view.
2. To set a breakpoint on the Click event handler declaration, click the mouse pointer in the gray area on the left edge of the command. The breakpoint appears as shown in Figure 5-25.

TIP: Another way to set a breakpoint is to place the insertion point on the target command, click Debug on the menu bar, then click Toggle Breakpoint. You can also place the insertion point on the target command and press F9.

---

3. Click Start Debugging to run the application. The project form appears.
4. Type 8 in the *How many do you want* to generate field, then click Generate Fibonacci Numbers. The execution arrow appears on the breakpoint.
5. To execute the current command, click the Step Into button on the IDE toolbar. Execution skips over the Dim statements because they do not contain executable

commands, and pauses on the first command under the `If..ElseIf..Else` decision structure, as shown in Figure 5-25.

TIP: Another way to execute the next command is to press F8.

---

6. Place the mouse pointer on howMany.Text, and note that a Tooltip appears that shows the item's current value, which is 8.
7. Press F8 to execute the current command. The execution arrow moves to the first command in the If decision structure.
8. Place the mouse pointer on the numberToGenerate variable, and note that its current value is zero.
9. Highlight the expression CInt(howMany.Text), place the mouse pointer on the highlighted expression, and note that its value is eight.
10. Continue to press F8 and examine variable values to view how execution proceeds and values change.
11. When you are ready to quit, click Continue on the IDE toolbar to continue execution until the event handler finishes. The message box appears and shows the incorrect result.
12. Click OK to close the message box, then close the application window.

While execution is paused at a breakpoint, you can edit the commands appearing in the Code editor. This allows you to immediately fix an error and confirm that the correction actually fixed the problem. To edit a command while debugging, rewrite the command in the Code editor while execution is paused. You can also reset the position of the execution arrow to run one or more commands again. To do this, right-click the command on which you want to reset the execution arrow, then click Set Next Statement.

The following steps show how to change one of the program commands and execute the command again to view the result of the change.

To edit and re-execute a command:

1. Click Start Debugging to run the application. The project form appears.
2. Type 8 in the *How many do you want to generate?* field, then click Generate Fibonacci Numbers. The execution arrow appears on the breakpoint.
3. Press F8 to execute the current command. Execution pauses on the first command in the `If..Else` decision structure.
4. Press F8 again to move to the next command, which assigns the contents of the form's text box to numberToGenerate variable.
5. Press F8 again to move to the next command, which is the second `If` decision structure that evaluates whether the value of the numberToGenerate variable is one. Move the mouse pointer onto any reference of the numberToGenerate variable in the Code editor, and confirm that its value is eight.
6. Press F8 again. Execution moves to the `ElseIf` command, which is what you expect because the value of numberToGenerate is not one.
7. Place the insertion point on the command that is two lines above the execution arrow, which is the `If` decision structure that evaluates whether the value of the numberToGenerate value is one. Replace the one with eight, so that the decision structure's condition is now true. The command should appear as follows:

```
If numberToGenerate = 8 Then
```

8. Make sure the insertion point is on the command you just changed. Right-click, then click Set Next Statement. The execution arrow moves up to the command you just changed.

9. Press F8 to execute the command again. The execution arrow moves to the command just below the `If` statement because the statement is now true.

10. Click the Continue button. The message box displays the Fibonacci series containing only the value zero as a result of your change.

11. Click OK to dismiss the message box, then close the application.

12. In the Code editor, reverse the change you made in the Code editor so that the line appears as it did before:

```
If numberToGenerate = 1 Then
```

Using the Immediate Window

While you are debugging, you can use the Immediate window to display current program values and to change program values during execution, as shown in Figure 5-26.

To display the Immediate window, click Debug on the menu bar, point to Windows, then click Immediate. To display a current program data value in the Immediate window, type a question mark (?), followed by the item name, then press Enter. To change a program value, type an assignment statement that resets the value, then press Enter. The following steps show how to open the Immediate window and use it to display and change a program value.

To use the Immediate window while debugging:

1. Clear the current breakpoint by clicking the red dot on the left side of the Code editor. The breakpoint no longer appears.

FIGURE 5-26   Using the Immediate window while debugging

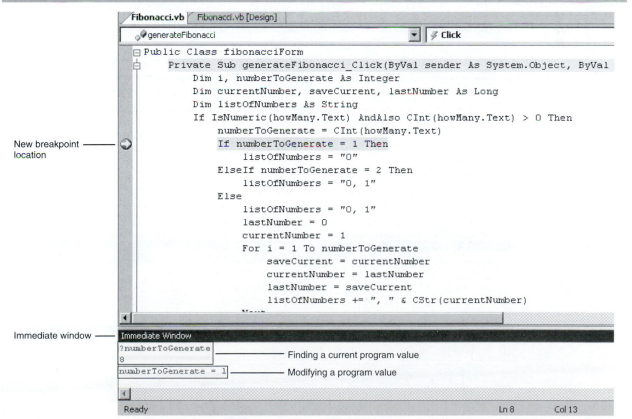

TIP: Another way to clear a breakpoint is to place the insertion point on the breakpoint, then press F9.

---

2. Set a new breakpoint on the program line which begins the inner `If` decision structure (see Figure 5-26).
3. Click the Start Debugging button, type 8 in the text box, then click Generate Fibonacci Numbers. The execution arrow appears on the breakpoint.
4. To open the Immediate window, click Debug on the menu bar, point to Windows, then click Immediate. The Immediate window appears at the bottom of the IDE.
5. Type ?numberToGenerate in the Immediate window, then press Enter. The current variable value, which is the same as the text box value, appears in the Immediate window.
6. To reset the variable value to a different value, type numberToGenerate = 15 in the Immediate window, then press Enter.
7. Place the insertion point on numberToGenerate on the current program line to confirm that the new value appears in the Tooltip.

Using the Locals Window

Another useful debugging window is the Locals window, shown in Figure 5-27. The Locals window displays all the current form variables and their associated values during program execution. As execution proceeds, values update automatically. To open the Locals window, click Debug on the menu bar, point to Windows, then click Locals.

FIGURE 5-27 Using the Locals window while debugging

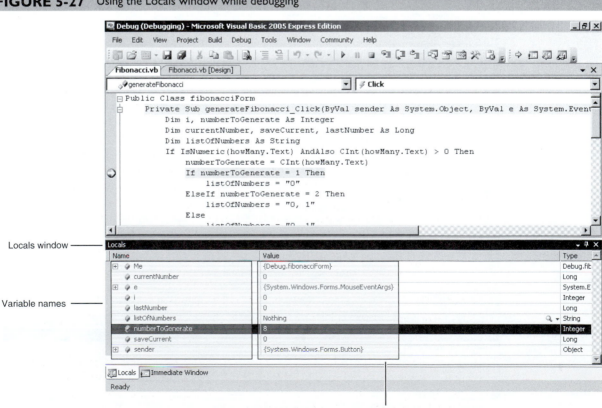

Locals window

Variable names

Variable values

FIGURE 5-28   Using the Watch window while debugging

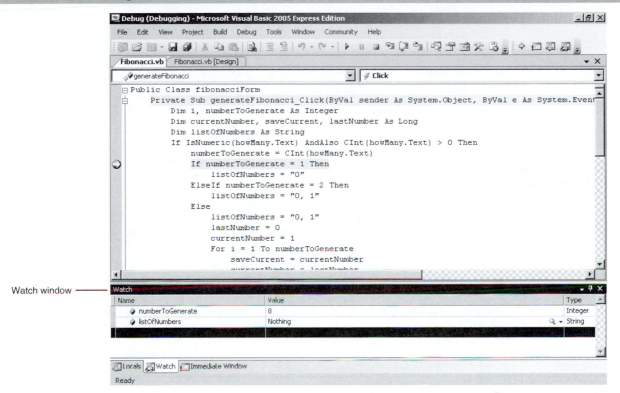

Watch window

Creating a Watch

For complex programs with many variables, the Locals window can display a very long list of variables and values. Usually you track only a few variables while debugging, and it can become hard to find the values you need in the Locals list. To create a list that is similar to the one in the Locals window but showing only selected expressions or variables, you create a watch. A *watch* tracks the value of a specific variable or expression during debugging and displays the result in the Watch window, as shown in Figure 5-28.

To create a watch, place the pointer on the variable you want to track or highlight the expression you want to track. Click Debug on the menu bar, then click QuickWatch. The QuickWatch dialog box opens and allows you to set and configure the watch. To delete a watch, right-click the watch in the Watch window, then click Delete Watch. The following steps demonstrate creating a watch in the Debug project.

To create a watch:

NOTE: The Debug project should be running and paused on the breakpoint, as shown in Figure 5-28. If it is not, repeat the previous set of steps.

---

1. To create a watch on the listOfNumbers variable, click the insertion point on the listOfNumbers variable anywhere in the Code editor, click Debug on the menu bar, then click QuickWatch. The QuickWatch dialog box opens and displays listOfNumbers in the Expression field.

2. Click Add Watch, then click Close. The Watch window opens and shows the new watch.

3. Press F8 to step through the program commands, and observe how the watch value changes as the program adds items to the list.

4. When you have seen enough, click Stop Debugging on the toolbar, then close the project.

VB has many powerful debugging features, and this section has provided an overview of the basics. The debugger aids development by helping you find errors, and you should use it regularly.

IN CONCLUSION . . .

This chapter provided a broad overview of the VB IDE and the VB programming language. It described the structure of the .NET environment, and you became familiar with the IDE. It showed how to make a project, which allowed you to become familiar with forms and controls and enabled you to learn how to write event handlers, procedures, and custom classes to perform a variety of programming tasks. At this point, you have the foundations you need in both database and application development to create Windows-based database applications, which the next chapter addresses.

SUMMARY

- The .NET framework provides the foundation for all .NET applications. It consists of the Common Language Runtime (CLR), which is an environment that provides services to manage application execution, and the Framework Class Libraries (FCL), which are libraries that contain code for creating common programming objects.

- When you compile a .NET program, the compiler first translates your source code into a Microsoft Intermediate Language (MSIL) assembly, which is a hardware-independent set of instructions. Before the assembly can execute, a JIT compiler must compile it into the binary code for a specific hardware platform.

- An integrated development environment (IDE) is an environment for developing programs that has multiple components and that displays multiple windows for performing different programming tasks. In the Visual Studio IDE, you create a project, which is a collection of files that comprise an application. A project contains one or more forms, and forms display controls that allow users to interact with the application. A solution is a complex application made up of multiple projects.

- In the IDE, the Solution Explorer allows you to access and view project components. The Properties window allows you to modify item properties in a project. The Toolbox allows you to create new form controls. The Code editor allows you to enter, modify, and debug program code.

- In Windows applications, program commands execute in response to events, which are user or system actions. Project components can have event handlers, which are programs that execute in response to specific events.

- In VB, procedures are named blocks of code that can receive parameters and that other procedures can call. Procedures include functions, which return a single value to the calling procedure, and subroutines, which manipulate data values but do not return a specific value.

- A public variable is defined in a class definition, persists during the entire life of the associated object, and can be read and modified anywhere in the application. A private variable is defined in terms of a class definition, persists during the entire life of the associated object, but can be read and modified only by procedures in its class. A Dim variable is local to a procedure or block; it persists and is visible only in its procedure.

- VB objects, such as controls and variables, have properties that allow you to specify and retrieve values about the object. Objects also have methods, which provide a way to act on or modify the object.

- Strong typing requires programmers to explicitly specify the data type of each expression in an operation and explicitly convert values into compatible types as needed. In VB, you enforce strong typing by setting the Option Strict setting to On in the IDE.

- VB provides composite data types, which are data types that store multiple scalar values. Important composite data types are arrays, array lists, and structures.
- In VB, you control program execution using the If . . . ElseIf . . . Else and Select . . . Case decision structures. You support exception handling using a Try . . . Catch . . . Finally block.
- VB supports a variety of pretest and posttest loops to support iterative operations. The For . . . Next loop performs an operation a set number of times, and the For Each . . . Next loop performs operations on every element in a collection.
- You can create custom classes in VB projects to perform application tasks. This is desirable because the code for an object class is a self-contained module that you can use in different applications and that multiple programmers can use.
- Complex projects often contain multiple forms. In a project with multiple forms, the startup form is the form that appears when the user starts the application. VB provides methods for showing and hiding subsequent forms and for referencing items on alternate forms.
- The VB IDE debugging features allow you to set breakpoints to pause program execution, step through commands and examine item values, and modify and re-execute program commands. You can use the Immediate, Locals, and Watch windows to monitor variables during execution.

KEY TERMS

Array   Composite data type that stores a list of data items all having the same data type

Array list   Composite data type storing a set of values that can be of any data type

Assembly   MSIL code before it is compiled into an executable program

Breakpoint   Debugging element that pauses execution on a specific command

By reference   Method of passing parameters in which the procedure passes a reference to the memory location that stores the parameter, and the original value can be changed by the called procedure

By value   Method of passing parameters in which the procedure passes a copy of the actual data value, and the original value remains unchanged

Code file   VB project file with a .vb extension that stores the programmer-provided code in a form

Code view   In the VB IDE, an editor that allows you to enter and view program code

Common Language Runtime (CLR)   .NET framework component that provides services to manage application execution regardless of the development programming language

Compiler   Program that decodes instructions written in a higher-level language and produces instructions in a lower-level language, such as assembly language

Composite data type   Data type that stores multiple scalar values

Control   Object in a visual application that displays information and allows users to interact with the application

Default event   Object event for which developers most commonly write an event handler

Designer file   VB file with a .Designer.vb extension that stores the code to represent the visual components of a form

Designer view   In the VB IDE, a graphical view of the form that allows you to add and position items such as text boxes and buttons

Dim variable   Local variable that persists from the time a procedure's execution begins until the time execution ends and that is visible only in its procedure

Dynamic link library   File with a .dll extension that is a code library that executable programs link to at run time

Elementary data type   VB data type that references a scalar data value of a specific size and format

Event   User or system action that may cause an event handler to execute

Event handler   Program that executes in response to specific events

Exception   Run-time error

Exception handlers   Commands to handle exceptions

Executable file   File that a computer can execute

Execution arrow   Debugging element that marks the command that executes next

Form   VB Windows project objects that contain the application items with which a user interacts, such as text boxes, buttons, and labels

Framework Class Libraries (FCLs)   .NET framework libraries that contain code for creating common programming objects

Function   VB procedure that returns a specific value to the calling procedure

Global Assembly Cache (GAC)   In the .NET framework, a location storing programs that multiple applications share

Glyph   Icon on the left side of an Intellisense list that differentiates between methods and properties

Hungarian notation   Standard object notation that specifies object names using a three-letter prefix, which specifies the object type, followed by a descriptive name made up of one or more words

Index Specifies an item's position in an array

Instantiate Action that creates an instance of an object from a class

Integrated development environment (IDE) Environment for developing programs that has multiple components and that displays multiple windows for performing different programming tasks

Intellisense list Code completion list that the IDE displays to provide argument values

Just-in-time (JIT) compiler Compiler that compiles an assembly for a specific hardware platform.

Literal Data value that you hard code in a program command

Member Individual data item in a structure

Message box Dialog box displaying a short message and one or more buttons that allow the user to take actions

Microsoft Intermediate Language (MSIL) Hardware-independent set of instructions that can be converted to native binary code that runs on a specific hardware platform

Modal form Form in a multiform application that commands all the application's attention and that must be closed or hidden before the user can interact with a different form

Multidimensional array Array that stores two or more data values

Namespace Naming scheme that uses a hierarchical dotted naming convention

Native assembly cache In the .NET framework, a location that stores stand-alone executable programs

Persistence Characteristic that specifies when a program allocates memory for a variable and when the program clears the memory for other uses

Private variable Variable defined in a class declaration that persists from the time its object is instantiated until the time it is destroyed, and that can be read and modified only by other procedures in its class

Procedure In VB, a named set of commands that can receive parameters and that other procedures can call

Project Collection of files that comprise a VB Windows application

Project file VB project file with a .vbproj extension that keeps track of the files and framework libraries the project uses

Project folder Folder that stores all a project's files and subfolders

Property Value that describes or controls an object's appearance and/or behavior

Public variable Variable defined in a class declaration that persists from the time its object is instantiated until the time its object is destroyed, and that is visible to all other application classes

Region Area in the Code editor that appears as a node you can collapse or expand

Resource file VB project file with a .resx extension that stores application resources

Scope Characteristic that specifies the procedures, modules, and classes in which a variable is visible

Solution VB Windows application made up of multiple projects

Solution file File with a .sln extension that keeps track of all the projects that a solution contains

Solution folder Folder that contains multiple project folders

Source code Program commands that programmers enter

Startup form Form that first appears when a user starts a Windows application

Strong typing Program setting that requires programmers to explicitly specify the data type of each expression in an operation and that explicitly converts values into compatible types as needed

Structure Composite data type that allows you to store and manipulate multiple related data items with different data types

Subroutine VB procedure that manipulates data values but does not return a specific value

Two-dimensional array Array that stores two columns of data values

Watch Debugging element that tracks the value of a specific variable or expression during execution

Weak typing Program setting in which a program automatically converts values to compatible data types

STUDY QUESTIONS

Multiple-Choice Questions

1. In VB, an event handler is an example of a:
   a. Class
   b. Method
   c. Function
   d. Subroutine

2. The best data type for storing all the data in the UniversityState table in Figure 3-2 is a(n):
   a. One-dimensional array
   b. Two-dimensional array
   c. Array list
   d. Structure

3. In a .NET Windows application that contains a single project, the file with an .sln extension is stored directly in the:
   a. Project folder
   b. Solution folder
   c. Bin folder
   d. None of the above

4. When you are debugging a VB project, what does the Immediate window allow you to do?
   a. View the value of a specific variable
   b. Automatically monitor the value of a specific variable
   c. Change the contents of a program command
   d. Both a and c

5. In VB, ToString is an example of a(n):
   a. Elementary data type
   b. Composite data type
   c. Property
   d. Method

```
Dim intMyNumber As Integer = 3
Do While intMyNumber < 6
   MessageBox.Show(intMyNumber.ToString)
   If intMyNumber = 6 Then Exit Do
   intMyNumber = intMyNumber + 1
Loop
```

6. In the preceding program code, how many times does the message box appear?
   a. 2
   b. 3
   c. 4
   d. 5

7. When you compile a .NET program, the compiler first translates your commands into a(n):
   a. Assembly
   b. Hardware-specific executable file
   c. Solution
   d. JIT DLL

8. In VB, a variable you declare in a procedure is always:
   a. Public
   b. Private
   c. Dim
   d. Protected

9. In a custom class, a _____ allows you to perform data validation whenever a data value is set.
   a. Public variable
   b. Private variable
   c. Method
   d. Property element

10. In VB, a(n) _____ is a named block of code that can receive multiple input parameters and that returns a single value.
    a. Procedure
    b. Function
    c. Subroutine
    d. Event handler
    e. Either a or b

11. _____ describes where a variable is visible, and _____ describes when the variable is visible.
    a. Scope, persistence
    b. Persistence, scope
    c. Public, private
    d. Private, public

True/False Questions

1. In a VB Windows application, you specify a project's startup form in the project's Property pages.
2. A JIT compiler creates an assembly.
3. A variable that you declare in a class declaration is never a private variable.
4. In the VB IDE, a project contains multiple solutions.
5. In a VB project, the Me object always refers to the startup form.
6. In the VB Code editor, a blue wavy line appears under your code when a compile error occurs.

Short Answer Questions

1. Suggest control names for the following form items:
   a. A check box that specifies whether enrollment in a course is open or closed.
   b. A command button that a user uses to select a specific student from a list of students
   c. A form that displays a list of available classes at Ironwood University
   d. An option button that specifies whether a student's gender is male
   e. A text box that allows a user to enter his or her user name
2. What is the VB line continuation character, and when should you use it?
3. List the three types of VB variables, and discuss their differences in terms of scope and persistence.
4. Describe the differences between weak typing and strong typing.
5. When should you pass procedure parameters by reference, and when should you pass them by value?
6. Describe the differences between an array, an array list, and a structure.
7. List an advantage of creating a custom class rather than a user-defined procedure to perform a programming task.
8. What is a modal form, and how do you display a modal form in an application?
9. What is a class property element, and when should you create one?

Guided Exercises

1. **Creating a Project That Contains Public, Private, and Dim Variables**
   In this exercise, you create a project that uses the form and message box in Figure 5-29. The form contains text boxes that allow the user to enter a value for a public, private, and Dim variable. When the user clicks the Show button, the program displays a message box that displays the different variable values.
   a. Create a new project named 5Exercise1, and save the project in your \SQLServer\ Solutions\Chapter5 folder. Then create a new form named frmExercise1.vb, and save the form in the project folder. Make sure that the project's Option Strict setting is set to On.

FIGURE 5-29   Exercise 5-1

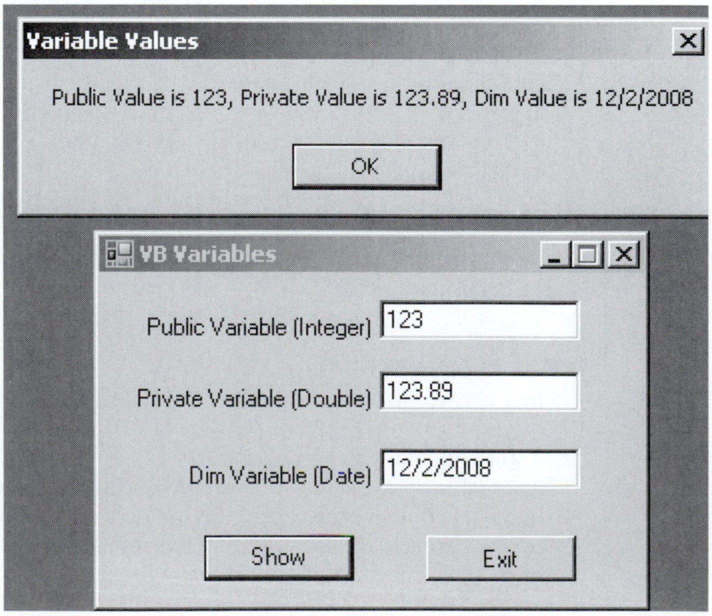

b. Configure the form properties as follows:

Property Name	New Value
Name	frm5Exercise1
FormBorderStyle	FixedSingle
MaximizeBox	False
StartPosition	CenterScreen
Size	298, 192
Text	VB Variables

c. Create the controls shown in Figure 5-29. Assign descriptive names to all the controls except the labels, and configure the controls as shown.

d. Declare a public variable named intPublic that uses the Integer data type.

e. Declare a private variable named dblPrivate that uses the Double data type.

f. Create an event handler associated with the Show Values button. Declare a Dim variable named datDimDate that uses the Date data type.

g. Add commands in the event handler to assign the text box values to the variables. (Hint: you will need to perform some data type conversions.)

h. Add a command to display the variable values in the message box as shown in Figure 5-29. You must reference the variables rather than the text box values in the command that displays the message box.

i. Create an event handler for the Exit button to close the application.

2. **Creating a Project That Uses an If . . . ElseIf . . . Else Decision Structure**

In this exercise, you create the form in Figure 5-30, which calculates and displays a salesperson's commission, which is based on the sales amount. The user enters the sales amount in the Sales Amount text box and clicks Calculate, and the application displays the commission amount in a message box as shown.

a. Create a new project named 5Exercise2, and save the project in your \SQLServer\ Solutions\Chapter5 folder. Then create a new form named frm5Exercise2.vb, and

FIGURE 5-30   Exercise 5-2

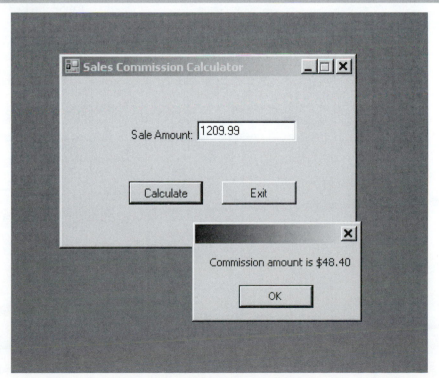

save the form in the project folder. Make sure that the project's Option Strict setting is set to On.

a. Configure the form properties as follows:

Property Name	New Value
Name	frm5Exercise2
FormBorderStyle	FixedSingle
MaximizeBox	False
StartPosition	CenterScreen
Size	298, 192
Text	Sales Commission Calculator

b. Create the controls shown in Figure 5-30. Assign descriptive names to all the controls except the labels, and configure the controls as shown.

c. Create an event handler for the Calculate button that calculates the commission based on the amount that the user enters in the Sales Amount field. Use an If. . . ElseIf. Else decision structure to determine the commission amount. If the sales amount is less than $500, the commission rate is 8%; if the sales amount is $500 or greater, but less than $1,000, the commission rate is 6%; and if the sales amount is $1,000 or greater, the commission rate is 4%.

d. Display the calculated commission amount in a message box as shown. (Hint: Use the FormatCurrency function to format the amount as shown.)

e. Create an event handler for the Exit button to exit the application.

3. **Creating a Project That Uses a Select . . . Case Decision Structure**

In this exercise, create a project that contains the form in Figure 5-31 that allows a user to enter a two-letter state abbreviation and a purchase amount and that then displays the state sales tax amount for the purchase.

a. Create a new project named 5Exercise3, and save the project in your \SQLServer\ Solutions\Chapter5 folder. Then create a new form named frm5Exercise3.vb, and save the form in the project folder. Make sure that the project's Option Strict setting is set to On.

b. Configure the form properties as follows:

Property Name	New Value
Name	frm5Exercise3
FormBorderStyle	FixedSingle
MaximizeBox	False
StartPosition	CenterScreen
Size	298, 192
Text	State Sales Tax Amounts

FIGURE 5-31   Exercise 5-3

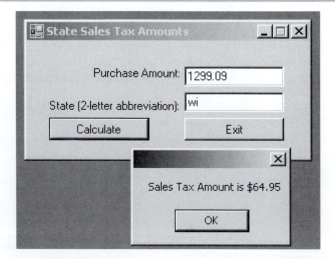

TABLE 5-13   Data for Exercise 5-3

State	Abbreviation	Tax %
MONTANA	MT	0
MICHIGAN	MI	6
CALIFORNIA	CA	7.25
COLORADO	CO	2.9
ILLINOIS	IL	6.25
IOWA	IA	5
MINNESOTA	MN	6.5
WISCONSIN	WI	5
WYOMING	WY	4

   c. Create the controls shown in Figure 5-31. Assign descriptive names to all the controls except the labels, and configure the controls as shown.

   d. Create an event handler for the Calculate button that contains a Select . . . Case decision structure that determines the sales tax rate based on the state of purchase. Use the data to create in Table 5-13 in your Select . . . Case structure.

   e. Add a command to the event handler to display the message box as shown. (Hint: Use the FormatCurrency function to format the amount as shown.)

   f. Create an event handler for the Exit button to exit the application.

4. **Creating a Project That Uses User-Defined Procedures and Loops**

In this exercise, you create a project that contains the form in Figure 5-32. This form generates what are called Apocalyptic numbers, which are numbers that you generate using the formula 2^n and that contain the sequence "666." The user can select how many numbers to generate using the form text boxes. If the user places a value in the Maximum N Value text box, the program examines that many numbers for the sequence. (For example, in Figure 5-32, the user types "600" in this text box; so the program examines the numbers from 2^1 to 2^{600} for the sequence. If the user places a value in the Numbers to Generate text box, the

FIGURE 5-32   Exercise 5-4

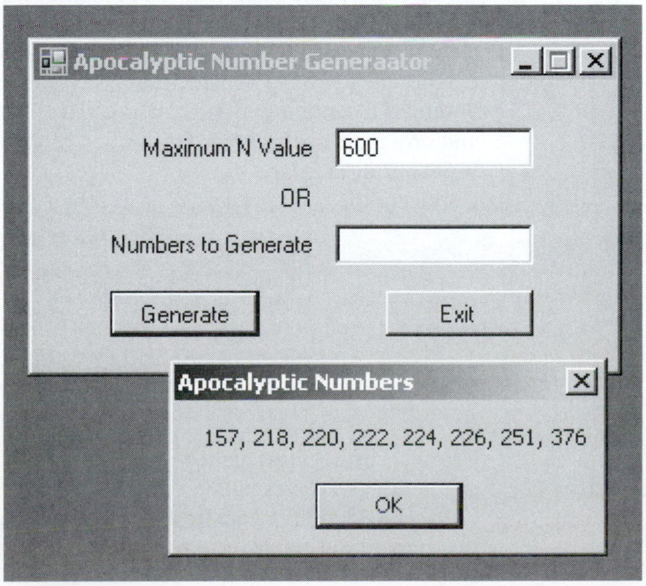

program generates exactly that many Apocalyptic numbers. For example, if the user types "5" in the text box, the program displays the first five values that appear in the message box in Figure 5-32.

a. Create a new project named 5Exercise4, and save the project in your \SQLServer\ Solutions\Chapter5 folder. Then create a new form named frm5Exercise4.vb, and save the form in the project folder. Make sure that the project's Option Strict setting is set to On.

b. Configure the form properties as follows:

Property Name	New Value
Name	frm5Exercise4
FormBorderStyle	FixedSingle
MaximizeBox	False
StartPosition	CenterScreen
Size	298, 192
Text	Apocalyptic Number Generator

c. Create the controls shown in Figure 5-32. Assign descriptive names to all the controls except the labels and configure the controls as shown.

d. Create a user-defined subroutine or function to generate the list based on the maximum value of N that the user enters in the first text box.

e. Create a second user-defined subroutine or function that generates the list based on the maximum number of list items to generate that the user enters in the second text box.

f. Create a Click event handler for the Generate button that uses a Try/Catch block. Throw an exception and display an appropriate message if the user enters no value in either of the text boxes or if the user enters a value in both text boxes.

g. Create an If . . . ElseIf . . . Else decision structure that evaluates which text box the user enters a value. If the user enters a value in the first text box, call the appropriate procedure, and if the user enters a value in the second text box, call the other procedure. Then display the output in a message box. Format the output as shown.

h. Create an event handler for the Exit button to close the application.

5. **Creating a Project That Contains a Custom Class**
In this exercise, create a project that contains a custom class that represents information in the SportEmployee table in the Sport Motors database (see Figures 3-3 and 3-4). Figure 5-33 illustrates the class definition.

The user will enter data values for the custom class items using the form in Figure 5-34. When the user clicks Save, the form instantiates a class object, sets the class items to the user-entered values, and calls the method that calculates the years of service. The form then displays the message box showing the object values.

a. Create a new project named 5Exercise5, and save the project in your \SQLServer\ Solutions\Chapter5 folder. Then create a new form named frm5Exercise5.vb, and save the form in the project folder. Make sure that the project's Option Strict setting is set to On.

b. Configure the form properties as follows:

Property Name	New Value
Name	frm5Exercise5
FormBorderStyle	FixedSingle
MaximizeBox	False
StartPosition	CenterScreen
Size	389, 211
Text	Sport Employees

c. Create a custom class named SportEmployee.vb. Create a region for public variables, and define the class's public variables as shown in Figure 5-33.

d. In the class definition, create a region for public methods, then create a public function that returns the employee's years of service that has an input parameter of the employee's hire date. (Hint: Use the DateDiff built-in function.)

FIGURE 5-33   Class definition for Exercise 5-5

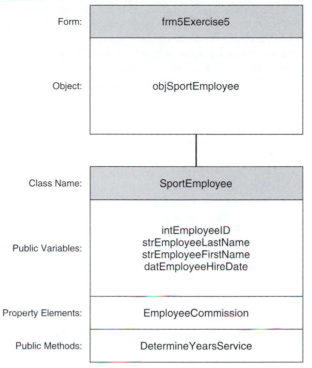

e. In the class definition, create a property element to represent the employee's commission, and create a corresponding private variable that has the Double data type. In the property element's Set procedure, confirm that the commission is not greater than 8%, and display an appropriate error message if a user tries to set the commission to a higher value. Allow the user to enter the commission as a percentage (such as "8"), but save the value as a decimal (such as "0.08").

FIGURE 5-34   Exercise 5-5

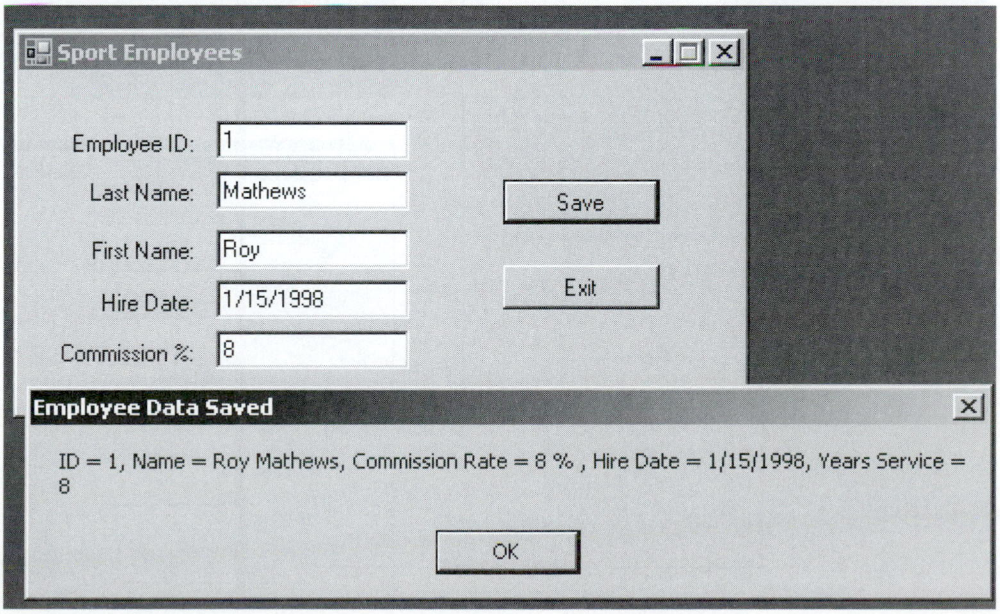

   f. Create a Click event handler for the Save button that creates a new object instance of the class, sets the instance's public variable values and property element value to the form text box values, calls the method that calculates the years of service, and then confirms the results in the message box as shown. Use a Try/Catch block to throw an exception if the user tries to set the commission to an illegal value.

   g. Create a Click event handler for the Exit button that exits the application.

6. **Creating a Project with Multiple Forms**

In this exercise, you work with a project that displays multiple forms, as shown in Figure 5-35. This application first displays the Ironwood University form, as shown in Figure 5-35. The user enters a Student ID and PIN value, and clicks Log On. The application then displays the Ironwood University Student Menu form, which allows the user to view a campus map or to view his or her personal data. The forms for this project have already been created for you.

   a. In Windows Explorer, copy the 5Exercise6 folder and all its contents from the SQLServer\Chapter5\Datafiles folder to your SQLServer\Chapter5\Solutions folder, and open the project.

   b. Specify the project startup form as frmMain.

   c. On the Main form, create a Click event handler for the Login button on the Main form that hides the current form and that shows the Student Menu form as a modal form. Allow the user to log on as either Student ID 1 or Student ID 2 in the Ironwood University database (see Figure 3-2). Use a Try/Catch block that throws an exception

FIGURE 5-35 Exercise 5-6

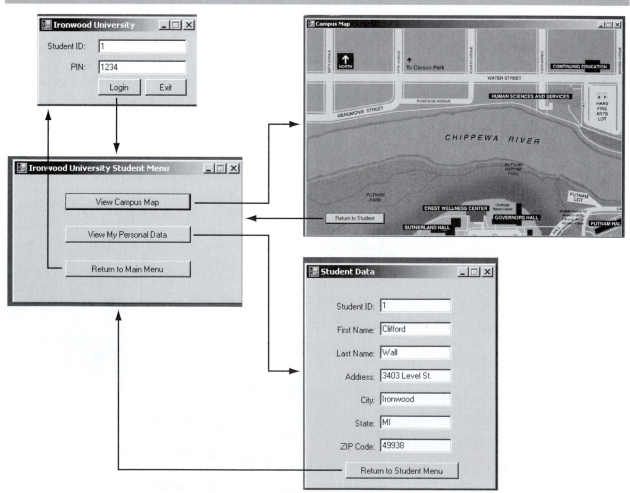

and displays an appropriate error message if the user enters any other Student ID value. (Any PIN value is acceptable. Hard code in the test for a Student ID value of 1 or 2.)

d. On the Main form, create a Click event handler for the Exit button that exits the application.

e. On the Student Menu form, create a Click event handler that displays the Campus Map as a modal form.

f. On the Student Menu form, create a Click event handler that displays the Student Data form as a modal form and that displays the student's associated data. Create a decision structure that displays the correct data from Figure 3-2 if the student logged on as Student ID 1 or as Student ID 2. (Do not try to do this from a database query; just look at the figure and use this information to hard code in the correct data for student 1 or student 2.)

g. On all forms with "Return to Student Menu" buttons, create Click event handlers that hide the current form and redisplay the Student Menu form.

7. **Debugging a Project**

In this exercise, debug the Debug project that you used earlier in the chapter. Recall from the section titled "Using the IDE's Debugging Features" that the form in Figure 5-27 allows you to generate a Fibonacci series, which is a number series that starts with zero and one as the first two numbers. To determine the third number, you add these numbers, and the result is one. You then add the values that are the last two numbers in the series (one and one) to determine the next value, which is two. You again add the last two numbers in the series (one and two) to determine the next value in the series, which is three. A list of the first eight Fibonacci numbers is (0, 1, 1, 2, 3, 5, 8, 13). To use the Debug project, type the number of Fibonacci numbers that you want to generate, then click Generate. The Fibonacci series then appears in a message box.

a. If you did not do this earlier in the chapter, copy the \SQLServer\DataFiles\Chapter5\Debug folder and all its contents to your \SQLServer\Solutions\Chapter5 folder. Then open the project.

b. Use the debugging features in the IDE to find and correct the errors.

CHAPTER 6

Creating VB .NET Database Applications

Learning Objectives

At the conclusion of this chapter, you will be able to:

■ understand how applications access data in .NET;

■ create and work with .NET data components;

■ describe different ways to display data;

■ use data-bound controls to create a variety of read-only database applications;

■ use data-bound controls to create forms that allow users to insert and update data;

■ create database applications that use program commands to process data;

■ create a database application that uses a combination of data-bound controls and program commands to process data;

■ learn how to retrieve database data asynchronously.

So far, you have learned how to create and work with SQL Server database tables. You have also become familiar with the Visual Studio 2005 or VB Express IDE and learned how to create Windows applications. This chapter pulls these topics together and describes how to use VB controls and other tools to create database applications.

In this chapter, you learn how to use data-bound controls, which are controls that enable a form to connect to a database and display database data. You also learn how to write program code to enable a form to interact with a database. This chapter focuses on a common set of methods and techniques that allow performing most database application tasks.

ACCESSING DATA IN .NET

To enable .NET applications to communicate with databases, Microsoft developed *ADO.NET,* which is a set of object classes that support database access. In this book, we use ADO.NET 2.x. ADO.NET 2.x retains and adds to the functionality contained in ADO.NET 1.x. ADO.NET 1.x was introduced in .NET 2002/2003. The following subsections describe ADO.NET 1.x and its ADO.NET 2.x extensions.

Data Access Features in ADO.NET 1.x

Figure 6-1 shows the ADO.NET 1.x data access architecture.

FIGURE 6-1   ADO.NET 1.x data access architecture

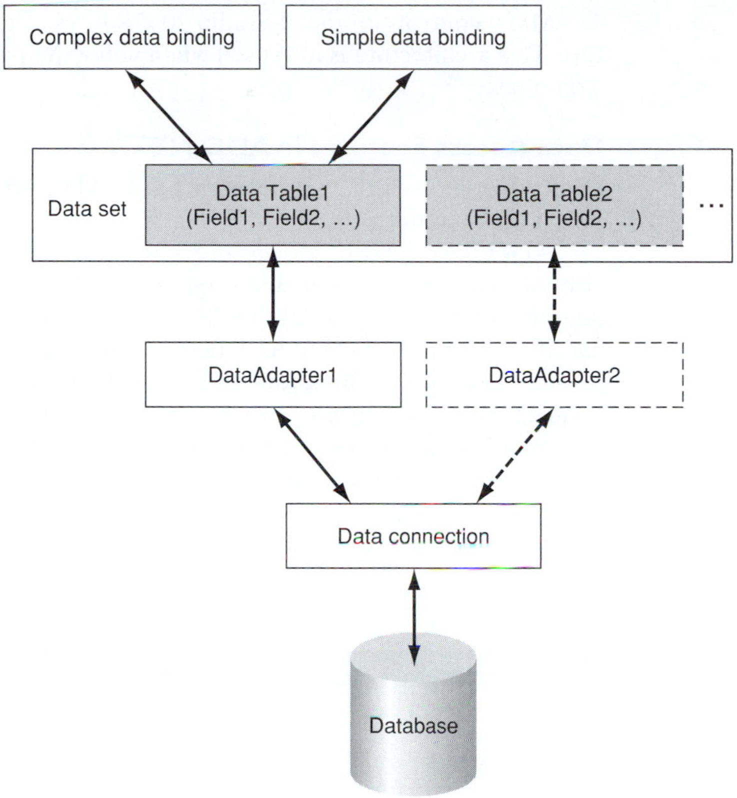

To enable communication between an application and a database, the application first makes a *data connection,* which specifies a communication path between the application and the database. A data connection object communicates with one or more data adapters. A *data adapter* is a form component that provides methods for retrieving and modifying data. It works in a disconnected fashion: It automatically opens the data connection, retrieves the data, and then automatically closes the connection after it receives all the data. This avoids keeping data connections open for long intervals, which helps the DBMS handle an increased number of data requests.

A data adapter stores retrieved data in a *data set* object. (Data sets are collections similar to the array lists described in Chapter 5.) Because the same data set object can simultaneously store data from several data adapters, a data set stores the retrieved data in separate *data table* objects that are in the data set.

After you fill a data table with retrieved data, you can manipulate the data using program commands, or you can *bind,* or attach, the data in a data table to VB form controls such as combo boxes, data grid views (which display data in a tabular format), or text boxes. Data binding automates tasks such as filling a combo box with retrieved data, displaying data in a text box, and updating data.

Simple data binding binds one field in a data table to a control. If several controls are bound to several columns in the same data table, they are automatically synchronized to display the same row in the data table at the same time.

Complex data binding binds a single control to multiple fields in a data table. For example, a data grid view control binds to an entire data table and displays all the table data in a tabular format. This control supports adding, updating, deleting, and viewing table data. Combo box and list controls support complex binding by displaying one field in a record while keeping track of the value of a different field in the same record.

Many controls in Visual Studio 2005 still use the original ADO.NET 1.x architecture. This architecture is also used when you write program commands to interact with a database.

Data Access Features in ADO.NET 2.0

Figure 6-2 shows the enhancements that ADO.NET 2.x provide to the .NET data access architecture.

ADO.NET 2.x uses a *data source* to interact with a database. A data source consists of a data connection, a strongly typed data set, and one or more pairs of table adapters and associated data tables. A *strongly typed data set* includes a schema that specifies information about its data fields, their data types, and their constraints, such as primary key relationships, foreign key relationships, and NOT NULL constraints. This enables the Code editor to provide Intellisense code completion lists when you write commands that reference the data set. It also allows the compiler to perform type checking and catch data entry errors.

A strongly typed data set contains one or more table adapters. A *table adapter* is a strongly typed wrapper, or interface, to a data adapter. (A data adapter is a form

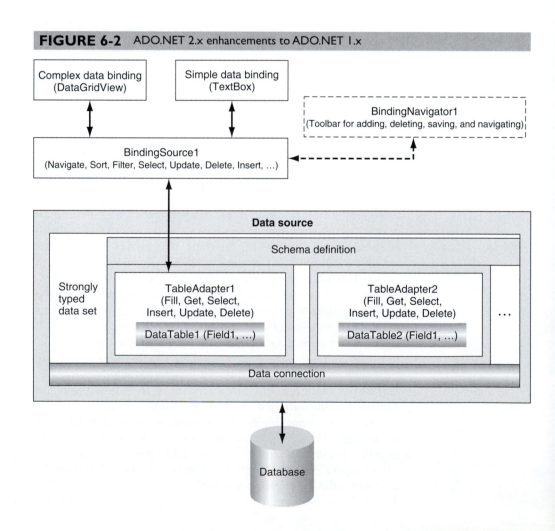

FIGURE 6-2   ADO.NET 2.x enhancements to ADO.NET 1.x

component that provides methods for retrieving and modifying data.) With a conventional data adapter, every form needs its own individually configured data adapter. With a table adapter, the same table adapter class can support multiple forms and/or multiple controls. A table adapter allows you to define multiple versions of data manipulation commands such as Fill, Get, Select, Insert, Update, and Delete. A table adapter has an associated data table, which is stored in the data source's data set.

A *binding source* is an intermediary that uses either simple or complex data binding to bind a control to a data table. The binding source performs all the data interaction operations, including navigating through records, sorting, filtering, and modifying. You can still write program commands to bind a control directly to a data set's data table, but it is easier and faster to use binding sources.

The *binding navigator* provides a user interface to the binding source, in the form of a toolbar, for tasks such as moving through records, adding new records deleting records and saving changes. The binding navigator in Figure 6-2 is shown in dashed lines because it is optional: a binding source does not always have an associated binding navigator. Although a binding navigator provides a lot of functionality, you usually need to write additional program code to complete the interface for most database applications.

CREATING AND MANAGING DATA ACCESS COMPONENTS IN THE VB IDE

The VB IDE provides a set of data designer tools to assist developers in creating database applications. This section describes how to create ADO.NET data access components and how to use IDE tools to work with these components.

Creating a Data Source

The first step in connecting a VB project to a database is to create a data source. This chapter creates all the example database application forms in a single project that uses a single data source referencing every table in the Ironwood University database. This is the only data source for all the project forms.

The following steps show how to create a new project and a new data source.

To create a new project and new data source:

1. Start VB Express or Visual Studio 2005, and create a new project named DBExamples. (Do not create a directory for the solution.) Save the project in the \SQLServer\Solutions\Chapter6 folder. Make sure that the project's Option Strict value is set to On.
2. To create a new data source, click Data on the menu bar, then click Add New Data Source. The Data Source Configuration Wizard opens.
3. On the *Choose a Data Source Type* page, select Database if necessary, then click Next.
4. On the *Choose your data connection* page, click New Connection. The Add Connection dialog box opens.
5. *If you are using either VB Express or VS 2005 and connecting to a local SQL Server Express database,* click Browse, navigate to \SQLServer\Databases\, select *yourDatabaseName*.mdf, then click Open.

    If you are using VS 2005 and connecting to a remote SQL Server database, open the Server name list, select your server name, select the authentication approach, and, if necessary, type the username and password that your instructor provides. Make sure that the *Select or enter a database name* option button is selected, open the Database name list, and select your database.

6. Click Test Connection. The "Test connection succeeded" message box should appear. Click OK, then click OK again.

HELP: If an error message stating "No database file was specified" appears, click the Advanced button, select the AttachDbFilename property, click the Ellipsis (. . .) button, then select the .mdf file again. Click Open and then click OK, then test the connection again.

NOTE: If you are using VS 2005 and connecting to a remote SQL Server database and you used SQL Server Authentication to connect, select the *Yes, include sensitive data in the connection string* option. This includes the username and password you used to connect in your project code and is necessary if you plan to work the example and exercises in this chapter.

---

7. On the *Choose your data connection* page, click Next.

8. *If you are using either VB Express or VS 2005 and connecting to a local database,* a message box opens and displays the message "The connection you selected uses a local data file that is not in the current project. Would you like to add the file to your project and modify the connection?" Click Yes to copy *yourDatabaseName.mdf* to the project folder.

NOTE: Selecting Yes in this step modifies the connection string to refer to the database file in the current project folder rather than in its original location. This way, you can copy the project folder and its contents to a different location. If you need to reset the database to its original contents due to inserts, updates, or deletes you have made while developing your program, do this by replacing the .mdf and .ldf files in your project folder with copies of the original .mdf and .ldf files from your \SQLServer\ Databases\ folder.

---

9. The *Save the connection string to the application configuration file* page appears. Make sure that "Yes, save the connection as" is checked, then click Next.

NOTE: A VB project stores data connection information in a file named app.config that the IDE creates and adds to your project when you create a data source.

---

10. The *Choose your database objects* page appears.

The *Choose your database objects* page allows you to select the database data objects that you want your project to be able to access. These objects can include all the tables, views, stored procedures, and functions in the database. After you select the objects, the IDE references them from a strongly typed data set. It also creates a table adapter that provides an interface for adding, updating, deleting, and viewing the data. It stores this information in an .xsd (XML schema definition) file, which captures information in a relational database schema such as table structures, data types, and relationships. This creates the strongly typed data set. (You will learn more about .xsd files in Chapter 9.)

Because this data source provides all the data throughout the chapter, you will select all the tables in the Ironwood University database.

To select the data source's database objects:

1. On the *Choose your database objects* page, open the Tables node. A list of all the database tables appears.
2. Scroll down the list, and check all the tables that begin with the word "University."
3. Accept the default DataSet name, then click Finish. (This step may take a few moments to complete because the system creates the .xsd file and initializes the data adapters and table adapters.)

Using the Data Designer Tools

After you create a data source, you can view its data using different data designer tools. The following subsections describe these tools.

Database Explorer

The *Database Explorer* provides a hierarchical view of all your data connections and the database objects that you can access in each connection. To open the Database Explorer, click View on the menu bar, then click Database Explorer. (VS 2005 users click View on the menu bar, then click Server Explorer.) Figure 6-3 shows the Database Explorer window.

> **NOTE:** If you are using VS 2005, the Database Explorer is included in the Server Explorer, which allows you to view and manage server connections along with database connections.

The Database Explorer displays each data connection as a node. When you open the connection node, you can view the connection's database objects, and when you open an object node, you can view the object's details. You can also use the Database Explorer to create a new connection and to create and manage the following database objects:

- **Database diagrams** are visual representations of a database that show tables, fields, primary keys, and foreign key links. (The visual representations of the

FIGURE 6-3 Database Explorer window

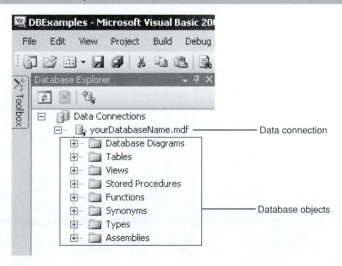

Ironwood University and Sport Motors databases in Figures 3-1 and 3-3 are database diagrams.)

- **Tables** displays nodes for all the database tables. In this node, you can create a new database table, modify the design of an existing table, and view and modify the table data.
- **Views** displays nodes for all the database views and allows you to create and modify views.
- **Stored Procedures, Functions, Synonyms, Types,** and **Assemblies** displays nodes for these objects and allows you to edit existing entries or create new ones.

The Database Explorer duplicates many of the functions you used in Management Studio to create and manage database objects. A notable exception, however, is that you cannot create a new database. (If you're using VS 2005's Server Explorer, you "can" create a new SQL Server database.)

Database Explorer is useful for viewing the current database objects and their properties, but it does not replace scripts used to create and manage these objects. When you make changes using Database Explorer, a record is not kept of what you have done. If you lose the database file, or if it becomes corrupted, you have no easy way to create it again. Scripts provide documentation of what is in a database and a way to restore a database to its original state. Although scripts are not a substitute for making backups of a production database, they are extremely useful in a development and testing environment.

Data Sources Window

The *Data Sources* window displays all your project's data sets and provides a hierarchical view of the data tables in each data set. Figure 6-4 shows the Data Sources window.

When you create a data source in a project, the default IDE window configuration automatically displays the Data Sources window on top of the Solution Explorer. You

FIGURE 6-4   Data Sources window

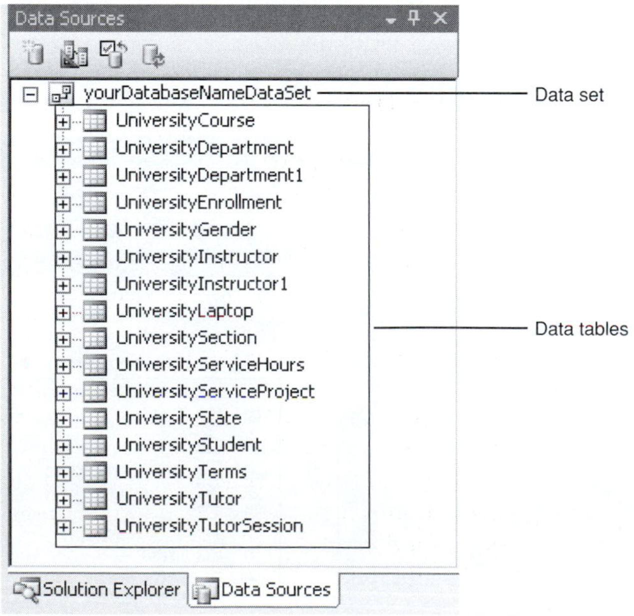

FIGURE 6-5 Operations in the Data Sources window

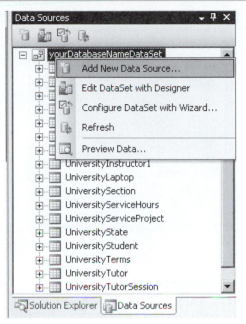

can toggle between the two windows using the bottom tabs. If the Data Sources tab does not appear automatically, you can display it by clicking Data on the menu bar, then clicking Show Data Sources. If the Data Sources window displays the text "Add New Data Source. . . ," then your project does not yet contain any data sources.

When you right-click anywhere in the Data Sources window, the menu shown in Figure 6-5 opens. This menu allows you to add a new data source or to edit existing data sets using the DataSet Designer.

The third menu choice, Configure DataSet with Wizard, displays the *Choose your database objects* page in the Data Source Configuration Wizard. (You used this page to select the database objects when you originally created the data source.) It is best to avoid this selection because it remakes the data source and overwrites any changes you have subsequently made to the data set using the DataSet Designer. The final menu choice, Preview Data, allows you to view the data in the data table but does not allow you to modify data.

TIP: You view and modify data from the Database or Server Explorer (not the Data Sources window or DataSet Designer) if you open a connection, open Tables, right-click a table, and select Show Table Data.

The Data Sources window is your primary interface for creating data-bound form controls. When a project form is open in Designer view, you can select a data table, then open a drop-down menu to display the choices shown in Figure 6-6.

These selections allow you to specify the type of data-bound controls that you want to add to the form. You can then drag a data table from the Data Sources window and drop it onto the form to create the data-bound control. By default, the data table appears as a data grid view control, which shows the data in a tabular format. If you select Details, the data-bound controls appear as individual text boxes for every table field.

FIGURE 6-6   Using the Data Sources window to create data-bound controls

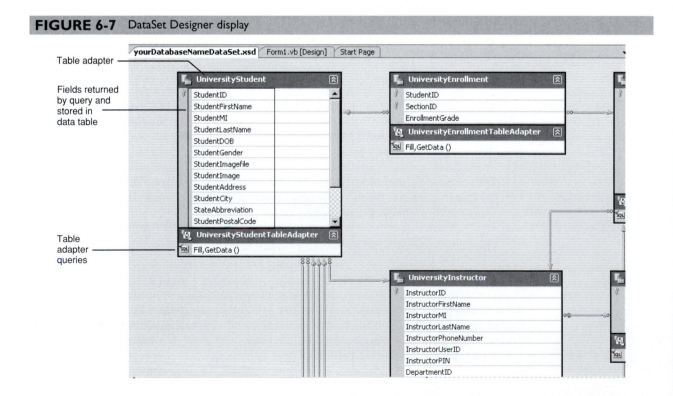

DataSet Designer

The *DataSet Designer* allows you to edit data tables and table adapters in a data source. To open the DataSet Designer, right-click a data source in the Data Sources window, then click Edit DataSet with Designer. The DataSet Designer displays a visual view of the data tables and their associated table adapters, as shown in Figure 6-7.

The DataSet Designer displays each of the table adapters as data table/query window pairs. The data table fields appear in the upper windowpane, and the table adapter's queries appear in the lower windowpane. You can move and resize the panes

FIGURE 6-7   DataSet Designer display

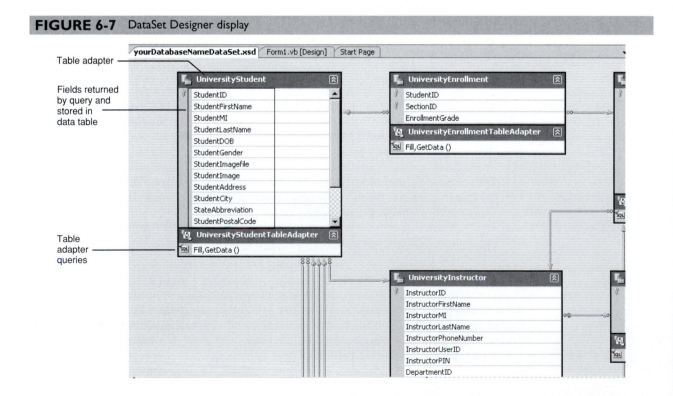

to improve the diagram's appearance. The lines that connect the windows represent primary key–foreign key relationships among the tables. You can drag the lines to align them with the correct fields in each data table.

The IDE automatically generates the Fill and GetData methods shown in Figure 6-7 when it creates the data source. These methods use a SQL query to retrieve all the data in the associated database table. You can generate additional table adapter queries if your applications need them.

COMMON DATABASE INTERFACES

After making a data source for a project, the next step is to create application interfaces for displaying and working with database data using controls such as text boxes, lists, and grids. Before describing the technical details for implementing these interfaces, we will explore the different types of user interfaces that database applications commonly use and suggest enhancements that these interfaces can include. This will help you understand the basic building blocks of database interfaces and assist you in designing interfaces for your database applications.

Database Interfaces

Table 6-1 summarizes common user interfaces for displaying database data.

NOTE: The interface examples that follow display data from the Ironwood University database (Figures 3-1 and 3-2).

The *single-record* data display (Figure 6-8) displays a single record on the form at a time.

TABLE 6-1	Common data display interfaces
Type	*Description*
Single-record	Displays a single record at a time
Tabular	Displays multiple records in a tabular format
Master-detail	Allows the user to select a master record, then displays detail values; often implemented by combining single-record and tabular displays.

FIGURE 6-8   Single-record display

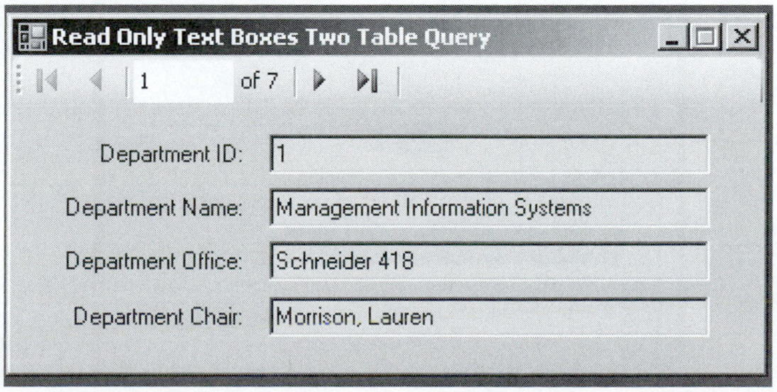

FIGURE 6-9   Tabular data display

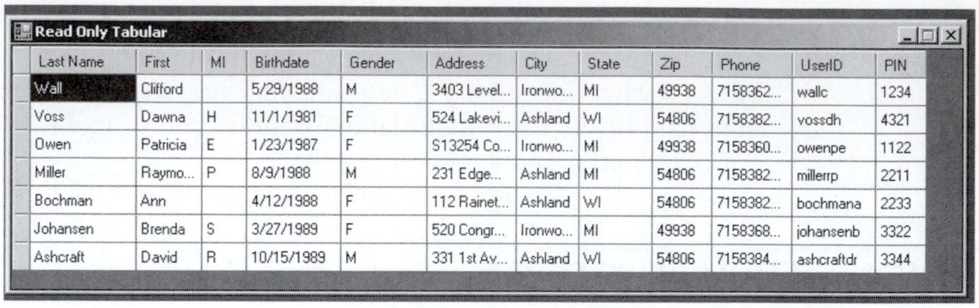

Last Name	First	MI	Birthdate	Gender	Address	City	State	Zip	Phone	UserID	PIN
Wall	Clifford		5/29/1988	M	3403 Level...	Ironwo...	MI	49938	7158362...	wallc	1234
Voss	Dawna	H	11/1/1981	F	524 Lakevi...	Ashland	WI	54806	7158382...	vossdh	4321
Owen	Patricia	E	1/23/1987	F	S13254 Co...	Ironwo...	MI	49938	7158360...	owenpe	1122
Miller	Raymo...	P	8/9/1988	M	231 Edge...	Ashland	MI	54806	7158382...	millerrp	2211
Bochman	Ann		4/12/1988	F	112 Rainet...	Ashland	WI	54806	7158382...	bochmana	2233
Johansen	Brenda	S	3/27/1989	F	520 Congr...	Ironwo...	MI	49938	7158368...	johansenb	3322
Ashcraft	David	R	10/15/1989	M	331 1st Av...	Ashland	WI	54806	7158384...	ashcraftdr	3344

The toolbar provides the control at the top of Figure 6-8 that is used for stepping through multiple records in the data set. This interface is used for inserting, updating, and deleting records. It can show data from one or more tables; Figure 6-8 displays data retrieved from two tables (UniversityDepartment and UniversityInstructor).

The *tabular* data display (Figure 6-9) shows multiple records at one time in a grid format. Users can use this interface for viewing, inserting, updating, and deleting record values. A tabular display might have horizontal or vertical scrollbars to show more data than fits on the form.

A *master-detail* data display (Figure 6-10) shows data values that have a one-to-many relationship. Recall that with a one-to-many relationship, a record in one table can have multiple associated records in another table. Figure 6-10 illustrates the one-to-many, or master-detail, relationship between the UniversityDepartment and UniversityCourse tables in Figure 3-1: a department offers multiple courses, but a particular course is offered by a single department. The UniversityDepartment table is the master table in the relationship, and UniversityCourse is the detail table in the relationship. Note that this data display combines a single-record display for the master records with a tabular display for the detail records. A master-detail display alternatively could use a tabular display for the master and a tabular display for the detail or possibly use a ListBox or ComboBox for the master and a tabular display for the detail.

FIGURE 6-10   Master-detail data display

Master record ———

Department Name: Accounting   Department Office: Schneider 419

Detail records ———

Name	Title	Credits
ACCT 201	Principles of Accounting	3
ACCT 312	Managerial Accounting	3

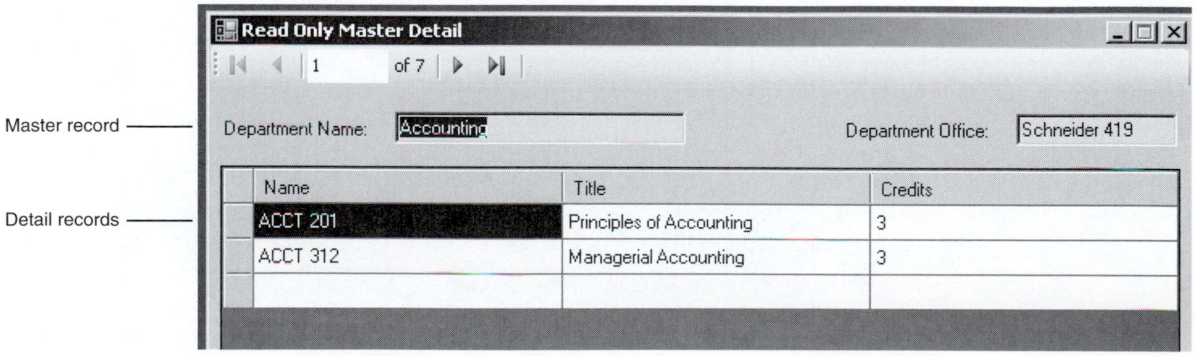

FIGURE 6-11   Form with image data

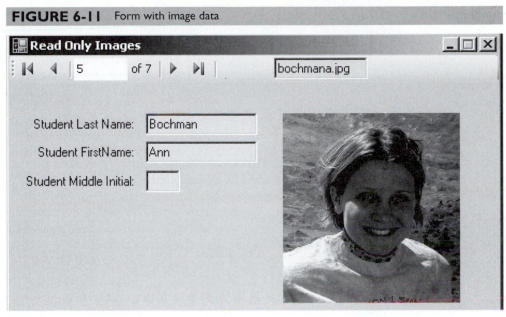

Photo courtesy of the authors.

Common Interface Enhancements

Most database applications provide enhancements that make it easier for users to display and work with data. You can include these enhancements in any of the basic data interfaces. The following subsections describe image data, text search, and pick list field enhancements.

Image Data

Most modern databases store image data, and database applications must be able to display these images. Figure 6-11 illustrates a form that displays image data.

There are two approaches for displaying image data in database applications: (1) *stored filenames,* in which you store the image file in a folder that is accessible to the database applications, and you store the image filename as a text string in the database; (2) *stored binary data,* in which you store the image as binary data in the database.

When you use the stored filenames approach, you store an image as a text string that references a filename and store the individual image files in a folder that database applications can access. Applications read the filename from the database and use this value to retrieve and display the image. The filenames in a folder must be unique. If duplicate filenames are needed, they can be organized into subfolders to avoid name conflicts. In this case, you would also store the names of subfolders along with filenames in the database. The advantage of this approach is that it makes it easy to write applications that display image data. The disadvantage of this approach is that someone may accidentally delete or rename the image files and subfolders without making the corresponding changes to the file and subfolder names stored in the database.

When you use the stored binary data approach, you do not need to worry about creating unique filenames or maintaining links between stored filenames and associated files. In addition, the database provides security and recovery features to safeguard the images. The disadvantage, however, is that the applications that display the images may be slower than applications that use the other approach. Most modern DBMS, including SQL Server, store images as "chunks" that fit on database pages. (A database page is a fixed-size internal storage unit.) Displaying an image usually requires the DBMS to reassemble these chunks into a stream of data that it writes to a temporary file that the application then displays. Because the other approach simply reads the file, it is usually faster.

So which approach should you use? If your applications display images frequently, use the file-based approach. If your applications do not display the images very often, if security is a concern, or if fault tolerance is needed, then store the images in the database.

NOTE: This book does not cover how to store and display binary images in a database. However, we have written two example programs for you to review if you need to use this approach. These files are included in the Datafiles\Chapter6 folder. The first one, SQLServerImageFields1, inserts and deletes images from a database and displays the images in a picture box. The second one, SQLServerImageFields2, inserts and deletes images from a database and displays the images in a DataGridView control.

Text Searches

The form in Figure 6-12 allows the user to perform a text search by entering a search value. When the user clicks Fill, the form retrieves one or more data values based on the search text.

You can configure this form to perform a partial search, in which the user enters one or more letters at the beginning of the search field, and the form retrieves all matching records. You can alternatively configure the form to perform a complete search, which retrieves only records that exactly match the search field text.

Pick List Field

Figure 6-13 illustrates a *pick list field,* which provides a selection for a field value in a data display. Usually, you create a pick list field for a field value that is a foreign key. The pick list may display a list of the foreign key values; however, it usually displays more descriptive values because foreign keys are usually surrogate key values that

FIGURE 6-12 Form that supports text searches

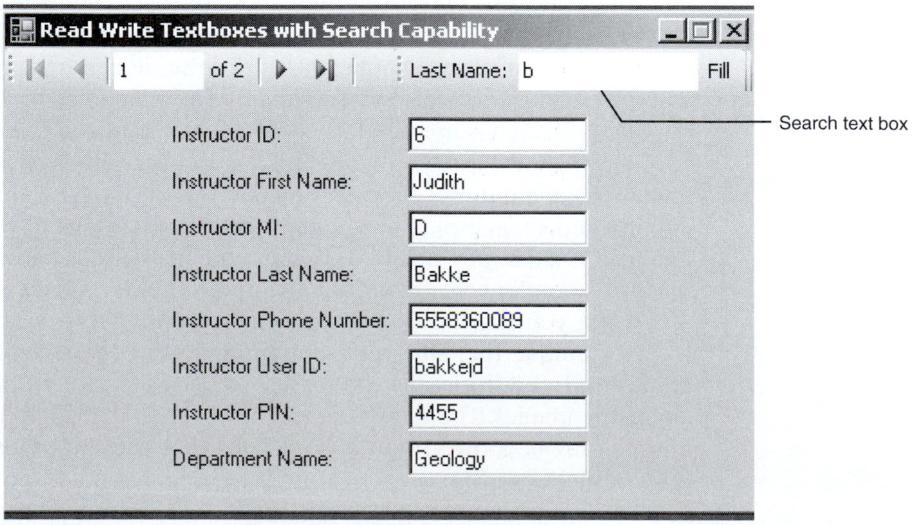

FIGURE 6-13   Pick list field

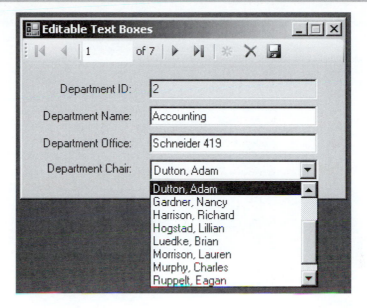

are not very descriptive. For example, Figure 6-13 shows records from the UniversityDepartment in a single-record data display. This table has a foreign key of ChairID, which references the UniversityInstructor table. This form displays concatenated instructor last and first name values in the pick list.

TIP: A ComboBox (as shown in Figure 6-13) or ListBox is sometimes used as the master display in a master-detail display. In this case, the pick list field value is usually a primary key instead of a foreign key.

WORKING WITH DATA-BOUND CONTROLS

So far, you have learned how VB applications access data, and you understand how to create data sources and work with IDE data controls. You are also familiar with how applications display database data. The next step is to create and configure data-bound controls to allow users to work with database data in applications.

In VS 2005/VB Express, the primary data-bound controls are text boxes and data grid views. Text boxes show data in a single-record format, and data grid views show data in a tabular format. *Data binding* creates links between controls on a form and data tables in a data source that allow the controls to display and update the current table data.

The following sections create a series of forms that demonstrate different ways of using data-bound controls to display data. First we demonstrate how to make forms that are read only and display database data but that do not allow users to change the data. Later, we make read-write forms that allow users to insert, update, and delete data records.

You will access all the project forms using a menu bar that provides a selection for each form. To create a menu bar, use a MenuStrip tool from the Toolbox. This provides an interface that creates horizontal and vertical menu choices, as shown in Figure 6-14.

FIGURE 6-14 Creating a MenuStrip control

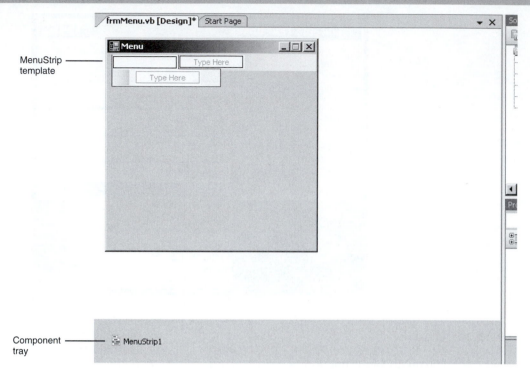

MenuStrip template

Component tray

The *MenuStrip* template allows you to enter the text for menu selections. To create the horizontal menu selections, type the top menu items horizontally across the strip. To create a child menu item, type its description below its associated parent menu item. As you enter menu items, additional "Type Here" template text boxes appear. After you create one or more child menu items, the next step is to create event handlers that execute when the user selects the item.

After you create a MenuStrip control, it appears in the Designer View Component tray. The Component tray provides a way to access form items (components) that are not visible on a form or that, like a MenuStrip, have multiple visible items. To select a single item, such as a single menu selection, select it on the form. To select the entire MenuStrip control, select it in the Component tray.

The following steps rename the default project form, create the MenuStrip control, and add the first menu selection and its first child menu item. You will create the rest of the menu items and their associated event handlers later.

To rename the project form and create the MenuStrip:

1. In the DBExamples project, open the Solution Explorer if necessary, and right-click Form1.vb. Rename the form to frmMenu.vb.
2. If necessary, open the form in Designer View, then modify the form properties as follows:

Property	*New Value*
FormBorderStyle	FixedSingle
MaximizeBox	False
StartPosition	CenterScreen

> **NOTE:** From this point forward, we refer to these properties as the *standard form property values*.

3. If necessary, change the form's Name property value to frmMenu and set the form's Text property value to Menu.
4. Open the Toolbox, scroll down to the Menus and Toolbars section, and double-click MenuStrip to add a menu to your form.
5. Place the insertion point in the "Type Here" text box in the tool strip, and type Read Only Examples.
6. Place the insertion point in the text box under Read Only Examples, and type Read Only Text Boxes. (You will add the rest of the menu selections later as you make additional forms.)
7. Save the project, then run the application.
8. Click Read Only Examples on the menu bar. The Read Only Text Boxes child menu item appears.
9. Close the application.

Read-Only Data-Bound Controls

This section describes how to create read-only data-bound controls, which are controls that allow users to view data but not to add new records or update values. (Read-only controls are easier to create and work with than read-write controls, which allow users to modify data.) We start with the easiest data display configuration, which is a single-record interface that shows data from a single table. The examples build on each other and become progressively more complex, and they use the following interface/table combinations: single-record from multiple tables; tabular from a single table; master-detail; and single-record with image.

Read-Only Single-Record Display from a Single Table

This section shows how to create the form in Figure 6-15, which displays all the fields in the UniversityDepartment table in a single-record display. This form contains text boxes and associated labels for each table field. It also contains the *BindingNavigator ToolStrip,* which allows users to step through the table records, shows the position of the record in the data table, and allows users to insert new records and delete existing records. (We disable these features in this form because it is a read-only form and because leaving them enabled introduces the need to perform data validation before

FIGURE 6-15   Form with a single-record display from a single table

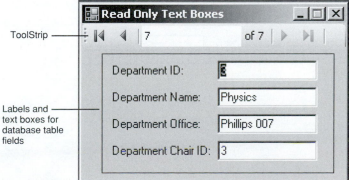

the user submits new data values to the database. We cover data validation later in this chapter.)

The following steps enable you to create a new form and modify its properties. Then we create data-bound text boxes for the UniversityDepartment table fields by selecting the table in the Data Sources window, then selecting the Details option. This instructs the IDE to display the data-bound controls as text boxes. Then we drag the data table from the Data Sources window and drop it onto the form.

To create a form with a single-record display from a single table:

1. To add a new form to the project, right-click the project in the Solution Explorer, point to Add, then click Windows form. Change the Name field value to frmReadOnlyTextboxes.vb, then click Add.
2. Set the new form's properties to the standard form property values for FormBorderStyle, MaximizeBox, and StartPosition.
3. If necessary, set the form's Name property value to frmReadOnlyTextboxes, and change the Text property value to Read Only Text Boxes.
4. Click the Data Sources tab on the bottom of the Solution Explorer to display the Data Sources window. If necessary, open the *yourDatabaseName*DataSet node.
5. Click the UniversityDepartment data table to display the drop-down list. Open the list, then select Details.
6. Drag the UniversityDepartment data table from the Data Sources window onto the form. The form should now look like Figure 6-16. If necessary, reposition the text boxes and resize the form.

When you add data-bound controls to a form, VB automatically creates a *ToolStrip,* which is a control that enables users to navigate among records, as well as to

FIGURE 6-16 Current Read Only Text Boxes form

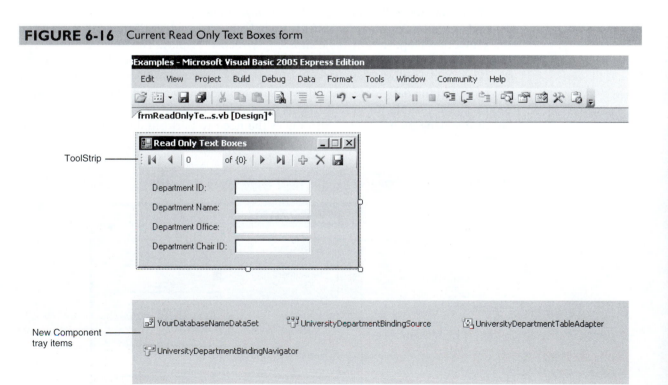

insert, update, and delete data values. The ToolStrip contains the following items, from left to right:

- **Move first** displays the first record in the data table.
- **Move previous** displays the record just before the current record.
- **Current position** shows the record number of the current record.
- **Total number of items** shows the number of records in the data table.
- **Move next** displays the record just after the current record.;
- **Move last** displays the last record in the data table.
- **Add new** creates a new blank record in the data table.
- **Delete** removes the current data table record.
- **Save Data** saves your changes and makes them permanent in the database.

VB also creates DataSet, BindingSource, TableAdapter, and BindingNavigator objects that appear in the Component tray. (Remember from Figure 6-2 that the ADO.NET 2.x architecture uses these components for data access.) VB also generates event handlers to load the data and to allow users to update records by changing values in the text boxes and then clicking the ToolStrip's Save Data button. Because this is a read-only form, we will delete the event handler for saving changes to data table items. We will also delete the Add New, Delete, and Save Data ToolStrip buttons.

To delete the event handler and ToolStrip buttons:

1. Select the Solution Explorer tab, select frmReadOnlyTextBoxes.vb in the Solution Explorer, then click the View Code button on the Solution Explorer toolbar to view the form in Code view.
2. In the Code editor, delete the code for the bindingNavigatorSaveItem_Click procedure, starting with Private Sub and ending with End Sub.

TIP: Do *not* delete the frmReadOnlyTextboxes_Load procedure. This code uses the table adapter's Fill method to open a connection to the database, retrieve the data specified in the table adapter's select query, and store it in the specified UniversityDepartment table adapter.

TIP: If you delete the components that were generated and placed in the component tray (Figure 6-16) and start over, this does not delete the code that was generated and placed in the Load or Click procedures. You need to delete this from the Code editor. Otherwise, this code is duplicated when you drag and drop the UniversityDepartment data table onto the form again.

---

3. Click the View Designer button on the Solution Explorer toolbar to view the form in Designer view. Right-click the Add New button (which displays a plus sign icon), then click Delete.
4. Delete the Delete button (which displays a red X) and the Save Data button (which displays a diskette).
5. Save the project.

To display the form from the startup Menu form, we add code to the Menu form to display the Read Only Text Boxes form, then redisplay the Menu form when the user closes the Read Only Text Boxes form. When we do this, we modify the mouse pointer that appears while the form is loading. Sometimes forms that contain data-bound controls can take a few moments to load because the application retrieves data from the database. During this delay, the user may become confused and think that the application is not working correctly. To avoid this confusion, continue to show the current form but display the mouse pointer as an hourglass. When the form with the data bound controls finishes loading, display it, and change the mouse pointer back to the regular arrow pointer. We use methods in the Cursors object class to modify the pointer shape.

To display the form from the startup Menu form:

1. To create the menu event handler, open frmMenu.vb in Designer view.
2. Double-click the Read Only Text Boxes menu selection to create its Click event handler. The form opens in Code view.
3. Add the following code to the event handler declaration:

```
'Change the current pointer to an hourglass
Me.Cursor = Cursors.WaitCursor
'Show the child form
frmReadOnlyTextboxes.ShowDialog()
'Redisplay the menu form after the user
'closes the child from
Me.Show()
'Restore the pointer to the default
Me.Cursor = Cursors.Default
```

4. Open frmReadOnlyTextboxes in the Code editor. Add the following command as the *last* line of the `frmReadOnlyTextboxes_Load` event-handling procedure:

```
frmMenu.Hide()
```

NOTE: From this point forward, we refer to these steps as the standard steps for creating a menu event handler and do not repeat them for each menu item.

5. Save the project, then run the application. The Menu form appears.

HELP: If the Read Only Text Boxes form appears, close the application, then make sure that frmMenu is the project Startup form.

6. Click Read Only Examples on the menu bar, then click Read Only Text Boxes. The Read Only Text Boxes form appears (and when this form appears the menu form should disappear) and displays the first record in the UniversityDepartment table.
7. Click Move Next on the ToolStrip to step through the table records.

TIP: If you move the mouse pointer onto the ToolStrip buttons, a ToolTip appears to describe each button.

8. Close the Read Only Text Boxes form, then close the Menu form.
9. Close all the open pages in the IDE Document window. Do not close the IDE.

Read-Only Single-Record Display from a Single Table

The previous example allows users to display data from a single table. In database applications, you often need to display data from multiple tables. For example, the application in Figure 6-15 would be a lot more informative if it displayed the name of the department chair rather than the department chair's ID value. In this section, we make the form in Figure 6-8, which shows the department chair's full name instead of the DepartmentChairID value.

To implement this, we create a new table adapter in the project. This table adapter contains a data set that includes the UniversityDepartment table data, along with the department chair's full name. We create this table adapter by joining the UniversityDepartment and UniversityInstructor tables.

New table adapters are created using the Table Adapter Configuration Wizard in the DataSet Designer. This wizard has a series of pages that allow you to select the table adapter's data connection and specify its SQL command. You can either type the SQL command directly or use Query Builder, which is a visual tool that automatically generates the SQL command. The following steps describe how to start the Table Adapter Configuration Wizard, start Query Builder, and select the query tables.

To start the wizard, open Query Builder, and select the query tables:

1. Click the Data Sources tab.
2. Click the Edit DataSet with Designer button on the Data Sources toolbar. The DataSet Designer opens.
3. Right-click in an open area of the DataSet Designer. (Do not right-click a data table or relationship). Point to Add, then click TableAdapter. The Table Adapter Configuration Wizard opens.
4. On the *Choose Your Data Connection* page, accept the current data connection string, then click Next.
5. On the *Choose a Command Type* page, make sure that the Use SQL statements option button is selected, then click Next.
6. On the *Enter a SQL Statement* page, click Query Builder.
7. In the Add Tables dialog box, select UniversityDepartment, press and hold the Ctrl key, then select UniversityInstructor. Click Add to add the tables to the Query Builder window, then click Close to close the Add Tables dialog box.
8. The Query Builder window opens and shows the selected tables. If necessary, resize the Query Builder window and the boxes that represent the tables.

Figure 6-17 illustrates the Query Builder window.

HELP: If you are using VB Express, the primary key–foreign key links may not appear. If this happens, create the links yourself by selecting the key field in one table, then dragging and dropping it onto the field in the related table. For this exercise, this means dragging and dropping DepartmentID from one table onto the other and dragging and dropping InstructorID from the UniversityInstructor table onto DepartmentChairID in the UniversityDepartment table.

The *Diagram pane* shows a visual view of the query tables and their fields. To select the query display fields, check the box next to the field name. The selected display fields then appear in the *Grid pane*. In the Grid pane, you can specify a sort order for the retrieved records and specify a filter (search condition) for the query. The *SQL pane* displays the text of the associated SQL command. When Execute is clicked, the records that the query retrieves appear in the *Results pane*.

The following steps show how to use Query Builder to select the query display fields, execute the query, and view the results. You can modify the query by concatenating the instructor name components together into a single field identified by an alias. (To concatenate text that a SQL command retrieves, use the plus sign (+) operator; to create an alias, type the alias after the field name.)

FIGURE 6-17 Query Builder window

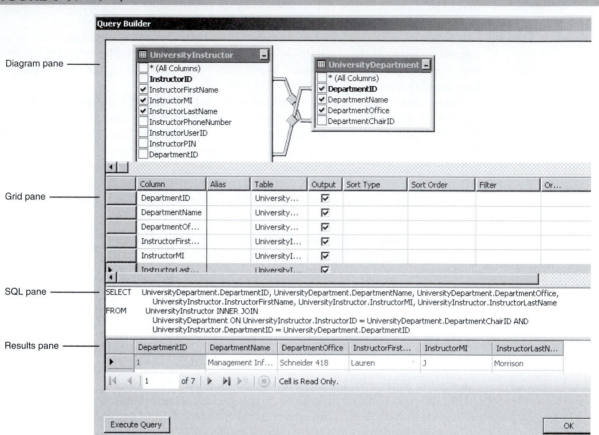

To create, execute, and modify the query:

1. In the Query Builder Display pane, check DepartmentID, DepartmentName, and DepartmentOffice in the UniversityDepartment table, and InstructorFirstName and InstructorLastName in the UniversityInstructor table. Note that the display fields appear in the Grid pane, and the SQL pane displays the revised SQL command.

2. Click Execute Query. The retrieved records appear in the Results pane. If necessary, resize the window and panes as needed so that the Query Builder window looks like Figure 6-17.

3. In the SQL pane, modify the first part of the SELECT clause in the SQL command to concatenate the last and first names as follows:

```
SELECT UniversityDepartment.DepartmentID,
UniversityDepartment.DepartmentName,
UniversityDepartment.DepartmentOffice,
UniversityInstructor.InstructorLastName +
', ' + UniversityInstructor.InstructorFirstName
AS InstructorFullName
```

4. Click Execute Query to test the modified query. The Results pane should now show the instructor name as a single formatted field.

5. Click OK to save the query and return to the wizard, which now displays the revised SQL command.

The steps for creating the table adapter are next. The default methods that the wizard creates to fill the table adapter with data, return the data table, and automatically update the underlying database table are accepted. Because this table adapter is created using joined tables, the methods that insert, update, and delete records from an underlying table do not work. (These methods work only for table adapters based on queries from a single table.) A results page will advise of this problem; this is expected and always appears when you create a table adapter that joins tables.

To complete the table adapter:

1. On the *Enter a SQL Statement* page, click Next.
2. On the *Choose Methods to Generate* page, accept creating the default methods for filling, returning, and updating the data set, then click Next.
3. The *Wizard Results* page appears, and displays warnings that the UPDATE and DELETE statements will not work. These warnings are expected because the action queries can be generated only for table adapters associated with a single table.
4. Click Finish. The new table adapter, named UniversityDepartment1, appears in the DataSet Designer window.
5. Close the DataSet Designer window, then save the project.

Now that the table adapter is complete, we can create the form that shows a single-record display from multiple tables, as shown in Figure 6-8. We will follow the same steps used in the previous exercise to create a single-record form that displays data from a single table.

To create the form that displays a single-record display from multiple tables:

1. Add a new form named frmReadOnlyTextboxesTwoTableQuery.vb to the project.
2. Set the new form's properties to the standard form property values. If necessary, change the Name value to frmReadOnlyTextboxesTwoTableQuery and set the Text value to Read Only Text Boxes Two Table Query.
3. To add the data-bound controls to the form, select the Data Sources tab, select UniversityDepartment1, open the list, and select Details. Then drag UniversityDepartment1 from the Data Sources window and drop it onto your new form. The labels, data-bound text boxes, and ToolStrip appear on the form. If necessary, reposition the controls on the form and resize it so that it looks like Figure 6-8.
4. Because this is a read-only form, open the form (frmReadOnlyTextboxesTwoTableQuery) in Code view and delete the bindingNavigatorSaveItem_Click procedure if it is present.
5. Open the form in Designer view, and delete the Add New, Delete, and Save Data buttons on the ToolStrip.
6. Save the project.

To test the form, you need to add the code to the menu form that displays the form from the menu bar.

To open the new form from the menu form:

1. To add the new menu selection to the Menu form, open the Menu form in Designer view, place the insertion point in the text box under the last entry, and type Read Only Text Boxes Two Table Query.
2. Create the Click event handler in the Menu form to call the frmReadOnlyTextBoxesTwoTableQuery form.

TIP: A quick way to add the code for this step is to copy it from the other menu item event handler, directly above the current event handler, and modify the form name in the command so that it refers to the new form.

---

3. Save the project, then run the application. Select Read Only on the menu bar, then click Read Only Text Boxes Two Table Query. The new form appears.
4. Use the ToolStrip to scroll through the records, then close both forms in the application.
5. Close all the open pages in the IDE Document window. Do not close the IDE.

Read-Only Tabular Display from a Single Table

So far, you have learned how to display data in a single-record format. In this section, we create a form that displays data from a single table in a tabular format using a data grid view control. To do this, select the table adapter in the Data Sources window as before, but instead of selecting Details, select DataGridView. The next sequence of steps shows how to create the form in Figure 6-9, which displays data from the UniversityStudent table.

To create the new form and add the data grid view control:

1. Create a new form named frmReadOnlyTabular.
2. Set the new form's properties to the standard form property values. If necessary, set the form's Name property to frmReadOnlyTabular, and set the Text value to Read Only Tabular.
3. Make sure that the form is open in Designer view.
4. To create the data grid control, open the Data Sources window, select UniversityStudent, open its list, and select DataGridView. Then drag UniversityStudent from the Data Sources window and drop it on the form. The DataGridView control appears on the form.

HELP: If a list arrow does not appear when you select the table adapter in the Data Sources window, make sure that you are displaying the form in Designer view.

---

5. Save the project.

To make the form read only, you must delete the event handler for updating data, and modify some of the data grid view control's properties. You must also delete the BindingNavigator control from the Components tray, which removes the ToolStrip from the form. In a read-only tabular form, you do not need the ToolStrip for navigating because you can scroll vertically through the records using scroll bars.

When you *dock* a control to a form, the control is attached to one or more edges of the form, and the control resizes to fit the containing form. Dock the DataGridView to the form by setting the control's Dock property to the value that represents the form edge to be docked to the form: Top, Bottom, Right, Left, or Fill (the last of which docks the control to all the form edges). The following steps modify the data grid view control to make it read only, then dock it to all the form edges.

To make the control read-only and to dock it to the form:

1. Open the form in Code view, and delete the code for the bindingNavigatorSaveItem_Click event handler.

2. Open the form in Designer view, select the new data grid view control, and modify its properties as follows:

Property	*New Value*
Name	dgStudent
AllowUserToAddRows	False
AllowUserToDeleteRows	False
AutoSizeColumnsMode	DisplayedCells
ReadOnly	True
RowHeadersWidth	20

3. Select UniversityStudentBindingNavigator from the component tray, right-click, then click Delete.

4. To dock the control to the form, select the UniversityStudentDataGridView control on the form, select the Dock property in the Properties window, and click the center square to set the Dock property value to Fill.

5. Resize the form by making it wider so that it displays as much of the data grid control's data columns as possible. (The amount the window can display depends on the resolution of the screen display. If all the columns are not visible, users will be able to view their data by scrolling in the data grid control.)

6. Save the project.

The next steps add the commands to view the new form from the menu form, test the application, and view the data in the data grid control.

To add the commands to view the new form and then test the application:

1. Add a new menu item to frmMenu that has the text Read Only Tabular, and modify the menu item's event handler so that it calls the frmReadOnlyTabular form.

2. Save the project, then run the application.

3. Select Read Only Examples on the menu bar, then click Read Only Tabular to display the form that contains the data grid view control. The form appears and displays all the fields in the UniversityStudent table.

4. Close the application.

The application does not yet look like Figure 6-9. The data grid control needs to be modified to suppress displaying all the table columns, and column headings need to be changed to display text other than the data table column names. Make these modifications by editing the columns that the data grid view control displays and by changing the HeaderText property of individual columns. The next set of steps show how to do this.

To change the data grid view control's appearance:

1. To suppress display of some of the table columns, open frmReadOnlyTabular in Designer view, right-click anywhere on the DataGridView except on one of the column headings, then click Edit Columns. The Edit Columns dialog box opens.

2. If necessary, select StudentID in the Selected Columns list, then click Remove. Repeat this step for the StudentImageFile, AdvisorID and StudentImage columns. (Do not close the Edit Columns dialog box yet.)

3. To change the column heading text, select StudentFirstName in the Selected Columns list, then change its HeaderText property value to First in the Bound Columns Property List.

4. Repeat step 3 for the following columns:

Column	New HeaderText Value
StudentMI	MI
StudentLastName	Last Name
StudentDOB	Birth Date
StudentGender	Gender
StudentAddress	Address
StudentCity	City
StateAbbreviation	State
StudentPostalCode	Zip
StudentPhoneNumber	Phone
StudentUserID	User ID
StudentPIN	PIN

5. Click OK to close the Edit Columns dialog box, then save the project.
6. Run the application, select Read Only Examples on the menu bar, then click Read Only Tabular. The form displays the modified data grid view display, as shown in Figure 6-9. (The form may not be the correct size for the data grid.)
7. Close the form, then close the menu form.
8. Modify the form size as necessary, then run the form again to check the changes.
9. Save the project, then close all the open pages in the IDE Document window. Do not close the IDE.

Creating a tabular data display that displays data from multiple tables requires a new table adapter based on a query that joins multiple tables. (You learned how to create a new table adapter that joined multiple tables in the section that described how to display data from multiple tables in a single-record display.) After you create the table adapter, select the new table adapter in the Data Sources window, open its list, select DataGridView, and create the data grid view control on the form.

Read-Only Master-Detail Display

A master-detail data display shows a one-to-many data relationship in which a record in one table can have multiple associated records in another table. This provides a "drill-down" view of data that allows you to move from high-level summary information to more detailed information. Figure 6-10 illustrates a master-detail display that shows data from the UniversityDepartment table in a single-record display, and related data from the UniversityCourse table in a tabular display. (A master-detail display could show the master records in a tabular display as well.)

When you create a data source that contains tables with foreign key relationships, VB automatically displays these relationships hierarchically in the Data Sources window, as shown in Figure 6-18. The Data Sources list shows data tables as nodes that contain table field names. When a master-detail relationship exists, the master table shows the detail table as an additional child node. For example, a UniversityDepartment offers multiple courses, so UniversityDepartment is the master table in the relationship and UniversityCourse is the detail table in the relationship. The Data Sources list displays the UniversityDepartment node that contains its table fields. It also contains the UniversityCourse table as a child node. Similarly, a UniversityCourse can have multiple associated sections. When you open the UniversityCourse node, the table fields appear, along with a node that represents the UniversitySection table.

To create a form that displays a master-detail relationship, drag the table adapter that displays the master record and drop it onto the form. To create the detail relationship, drag the table adapter that appears below the master record and drop it onto the

FIGURE 6-18   Master-detail relationships in the Data Sources window

Master record ——

Detail records ——

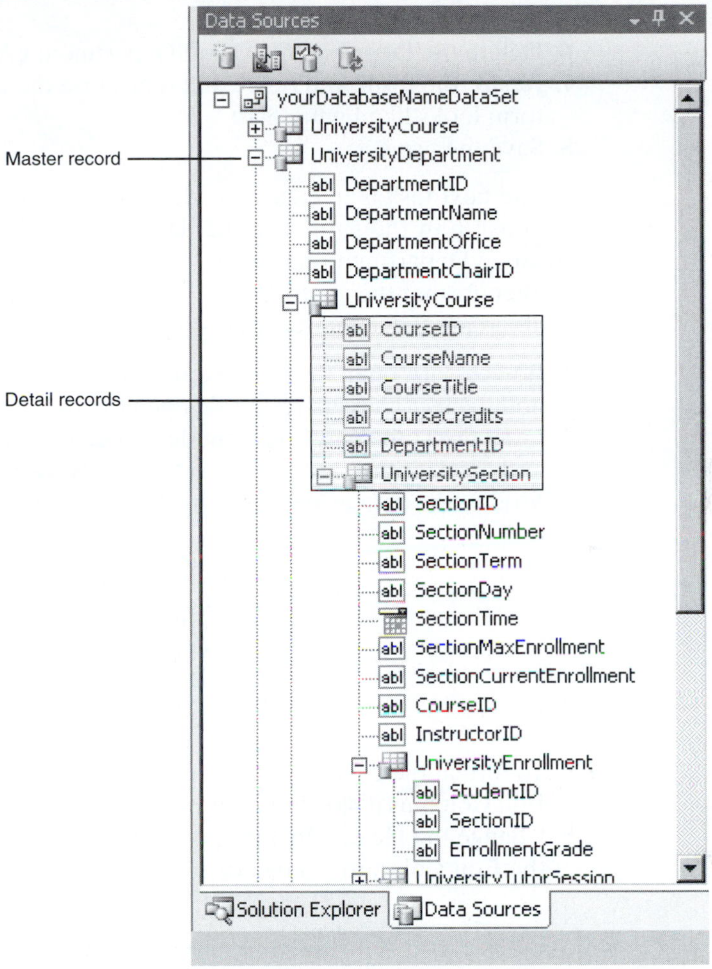

form. This preserves the relationship and automatically adds the synchronizing code between the master and detail components.

The following steps create the form with the master-detail data display in Figure 6-10. First you create the master record selections as read-only text boxes that use a single-record display.

To create the master-detail display form and master record selections:

1. Create a new form named frmReadOnlyMasterDetail. Set the new form's properties to the standard form property values. If necessary, set the form's Name property to frmReadOnlyMasterDetail, and set the Text value to Read Only Master Detail.

2. To display the master records in a single-record display, open the Data Sources window, select UniversityDepartment, open its list, and click Details.

3. Drag UniversityDepartment from the Data Sources window and drop it onto the form.

4. Open the form in Code view, and delete the bindingNavigatorSaveItem_Click procedure.

5. Open the form in Designer view, and delete the Add New, Delete, and Save Data buttons on the ToolStrip. (You may need to make the form wider to display all the ToolStrip buttons.)
6. Delete the Department ID and Department Chair ID labels and text boxes.
7. Resize the form, and resize and reposition the labels and text boxes so that the form looks like Figure 6-10.
8. Save the project.

The next task is to create the detail record display. To represent the master-detail relationship in the form, use the data table in the Data Sources window under the UniversityDepartment data table. Display the detail records in a data grid view control, then format the control.

To create the detail record display:

1. If necessary, open the Data Sources window. Open the UniversityDepartment node, select UniversityCourse, open the list, and select DataGridView.
2. Drag the UniversityCourse node that currently displays the selection list arrow, and drop it onto the form. The data grid view control appears on the form.
3. Modify the data grid view control's properties as follows:

Property	New Value
AllowUserToAddRows	False
AllowUserToDeleteRows	False
AutoSizeColumnsMode	Fill
ReadOnly	True
RowsHeaderWidth	20

4. To format the data grid view control, right-click it, then click Edit Columns. In the Edit Columns dialog box, remove the CourseID and DepartmentID columns.
5. Change the HeaderText property of the following columns, then click OK to close the Edit Columns dialog box.

Column	New Header Text
CourseName	Name
CourseTitle	Title
CourseCredits	Credits

6. Resize and reposition the data grid control so that it looks like the one in Figure 6-10.
7. Create a label control and position it on the left edge of the form, just above the data grid view control. Changes its properties as follows:

Property	New Value
Font	12-point Microsoft Sans Serif Bold
Text	Courses

8. In the frmMenu form, add a new menu item under the previous selection that has the text Read Only Master Detail, and modify the menu item's event handler so that it calls the frmReadOnlyMasterDetail form.
9. Save the project, then run the application.
10. Select Read Only Examples on the menu bar, then click Read Only Master Detail to display the master-detail display. The form appears, displaying the first record in the UniversityDepartment table (Management Information Systems) and all its associated courses from the UniversityCourse table.

11. Click Move Next on the ToolStrip. The next UniversityDepartment record (Accounting) appears, along with its associated courses.
12. Continue to click Move Next to view all the department records and their associated courses.
13. Close the application, and close all the open pages in the IDE Document window. Do not close the IDE.

Read-Only Single-Record Display with Images

This section shows how to create the form in Figure 6-11, which displays a student's first and last name in text boxes, along with his or her image. The form uses the stored filename approach, which retrieves the image filename from the database and then displays the associated image file.

To display an image on a VB form, use a *picture box* control, which is a control that displays a graphic image file. VB picture box controls can display graphic images with the following file formats: bitmap (.bmp), JPEG (.jpg), metafile (.wmf), GIF (.gif), and icon (.ico). The next set of steps create a new form that displays the student's first and last name and image file fields in a single-record format and that contains a picture box control showing the student's image file.

To create the form and text box items:

1. Create a new form named frmReadOnlyImages.
2. Set the new form's properties to the standard form property values. If necessary, set the form's Name property to frmReadOnlyImages and set the Text value to Read Only Images.
3. Open the Data Sources window, select the UniversityStudent data table, open the list, and select Details.
4. Open the UniversityStudent node. Select the StudentLastName node (which appears as a text box), then drag and drop it onto the form. The field appears on the form as a text box and label.
5. Repeat the previous step for the StudentFirstName, StudentMI, and StudentImagefile nodes.
6. Move the text box for the Student Imagefile to the top of the form, on the binding navigator control, as shown in Figure 6-11.
7. Delete the Student Imagefile: label.
8. Open the form in Code view, and delete the bindingNavigatorSaveItem_Click procedure.
9. Open the form in Designer view, and delete the Add New, Delete, and Save Data buttons on the ToolStrip.
10. Save the project.

The next task is to create the picture box control to display the image. You first configure the picture box to resize the image automatically so that it conforms to the picture box control's size by setting its SizeMode property to Zoom. Then you create an event handler that is associated with the TextChanged event of the StudentImagefile text box. When the user moves to a new student record and the filename changes, the event handler sets the picture box's ImageLocation property, which specifies the image folder path and filename, to the new data value.

How do you reference the location of the image files in the application's file system? Place the student image files in a subfolder of the project's Debug folder, named Images\Student. The project's Debug folder holds the project assembly files during project development and becomes the application's startup path when the application runs. The application's *startup path* is the location that stores the project's assembly files. Reference folders in the project's startup path, which is the Debug folder, using the following general syntax:

```
Application.StartupPath & "\folderpath\filename"
```

For example, use the following command to reference the \Images\Student\ vossd.jpg file in the project's Debug folder:

```
Application.StartupPath & "\Images\Student\vossd.jpg"
```

To create and configure the picture box control:

1. Open the form in Designer view, open the ToolBox, and double-click the PictureBox control to add it to the form. Resize the form and picture box, and reposition the form controls so that they look like Figure 6-11.
2. Modify the picture box's properties as follows:

Property Name	New Value
Name	picStudent
SizeMode	Zoom

3. Copy the \SQLServer\Datafiles\Chapter6\Images folder and all its contents to your \SQLServer\Solutions\Chapter6\DBExamples\bin\Debug\ folder.
4. To create the event handler, open the form in Code view, open the Class list, select StudentImagefileTextBox, then open the Events list and select TextChanged. The new event handler declaration appears in the Code editor.
5. Add the following command to the event handler to display the new image in the picture box:

```
picStudent.ImageLocation = Application.StartupPath & _
                    "\Images\Student\" & _
                    StudentImagefileTextBox.Text
```

6. Add a new menu item under the previous selection with the text Read Only Images, and modify the menu item's event handler so that it calls the frmReadOnlyImages form.
7. Save the project, then run the application.
8. Select Read Only Examples on the menu bar, then click Read Only Images to display the new form. The form appears and displays the first student record (Clifford Wall) and his associated image.
9. Click Move Next on the ToolStrip. The next student record (Dawna Voss) appears, along with her image.
10. Continue to click Move Next to view all the student records and their associated images.

Close the application, and close all the open pages in the IDE Document window. Do not close the IDE.

TIP: If you do not want the image filename to appear on the form, you can delete the label, then set its Location property coordinates to negative values, such as −200, −200. This positions the text box outside the visible portion of the form.

Read-Only Single-Record Display with Search Field

Finding a specific record by scrolling through all the data table values is not reasonable when a table contains a large number of records. One solution is to create a text search field that allows the user to enter a search value and has the form retrieve the matching record(s). This section shows how to create the form in Figure 6-12, which displays a *Fill ToolStrip,* a ToolStrip control that contains a search text box allowing a user to enter one or more characters for an instructor's last name and then click a link that fills the form with data based on the search value. The form retrieves all instructor records that match the search string.

To create this form, create a table adapter that contains a parameter query. In a VB Windows application, a *parameter query* is a query that receives a search value from a form control, such as a text box. To create a parameter query, use the following general syntax in the query search condition:

```
WHERE SearchColumn Operator @VariableName
```

For example, the following query prompts the user to enter a search condition for one or more characters at the beginning of the instructor's last name value:

```
WHERE InstructorLastName LIKE @LastNameSearchString + '%'
```

TIP: The plus sign (+) is the SQL concatenation operator, and the percent sign (%) is the SQL wildcard character that represents any number of characters.

The following steps create the form in Figure 6-12, which shows a single-record display of the fields in the UniversityInstructor table. This requires a new table adapter named UniversityInstructorSearch that is based on a parameter query using a parameter named @LName to reference the value the user enters in the fill ToolStrip search text box. The query uses the LIKE condition operator, which matches partial text strings. It concatenates the % wildcard character to the text box value to allow the user to a partial search string.

To create the form and table adapter:

1. Create a new form named frmReadOnlySearch. Set the new form's properties to the standard form property values for FormBorderStyle, MaximizeBox, and StartPosition. If necessary, set the form's Name property to frmReadOnlySearch, and set the Text value to Read Only Search.
2. To create the new table adapter, open the Data Sources window, and click Edit DataSet with Designer on the toolbar to open the DataSet Designer.
3. Create a new table adapter that uses the following parameter query to retrieve the table data:

```
SELECT InstructorID, InstructorFirstName,
       InstructorMI, InstructorLastName,
       InstructorPhoneNumber, InstructorUserID,
       InstructorPIN, DepartmentName
FROM UniversityInstructor
INNER JOIN UniversityDepartment
ON UniversityInstructor.DepartmentID =
   UniversityDepartment.DepartmentID
WHERE InstructorLastName Like @LName + '%'
ORDER BY InstructorLastName, InstructorFirstName
```

4. Right-click the new table adapter, click Rename, and change the name to UniversityInstructorSearch.
5. Close the DataSet Designer window, and click Yes to save your changes.
6. Save the project.

The next step is to bind the table adapter to the form. The following steps show how to display the data using a single-record display and how to delete the code and buttons as necessary to make the form read only. They also modify the parameter name on the Fill ToolStrip from "LName" to "Last Name." Finally, they add the commands to run the form from the Menu form, and test the form.

To bind the table adapter to the form and test the form:

1. In the Data Sources window, select UniversityInstructorSearch, open the list, and click Details.
2. Drag UniversityInstructorSearch and drop it onto the form. The data table text boxes and labels appear on the form, along with the Fill ToolStrip.
3. To allow repositioning the Fill ToolStrip to the top of the form, select the Fill ToolStrip in the component tray, and change its Dock property to None. Then select the entire Fill ToolStrip (not its individual components) and drag it to the top of the form on the right side of the binding navigator.
4. Resize and reposition the form and form items so that the form looks like Figure 6-12.
5. Open the form in Code view and delete the bindingNavigatorSaveItem_Click procedure.
6. Open the form in Designer view, and delete the Add New, Delete, and Save Data buttons on the ToolStrip.
7. Select LName text label on the Fill ToolStrip. (This is the ToolStripLabel control.) Change its Text property value to Last Name:.
8. Add a new menu item to frmMenu under the previous selection with the text Read Only Search, and modify the menu item's event handler so that it calls the frmReadOnlySearch form.
9. Save the project, then run the application.
10. Select Read Only Examples on the menu bar, then click Read Only Search to display the new form. The form opens but does not yet display any data.
11. Type "b" in the Fill ToolStrip text box, then click Fill on the Fill ToolStrip. The form retrieves records for two instructors, both of whom have last names that begin with "b."
12. To retrieve all the instructor records, delete all the text in the search text box, then click Fill. The form retrieves all the instructor records.
13. Close both application forms.
14. Close all open pages in the Document window. Do not close the IDE.

Read-Write Data-Bound Controls

So far, you have learned how to create a variety of read-only data-bound controls. Creating read-write data-bound controls that enable users to update data adds complexity because it introduces the need to perform data validation before the user submits new data values to the database. In a database application, *data validation* confirms that the user enters field values with specific data types, provides values for fields with NOT NULL constraints, and enters legal primary and foreign key values.

This section describes a series of forms that use read-write data-bound controls. The forms start simple and become more complex as follows: single-record display from a single table; enhanced single-record display that uses a pick list and allows users to cancel editing operations; tabular display from a single table that uses a pick list and data validation; updatable master-detail; and finally updatable master-detail that allows you to cancel edits in progress. As before, you create these forms in the DBExamples project created earlier in the chapter.

Read-Write Issues When Connecting to a Microsoft SQL Server Database File

If you are using VB Express, you are limited to connecting to Microsoft SQL Server database files when adding a project Data Source. If you are using VS 2005, you have the option of connecting either to a SQL Server database file or to a remote SQL Server database. Whenever you choose to connect to a file rather than a remote server, a few issues related to inserting, updating, and deleting can cause some confusion.

Earlier in this chapter, you were instructed to click Yes when adding a connection to a database file to your project and the following message appeared: "The connection you selected uses a local data file that is not in the current project. Would you like to add the file to your project and modify the connection?" When you did this, the IDE copied the database .mdf and .ldf files into the project's application path (Debug) folder. This worked well as long as the forms were read only. However, when you make forms that change the database data, a problem occurs. As you test your program and make changes to the database, everything appears to work correctly. After you exit your application and then restart it, however, your changes to the database are not saved, and the database is in its original condition.

This happens because your program is always editing the copy of the .mdf and .ldf files that the IDE stores in the project's application path folder. Each time you start your program, the IDE recopies the database files into your project's application path folder. Microsoft's intent is to ensure the developer is always working with a "fresh" copy of the data. (This does not affect a completed application because its users are not running it through the VB Express or VS 2005 IDE, but run the program's assembly file directly.)

We strongly recommend modifying this default IDE behavior because in many situations you need to run your program, modify the database data, then recheck the data to ensure that the program worked correctly and the changes were really made. For example, sometimes the IDE does not display an error message to let you know that an update failed, so the only way to confirm the update is to stop the application, restart it, and see if the changes appear. The Database Explorer or the Data Sources window also displays the data from the database files stored in the project's Debug folder.

The solution is to prevent the IDE from copying the database files from the project's root folder to the project application path folder. You can do this by first selecting the database .mdf file in the Solution Explorer, displaying its Properties window, and changing its *Copy to Output Directory* property from *Copy always* to *Do not copy*. After changing this property, then copy the original database .mdf and .ldf files to the project's application path (Debug) folder. (If you copy these files *before* changing this property, the IDE deletes the files from the project application path folder when you change the property, and the program fails when it tries to access the files.)

The following steps show how to perform the steps to configure your IDE not to copy the database files each time the application starts.

NOTE: Perform these steps only if you are connecting to a local database using the database .mdf file.

To modify your project to avoid copying the database files:

1. *If you are using VB Express or VS 2005 and connecting to a database file,* open the Solution Explorer and select *yourDatabaseName.*mdf.

2. In the Properties window, change the Copy to Output Directory property value to Do not copy. Leave all other properties unchanged.

TIP: A project's data source also has a Copy to Output Directory property. Make sure you have selected the .mdf file in the Solution Explorer and not the .xsd file.

---

3. In Windows Explorer, copy the *yourDatabaseName*.mdf and yourDatabaseName_log.ldf files from your project's root folder to the project's bin\Debug folder, and confirm overwriting the existing files.
4. Save the application, run the project, click Read Only Examples on the menu bar, then click Read Only Text Boxes to confirm that the project is working correctly.

HELP: If an error occurs, click Stop Debugging on the toolbar, repeat step 3, then run the project again. The project should run correctly.

---

5. Close the application.

TIP: If you are working with a large database file that is hundreds of megabytes or gigabytes in size, modifying the project to avoid copying the file is essential. Otherwise every time you try to test your application from the IDE, it copies the file from the project root folder to the bin\Debug folder, and this can take quite awhile.

Read-Write Single-Record Display from a Single Table

This section creates the form in Figure 6-15, which shows all the fields from the UniversityDepartment table in a single-record display. This time, we do not disable the data-bound controls' editing features to make it an editable form. This illustrates some of the problems that can occur if you do not include data validation in a form.

To create a read-write single-record display form:

1. Create a new form named frmReadWriteTextBoxes. Set the new form's properties to the standard form property values. If necessary, set the form's Name property to frmReadWriteTextboxes, and set the Text value to Read Write Text Boxes.
2. In the Data Sources window, select UniversityDepartment, open its list, click Details, then drag the data table and drop it onto the form. If necessary, resize the form and reposition the labels and text boxes so that they are centered on the form.

That's it; you are done with the form! You are probably thinking, "Why did we go to extra work earlier to disable editing?" To answer this question, we create a new menu item on the MenuStrip control, then run and test the form to see the problems.

To create the menu item and test the form:

1. Open frmMenu.vb in Designer view, and add a new top-level menu item on the right edge of Read Only Examples with the text Read Write Examples.
2. Create a new menu item under Read Write Examples with the text Read Write Text Boxes. Perform the steps for adding the commands to call the new form (which is frmReadWriteTextBoxes) from the menu form and to hide the menu form from the new form.
3. Save the project, then run the application.
4. On the Menu form, select Read Write Examples on the menu bar, then click Read Write Text Boxes. The new form appear, and displays the first UniversityDepartment record.

5. Click Add New on the ToolStrip. A new blank record appears in the form, and displays the next DepartmentID value from the table's identity column.

6. Add the following values to the form text boxes:

Text Box	*New Value*
Department ID	(Do not change)
Department Name	Sociology
Department Office	Schneider 423
Department Chair ID	6

7. Click Save Data on the ToolStrip. Nothing appears to happen, but in this case, that is a good sign because it means that the form saved the data to the database. If an error message appears, there is a problem, and the record is not saved. However, it would have been nice to have some positive feedback.

TIP: Until you click Save Data, the form does not update the database.

---

8. Click Move Previous several times to scroll backward through the table records. Then, click Move Last to move to the last record, which is the record you just added.

So far, so good—right? Aside from not getting any positive feedback when you saved the record, the form seems to work pretty well. However, things do not go so well if you enter incorrect data values, as you will see next.

To see what happens when you enter incorrect data values:

1. Click Add New again, and enter the following new record values. Note that the Chair ID value (20) is an illegal foreign key value because it does not exist in the parent (UniversityInstructor) table.

Text Box	*New Value*
Department ID	(Do not change)
Department Name	Astronomy
Department Office	Phillips 223
Department Chair ID	20

2. Click Save Data. This time, execution pauses for a few seconds, then the Code editor window opens, with execution stopped on a system-generated command. The following error message appears:

> The INSERT statement conflicted with the FOREIGN KEY constraint "FK_UniversityDepartment_DepartmentChairID". The conflict occurred in database (description of the database filename, tablename, and fieldname). The statement has been terminated.

3. Click Stop Debugging on the IDE toolbar to end program execution.

If a user was using a compiled version of this program, the same error message would appear in a message box, and the program would terminate after the user clicked OK to close the message box. The user would lose unsaved work.

The data source for the UniversityDepartment data table is strongly typed. As a result, the application performs data validation when you attempt to save a new record or navigate to a different record. If the validation fails, a system error occurs and execution terminates. The system generated this error as a result of the value that the user entered for the Department Chair ID foreign key value. A foreign key value must exist in the table in which the field is a primary key. The DepartmentChairID column references the InstructorID column in the UniversityInstructor table. If you look at Figure 3-2, you see that InstructorID 20 does not exist.

Another data entry error occurs if the user creates a new record, then changes his or her mind and tries to cancel the operation. We try this next.

To try to enter a new record and then cancel the operation:

1. Run the application again, open the Read Write Text Boxes form, then click Add New. A new blank record appears in the form.
2. Assume that you changed your mind about adding a new record, so instead of entering data values, click Move Previous. Once again, execution stops, and the following error message appears:

    Column 'DepartmentName' does not allow nulls.

3. Click Stop Debugging on the IDE toolbar to end program execution.

In this example, the form generated an error because DepartmentName has a NOT NULL constraint. When you navigated to a different record, the application assumed that you wanted to save the values as you left them, with NULL values in each field except DepartmentID, and generated the validation error. You could have clicked Delete on the ToolStrip to cancel the Add New operation, but most users would not know to do this. Similarly, if you edit a record by changing the value in a text box, then change your mind and want to restore the original value, you cannot cancel the editing operation.

Finally, a data validation error occurs if the user tries to delete or change a record's primary key value. Recall that in a database, every record must have a unique primary key value. If you delete the primary key or change the primary key to a value that is not unique, an error occurs, as you will see next.

To try to delete the primary key value:

1. Run the application again, and open the Read Write Text Boxes form. The first record in the data table appears.
2. Delete the value in the Department ID text box, which is the record's primary key, then click Save Data. A message box opens that displays the message "Validation errors occurred." Click OK to close the message box.
3. Try to navigate to another record by clicking one of the buttons on the ToolStrip. Note that at this point, the application seems to be locked up. The form's internal data validation requires the user to enter a value in the text box associated with the table's primary key.
4. Type 1 in the Department ID, then click Move Next. The form is operational again.
5. Close the application.

Enhanced Read-Write Single-Record Display

As you can see, the unmodified read-write form works for read-write operations, but it allows users to enter illegal foreign key values, suffers from a lack of positive feedback when an operation is successful, does not allow users to cancel editing operations, and allows users to enter and/or change primary key values. This section adds enhancements to the previous form to address these issues.

Creating a Pick List Field   The first problem we address occurs when the user enters a foreign key value that does not exist in its parent table. The form could avoid this error by allowing the user to select only valid values from a pick list field. In this form, the pick list displays instructor names from which the user can choose a value. The associated (and valid) InstructorID is associated with the table's DepartmentChairID field.

To create the pick list field shown in Figure 6-13, first create a table adapter whose SQL query retrieves the data values that the pick list displays. Then delete the existing text box and replace it with a combo box control, which is a drop-down list that displays the current selection.

A combo box's DataSource property specifies the binding source to the data set whose data appears in the list. Its DisplayMember and ValueMember properties specify table adapter fields. The DisplayMember specifies the field whose value appears in the combo box, and the ValueMember usually specifies the primary key field for the displayed value. For example, suppose you have a combo box that displays instructor last names and then provides InstructorID foreign key values. The DisplayMember value would be InstructorLastName, and the ValueMember value would be InstructorID.

Sometimes when you create a pick list field, its current selection needs to synchronize with the other form values when editing existing entries. For example, in Figure 6-13, when the form displays the data for the Management Information Systems department, the combo box needs to display the correct department chair name. To synchronize the value that appears in the combo box with the other form values, which are bound to a different data table, set the combo box's DataBindings—SelectedValue property to the related field in the other data table's data bindings list. In the form in Figure 6-13, set the combo box's DataBindings—SelectedValue property to the DepartmentChairID field in the UniversityDepartment data bindings list.

The following steps show how to create a table adapter whose query retrieves instructor first and last names, concatenates them into a single value, and sorts them alphabetically, as shown in Figure 6-13. You can delete the existing Department ID text box and replace it with a combo box. Finally, you can bind the new combo box to a table adapter by dropping the table adapter onto the combo box, which automatically configures the combo box's DataSource, DisplayMember, ValueMember and DataBindings—SelectedValue properties.

To add a pick list to the form:

1. Create a new table adapter using the following SQL query:

```
SELECT InstructorID, InstructorLastName +
        ',' + InstructorFirstName AS Name
FROM UniversityInstructor
ORDER BY InstructorLastName, InstructorFirstName
```

2. Open frmReadWriteTextboxes in Designer view, and delete the Department Chair ID text box.
3. Change the Text property of the Department Chair ID label to Department Chair.
4. Open the Toolbox, select the ComboBox control, and create a new combo box control on the form on the right edge of the Department Chair label.
5. Change the new combo box's properties as follows:

Property	*New Value*
Name	cboDepartmentChair
DropDownStyle	DropDownList

6. To bind the combo box to the table adapter, drag UniversityInstructor1 (which is the table adapter that you made in step 1 if you kept the default name) from the Data Sources window and drop it onto the new combo box. This step should automatically configure the combo box and bind it to the UniversityInstructor1 table adapter.

7. Select the new combo box, then click its Property tab (on the top right corner of the combo box) to open its Tasks list. If necessary, set the properties as follows:

Property	*Value*
DataSource	UniversityInstructor1BindingSource
DisplayMember	Name
ValueMember	InstructorID
SelectedValue	UniversityDepartmentBindingSource-DepartmentChairID

TIP: Sometimes these properties are automatically assigned and sometimes you must assign them manually.

8. Save the project, then run the application and open the form. The form displays the record for the Management Information Systems department, and shows "Morrison, Lauren" as the department chair.
9. Open the Department Chair combo box. The list appears, as shown in Figure 6-13.
10. Select another list item, then close the list. The selected item appears in the form as the new Department Chair value.
11. Click Save Data to save your changes, then close the application.

TIP: There is another way to create a pick list, but you should not use it: prior to dragging the table adapter to the form, select the field to be used as a pick list in the Data Sources window, open its combo box, and select ComboBox from the list. This generates a combo box rather than a text box for the field on the form when the table adapter is dragged and dropped on the form. You can then configure the combo box properties. However, this combo box does not work properly and causes a variety of run-time errors at inopportune times. This seems to be a bug in the IDE that will probably be corrected in a future version.

Providing Feedback   Another problem with the unmodified read-write form is the lack of positive feedback when the user successfully inserts a new record. To address this, the following steps show how to create a message box in the Save Data button's Click event handler.

To provide feedback when a user inserts or updates a record:

1. Open the frmReadWriteTextBoxes form in Code view, and modify the code in the bindingNavigatorSaveItem_Click event handler to match the following shaded code. (You do not need to use the line continuation character to break the update command into two lines, but we did this to make it fit on this page.)

```
If Me.Validate() Then
  Me.UniversityDepartmentBindingSource.EndEdit()
  Me.UniversityDepartmentTableAdapter.Update( _
    Me.YourDatabaseNameDataSet.UniversityDepartment)
  MessageBox.Show("Successfully saved your changes")
Else
  MessageBox.Show("Unable to save your changes")
End If
```

2. Save the project, then run the application and open the form.

3. Click Add New to insert a new blank record, then add a record with the following data values:

Text Box	New Value
Department ID	(Do not change)
Department Name	Psychology
Department Office	Hibbard 610
Department Chair	Bakke, Judith

4. Click Save Data. The "Successfully saved your changes" message box appears. Click OK to close the message box.
5. Change the Department Chair value to Buck, Ted; the click Save Data. The message box appears after saving the update operation. Click OK to close the message box, then close the application forms.

Canceling Editing Operations   Another problem occurs when a user inserts a new record or begins to update an existing record, then wants to cancel the operation. Our solution is to create an event handler that executes whenever the user clicks one of the navigation buttons (Move First, Move Next, Move Previous, or Move Last.) The event handler calls the binding source's CancelEdit method, which cancels in-progress insert or update operations.

The following steps show how to create an event handler declaration for the Move event for one of the navigation buttons, and then modify the event handler declaration so that it handles the Move event for all the navigation buttons.

To create an event handler that cancels an in-progress editing operation:

1. To create the event handler declaration, open the frmReadWriteTextBoxes form in Code view, open the Objects list, and select BindingNavigatorMoveFirstItem. Then open the Events list and select Click. (We create the event handler for the Move First button, then modify it so that it handles the Click event for all buttons.)
2. The event handler declaration appears in the Code editor. Modify the event handler by adding the shaded code as follows, so that it handles all the navigation events:

```
Private Sub bindingNavigatorMove_Click(...) _
            Handles bindingNavigatorMoveFirstItem.Click, _
                  bindingNavigatorMoveLastItem.Click, _
                  bindingNavigatorMoveNextItem.Click, _
                  bindingNavigatorMovePreviousItem.Click, _
                  bindingNavigatorPositionItem.Click
   UniversityDepartmentBindingSource.CancelEdit()
End Sub
```

3. Save the project, then run the application and open the form.
4. To test if you can cancel an insert operation, click Add New on the ToolStrip. Then click Move previous. No error occurs, and the form displays the previous data table record.
5. To test whether you can cancel an update operation, delete the department name value of the current record, then click Move Previous. The form displays the previous record. Click Move Next. The form displays the record in which you deleted the department name value, and the value appears again.
6. Close the application.

Preventing Users from Changing Primary Key Values   A final concern lies in a user's ability to change primary key values in both new and existing records. To address this

FIGURE 6-19 Read-write form with a tabular display

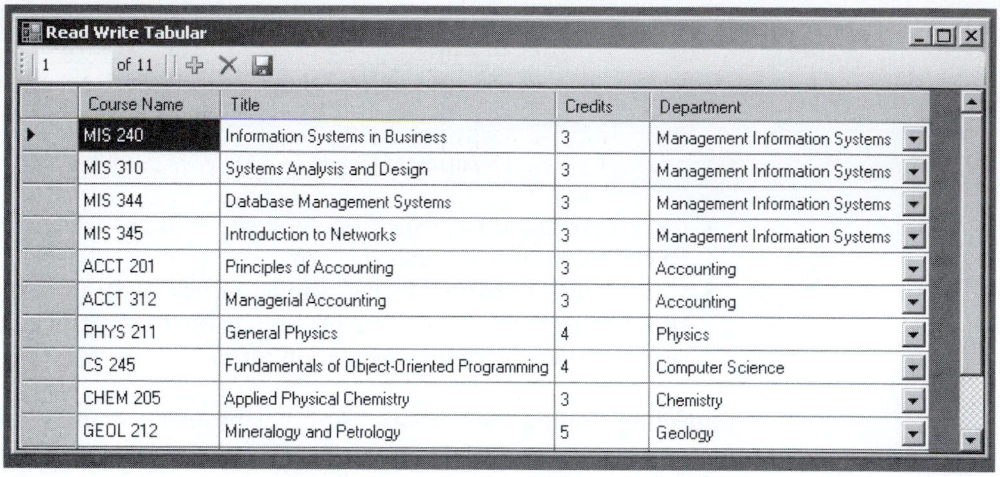

problem, we configure the text box corresponding to the data table's primary key so that its value cannot be changed by modifying its Read Only property value to True.

To make the primary key text box read-only:

1. Open the frmReadWriteTextBoxes form in Designer view, select the Department ID text box, and change its ReadOnly property value to True. The text box background color changes to gray, which indicates that the user cannot edit the value.
2. Save the project, run the application, and open the form. The first record appears.
3. Try to delete the Department ID value, and note that you cannot edit the value.
4. Close both application forms, then close all open pages in the IDE Document window. Do not close the IDE.

Read-Write Tabular Display

This section shows how to create a read-write form that displays data in a tabular format. This form, which appears in Figure 6-19, displays data from the UniversityCourse data table in a data grid view control.

This form allows users to view course data and to insert and update data values. It contains a pick list field for the Department data that presents a list of department names from which the user can select a value. We create this form just as we created the read-only tabular display form. The control automatically displays a new blank record at the bottom of the grid for inserting a new record, and it automatically saves new or updated record values when a user navigates to a different record.

To create a read-write form with a tabular display:

1. Create a new form named frmReadWriteTabular. Set the new form's properties to the standard form property values, set the form's Name property to frmReadWriteTabular, and set the Text value to Read Write Tabular.
2. In the Data Sources window, select UniversityCourse, open its list, and select DataGridView.
3. Select UniversityCourse, then drag it and drop it onto the form.
4. Select the data grid view control, and modify its properties as follows:

Property	*New Value*
Name	dgCourse
AutoSizeColumnsMode	AllCells
Dock	Fill

5. Right-click the data grid view control, then click Edit Columns. Modify the following column properties, then click OK to save your changes.

Column	Property	Value
CourseID	Visible	False
CourseName	HeaderText	Course Name
CourseTitle	HeaderText	Title
CourseCredits	HeaderText	Credits
DepartmentID	HeaderText	Department

6. Save the project.

Creating a Pick List in a Tabular Display   To create a pick list field in a tabular display, open the Edit Columns dialog box, select the target column, then set its ColumnType property to DataGridViewComboBoxColumn. You can then set the combo box's DataSource, DisplayMember, and ValueMember properties to the appropriate binding source and field names. The following steps show how to create a pick list field for the Department column that displays the department names, and returns the DepartmentID value.

To create a pick list in a data grid view control:

1. Open the form in Designer view, right-click the data grid view control, then click Edit Columns. Select the Department column, and change the ColumnType property value to DataGridViewComboBoxColumn.
2. To specify the combo box's data source, select the Department column's DataSource property, open the list, open the Other Data Sources node, open the Project Data Sources node, open the *yourDatabaseName*DataSet node, then select UniversityDepartment.

HELP: The DataSource property does not appear until you set the ColumnType to DataGridViewComboBoxColumn.

3. To specify the data that the combo box displays, select the DisplayMember property, open the list, and select DepartmentName.
4. To specify the data value that the form associates with the selection, select the ValueMember property, open the list, and select DepartmentID.
5. Click OK to close the Edit Columns dialog box. The Department column now displays a list.

HELP: If you run your form now and, after you exit the application, the Form Designer displays numerous errors, proceed to the HELP: section following the next set of steps.

Next add the commands to display the form from the Menu form, then run and test the form. You will perform an illegal action on purpose to trigger a data validation error and to see how the form handles it.

To display the form from the Menu form and to run and test it:

1. Open frmMenu.vb in Designer view, and add a new menu item under Read Write Examples with the text "Read Write Tabular." Then add the commands to call the frmReadWriteTabular from the menu form and hide the menu form from frmReadWriteTabular.
2. Save the project, then run the form, which displays the records from the UniversityCourse table.

3. Scroll to the bottom record, which is blank, and enter the following data values:

Column	Value
Course ID	(Accept the identity column value)
Course Name	CS 163
Title	Introduction to C++ Programming
Credits	3
Department	Computer Science

4. Click Save Data to save the change.
5. Place the insertion point on CS 163 (which is the Course Name value that you just inserted), click again to open the field in editing mode, then delete the value.
6. Click Save Data. A message box displays a lengthy and cryptic error message that appears to have something to do with a NOT NULL exception.
7. Click OK to close the message box, then close the application forms.

HELP: If after exiting the application, the Form Designer displays numerous errors instead of the frmReadWriteTabular form and its controls, perform the following steps: (1) Open the Solution Explorer and click the Show All Files button. (2) Expand the frmReadWriteTabular node. (3) Double-click frmReadWriteTabular.Designer.vb to display it in the Code editor, then add a blank line at the top of the file. This causes the IDE to clear the errors.

Creating an Event Handler to Display Custom Error Messages   If we were unconcerned about showing users cryptic system error messages like that in step 6 above, we could stop here. We cannot subject users to this sort of abuse, however, so we create a DataError event handler for the data grid view control. This event handler enables you to display custom error messages instead of system-generated messages.

You create a DataError event handler by opening the form in Code view, selecting the data grid view control as the object, then selecting the DataError event. The `Me.Validate()` method calls this event handler. The first command we add to the event handler prevents running the code to update the database. Next, a Select. . .Case decision structure tests for an error in each of the data grid columns and displays a message box that describes the error (or errors) that most likely occurred for the column. For example, the Course Title column is a required value, so the user must enter a value. The Credits column is a number value, so the user must enter an integer number.

The following steps create a DataError event handler for the frmReadWriteTabular form to provide custom error messages.

To create a DataError event handler:

1. Open frmReadWriteTabular in Code view, select dgCourse in the Objects list, then select DataError in the Events list. The DataError event handler declaration appears.

TIP: Another way to create the error handler declaration is to select the data grid view control, select the Events (lightening bolt) button on the Properties window toolbar, scroll down to the DataError event, then double-click it.

---

2. Add the following outlined code to the event handler declaration:

```
'Cancel updating the database
e.Cancel = True
'Select the correct error and
'display the appropriate message
Select Case dgvCourse.Columns _
  (e.ColumnIndex).DataPropertyName
  Case "CourseName"
    MessageBox.Show _
      ("Course Name is required and " & _
       "must be less than 10 characters" & _
       vbCr & "Press Esc to cancel editing", _
       "Data Error", MessageBoxButtons.OK, _
       MessageBoxIcon.Information)
  Case "CourseTitle"
    MessageBox.Show("Title is required and " & _
      "must be less than 200 characters" & _
      vbCr & "Press Esc to cancel editing", _
      "Data Error", MessageBoxButtons.OK, _
      MessageBoxIcon.Information)
  Case "CourseCredits"
    MessageBox.Show("Please enter a valid " & _
      "number between 1 and 10 " & _
      vbCr & "Press Esc to cancel editing", _
      "Data Error", MessageBoxButtons.OK, _
      MessageBoxIcon.Information)
  Case Else
    MessageBox.Show("Unknown error: " & _
      e.Exception.Message & _
      vbCr & vbCr & "Press Esc to cancel " & _
       "editing", "Data Error", _
       MessageBoxButtons.OK, _
      MessageBoxIcon.Information)
End Select
```

3. Save the project, then run the application and open the form.
4. Select the Course Name value for the first record (MIS 240), click the value again to open it for editing, then delete the value. Click the Save Data button. The message box opens and displays the custom message.
5. Click OK to close the message box. (If you selected a different row in the grid to apply the change, you need to press Esc to cancel the editing operation.) The form displays the original data value.
6. Close both application forms, and close all open pages in the IDE Document window. Do not close the IDE.

Read-Write Master-Detail Display

Recall that a master-detail data display shows a one-to-many data relationship in which a record in one table can have multiple associated records in another table. Depending on your application's needs, you can design a read-write master-detail display to allow editing in the detail section only or to allow editing in both the master list and the detail section. This section shows how to create the form in Figure 6-20, which allows editing in both the master and detail display.

The following steps show how to create the master section of the form, which displays UniversityDepartment data in a single-record display. Then the data-bound controls are added to the form, as well as the commands to display the form from the Menu form.

FIGURE 6-20 Read-write form with a master-detail display

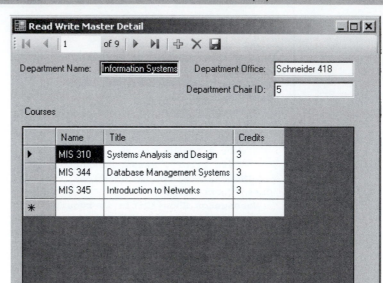

NOTE: These steps do not add enhancements such as pick lists to display foreign key values, messages confirming update operations, and error handling. However, you would add these to a finished application.

To create the form, add the master section's data bound controls, and add the commands to display the form:

1. Create a new form named frmReadWriteMasterDetail. Set the new form's properties to the standard form property values, set the form's Name property to frmReadWriteMasterDetail, and set the Text value to Read Write Master Detail.
2. In the Data Sources window, open the UniversityDepartment node, then drag the following fields and drop them onto your form to create the data-bound text boxes: DepartmentName, DepartmentOffice, DepartmentChairID.
3. Resize and reposition the form and text boxes so that the master section of your form looks like Figure 6-20.
4. Open frmMenu.vb in Designer view, and add a new menu item below Read Write Examples that has the text Read Write Master Detail, and add the commands to call the frmReadWriteMasterDetail form from the menu form.
5. Save the project.

The next step is to add the detail section to the form. We create and configure a data grid view control that displays data from the UniversityCourse table adapter.

To create the form's detail section:

1. In the Data Sources window, open the UniversityDepartment node, select the UniversityCourse node below it, open the list, and click DataGridView.
2. Drag the UniversityCourse data table and drop onto your form.
3. Change the new data grid view control's Name property value to dgCourse and its AutoSizeColumnsMode value to DisplayedCells.

4. Right-click the data grid view control, then click Edit Columns. Modify the column properties as follows, then click OK to save your changes.

Column	Property	New Value
CourseID	Visible	False
CourseName	HeaderText	Name
CourseTitle	HeaderText	Title
CourseCredits	HeaderText	Credits
DepartmentID	Visible	False

5. Create a new Label control and set its Text property value to Courses. Position it over the DataGridView, as shown in Figure 6-20.

6. Resize and reposition the form controls to look like Figure 6-20.

7. Save the project.

Currently, you can use the form to view master-detail records and to insert and update data in the form's master section. However, the form does not yet insert and update detail records. Why? The IDE added the BindingNavigator control and the bindingNavigatorSaveItem_Click event handler to the form when you created the form's master section. However, when you added the detail section later, the IDE did not add the code to update changes in the detail section. To enable updates in the detail section, you must add a command to the `bindingNavigatorSaveItem_Click` procedure to update the UniversityCourse table adapter. The following steps show how to do this.

To add the command to update the table adapter, then test the form:

1. Open the frmReadWriteMasterDetail form in Code view, and add the following command as the last command in the bindingNavigatorSaveItem_Click procedure:

```
Me.UniversityCourseTableAdapter.Update( _
    Me.YourDatabaseNameDataSet.UniversityCourse)
```

NOTE: You can omit the line continuation character if you place all this in one line of code.

2. Save the project, then run the application and open the form. The form appears, as shown in Figure 6-20.

3. Click Add New on the ToolStrip to add a new master record. A new blank record appears.

4. Type the following data values for the new department, then click Save Data.

Field	Value
Department ID	(accept value from identity column)
Department Name	Art
Department Office	FA 113
Department Chair ID	1

5. Add the following detail record in the Course data grid view, then click Save Data to save the change:

Column	Value
Title	ART 113
Name	2-D Specialized Art
Credits	3

6. Exit both application forms, then run the application again and open the Read Write Master Detail form and confirm that your new master and detail records exist.

7. Close the application forms, then close all open pages in the IDE Document window. Do not close the IDE.

NOTE: If you try to delete the Art Department without first deleting the ART 113 course, an error occurs because adding the ART 113 course creates a record in the UniversityCourse table with a foreign key linking it to the Art Department in the UniversityDepartment table. If you first delete the ART 113 course and *then* delete the ART Department, the deletion works. As you can see, additional error handling and user messages are needed before this is truly a user-friendly application.

USING PROGRAM COMMANDS TO MANIPULATE DATA

Data-bound controls provide a great way to make applications quickly, but sometimes these controls do not provide the flexibility applications require. Data-bound controls are limited by being tightly bound to database tables, and they cannot handle inserts, updates, and deletes if they display data from a table adapter that joins multiple tables. Data-bound controls are also not well suited for tasks such as querying a database to verify a user's identity when he or she enters a user ID and password.

Consider the case when a student enrolls at Ironwood University and wants to register for courses. An application needs to allow a student to select a term, view available courses and course sections from the UniversityCourse and UniversitySection tables, and then insert records in the UniversityEnrollment table. You could create data-bound controls for all these tables, but the application would become cumbersome and confusing with multiple master-detail relationships appearing on the same form. The best approach for forms that manipulate data from a variety of different tables is to create controls manually, then use program code to perform the underlying database queries.

This section demonstrates how to create data components and execute queries. The following section describes how to connect to a database using program commands. The sections that follow provide instructions for creating and configuring forms that use program commands to display database data and interact with the database.

Creating Data Components Using Program Commands

Recall from Figure 6-1 that ADO.NET 1.x uses a data connection and data adapter to create a data set. So far, you have created these components using wizards. Now we show how to create these components using program commands.

Data Connection

Recall that a data connection specifies a communication path between the database and an application. The command to create a data connection object has the following general syntax:

```
{Private|Public|Dim} ConnectionName As New Data.SqlClient.SqlConnection
```

After you create a connection object, you must set its *connection string,* which specifies how to connect to a specific database. The connection string identifies the database server, database instance on the server, target database (such as your DatabaseName.mdf), and security information. The following command specifies the connection string for a SQL Server Express datafile (as opposed to a remote SQL Server database):

```
ConnectionName.ConnectionString = _
  "Data Source=.\SQLEXPRESS;" & _
  "AttachDbFilename=|DataDirectory|\" & _
  "yourDatabaseName.mdf;" & _
  "Integrated Security=True;"
```

This command has the following components:

- **`"Data Source=.\SQLEXPRESS;"`** specifies the database server as an instance of SQLExpress running on the local computer. The dot/backslash (.\) syntax references the local computer.
- **`"AttachDbFilename=|DataDirectory|\yourDatabaseName.mdf;"`** specifies the folder path and filename of the database .mdf file. The `|DataDirectory|` specification directs the application to look for the database datafile in the same directory as the current application, which is the folder that stores the project's compiled assembly file. In this book, you always work in the development environment and use the Debug mode for compiling; so this folder is *ProjectFolder*\Bin\Debug.
- **`"Integrated Security=True"`** specifies that the connection uses Windows authentication to enable database access.

The connection string for a remote SQL Server database is somewhat easier. Often, full (non-Express) SQL Server installations do not name their database instance. To connect to a remote database, you need to specify only the database server name. For example, the following command creates the connection string for a remote SQL Server database in which the server name is CompanyDatabaseServer:

```
connectionName.ConnectionString = _
  "Data Source= CompanyDatabaseServer;" & _
  "Initial Catalog=yourDatabaseName;" & _
  "Integrated Security=True"
```

If the remote SQL Server database instance *is* named, the preceding connect string becomes:

```
connectionName.ConnectionString = _
  "Data Source= " & _
    "CompanyDatabaseServer\instanceName;" & _
    "Initial Catalog=yourDatabaseName;" & _
    "Integrated Security=True"
```

NOTE: Notice there is no AttachDBFilename section in these connection strings. For them to work property, the database must be *attached* to the SQL Server DBMS, which means that the database is available and running on the DBMS. If an .mdf file is attached to a server, the DBMS knows the location of the .mdf file in its file system, so you do not need to specify its location. A database administrator might detach a database from a DBMS instance to perform maintenance activities on the database.

Sometimes programs connect to a database through an account managed by SQL Server authentication rather than through Windows authentication. (This requires the DBA to create user accounts and passwords for each user.) In this case, the connection string for a remote SQL Server database becomes:

```
connectionName.ConnectionString = _
  "Data Source= CompanyDatabaseServer;" & _
  "Initial Catalog=yourDatabaseName;" & _
  "Persist Security Info=True;" & _
  "User ID=userID;Password=userPassword"
```

NOTE: If the preceding connection string connects to a named SQL Server instance, you must follow the server name with the instance name.

NOTE: In this book, our examples use a SQL Express file-based connection string. If you are connecting to a remote database, you need to change your connection string based on your database configuration.

You can find your database's connection string by looking in one of several project configuration files that the IDE generates when you use a wizard to create a new data source. One file is app.config, which is in the project folder. You can open this file in a text editor, copy the connection string, and then paste it directly into your Code editor window. Another place to find your database's connection string is in the project's Property pages. You can find this by opening the project's Property pages and selecting the Settings tab.

Data Adapter

A *data adapter* provides methods for retrieving and modifying data. The command to create a data adapter object uses the following syntax:

```
{Private|Public|Dim} AdapterName As New Data.SqlClient.SqlDataAdapter
```

A data adapter has one or more associated *SQL command objects,* which specify SELECT, INSERT, UPDATE, and DELETE queries for the adapter. Because you often do not perform all these operations with a given data adapter, the system does not immediately create these SQL command objects and allocate memory for them. As a result, before you can perform *any* database actions with a data adapter, you must first create a SQL command object, assign a query to its SQL command text, and assign it to the data adapter's associated command property. After doing this, the last step to make it operational is to assign a data connection object to the data adapter. The following commands perform these steps:

```
'Create the SQL command object
{Private|Public|Dim} CommandName As New Data.SqlClient.SqlCommand
'Assign the SQL command text to the object
CommandName.CommandText = "SQLCommandText"
'Assign the SqlCommand object to the data adapter
AdapterName.TypeCommand = CommandName
'Assign a connection to the SQL Command object
AdapterName.SelectCommand.Connection = ConnectionName
```

In this syntax, "*SQLCommandText*" can be any SQL command, including DDL, DML, and transaction control commands. A data adapter can have several associated

SQL command objects that you create depending on your application's needs. The *Type*Command property is SelectCommand, UpdateCommand, InsertCommand, or DeleteCommand.

Data Set

A *data set* is a container that stores data retrieved by a data adapter. Use the following general syntax to create a data set object:

```
{Private|Public|Dim} DataSetName As New Data.DataSet
```

You use the data adapter's Fill method to fill the data set. The Fill method opens the connection, executes the SQL command, retrieves the data, and places it in the data set. The Fill method has the following general syntax:

```
AdapterName.Fill(DataSetName, "DataTableName")
```

In this syntax, "*DataTableName*" creates a data table in the data set. The data table is not typed. Unlike a project data source, it does not store any information about the data types or table or column constraints that enable it to perform data validation later.

The following commands show how to put all this together and retrieve data from the UniversityStudent table:

```
'Declare the data components
Dim cnStudent As New Data.SqlClient.SqlConnection
Dim daStudent As New Data.SqlClient.SqlDataAdapter
Dim sqlCommand As New Data.SqlClient.SqlCommand
Dim dsStudent As New Data.DataSet

'Create the connection string
cnStudent.ConnectionString = "Data Source=.\SQLEXPRESS;" & _
   "AttachDbFilename=|DataDirectory|\yourDatabaseName.mdf;" & _
   "Integrated Security=True;"

'Create the SQL command
sqlCommand.CommandText = _
   "SELECT StudentLastName, StudentFirstName " & _
   "FROM UniversityStudent"

'Configure the data adapter
daStudent.SelectCommand = sqlCommand
daStudent.SelectCommand.Connection = cnStudent

'Fill the data set
daStudent.Fill(dsStudent, "nameDataTable")
```

Creating a Form That Uses Program Commands to Retrieve Data

This section shows how to create the form in Figure 6-21, which uses program commands to retrieve and display database data.

When the user clicks Retrieve, the form executes program commands to retrieve the last and first names of students in the UniversityStudent table and display them in a list. We add a list box and button control to the form, then create an event handler for the button. This event handler contains commands to create a data connection, data adapter, and data set, then executes the query and fills the data set. The event handler then uses the list box's AddItem method to populate the list box with the data set contents.

FIGURE 6-21 Form that uses program commands to retrieve and display database data

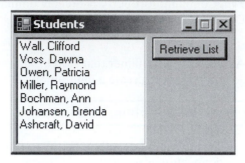

To create a form that uses program commands to retrieve data:

1. Create a new form named frmProgramCodeStudents. Set the new form's properties to the standard form property values. Set the form's Name property to frmProgramCodeStudents, and the Text value to Students.
2. Open the Toolbox and create a ListBox and a Button control on the form. Resize and reposition the form and form controls so that your form looks like Figure 6-21.
3. Change the list box's Name property value to lstStudents and its Locked property value to True.
4. Change the button's Name property value to btnRetrieve and its Text property value to Retrieve.
5. Create a Click event handler for btnRetrieve that has the following commands. Be sure to change the data connection connect string as necessary for your database connection.

```
'Create the data objects
Dim cnStudent As New Data.SqlClient.SqlConnection
Dim daStudent As New Data.SqlClient.SqlDataAdapter
Dim sqlCommand As New Data.SqlClient.SqlCommand
Dim dsStudent As New Data.DataSet

'Clear the current list contents
lstStudents.Items.Clear()

'Create the data connection
cnStudent.ConnectionString = "Data Source=.\SQLEXPRESS;" & _
    "AttachDbFilename=|DataDirectory|\yourDatabaseName.mdf;" & _
    "Integrated Security=True;"

'Create the SQL Command
SqlCommand.CommandText = _
    "SELECT StudentLastName, StudentFirstName, " & _
    "StudentMI " & _
    "FROM UniversityStudent"

'Create and configure the data adapter
daStudent.SelectCommand = sqlCommand
daStudent.SelectCommand.Connection = cnStudent

'Fill the data set
daStudent.Fill(dsStudent, "NameList")
'Place the data set contents in the list box
If dsStudent.Tables("nameList").Rows.Count > 0 _
    Then
        Dim studentRow As Data.DataRow
```

```
      For Each studentRow In dsStudent.Tables("NameList").Rows
          lstStudents.Items.Add _
              (studentRow.Item("StudentLastName").ToString & _
              ", " & _
              studentRow.Item("StudentFirstName").ToString)
    Next
End If
```

6. Open frmMenu.vb in Designer view, and add a new top-level menu item that has the text Program Examples. Add a menu selection under Program Examples that has the text Student List. Create an event handler for the new menu item to call the frmProgramCodeStudents form from the menu form.
7. Save the project, then run the application and open the form.
8. Click Retrieve. The student names appear in the list.
9. Close the application forms.
10. Close all open pages in the IDE Document window. Do not close the IDE.

Creating a Login Form That Uses Parameter Queries to Accept Inputs

Sometimes you need to create applications that allow users to enter data values serving as search conditions for database queries. This section shows how to use program commands to implement the Student Login form in Figure 6-22.

In this form, the student enters values in the User ID and PIN fields, then clicks Login. The form verifies that the User ID/PIN combination is valid by querying the UniversityStudent table. If the combination is valid, the next application form appears. If the combination is not valid, an error message appears.

NOTE: In a production environment, the application would probably give the user three tries to correctly enter the User ID/PIN combination. To simplify it, our example allows only one chance.

To allow queries to interact with user inputs, configure the SQL command object's command text as a parameter query. When you create a parameter query in a form that performs database processing using program commands, bind each parameter to an associated form control value by adding the parameter variable name and its value to a parameter list. To do this, use the following general syntax:

```
CommandName.Parameters.Add(New Data.SqlClient.SqlParameter _
                          ("VariableName", ControlValue))
```

FIGURE 6-22   Student Login form that processes user inputs

For example, the following commands create a parameter query that retrieves a StudentID value based on values that a user inputs for StudentUserID and StudentPIN. The parameter query contains variables for the StudentUserID and StudentPIN values, then binds these parameter variables to associated form controls:

```
'Create the parameter query
sqlCommand.CommandText = _
  "SELECT StudentID " & _
  "FROM UniversityStudent " & _
  "WHERE StudentUserID=@sID " &
  "AND StudentPIN = @sPIN"
'Bind the parameter variables to form controls
sqlCommand.Parameters.Add(New Data.SqlClient.SqlParameter _
                          ("sID", txtUserID.Text))
sqlCommand.Parameters.Add(New Data.SqlClient.SqlParameter _
                          ("sPIN", txtPIN.Text))
```

To execute this query, first open the data connection using the connection's Open method, which has the following syntax:

```
ConnectionName.Open()
```

TIP: Data adapters automatically open a connection, retrieve data, and close the connection. SQL command objects require doing this explicitly.

Then use the SQL command object's ExecuteScalar() method to execute the query. ExecuteScalar() returns the first cell/column for the first row that the query retrieves. (Use this method to determine whether a query returns any value when you do not care if it returns more than one row.) If the query does not return a value, the method returns NULL. The ExecuteScalar() method uses the following general syntax:

```
ReturnVariable = SqlCommand.ExecuteScalar()
```

After executing the query, you explicitly close the data connection using the connection's Close() method:

```
ConnectionName.Close()
```

The following steps create the Student Login form in Figure 6-22. We add the code to create and configure the data connection and adapter and to create the SQL command object's command text as a parameter query. We execute the query in a Try/Catch block, and display a message describing the success or failure of the login attempt.

To create the Login form:

1. Create a new form named frmProgramCodeLogin. Set the new form's properties to the standard form property values. Set the form's Name property to frmProgramCodeLogin, and set the Text value to Student Login Form.
2. Add the label, text box, and button controls shown in Figure 6-22 to the form. Configure the label control's Text property as shown.
3. Set the Name property of the first text box to txtStudentID and the Name property of the second text box to txtPIN. Set the Name property of the button to btnLogin and its Text property to Login.
4. Set the txtPIN text box's PasswordChar value to * (asterisk).

5. Resize the form, and resize and reposition the controls so that the form looks like Figure 6-22.

6. Create a new event handler for the Login button's Click event, and add the following commands to create and configure the data components. Change the connection string as necessary to connect to your database.

```
'Declare the data components
Dim cnStudent As New Data.SqlClient.SqlConnection
Dim sqlCommand As New Data.SqlClient.SqlCommand
'Declare a local variable to reference
'the retrieved StudentID value
Dim lngStudentID As Long
'Create the connection string
cnStudent.ConnectionString = "Data Source=.\SQLEXPRESS;" & _
   "AttachDbFilename=|DataDirectory|\"yourDatabaseName.mdf;" & _
   "Integrated Security=True;User Instance=True"
'Assign the command to the connection
sqlCommand.Connection = cnStudent
'Create the SQL Command object
'as a parameter query
sqlCommand.CommandText = _
   "SELECT StudentID " & _
   "FROM UniversityStudent " & _
   "WHERE StudentUserID=@sID AND " & _
   "StudentPIN = @sPIN"
'Associate the parameters with form controls
sqlCommand.Parameters.Add(New Data.SqlClient.SqlParameter _
                      ("sID", txtStudentID.Text))
sqlCommand.Parameters.Add(New Data.SqlClient.SqlParameter _
                      ("sPIN", txtPIN.Text))
Try
   'Open the connection
   cnStudent.Open()
   'Execute the query
   lngStudentID = CLng(sqlCommand.ExecuteScalar)
   If lngStudentID <> 0 Then
     MessageBox.Show("Login succeeded")
   Else
     MessageBox.Show("Login failed" & vbCr & _
         "Hint: a valid login is wallc - 1234" & _
         vbCr & "Look in the UniversityStudent " & _
         "table for more logins")
     Me.Dispose()
   End If
Catch ex As Exception
     MessageBox.Show(ex.Message)
Finally
     'Close the connection
     cnStudent.Close()
End Try
```

7. Save the project.

8. Open the Menu form in Designer view. Open the Program Examples menu item, then add a new menu item that has the text Login Form. Add the commands to call the frmProgramCodeLogOn from the menu form.

9. Save the project, run the application, and open the form. The Login form appears.

10. To test for a successful login attempt, type wallc in the Student ID field and 1234 (which is the correct PIN, as shown in Figure 3-2) in the PIN field, then click

Login. The "Login succeeded" message box appears. Click OK to close the message box.

11. To test for an unsuccessful login attempt, change the PIN field value to 1111 (which is an incorrect PIN), then click Login. The "Login failed" message box appears.

12. Click OK, exit the application, then close all open windows in the IDE Document window. Do not close the IDE.

CREATING A FORM COMBINING DATA-BOUND CONTROLS AND PROGRAM COMMANDS

So far, you have learned to create database applications that use data-bound controls that wizards create and, separately, to use program commands to retrieve and process data. In this section, you will learn how to create a form that combines both approaches. We will create the form in Figure 6-23, which allows students to enroll in course sections.

When the form opens, the user selects a term. The form then displays an alphabetical list of departments and the courses they offer for the selected term, along with the associated course section offerings. The user can select a course section and add it to his or her schedule. To create the form, we create data-bound controls to display the term, course section, and student schedule data. The Add Course button uses program controls to add the selected course section to the student's schedule.

To create the Course Enrollment form and its new table adapters:

1. Create a new form named frmCourseEnrollment. Set the new form's properties to the standard form property values. Set the form's Name property to frmCourseEnrollment, and set the Text value to Course Enrollment.

2. To display the data in the course term's combo box, create a new table adapter named UniversityTerms that uses the following query:

```
SELECT DISTINCT SectionTerm FROM UniversitySection
```

FIGURE 6-23   Course enrollment form

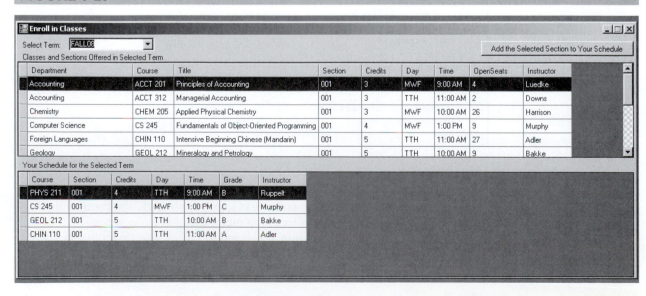

3. To display the course section information, create a new table adapter named SectionInformation that uses the following SQL query:

```
SELECT SectionTerm, DepartmentName,
       CourseName, CourseTitle, CourseCredits,
       InstructorLastName, SectionDay, SectionTime,
       SectionNumber, UniversitySection.SectionID,
       SectionMaxEnrollment -
         UniversitySection.SectionCurrentEnrollment
         AS OpenSeats
FROM UniversitySection
     INNER JOIN UniversityCourse
     ON UniversitySection.CourseID =
        UniversityCourse.CourseID
     INNER JOIN UniversityDepartment
     ON UniversityCourse.DepartmentID =
        UniversityDepartment.DepartmentID
     INNER JOIN UniversityInstructor
     ON UniversitySection.InstructorID =
        UniversityInstructor.InstructorID
ORDER BY SectionTerm, DepartmentName, CourseName
```

4. To create a relationship between the UniversityTerms and SectionInformation table adapters, right-click UniversityTerms, point to Add, then click Relation. The Relation dialog box opens.

5. Select UniversityTerms in the Parent Table list. Click the box under Key Columns, open the list, and select SectionTerm as the linking field in the parent table.

6. Select SectionInformation in the Child Table list. Click the box under Foreign Key Columns, open the list, and select SectionTerm as the linking field in the child table. Then click OK to save the relation and close the Relation dialog box.

7. Close the Data Set Designer window, and click Yes to save your changes.

Next, we create the data-bound controls to display the table adapter data tables. We configure the controls so that they are read only. Then we add commands to display the form from the Login form and run the form.

To create and configure the data-bound controls and run the form:

1. Open frmCourseEnrollment in Designer view.

2. Create a Label control on the form, and change its Text property value to Select Term:.

3. Create a ComboBox control on the form, and change its properties as follows:

Property	New Value
Name	cboTerm
Data Source	UniversityTerms
Display Member	SectionTerm
Value Member	SectionTerm

4. Resize and reposition the label and combo box as shown in Figure 6-23.

5. In the Data Sources window, open the UniversityTerms node, select SectionInformation, open the list, and select DataGridView. Drag SectionInformation and drop it onto the form under the Section Term combo box.

6. Change the data grid view control's property values as follows:

Property	New Value
Name	dgSectionInformation
AllowUserToAddRows	False
AllowUserToDeleteRows	False
AutoSizeColumnsMode	Displayed Cells
ReadOnly property	True
RowHeadersWidth	15
SelectionMode	FullRowSelect

7. Right-click the data grid view control and then click Edit Columns. Select the SectionTerm column, then click Remove.

8. Order the columns as shown in the following list, and change the column properties as shown:

Column	Property	New Value
DepartmentName	HeaderText	Department
CourseName	HeaderText	Course
CourseTitle	HeaderText	Title
SectionNumber	HeaderText	Section
CourseCredits	HeaderText	Credits
SectionDay	HeaderText	Day
SectionTime	HeaderText	Time
OpenSeats	HeaderText	Open Seats
InstructorLastName	HeaderText	Instructor
SectionID	Visible	False

9. Select the SectionID column, and change its Name property value to SectionID. This step is important, because this value serves as part of the primary key when the student selects a section and adds it to his or her schedule.

10. Select the Time column, select its DefaultCellStyle property, click the Ellipsis (...) button, select Format, click the Ellipsis (...) button, select Date Time, then select the time value that has the format H:MM AM|PM.

NOTE: The time format appears as your current system time. For example, if it is 1:15 p.m., select this value.

---

11. Click OK three times to close from the Edit Columns dialog.

12. Resize the form, then resize and reposition the form controls so that the top part of your form looks like Figure 6-23.

13. To display the form from the Login form, open frmProgramCodeLogin in Code view, and modify the If/Else decision structure that validates the login as shown in the following code. (Delete the existing command that displays the MessageBox showing the message "Login succeeded.")

```
If lngStudentID <> 0 Then
   frmcourseEnrollment.lngStudentID = lngStudentID
   frmCourseEnrollment.ShowDialog()
Else
```

14. Open the Course Enrollment form (frmCourseEnrollment) in Code view, and add the following highlighted code to the form's class declaration to create the lngStudentID variable that the frmProgramCodeLogin form references:

```
Public Class frmCourseEnrollment
   Public lngStudentID as Long
```

15. Save the project, run the application, and open the Login form. Type wallc in the Student ID field and 1234 in the PIN field, then click Login. The Course Enrollment form opens.
16. Close the application, then resize the form and data grid control as necessary.

Next we create the table adapter that displays a student's schedule information. This is a master-detail relationship with the UniversityTerms table adapter as the master and with the table adapter that retrieves the student's schedule as the detail. This ensures that only classes from the selected term appear in the student's schedule.

To create the student schedule table adapter:

1. Create a new table adapter named StudentSchedule that uses the following SQL query:

```
SELECT CourseName, CourseCredits,
       EnrollmentGrade, SectionNumber,
       SectionDay, SectionTime, InstructorLastName,
       SectionTerm, UniversityEnrollment.StudentID
FROM UniversitySection
    INNER JOIN UniversityCourse
    ON UniversitySection.CourseID =
       UniversityCourse.CourseID
    INNER JOIN UniversityInstructor
    ON UniversitySection.InstructorID =
       UniversityInstructor.InstructorID
    INNER JOIN UniversityEnrollment
    ON UniversitySection.SectionID =
       UniversityEnrollment.SectionID
WHERE StudentID = @studentID
```

2. To create the relationship between the StudentSchedule and UniversityTerms table adapters, right-click StudentSchedule, point to Add, then click Relation. The Relation dialog box opens.
3. Select UniversityTerms in the Parent Table list. Click the box under the Key Columns, open the list, and select SectionTerm as the linking field in the parent table.
4. Select StudentSchedule in the Child Table list, open the Foreign Key Columns list, and select SectionTerm.
5. Close the DataSet Designer window, then click Yes to save your changes.

Now we add the data-bound controls to display the student schedule information. We modify the form Load event that fills the data adapter so that it uses the current student as its parameter. (This is what the lngStudentID variable that we created before is used for.)

To create and configure a data grid view to display the schedule information:

1. Open frmCourseEnrollment in Designer View. In the Data Sources window, open the UniversityTerms node, select StudentSchedule, open its list, and select DataGridView. Then drag and drop StudentSchedule onto the frmCourseEnrollment form below the other data grid view.
2. Open the frmCourseEnrollment form in Code view, copy the following command from the Try block of the FillToolStripButton_Click event handler, then paste it as the last line of code in the Load event handler:

```
Me.StudentScheduleTableAdapter.Fill _
    (Me.YourDatabaseNameDataSet.StudentSchedule, _
    CType(StudentIDToolStripTextBox.Text, Long))
```

3. Delete the FillToolStripButton_Click the event handler.

4. Modify the command you pasted into the Load event handler to use lngStudentID as follows:

```
Me.StudentScheduleTableAdapter.Fill _
    (Me.YourDatabaseNameDataSet.StudentSchedule, _
    lngStudentID)
```

5. Open the form in Designer view, and delete the FillToolStrip that was added when you dropped the StudentSchedule table adapter on frmCourseEnrollment. (This FillToolStrip appears at the top of the form, with "studentID:" as a text box label.)

6. Change the bottom data grid view control's property values as follows:

Property	New Value
Name	dgCurrentCourseSchedule
AllowUserToAddRows	False
AllowUserToDeleteRows	False
AutoSizeColumnsMode	Displayed Cells
ReadOnly	True
RowHeadersWidth	15
SelectionMode	FullRowSelect

7. Modify the bottom data grid view's column properties so that they look like Figure 6-23.

8. Run the application and log onto the enrollment form using Student ID wallc and PIN 1234. The course sections and student Clifford Wall's schedule for the FALL08 term appear in the form.

9. Open the Select Term combo box and select SPR09. The course section offerings change. Note that student Walls is not enrolled in any courses for this term.

10. Select the SUMM08 term. Note that student Walls is enrolled in one course for this term.

11. Close the form applications.

To finish the form, we need to add the Add Course button in Figure 6-23, which enables students to add new courses to their schedules. This button has an event handler that uses program commands to insert the student's course section selection into the UniversityEnrollment table. To implement this, we use the same commands as before to create a data connection, data adapter, and SQL command object. This time, the SQL command object uses an INSERT action query that inserts the current student ID and selected course section ID into the UniversityEnrollment table. For the student ID value, the INSERT query references the txtStudentID text box value. For the selected course SectionID value, the query references the SectionID cell in the data grid view's selected row, using the following syntax:

```
DataGridViewName.CurrentRow.Cells("Name").Value
```

NOTE: The ("Name") used in this command is the (Name) property shown in the Edit Columns dialog.

To execute queries that insert, update, or delete data, we use a SQL command object's ExecuteNonQuery method. This method returns an integer representing the number of database rows that the query affects. If the command fails, the method returns the value −1. You might use the following commands to execute an action query, then display a message box displaying how many rows the query affected:

```
Dim intRowsAffected As Integer
intRowsAffected = sqlCommand.ExecuteNonQuery()
MessageBox.Show(CStr(intRowsAffected) & "row(s) affected.")
```

To add the Add Courses button and event handler:

1. Open the frmCourseEnrollment form in Designer view, and create a new Button control. Change the button name to btnAddCourses, and change its Text value to Add Courses.
2. Create an event handler for the button's Click event that has the following commands. Be sure to change the database connection string for your database.

```
'Declare the data components
Dim cnCourseEnrollment As _
New Data.SqlClient.SqlConnection
Dim sqlCommand As New Data.SqlClient.SqlCommand

'Create the connection string
cnCourseEnrollment.ConnectionString = _
  "Data Source=.\SQLEXPRESS;" & _
  "AttachDbFilename=|DataDirectory|\" & _
  "yourDatabaseName.mdf;" & _
  "Integrated Security=True;User Instance=True"

'Assign the command to the connection
sqlCommand.Connection = cnCourseEnrollment

'Assign the student's ID
'to the studentID parameter
sqlCommand.Parameters.Add _
  (New Data.SqlClient.SqlParameter("studentID", _
  lngStudentID))

'Assign the selected SectionID
'to the sectionID parameter
sqlCommand.Parameters.Add _
  (New Data.SqlClient.SqlParameter("sectionID", _
  CStr(dgSectionInformation.CurrentRow.Cells _
    ("SectionID").Value)))

'Create the SQL Command object
'as a parameter query
sqlCommand.CommandText = _
    "INSERT INTO UniversityEnrollment " & _
    "(StudentID, SectionID) " & _
    "VALUES (@studentID, @sectionID)"
Try
  'Open the connection
  cnCourseEnrollment.Open()

  'Execute the query
  sqlCommand.ExecuteNonQuery()

  'Update the section's current enrollment
  sqlCommand.CommandText = _
        "UPDATE UniversitySection " & _
        "SET SectionCurrentEnrollment = " & _
        "SectionCurrentEnrollment + 1 " & _
        "WHERE SectionID = @sectionID"
  sqlCommand.ExecuteNonQuery()
```

```
Catch ex As Exception
  MessageBox.Show(ex.Message)
Finally
  'Close the connection
  cnCourseEnrollment.Close()
End Try

'show the changes in the grids by refilling them
StudentScheduleTableAdapter.Fill _
  (YourDatabaseNameDataSet.StudentSchedule, _
  lngStudentID)
SectionInformationTableAdapter.Fill( _
  YourDatabaseNameDataSet.SectionInformation)
```

3. Save the project, then run the application. Login to the application as student wallc as before.
4. Select the SPR09 term. Select Section 1 of GEOL212 in the course section's data grid view, then click Add Course. The new course appears in the student schedule, and the open seats for GEOL212 has been reduced to 5 from its original 6. Click OK to close the message box.

HELP: If an error message appears stating that column name SectionID cannot be found, click OK, close the application, then right-click the section information data grid control and open its columns for editing. Select the SectionID column, and change its Name property value to SectionID.

---

5. Close the application forms.
6. Close all open windows in the IDE Document window.

RETRIEVING DATA ASYNCHRONOUSLY

Until now, we have allowed an application to "hang" while it retrieves data. When this happens, the user just has to wait until the application finishes retrieving the data. This is not a big issue with small database tables like those we have been using—but how many "real world" tables contain fewer than 50 records? Sometimes data retrieval operations can take a long time, and a user might want to abort the operation and do something else. An alternate approach is to have the application retrieve the data *asynchronously,* that is, the application retrieves the data in the background. All of the form controls remain active, allowing the user to perform other application tasks. The following sections describe how to create asynchronous operations in .NET using the BackgroundWorker component, the test database we use to illustrate these operations, and the steps for creating an asynchronous database application.

.NET BackgroundWorker

The .NET IDE has a new component, called *BackgroundWorker,* that allows you to create asynchronous operations. BackgroundWorker runs code separately from the rest of the form code. This separate process is called a *thread.* BackgroundWorker provides methods and events for starting the thread, specifying the code to run in it, and reporting back when it is finished. You create a thread by calling BackgroundWorker's `RunWorkerAsyn()` method. As soon as you call this method, it triggers BackgroundWorker's `DoWork` event. You place the code to be processed in the BackgroundWorker's thread in this event handler. When the code in the thread finishes running, the Backgroundworker's `RunWorkerCompleted` event fires. This is where you place the commands to display the retrieved data.

FIGURE 6-24   GeoData database tables

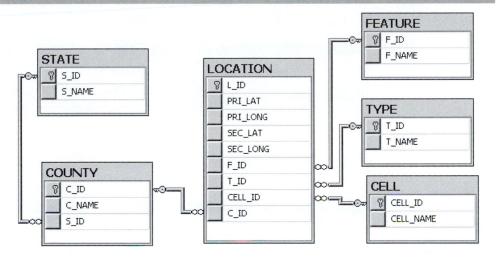

GeoData Test Database

To demonstrate asynchronous data retrievals, we need to use a large database that contains many records and introduces an appreciable delay during retrievals. We use a database that displays geographic data copyrighted by the United States Geological Survey (USGS).

> **NOTE:** You can obtain the source data for this database at http://geonames .usgs.gov/geonames/stategaz/index.html. Its use is allowed as long as the USGS is cited as its source.

The USGS distributes this data in text files, so we designed and implemented a SQL Server database named GeoData (GeoData.mdf) to store the data. Our GeoData database stores the geographic information from three states: West Virginia, Wisconsin, and Wyoming (we were in a "W" mood at the time). This file is approximately 22 megabytes in size and has six tables, as shown in Figure 6-24.

The GeoData database tables represent geographic data organized by states, counties, and locations. A location is a specific place on a map and represents a feature (such as the city Eau Claire, Wisconsin.) A location is of a specific type (such as a reservoir or city) and appears in a specific cell on a geographic map. The database's largest table is LOCATION, which contains 99,181 records. (We did not include all the available USGS data because this creates a database over 321 megabytes in size.)

Creating an Asynchronous Database Application

The following steps show how to create the GeoData database application in Figure 6-25. While the form retrieves data, it displays the message "Retrieving data—Cancel?" If the user clicks this button during the retrieval operation, the application cancels the data retrieval and displays the previous menu form. After the form retrieves all the data, it displays the data in a data grid view control.

To create this form, add a new data source that connects to the GeoData database to the DBExamples project, add a table adapter that retrieves data from GeoData database tables, and add a data grid view control to display the data. The following steps show how to do this and how to run the project without adding the asynchronous data retrieval components to experience the retrieval delay that occurs.

FIGURE 6-25 GeoData database application

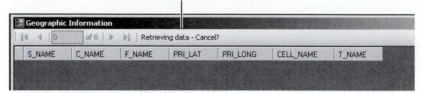

This button is active while retrieving data.

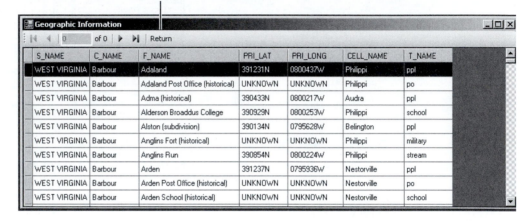

After the data is retrieved, the button's text changes to "Return."

To add a new data source and create the GeoData form:

1. Click Data on the menu bar, then click Add New Data Source. Make sure Database is selected, then click Next.
2. Click New Connection.
   If you are connecting to a local database, click Browse, navigate to the \SQLServer\Datafiles\Databases folder, select GeoData.mdf, then click Open.
   If you are connecting to a remote database, select your authentication method, select your server, then select the GeoData database. Use the steps you used before to finish creating the data source.
3. Click Test Connection, click OK, then click Next. On the *Choose your database objects* page, select all six of the GeoData tables, then click Finish.
4. *If you are connecting to a local database file,* select GeoData.mdf in the Solution Explorer, open the Properties window, and set its Copy to output directory property to Do not copy. In Windows Explorer, copy the GeoData.mdf and GeoData_log.ldf database files from the project's root folder to the project's bin\Debug folder.
5. Open the Data Sources window, select GeodataDataSet, then click Edit Dataset with Designer on the toolbar to open the Data Set Designer.
6. Create a new table adapter named AllInfo using the following SQL query, then close the Data Set Designer window and click Yes to save your changes.

```
SELECT STATE.S_NAME, COUNTY.C_NAME,
       FEATURE.F_NAME, LOCATION.PRI_LAT,
       LOCATION.PRI_LONG, CELL.CELL_NAME, TYPE.T_NAME
FROM STATE
     INNER JOIN COUNTY
       ON STATE.S_ID = COUNTY.S_ID
     INNER JOIN LOCATION
```

```
        ON COUNTY.C_ID = LOCATION.C_ID
    INNER JOIN FEATURE
        ON LOCATION.F_ID = FEATURE.F_ID
    INNER JOIN TYPE
        ON LOCATION.T_ID = TYPE.T_ID
    INNER JOIN CELL
        ON LOCATION.CELL_ID = CELL.CELL_ID
ORDER BY STATE.S_NAME, COUNTY.C_NAME, FEATURE.F_NAME
```

7. Create a new form named frmGeoData. Set the form's properties to the standard form properties, and set the form's Text property to Geographic Information.

8. Open the Data Sources window, select AllInfo, then open the list and select DataGridView. Drag AllInfo and drop it on your form to create a data grid view control.

9. Modify the data grid view's properties as follows:

Property	New Value
Name	dgGeoData
AllowUserToAddRows	False
AllowUserToDeleteRows	False
AutoSizeColumnsMode	Displayed Cells
Dock	Fill
ReadOnly	True
RowHeadersWidth	15
SelectionMode	FullRowSelect

10. Delete the Add, Delete, and Save buttons on the form's ToolStrip.

11. To add the button to the binding navigator to allow the user to close the window and stop the query, select the ToolStrip, open the Add ToolStripButton combo box on the right side of the ToolStrip, then select Button.

12. With the new button selected, open the Properties window and set the following property values:

Property	New Value
Name	btnReturn
DisplayStyle	Text
Text	Return

13. Double-click the Return button to create its Click event handler, then add the following command to the event handler:

```
Me.Close()
```

14. Add a new menu entry to frmMenu under Read Only Examples that has the text GeoData. Add the following commands to your GeoData menu choice's Click event handler to call the form:

```
frmGeoData.ShowDialog()
Me.Show()
```

15. Add `frmMenu.Hide()` as the last line of code in frmGeoData's Load event handler.

16. Save the project, then run the application and open the form. Your form appears to hang for however long it takes to retrieve the data in the frmGeodata's Load

event handler. (To confirm this, select a different menu choice while you wait.) After 30 seconds or so, the form appears and displays the data in the data grid view control.

17. Close the application windows.

To enable the user to cancel the data retrieval operation, we configure the form to retrieve the data asynchronously using a BackgroundWorker component. When a user runs the form, the form immediately opens. However, the data grid view control does not display the data until all the data has been retrieved. The BackgroundWorker starts a new thread, which retrieves the data. While waiting, the user has the option of canceling the retrieval and returning to the previous menu form.

The following steps modify the form to retrieve the data asynchronously. First, the steps set dgGeodata's DataSource property to Nothing; this is necessary because the control is filled using a different thread from the one that created it. The next steps set the Return button's Text property to display the message "Retrieving data—Cancel?" Finally, the steps start the BackgroundWorker's thread from a Try/Catch block in the form's Load event handler. The Try/Catch block is needed because even if the user cancels the data retrieval, the BackgroundWorker thread continues working because it is using a different thread from the form's thread.

To configure the GeoData form to use asynchronous data retrieval:

1. Open frmGeoData in Designer view. Open the Toolbox, and drag a BackgroundWorker component onto the form's component tray.

2. Select BackgroundWorker1 in the form's component tray, display the Properties window, and change its name to bwGeoData.

3. Display frmGeoData in Code view, and change the code in its Load event handler to the following:

```
Private Sub frmGeodata_Load(...
  dgGeodata.DataSource = Nothing
  btnReturn.Text = "Retrieving data - Cancel?"
  Try
    bwGeodata.RunWorkerAsync()
  Catch
  End Try
  frmMenu.Hide()
End Sub
```

4. To create the DoWork event handler to fill the data set, open the form's Objects list and select bwGeoData, then open the Events list and select DoWork. Add the following command to the event handler:

```
AllInfoTableAdapter.Fill(Me.GeoDataDataSet.AllInfo)
```

5. To create the RunWorkerCompleted event handler to display the data, open the Objects list and select bwGeoData, then open the Events list and select RunWorkerCompleted. Add the following highlighted commands to the event handler:

```
dgGeodata.DataSource = AllInfoBindingSource
btnReturn.Text = "&Return"
```

6. Save the project, then run the application and open the GeoData form. The form button displays "Retrieving Data—Cancel?" as the form retrieves the data. After about half a minute, the data appears in the form.

7. Click Return to close the form, then open it again. This time, click Retrieving data—Cancel? to cancel the data retrieval operation and redisplay the menu form.

8. Close the application.

What if the user cancels the retrieval operation, then immediately reopens the form before the BackgroundWorker's thread finishes? An error occurs, because the form's Load event handler tries to start the BackgroundWorker thread again, but it is already running. You cannot stop a Fill operation while it retrieves data using commands in a BackgroundWorker thread. This is a performance concern because the thread continues to place a processing load on the SQL Server database process retrieving the data. When you are connecting to a local database file, this load is on the local computer and might slow it down slightly; however, if you are connecting to a remote server, the server's performance is adversely affected because it continues processing the data retrieval request.

IN CONCLUSION . . .

In this chapter, you learned different ways to display data in Windows applications. You also learned how to create Windows-based database applications using both data-bound controls and program commands. Data-bound controls make it easy to create a variety of applications that allow users to view and update data. Sometimes the data-bound controls do not provide the flexibility your application needs, however, so you need to write program code to process data. You have also learned how to create a Windows application that retrieves data asynchronously and allows users to cancel data retrieval operations.

You now have the knowledge you need to create basic database applications. Future chapters focus on adding reporting functions to your applications, creating Web-based applications, and using database data in an XML format.

SUMMARY

- ADO.NET is a set of object classes that allow .NET applications to communicate with databases.
- The original ADO.NET 1.x version uses a data connection to create a communication path between the application and the database. The data connection communicates with one or more data adapters, which provide methods for processing data. The data adapter stores retrieved data in a data set.
- After an application retrieves data into a data set, you can bind the data to a control. Simple data binding binds one field to a control. Complex data binding binds multiple fields to a control.
- VS 2005 supports enhanced ADO.NET 2.x, which adds a data source object to specify a data connection and to create a strongly typed data set. A strongly typed data set stores information about the retrieved data's data types and constraints. It also contains one or more table adapters, which are interfaces to data adapters storing data tables.

- The VB IDE provides data designer tools to allow you to view and manipulate data components. The Database Explorer displays all project data connections and their underlying objects. The Data Sources window displays a project's data sets and underlying data tables, and it is the primary interface for creating data-bound controls. The Data Set Designer allows you to create and edit data tables and table adapters in a data source.
- Database applications use single-record displays, which show one record at a time; tabular displays, which show multiple records at a time in a table; and master-detail displays, which show master-detail (one-to-many) relationships by displaying a master record in one part of the display, as well as associated detail records in another part of the display.
- Enhancements to the basic data interfaces include displaying image data, showing foreign key values in pick lists, and allowing users to perform text searches for record values.

- To store and display image data, you can use either the stored binary data approach, which stores the images as binary data values, or the stored filename approach, which stores text strings that represent the image file locations in a server file system.
- In VS 2005/VB Express, the primary data-bound controls are text boxes, which show data in a single-record display, and data grid views, which show data in a tabular display.
- When you add data-bound controls to a form, VB automatically creates a ToolStrip, which is a control that allows users to navigate in a data set and modify data values.
- To create a form that displays a master-detail relationship using data-bound controls, drag the table adapter that displays the master record from the Data Sources window and then drop it onto the form. To create the detail relationship, drag the table adapter below the master table adapter in the Data Sources window and drop it on the form.
- To create a form that allows users to find a specific record using a text search, create a parameter query, which is a query that receives a search condition value from a form control.
- Forms that contain data-bound controls that enable users to change database values require enhancements to avoid user errors, add meaningful confirmation and error messages, allow users to cancel editing operations, and validate input data.
- Forms with data-bound controls may not have the flexibility that some applications require for working with multiple tables or processing data in nontraditional ways. In these cases, you need to use program commands to create data-processing components and process data.
- You can create applications that use data-bound controls, in conjunction with program commands, to display and process data.
- An application can retrieve data asynchronously, that is, retrieve data in the background while enabling the user to perform other application tasks. To set up an asynchronous database application, create a BackgroundWorker component that retrieves the data using a separate program thread.

KEY TERMS

Asynchronous data retrieval Retrieval of data in a separate application thread while allowing the user to simultaneously perform other tasks

Bind Attachment of data in a data table to a form control

Binding Navigator Toolbar that provides a user interface to allow users to work with a data-bound control

Binding source Interface that binds a control to a data table

Complex data binding Binding of a control to multiple fields in a data table

Data adapter Data component that provides methods for retrieving and modifying data

Data binding Binding that creates a link between controls on a form and data in a data source

Data connection Data component that specifies a communication path between the application and the database

Data set Data component that stores one or more data tables

Data table Data component that stores the data retrieved by a data adapter

Data validation Act of confirming that user-entered data values are valid

Dock Attachment of a control to one or more edges of a form

Master-detail display Database interface that displays data values with a master-detail (one-to-many) relationship

Parameter query Query that receives a search value using an input parameter

Pick list field Field in a database interface that provides selections for a data value

Picture box control Control that displays a graphic image file

Simple data binding Binding of one field in a data table to a control

Single-record display Database interface that displays a single record at a time

Stored binary data approach Approach for displaying image data in which the database stores the binary data of an image

Stored filenames approach Approach for displaying image data in which the database stores a text string that represents the image file location in the server file system

Strongly typed data set Data storage container with a schema that specifies information about data fields, data types, and constraints

Table adapter Strongly typed interface to a data adapter

Tabular display Database interface that displays multiple records in a table format

Thread Separate process in a form that can support asynchronous data retrievals

STUDY QUESTIONS

Multiple-Choice Questions

1. In a read-write data grid view control, you create a _____ to trap system errors and provide informative error messages.
   - a. Try/Catch block
   - b. DataError event handler
   - c. OnError program block
   - d. Data validation program block

2. When you create a data-bound control based on a table adapter that uses a parameter query, the IDE automatically creates a:
   - a. MenuStrip
   - b. Data adapter
   - c. Parameter list
   - d. Fill ToolStrip

3. When you create a connection object using program commands, the connection string can specify:
   - a. The database server name
   - b. The path to the database application
   - c. The path to the database .mdf file
   - d. Both a and c

4. You use a data grid view data-bound control to display data in a _____ format.
   - a. Single-record
   - b. Tabular
   - c. Master-detail
   - d. Both b and c

5. In a combo box, the _____ property specifies that value that appears in the combo box, and the _____ property specifies the primary key of the displayed value.
   - a. DisplayMember, ValueMember
   - b. ValueMember, DisplayMember
   - c. DisplayMember, DisplayValue
   - d. DisplayValue, DisplayMember

6. To create a data grid view control that shows data from multiple tables, you must base the control on a table adapter:
   - a. Whose query joins multiple tables
   - b. That has a relation to another table adapter
   - c. That uses a parameter query
   - d. Whose FillBy method has been modified.

7. A _____ specifies a communication path between a database application and a database server.
   - a. Data connection
   - b. Data adapter
   - c. Table adapter
   - d. Data binding

8. To create a data-bound control that receives search condition inputs from other form control values, you must base the control on a table adapter that uses:
   - a. Programmatic data controls
   - b. A parameter list
   - c. A parameter query
   - d. A relation

9. A data-bound control must be associated with a strongly typed data set in order to perform _____ operations.
   - a. INSERT
   - b. UPDATE
   - c. Text search
   - d. Data validation

10. You use pick list fields to display data values for fields that represent _____ key values.
    - a. Primary
    - b. Foreign
    - c. Surrogate
    - d. Composite

True/False Questions

1. In a master-detail display, you always display the master record using a single-record display.
2. In the IDE, you use either the Data Sources window or the DataSet Designer to create new table adapters.
3. A master-detail data display usually displays data from two database tables.

4. You can create a pick list field in a tabular data display.
5. ADO.NET 1.x supports only simple data binding, while ADO.NET 2.0 supports only complex data binding.
6. In a master-detail display, if the user deletes a master record that has associated detail records, an error occurs.

Short Answer Questions

1. List two situations in which you need to use program commands rather than data-bound controls to create database applications.
2. List an advantage and a disadvantage of using the stored filename approach for storing and displaying image data. Then list an advantage and a disadvantage of using the stored binary data approach.
3. Describe the differences between the ExecuteScalar() and ExecuteNonQuery() functions and the values each function returns.
4. Describe the difference between simple data binding and complex data binding.
5. How do you modify a data-bound control to make it read only?
6. How do you create data-bound controls that have a master-detail relationship?
7. List three problems that you need to address when you create read-write data-bound controls.
8. What does the VB IDE place in the Component tray?
9. List two places where you can find the connection string specification for your database.
10. Write a command to create a SQL command object. Write a command to set its command text to retrieve the first and last names of all students who live in the state that the user enters in a form text box named txtState. Then write the command to associate the parameters with the form text box.
11. Define asynchronous data retrieval, and describe when you need to use it.

Guided Exercises

All the following exercises use the Sport Motors database, which Figures 3-2 and 3-4 illustrate.

1. **Creating a Project with a Data Source and Menu**
    This exercise creates a project that stores the forms for all the chapter's guided exercises.
    a. Create a new project named DBExercises, and save it in your \SQLServer\Solutions\Chapter6 folder. Do not create a directory for the solution, and make sure that the project's Option Strict setting value is on.
    b. In the project, create a new data source that uses the *yourDatabaseName* database. (If you are connecting to a local database, reference the *yourDatabaseName*.mdf file. If you are connecting to a remote database, use the connection information that your instructor provides.) Include both the University and SportMotors database tables in the data source.
    c. Rename the project's default form frmMenu, and configure the form using the standard form properties you used in the chapter tutorials. Change the form's Text property value to Chapter 6 Guided Exercises.
    d. Create a MenuStrip control on frmMenu that displays menu choices calling the forms for the rest of the exercises. Create top-level menu items that display the following selections: Read-Only Exercises, Read-Write Exercises, and Program Code Exercises.
2. **Creating a Form with a Read-Only Single-Table Display That Displays Image Data**

    NOTE: This exercise assumes that you have completed Exercise 6-1.

    In this exercise, you create the form in Figure 6-26, which allows Sport Motors employees to view inventory items.
    a. Create a new form in the DBExercises project named frmExercise2.vb. Configure the form using the standard form properties that you used in the chapter. Change the form's Text property to Exercise 6-2.
    b. Add a new menu selection under the Read-Only Exercises menu item in the project frmMenu form that has the text "Exercise 6-2," then add all the necessary commands to make the menu selection display the frmExercise2 form and hide the menu form.

FIGURE 6-26   Exercise 6-2

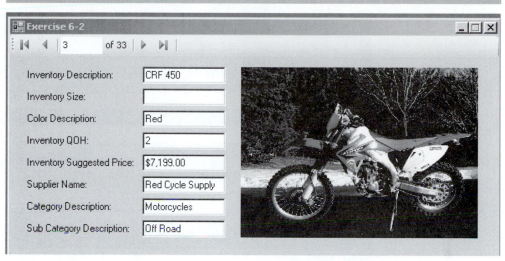

c. Create a new table adapter and associated data table that displays the fields shown in Figure 6-26 by joining the SportInventory, SportSupplier, SportCategory, and SportSubCategory tables. Rename the data table SportInventoryJoin and the table adapter SportInventoryJoinTableAdapter.

d. Create and configure the data-bound single-record read-only display controls shown in Figure 6-26 using the SportInventoryJoin data table.

e. Copy the Images folder and files from the SQLServer\Datafiles\Chapter6 folder to the project folder's \bin\Debug folder. Then add a picture box control to display the inventory images, as shown in Figure 6-26. Reference the image filename using the stored filename approach. Configure the form so that the text box displaying the image filename does not appear on the form.

3. **Creating a Read-Only Master-Detail Display with a Text Search Field**

NOTE: This exercise assumes that you already completed Exercise 6-1.

In this exercise, you create the form in Figure 6-27, which allows Sport Motors employees to enter a search value for an order date or leave it blank to retrieve all orders, then view information about the orders.

a. Create a new form in the DBExercises project named frmExercise3.vb. Configure the form using the standard form properties you used in the chapter. Change the form's Text property to Exercise 6-3.

b. Add a new menu selection under the Read-Only Exercises menu item in the project frmMenu form with the text Exercise 6-3, then add all the necessary commands to make the menu selection display the frmExercise3 form and hide the menu form.

c. Create a new table adapter and associated data table that displays the fields shown in the master record block in Figure 6-27 by joining the SportOrder, SportCustomer, and SportEmployee tables. Configure the query as a parameter query that uses the OrderDate field as a parameter value. Rename the data table SportOrderSearch and the table adapter SportOrderSearchTableAdapter.

d. Create the master data grid view based on the SportOrderSearch data table, and modify the data grid view columns as shown in Figure 6-27. Be sure to format the OrderDate as shown. Configure the data grid view so it is read only.

e. Create a new table adapter and associated data table that displays the fields shown in the detail record block in Figure 6-27 by joining the SportOrderDetail and SportInventory tables. Rename the data table SportOrderDetailJoin and the table adapter SportOrderDetailJoinTableAdapter. (Hint: To display the Unit Price values as currency, use the SQL Style function in the table adapter query.)

FIGURE 6-27 Exercise 6-3

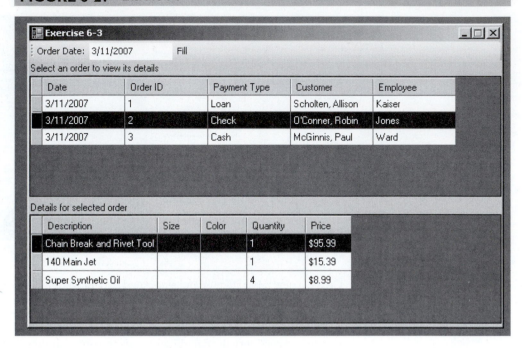

f. Create a relation between the two new data tables. Specify SportOrderSearch as the parent table and SportOrderDetail as the child table, and join the tables on the OrderID field.
g. Create the detail data grid view based on the SportOrderDetailJoin data table, and modify the data grid view columns as shown in Figure 6-27. Format the price as shown, using the DefaultCellStyle property. Configure the data grid view so that it is read only.

4. **Creating a Read-Write Single-Record Display**

NOTE: This exercise assumes that you already completed Exercise 6-1.

In this exercise, you create the form in Figure 6-28, which allows Sport Motors employees to enter and update customer data.
a. Create a new form in the DBExercises project named frmExercise4.vb. Configure the form using the standard form properties you used in the chapter. Change the form's Text property to Exercise 6-4.
b. Add a new menu selection under the Read-Write Exercises menu item in the project frmMenu form that has the text Exercise 6-4, then add all the necessary commands to make the menu selection display the frmExercise4 form and hide the menu form.
c. Create and configure the data-bound single-record display controls shown in Figure 6-28 using the SportCustomer data table.
d. Display the StateAbbreviation field as a pick list based on the SportState data table. Display the StateName in the combo box, and specify StateAbbreviation as the associated data value.
e. Add a message box to confirm when the database successfully saves a user's changes.
f. Create an event handler to cancel in-progress editing operations.
g. Configure the text box that displays the table's primary key so that it is read only.

5. **Creating a Read-Write Master-Detail Display**

NOTE: This exercise assumes that you already completed Exercise 6-1.

FIGURE 6-28 Exercise 6-4

In this exercise, you create the form in Figure 6-29, which allows Sport Motors employees to view, enter, and update department and employee data.

a. Create a new form in the 6DBExercises project named frmExercise5.vb. Configure the form using the standard form properties you used in the chapter. Change the form's Text property to Exercise 6-5.

b. Add a new menu selection under the Read-Write Exercises menu item in the project frmMenu form that has the text Exercise 6-5, then add all the necessary commands to make the menu selection display the frmExercise5 form and hide the menu form.

FIGURE 6-29 Exercise 6-5

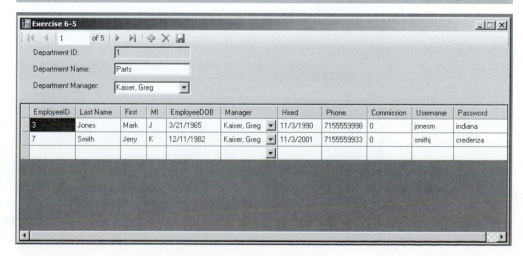

c. Create and configure the data-bound single-record display controls for the master record as shown in Figure 6-29, using the SportDepartment data table. Create a pick list field to display the department manager's last and first names, as shown. (You need to create a new table adapter to concatenate the data values.) Add a message box to confirm successful editing operations. Disable the primary key text box, and add an event handler to cancel in-progress editing.

d. Create and configure the data grid view for the detail records as shown in Figure 6-29, using the SportEmployee table.

e. Create a DataError event handler for the data grid view control to advise the user of the following data validation constraints:

Column	*Constraint(s)*
Last Name	Cannot be NULL
DOB	Must be a valid date
Hire Date	Must be a valid date
Commission	Must be a number between 0 and 1; cannot be NULL

6. **Creating a Master-Detail Display with a Text Search Field That Uses Program Commands to Update Data**

NOTE: This exercise assumes that you already completed Exercise 6-1.

In this exercise, you create the form in Figure 6-30, which allows Sport Motors employees to enter a search value for a supplier and then view information about all inventory items associated with the supplier. When a new shipment of a selected item is received, the employee enters the number of items in the shipment, and program commands automatically update the item's quantity on hand by the given amount.

a. Create a new form in the 6DBExercises project named frmExercise6.vb. Configure the form using the standard form properties you used in the chapter. Change the form's Text property to Exercise 6-6.

FIGURE 6-30   Exercise 6-6

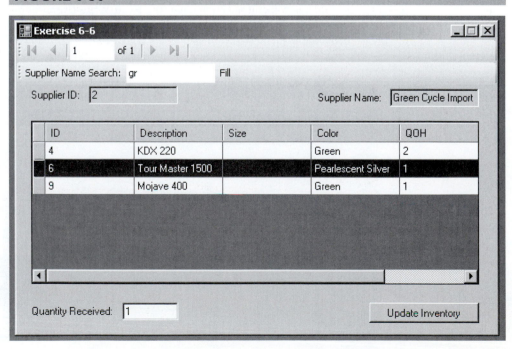

b. Add a new menu selection under the Program Code Exercises menu item in the project frmMenu form that has the text Exercise 6-6, then add all the necessary commands to make the menu selection display the frmExercise6 form and hide the menu form.

c. Create a new table adapter and associated data table that displays the fields shown in the master record block in Figure 6-30. Configure the query as a parameter query that uses the SupplierName field as a parameter value. Structure the query so that the user can enter any characters from the left side of the SupplierName value and the query retrieves all suppliers whose name matches the entered characters. Rename the data table SportSupplierSearch and the table adapter SportSupplierSearchTableAdapter.

d. Create the master data-bound text boxes based on the SportOrderSearch data table, and configure the controls so that they are read only.

e. Create a data grid view that displays the fields shown in the detail record block in Figure 6-30 using the SportInventory data table. (Hint: To display the Unit Price values as currency, modify the field in the table adapter query using the SQL CONVERT function.) Configure the data grid as read only, and edit its columns as shown.

f. Create the Quantity Received label and text box, as well as the Update Inventory button.

g. Create an event handler for the Update Inventory button, which uses program commands to update the inventory quantity on hand of the selected inventory item by the amount the user types into the Quantity Received text box. Be sure to refresh the data grid display to show the updated inventory amount. (Hint: Reference the inventory item using the following syntax:

```
DataGridViewName.Cells("InventoryID").Value)).
```

7. **Creating the Sport Motors Customer Order Application**

NOTE: This exercise assumes that you already completed Exercise 6-1.

In this exercise, you create the Sport Motors Customer Order application. When the application first opens, it displays the Login form in Figure 6-31. After a successful login, the application displays a form that allows the employee to create a new customer order, as shown in Figure 6-32.

When the Customer Order form first opens, the employee clicks the New Order button, and a new Order ID value appears. The employee selects the order date, customer, employee, and payment type from the form combo boxes, then clicks Save Order to save the order record. The employee selects the target inventory item, specifies the item quantity and sale price in the form text boxes, and then clicks on Add selected item to existing order. The item then appears in the Order Details data grid view.

FIGURE 6-31   Exercise 6-7 Login form

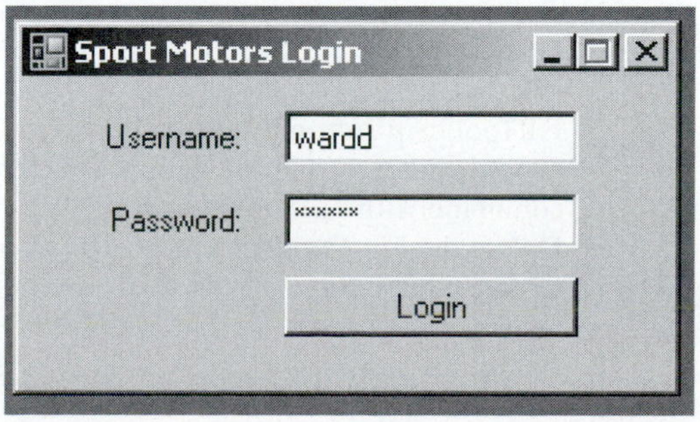

FIGURE 6-32 Exercise 6-7 Customer Order form

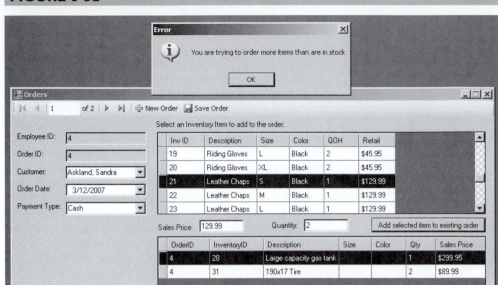

a. Create a new form in the DBExercises project named frmExercise7Login.vb. Configure the form as shown in Figure 6-31.

b. Create a second form in the DBExercises project named frmExercise7Orders.vb. Configure the form as shown in Figure 6-32.

c. Add a public form variable named lngEmployeeID of type Long to frmExercise7Orders.vb.

d. Add a new menu selection under the Program Code Exercises menu item in the project frmMenu form that has the text Exercise 6-7, then add all the necessary commands to make the menu selection display the frmExercise7Login form.

e. Add program commands to frmExercise7Login's Login button to create a database connection and confirm that the employee username/password combination is valid. If it is valid, assign the retrieved EmployeeID to frmExercise7Orders' lngEmployeeID variable, display the New Order form, and hide the Login form. When the user closes the Customer Order form, do not redisplay the Login form; instead, make sure the Login form is disposed of and redisplay the Menu form. If the username/password combination is not valid, display an appropriate message box and exit the application.

f. Create a new table adapter named SportOrderByEmployeeID to display all the SportOrder fields. Display only orders associated with the current employee. (Hint: Use a parameter query.)

g. Delete the Delete button from the BindingNavigator control, and configure the Add New and Save Data buttons as shown in Figure 6-32. (Hint: Use the DisplayStyle and Text properties.)

h. Open the form in Code view, and copy the line of code starting with `Me.SportOrderByEmployeeIDTableAdapter.Fill` from the FillToolStripButton_Click event and make it the first line of code in the form's Load event handler. Replace `CType(EmpIDToolStripTextBox.Text, Long)` in the Fill command with `lngEmployeeID`.

i. Delete the Fill ToolStrip control. (Do not delete the BindingNavigator control.)

j. Create combo boxes to display formatted customer names and order payment types as shown.

k. Add error handling to the code in the FillToolStrip's Save button event handler to ensure that the order ID and order date values are valid.

FIGURE 6-33   Exercise 6-8 Enhanced Customer Order form

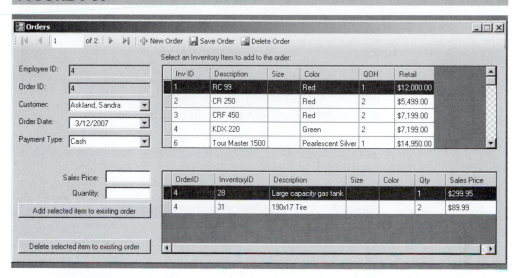

l. Display Inventory items in a read-only data grid view based on the SportInventory table adapter. Configure it to show the columns in the top grid in Figure 6-32.

m. Create a new table adapter named SportOrderDetailJoin that retrieves data from the SportOrderDetail and SportInventory tables to display the data in the lower data grid view.

n. Add a new relation to create a master-detail relationship between the employee and order table adapters.

o. Add code preventing adding a new item if the user has clicked the New Order button without successfully clicking the Save Order button. Hint: One way to do this is to make a Boolean module level variable named `blnAddingOrder` that is initially False. Set it to True in the Add Order event handler and back to False in the Save Order event handler.

p. The Add button's event handler should ensure the entered price and quantity are valid values, check the QOH for the selected inventory item and prevent adding it if the QOH is zero, check the desired quantity against the QOH, and, if greater, prevent adding the item to the order.

q. The Add button event handler should insert the new order detail entry into SportOrderDetail using program commands and update SportInventory's InventoryQOH field to reduce it by the amount added to the order.

8. **Enhancing the Customer Order Form to Allow Deleting Orders and Order Items**

NOTE: This exercise assumes that you have completed Exercises 6-1 and 6-7.

This exercise enhances the Customer Order form in Exercise 6-7 by allowing employees to delete orders and order items, as shown in Figure 6-33.

a. Enhance frmExercise7Orders to match Figure 6-33 by adding the code needed to delete records from the SportOrderDetail and SportOrder tables.

b. Use appropriate error handling to ensure that a user has selected an item before deleting it and that a user cannot delete an item until he or she has first deleted all the order's items.

9. **Creating an Application to Asynchronously Retrieve Data**

NOTE: This exercise assumes that you have completed Exercise 6-1.

This exercise creates the form in Figure 6-34, which allows the user to enter a search string specifying one or more letters in a state name.

FIGURE 6-34   Exercise 6-9

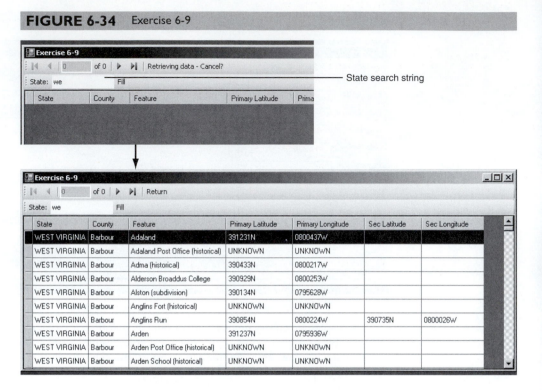

When the user clicks Fill, the form asynchronously retrieves the data values for the state as shown and displays the "Retrieving data—Cancel?" button. When the data retrieval operation is completed, the form displays the retrieved data in the data grid view control and the button displays the label Return, which closes the form and redisplays the Menu form.

a. Create a new form in the DBExercises project named frmExercise9geodata.vb. Configure the form using the standard form properties used in the chapter. Change the form's Text property to Exercise 6-9.

b. Add a new menu selection under the Read-Only Exercises menu item in the project frmMenu form that has the text Exercise 6-9, then add all the necessary commands to make the menu selection display the frmExercise9 form.

c. Add a new data source to your DBExercises project for the GeoData.mdf database (This file is in the \SQLServer\Datafiles\Databases folder).

d. Create a new table adapter and associated data table named FeaturesByState that displays the fields shown in Figure 6-34. The table adapter should use a parameter query that enables the user to search by the state name using a partial text string.

e. Create and configure the data grid view control shown in Figure 6-34 using the FeaturesByState data table.

f. Modify and add code as needed to make the form retrieve the data asynchronously.

CHAPTER 7

Creating Database Reports

Learning Objectives

At the conclusion of this chapter, you will be able to:

- describe commonly used database report layouts;

- create and format a simple report that displays data from a single table;

- create reports that display data from multiple database tables;

- implement reports with master-detail layouts;

- include summary data and calculated values in reports;

- pass parameter values from forms to reports.

You have learned how to create Windows-based database applications that allow users to work with database data. In this chapter, you will learn how to use Crystal Reports Designer to create a variety of database reports that you can display in the Windows applications that you create using the Visual Studio 2005 or VB Express IDE.

A *report* is a summary view of database data that users can view on a computer screen, print on paper, or send as an e-mail message. A report displays database data and often displays summary information or calculated values to help managers analyze data and make decisions. A report might list current enrollments in all Ironwood University courses for a specific term, present a line chart to show enrollment trends over the past two years, or display a student transcript that shows the student's total course credits and cumulative grade point average.

In this book, you will use an embedded version of the Crystal Reports Designer application that you can run from within Visual Studio 2005. This is a visual application that uses wizards and dialog boxes to allow you to create reports. Traditionally, Crystal Reports Designer is a stand-alone application. Microsoft has embedded a version of Crystal Reports in Visual Studio 2005. The embedded version has fewer features and functions than the stand-alone version, but the embedded version has enough functionality to make a variety of database reports.

NOTE: VB Express does not include the embedded version of Crystal Reports. If you are using VB Express, you will not be able to complete the tutorials or exercises in this chapter.

COMMON DATABASE REPORT LAYOUTS

This section introduces common report data layouts. This will help you understand the types of reports you can make with Crystal Reports and help you design reports for your own applications. Figure 7-1 illustrates the most common report layout, which shows data from a single table in a tabular format. Reports can easily display data from multiple tables in a tabular format as well.

Often reports display data in a master-detail format, in which one or more fields for a single master record appear, followed by detail records in a tabular format. The report repeats the master record and associated detail records as many times as necessary. Figure 7-2 shows a master-detail report with a master group and a set of associated detail records.

The report in Figure 7-2 has a single master-detail relationship. It lists all tutors from the UniversityTutor table, along with the details of all their tutoring sessions, from the UniversityTutorSession table. It lists two different master records (tutors Cheryl and Michael), and each tutor has multiple tutoring sessions.

Many times, reports have multiple master-detail relationships. Figure 7-3 shows a master-detail report with two master groups. This report shows that an Ironwood University department offers multiple courses, and a course has multiple associated course sections. In this report, the data for each department appears on a different report page.

The embedded version of Crystal Reports allows you to display reports on Windows forms. This chapter illustrates how to create reports using a single VB project that contains separate forms to display each report. The reports are accessed using pull-down menus on the project's startup form. The following steps show how to create a VB project and create a MenuStrip control on the project's startup form. Then, you create the form that displays the first report, which uses a tabular display.

FIGURE 7-1   Single-table tabular report

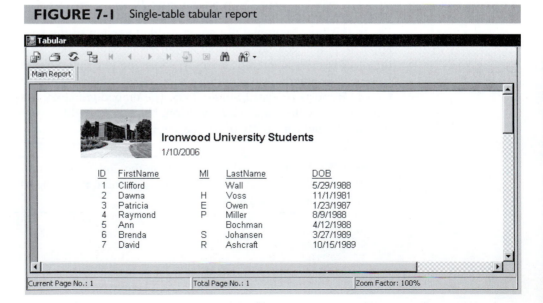

FIGURE 7-2 Master-detail report

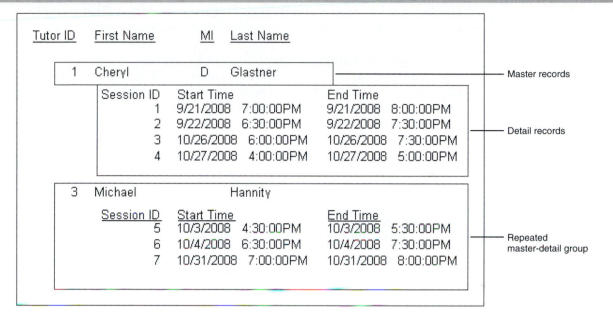

To create the VB project to display the chapter tutorial reports:

1. In the Visual Studio 2005 IDE, create a new Windows application project named DBReports. Save the project in your \SQLServer\Solutions\Chapter7 folder. Do not create a separate solution folder for the project.

2. Open the Solution Explorer if necessary, and rename the default form to frmMenu.vb.

3. If necessary, open the form in Designer view. Modify the form properties as follows:

Property	New Value
FormBorderStyle	FixedSingle
MaximizeBox	False
StartPosition	CenterScreen

FIGURE 7-3 Master-detail report with two master groups

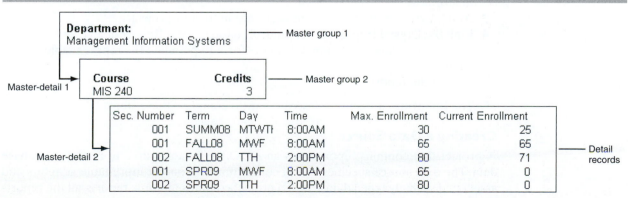

NOTE: From this point forward, we refer to these properties as the *standard form property values*. Whenever you are instructed to set a form's properties to the standard form property values, use these values.

4. Set the form's Text property value to Report Examples.
5. Open the Toolbox, scroll down to the Menus and Toolbars section, then double-click MenuStrip to add a menu to your form. Place the insertion point in the *Type Here* text box in the tool strip, then type Simple Reports.
6. Place the insertion point in the text box under Simple Reports, and type Tabular. (You will add the rest of the menu selections later as you make new forms.)
7. Add a new form to the project named frmTabular.vb. Change the form's properties to the standard form property values. Change the form's Text property value to Tabular.
8. To call the Tabular form from the menu form, open the Menu form in Designer view, open the Simple Reports menu item, double-click Tabular to create a new event handler, then add the following command to the event handler:

```
'Change the current pointer to an hourglass
Me.Cursor = Cursors.WaitCursor
'Show the child form
frmTabular.ShowDialog()
'Redisplay the menu form after
'the user closes the child from
Me.Show()
'Restore the pointer to the default
Me.Cursor = Cursors.Default
```

9. Save the project.

NOTE: For the rest of the chapter, repeat these steps to create new forms and to call the forms from the Menu form.

CREATING A SINGLE-TABLE TABULAR REPORT

To create a report in a form, you will perform the following steps:

1. Create a data source in the project.
2. Create the form to display the report, and add a Crystal Report viewer control to the form.
3. Add a Crystal Report object class definition to your project.
4. Link the Crystal Report viewer control to the Crystal Report object, and add data components and commands to the form to populate the report's table adapter.
5. Format the report.

The following subsections describe how to complete these steps.

Creating a Data Source

A project that contains reports uses an ADO.NET data source to retrieve database data. The data source specifies a data connection and one or more table adapters and associated strongly typed data sets. If a project contains multiple reports, all the reports can use the same data source. The steps to create the data source are exactly the same as the ones you used in Chapter 6 to create data sources to retrieve and process database data in VB forms. Now you will create the project data source.

To create the data source:

1. To create a new data source, click Data on the menu bar, then click Add New Data Source. The Data Source Configuration Wizard opens.
2. On the *Choose a Data Source Type* page, select Database if necessary, then click Next.
3. On the *Choose your data connection* page, click New Connection. The Add Connection dialog box opens.
4. *If you are connecting to a local SQL Server Express database,* click Browse, navigate to \SQLServer\Databases\, select *yourDatabaseName*.mdf, and then click Open.

   If you are connecting to a remote SQL Server database, select Microsoft SQL Server from the Data source list, click Continue, type or select your server name in the Server name field, select the authentication approach, and if necessary type the username and password that your instructor provides, select the Select or enter a database name option button, open the list, and select your database.
5. Click Test Connection. The "Test connection succeeded" message box should appear. Click OK, click OK again, and then click Next.

NOTE: If you see a message saying "No database file was specified," click the Advanced button and enter the path to the .mdf file in the AttachDbFilename box.

---

6. *If you are connecting to a local database,* a message box opens and displays the message "The connection you selected uses a local data file that is not in the current project. Would you like to add the file to your project and modify the connection?" Click Yes to copy *yourDatabaseName.mdf* to the project folder.
7. The *Save the connection string to the application configuration file* page appears. Make sure that "Yes, save the connection as is" is checked, and then click Next.
8. The *Choose your database objects* page appears. Open the Tables node. A list of all the database tables appears. Scroll down the list, and check all the tables that begin with the word "University." You will select a total of thirteen tables.
9. Accept the default data set name, then click Finish. (This step may take a few moments to complete because the system creates the .xsd file and initializes the data and table adapters.)

Creating a Report Viewer Control

A *Crystal Report viewer* is a form control that displays a report, along with controls for working with the report. To create a Crystal Report viewer control, open the Toolbox and select the CrystalReportViewer control tool.

To create the report viewer control:

1. Select the frmTabular.vb[Design] tab to display the form in Designer view.
2. To create the CrystalReportViewer control, open the Toolbox, scroll down to the Crystal Reports node, open the node if necessary, and click CrystalReportViewer.
3. Move the mouse pointer onto the form, and draw a rectangle to represent the report viewer. The CrystalReportViewer appears and looks like Figure 7-4.

The Crystal Report viewer control automatically docks to the form and fills the form's surface. By default, it displays a toolbar to allow the user to interact with the report and navigate to different report records. It also displays a *Group pane,* which

FIGURE 7-4 Crystal Report viewer control

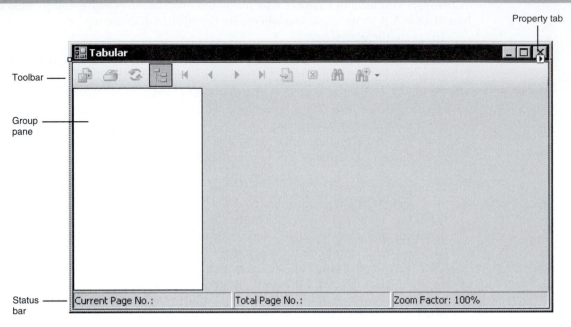

allows the user to collapse or expand report details in master-detail reports, and a *Status bar,* which shows the report page count and current page number. You can click the *Property tab,* which is the small arrow in the top right corner of the control. This action displays menu choices that allow you to hide one or more default components or undock the control from the form.

Always change the Name property value of a Report viewer control. You can also configure other properties to controls its appearance. The following steps show how to use Property tab selections to hide the Group pane and undock the control. They also modify the report viewer control's Name property.

To modify the report viewer control:

1. Click the Property tab in the top right corner of the form. The CrystalReportViewer Tasks list opens. Clear the Display Group Tree check box, and click Undock in the parent container. (You typically do not display the Group Tree pane except in master-detail reports.)
2. Select the report viewer control in the form, and change its Name property value to crvStudent.
3. Save the project.

Creating the Report Object Class Definition

A *Crystal Report object class definition* is a form item that specifies the report contents and format. To create it, add a new Crystal Report item to your form, then configure its properties. You can configure the report object class manually or by using a wizard. It is easier to use the wizard, so that is how we will do it. Now you will add the report object class.

To add the Crystal Report object class:

1. Right-click the DBReports node in the Solution Explorer window, point to Add, and then click New Item.

2. Select Crystal Report in the Templates window, change the Name field value to rptStudent.rpt, and then click Add. The rptStudent page appears in the Document window, and the Crystal Reports Gallery wizard opens.

HELP: If the Crystal Reports End-User License Agreement window opens, select the *I accept the agreement* option button, and then click OK.

The Crystal Reports Gallery presents you with options for starting a wizard to create the report, creating a blank report and specifying its components manually, or creating a report from an existing report. Creating a report from an existing report allows you to build on previous reports and copy their styles and formats. The Gallery also allows you to select a standard, cross-tab, or mailing label report display format.

If you select the option of starting a wizard, the Report Creation Wizard opens. The Report Creation Wizard has the following pages:

1. **Data** allows you to specify the data tables that provide data values for the report.
2. **Fields** allows you to specify the data table fields.
3. **Grouping** allows you to specify master-detail relationships and how you wish to group report data.
4. **Record Selection** allows you to specify search conditions to display selected data values on the report.
5. **Report Style** allows you to select from a list of predefined styles to specify data formatting styles, shading, and colors.

The following steps show how to start the wizard and create the single-table tabular report in Figure 7-1.

To start the wizard and create the single-table tabular report:

1. In the Crystal Reports Gallery dialog box, make sure that the Using the Report Wizard option button is selected and that the Standard display is selected, and then click OK. The Standard Report Creation Wizard opens, and the *Data* page appears.
2. On the *Data* page, open the Project Data node, open the ADO.NET DataSets node, open the DBReports.*yourDatabaseName*DataSet node, select UniversityStudent, and then click the Add item button, which is a single right-pointing arrow. The *yourDatabaseName*DateSet node and the UniversityCourse data table appear in the Selected Tables list. Click Next.
3. On the *Fields* page, open the UniversityStudent node in the Available Fields list. Select StudentID, press and hold Ctrl, and then select StudentFirstName, StudentMI, StudentLastName, and StudentDOB. Click the Add item button. The selected fields appear in the Fields to Display list. Click Next.
4. You will not specify any master-detail groupings, so do not do anything on the *Grouping* page, and click Next.
5. You will not specify a search condition, so do not do anything on the Record *Selection* page, and click Next.
6. On the *Report Style* page, make sure that Standard is selected in the Available Styles list, then click Finish. The embedded Crystal Reports IDE windows appear, as shown in Figure 7-5.

HELP: If your display does not look like Figure 7-5, click Window on the menu bar, and then click Reset Window Layout.

FIGURE 7-5 Embedded Crystal Reports IDE windows

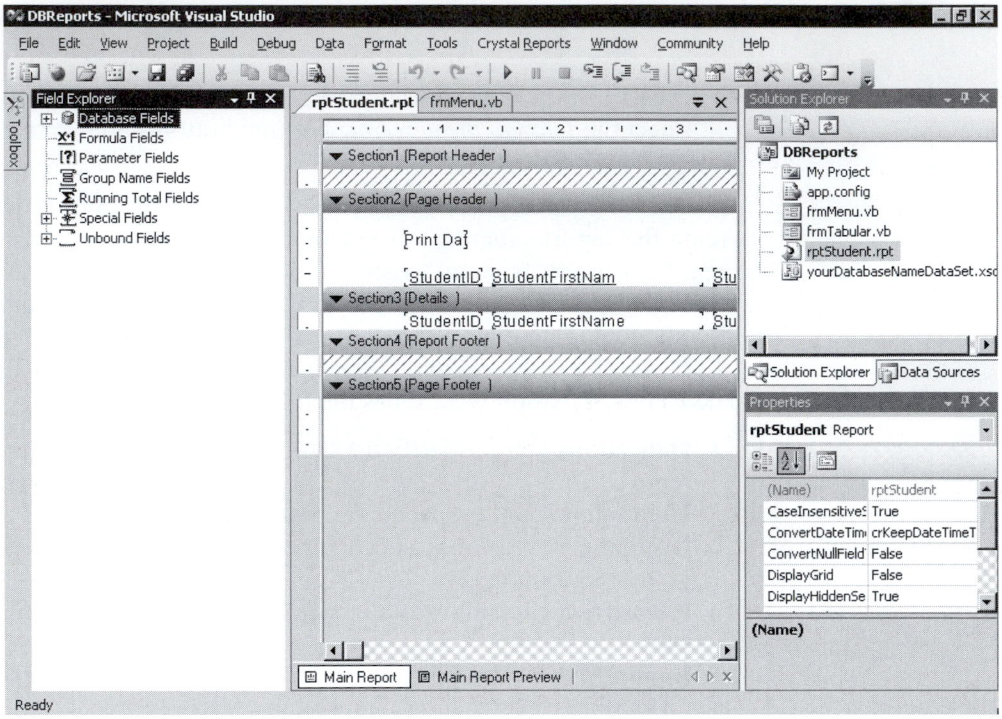

Report IDE windows

The VS 2005 IDE for creating a Crystal Report allows you to modify the report that the wizard creates. It contains the *Field Explorer,* which displays a hierarchical view of the report fields. The IDE document window displays the report in Designer view, which shows the report layout sections and components, and in Previewer view, which shows how the report will appear to the user.

The Field Explorer displays the following nodes to represent the different types of report fields:

1. **Database fields** display retrieved database data.
2. **Formula fields** display values that are calculated by applying formulas to database field values.
3. **Parameter fields** allow users to input values that the report uses as search conditions to filter data.
4. **Group name fields** allows users to work with groups of fields in master-detail relationships.
5. **Running total fields,** also called summary fields, display a running total of a numeric database or formula field value.
6. **Special fields** provide templates to display values such as the current date, time, page number, and the like.
7. **Unbound fields** are not bound to a database field and are used to store report values such as values used in formulas.

You can add new fields to the report layout by selecting a field in the Field Explorer, then dragging it and dropping it onto the report in Designer view. Designer view shows the different report sections and displays the report components as objects. The *report sections* organize the report items and specify where the report displays

FIGURE 7-6   Report sections

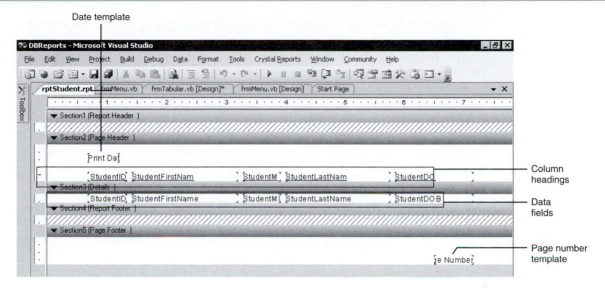

items and how often the items appear. Figure 7-6 illustrates the report sections and components.

A Crystal Report has the following sections:

1. **Report header** displays items that appear once at the beginning of the report. Normally, you place the report title in this section, along with objects you want to display only once in the report, such as charts or letterhead images.
2. **Page header** displays items that appear at the top of each report page. This section might display page numbers, column headings, the total number of records that the report displays, or the date you generate the report.
3. **Details** displays the report data values. Items that you place in this section repeat once for each record.
4. **Report footer** displays items that appear once, at the end of the report. You might place summary values or a message indicating the end of the report in this section.
5. **Page footer** displays items that appear at the bottom of each report page. As with the page header, you might place page numbers, the total number of records that the report displays, or the date the report was generated.

Figure 7-6 shows the default items that appear in each report section. The report header and report footer are disabled and shaded. The page header displays the *date template,* which is a special field displaying the current date on the generated report and the column headings for the report data. The details section displays database fields that correspond to each report data column. The report footer does not display any items, and the page footer displays the page number template, which is a special field displaying the current page number.

To view the report in Previewer view, which is how the report appears to the user, click the Main Report Preview button in the bottom left corner of the report. To return to Designer view, click the Main Report button. Previewer view shows "template" data, not the actual data that the report displays when it appear on a Windows form or is printed.

Linking the Report to the Report Viewer Control and Adding the Data Components

To display a report on a Windows form, you must configure the form to link the report's object class to the Crystal Report viewer control that you created earlier. This creates an instance of the report object class in the project and displays the report in the viewer. To link the report class to the viewer, you must modify the viewer control properties, add data components to the form, and modify code to the form's Load event handler, which retrieves the data and loads it into the report viewer control.

When you create a data-bound control in a Windows form, the IDE uses a data set, table adapter, and binding source. When you used data-bound controls in Chapter 6, the IDE created these components automatically. When you create a Crystal Report viewer in a form, you must create and configure the components manually. The following steps show how to add a data set and binding source to the form and how to configure the items to work with the report viewer control.

To link the report to the report viewer control and create the data components:

1. To link the report to the report viewer control, open frmTabular in Designer view. Select the CrystalReportViewer control, select its ReportSource property, open the list, and select DBReports.rptStudent. The IDE creates an instance of the rptStudent object class, displays rptStudent1 in the Component tray, and displays the report in the report viewer control.

TIP: rptStudent1 is an object instance of the rptStudent object class.

HELP: At this point, the report displays template data rather than data that it will retrieve from the database.

---

2. To create the data set component, open the Toolbox, scroll to the Data node, select the DataSet tool, then drag it and drop it onto the form's Component tray. The Add Dataset dialog box opens.
3. In the Add Dataset dialog box, make sure that the Typed dataset option button is selected and that the dataset name is DBReports.*yourDatabaseName*DataSet. Then click OK. A new data set named *YourDatabaseName*DataSet1 appears in the Component tray.
4. To create the binding source, open the Toolbox, select the BindingSource tool, and then drag and drop it onto the form's Component tray. A new binding source named BindingSource1 appears in the Component tray.
5. Select BindingSource1 in the Component Tray, select its DataSource property in the Properties window, open the list, open the Other Data Sources node, open the Project Data Sources node, and then select *yourDatabaseName*DataSet1.
6. Select the binding source's DataMember property, open the list, and select UniversityStudent. This creates a new Table Adapter form component named UniversityStudentTableAdapter, which appears in the form's Component tray.
7. Open frmTabular in Code view. When you created the table adapter, the IDE added a command to the form's Load event handler to call the table adapter's Fill method. Add the following command, which specifies that the new data set is the report's data source, as the last command in the Load event handler:

```
rptStudent1.SetDataSource(Me.YourDatabaseNameDataSet1)
```

FIGURE 7-7   Report formatting issues

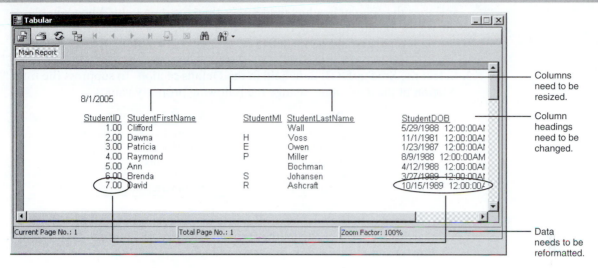

8. Run the application. Select Simple Reports on the menu bar, then click Tabular. The report looks something like the one in Figure 7-7. (You may need to resize the form and/or the report viewer control to display all the report columns without scrolling.) The report formatting needs some fine-tuning, which the next section addresses.
9. Close the application forms.

Formatting a Report

Figure 7-7 highlights some of the formatting issues that you often need to address with new reports. First, some of the data value formats need to be changed: the StudentID values, which should be integers, appear with two decimal places, and the dates appear in the default SQL Server format, which includes a time component. Also, the column headings, which are the same as the database field names, need to be revised, and the columns need to be resized. Additionally, reports often display *boilerplate objects,* which are text and graphic objects that enhance the report's appearance and that do not depend on the data that the report displays. The following subsections address these issues.

As you modify the report formatting, run the form and view the results of your changes. It is important to note that you *must* save the report object (.rpt) file each time you make a change, or the changes will not appear when you run the form.

Modifying Report Data Formats

To modify the format in which a report displays data, display the report in Designer view, select the data field in which you want to change the data format, then modify the field's data properties. The following steps show how to modify the StudentID values so that they appear as integers with no decimal values and the StudentDOB values so that they do not display the time component of the date value.

To modify the report's data formats:

1. Select the rptStudent.rpt tab to display the report in Designer view. (Recall from Figure 7-6 that this view shows the report sections and components.)
2. To modify the StudentID data format, select the StudentID data field in the Details report section. Selection handles appear around the field. In the Properties window, change the Decimal Places property value to **0**.

CAUTION: Do not select an item in the Page Header section, because this specifies the column heading field rather than the data field. When you place the mouse pointer on a report field, a ToolTip appears that describes whether the item is a data field or a heading.

3. Select the StudentDOB data field in the Details section. To suppress the time portion of the date value, change the following property values:

Property	New Value
Am String	(deleted)
HourType	crNoHour
MinuteType	crNoMinute
Pm String	(deleted)
SecondType	crNumericNoSecond

4. Run the application, click Simple Reports on the menu bar, and then click Tabular. The report appears in the form and displays the correct data formats for StudentID and StudentDOB, as shown in Figure 7-1.

HELP: If your changes do not appear when you run the form, make sure that you saved the report object.

5. Close the application forms.

Changing the Column Headings

Note in Figure 7-7 that the report column headings default to the database field names. To modify the column heading text, select the heading in the Page Heading report section, right-click, and then click Edit Text Object to open the text for editing.

To change the column headings:

1. In rptStudent.rpt in Designer view, select the StudentID field in the Page Headings section. Selection handles appear around the heading.
2. Right-click, then click Edit Text Object to open the heading for editing, and change the text to ID.
3. Modify the other column headings as shown in Figure 7-1, then run the application and open the form to confirm that your column headings look like those in Figure 7-1.
4. Close the application forms.

Resizing and Repositioning the Report Columns

The report column width is fixed at design time, and sometimes you need to make the columns wider or narrower to accommodate retrieved data values. To change a column's width, select the report column and then resize it. It is best to resize both the column heading and data field at the same time, so that their widths are the same. Now make the ID, First and Last Name, MI, and DOB columns narrower, and reposition the report columns.

To resize and reposition the report columns:

1. In rptStudent.rpt in Designer view, select the ID field in the Page Header section, press and hold Ctrl, and then select StudentID in the Details section. Selection handles appear around both fields. Place the mouse pointer on the right edge of either selected field, and resize the fields to make them narrower.
2. With both fields still selected, reposition the fields by dragging them to the left side of the report.

3. Repeat steps 1 and 2 for the First Name, MI, Last Name, and DOB fields. Make sure that the column heading text is still visible in the resized columns.

4. Run the application, open the Simple Report form, and view the resized and repositioned columns. If necessary, adjust the column sizes and positions so that your report looks like Figure 7-1.

TIP: To align fields, select the first field, press and hold Ctrl, right-click, point to Align, and then select the alignment style (Lefts, Centers, Rights, or To Grid.)

HELP: If your changes do not appear when you run the form, check to see that you saved the report object before you ran the form.

Adding Boilerplate Objects

Boilerplate objects are report items that always appear the same, regardless of the data that the report displays. Boilerplate objects such as titles and graphic images make reports more attractive and informative. By default, the Crystal Report Creation Wizard creates the boilerplate date and page number templates on the report. Now you will add the "Ironwood University Students" title and graphic image to the page header section.

To add the boilerplate objects to the report:

1. In rptStudent.rpt in Designer view, move the mouse pointer onto the bottom edge of the Page Header section, and drag the mouse pointer down to make the Page Header section about 1.2 inches long. Then reposition the column headings so that they are on the bottom edge of the Page Header section.

2. Move the date template so that it is in the approximate position shown in Figure 7-1.

3. To add the report title, right-click anywhere on the report in Designer view, point to Insert, and then click Text Object. A new text object appears. Move the object into the Page Header section, and place it in the approximate position of the "Ironwood University Students" report title in Figure 7-1.

4. If necessary, select the text object, right-click, and then click Edit Text Object. The insertion point appears in the text object. Type Ironwood University Students.

5. Make sure that the text object is still selected. In the Properties window, select the Font property, click the ellipsis button (which displays ". . ."), select a 12-point Arial Bold font, and then click OK.

6. Resize the title text object, and reposition it so that its right edge aligns with the right edge of the Page Header and Details fields.

7. To add the graphic image to the report, right-click anywhere on the report in Designer view, point to Insert, and then click Picture. Navigate to the SQLServer\Datafiles\Chapter7 folder, select Ironwood.jpg, and then click Open. Move the mouse pointer onto the Page Header section, and drop the picture object onto the Page Header section. Resize and reposition the picture object and other Page Header objects so that they look like Figure 7-1. (You may need to resize the Page Header section also.)

8. Run the application and open the Tabular form. If necessary, close the application forms, then adjust the form and/or report items to make them look like those in Figure 7-1.

9. Close the application, and close all open windows in the Document window. Do not close the IDE.

CREATING A REPORT THAT DISPLAYS DATA FROM MULTIPLE TABLES

To create a report that displays data from multiple tables, first create a table adapter and associated data table using a join query to retrieve and store the report data. Then, follow the same steps as you did in the previous section to create the report viewer control and report, and to link the report viewer to the report. The following steps show how to create the report in Figure 7-8 that displays data from both the UniversityLaptop and UniversityStudent tables and lists all laptop computers along with the name of the student assigned to each computer.

To create the report form and report viewer control:

1. Create a new form named frmTabularMultipleTables.vb. Set the form properties to the standard form property values. Change the form's Text property to Tabular-Multiple Tables.
2. Add a new menu selection to the Menu form under the Simple Reports selection that has the text Tabular-Multiple Tables. Add the commands to display the new form from the Menu form.
3. To create the report viewer control, open the frmTabularMultipleTables form in Designer view, open the Toolbox, and create a new CrystalReportsViewer control on the form. Click the report viewer control's Property tab, hide the Group tree, and undock the control from the form. Change the report viewer control's Name property value to crvLaptopStudent.

The next step is to create the table adapter that retrieves the report data by joining the two tables. To create the table adapter, open the DataSet Designer and create a new table adapter and associated data table that retrieves the data the report displays.

FIGURE 7-8   Multiple-table tabular report

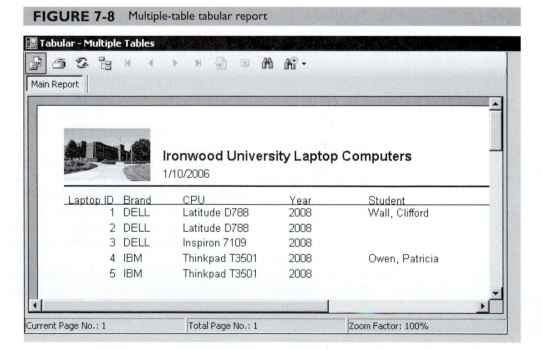

Laptop ID	Brand	CPU	Year	Student
1	DELL	Latitude D788	2008	Wall, Clifford
2	DELL	Latitude D788	2008	
3	DELL	Inspiron 7109	2008	
4	IBM	Thinkpad T3501	2008	Owen, Patricia
5	IBM	Thinkpad T3501	2008	

Ironwood University Laptop Computers
1/10/2006

Current Page No.: 1   Total Page No.: 1   Zoom Factor: 100%

To create the table adapter:

1. Open the Data Sources window by clicking Data on the menu bar, then clicking Show Data Sources. Click on Edit Dataset with Designer on the Data Sources toolbar to open the Data Set Designer.
2. Right-click in any open area in the Data Set Designer window, point to Add, and then click Table Adapter. Accept the project data source's connection, then click Next. Accept the *Use SQL Statements* option, and then click Next.
3. Type the following command in the SQL Statement field.

```
SELECT LaptopID, LaptopBrand, LaptopCPU,
       LaptopYear, StudentLastName + ', ' +
       UniversityStudent.StudentFirstName AS StudentName
FROM UniversityLaptop
LEFT OUTER JOIN UniversityStudent
ON UniversityLaptop.StudentID = UniversityStudent.StudentID
```

TIP: This command uses an outer join to display all laptop computers, even those not assigned to students.

4. Click Next two times, and then click Finish. The new data table, which is named UniversityLaptop1, appears in the Data Set Designer window. Right-click the data table, click Rename, and change the data table's name to UniversityLaptopStudent.
5. Close the Data Set Designer window, and click Yes to save your changes.

The following steps describe how to create the report object and specify its structure using the Report Creation Wizard. They specify the data source as the new UniversityLaptopStudent data table.

To create the report object:

1. In the Solution Explorer, create a new Crystal Report item named rptLaptopStudent.rpt. When the Crystal Reports Gallery dialog box opens, accept the default selections, and then click OK.
2. On the Data page, open the Project Data node, open the ADO.NET DataSets node, open the DBReports.*yourDatabaseName*DataSet node, select UniversityLaptopStudent, click the Add item button to move the selection to the Selected Data Sources list, and then click Next.

HELP: If UniversityLaptopStudent does not appear in the data set, right-click the data set, and then click Refresh.

3. On the Fields page, open the UniversityLaptopStudent node, then click the Add all items button, which appears as two right-pointing arrows, to move all the items to the Fields to Display list. Click Next.
4. On the Grouping page, click Next; on the Record Selection page, click Next.
5. On the Report Style page, select Maroon/Teal Box, then click Finish. The report appears in Designer view.
6. To link the report to the report viewer control, open frmTabularMultipleTables in Designer view, and set the report viewer control's ReportSource property value to DBReports.rptLaptopStudent. The report fields appear in the report viewer control. (Recall that the report viewer control displays the template data values at this point.)

The final step is to create the report's data components. To do this, manually create a form data set and binding source. Then link the new table adapter to the form's binding source.

To create the report's data components and view the report:

1. Open the Toolbox and create a new Dataset object on the form's Component tray. Accept the data set's default property values.
2. To create the binding source component, open the Toolbox and create a new binding source on the form's Component tray. Change the binding source's Data Source property value to *yourDatabaseName*DataSet1, and change its Data Member property value to UniversityLaptopStudent.
3. Open frmTabularMultipleTables in Code view, and add the following command as the last command in the Load event handler:

```
rptLaptopStudent1.SetDataSource(Me.YourDatabaseNameDataSet1)
```

4. Run the application and open the Tabular-Multiple Tables form. The report appears in the report viewer control. Close the application forms.
5. Modify the report format and add the boilerplate objects as shown in Figure 7-8 to finish the report.
6. Close all open pages in the browser window. Do not close the IDE.

CREATING A MASTER-DETAIL REPORT WITH A SINGLE MASTER-DETAIL RELATIONSHIP

To create a report that displays master-detail data, create a table adapter and associated data table that retrieves and stores all the report data, including both the master and detail records. Then create a report viewer control on the form, just as you did before, and link it to the report viewer control on the form, and create the data components to link the viewer to the report.

When you create the report object for a master-detail report, you must specify *report groups,* which are sections that specify the column headings, detail data, and summary data that repeat for each record in a section of a master-detail report. A report that has a single master record with a single set of related detail records contains two groups: one the master record and one for the detail records. Figure 7-9 illustrates the report groups in the master-detail report in Figure 7-2, which displays data from the UniversityTutor and UniversityTutorSession tables.

Figure 7-9 shows that the master group contains the data fields for a master record (such as tutor Cheryl Glastner), as well as the column headings for her detail records. The detail column headings repeat for each master record. The detail group contains the data fields for each detail record, which is the data for each individual tutoring session.

NOTE: Technically, you do not need to create a separate group for the detail records because they can appear in the report's Details section. However, creating a separate group makes the report structure more explicit.

FIGURE 7-9 Report groups for a master-detail report with a single master group

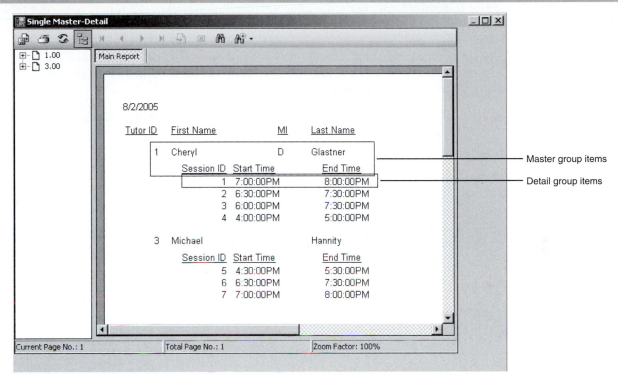

The following subsections describe how to make the master-detail report form and viewer control, create the table adapter, create the report object with the master-detail groups, and link the report object to the viewer. The final subsection describes how to format the master-detail report.

Creating the Master-Detail Report Form and Viewer Control

The following steps show how to create the form and menu item to display the form, and create the report viewer control.

To create the report form and report viewer control:

1. Create a new form named frmSingleMasterDetail.vb. Set the form properties to the standard form property values. Change the form's Text property value to Single Master-Detail.

2. Add a new top-level menu selection on the Menu form that has the text "Master-Detail Reports." Then add a new menu item under Master-Detail Reports with the text "Single Master-Detail." Then add the commands to the Menu form to display the new form from this menu selection.

3. To create the report viewer control, open the frmSingleMasterDetail form in Designer view, open the Toolbox, and create a new CrystalReportsViewer control on the form. Click the report viewer control's Property tab, and undock the control from the form. Resize the viewer control to fill the form, and change the report viewer control's Name property value to crvTutorSessions. (You display the Group Tree pane in this report because it is a master-detail report.)

Creating the Table Adapter

The following steps create the table adapter that retrieves the report data. The table adapter joins the UniversityTutor and UniversityTutorSession tables, retrieving both the master and detail records. The table adapter and data table must include the primary key fields for both groups, even though the report does not display the values, because the report uses the primary key values to sort the data into its groups.

To create the table adapter:

1. Open the Data Set Designer, and create a new table adapter that uses the following SQL statement:

```
SELECT UniversityTutor.TutorID, TutorFirstName,
       TutorMI, TutorLastName, TutorSessionID,
       TutorSessionStartTime, TutorSessionEndTime
FROM UniversityTutor
INNER JOIN UniversityTutorSession ON
UniversityTutor.TutorID = UniversityTutorSession.TutorID
```

2. Rename the data table to UniversityTutorSessionDetail, close the Data Set Designer window, and click Yes to save your changes.
3. Save the project.

Creating the Report Object Class and Specifying the Master-Detail Groups

The next step is to create the report object class, specify its structure using the Report Creation Wizard, and specify its data source as the new UniversityTutorSessionDetail data table. On the Grouping page, you will create the two report groups shown in Figure 7-9. You will also create a master group based on the TutorID field and a second group based on the TutorSessionID field.

To create the report object and specify the master and detail groups:

1. Open the Solution Explorer, and create a new Crystal Report object class named rptTutorSessions.rpt. When the Crystal Reports Gallery dialog box opens, accept the default selections, and then click OK.
2. On the Data page, open the Project Data node, open the ADO.NET DataSets node, open the DBReports.*yourDatabaseName*DataSet node, select UniversityTutorSessionDetail, click the Add item button to move the selection to the Selected Data Sources list, and then click Next. (If this selection does not appear in the data set, right-click it, and then click Refresh.)
3. On the Fields page, open the UniversityTutorSessionDetail node, then click the Add all items button, which appears as two right-pointing arrows, to move all the items to the Fields to Display list. Click Next.
4. On the Grouping page, select UniversityTutorSessionDetail.TutorID, and then click Add item. The TutorID field appears in the Group By list as the master group's identifier.
5. To add the detail group, select UniversityTutorSessionDetail.TutorSessionID, and then click Add item. The TutorSessionID field appears in the Group By list as the detail group's identifier. Your completed Grouping page should look like Figure 7-10. Click Next.

FIGURE 7-10   Specifying the report groups

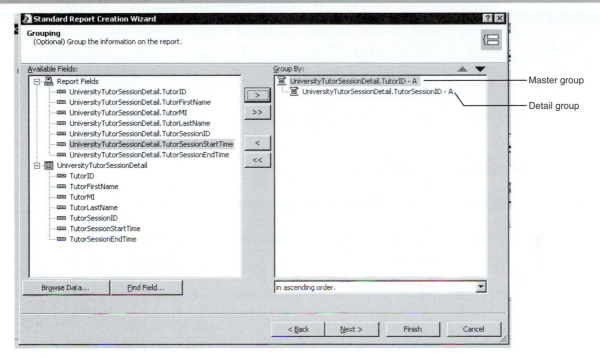

TIP: The "A" that follows the group names specifies that the report will display the records in the group in ascending order. To display report records in descending order, open the list below the Group By list, and select "in descending order."

The next wizard page allows you to select summary columns. You can create summary columns for each group to perform the standard SQL group functions (SUM, COUNT, AVG, and so forth), as well as a variety of other functions. By default, the Report Creation Wizard creates summary columns to sum all numeric report columns. The following steps remove the summary columns because this report does not display any summary information. They also finish creating the report object and link the report to the report viewer on the form.

To remove the summary columns and finish the report object:

1. On the Summaries page, select the Sum of UniversityTutorSessionDetail.TutorID in the Summarized Fields list, and then click Remove item (which appears as a left-pointing single arrow) to remove the summary column.
2. Repeat step 1 for the three other summary columns in the Summarized Fields list, and then click Next.
3. On the Record Selection page, click Next.
4. On the Report Style page, select Standard, and then click Finish. The report appears in Designer view, as shown in Figure 7-11.
5. Save the project.

Formatting a Master-Detail Report

The report now displays a group header section and a group footer section for each report group. In Figure 7-11, Group Header 1 represents the master group's group

FIGURE 7-11 Report with group sections

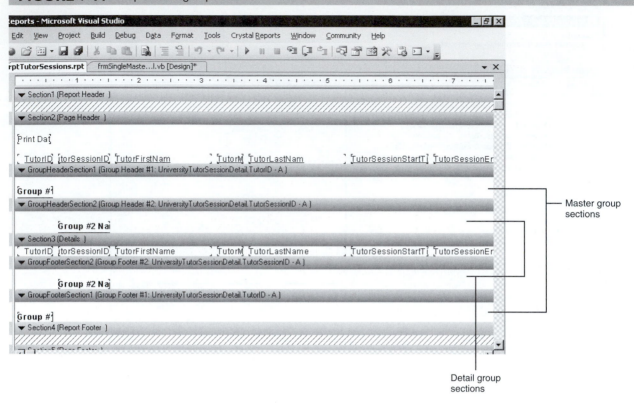

Master group sections

Detail group sections

header section, and Group Header 2 represents the detail group's group header section. The group footer sections are similarly labeled. Every report item (such as a column heading or a data field) that appears in the Group Header 1 section appears once for every master record. Every report item that appears in the Group Header 2 section appears once for every detail record.

The wizard automatically places *group name fields* in the group header and footer sections. The group name fields, which appear as Group 1 Name and Group 2 Name, are text objects that identify the groups.

To make the master-detail data fields and column headings display correctly, you need to move the column headings and data fields into the correct group sections. Here is a general strategy for formatting master-detail reports that do not contain summary fields:

1. Move the master column headings to the Page Header section so that they appear once, at the top of every report page.
2. Move the master fields to the Group Header 1 section, to display each master record once. Move the detail column headings to the Group Header 1 section because they appear once for every master group.
3. Move the detail fields to the Group Header 2 section to display each detail record once.
4. Delete the group name fields.
5. Resize the group footer sections to display or hide white space under each report group data as needed.

FIGURE 7-12   Formatted master-detail report sections

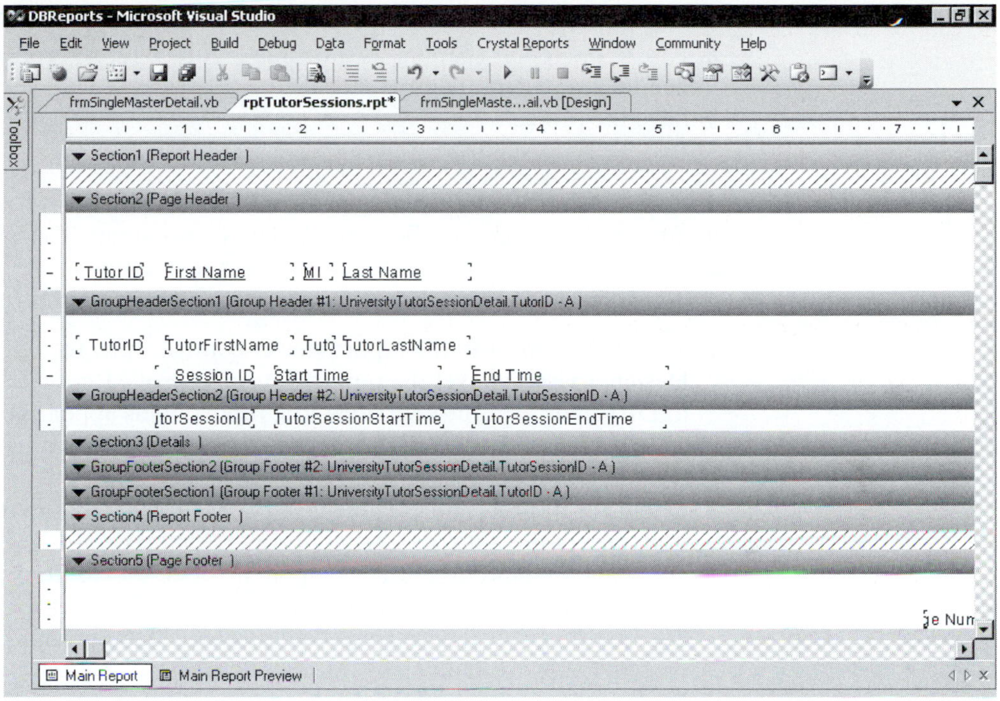

The following steps format the report. They confirm that the master column headings are in the Page Header section and move the master fields (TutorID, TutorFirstName, TutorMI, TutorLastName) to the Group Header 1 section. They move the detail column headings to the Group Header 1 section. They also move the detail data fields (TutorSessionID, TutorSessionStartTime, TutorSessionEndTime) to the Group Header 2 section. Finally, they format the report by deleting the group header names and resizing the report footer sections so that they do not display any white space under the report data. The formatted report sections ultimately look like Figure 7-12.

To format the master-detail report:

1. Make sure that the master column headings (TutorID, TutorFirstName, TutorMI, TutorLastName) are in the Page Header section.
2. Move the detail column headings (TutorSessionID, TutorSessionStartTime, TutorSessionEndTime) from the Page Header section to the Group Header 1 section.

CAUTION: Be sure to move the column headings. Do not move the data fields, which are currently in the Details section. You can place the mouse pointer on a field, and a ToolTip appears to show whether the field is a heading or a data field.

---

3. Delete the Group 1 Name and Group 2 Name group name fields from the group header and footer sections. (You will delete a total of four items.)
4. Move the master data fields (TutorID, TutorFirstName, TutorMI, TutorLastName) from the Details section to the top of the Group Header 1 section, as shown in Figure 7-12.

5. Modify the text of the column headings as shown in Figure 7-12.
6. Select the TutorID data field, and change its Decimal Places property value to 0.
7. Repeat step 6 for the TutorSessionID data field.
8. Resize the report sections as shown in Figure 7-12, and reposition the column headings and data fields as shown.
9. Save the project.

Creating the Report Data Components

The final task is to create the report's data components. Then you will run the form, view the report data, and fine-tune the report formatting.

To create the report's data components then view the report:

1. To link the report to the report viewer control, open frmSingleMasterDetail in Designer view, and set the report viewer control's ReportSource property value to DBReports.rptTutorSessions. The report fields appear in the report viewer control. If necessary, resize the form and/or report viewer control so that all the form fields are visible.
2. Open the Toolbox and create a new Dataset object on the form's Component tray. Accept the data set's default property values.
3. To create the binding source component, open the Toolbox, and create a new binding source on the form's Component tray. Change the binding source's Data Source property value to *yourDatabaseName*DataSet1, and its Data Member property value to UniversityTutorSessionDetail.
4. Open frmSingleMasterDetail in Code view, and add the following command as the last command in the Load event handler:

```
rptTutorSessions1.SetDataSource(Me.YourDatabaseNameDataSet1)
```

5. Run the application. Click Master-Detail on the menu bar, and then click Single Master-Detail to open the form.
6. Modify the report format as necessary to make your report look like Figure 7-2.
7. Close the application windows, and then close all open pages in the IDE browser window. Do not close the IDE.

CREATING A MASTER-DETAIL REPORT WITH MULTIPLE MASTER-DETAIL RELATIONSHIPS

Reports can display data values that have multiple master-detail relationships. For example, the report in Figure 7-3 has two master-detail relationships: a department offers multiple courses, and a course has multiple associated course sections. To create this report, create a table adapter and associated data table that retrieves and stores all the data for all the master and detail groups. Then create a report viewer control on the form, link it to the report viewer control on the form, and create the data components to link the viewer to the report. Finally, format the report.

Creating the Master-Detail Report Form and Viewer Control

The following steps show how to create the form and menu item to display the form and to create the report viewer control on the form.

To create the report form and report viewer control:

1. Create a new form named frmMultipleMasterDetail.vb. Set the form properties to the standard form property values. Change the form's Text property value to Multiple Master-Detail.
2. In the frmMenu form, add a new menu item under Master-Detail Reports that has the text Multiple Master-Detail. Then add the commands to the Menu form to display the new form from this menu selection.
3. To create the report viewer control, open the frmMultipleMasterDetail form in Designer view, open the Toolbox, and create a new CrystalReportsViewer control on the form. Resize the viewer control to fill the form, and change the report viewer control's Name property value to crvDepartmentCourses. Hide the Group Tree pane.

Creating the Table Adapter

The next task is to create the table adapter that retrieves the report data. The table adapter joins the UniversityDepartment, UniversityCourse, and UniversityCourseSection tables, and retrieves all the master and detail records. The table adapter and data table must include the primary key fields for the master and detail groups, even though the report does not display all the key fields, because the report uses the primary key values to sort the data into its groups.

To create the table adapter:

1. Open the Data Set Designer, and create a new table adapter that uses the following SQL statement:

```
SELECT UniversityDepartment.DepartmentID,
       DepartmentName, UniversityCourse.CourseID,
       CourseName, CourseCredits,
       UniversitySection.SectionID, SectionNumber,
       SectionTerm, SectionDay, SectionTime,
       SectionMaxEnrollment, SectionCurrentEnrollment
FROM UniversityCourse
INNER JOIN UniversityDepartment
ON UniversityCourse.DepartmentID = UniversityDepartment.DepartmentID
INNER JOIN UniversitySection
ON UniversityCourse.CourseID = UniversitySection.CourseID
```

2. Rename the data table to UniversityDepartmentCourses, then close the Data Set Designer window and click Yes to save your changes.
3. Save the project.

Creating the Report Object Class and Specifying the Master-Detail Groups

The next step is to create the report object class and specify its structure using the Report Creation Wizard. Specify its data source as the new UniversityDepartmentCourses data table. On the Grouping page, you create the three report groups: you will create a master group based on the DepartmentID field, a second master group based on the CourseID field, and a third group based on the SectionID field.

To create the report object:

1. Open the Solution Explorer and create a new Crystal Report item named rptDepartmentCourses.rpt. When the Crystal Reports Gallery dialog box opens, accept the default selections, and then click OK.
2. On the Data page, refresh the Project Data if necessary, select UniversityDepartmentCourses, click the Add item button to move the selection to the Selected Data Sources list, and then click Next.
3. On the Fields page, open the UniversityDepartmentCourses node, click Add all items to move all the items to the Fields to Display list, and then click Next.
4. On the Grouping page, to add the first master group, select UniversityDepartmentCourses.DepartmentID, and then click Add item.
5. To add the next master group, select UniversityDepartmentCourses.CourseID, and then click Add item.
6. To add the detail group, select UniversityDepartmentCourses.SectionID, and then click Add item. The Group By list should show DepartmentID, CourseID, and SectionID, in that order, as the report groups. Click Next.
7. On the Summaries page, remove all the summary fields, and then click Next.
8. On the Record Selection page, click Next.
9. On the Report Style page, select Standard, and then click Finish. The report appears in Designer view.
10. Save the project.

Formatting the Multiple Master-Detail Report

The next step is to move the master and detail column headings and fields into the correct report sections, and format the data fields and column heading text. The following steps format the report so that it looks like Figure 7-13.

FIGURE 7-13   Formatted multiple master-detail report

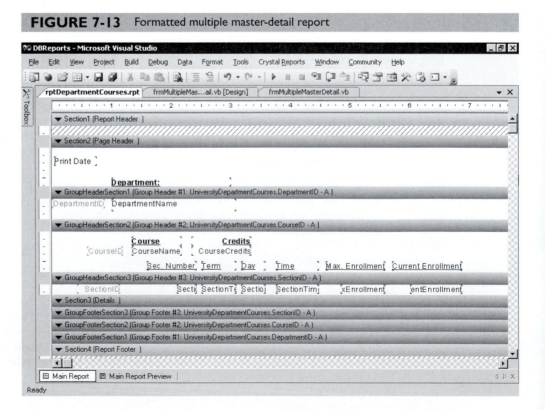

To format the multiple master-detail report:

1. Delete the group name fields (Group 1 Name, Group 2 Name, Group 3 Name) in all group header and footer sections.
2. Move the DepartmentID and DepartmentName data fields from the Details section to the Group Header 1 section.
3. Delete the DepartmentID, CourseID, and SectionID field headings from the Page Header section.

HELP: If you accidentally delete a data field, you can open the Database Fields node in the Field Explorer, drag the field, and then drop it onto the report in Designer view.

---

4. To make the DepartmentID field so it does not appear on the report, select the DepartmentID data field, and change its Suppress property value to True. The data field appears disabled. Repeat this step for the CourseID and SectionID data fields.
5. Move the CourseName and CourseCredits field headings to the Group Header 2 section. Change the header text of CourseName to Name, and change CourseCredits to Credits. Change the field headings to a bold font.
6. Move the CourseID, CourseName and CourseCredits data fields to the Group Header 2 section.
7. Move the SectionNumber, SectionTerm, SectionDay, SectionTime, SectionMaxEnrollment, and SectionCurrentEnrollment field headings to the Group Header 2 section. Change the column heading text as shown in Figure 7-13, and resize and reposition the columns as necessary.
8. Move the SectionID, SectionNumber, SectionTerm, SectionDay, SectionTime, SectionMaxEnrollment, and SectionCurrentEnrollment data fields to the Group Header 3 section. Resize and reposition the fields as necessary so that they appear under their associated column headings.
9. Select the SectionTime data field, and change its properties as follows:

Property	New Value
DayType	crNoDay
MonthType	crNoMonth
SecondType	crNumericNoSecond
YearType	crNoYear

10. Resize the report sections so that they appear as shown in Figure 7-13, and then save the project.

Creating the Report Data Components

The final task is to create the report's data components. Then you run the form, view the report data, and fine-tune the report formatting.

To create the report's data components then view the report:

1. To link the report to the report viewer control, open frmMultipleMasterDetail in Designer view and set the report viewer control's ReportSource property value to DBReports.rptDepartmentCourses. The report fields appear in the report viewer control. If necessary, resize the form and/or report viewer control so that all report fields appear.
2. Open the Toolbox and create a new Dataset object on the form's Component tray. Accept the data set's default property values.

3. Open the Toolbox, and create a new binding source on the form's Component tray. Change the binding source's Data Source property value to *yourDatabaseName*DataSet1 and its Data Member property value to UniversityDepartmentCourses.

4. Open frmMultipleMasterDetail in Code view, and add the following command as the last command in the Load event handler:

```
rptDepartmentCourses1.SetDataSource(Me.YourDatabaseNameDataSet1)
```

5. Save the project, and then run the application. Click Master-Detail on the menu bar, and then click Multiple Master-Detail to open the form.

6. Modify the report format as necessary to make your report look like Figure 7-3.

7. Close the application windows.

Placing Report Groups on Different Pages

Sometimes in master-detail reports, you create page breaks to format the report or to facilitate distributing the report to different people. In the master-detail report in Figure 7-3, you place the data for each DepartmentID group on a separate page. To implement this, select the group footer after which you want to place the page break, and then change its PageBreakAfter property value to true. For this report, you place the page break after Group Footer Section 1.

To create the report page breaks:

1. Open rptDepartmentCourses in Designer view, select GroupFooterSection1, and change its NewPageAfter property value to True.

2. Save the project, and then run the application. Click Master-Detail on the menu bar, and then click Multiple Master-Detail to open the form. Note that the course data for each department now appears on a different report page.

3. Click the Go to Next Page button on the report toolbar to scroll through the report pages, and then close the application windows.

ADDING SUMMARY AND FORMULA FIELDS TO A REPORT

Reports often contain summary information to help managers view performance data and identify trends. This summary information may involve a simple summary operation, such as summing a column of data values, or it may involve a calculation, such as calculating a student's grade point average or a salesperson's commission for the month or year. The following sections describe how to create summary and formula fields in a report.

Summary Fields

A Crystal Report summary field summarizes retrieved data using one of the SQL summary functions or a statistical operation such as finding the standard deviation of a data set. You can create a summary field in the Report Creation Wizard when you first make the report, or you can add a summary function field to an existing report. In this section, you will add the summary fields shown in Figure 7-14, which show the maximum and current enrollments for each course.

To create a summary field, insert the summary field in the report, and then specify which field is being summarized, the type of summary operation, and the report group

FIGURE 7-14 Summary fields

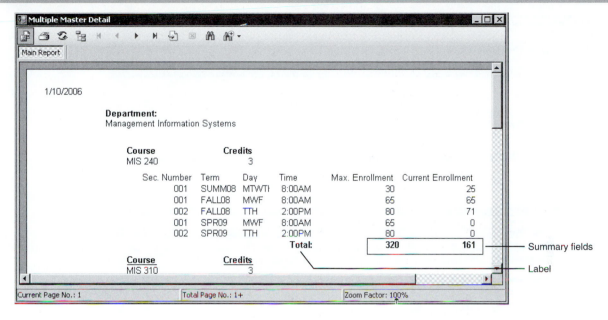

that will contain the summary field. To determine the report group that contains a summary field, consider how you would describe the summary total. For example, you would describe the summary field that sums the current enrollments for each course as "Total course enrollment for Course X," so you place the summary field in Group 2, which contains the CourseID and CourseName data fields, because each course has a single total enrollment. To create a summary field that would sum all the enrollments for an entire department, place the summary field in Group 1, which contains the DepartmentID and DepartmentName data fields.

To create the summary fields:

1. If necessary, open rptDepartmentCourses in Designer view. Right-click anywhere on the report, point to Insert, and then click Summary. The Insert Summary dialog box opens.
2. To specify the field that is being summarized, open the "Choose the field to summarize" list and select UniversityDepartmentCourses.SectionMaxEnrollment.
3. To specify the summary operation, open the Calculate the summary list and select Sum, which is the default operation.
4. To specify the report group that contains the summary field, open the Summary Location list, and select Group 2, which is the CourseID group.
5. Click OK. The new summary field appears in Group Footer 2 and directly below the SectionMaxEnrollment data field above.
6. Repeat steps 1 through 5 to create the summary field for the SectionCurrentEnrollment field.
7. To create the label for the summary fields, right-click anywhere on the report in Designer view, point to Insert, and then click Text Object. Place the new text object in the Group Footer 2, on the left edge of the SectionMaxEnrollment summary field, as shown in Figure 7-15.
8. Type Total: as the object's text, change the object's font to a bold font, then resize and reposition the text object as necessary. Your report layout should look like Figure 7-15.

FIGURE 7-15 Report layout with summary fields and label

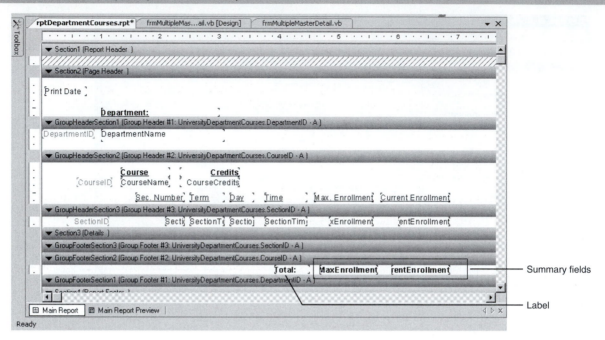

9. To format the SectionMaxEnrollment summary field, select the field, and change its DecimalPlaces property value to 0.
10. Repeat step 9 for the SectionCurrentEnrollment summary field.
11. Save the project, then run the application and open the form. Your summary fields should look like Figure 7-14.
12. Close the application forms.

Formula Fields

A formula field contains a formula or function that manipulates report data. It can perform a simple arithmetic operation, such as adding two field values. It can also perform complex processing, such as calculating a student's grade point average based on the student's courses and associated grades. Figure 7-16 illustrates formula fields in the course section report you have been working on.

FIGURE 7-16 Report with formula fields

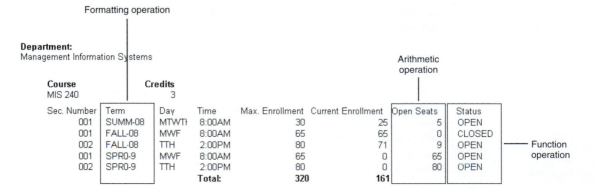

In Figure 7-16, the Open Seats formula field displays the difference between the maximum and current enrollment values for each course section. The Status formula field evaluates whether the section has any open seats and displays the text "OPEN" if the section has open seats or "CLOSED" if the section does not.

The Term column illustrates how to use a formula field to format a data value. Recall that in the database, the SectionTerm data field stores the data value as a string of characters, such as "SUMM08". The formula field formats the value by placing a hyphen after the first four characters of the term, so it appears as "SUMM-08".

To create a new formula field, right-click the Formula Fields node in the Field Explorer, and then click New. A dialog box opens that prompts you to name the formula field. Formula field names can contain letters, numbers, and underscores, but they cannot contain blank spaces.

After you name the formula field, use the Formula Editor window to specify the formula or function whose result the formula field displays. Figure 7-17 illustrates the Formula Editor window's components.

The Formula Editor toolbar contains buttons that allow you to create and save formula columns and to configure the Formula Editor windows. The *Workshop tree* displays nodes that allow you to access existing formula columns, as well as existing report sections and their contents. The *Field tree* displays all the report fields, including data fields, summary fields, and other formula fields. The *Function tree* displays all the built-in Crystal Report functions that you can use in formulas. The *Operator tree* displays built-in arithmetic, string, and other functions that you can use in formulas.

The *Formula Text editor* displays the commands for the formula or function whose result the formula field displays. You can type a formula or function directly into the Formula Text editor pane. You can also double-click fields, built-in functions, and/or build-in operators in the Formula Editor windows, displaying and editing them in the Text editor. The Text editor requires field names to appear in braces ({}) and displays reserved words in program commands in blue text.

FIGURE 7-17   Formula Editor window

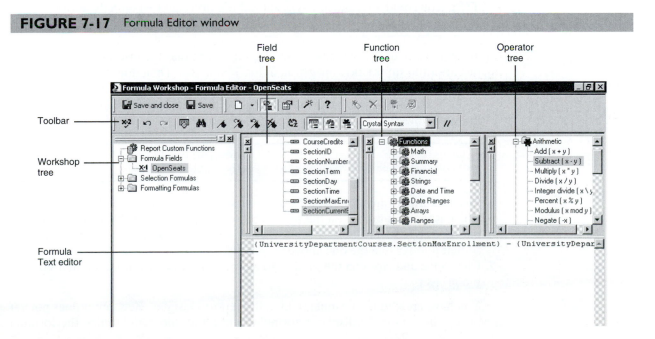

The following subsections describe how to create different types of formula fields. The first section describes how to use an arithmetic operation in a formula, the next describes how to write a function whose return value the formula column displays, and the final section describes how to use a formula field to format a data value by embedding formatting characters.

Arithmetic Operations

To create the formula field that displays the number of open seats in each course section, specify the formula, which is the difference between the maximum and current enrollment values for each course section, in the Formula Editor.

To create a formula field that uses an arithmetic operation:

1. If necessary, open rptDepartmentCourses in Designer view. Right-click Formula Fields in the Field Explorer, and then click New. (If the Field Explorer is not open in your IDE, click Crystal Reports on the menu bar, and then click Field Explorer.)
2. Type OpenSeats in the Name field, and then click Use Editor. The Formula Editor window opens, as shown in Figure 7-17.

NOTE: Many of the features of the Formula Expert are disabled in the embedded version of Crystal Reports.

---

3. To create the formula, open the *yourDatabaseName*DataSet node in the Field tree window, open the UniversityDepartmentCourses node, and then double-click SectionMaxEnrollment. The field name appears in the Text editor, with its name enclosed in braces, as shown in Figure 7-17.
4. To specify the arithmetic operator, which is the subtraction operator, make sure that the insertion point is just after the closing brace for the SectionMaxEnrollment node. Then open the Operators node in the Operator tree window, open the Arithmetic node, and double-click Subtract. The subtraction operator appears in the Text editor window, just after the SectionMaxEnrollment field.

TIP: You could alternatively type the subtraction sign ($-$) directly in the Text editor window.

---

5. To specify the next field in the formula, make sure that the insertion point is just after the subtraction operation in the Text editor. Then double-click the SectionCurrentEnrollment node in the Field tree. The field specification appears in the Text editor. Your completed formula specification should appear all on one line as follows:

```
{UniversityDepartmentCourses.SectionMaxEnrollment} -
{UniversityDepartmentCourses.SectionCurrentEnrollment}
```

6. To check the formula syntax for errors, click the Check button on the toolbar, which is the first button on the second button row. When the "No errors found" message appears, click OK. If this message does not appear, correct the formula so that it looks like the one above.
7. Click Save and close on the toolbar to close the Formula Editor, and then save the project.

You have created the formula field in the report Designer view, but it does not yet appear on the report. To display a formula field on a report, right-click the formula field, and then click Insert to Report. You then drop the formula field object onto the report section in which it will appear. The OpenSeats formula column appears beside each course section data row, so you drop it next to the SectionCurrentEnrollment data field in the GroupHeaderSection3. You also create a column heading for the formula column in the GroupHeaderSection2.

To place the formula field on the report and create the column heading:

1. Right-click OpenSeats in the Field Explorer, and then click Insert to Report. When you move the pointer across the report sections, the pointer appears with a report object.
2. Drop the report object in GroupHeaderSection3, on the right edge of the SectionCurrentEnrollment data field. (You may have to scroll to the right edge of the report to do this. You may also have to move the report data fields in GroupHeaderSection3 to make room for the formula column.)
3. To format the formula field's data, select it, and then change its DecimalPlaces property value to 0. To align the data with the right-edge of the column, select its HorAlignment property and set its value to crRightAlign.
4. To create the column heading, right-click anywhere on the report, point to Insert, and then click Text Object. Drop the new text object into GroupHeaderSection2, just above the new formula column.
5. Type Open Seats for the text object's text, then resize and reposition the text object as necessary.
6. Save the project, and then run the application. The Open Seats formula column should look like the column in Figure 7-16. If necessary, adjust the column's size and position.
7. Close the application forms.

User-Defined Functions

You can create formula columns that return values you write using the BASIC programming language. These functions can perform fairly sophisticated programming operations that involve assignment statements, decision control structures, and loops.

NOTE: It is beyond the scope of this chapter to cover BASIC programming, but you can find examples in the IDE online help system by searching for Crystal Reports, and then selecting Formula reference.

To illustrate a simple function, you will create the Status formula field in Figure 7-16, which evaluates the value of the OpenSeats formula column. If its value is 0, the Status formula field displays the value "CLOSED"; if its value is greater than 0, the field displays "OPEN." This function will use an `If/Then` decision control structure, which has the following syntax:

```
If Condition Then
    FormulaFieldDisplayValue
Else
    FormulaFieldDisplayValue
```

In this syntax, *Condition* specifies an expression that evaluates as either true or false. The *FormulaFieldDisplayValue* specifies the value that the formula field will display. In this formula column, the *Condition* evaluates the value of the @OpenSeats formula field, and this specification must appear in braces.

To create the formula column that uses an `If/Then` decision control structure:

1. In rptDepartmentCourses in Designer view, right-click Formula Fields in the Field Explorer, then click New. Type SectionStatus in the Name field, and then click Use Editor.
2. Type the following commands in the Text editor to specify the function:

```
If {@OpenSeats} = 0 Then
    'CLOSED'
Else
    'OPEN'
```

TIP: To insert a field name in a command, double-click the field in the Field tree window.

---

3. Click Check on the toolbar to check for errors, correct any errors, and then click OK when the message appears stating that no errors were found. Then click Save and close.
4. Right-click SectionStatus in the Field Explorer, and then click Insert to Report. Drop the report object in GroupHeaderSection3, on the left edge of the OpenSeats formula field. (You may have to move the report data to make room for the new formula column.)
5. Create a new column heading for the formula field with the text "Status".
6. Save the project, and then run the application. The Open Seats formula column should look like the one in Figure 7-16. If necessary, adjust the column's size and position.
7. Close the application forms.

Formatting Data Values

Often databases store values such as telephone numbers, postal codes, and social security numbers as number characters without embedded formatting characters. This enables application developers to format the data appropriately for each application. To make applications more attractive and readable, it is a good practice to insert formatting characters into these values.

To modify the format of a data field in Crystal Reports, use the Picture function, which is a built-in function with the following format:

```
Picture(DataValue, "FormattedValue")
```

In this syntax, *DataValue* represents the input data and can be a data field name or an actual data value. *FormattedValue* represents the *format mask,* or output data format, of the data value. For a text data value, represent data characters as the letter x. For a number data value, represent digits using the number 9. Table 7-1 illustrates how you use the Picture function to format text and number data values.

The following steps show how to use the Picture function to modify the format of the SectionTerm column. You create a formula column that places a hyphen after the first four characters of the term code. Then you change the SectionTerm data field's Suppress property to True, so that the actual SectionTerm values do not appear. Finally, you place the new formula field, which contains the formatted values, on top of the SectionTerm data field. As a result, the formatted values appear in place of the actual data values.

TABLE 7-1	Using the Picture function to format data values	
Input Data Value	**Picture Function Syntax**	**Output Data Value**
StudentPhoneNumber = 7159362331	`Picture({StudentPhoneNumber}, "(xxx) xxx-xxxx")`	(715) 936-2331
SectionID = 3	`Picture({SectionID}, "-9-")`	-3-

To create a formula field to insert formatting characters:

1. Create a new formula field named FormattedTerms, and type the following commands in the Text editor to specify the function. (This command should appear on a single Text editor line).

```
Picture({UniversityDepartmentCourses.SectionTerm},
        "xxxx-xx")
```

2. To hide the current SectionTerm value, select the SectionTerm data field in the GroupHeaderSection3, and change its Suppress property value to True.
3. Right-click FormattedTerms in the Field Explorer, and then click Insert to Report. Drop the report object in the GroupHeaderSection3, on top of the SectionTerm data field. (You may need to adjust the formula field column width and adjust the spacing and position of the data fields and headings.)
4. Save the project, and then run the application. The FormattedTerms formula column should look like the one in Figure 7-16. If necessary, adjust the column's size and position.

NOTE: In this example, "SPR09" is not formatted correctly because it contains a three-character prefix before the term year. This illustrates the need to carefully design data codes in your database to ensure consistent formatting. To correct this problem, you would need to write a custom function to parse the data value, find the number characters, and place the formatting character just before them.

---

5. Close the application forms, and then close all open pages in the IDE document window.

CREATING A REPORT THAT ACCEPTS AN INPUT PARAMETER

You usually integrate database reports with other applications. For example, you might create an application that allows a student to enroll in courses, and then prints a report showing the student's schedule. A different application might create a customer order, and then create a report to represent a receipt for the customer's purchases. To enable reports to interact with applications, they must accept input parameters to specify input values such as the student ID number or the customer's order ID value.

To create a report that accepts one or more input parameters, base the report on a table adapter and data table that uses a parameter query. (Remember that a parameter query uses one or more variables to represent search condition values.) In this section, you will create the report in Figure 7-18, which allows the user to select a Department

FIGURE 7-18 Report that accepts an input parameter

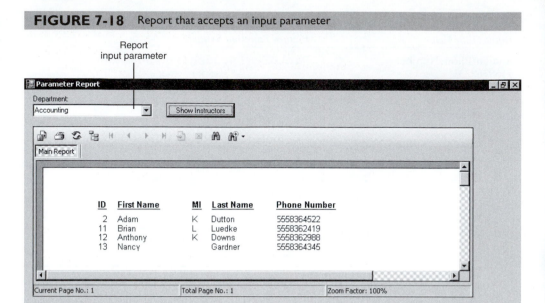

Name from a combo box. When the user clicks Show Instructors, the report shows the instructors for the selected department.

To create a report that accepts an input parameter, the steps are similar to those used to create any report: first create the form and the report viewer control. Then create a table adapter and associated data table that retrieves and stores the report data. This time, the table adapter uses a parameter query. As before, link the table adapter to the report viewer control and create the data components to link the viewer to the report. Finally, format the report. The following sections illustrate these steps for the report in Figure 7-18.

Creating the Report Form and Viewer Control

The following steps show how to create the form, the menu item to display the form, and the report viewer control. They also show how to create the data-bound combo box, which displays the DepartmentName values, and the Show Instructors button.

To create the report form and controls:

1. Create a new form named frmParameterReport.vb. Set the form properties to the standard form property values, and change the form's Text property value to Parameter Report.
2. In the frmMenu form, add a new top-level menu item that has the text "Parameter Report." Then add the commands to display the new form from this menu selection on the Menu form.
3. To create the combo box that allows the user to select a department name, create a new ComboBox and Label control on the form. Change the combo box's Name property value to cboDepartment and the label's Text property value to Department:.
4. To bind the combo box to the data source, open the Data Sources window, and drag the UniversityDepartment node from the Data Sources window and drop it onto the combo box.
5. Create a new Button control, and place it on the right side of the combo box. Change its Name property value to btnShowInstructors, and its Text property value to Show Instructors.

6. Create a new CrystalReportsViewer control on the form. Resize the viewer control to fill the form, configure the viewer control so that it does not display the Group tree, and change the report viewer control's Name property value to crvDepartmentInstructors.
7. Save the project.

Creating the Table Adapter

The next step is to create the table adapter that retrieves the report data. The table adapter retrieves the UniversityInstructor fields shown in Figure 7-18 and has a search condition that specifies a parameter variable for the DepartmentID field.

To create the table adapter:

1. Open the Data Set Designer, and create a new table adapter named InstructorParameter that uses the following SQL statement:

```
SELECT InstructorID, InstructorFirstName,
       InstructorMI, InstructorLastName,
       InstructorPhoneNumber
FROM UniversityInstructor
WHERE DepartmentID = @SelectedDepartment
```

2. Save the project.

Creating the Report Object Class

The next step is to create the report object class using the Report Creation Wizard and to specify its data source as the new InstructorParameter data table.

To create the report object:

1. Open the Solution Explorer, and create a new Crystal Report object class named rptInstructorParameter.rpt. When the Crystal Reports Gallery dialog box opens, accept the default selections, and then click OK.
2. On the Data page, refresh the Project Data node, open the ADO.NET DataSets node, open the DBReports.*yourDatabaseName*DataSet node, select InstructorParameter, click the Add item button to move the selection to the Selected Data Sources list, and then click Next.
3. On the Fields page, open the InstructorParameter node, and then click the Add all items button. Click Next.
4. You will not create any report groups, so on the Grouping page, click Next. On the Record Selection page, click Next. On the Report Style page, select Standard, and then click Finish. The report appears in Designer view.
5. Save the project.

Creating the Report Data Components

As before, the final task is to create the report's data components. In this form, you do not need to create a data set because the IDE already created one for the data-bound combo box. You still need to create a new binding source for the report, however. Link the new table adapter to the report's binding source, and create commands in the form's Load event to fill the report's table adapter with data based on the current selection in the Department Name combo box. Also create a Click event handler for the Show Instructor button, which refills the report table adapter with data using the input parameter, and then refreshes the report display.

To create the report's data components:

1. To link the report to the report viewer control, open frmParameterReport in Designer view, and set the report viewer control's ReportSource property value to DBReports.rptInstructorParameter. If necessary, resize the form and/or report viewer control so that all report fields are visible.

2. Open the Toolbox, and create a new binding source on the form's Component tray. Change the binding source's Data Source property value to *yourDatabaseName*DataSet and its Data Member property value to InstructorParameter.

3. Open frmParameterReport in Code view, and add the following command as the last command in the Load event handler:

```
rptInstructorParameter1.SetDataSource(Me.YourDatabaseNameDataSet)
```

To finish the form, you will add commands to fill the table adapter and to refresh the report display based on the user's department name selection. Place these commands in the form's Load event handler, so that the report displays data when it first opens. Also place these commands in the Show Instructor button's Click event handler.

Recall from Chapter 6 that to fill a table adapter based on a parameter query, you pass the parameter value to the table adapter's Fill method. To specify the parameter value, you reference the combo box's SelectedValue property, which represents the DepartmentID value of the combo box's current selection. Then refresh the report viewer control on the form, using the viewer control's RefreshReport method.

To add the commands to fill the table adapter and refresh the report display:

1. In frmParameterReport in Code view, add the following commands so that they appear as the last commands in the form's Load event handler:

```
'Fill the table adapter
Me.InstructorParameterTableAdapter.Fill _
    (Me.YourDatabaseNameDataSet.InstructorParameter, _
    CLng(cboDepartment.SelectedValue))
'Refresh the report viewer control
crvDepartmentInstructors.RefreshReport()
```

2. Create a Click event handler for the btn ShowInstructor button, then add the commands in step 1 to the event handler.

3. Save the project, and then run the application. Click Parameter Report on the menu bar to open the form. The instructors for the first department (Management Information Systems) appear on the report.

4. Open the Department list, and select Accounting. The report now lists the Accounting instructor names.

5. Close the application forms, then format the report as necessary to make it look like Figure 7-18.

IN CONCLUSION . . .

This chapter shows how to use Crystal Reports to create reports to display summary snapshots of database data. Many other applications exist to create database reports, but they all structure reports using similar layouts and follow the concept of placing master-detail report items in different report sections to specify how the report data appears to the user. Most reporting tools have features that allow you to create summary and formula fields and to pass input parameters to filter report data.

SUMMARY

- A report is a summary view of database data that users can view on a computer screen, print on paper, or send as an e-mail message. A report displays database data and often displays summary information or calculated values to help managers make decisions.
- A report can display data from one or more database tables in a tabular layout or a master-detail layout where a master record has multiple related detail records. A report can also display multiple master-detail relationships.
- You display a Crystal Report in a VB form using a Crystal Report viewer control, which is a control that displays a report, along with controls for working with the report.
- You create a Crystal Report object class definition in a project to specify a report's contents and format.
- In the VS 2005 IDE, the Field Explorer displays a hierarchical view of the report fields. The IDE document viewer shows the report in Designer view, which

shows the report sections and components, or Previewer view, which shows how the report will appear to the user.
- Report sections organize the report items and specify where the report displays items and how often the items appear.
- To enhance a report's appearance add boilerplate objects, which are text and graphic objects that do not change based on the report's data.
- In a report that displays master-detail data, create a report group for every master and detail data group. To format the report, place the items that repeat for every group in the group header section.
- A summary field performs a summary operation on a set of retrieved data values, and a formula field performs a calculation or program operation on a data value.
- To create a report that displays data, based on user inputs, create the report from a table adapter that uses a parameter query.

KEY TERMS

Boilerplate object   Report object containing text or graphics that enhance report appearance and do not change based on the data that the report displays

Crystal Report object class definition   Form item that specifies the report contents and format

Crystal Report viewer   Form control that displays a report, along with controls for working with the report

Date template   Report field that displays the current date on a generated report

Details section   Report section that displays the report data values

Formula field   Report field that performs a calculation or program function on a retrieved data value

Group name fields   Text objects that label report groups

Page footer   Report section that displays items appearing at the bottom of each report page

Page header   Report section that displays items appearing at the top of each report page

Report   Summary view of database data that users can view on a computer screen, print on paper, or send as an e-mail message

Report footer   Report section that displays items appearing once at the end of the report

Report groups   Report sections that specify the column headings, detail data, and summary data that repeat for each record in a section of a master-detail report

Report header   Report section that displays items appearing once at the beginning of the report

Report sections   Groupings that specify where the report displays items and how often the items appear

Summary field   Report field that summarizes a set of retrieved data

STUDY QUESTIONS

Multiple-Choice Questions

1. A page number is an example of a(n):
   - a. Data field
   - b. Parameter field
   - c. Unbound field
   - d. Boilerplate object

2. To create a report that lets the user specify a search condition using a form control, you must:
    a. Create a data-bound control on the form
    b. Base the report on a parameter query
    c. Create a master-detail report, and use the search condition to specify the master record value
    d. All of the above
3. A Crystal Report _____ specifies the contents and format of a specific report.
    a. Viewer control
    b. Table adapter
    c. Data set
    d. Object class definition
4. In a tabular report, the column headings appear in the report's _____ section.
    a. Report header
    b. Page header
    c. Details
    d. Report footer
    e. Page footer
5. Usually you display the Crystal Report viewer control _____ only on master-detail reports.
    a. Toolbar
    b. Group tree pane
    c. Status bar
    d. Property tab
6. When you create a master-detail report, the report's table adapter should retrieve:
    a. Only the master records
    b. Only the detail records
    c. Both the master and detail records

True/False Questions

1. You usually put a summary field in a group or page footer section.
2. All the reports in a project can use the same data source.
3. When you create a formula field, you enclose the entire formula expression in braces.
4. A tabular report displays data from a single database table, and a master-detail report displays data from two or more tables.

Short Answer Questions

1. Describe the differences between a form and a report.
2. List the steps for creating a Crystal Report in a VB project.
3. When viewing a report in Designer view, how can you tell the difference between a field heading and a data field?
4. What is the difference between a summary field and a formula field?
5. How many group sections would you create for a report based on the following query? Defend your answer.

```
SELECT UniversityEnrollment.StudentID,
       StudentLastName, UniversityCourse.CourseID,
       CourseName, UniversitySection.SectionID,
       SectionNumber, SectionTerm, EnrollmentGrade
FROM UniversityEnrollment
INNER JOIN UniversityStudent
ON UniversityStudent.StudentID = UniversityEnrollment.StudentID
INNER JOIN UniversitySection
ON UniversityEnrollment.SectionID = UniversitySection.SectionID
INNER JOIN UniversityCourse
ON UniversitySection.CourseID = UniversityCourse.CourseID
WHERE UniversityStudent.StudentID = 1
ORDER BY SectionTerm
```

Guided Exercises

All the following exercises use the Sport Motors database, which Figures 3-2 and 3-4 illustrate.

1. **Creating a Project with a Data Source and Menu**

   This exercise creates a project that stores the solutions for all of the chapter's guided exercises.

   a. Create a new project named ReportExercises, and save it in your \SQLServer\ Solutions\Chapter7 folder. Do not create a directory for the solution, and make sure that the project's Option Strict setting value is On.

   b. In the project, create a new data source that uses the *yourDatabaseName* database. (If you are connecting to a local database, reference the *yourDatabaseName*.mdf file. If you are connecting to a remote database, use the connection information that your instructor provides.) Include only the Sport Motors database tables in the data source.

   c. Rename the project's default form frmMenu, and configure the form using the standard form properties described in the chapter tutorials. Change the form's Text property value to Chapter 7 Exercises.

   d. Create a MenuStrip control on frmMenu that displays menu choices calling the forms for the rest of the exercises. Create top-level menu items that display the following selections: Tabular Reports, Master-Detail Reports, and Parameter Reports.

2. **Creating a Tabular Report From a Single Table**

NOTE: To complete this exercise, you must first complete Exercise 7-1.

In this exercise, you create the form in Figure 7-19, which displays a report that shows Sport Motors inventory items.

   a. Create a new form in the 7DBReportExercises project you created in Exercise 7-1. Name the new form frmExercise2.vb. Configure the form using the standard form properties you used in the chapter. Change the form's Text property to Exercise 7-2.

   b. Add a new menu selection under the Tabular Reports menu item in the project's frmMenu form with the text Exercise 7-2, and then add all the necessary commands to make the menu selection display the frm7Exercise2 form.

FIGURE 7-19   Exercise 7-2

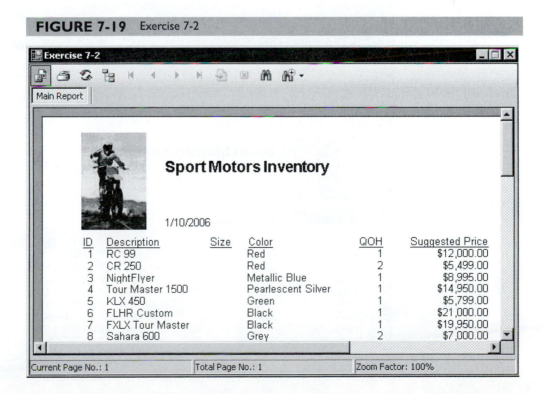

   c. Create a Crystal Report viewer control on the form. Name the control crvInventory, and configure the viewer as shown in Figure 7-19.

   d. Add a new Crystal Report object class named rptInventory to the project. Configure the object class to define the report in Figure 7-19.

   e. Link the report to the viewer control, and create the form data components to display the report data.

   f. Format the report so that it looks like Figure 7-19. For the graphic image, use an image of your choice, or use motox1.jpg, which is in the \SQLServer\DataFiles\Chapter7 folder.

3. **Creating a Tabular Report from Multiple Tables**

NOTE: To complete this exercise, you must first complete Exercise 7-1.

In this exercise, you create the form in Figure 7-20, which displays a report about Sport Motors employees that contains data from multiple tables.

   a. Create a new form in the ReportExercises project you created in Exercise 7-1. Name the new form frmExercise3.vb. Configure the form using the standard form properties you used in the chapter. Change the form's Text property to Exercise 7-3.

   b. Add a new menu selection under the Tabular Reports menu item in the project's frmMenu form that has the text Exercise 7-3, and then add all the necessary commands to make the menu selection display the frmExercise3 form.

   c. Create a Crystal Report viewer control on the form. Name the control crvEmployeeDetails, and configure the viewer as shown in Figure 7-20.

   d. Create a new table adapter named EmployeeDetails that joins the SportEmployee and SportDepartment tables and that displays the fields shown in Figure 7-20. Order the records by the EmployeeLastName field.

   e. Add a new Crystal Report object class named rptEmployeeDetails to the project. Configure the object class to define the report shown in Figure 7-20.

   f. Link the report to the viewer control, and add the form data components to display the report data.

FIGURE 7-20 Exercise 7-3

FIGURE 7-21   Exercise 7-4

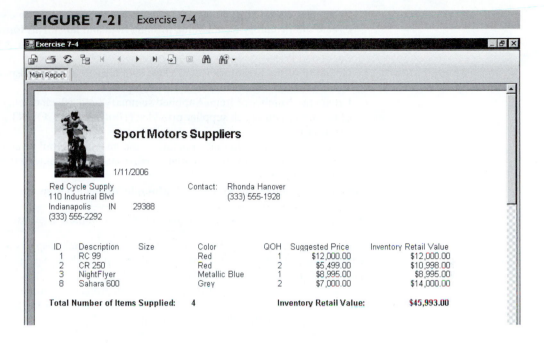

g. Format the report so that it looks like Figure 7-20. Create a formula field to format the EmployeeHomePhone data field as shown. For the graphic image, use an image of your choice, or use motox1.jpg, which is in the \SQLServer\DataFiles\Chapter7 folder.

4. **Creating a Master-Detail Report**

NOTE: To complete this exercise, you must first complete Exercise 7-1.

In this exercise, you create the form in Figure 7-21, which displays a master-detail report that displays information about Sport Motors suppliers and their associated inventory items.

a. Create a new form in the ReportExercises project you created in Exercise 7-1. Name the new form frmExercise4.vb. Configure the form using the standard form properties you used in the chapter. Change the form's Text property to Exercise 7-4.

b. Add a new menu selection under the Master-Detail Reports menu item in the project's frmMenu form with the text Exercise 7-4, and then add all the necessary commands to make the menu selection display the frmExercise4 form.

c. Create a Crystal Report viewer control on the form. Name the control crvSupplierInventory, and configure the viewer as shown in Figure 7-21.

d. Create a new table adapter named SupplierInventory that joins the SportSupplier and SportInventory tables and that displays the fields for the report in Figure 7-21. Order the records by the SupplierName field. (You will create a formula field to calculate the Inventory Retail Value fields, along with summary fields to calculate the Number of Items Supplied and Total Inventory Retail Value fields, so you do not need to retrieve these values in the query.) Be sure to include the SupplierID and InventoryID fields in the query because you will base the report groups on these values.

e. Add a new Crystal Report object class named rptSupplierInventory to the project. Configure the object class to define the report as shown in Figure 7-21. Create report groups to display the supplier and inventory information in separate groups.

f. Link the report to the viewer control, and add the form data components to display the report data.

g. Format the report so that it looks like Figure 7-21. Create formula columns to format the telephone numbers as shown. For the graphic image, use an image of your choice, or use motox1.jpg, which is in the \SQLServer\DataFiles\Chapter7 folder.

h. Configure the report so that the data for each supplier appears on a separate report page.

i. Create the Inventory Retail Value formula field and label. This formula field calculates the retail value of each inventory item. Calculate the retail value as QOH times Suggested Price.

j. Create the Total Inventory Retail Value summary field, which displays the total retail value of the on-hand inventory for each supplier.

k. Create the Number of Items Supplied summary field, which displays the total number of inventory items each supplier provides. (Hint: Use the COUNT group summary function.)

l. Create a summary field that summarizes the inventory retail value for all suppliers, and display it in the report footer. Create a corresponding label with the text "Inventory Retail Value for All Suppliers."

5. **Creating a Master-Detail Report with Multiple Master Sections**

NOTE: To complete this exercise, you must first complete Exercise 7-1.

In this exercise you create the form in Figure 7-22, which displays a master-detail report with multiple master sections that shows information about Sport Motors customers and their associated orders and order detail lines.

a. Create a new form in the DBReportExercises project you created in Exercise 7-1. Name the new form frmExercise5.vb. Configure the form using the standard form properties you used in the chapter. Change the form's Text property to Exercise 7-5.

b. Add a new menu selection under the Master-Detail Reports menu item in the project's frmMenu form with the text Exercise 7-5, and then add all the necessary commands to make the menu selection display the frmExercise5 form.

c. Create a Crystal Report viewer control on the form. Name the control crvCustomerOrders, and configure the viewer as shown in Figure 7-22.

d. Create a new table adapter named CustomerOrders that joins the SportCustomer, SportOrder, SportOrderDetail, and SportInventory tables and that retrieves the fields required by the report in Figure 7-22. Order the records by the CustomerLastName field. (You will create formula fields that calculate the Extended Total and 6% Sales Tax field values, along with summary fields that calculate the Subtotal and ORDER TOTAL field values, so you do not need to retrieve these values in your query.)

FIGURE 7-22 Exercise 7-5

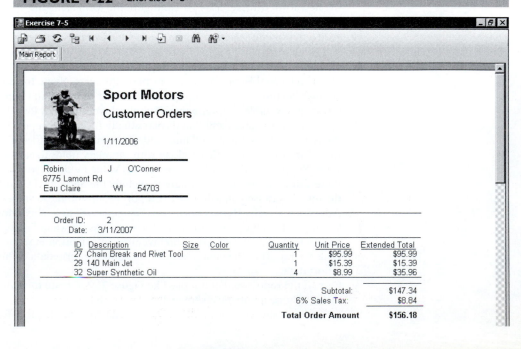

e. Add a new Crystal Report object class named rptCustomerOrders to the project and configure the object class to define the report as shown in Figure 7-22.

f. Link the report to the viewer control, and add the form data components to display the report data.

g. Format the report so that it looks like Figure 7-22. Create a formula column to format the telephone number as shown. For the graphic image, use an image of your choice, or use motox1.jpg, which is in the \SQLServer\DataFiles\Chapter7 folder.

h. Configure the report so that the data for each customer appears on a separate report page.

i. Create the Extended Total formula field and label, which displays the quantity times price for each order detail line.

j. Create the Subtotal summary field and label, which sums the extended total values.

k. Create the Sales Tax formula field and label, which displays the order's sales tax. Calculate sales tax as 6% of the order subtotal value.

l. Create the Order Total formula field and label, which sums the subtotal and the sales tax.

6. **Creating a Tabular Report with an Input Parameter**

NOTE: To complete this exercise, you must first complete Exercise 7-1.

In this exercise, you create a form that contains a master-detail data display showing merchandise categories and related subcategories. When the user selects a category in the combo box and clicks on Show Merchandise in Category, the report in Figure 7-23 appears, which shows data about all inventory items in the selected category.

a. Create a new form in the DBReportExercises project you created in Exercise 7-1. Name the new form frmExercise6.vb. Configure the form using the standard form properties you used in the chapter. Change the form's Text property to Exercise 7-6.

FIGURE 7-23 Exercise 7-6

b. Add a new menu selection under the Parameter Reports menu item in the project's frmMenu form with the text Exercise 7-6, then add all the necessary commands to make the menu selection display the frmExercise6 form.

c. Create a combo box, label, and Display Items button on the form as shown. Configure the combo box to display the CategoryDescription field value from the SportCategory table, and specify CategoryID as the combo box's ValueMember property.

d. Create a Crystal Report viewer control on the form. Name the control crvCategoryInventory, and configure the viewer as shown in Figure 7-23.

e. Create a new table adapter named CategoryInventory that displays the fields shown in Figure 7-23. This table adapter uses a query that accepts an input parameter variable for the CategoryID field value.

f. Add a new Crystal Report object class named rptCategoryInventory to the project. Configure the object class to define the report as shown in Figure 7-23, based on the CategoryInventory table adapter.

g. Link the report to the viewer control, and add the form data components to display the report data.

h. Add the commands to the form's Load event handler to link the report to the table adapter, fill the table adapter by passing to it the combo box selection value, and refresh the report display.

i. Create a Click event handler that contains the commands to fill the table adapter and refresh the report display.

j. Format the report so that it looks like Figure 7-23. For the graphic image, use an image of your choice, or use motox1.jpg, which is in the \SQLServer\DataFiles\Chapter7 folder.

7. **Creating a Master-Detail Report with an Input Parameter**

NOTE: To complete this exercise, you must first complete Exercise 7-1.

In this exercise, you create a form that contains a master-detail data display of Sport Motors daily sales information. The user inputs a start date and end date on the form and clicks Show Sales, and the report in Figure 7-24 appears, which shows data for all sales during the specified time period.

a. Create a new form in the DBReportExercises project you created in Exercise 7-1. Name the new form frmExercise7.vb. Configure the form using the standard form properties you used in the chapter. Change the form's Text property to Exercise 7-7.

b. Add a new menu selection under the Parameter Reports menu item in the project's frmMenu form with the text Exercise 7-7, and then add all the necessary commands to make the menu selection display the frmExercise7 form.

c. Create the text boxes, labels, and button on the form as shown. Add commands to the form's Load event handler so that when the form first opens, it displays the current date. [Hint: Initialize the text box's Text property values in the form's Load event handler using the Today() function.]

d. Create a Crystal Report viewer control on the form. Name the control crvDailySales, and configure the viewer as shown in Figure 7-24.

e. Create a new table adapter named DailySales that displays the fields required to create the report in Figure 7-24. The table adapter needs to retrieve the DetailQuantity and DetailUnitPrice values for each order detail line to calculate the Order Total summary field. (You will create a report summary field to calculate the Daily Total field value, so the query does not need to retrieve this value.) Structure the query to accept input parameter values for the OrderDate value such that the order date is greater than or equal to the Start Date value and less than or equal to the End Date value.

f. Add a new Crystal Report object class named rptDailySales to the project. Configure the object class to define the report shown in Figure 7-24 based on the DailySales table adapter. (Hint: Create report groups for the order date and for each order ID.)

g. Create a formula field named ExtendedTotal that calculates the product of the DetailQuantity times the DetailUnit price for each order detail line. (This field will not appear on the report, but you will use it to calculate the Order Total summary field.)

FIGURE 7-24   Exercise 7-7

h. Create a summary field that sums the ExtendedTotal formula field values for each order. Create the Order Total label as shown in Figure 7-24, and position the summary field under the label.

i. Create a summary field that sums the ExtendedTotal formula field values for all orders on each day. Create the Daily Total label as shown in Figure 7-24, and position the summary field beside the label.

j. Configure the report to display each day's orders on a separate report page. (Hint: To display each day separately, select the report group for the data organized by OrderDate, right-click, click Group Expert, click Options, and then configure the report so that it displays the section for each day.)

k. Link the report to the viewer control, and add the form data components to display the report data.

l. Add the commands to the form's Load event handler to fill the table adapter by passing to it the text box values and to refresh the report display. You will need to change the text box values to a date data type using the CDate() function.

m. Create a Click event handler that contains the commands to fill the table adapter and refresh the report display.

n. Format the report so that it looks like Figure 7-24. For the graphic image, use an image of your choice, or use motox1.jpg, which is in the \SQLServer\DataFiles\Chapter7 folder.

CHAPTER 8

Creating Web-Based Database Applications Using ASP.NET

Learning Objectives

At the conclusion of this chapter, you will be able to:

- describe the architecture of the World Wide Web and Web-database applications;

- understand the structure of an ASP.NET Web application;

- create an ASP.NET Web site;

- create Web database forms that allow users to process database data using single-record, tabular, and master-detail displays;

- enhance Web database forms with pick lists, validation controls, and images.

NOTE: To complete the tutorials and exercises in this chapter, you need to use either Visual Web Developer 2005 Express (which we refer to as VWD Express) or VS 2005. If you are using VS 2005, reconfigure it for Web projects using the steps that the chapter provides.

Web-based database applications provide an easy and reliable way to distribute database applications to users. With a Web-based database application, the application interface runs on a Web browser on the client's workstation, and accesses Web pages and/or database data from a remote server. Most people have browsers and are familiar with using Web pages, so administrators do not have to worry about users having adequate hardware and software to run database applications or about user training. It is very easy to distribute upgrades to Web-based database applications by simply deploying them on the Web server. As a result, many organizations are moving to Web-based database applications. Therefore, it is important to understand how these applications work and how to create them. This chapter introduces Web concepts and Web-database concepts. It also provides an overview of ASP.NET, which is the .NET component for creating Web applications, and describes how to create a variety of Web applications that interact with databases.

To create ASP.NET Web pages, you will use the VB programming language. Many of the Toolbox controls that you will use in ASP.NET are similar to the ones you used to create Windows applications, but they have been redesigned to work in a Web environment. The underlying database architecture is also similar, but ASP.NET provides a number of new data-bound controls for the Web environment.

INTRODUCTION TO THE WORLD WIDE WEB

The *World Wide Web,* which most people call the *Web,* is a network of server and client computers that share information. The following subsections describe the architecture of the Web, explore Web addresses, and discuss Hypertext Markup Language (HTML).

Web Architecture

Figure 8-1 illustrates the basic components and operations of the World Wide Web. Recall that a server is a computer that shares resources, and a client is a program that requests and uses server resources. On the Web, client computers run *Web browsers,* which are applications that request Web pages. There are many browsers in use today, including Microsoft Internet Explorer, FireFox, Safari, and Opera.

The client's Web browser sends a request for a Web page over the network to a Web server. A *Web server* is a computer running special Web server software that services client requests for Web pages. The Web server finds the requested Web page in its file system and sends it to the client browser.

TIP: You can create a Web server on just about any networked computer by installing and configuring a Web server process. For a busy Web site, however, you need to use a dedicated server with multiple processors and hard drives, or even multiple servers. Here is an interesting piece of industry gossip: Google does not publicize the number of servers supporting its Web site; however, in 2005 Google was thought to use between 100,000 and 165,000 servers. Some 2006 estimates place the number at over 200,000—all supporting what appears to users as a single Web site.

A *network* is a communication path between a sender and a receiver. The sender and receiver might communicate using electromagnetic signals over a phone wire, light pulses over a fiber optic cable, or smoke signals through the air. As a Web application developer, you do not need to understand how the network physically transmits data. However, the speed with which the network transmits the data matters; so a smoke signal is a poor choice.

A *Web page* is a file with an .html or .htm extension that contains hypertext markup language (HTML) commands, which are commands that specify the appearance and contents of a Web page.

FIGURE 8-1   Web components and operations

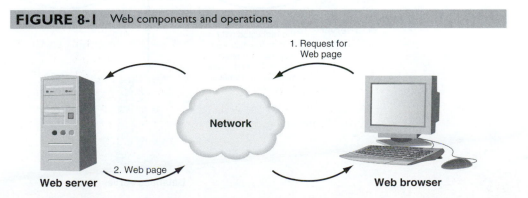

Web server   Web browser

TIP: Different browsers sometimes display Web pages differently. When you create Web applications using ASP.NET, the application recognizes the client browser type, and tries to adjust the Web page's appearance accordingly. However, pages created using ASP.NET (or any other technology for that matter) do not always display correctly on browsers other than the Internet Explorer (or whatever browser was originally used to test the page while it was developed). To ensure that Web pages display correctly on different Web browsers, you need to test them using every browser you anticipate will be used to display the page. Then, if needed, you can add commands to the Web page to detect the type and version of browser requesting a page and modify the Web page accordingly. This book does not address browser compatibility issues.

The VS 2005/VWD Express IDE provides a built-in Web server to allow testing Web applications during development. This enables testing potentially buggy applications without affecting a production server on which other users depend.

ASP.NET enables creating a rich user interface with highly interactive controls that are similar to the Windows applications you made in Chapters 5 and 6. This high degree of user interaction sometimes requires many "round trips" between the Web server and Web browser. The browser must transmit user inputs to the server, and the server must send different Web pages to the browser in response to these inputs. As a result, ASP.NET pages work best on fast networks that can transmit a lot of data in short time intervals.

When a Web site stores and manages data using a database, it commonly uses the architecture shown in Figure 8-2. In the Web-database architecture, the database server process runs on a separate server from the Web server process. The Web server receives the browser request as before, but this time it runs a program that performs the requested data operations. Distributing the database server process and the Web server process across multiple servers improves system performance.

For a data retrieval operation, the Web server sends the SELECT query to the database, receives the requested data, inserts the data values into the Web page, then

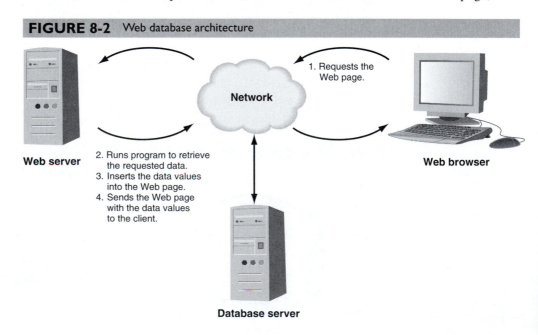

FIGURE 8-2 Web database architecture

sends the formatted Web page to the client. For an insert, update, or delete operation, the Web server forwards the action query to the database, receives the database response, then forwards the response to the client in a Web page.

NOTE: If you are running SQL Express on a local database, you are running your database server and Web server on the same computer. This provides an excellent development and testing configuration for creating Web database applications. The only drawback is that you cannot test the scalability of your application in terms of how it will respond to multiple users processing large amounts of data.

Web Addressing Concepts

To understand how Web servers communicate with client browsers, you need to understand Web addressing. The following subsections describe the components of a Web address: communication protocols, Uniform Resource Locators (URLs), and ports.

Communication Protocols

To enable communication between servers and browsers, the Web uses communication protocols. A *communication protocol* is an agreement between a sender and a receiver that specifies how they will format, send, and receive data. The primary communication protocol used by all Internet traffic, including e-mail messages, file transfers, and Web pages, is the *Internet Protocol (IP)*. The Internet is a global network composed of many smaller networks linked through IP.

IP creates unique addresses for networked computers. Every computer on the Internet must have a unique address to enable communications. An IP address consists of a series of numbers separated by periods, such as 68.115.71.53. Because people have trouble remembering numeric IP addresses, many IP addresses have associated *domain names,* which are human-friendly names that reference a numeric IP address. Examples of domain names are www.google.com and www.uwec.edu. When you type a domain name in your Web browser's Address field, a special server called a *domain name server* converts the domain name to its associated numeric IP address.

When you type a Web server domain name in the Address field of your browser, it usually includes the prefix *http:* which stands for HyperText Transfer Protocol. *HyperText Transfer Protocol* (*HTTP*) is a communication protocol that works with and on top of IP. It coordinates the messages between a browser and Web server and determines how the Web server sends text and images to browsers.

TIP: Most browsers support protocols other than HTTP, such as File Transfer Protocol (FTP), which allows the browser to connect to and exchange information with an FTP server for transferring files.

Uniform Resource Locators

When you request a Web page in a Web browser, the value you type in the browser's Address field is called a *Uniform Resource Locator* (*URL*). Figure 8-3 illustrates the components of a URL.

FIGURE 8-3   URL components

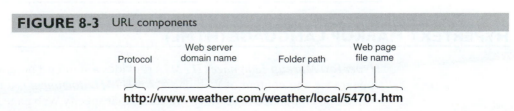

The first component in a URL is the communication protocol, usually `http://`. Next comes the Web server domain name or IP address; you can use either one interchangeably. This is optionally followed by the folder path and name of the requested Web page file. The folder path specifies the Web page's location in the Web server's file system. This may be an actual folder, or a *virtual directory,* which references a folder that can be located anywhere in the Web server's file system.

NOTE: This book uses the terms "directory" and "folder" interchangeably.

The folder path and Web page filename are optional. If a URL does not include a folder path and filename, the Web server returns its *default document,* which is a home page from which users can navigate to find more specific information.

How do you specify a Web page URL when you are developing Web applications in the ASP.NET IDE using the test Web server? The IP protocol has a special address to reference the local workstation. The numeric address is 127.0.0.1 and is called the *local loopback address* because it "loops back" to itself. You can alternatively reference the local loopback address using the domain name *localhost.* An example URL that requests a Web page on a Web server running on the same computer is `http://localhost/MyFolder/myPage.aspx`.

NOTE: Although "127.0.0.1" and "localhost" reference the same location, you should use localhost rather than the numeric address because applications sometimes block addresses that use 127.0.0.1.

Ports

A computer that runs a Web server process can also run other server processes at the same time. For example, a single computer could simultaneously run a Web server, database server, and e-mail server. In this situation, a server's IP address needs to include the "address" of the desired server process as well as the physical computer address. The address for a server process is called a *port.* A port is a value that references a server process using a number between zero and 65,535. The IP protocol specifies a standard port number for common server processes such as e-mail servers (Port 25), Web servers (Port 80), and FTP servers (Port 21).

A server maintains an *IP port table,* which contains port numbers in one column and main memory locations of associated server processes in the second column. The port number is fixed, but the main memory location, where the associated process runs, varies and is written to the table at the time the process starts.

Server administrators can use alternate port numbers to identify server processes. This becomes necessary if a computer runs two similar server processes, such as two e-mail servers or two Web servers. If a Web administrator assigns a Web server to a port number other than 80, the URL that references the Web server must include the port number using the following syntax: `http://WebServerName:PortNumber/. . . .` For example, the following URL specifies a Web server running on the local workstation using port number 1685:

```
http://localhost:1685/WebExamples/Default.aspx
```

HYPERTEXT MARKUP LANGUAGE (HTML)

HyperText Markup Language (*HTML*) provides a standard notation for specifying the appearance and content of Web pages. An *HTML document* is a text file that consists of text and embedded tags, which are codes that specify Web page formatting and links to other pages. An HTML document can have an .htm or .html extension. This book does not provide an HTML primer, but we will introduce the concepts of tags, HTML document structure, and HTML forms.

Tags

A *tag* is a formatting code that encloses a Web page element, such as a line of text or an image, and instructs the browser how to process or display the item. The general syntax of an HTML tag is as follows:

```
<TagName>Element</TagName>
```

HTML tags appear in angle brackets (<>). Place the opening tag just before the element you want to format. The closing tag marks the end of the formatting or section. A closing tag is always prefaced by a front slash (/). For example, the following tag instructs the browser to place the text it encloses in a strong (**boldface**) font:

```
<strong>This is bolded text.</strong>
```

Sometimes tags are one-sided tags because they do not enclose an element but instead instruct the browser to perform a one-time action, such as placing a line break on a page, as follows (a browser will display this as a single line followed by a line break after the words "a line break"):

```
<strong>This is bolded text followed
by a line break.</strong><br>
```

HTML Document Structure

Figure 8-4 shows the general structure of an HTML document. An HTML document begins with an opening <html> tag and ends with a closing </html> tag. Next comes the *heading section,* which is enclosed in <head> tags. The heading section can contain special tags that instruct the browser how to display the document. The heading section also contains the <title> tag, which assigns the text that appears at the top of the browser's window. The final section of an HTML document is the *body section,* which is enclosed in <body> tags, and contains all the Web page's content and format tags.

An HTML document can contain *client-side script* commands, which are program commands that the browser executes. Client-side scripts are usually written with scripting languages such as JavaScript or VBScript. Client-side scripts can support processing such as arithmetic calculations and data validation.

FIGURE 8-4   HTML document structure

```
<html>
  <head>
    <title>Web_page_title</title>
  </head>
  <body>
    Web_page_body_elements
  </body>
</html>
```

HTML Forms

Web-based database applications often use *HTML forms*, which are enhancements to HTML documents containing controls such as text boxes and buttons that allow users to enter inputs and interact with the Web page. These controls, called *inputs*, allow users to submit data values to the Web server for processing by a server-side program. A *server-side* program runs on the Web server and can process form inputs in different ways, including retrieving or modifying database data.

Tags can have *attributes*, which are values that modify the tag. An opening form tag has an ID attribute, which specifies an identifier that uniquely identifies the form in the application. A form tag also has an action attribute, which specifies the program that processes the form when the user submits it to the Web server. For example, the following form tag creates a form named frmCustomer and calls a program named insertCustomer.aspx to process the form inputs when the user submits the form:

```
<form  id=frmCustomer  action=insertCustomer.aspx>
     FormElements
</form>
```

The following tag creates a button input that displays the text "Submit," and its Click event calls a JavaScript client-side program named "validateDate()":

```
<input  type="button"
onclick="validateDate();"  value="Submit">
```

HTML is a large topic, and there are many comprehensive books and Web-based references on this topic. You do not need to be an HTML expert to develop Web database applications using VS 2005/VWD Express because the IDE automatically generates the HTML tags and form elements. This HTML introduction is necessary, however, to enable you to understand the vocabulary used in the chapter on ASP.NET applications.

TIP: Although you don't need to be an HTML expert to work with ASP.NET, virtually all experienced Web developers are proficient with HTML. It's an important skill to add to your resume.

INTRODUCTION TO ASP.NET

Initially, Web pages did not contain forms that allowed users to interact with applications and process user inputs. The first technology to create server-side programs to process user inputs was the Common Gateway Interface (CGI) protocol. Developers could write executable programs using many different programming languages, and, as long as the programs followed CGI protocols, the Web server could receive user form inputs, process them, and send a response back to the user's browser. If performance had not been an issue, this might have been the only technology that ever evolved, and we would all still be writing and using CGI-based programs today. Performance was an issue, however, because CGI did not work well for Web sites that needed to service large numbers of users.

In response, vendors developed new technologies such as Active Server Pages (ASPs) and Java Server Pages (JSPs). Both ASPs and JSPs improve performance over CGI, but neither provides the rich support that developers have come to expect from Visual Studio and other visual IDEs. To address this issue, Microsoft developed

ASP.NET, which provides adequate performance for high-volume Web sites, along with an IDE that allows developers to create complex interactive Web applications quickly and easily.

NOTE: ASP.NET 2.0 (delivered with VS 2005 and Visual Web Developer Express) can now take advantage of the full memory address space available with newer 64-bit processors. In addition, ASP.NET 2.0 also has new database caching features that enable developers to automatically cache database content in the Web site and update the cache as needed whenever the back-end database changes.

This section provides an overview of the ASP.NET technology. The following subsections describe how ASP.NET processes Web pages, structures Web application files, and organizes a Web site.

ASP.NET Web Page Processing

Figure 8-1 showed that in basic Web processing, browsers request Web pages from Web servers, and Web servers deliver Web page files to browsers. How does a Web server know when a user submits an HTML form that contains inputs? How does the server create a Web page that responds to these inputs? The answer lies in the type of Web page file that the browser requests. If a browser requests a file with an .htm or .html extension, the Web server knows to deliver a *static Web page,* which is a Web page whose content is fixed at design time and does not depend on user inputs. If the browser requests a Web page with a different extension, and the Web server understands how to process the file type, then the server processes it as a dynamic Web page. A *dynamic Web page* is a Web page that the Web server creates based on user inputs.

TIP: Many people use the phrase "dynamic Web page" to describe Web pages that use client-side processing to animate images or text. In this book, we define dynamic Web pages as pages that use server-side processing to generate their content.

Recall that an HTML form tag has an action attribute specifying the program that runs when the user submits the form to the Web server. With older technologies such as ASP and JSP, the developer creates an HTML document to define the form controls, then creates a second ASP or JSP dynamic Web page to define the program commands that process the form inputs and display the Web page the user receives in response to the form inputs.

Figure 8-5 illustrates traditional (non-ASP.NET) dynamic Web page processing. With traditional (non-ASP.NET) dynamic Web page processing, the client Web browser first submits form inputs and a request for a dynamic Web page to a Web server. The server receives the request, and processes the dynamic Web page file using the form inputs as parameters. If the dynamic Web page processing involves database operations, the Web server opens a connection to the database and requests the desired data or forwards the action query. It then creates a formatted HTML document that might contain retrieved data or a confirmation message describing the status of an action query.

ASP.NET uses a different processing approach, which Figure 8-6 illustrates. With ASP.NET, the client browser initially requests the ASP.NET Web page, which is called a *Web form.* The Web server processes the request and delivers an HTML document representing the Web form in its initial state. The user interacts with the Web form by entering values or performing actions that cause event handlers to execute.

FIGURE 8-5 Traditional dynamic Web page processing

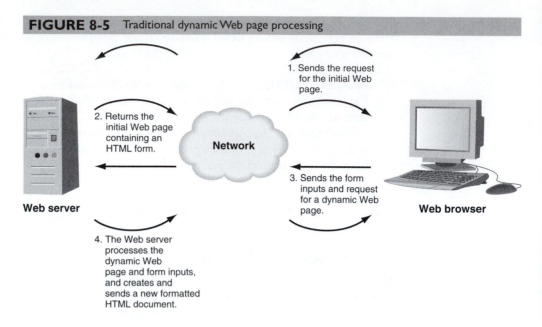

Certain events cause the browser to send, or *post,* the Web form back to the server for processing. When the browser posts the Web form back to the server, the server processes all the accumulated event handlers along with the user inputs. These event handlers and inputs might involve opening a connection to a database and executing a database query. ASP.NET then creates, or renders, a new HTML document based on the event handler results. The user can interact with the document again and the browser again keeps track of inputs and events, eventually posting the Web form back to the server for more processing. This process of repeatedly raising events and posting the same Web form back to the server is called *postback processing.* Figure 8-6's postback loop illustrates the process of the user repeatedly interacting with the Web form, and then posting it back to the server multiple times.

Why does the browser not post the form back to the server for every user action? The answer involves performance. If the browser posts the form back to the server

FIGURE 8-6 ASP.NET Web page processing

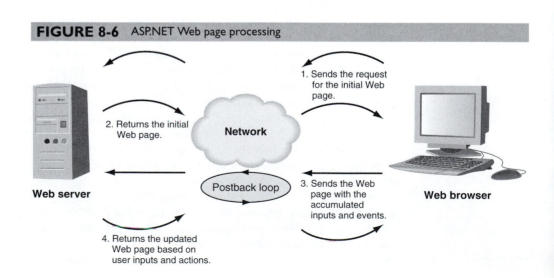

every time the user types a character or selects a value from a list, the frequent round trips between the browser and server could bring processing to a halt.

When a page is posted back, how does the server know which event handlers to process and which inputs have changed? When ASP.NET sends a Web form to a user's browser, it includes a hidden input in the Web page. This input, called the *ViewState* input, stores all the current values for a form's controls. When the browser posts the Web form back to the server, the server compares the original values stored in the ViewState input to the current input values in the submitted form and runs the required event handlers based on the changes. For example, if a list's current selection is different from what it was initially, ASP.NET knows to run the event handler associated with changing the list's value.

Web Form Files

An ASP.NET Web form consists of HTML tags and elements, along with commands that define Web form controls, called *server controls,* such as text boxes and buttons. It also contains program commands that perform server-side processing. ASP.NET places the HTML and server control definitions in the Web form file, which has an .aspx file extension. It places program commands for the Web form's server-side event handlers in an associated file called a *code file,* which has the same name as the Web form file, but has an .aspx.vb extension. Keeping the Web form HTML contents and ASP.NET control definitions in a separate file from the VB event handler commands makes the Web form more modular and easier to understand and maintain.

Figure 8-7 illustrates the Web form files, and the following subsections discuss their contents.

FIGURE 8-7   ASP.NET Web form files

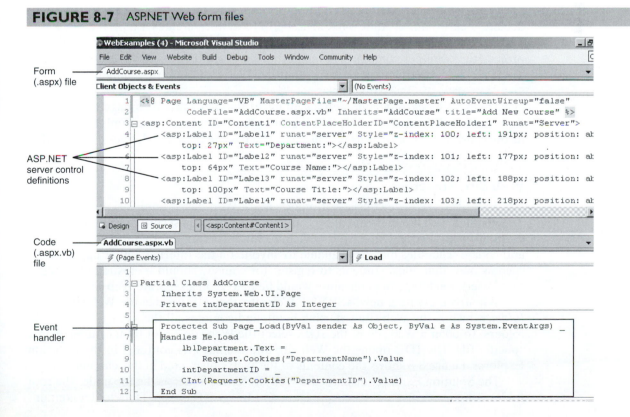

.aspx Files

The left pane in Figure 8-7 shows the contents of the .aspx file. The first line is a *page directive,* which specifies how ASP.NET processes the Web page. This command is within *command delimiter tags* (`<% @` and `%>`), which instruct ASP.NET to execute the command rather than display it as text on the Web page. The Web page's `Language` specification specifies the programming language in which the page's event handlers and other programs are written. The `AutoEventWireup` specification specifies how the Web page links its event-handling procedures to its ASP.NET controls. When this value is false, the `Handles` attribute at the end of an event handler specifies the event for which the procedure executes.

The `Codefile` specification links the .aspx file to the aspx.vb file that stores the Web page's event-handling commands, which appear in the right-hand pane. The `inherits` specification merges the class that stores the Web page's HTML and ASP.NET controls with the AddCourse class for event handling.

The HTML tags and elements look like those in any Web page. The ASP.NET control definitions, which define Web page controls such as text boxes and buttons, are special tags that begin with an `asp:` prefix. Browsers do not understand `asp:` tags, so ASP.NET translates these tags into the associated HTML form control tags when it renders the Web page's HTML document. ASP.NET provides many controls that do not exist in standard HTML forms, but ASP.NET manages to render these controls by combining standard HTML form controls with client-side JavaScript procedures. As a result, ASP.NET controls look and work much like the equivalent controls in a Windows application.

Code Files

The right pane in Figure 8-7 shows the contents of the Web page's .aspx.vb file, which is also called its code file. Recall that a Web page's code file contains event handlers for processing user actions. The first command uses the `Partial` keyword to declare a class named AddCourse. The Partial keyword creates a partial class, which allows a single class to be split into several separate files. When you compile the project, the compiler combines all the partial classes and treats them as a single class. The `Inherits` command specifies that the Web page inherits elements from the `System.Web.UI.Page` object class.

The next block of a code defines an event handler for a Web page control. The `Protected` keyword specifies that the subroutine can be accessed only from within its own partial class or from its parent class, which is the class that defines the ASP.NET controls in the .aspx file.

Web Site Structure

An ASP.NET *Web site* consists of one or more Web-based applications. Within an organization, you might create different Web sites based on security requirements. For example, at Ironwood University, applications that contain information about courses and course schedules may be available to anyone on the Internet. Other applications, such as ones that allow students to register for courses, should be restricted to registered users. Each type of application would be placed on a separate Web site.

When you create a new ASP.NET Web site, the IDE creates the Web site's *root folder,* which is the Web site's starting point, and contains all the site's files and subfolders. To open a Web site in the IDE, select the Web site's root folder rather than a specific file. The IDE opens the Web site and displays its contents in the Solution Explorer. Figure 8-8 shows the contents of the Web site created in this chapter.

The Solution Explorer displays the Web site's root folder as the top node. The root folder contains two subfolders: App_Data and Images. The App_Data folder contains

FIGURE 8-8 Web site components

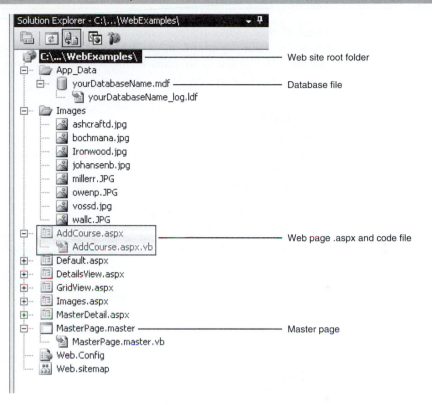

the Web site's database file, and the Images folder contains the image files that the Web site displays. The App_Data folder is a new feature in ASP.NET that improves security for a local database that runs on a Web server. With a public Web site, someone with malicious intentions might be able access and a compromise a local database file that the Web server stores. The App_Data folder provides a secure location for local database files, because the Web server protects the contents of this folder and prevents Web site users from accessing, deleting, or copying it.

The Images folder provides a central location for the Web site's image files. This organizes the files on the Web server and creates a straightforward and logical folder path for image links.

CAUTION: You should not store image files or any other files other than database files in the App_Data folder, because the Web server will not allow them to be linked to Web pages.

The Solution Explorer also displays nodes for each of the Web site's Web form .aspx files and their associated code files. The root folder stores both file types, and the Solution Explorer display uses an arrow to indicate the relationship between the Web form file and its code file.

A *master page* is a template that contains items appearing on all the site's Web pages. It contains the HTML document codes for all the Web site pages, as well as links to all the other Web forms. The web.config file stores storing application settings, such as the text for the connection string to the database. The Web.sitemap file creates a site map, which is a hierarchical display containing navigational links to the Web site's pages.

CREATING AN ASP.NET WEB SITE

The following section shows how to create an ASP.NET Web site containing Web forms for database applications. The VWD IDE is very similar to the VB IDE, so you are already familiar with many of the windows, features, and procedures for creating and working with applications.

Creating a New Web Site

A Web site is similar to a VB project: it contains one or more Web forms, as well as other components to support the forms. When you create a Web site, you specify the site's root folder.

To create a Web site:

1. Start VS 2005 or VWD Express.

NOTE: If you are using VS 2005, you need to configure it for Web development by performing the following steps: Select Tools on the menu bar, and then select Import and Export Settings. On the Import and Export Settings Wizard Welcome page, select the Reset all settings option button, and then click Next. On the Save Current Settings page, select the "No, just import new settings, overwriting my current settings" option button, and then click Next. On the Choose a Default Collection of Settings page, select the Web Development Settings node, then click Finish. When the Reset Complete page appears, click Close to close the wizard.

---

2. To create the new Web site, click File on the menu bar, and then click New Web Site. The New Web Site dialog box opens.
3. Select the ASP.NET Web Site template, and then click Browse. Navigate to your \SQLServer\Solutions\Chapter8 folder, and then click Open. Type \WebExamples at the end of the folder path to create the Web site root folder. If you are saving your solutions to your C:\ drive, your complete folder path would appear as C:\SQLServer\Solutions\Chapter8\WebExamples.
4. Click Yes to confirm creating a new folder, then click OK to create the Web site. The Default.aspx Web form appears in the IDE Document window, and the new Web site's root folder appears in the Solution Explorer.
5. Click the Save All button to save the project.

Figure 8-9 illustrates the VWD IDE. The VWD IDE is similar to the VB IDE: it contains the Solution Explorer, which allows you to view and access Web site components; the Toolbox, which allows you to create form components and controls; the Properties window, which allows you to set item properties; and the Document window, which allows you to work with different components in the site.

When you open a Web form .aspx file in the IDE, you can view it in *Design view* (also called Designer view), which shows how the Web form will appear to the user, and in *Source view,* which shows the HTML source code for the form. You can use the *Web form view tabs* on the left bottom corner of the Document window to toggle between Design and Source view.

You can also view the Web form's code file, which contains the program commands for the form's event handlers. When you select a Web form in the Solution Explorer and then click the View Code button on the Solution Explorer toolbar, the form's code file opens.

FIGURE 8-9   Visual Web Developer IDE

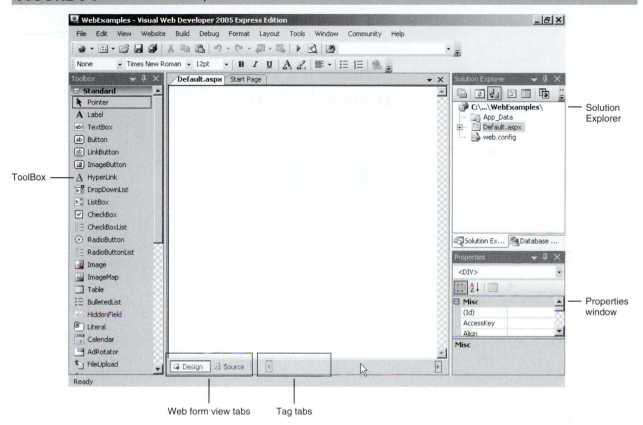

Web form view tabs   Tag tabs

The *Tag tabs* in Figure 8-9 appear when a form is displayed in Design or Source view. These buttons represent different tags in the form. When you select a specific tag tab and then enter text or an image item on the form in Design view, the IDE inserts the item in the selected tag.

The Default.aspx Web form represents the Web site's default document. (Recall that a default document is a Web site's home page and is usually the starting point for navigating to other Web pages on the site.) When you view Default.aspx in Source view, you see that it contains a page directive telling the server how to run the form, as well as the general tags for an HTML document.

Creating the Home Page

Now you will create the Web site's home page, which will look like Figure 8-10. The home page displays a title and image, and a site map that allows users to navigate to other Web forms. The site map displays nodes for the different Web forms that you will create in the chapter. The site map will appear on the Web site's master page, which is a master template for all the site's pages. The following subsections describe how to create the master page and site map and configure the home page.

Creating the Master Page

In an ASP.NET Web site, recall that a master page defines the layout and appearance of all a Web site's pages. Creating a master page ensures that all the site's pages have a consistent appearance. It also saves time and effort because you need to define the

FIGURE 8-10   Web site home page

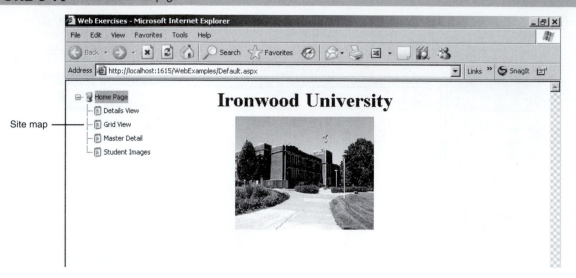

Site map

master page items only once. A master page can contain static text, graphic images, and Web server controls such as text boxes and buttons.

After you create the master page, you add new Web forms to the site as content pages. A *content page* links to a master page, and displays the specific content of the Web form. Every master page or content page contains a *content placeholder* control. This is an ASP.NET control that defines the area where you place the controls that appear on the individual Web forms.

The following steps configure the IDE so that it always displays new Web forms in Design view, and adds the master page to the Web site.

To configure the IDE and create the Web site master page:

1. To configure the IDE to display new Web forms in Design view, select Tools on the menu bar, select Options, select General in the left window pane, select the Design View option button, and then click OK.
2. To create the master page, right-click the Web site root folder in the Solution Explorer, and then click Add New Item.
3. Select the Master Page template, and check the *Place code in separate file* check box.

TIP: Do not clear the *Place code in a separate file* check box. If it is cleared, the IDE places the file's event handler commands in the .aspx file rather than in a separate .aspx.vb file. This is not a good practice because it makes the Web form less modular and harder to maintain.

---

4. Accept the default values in the *Name* field and *Language* list, and then click Add. The Masterpage.master file appears in the Document window in Design view, and shows a ContentPlaceHolder control.
5. Save the project.

Creating the Web Site Map

A *Web site map* is a tree structure that shows the layout of the Web site forms and allows users to navigate to any form by clicking on the associated node. Figure 8-10 shows the Web site map for the current Web site.

To create a Web site map, you must define a class containing XML elements that define the Web site's structure.

NOTE: XML, which stands for eXtensible Markup Language, defines a standard way to structure and store data in text files by defining data elements using HTML-style tags that define the data's structure. You will learn more about XML in Chapter 9.

To create the site map, define a *siteMapNodes* element for each tree node. Each element specifies the Web form's file name, the title on the site map, and a description in a ToolTip when the user places the mouse pointer on the site map node. Nest the elements to create the hierarchical structure. The default document, or home page, is the parent object, and subsequent forms are the child objects.

In the site map's XML file, define each node using the following general syntax:

```
<siteMapNode url="~/FormFileName"
             title="TitleSpecification"
             description="DescriptionSpecification">
```

In this syntax, `url` specifies the Web form's .aspx file. Preface the file name with a tilde followed by a front slash (~/), which indicates that the file is in the Web site's root folder. The `title` attribute is a text string that specifies the node title text in the site map. The `description` attribute specifies a more detailed text string description of the node that appears in a ToolTip when the user places the mouse pointer over the node. Now you will create the class that specifies the contents of Web site map in Figure 8-10.

To create the site map class:

1. In the Solution Explorer, right-click the Web site root folder, and then click Add New Item.
2. In the Add New Item dialog box, select the Site Map template, accept the default file name, and then click Add. The Web.sitemap file opens in the Document window.
3. Modify the template file by defining the Web site's siteMapNodes as follows. (Only modify the <siteMapNode> tags. DO NOT delete the <?xml> or <siteMap> tags in the file.)

```
<siteMapNode  url="~/Default.aspx"  title="Home   Page"
             description="ASP.NET   Examples">
    <siteMapNode  url="~/DetailsView.aspx"  title="Details   View"
             description="DetailsView   Example"  />
    <siteMapNode  url="~/GridView.aspx"  title="Grid   View"
             description="GridView   Example"  />
    <siteMapNode  url="~/MasterDetail.aspx"  title="Master   Detail"
             description="Master   Detail   Example"  />
    <siteMapNode  url="~/Images.aspx"  title="Student   Images"
             description="Student   Image   Example"  />
</siteMapNode>
```

4. Save the project.

Displaying the Web Site Map on the Master Page

To display the site map on the master page, open the master page in Design view and create a TreeView control. A *TreeView control* displays hierarchical data items in a tree structure with nodes and branches. Then link the TreeView control to the site map file.

To create the TreeView control to display the site map:

1. Select the MasterPage.master tab in the Document window to open the master page in Design view.

2. If necessary, open the Toolbox, open the Navigation node, select the TreeView control, and then drag it and drop it onto an open area on the Web form that is *not* on the WebContentPlaceholder control. The TreeView control appears on the Web form.

CAUTION: If you place the TreeView control on the master page's content placeholder control, it will not appear on the other Web forms.

---

3. Make sure that the TreeView control is selected, and change its ID property value to tvSiteMap.
4. To link the TreeView control to the class that defines the site map contents, open the tvSiteMap's DataSourceID property list, select New Data Source, select the Site Map data source, and then click OK. The node titles appear in the control, the SiteMapDataSource1 item appears on the form, and the site map displays the nodes you defined earlier.

TIP: You can also specify the TreeView's DataSourceID by clicking the Property tab found in the upper right corner of the control, and then opening the Choose Data Source list.

NOTE: In the VWD IDE, Web form components that do not have a visual representation appear directly on the form in Design view, rather than in the Component tray, as they did in VB.

---

5. To format the site map control, click the TreeView control's Property tab, which appears as a right-pointing arrow in the top right corner of the control. This opens the control's Tasks list.
6. Click AutoFormat, scroll down, select XP File Explorer, and then click OK. This formats the site map using server and page icons.
7. Open the TreeView control's Tasks list again, and check the Show Lines check box.
8. Drag your site map to the top left edge of the form, and then drop it. The site map appears in the top left corner of the form, and the ContentPlaceholder appears in the middle of the form. Your master page should look like Figure 8-11.
9. Save the project.

Creating and Formatting the Home Page

The next step is to create the Web site's home page and link it to the master page. The easiest way to do this is to delete the existing Default.aspx Web page and create a new content page to serve as the home page. (Recall that a content page links to a master page and contains the content for a specific Web form.)

Alternatively, you could delete the existing tags on the Default.aspx page and add the commands to link it to the master page. If you have already created a home page and want to turn it into a content page, this is a reasonable approach. In this case, however, the home page is blank, so it is easier to create a new one that already links to the master page. Now you will delete the existing Default.aspx page and create a new Web form that will be the site's home page. You will specify the new form as the Web site's Start page, so that it always appears first when you run the project.

To delete the Default.aspx page and create a new form that links to the master page:

1. In the Solution Explorer, select Default.aspx, right-click, click Delete, and then click OK to confirm the deletion.

FIGURE 8-11   Web site master page

Site map —

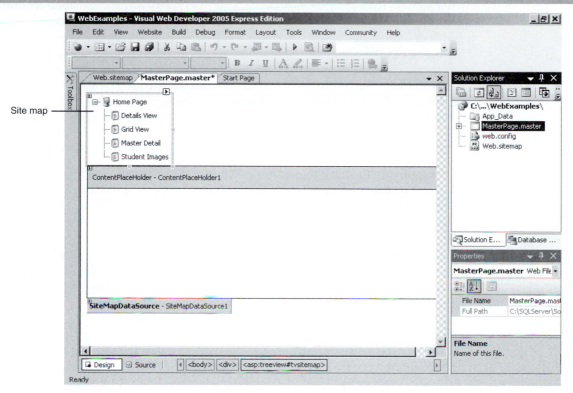

2. Right-click the Web site root folder, click Add New Item, and select the Web Form template.
3. Accept the default file name, which is Default.aspx, and make sure that the *Place code in a separate file* check box is checked.
4. To specify that the new Web form is a content page that links to the existing master page, check the Select master page check box, and then click Add.
5. In the Select a Master Page dialog box, make sure that the Web site root folder is selected in the Project folders list, and that MasterPage.master is selected as the master page, then click OK. The new content page appears in Design view and displays a content placeholder control. The site map should appear in the top left corner of the form. (It appears disabled.)
6. To specify the new form as the Web site's Start page, right-click Default.aspx in the Solution Explorer, and then click Set as Start Page.
7. To change the Web form's title, which is the text that appears in the browser title bar, click anywhere on the form to select it, then change the form's Title property to Web Exercises.
8. Save the project.

Adding Items to Web Forms

Adding a new control to a Web form is similar to adding a new control to a VB form: select the control in the Toolbox, then drag it and drop it onto the form. However, VWD positions items on the form differently. Whenever you create a new control, VWD places it in the top left corner of the form. To position the item, you need to understand its positioning attribute.

There are two basic positioning options for Web form items: absolute and relative. When an item uses *absolute positioning,* you can specify its exact position by dragging and dropping it into place on the form. When an item uses *relative positioning,* an item resides in a container object, such as a window pane. You drag the item directly from the Toolbox to the container object, and then set its position attribute to Relative. The item then moves to the specified container.

By default, the IDE does not set a positioning attribute for new controls. Now you will configure your IDE to use absolute positioning for new controls. Then you will add the content to the home page. You will add the Ironwood University label and photo to the page, as shown in Figure 8-10.

To configure the form to use absolute positioning and create the home page items:

1. To configure the form to use absolute positioning for new controls, click anywhere on the form to select it, click Layout on the menu bar, point to Position, and then click Auto-position options. In the Options dialog box, check the *Change positioning to the following for controls* check box. Make sure Absolutely positioned is selected in the list, and then click OK.
2. To add the Ironwood University label, make sure that Default.aspx is open in Design view, open the Toolbox, select the Label control, and drag it from the Toolbox and drop it onto the content placeholder control. The label appears in the top left corner of the form.
3. Change the Text property value to Ironwood University.
4. Open the label's Font property node, and change the Bold property value to True and the Size property value to XX-Large. Reposition the label so that it is in the top and center of the form, as shown in Figure 8-10.
5. To create the image, open the Toolbox, select the Image tool, and then drag it and drop it onto the content placeholder. An image placeholder appears in the top left corner of the form. (You may have to scroll to the left in the Document window to see the image placeholder.)
6. Resize the image placeholder so that it appears centered under the Ironwood University label. (You will fine-tune its position later.)
7. Save the project.

To finish the home page, you will copy the Web site image files to your Web site root folder. Then you will configure the image control so that it displays the Ironwood University photo. Then you will run the project and view your home page. When you run a project, the IDE automatically saves the project files.

To configure the image control and run the project:

1. To copy the image files, open Windows Explorer and copy the Images folder and its contents from your SQLServer\DataFiles\Chapter8 folder into your SQLServer\Solutions\Chapter8\WebExamples folder.
2. Select the Web site root folder in Solution Explorer, right-click, and then click Refresh Folder. The Images folder appears as a subfolder of the Web site.
3. To configure the image, select the image control in Design view, click its ImageUrl property in the Properties window, click the Ellipsis button (. . .), select the Images folder in the Project folders list, select Ironwood.jpg, and then click OK. The image appears on the form.

TIP: The ImageURL property value appears with a tilde and forward slash (~/) before the folder path and file name, which indicates that the folder and file are in Web site's root folder.

---

4. Adjust the image size and position so that it looks similar to Figure 8-10.

5. To run the project, click the Start Debugging button on the IDE toolbar. When the Debugging Not Enabled dialog box opens, accept the default option to add a new Web.config file and enable debugging, and then click OK. The Web site's home page opens in a browser window, as shown in Figure 8-10. Currently, only the Home Page link is enabled on the site map, because you have not yet created the site's other Web forms.

6. To stop the application, close the browser window.

CREATING WEB DATABASE FORMS

This section describes how to create Web forms that interact with databases. The first subsection describes in general how ASP.NET enables Web pages to access database data. Later subsections describe how to create Web forms that display data in single-record, tabular, and master-detail displays, as well as how to create a Web form that displays image data. You will add additional functionality to these Web forms with pick lists and validation controls.

Web-Database Connectivity

ASP.NET relies on ADO.NET to connect to databases and process database queries. (In Chapter 6 we explained that ADO.NET is a set of .NET object classes that support database access.) Web forms use many of the same ADO.NET data components as VB applications.

ASP.NET provides data-bound server controls that support complex data binding. (Simple data binding binds a control to one field in a data table, and complex data binding binds a control to multiple data table fields.) ASP.NET does not support simple data binding, but this is not a limitation, because you can use complex data binding to achieve the same results.

ASP.NET provides two different approaches to implement complex data binding. Figure 8-12 illustrates these approaches.

The first data access approach, which the left side of Figure 8-12 illustrates, uses a SQL data source control. A *SQL data source* control specifies a database connection, uses a SQL query to specify the records that the data source contains, and has associated queries to perform insert, update, and delete action queries. You create a new SQL data source for every data-bound control on a Web form. A SQL data source control does not use the Data Source/DataSet Designer/Table Adapter model used with VB Express and Windows applications, and it does not create a strongly typed data set to maintain data integrity or validate data.

The right side of Figure 8-12 illustrates the second data approach, which is called the *object data source* approach. With an object data source, the developer creates a custom class that defines a strongly typed data set with one or more associated table adapters. It uses table adapter and/or custom class methods to process the data. This approach is much more difficult to implement than the SQL data source method; however, it is preferable for N-tier systems that separate business rules from database and user interface operations. The custom class can run on different servers from the Web server and distribute processing over multiple servers.

In this book, we use SQL data source controls to bind data to controls. As a result, you will not create table adapters and data tables as you did in previous chapters. The following subsections describe how to use SQL data sources to create data-bound controls that display and process data using the data display options you learned about in Chapter 6: single-record displays, tabular displays, and master-detail displays.

FIGURE 8-12   ASP.NET data-binding approaches

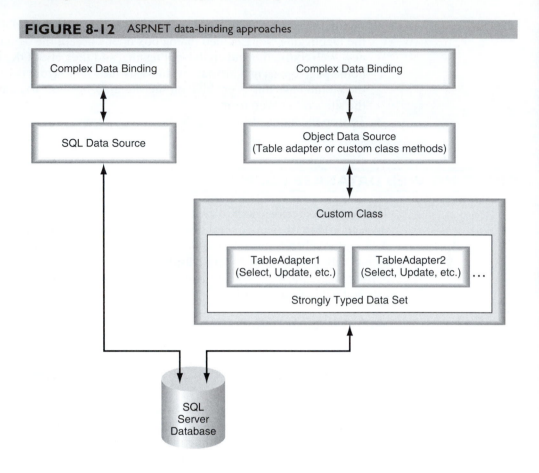

Read-Write Single-Record Display

This section shows how to create the form in Figure 8-13, which uses a data-bound control to support a read-write single-record display. This Web form displays data from the UniversityDepartment table using a *DetailsView* control, which is a server control that creates a single-record display. By default, a DetailsView control displays page links, which the user can click to navigate to a different page (or record). We have enhanced the control by creating navigation buttons to allow users to step through the retrieved values, along with a position locator label that displays the current record number and total number of records.

When the user clicks the Edit link on a record, the record opens for editing, as shown in Figure 8-14. When the user opens a record for editing, text boxes appear for the Name and Office values, and a pick list appears for the Chair value. After editing, the user clicks Update to save changes to the database and redisplay the form in Figure 8-13 with the updated value. When the user clicks the New link on the form in Figure 8-13, the form opens for inserting records, displaying blank text boxes for adding new Name and Office values and a pick list for selecting the Chair value.

The following steps create the Web form that displays this data. The form contains a *DetailsView control,* which is a data-bound server control that creates a single-record display of database data.

To create the Web form with the DetailsView control:

1. Right-click the Web site root folder, click Add New Item, and select the Web Form template. Change the file name to DetailsView.aspx, and make sure that the

FIGURE 8-13   Web form with read-write single-record display

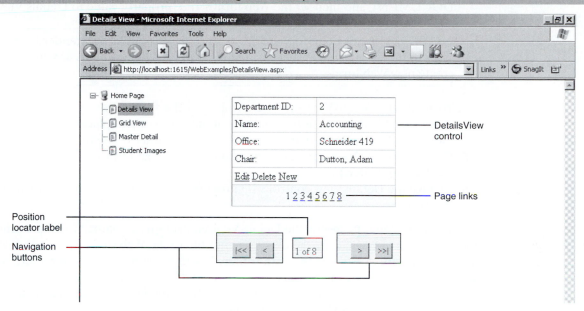

Place code in a separate file check box is checked. Check the Select master page check box, and then click Add.

HELP: If the Add New Item selection is not displayed, be sure that the browser window is closed and the application is not currently running.

2. In the Select a Master Page dialog box, make sure that the Web site root folder is selected in the Project folders list and that MasterPage.master is selected as the master page, and then click OK. The new content page appears in Design view, and displays a content placeholder control. The site map should appear on the top left corner of the form.

FIGURE 8-14   Single-record display opened for editing

⊟ 🖳 Home Page		
📄 Details View	**Department ID:**	2
📄 Grid View		
📄 Master Detail	**Name:**	Accounting
📄 Student Images	**Office:**	Schneider 419
	Chair:	Dutton, Adam ▼
	Update Cancel	
	1 2 3 4 5 6 7	
	|<< < 1 of 7 > >>|	

3. In the Properties window, make sure the top of the Properties window displays DOCUMENT, and then set the Web form's Title property value to Details View.

NOTE: From this point forward, we refer to these steps as the standard steps for creating a new Web form, and you will follow these steps as you create new Web forms.

---

4. To create the DetailsView server control, open the Toolbox, open the Data node, select the DetailsView control, and drag it onto the content placeholder area of the form. The new control appears in the top left corner of the form.
5. Drag the DetailsView control to the middle of the Web form. (You will fine-tune its placement later.)
6. Change the DetailsView control's ID property value to dvDepartment, then save the project.

The next step is to specify the DetailsView control's data source. If you are using a local database, you will copy the database .mdf file to the Web site's App_Data folder, and then specify this file as the data source. If you are connecting to a remote SQL server database, specify the connect string as you did in previous chapters. Then you will configure the data source to retrieve all the data from the UniversityDepartment table.

To specify the DetailsView control's data source:

1. *If you are connecting to a local SQL Server Express database,* copy *yourDatabaseName.mdf* from \SQLServer\Databases to SQLServer\Solutions\Chapter8\WebExamples\App_Data.

   If you are connecting to a remote SQL Server database, skip this step.

2. To configure the control's data source, click the Property tab on the top right corner of the control to open the control's Tasks list. Open the Choose Data Source list, and select New data source. The Data Source Configuration Wizard opens, and displays the Choose a Data Source Type page.
3. Select Database. In the *Specify an ID for the data source* field, type sdsDepartment, and then click OK. The *Choose Your Data Connection* page appears.
4. On the *Choose Your Data Connection* page, click New Connection. The Add Connection dialog box opens.
5. *If you are connecting to a local SQL Server Express database,* select Microsoft SQL Server Database File, click Continue, click Browse, navigate to \SQLServer\Solutions\Chapter8\WebExample\App_Data\, select *yourDatabaseName*.mdf, and then click Open.

   If you are connecting to a remote SQL Server database, select Microsoft SQL Server from the *Data source* list, click Continue, type or select your server name in the *Server name* field, select the authentication approach and if necessary, type the username and password that your instructor provides, select the *Select or enter a database name* option button, open the list, and select your database.
6. Click Test Connection. The Test connection succeeded message box should appear. Click OK, click OK again, and then click Next.

HELP: If an error message stating "No database file was specified" appears, click the Advanced button, select the AttachDbFilename property, click the Elipsis (. . .) button, and then select the .mdf file again. Click Open and then click OK, then test the connection again.

---

7. *If you are using either VB Express or VS 2005 and connecting to a local database,* the Save the connection string to the application configuration file page appears. Make sure that *Yes, save the connection as* is checked, then click Next.

8. In the *Configure the Select Statement* dialog box, select UniversityDepartment in the Name list, then check the DepartmentID, DepartmentName, DepartmentOffice, and DepartmentChairID check boxes.

9. To sort the data, click the ORDER BY button, open the Sort by list, and select DepartmentName. Make sure that the Ascending option button is selected, and then click OK.

10. To enable insert, update, and delete operations in the data source, click the Advanced button. Check the Generate INSERT, UPDATE, and DELETE statements check box, and then click OK.

11. Click Next, then click Test Query. The test query should retrieve all the table data.

12. Click Finish. The new sdsDepartment data source appears as a component on the Web form.

NOTE: From this point forward, we refer to steps 2 through 10 as the standard steps for creating a SQL data source, and you will follow them as you create new SQL data sources.

The next task is to configure the DetailsView control. The following steps show how to specify that it will support paging (navigation), as well as insert, update, and delete operations, and format the control by changing its format style. Then you will run the project and test the form.

To configure and format the DetailsView control and run the form:

1. Click the Property tab on the dvDepartment control to open the control's Tasks list. Check the Enable Paging, Enable Inserting, Enable Editing, and Enable Deleting check boxes.

HELP: If these check boxes do not appear, then you did not configure the SQL data source to support these operations. To correct this problem, edit the SQL data source by opening its Properties tab, selecting Configure Data Source, and repeating Steps 10-12 in the last set of steps.

---

2. Open the dvDepartment control's Tasks list, select Auto Format, select Autumn in the Select a scheme list, and then click OK.

3. Resize and reposition the DetailsView control so that it looks similar to Figure 8-13. (Your control does not yet display the navigation buttons.)

4. Run the project. The Web site's home page appears.

5. Select the Details View node on the site map to display the Details View Web page.

6. Click the page links at the bottom of the control to scroll through the records.

7. To update a record, select Page 2 (Chemistry). Click Edit to open the form for editing, change the office location to Phillips 221, then click Update. The Web form updates the record.

8. To add a record, click New. A new blank record appears. Type "Women's Studies" for the Department name, "Hibbard 620" for the Office Location, and "3" for the Chair ID value. Then click Insert.

9. To view your new record, select the last page link.

10. Close the browser window.

Creating a Pick List

Now you will create the pick list to display the Department Chair values. To display a field value as a pick list, modify the data source to retrieve the pick list values, then convert the field to a combo box that displays the retrieved values.

Modifying the SQL Data Source   The first step in adding a pick list to a Web form data-bound control is to modify the existing control's SQL data source query so that it displays the foreign key values of existing records, using the values that the user ultimately selects from the pick list. For the form in Figure 8-13, this requires joining the UniversityDepartment table with the UniversityInstructor table to display the department chair first and last names rather than the Chair ID values.

Why did we not join the tables and retrieve the foreign key values when we first created the control? When you create a SQL data source based on a single database table, the wizard automatically generates INSERT, UPDATE, and DELETE statements for the data source, then uses these statements to implement the control's insert, update, and delete operations. If you create a SQL data source that joins two or more tables, the wizard cannot generate the action queries, so the data source cannot support action query operations.

NOTE: You can create these action queries manually in a SQL data source, but this is complicated and error-prone. It is far easier to base the SQL data source on a single table and let the IDE create the action queries, then subsequently modify the SQL data source's SELECT query to display foreign key data values.

The following steps edit the data-bound control's data source so that its SELECT query retrieves instructor first and last names from the UniversityInstructor table and displays the names instead of the Chair ID values.

To edit the control's SQL data source:

1. In the DetailsView.aspx Web form in Design view, select the dvDepartment control, and click its Property tab to open its Tasks list.
2. Click Configure Data Source. The Configure Data Source wizard opens. On the *Choose Your Data Connection* page, click Next.
3. On the *Configure the select statement* page, select the Specify a custom SQL statement or stored procedure option button, and then click Next.
4. On the Define Custom Statements or Stored Procedures page, modify the SQL Statement so that it appears as follows:

```
SELECT   UniversityDepartment.DepartmentID,
         DepartmentName,  DepartmentOffice,
         DepartmentChairID,
         InstructorLastName  +  ',  '  +  InstructorFirstName
         As  DepartmentChair
FROM  UniversityDepartment
      INNER  JOIN  UniversityInstructor
      ON  UniversityDepartment.DepartmentChairID  =
         UniversityInstructor.InstructorID
ORDER  BY  UniversityDepartment.DepartmentName
```

5. Click the UPDATE tab, and note that the SQL query has not changed and still updates only the fields in the UniversityDepartment table. Repeat this step for the INSERT and DELETE tabs, and note that these queries still operate only on the UniversityDepartment table as well.

6. Click Next, and then click Test Query. If you typed the query correctly, the query data appears and now displays the Department Chair names.
7. Click Finish, and then click the Yes button to refresh the data source fields. Note that the control now displays the new DepartmentChair field as well as the DepartmentChairID field.
8. Open the dvDepartment control's Tasks list, and recheck the Paging, Inserting, Editing, and Deleting check boxes. (When you reconfigured the data source, the IDE cleared these boxes.)

NOTE: Repeat this step whenever the Insert, Edit, or Delete links no longer appear in a DetailsView control.

---

9. Run the project, confirm that the instructor names appear in the records, and then close the browser window.

HELP: If the data fields no longer appear in the DetailsView control, open the control's Tasks list, click Edit Fields, select each field in the Available fields list, and click Add to add the DepartmentID, Name, Office, ChairID, and Chair fields to the Selected fields list. Then click OK.

Modifying the Field Properties

The next step is to change the column headings. When you create a data-bound control in a Web form, all its fields are called *bound fields*. You can edit bound field properties by changing their headings, making them so that they do not appear on the form, and so forth. To edit bound field properties, use the Fields dialog box in Figure 8-15.

In the Fields dialog box, select the field you want to modify in the Selected fields list and modify the selected field's properties in the BoundField properties list. The following steps open the Fields dialog box, suppress displaying the DepartmentChairID field, and change the control's column headings.

To modify the field properties:

1. In the DetailsView.aspx Web form in Design view, select the dvDepartment control, click its Property tab to open its Tasks list, and then click Edit Fields. The Fields dialog box opens.
2. To suppress displaying the Department Chair ID value, select DepartmentChairID in the Selected fields list, and set its Visible property to False.
3. To modify the DepartmentID label, select DepartmentID in the Selected fields list, then change the HeaderText property value to Department ID:.
4. Repeat Step 3 to change the DepartmentName field's label to Name:, the DepartmentOffice field's label to Office:, and the DepartmentChair field's label to Chair:. Do *not* close the Fields dialog box yet.

Creating and Configuring the Pick List

This section describes how to modify the DetailsView control so that it displays the pick list showing department chair name values when the user inserts a new record or updates an existing record. To display a bound field as a pick list, you must convert the bound field to a template field. A *template field* has an associated HTML template, made of HTML form tags and elements, that the IDE places in the rendered version of the HTML document. This template specifies the field's appearance and enables you to display the field using a different type of control and to add validation controls for the field. A template field retains its original data binding. When you convert a field to

FIGURE 8-15   Fields dialog box

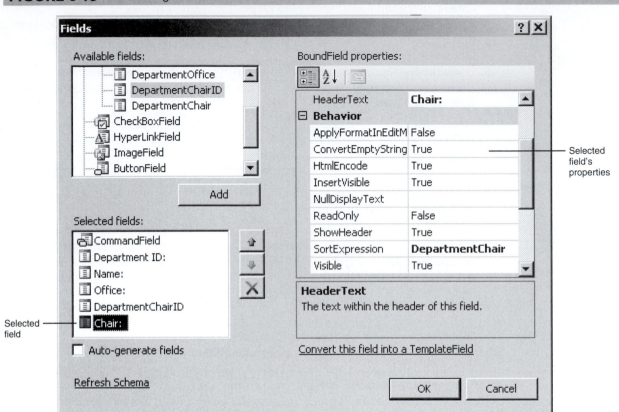

a template field, it is no longer a bound field, so its properties no longer appear in the BoundField properties list.

To convert a bound field into a template field, select the field in the Selected fields list, then click the *Convert this field into a TemplateField* link. The following steps show how to convert the DepartmentChair field to a template field.

To convert the DepartmentChair field to a template field:

1. In the Fields dialog box, select Chair: in the Selected fields list, then click the *Convert this field into a TemplateField* link.

CAUTION: After you convert a bound field to a template field, you cannot change it back.

---

2. Click OK to close the Fields dialog box. The Chair field no longer appears on the control.

To create the pick list that displays the Department Chair values, you must create a query to retrieve the data values that the pick list displays. The next steps show how to do this.

To create the pick list data source:

1. Open the Toolbox, scroll down to the Data section, and then drag a SqlDataSource from the Toolbox onto the ContentPlaceholder section on the Web form.

2. Change the ID property value of the new SqlDataSource control to sdsDepartmentChair.
3. Open the sdsDepartmentChair's Tasks list, and select Configure Data Source. The Data Source ConfigurationWizard opens.
4. On the *Choose Your Data Connection* page, open the connection string list, select yourDatabaseNameConnectionString, and then click Next.
5. On the *Configure the select statement* page, select the *Specify a custom SQL statement or stored procedure option* button, and then click Next.
6. On the *Define custom statements or stored procedures* page, type the following SQL SELECT command, and then click Next.

```
SELECT  InstructorID,  InstructorLastName  +  ',  '  +
        InstructorFirstName  as  DepartmentChair
FROM  UniversityInstructor
ORDER  BY  InstructorLastName,  InstructorFirstName
```

7. Click Test Query to confirm that the query retrieves the instructor ID and formatted name values, and then click Finish.

The next task is to open the Template Editor and configure the template field as a pick list. After you create a template field, specify its properties using the Template Editor, which Figure 8-16 illustrates.

FIGURE 8-16   Template Editor

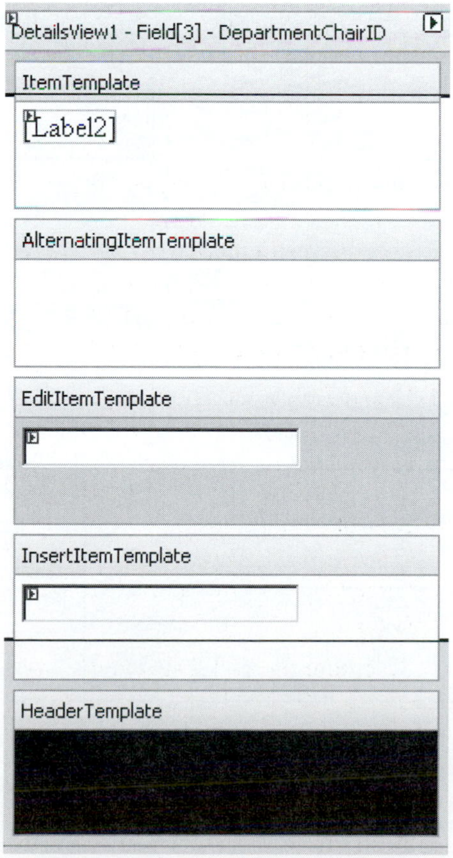

The Template Editor allows you to modify the contents and appearance of the following sections of a template field:

- **ItemTemplate** specifies the text and formatting for an existing field when the user is viewing the data.
- **AlternatingItemTemplate** applies only to a tabular display and specifies alternate text and formatting for every other field when a user is viewing the data.
- **EditItemTemplate** specifies the field's text and formatting when the user opens a record for editing.
- **InsertItemTemplate** specifies the field's text and formatting when the user inserts a new record.
- **HeaderTemplate** specifies the text and formatting that appear at the top of the field.

Figure 8-17 illustrates the steps for configuring the template field as a pick list. The DepartmentChair template field displays a pick list when the user opens the item for editing or inserts a new record. Therefore, delete the current contents in the EditItemTemplate and InsertItemTemplate sections, and replace their contents with a DropDownList control that displays the formatted DepartmentChair name values.

To configure the Department Chair value as a pick list:

1. To open the Template Editor and configure the new template field, open the dvDepartment control's Tasks list, then click Edit Templates. To display all the

FIGURE 8-17 Creating the pick list

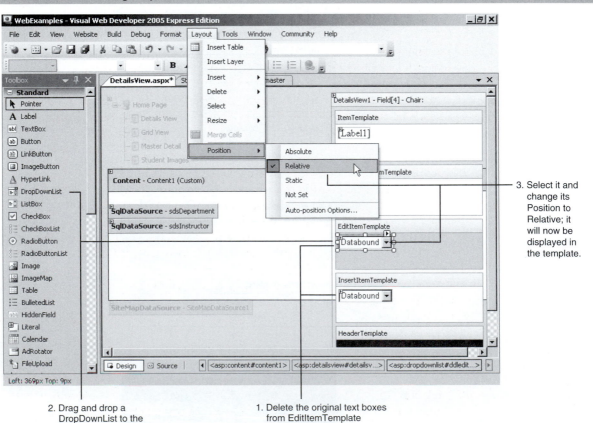

2. Drag and drop a DropDownList to the EditItemTemplate area.

1. Delete the original text boxes from EditItemTemplate and InsertItemTemplate.

3. Select it and change its Position to Relative; it will now be displayed in the template.

template sections, open the Display list, then select Field[4]—Department Chair. (Your field number may be different if you changed the order of the data fields.)

TIP: Another way to open the Template Editor is to right-click the control, point to Edit Template, and then click Field[4]—Department Chair.

---

2. Delete the text boxes from the InsertItemTemplate and EditItemTemplate sections.
3. Open the Toolbox, select the DropDownList control, then drag it from the Toolbox and drop it onto the EditItemTemplate area in the Template Editor. By default, the control appears in the top left corner of the template.
4. To fix its position in the EditItemTemplate, make sure that the new DropDownList control is selected, click Layout on the menu bar, point to Position, then click Relative. The list appears in the EditItemTemplate.
5. Change the DropDownList's ID property value to ddlEditChairNames.
6. Click the Property tab on the DropDownList control to open its Tasks list and select Choose Data Source. Open the *Select a data source* combo box and select sdsDepartmentChair. Open the *Select a data field to display* in the DropDownList and select DepartmentChair.
7. Confirm that InstructorID appears as the list selection in the *Select a data field for the value of the DropDownList,* then click OK.
8. To bind the DropDownList control's selected value to the data value that appears in the DetailsView control, click the Property tab on the DropDownList control and select Edit Databindings. Make sure SelectedValue is selected from the Bindable Properties list, open the Bound to list, and select DepartmentChairID from the list of available data values in the DetailsView control.
9. Click OK, and then save the project.

You have now created the pick list that will appear when the user opens the form for editing. You still need to create the pick list that will appear when the user inserts a new record. Rather than repeat all the steps, you can copy the existing DropDownList control in the EditItemTemplate, paste it into the InsertItemTemplate, and change the ID property of the pasted list control. Then run the project and test your pick lists.

To copy the list control to the InsertItemTemplate and then run the project:

1. In the Template Editor, select the DropDownList control.
2. Click Edit on the menu bar, and then click Copy.
3. Place the insertion point in the InsertItemTemplate, click Edit on the menu bar, and then click Paste. The newly copied DropDownList control appears in the upper left corner of the Template Editor.
4. To fix the new DropDownList control's position in the EditItemTemplate, make sure that the new DropDownList control is selected, click Layout on the menu bar, point to Position, and then click Relative.
5. Select the newly pasted DropDownList control, and change its ID property value to ddlInsertChairNames.
6. Click the Property tab on the Template Editor to open its Tasks list, and then click End Template Editing.
7. Run the project, select Details View on the site map, and then click Edit on the DetailsView control. Note that the Chair field now appears as a pick list. Click Cancel.
8. Click New to insert a new record and confirm that the Chair field appears as a pick list in this mode also. Click Cancel, and then close the browser window.

Validating User Inputs

Data validation confirms that the user enters data values with the correct data type, provides values for all fields with NOT NULL constraints, and enters valid primary and foreign key values. Currently, the Details View Web form validates some data: it does not allow the user to directly enter or edit the Department ID primary key, and it forces the user to select a valid Chair foreign key value using a pick list. However, it does not validate required fields or data types. The UniversityDepartment database table definition specifies that the DepartmentName and DepartmentChairID fields cannot be NULL and are limited to a maximum of 30 characters, so the form needs to validate these fields as well.

ASP.NET provides *validation controls,* which are server controls that you associate with template fields to restrict field input values. When you create a validation control, ASP.NET places commands in the rendered HTML document that call client-side JavaScript functions and validate the user inputs while the form is running.

ASP.NET validation controls include:

- **RequiredFieldValidator** determines whether a user entered any value.
- **RangeValidator** determines whether the input value is within a specific lower and/or upper bound.
- **CompareValidator** determines whether the input value matches one or more allowable values.

Validation controls typically display an error message directly on the form when the user enters an incorrect input. Figure 8-18 shows an example of a validation control error message that appears when the user tries to update a record and does not provide a value for the Office field.

Validation controls are associated with template fields. Therefore, bound fields have to be converted to template fields before you can create validation controls for them. The following steps show how to convert the DepartmentName and DepartmentOffice bound fields to template fields, and create a RequiredFieldValidator control for the DepartmentName field. You will validate that the user supplies a value both when inserting a new record and when editing an existing record, so you will create a validation control in both the EditItemTemplate and the InsertItemTemplate areas.

FIGURE 8-18   Validation control error message

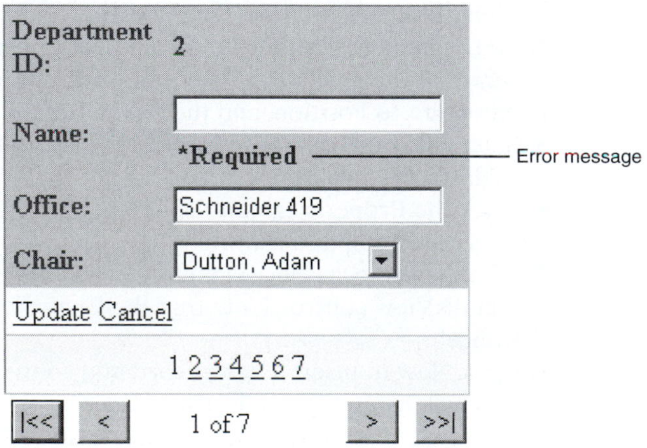

To convert the fields to template fields and add the RequiredDataValidator controls:

1. To convert the DepartmentName and DepartmentOffice fields to template fields, click the dvDepartment's Property tab to open its Tasks list, and then click Edit Fields to open the Fields dialog box.
2. Select Name from the Selected fields list, then click *Convert this field into a TemplateField*.
3. Repeat Step 2 for the Office field, and then click OK to close the Fields dialog box.
4. To open the DepartmentName template field in the Template Editor, right-click the dvDepartment control, point to Edit Template, and then click dvDepartment Field [1]—DepartmentName. (Your field number may be different.)
5. To create the RequiredFieldValidator control for the DepartmentName template field, open the Toolbox, open the Validation node, select the RequiredFieldValidator control, and drag it and drop it into the EditItemTemplate area. The control appears in the top left corner of the Template Editor.
6. With the RequiredFieldValidator control selected, click Layout on the menu bar, point to Position, and then click Relative. The control moves to the EditItemTemplate section.
7. Select the text box in the EditItemTemplate section, click Layout on the menu bar, point to Position, and then click Relative. Move the text box and validator control so that they appear as shown in Figure 8-18.
8. Set the validation control's ControlToValidate property value to TextBox1 and its ErrorMessage property value to *Required.
9. Repeat steps 5 through 8 for the InsertItemTemplate section.

To ensure that the user enters values with no more than 30 characters in the DepartmentName and DepartmentOffice fields, you will set the MaxLength property of these template fields to 30. Then you will run the project and test your validation controls.

To change the field MaxLength values and run the project:

1. With the DepartmentName template field still open in the Template Editor, select the text box in the EditItemTemplate area, press and hold Shift, and then select the text box in the InsertItemTemplate area. Selection handles should appear around both text boxes. Change the MaxLength property in the Properties window to 30.
2. Click the Template Editor Property tab to open its Tasks list, open the Display list, and select Field[2]—Office to open its template field in the Template Editor.
3. Repeat steps 1 and 2 for the DepartmentOffice template field.
4. Open the Template Editor Tasks list, then click End Template Editing.

HELP: If the Edit, New, and Delete links no longer appear in the DetailsView control, open the Tasks list and check the Enable Inserting, Enable Editing, and Enable Deleting check boxes.

---

5. Run the project and select the Details View link on the site map.
6. To test the RequiredFieldValidator control, click Edit to open the first record for editing, delete the Department Name value, and then click Update. The "*Required" error message should appear, as shown in Figure 8-18.
7. To test the MaxLength property constraint, try to type a value that is longer than 30 characters in the Department Name field. Note that you cannot type more than 30.
8. Click Cancel to cancel your changes, and then close the browser.

This Web form's data validation is not comprehensive. For example, if you attempt to delete a department with a child record in another table, a cryptic system error message appears stating that the operation failed. Fixing this problem requires additional coding, which we will address in a later section.

Creating Navigation Buttons

Currently users navigate through the data records using the page links at the bottom of the control. The next task is to add the navigation buttons shown in Figure 8-13, along with the position locator label that displays the current record number and total number of records.

To create the navigation buttons, you will add Button server controls to the form. To create the position locator label, you will add a Label server control.

To add the navigation buttons and position locator label:

1. With DetailsView.aspx open in Design view, open the Toolbox, open the Standard node, select the Button control, and drag and drop it onto the form. A button appears in the top left corner of the form.

2. Drag the button to the approximate position of the left-most button in Figure 8-13, and resize it as shown. (You will fine-tune its size and position later.) Then create three more button controls, and resize and reposition them as shown in Figure 8-13.

3. To ensure that the buttons have a uniform height and width, select the first button, press and hold Shift, and then select the remaining three buttons.

4. In the Properties window, change the Height property value of the button group to 25px and the Width property value to 30px.

5. To align the buttons, select all the buttons, click Format on the menu bar, point to Align, and then click Tops. Reposition the button group if necessary.

6. Moving from left to right, change the buttons' ID and Text property values as follows:

ID	*Text*
btnFirst	|<<
btnPrevious	<
btnNext	>
btnLast	>>|

7. To create the position locator label, select the Label control in the Toolbox and drop it onto the form. Resize and reposition it as shown in Figure 8-13.

8. Change the label's ID property value to lblPosition, and delete its Text property value.

Now you will create event handlers for the navigation buttons to allow the user to step through the records. The navigation button event handlers will use the DetailsView control's PageIndex and PageCount properties. The PageIndex property specifies the current page (record) appearing in the control, and the PageCount property specifies the total number of pages (records) that the control contains. Whenever the user clicks on one of the navigation button, the button's event handler changes the control's PageIndex property value to move to the desired record. The PageIndex value is zero-based; so the first record's index is zero, the second record's index is one, and so forth.

To create the navigation button event handlers:

1. With the DetailsView.aspx form open in Design view, double-click btnFirst. The code file opens and displays a new Click event handler declaration for the button.

2. Add the following command to the event handler, which sets the DetailsView control so that it displays the first record:

```
dvDepartment.PageIndex = 0
```

3. To create the event handler for btnPrevious, open the Objects list in the Code editor, and select btnPrevious. Then open the Declarations list, and select Click. Add the following command to the new event handler declaration, which sets the PageIndex property to the record just before the current record. If the control is currently on the first page, then the event handler does nothing.

```
If  dvDepartment.PageIndex > 0  Then
    dvDepartment.PageIndex -= 1
End If
```

4. Create a Click event handler for btnNext that contains the following commands. Note that if the control is currently on the last record, the event handler does nothing.

```
If  dvDepartment.PageIndex < dvDepartment.PageCount - 1  Then
    dvDepartment.PageIndex += 1
End If
```

5. Create a Click event handler for btnLast that has the following command, which sets the PageIndex property to the last record.

```
dvDepartment.PageIndex = dvDepartment.PageCount - 1
```

6. Save the project.

The final task is to create an event handler that updates the position locator label. You will associate this event handler with the DetailsView control's Databound event, which executes each time the control's page changes. The event handler will display the current PageIndex and PageCount property values in the label. Because the PageIndex value is zero-based, the event handler will add one to its value.

To create the event handler for the position locator label:

1. In the Code editor, select dvDepartment in the Objects list, and select DataBound in the Declarations list. The event handler declaration appears in the Code editor.
2. Add the following command to the event handler, which updates the position locator label's Text property whenever the user navigates to a new record:

```
lblPosition.Text = _
    CStr(dvDepartment.PageIndex + 1) & " of " & _
    dvDepartment.PageCount.ToString
```

3. Run the project and select Details View in the site map.
4. Test the navigation buttons to confirm that they scroll through the records and to make sure that the position locator label updates correctly. (You may need to move the buttons down on the Web form so they appear correctly when the user opens a record for editing.)
5. Close the browser window, and then close all open pages in the Document window. Do not close the IDE.

Read-Write Tabular Display

To create a tabular data display on a Web form, use an ASP.NET *GridView control*, which allows users to edit and delete record values. In this section, you will create the

FIGURE 8-19 Web form with read-write tabular data display

	LastName	FirstName	MI	Phone	UserID	Department
Edit	Adler	Diane	O	5558365960	adlerdo	Foreign Languages
Edit	Bakke	Judith	D	5558360089	bakkejd	Geology
Edit	Buck	Ted		5558362531	buckt	Management Information Systems
Edit	Downs	Anthony	K	5558362988	downsak	Accounting
Edit	Dutton	Adam	K	5558364522	duttonak	Accounting
Edit	Gardner	Nancy		5558364345	gardnern	Accounting
Edit	Harrison	Richard	P	5558364901	harrisrp	Chemistry
Edit	Hogstad	Lillian	S	5558366946	hogstadls	Management Information Systems
Edit	Luedke	Brian	L	5558362419	luedkebl	Accounting
Edit	Morrison	Lauren	J	5558362243	morrislj	Management Information Systems

1 <u>2</u>

form in Figure 8-19, which displays data from the UniversityInstructor and UniversityDepartment tables in a tabular display.

> **NOTE:** A GridView does not support adding new records. You will learn how to add new records to a tabular display later in the chapter.

A user can view the records and open a record for editing by clicking the Edit link on the left side of the record. Figure 8-20 shows the display of a record opened for editing. In this display, the data fields appear as text boxes and/or pick lists whose values the user can modify. When the user clicks Update, the control saves the changes and redisplays the form in Figure 8-19. The following subsections describe how to

FIGURE 8-20 Tabular data display opened for editing

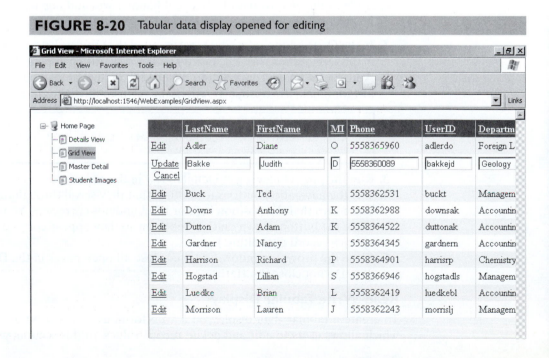

create a form with a GridView data-bound control, add a pick list to display foreign key values, and add validation controls.

Creating a GridView Control

The following steps show how to create a new Web form in your project, add a GridView control to the form, and configure its properties. Then they create an associated data source that retrieves data values from the UniversityInstructor table.

To create a new Web form and GridView control:

1. Follow the standard steps for creating a new Web form that were presented earlier in the chapter. Save the Web form as GridView.aspx, place the code in a separate file, and use the project's master page. Change the form's Title property value to Grid View.
2. To create the GridView control, open the Toolbox, open the Data node if necessary, select the GridView control, and then drag the control from the Toolbox onto the content area of the form. Resize and reposition the GridView control so that it looks approximately like Figure 8-19.
3. Change the control's ID property value to gvInstructor, open the HeaderStyle property node, and set the HeaderStyle's HorizontalAlign property to Left.
4. Click the Property tab on gvInstructor to open its Tasks list. Select Auto Format, select the Sand & Sky formatting scheme, and then click OK.
5. To create a data source for the control, open the Tasks list, open the Choose Data Source list, then click New Data Source.
6. Follow the standard steps for creating a new SQL data source outlined earlier in the chapter. Change the data source ID value to sdsInstructor, select the UniversityInstructor data table, and include all the table's fields. Order the data by InstructorLastName and then by InstructorFirstName. Be sure to click the Advanced button and generate the INSERT, UPDATE, and DELETE queries.
7. Run the project and click the Grid View node on the site map. Currently, the form displays data from the UniversityInstructor table only.
8. Close the browser window.

The next step is to modify the data source so that it joins the UniversityInstructor and UniversityDepartment tables to display the DepartmentName values. (Recall that you do not initially create join queries for read-write data-bound controls because this does not allow you to edit the control's contents.) After you modify the data source, you will format the control's column headings.

To modify the data source to retrieve the UniversityDepartment data and format the column headings:

1. If necessary, click the control's Property tab to open its Tasks list, then click Configure Data Source. Accept the current data connection value, and then click Next.
2. Select the *Specify a custom SQL statement or stored procedure option* button, and then click Next.
3. Type the following query in the SQL Statement field to join the UniversityDepartment and UniversityInstructor tables and to display the DepartmentName field:

```
SELECT  UniversityInstructor.InstructorID,
        InstructorFirstName,  InstructorMI,
        InstructorLastName,  InstructorPhoneNumber,
        InstructorUserID,
        UniversityInstructor.DepartmentID,  DepartmentName
```

```
FROM  UniversityInstructor
      INNER  JOIN  UniversityDepartment
      ON  UniversityInstructor.DepartmentID  =
          UniversityDepartment.DepartmentID
ORDER  BY  InstructorLastName,  InstructorFirstName
```

4. Click Next, click Test Query to confirm that you entered the query correctly, and then click Finish.
5. When the dialog box opens asking if you want to refresh the fields and keys, click Yes.
6. Open the control's Tasks list, and then check the Enable Paging, Enable Sorting, and Enable Editing check boxes. (Do not check the Enable Deleting and Enable Selection check boxes.)

HELP: If the field names and template values no longer appear in the control, open the Fields dialog box and add the fields back to the control.

---

7. To format the columns, open the control's Tasks list, and select Edit Columns to open the Fields dialog box. Select the InstructorID field and set its Visible property value to False, then select the DepartmentID field and set its Visible property value to False.
8. To change the order of the fields in the GridView control, select InstructorLastName, and then click the Up arrow two times so that it appears just before InstructorFirstName.
9. Change the HeaderText property for each visible field (all fields except InstructorID and DepartmentID) to match what appears in Figure 8-19.
10. Convert all visible fields into template fields, and then click OK to close the Fields dialog box.
11. Run the project and click Grid View on the site map. The Web form should look something like Figure 8-19. (You may need to resize the control.)
12. In Design view, resize and reposition the GridView control if necessary.

Creating a Pick List

Next, you will create the pick list that appears when the user opens the control for editing. You will follow the same steps you performed earlier to create the pick list in the DetailsView control: open the DepartmentName template field in the Template Editor and create a DropDownList control. Then you will create an associated SQL data source that retrieves the department name values.

To create the pick list:

1. Drag a SqlDataSource from the Toolbox onto the page. In its Tasks dialog (which is initially displayed after dropping it on the page), select Configure Data Source. The Data Source ConfigurationWizard opens.
2. On the *Choose Your Data Connection* page, open the connection string list, select yourDatabaseNameConnectionString, and then click Next.
3. On the *Configure the select statement* page, select the Specify a custom SQL statement or stored procedure option button, and then click Next.
4. On the *Define custom statements or stored procedures* page, type the following command in the SQL SELECT field, and then click Next.

```
SELECT  DepartmentID,  DepartmentName
FROM  UniversityDepartment
ORDER  BY  DepartmentName
```

5. Click Test Query to confirm that the query retrieves the DepartmentID and DepartmentName values, and then click Finish.

6. Change the ID property value of the new SqlDataSource to sdsDepartmentName.

7. To open the Template Editor and configure the new template field, click the GridView control's Property tab to open its Tasks list, and then click Edit Templates. To display all the template sections, open the Display list, and then select Field[8]—Department.

8. Delete the text box from the EditItemTemplate area.

9. Open the Toolbox, select the DropDownList control, then drag it and drop it onto the EditItemTemplate area in the Template Editor. Change its layout position to Relative so that the list appears in the EditItemTemplate area.

10. Select the DropDownList control, and set its ID property value to ddlDepartment and its Width property value to 230px.

11. Click the Property tab on the DropDownList control to open its Tasks list, then select Choose Data Source. The Data Source ConfigurationWizard opens. Open the *Select a data source* combo box and select sdsDepartmentName. Open the *Select a data field* to display in the DropDownList list, and select DepartmentName.

12. On the Choose Data Source page, open the *Select a data field* to display in the DropDownList list, and select DepartmentName.

13. Confirm that DepartmentID appears as the selection in the *Select a data field for the value of the DropDownList* list, and then click OK.

14. To bind the DropDownList control's selected value to the data value that appears in the DetailsView control, open the DropDownList control's Tasks list, and select Edit DataBindings. Make sure SelectedValue is selected from the Bindable Properties list, open the Bound to list, and select DepartmentID.

15. Click OK.

16. Open the Template Editor's Tasks list, and then click End Template Editing to close the Template Editor.

17. Run the project and click Grid View on the site map. Click Edit on the first displayed record to open it for editing, and open the Department pick list to confirm that it displays the department name values.

18. Click Cancel to close the record, and then close the browser window.

Resizing the Edit Columns and Adding Data Validation

The following steps show how to configure the data properties of the template fields to modify the field widths when the control is opened for editing and how to add validation controls to validate input values. Table 8-1 shows the fields in the GridView control, summarizes their data types and maximum lengths, and shows whether they are required.

TABLE 8-1 GridView column constraints

Field Name	Data Type	Max Length	Required
InstructorID	bigint		Yes (identity)
InstructorLastName	varchar	30	Yes
InstructorFirstName	varchar	30	Yes
InstructorMI	varchar	1	No
InstructorPhoneNumber	varchar	10	No
InstructorUserID	varchar	10	Yes

TIP: You can find the information in Table 8-1 by looking at the .sql script file that creates the databases and tables. Another way to view this information is to open the Database Explorer (View/Database Explorer), open the connection, tables, desired field, and then view its properties in the Properties window.

Now you will configure the template fields so that their MaxLength property values match their database table definitions. You will also modify the template field Width property values to resize the display widths when the fields are opened for editing. You will create the RequiredFieldValidator controls for the required fields, and you will create a RangeValidator control for the Phone field to confirm that the user enters a value that is a valid telephone number. Even though the database stores this value as a text (varchar) value, you will validate it as a number to ensure that the user enters a 10-digit number expression.

To configure the MaxLength and Width property values and create the validation controls:

1. Open the Last Name template field in the Template Editor, select the text box in the EditItemTemplate area, and set its MaxLength property value to 30 and its Width property value to 100px.
2. Repeat step 1 for the following template fields:

Template Field	MaxLength	Width Value
First Name	30	100px
MI	1	10px
Phone	10	90px
User ID	10	60px

3. Open the Last Name template field in the Template Editor, open the Toolbox, select the RequiredFieldValidator control, and drop it onto the EditItemTemplate area. Click Layout on the menu bar, point to Position, and then click Relative. Set its ControlToValidate property to TextBox1, and its ErrorMessage property to *Required. Place the control on the right edge of the text box.
4. Repeat Steps 3 and 4 for the following template fields:

Template Field	ControlToValidate	Message
First Name	TextBox2	*Required
User ID	TextBox5	*Required

NOTE: You should change the ControlToValidate value to the value that appears in the ControlToValidate list in the Properties window if it is different than the value shown.

---

5. To create the RangeValidator control for the Phone field, open the Phone template field in the Template Editor, open the Toolbox, select the RangeValidator control, and drag it onto the form and drop it onto the EditItemTemplate area of the Template Editor. Click Layout on the menu bar, point to Position, and then click Relative.

FIGURE 8-21 Initial GridView control with unaligned text boxes

	LastName	FirstName	MI	Phone
Edit	Adler	Diane	O	5558365960
Update Cancel	Bakke	Judith	D	5558360089
Edit	Buck	Ted		5558362531
Edit	Downs	Anthony	K	5558362988
Edit	Dutton	Adam	K	5558364522
Edit	Gardner	Nancy		5558364345
Edit	Harrison	Richard	P	5558364901

Unaligned text boxes →

6. Modify the RangeValidator control's property values as follows:

Property	New Value
ControlToValidate	TextBox4 (or whatever appears in the ControlToValidate list)
ErrorMessage	*Numbers Only
MaximumValue	9999999999
MinimumValue	1000000000
Type	Double

7. Change the text box's layout position to Relative, and then move the validation control so that it appear on the right edge of the text box.
8. Close the Template Editor.
9. Run the project, select Grid View on the site map, and then select Edit in the first record. Your initial result should show that a row opened for editing looks something like Figure 8-21. Note that the editing text boxes are not horizontally aligned.
10. Close the browser window.

Why did this happen? The problem is that the template fields leave space for the validation control error messages below the text boxes, even when the messages do not appear. Figure 8-22 shows how the GridView appears when the user enters illegal data

FIGURE 8-22 Error message positions

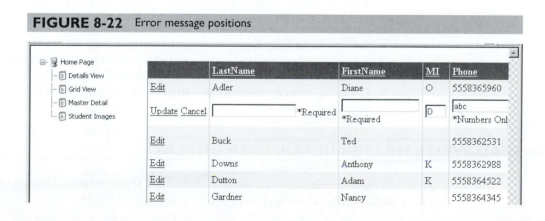

values and the validation control messages appear. Even though you carefully placed the validation messages on the right edge of the template field text boxes, they now appear below the text boxes. ASP.NET does not display validation control error messages in a consistent way.

To finish this form, you need to format the template fields so that the validation control messages always appear below the template field text boxes. You also need to format the fields that do not have validation controls so that they have space below them and align horizontally with the fields having validation controls. To do this, you will add a line break between each textbox and validation control. You will also place a line break after the items that do not have validation controls, which includes the column displaying the Edit link, along with the MI and Department columns. You must convert the first column in the control, which displays the Edit link, to a template field.

To add a line break to the template fields:

1. To convert the column that displays the Edit link to a template field, click the Property tab on the gvInstructor control to open its Tasks list, click Edit Columns, select Edit, Update, Cancel in the Selected fields list, and then click *Convert this field into a TemplateField*. Then click OK.
2. Right-click gvInstructor, point to Edit Template, and then select Column [0] to open the first GridView template field for editing. Place the insertion point between the Update and Cancel links in the EditItemTemplate area, and then press Enter to put a line break between the links and display them on two separate lines, with the Cancel link below the Update link.
3. Click the Property tab on the Template Editor, open the Display list, and select Column [2]—Last Name. Place the insertion point just after the text box in the EditItemTemplate area, and then press Enter to display the "*Required" error message on the line below the text box.

NOTE: For this technique to work correctly, the layout position of the text box must be Not Set and the layout position of the validation control must be Relative.

---

4. Repeat Step 3 for the First Name, Phone, and User ID template fields.
5. To add the blank line for the MI template field, which does not have a validation control, click the Property tab on the Template Editor, open the Display list, and select Column [4]—MI. Place the insertion point just after the text box in the EditItemTemplate area, press Enter, then press the Spacebar to add a blank space after the line break.

NOTE: If you enter a line break and do not place anything on it (we added a space), the IDE ignores it when rendering the HTML document.

---

6. Repeat step 5 for the Department template field, then click the Property tab on the Template Editor, and click End Template Editing.
7. Run the project, select Grid View on the site map, and then click Edit on the first record. The editing controls should now align horizontally.
8. Close the browser window, and then close all open pages in the IDE Document window.

READ-WRITE MASTER-DETAIL DATA DISPLAY

In this section, you will create a Web form that contains the read-write master-detail data display shown in Figure 8-23.

FIGURE 8-23 Read-write master-detail Web form

Master Detail - Microsoft Internet Explorer
File Edit View Favorites Tools Help
Back Search Favorites
Address http://localhost:1546/WebExamples/MasterDetail.aspx
Home Page
Details View
Grid View
Master Detail
Student Images
Select Department: Accounting
Add New Course
Name Title Credits
Edit Delete ACCT 201 Principles of Accounting 4
Edit Delete ACCT 312 Managerial Accounting 3
Edit Delete ACCT 315 Accounting Systems 3
Edit Delete ACCT 450 Accounting Seminar 3
Master records
Add New Course button
Detail records

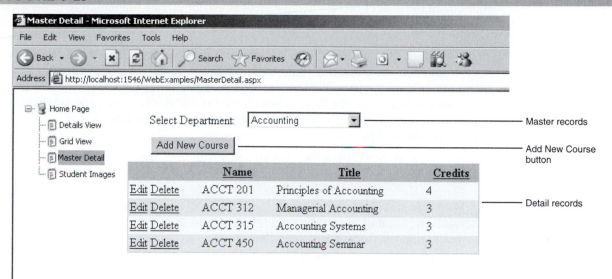

In this Web form, the user selects a department name from a list and the related courses that the department offers appear in a tabular display. When the user clicks Add New Course, the Web form in Figure 8-24 opens, which allows the user to add a new course for the selected department.

Creating the Web Form and Master List

The data configuration in Figure 8-23 poses a new challenge by displaying the master records in a list. Recall from Figure 8-6 how ASP.NET processes Web pages: the user enters inputs and performs events, which are ultimately posted to the Web server for processing. Some events, such as clicking a button, cause an immediate postback event. Other events, such as selecting a list item, accumulate and are processed when the form

FIGURE 8-24 Web form to add a new detail record

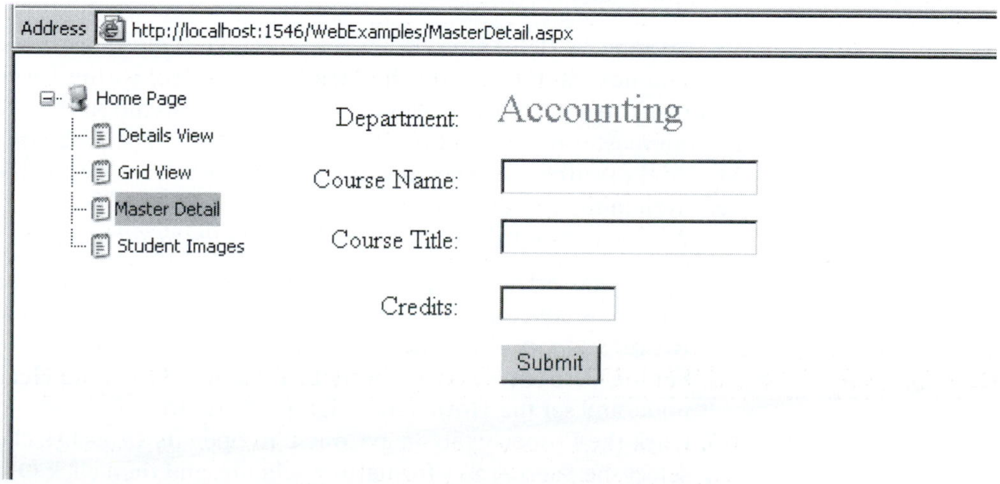

Address http://localhost:1546/WebExamples/MasterDetail.aspx
Home Page
Details View
Grid View
Master Detail
Student Images
Department: Accounting
Course Name:
Course Title:
Credits:
Submit

is ultimately posted back to the server. As a result, when the user selects a new department from the master list, the detail display does not update immediately.

One solution to this problem is to have the user select the department from the list, then click a Refresh button to trigger the postback event and refresh the data display. However, our goal is to have Web forms behave as much like Windows applications as possible, so that is not a satisfactory solution. Instead, we will force a postback event for the list by setting its AutoPostBack property set to True.

Now you will create the Web form with the list that displays the department values. You will set the list control's AutoPostBack property value to True.

To add the Web form and create the master list:

1. Follow the standard steps for creating a new Web form that were presented earlier in the chapter. Save the Web form as MasterDetail.aspx, place the code in a separate file, and use the project's master page. Change the form's Title property value to Master Detail. Configure the form to use absolute positioning for new form controls.
2. Open the Toolbox, select the Label control, and drag it and drop it onto the content area of the form. Change its Text property to Select Department:, and resize and reposition it as shown in Figure 8-23.
3. Open the Toolbox, select the DropDownList control, and drag it and drop it onto the content area of the form. Set its ID property to ddlDepartment, and resize and reposition it as shown in Figure 8-23.
4. Click the Property tab on ddlDepartment to open its Tasks list, click Choose Data Source, and follow the standard steps for creating a new SQL data source. Name the new data source sdsDepartment, specify its table as UniversityDepartment, select the DepartmentID and DepartmentName columns as the data sources, and order the values by DepartmentName. Do not specify to generate the INSERT, UPDATE, and DELETE statements. Set the Display field value to DepartmentName and the Value field to DepartmentID.
5. If necessary, click the ddlDepartment Property tab to open the Tasks list, and check the Enable AutoPostBack check box.

   TIP: Another way to set the AutoPostBack property to True is to select the control in Design view, and then set its AutoPostBack property to True in the Properties window.

6. Run the project, click Master Detail in the site map, and confirm that the list displays the department names.
7. Close the browser window.

Creating the Detail GridView

The next step is to add the GridView control to the form to display the detail records. You will create a GridView control as you did in the previous section. To create the master-detail relationship, you will create a search condition in the control's SQL data source that specifies the GridView's DepartmentID value as the current selection in the form's list control.

To create the GridView control to display the detail records:

1. In the MasterDetail.aspx form in Design view, open the Toolbox, select the GridView control, and drag it and drop it onto the content area of the form. Resize and reposition the control as shown in Figure 8-23.
2. Set the GridView's ID property to gvCourse. Open the HeaderStyle property node, and set the HorizontalAlign property to Left.
3. Click the Property tab on gvCourse to open its Tasks list, click Auto Format, select the Sand & Sky formatting scheme, and then click OK.

4. On the gvCourse's Tasks list, open the Choose Data Source list, then select Add New Data Source. Select Database as the data source, type sdsCourse as the data source name, and then click OK.

5. Select yourDatabaseNameConnectionString as the connection string, select UniversityCourse as the table name, and include all its fields.

6. To specify the master-detail relationship between the master list and detail GridView control, click WHERE. The Add WHERE clause dialog box opens.

7. Open the Column list, which specifies the search condition column in the GridView control, and select DepartmentID.

8. Open the Operator list and select =.

9. Open the Source list, which specifies the search condition value, and select Control. This specifies that the search condition comes from a control on the form.

10. Open the ControlID list, and select ddlDepartment.

11. Click Add, and then click OK.

12. On *the Configure the SQL Statement* page, click ORDER BY, open the Sort by list, select CourseName, and then click OK.

13. On the *Configure the SQL Statement* page, click Advanced, check the *Generate INSERT, UPDATE, and DELETE statements* check box, click OK, click Next, and then click Finish.

HELP: If you click the Test Query button, you will see a dialog box allowing you to enter the value for the department id that is supplied from the pick list when the form runs.

---

14. In the dgCourses Tasks list, check the Enable Sorting, Enable Editing, and Enable Deleting check boxes.

15. Run the project, and select Master Detail on the site map. Select different departments in the list, and confirm that the GridView control correctly displays the selected detail records.

16. Close the browser window.

Now you will format the GridView. You will hide the CourseID and DepartmentID column values, and modify the column headings. Then you will run the project and check the formatting.

To format the GridView and run the project:

1. If necessary, click the dgCourse Property tab to open its Tasks list, and then click Edit Columns.

2. Set the CourseID and DepartmentID fields' Visible property to False.

3. Modify the HeaderText property of the following fields:

Field	HeaderText
CourseID	Course ID
CourseName	Name
CourseTitle	Title
CourseCredits	Credits.

4. Run the project, select Master Detail in the site map, and confirm that the master and detail records display correctly.

5. Close the browser window, and modify the GridView control's size and position if needed.

When you create a GridView control that displays detail records in a master-detail relationship, its UPDATE query attempts to update the master record field. Before you can use the GridView to update records, you must modify the UPDATE query by deleting this part of the query. You will do this next, then run the form and confirm that it updates the existing course records correctly.

To modify the UPDATE query and test the form:

1. If necessary, select the gvCourse Property tab to open its Tasks menu, click Configure Data Source, and then click Next.
2. On the Configure the Select Statement page, select the *Specify a custom SQL statement or stored procedure option* button, click Next, click the UPDATE tab, and then modify the query by removing the reference to the DepartmentID field so that the query appears as follows:

```
UPDATE   [UniversityCourse]
SET   [CourseName]   =   @CourseName,
      [CourseTitle]  =   @CourseTitle,
      [CourseCredits]  =   @CourseCredits
WHERE   [CourseID]   =   @CourseID
```

3. Click Next, click Next again, and then click Finish.
4. Run the project, select Master Detail on the site map, click the Edit link on the first course record, change the Credits value to 4, and then click Update. The record should update successfully.
5. Close the browser.

Creating a Form to Insert New Detail Records

A GridView control does not allow users to insert new records. To enable users to insert new detail records, you will create the Add New Course button shown in Figure 8-23 and an associated event handler that displays the form in Figure 8-24, which lets the user to add a new course for the selected department.

This requires learning how to call a second form from the current form. It also requires passing a variable value to the second form, because the selected Department ID value is a foreign key in the new course record.

To display a second Web form from the current form, use the following general syntax:

```
Server.Transfer("NewWebFormName.aspx")
```

To display a second HTML file (not a Web form .aspx file) from the current form, use a different command:

```
Response.Redirect("NewHTMLDocument.htm")
```

You can use Response.Redirect to display a Web form .aspx file, but to improve system performance, you should always use Server.Transfer with .aspx files. Response.Redirect is slower because it does not immediately send a page to a browser. Instead, it sends a message to the browser asking it to send a request back to the Web server for the new page.

Different approaches exist for passing data values from one Web page to another. One approach is to create a *session variable,* which is a variable that the server (not the browser) stores as long as a new page or postback from the browser is received within a specific time interval, typically 20 minutes. Web sites sometimes use session variables to store information that is not required for very long, such as information about the contents of a user's shopping cart. A drawback of using session variables is that if users are distracted and do not request a new page or postback in 20 minutes, they lose their selections.

Another approach is to create a *cookie,* which can contain multiple data values. Cookies can be *temporary,* lasting until the user closes the browser, or *persistent,* that is, available whenever the user connects to the Web site that creates the cookie, even after closing and reopening the browser. Temporary cookies reside in the client's main memory, and persistent cookies are stored in the client's file system. The only Web site that can access a cookie is the Web site that originally creates the cookie. Web sites often use cookies to maintain information over extended periods of time, such as user names and passwords to enter a Web site or shopping or search preferences.

In this book, we use temporary cookies to pass data values between Web forms, because they are more versatile and persistent than session variables. The general syntax to create a temporary cookie is:

```
Response.Cookies("CookieName").Value  =  "CookieValue"
```

The general syntax to retrieve the value of an existing cookie is:

```
Request.Cookies("CookieName")
```

Now you will create the AddCourse Web form in Figure 8-25.

FIGURE 8-25   AddCourse.aspx Web form controls

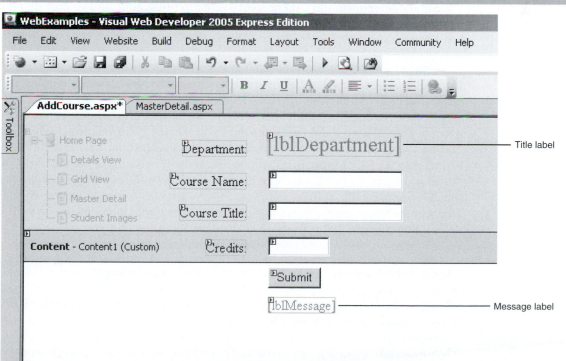

This form contains text boxes that correspond to the UniversityCourse table fields and uses a Button control that contains program commands to create the required data components and execute the INSERT query. It also contains a Title label to display the currently selected department and a Message label to display system messages.

To create the AddCourse Web form:

1. Follow the standard steps for creating a new Web form. Save the Web form as AddCourse.aspx, place the event handler code in a separate file, and use the project's master page. Change the form's Title property value to Add New Course.
2. Create the text boxes, button, and label controls shown in Figure 8-25. (The department name, such as "Accounting," appears in the Title label control that automatically displays the selected department name when the form runs.) Be sure to use absolute positioning for all form controls.
3. To configure Title label, change its ID property to lblDepartment, ForeColor to a green shade, and delete its Text value. Open its Font property node, open the Size list, and select X-Large.
4. To configure the Message label, change its ID property to lblMessage, the ForeColor to a green shade, and Visible to True, and then delete its Text value.
5. Modify the Text property of the labels as shown in Figure 8-24.
6. Modify the text box properties as follows:

Text Box	*ID Value*	*MaxLength Value*
Course Name	txtName	10
Course Title	txtTitle	200
Credits	txtCredits	1

7. Set the Submit button's ID property value to btnSubmit, and change its Text property to Submit.
8. Save the project.

The following steps add the Add New Course button to the MasterDetail.aspx Web form. The button's event handler creates cookies to store the selected department's DepartmentID value, which the form uses in its INSERT query, and the DepartmentName value, which appears at the top of the AddCourse.aspx Web form. The event handler also contains the command to display the AddCourse.aspx Web form.

The AddCourse.aspx Web form contains the declaration for a Private variable to represent the DepartmentID value. You will also add commands to the AddCourse.aspx form's Load event handler to retrieve the cookie values and to assign the DepartmentID cookie value to the variable, as well as to display the DepartmentName cookie value and display it in the Title label. Then you will run the project and confirm that the new form displays correctly.

To create the button and commands to display the detail form:

1. Click the MasterDetail.aspx tab in the Document window to display the master form in Design view.
2. Open the Toolbox, select the Button control, and then drag it from the Toolbox and drop it onto the master form's content area. Set the button's layout position to Relative.
3. Set the button's ID property value to btnAddCourse and its Text property value to Add New Course. Resize and reposition the button as necessary so that your form looks like Figure 8-23.

4. Double click the new button to open the form's code file and create a Click event handler declaration. Add the following commands to the declaration:

```
'Create the cookies storing the selected department values
Response.Cookies("DepartmentID").Value = ddlDepartment.Text
Response.Cookies("DepartmentName").Value = _
                    ddlDepartment.SelectedItem.Text
'Display the new form
Server.Transfer("AddCourse.aspx")
```

5. Click the AddCourse.aspx tab in the Document window to display the Web form in Design view. Double-click in any empty area of the form to open the form's code file and create a form Load event handler declaration.

TIP: Another way to create a form Load event handler declaration is to open the code file, select Page Events in the Objects list, and then select Load in the Events list.

---

6. Add the following highlighted commands to the code file:

```
Partial Class AddCourse
  Inherits System.Web.UI.Page
  Private intDepartmentID As Integer
  Protected Sub Page_Load(...
    lblDepartment.Text = Request.Cookies("DepartmentName").Value
    intDepartmentID = CInt(Request.Cookies("DepartmentID").Value)
  End Sub
End Class
```

7. Run the project, and select Master Detail in the site map.
8. Click Add New Course. The AddCourse.aspx Web form should appear and display "Accounting" in the Title label.
9. Close the browser window.

To complete the form, you need to create an event handler for the Submit button to insert the record in the database. Using the same VB commands you learned in Chapter 6, you will create a connection and its associated objects and insert a record. Then you will specify the SQL command as a parameter query and bind the parameters to the form control values.

To create the event handler to insert the record:

1. Select the AddCourse.aspx tab in the Document window to view the Web form in Design view, and then double-click the Submit button to create a Click event handler declaration.
2. Add the following commands to insert the record:

NOTE: If you are connecting to a remote SQL Server database, you need to modify your connection string.

```
'Declare the data components
Dim cnCourse As New Data.SqlClient.SqlConnection
Dim sqlCommand As New Data.SqlClient.SqlCommand
'Create the connection string
cnCourse.ConnectionString = "Data Source=.\SQLEXPRESS;" & _
    "AttachDbFilename=|DataDirectory|\yourDatabaseName.mdf;" & _
    "Integrated Security=True;User Instance=True"
```

```
'Assign the command to the connection
sqlCommand.Connection = cnCourse
'Create the SQL Command object as a parameter query
sqlCommand.CommandText = _
  "INSERT INTO UniversityCourse " & _
  "(CourseName, CourseTitle, CourseCredits, DepartmentID) " & _
  "VALUES(@CourseName, @CourseTitle, @CourseCredits, " & _
      "@DepartmentID)"
'Associate the parameters with form controls
sqlCommand.Parameters.Add(New Data.SqlClient.SqlParameter _
                    ("CourseName", txtName.Text))
sqlCommand.Parameters.Add(New Data.SqlClient.SqlParameter _
                    ("CourseTitle", txtTitle.Text))
sqlCommand.Parameters.Add(New Data.SqlClient.SqlParameter _
                    ("CourseCredits", txtCredits.Text))
sqlCommand.Parameters.Add(New Data.SqlClient.SqlParameter _
                    ("DepartmentID", intDepartmentID))
Try
  'Open the connection
  cnCourse.Open()
  'Execute the query
  sqlCommand.ExecuteNonQuery()
  'Display the confirmation message label
  lblMessage.Text = "Added " & txtName.Text
  'Reset the form controls
  txtName.Text = ""
  txtTitle.Text = ""
  txtCredits.Text = ""
Catch ex As Exception
  lblMessage.Text = ex.Message
Finally
  'Close the connection
  cnCourse.Close()
End Try
```

3. Run the project, click Master Detail on the site map, and then click Add New Course.
4. Type "ACCT 315" in the Name field, "Accounting Systems" in the Title field, and "3" in the Credits field, and then click Submit. The Message label should appear and confirm that the record was added.
5. Click Master Detail on the site map. The new record should now appear in the GridView.
6. Close the browser window.

Preventing Users from Deleting Master Records

Referential integrity constraints prevent users from deleting a master record that has related detail records. For example, in the form in Figure 8-24, if the user clicks the Delete link for ACCT 201, an error page appears because ACCT 201 has associated course sections in the UniversitySection table.

To prevent users from seeing a cryptic system-generated error page when trying to delete a master record with related detail records, you will create an event handler for the GridView control's RowDeleting event that executes when the user clicks the Delete link. This event handler cancels the delete operation, then tries to delete the record programmatically. If the deletion fails, the event handler displays a more appropriate message. You will also create a label on the MasterDetail.aspx Web form to display a message if the deletion fails.

To create an event handler to prevent users from deleting master records:

1. Select the MasterDetail.aspx tab to open the Web form in Design view.

2. Open the Toolbox, select the Label control, and drag it and drop it onto the form content area. Change its layout position to Relative, then move the label so that it appears on the right edge of the Department Name list. Change the label's ID property to lblMessage and its ForeColor property to a green shade, and then delete its Text property value.

3. Select the MasterDetail.aspx.vb tab to open the form's code file.

4. To create the RowDeleting event handler, select gvCourse in the Objects list, and select RowDeleting in the Events list. The event handler declaration appears in the Code editor.

5. Add the following commands to create the event handler. Change the connection string as necessary for your database connection.

```
'Cancel the deletion
e.Cancel = True
'Declare the data components
Dim cnCourse As New Data.SqlClient.SqlConnection
Dim sqlCommand As New Data.SqlClient.SqlCommand
'Create the connection string
cnCourse.ConnectionString = "Data Source=.\SQLEXPRESS;" & _
  "AttachDbFilename=|DataDirectory|\yourDatabaseName.mdf;" & _
  "Integrated Security=True;User Instance=True"
sqlCommand.Connection = cnCourse
'Create the SQL command as a parameter query
sqlCommand.CommandText = _
  "DELETE FROM UniversityCourse WHERE CourseID = CourseID"
'Assign the parameter value to the query
sqlCommand.Parameters.Add (New Data.SqlClient.SqlParameter _
                    ("CourseID", e.Keys("CourseID")))
Try
  'Open the connection and execute the query
  cnCourse.Open()
  sqlCommand.ExecuteNonQuery()
Catch ex As Exception
  'display the error message in the label
  lblMessage.Text = "Delete failed because " & _
                  e.Values("CourseName").ToString & _
                  " has sections assigned to it"
  lblMessage.Visible = True
Finally
  cnCourse.Close()
End Try
'Refresh the GridView
gvCourse.DataBind()
```

6. Run the project, and then click Master Detail on the site map.

7. Click the Delete link for ACCT 201. The error message should appear because the course has associated sections.

8. Close the browser window, then close all open pages in the IDE Document window.

DISPLAYING IMAGES

Web pages provide an good way to display and distribute image data. This section describes how to create the Web form in Figure 8-26, which displays student images.

This Web form is a read-only single-record display that uses a DetailsView control to allow users to scroll through student records and display student images. The following steps create the new form and the DetailsView control to display the form items.

FIGURE 8-26   Web form with image data

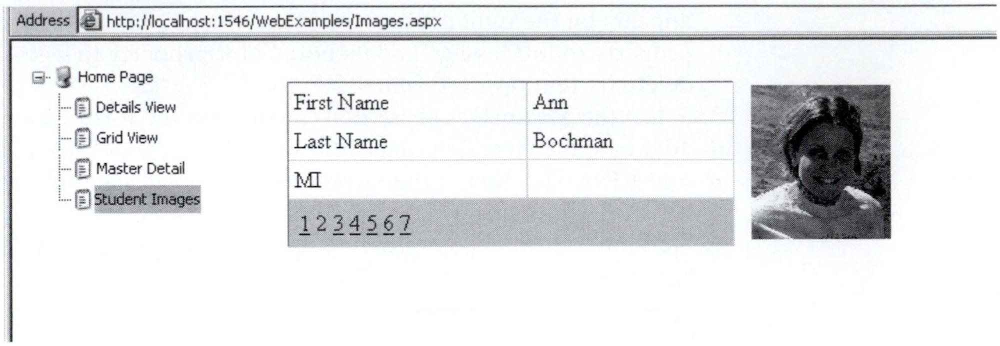

Photo courtesy of the authors.

To create the form and DetailsView control:

1. Follow the standard steps for creating a new Web form. Save the Web form as Images.aspx, place the code in a separate file, and use the project's master page. Change the form's Title property value to Student Images.
2. Open the Toolbox, select the DetailsView control, drag it from the Toolbox, and drop it onto the form's content area. Set the control's ID property value to dvStudent, and resize and reposition the control so that it looks approximately like Figure 8-26.
3. To create the control's SQL data source, follow the standard steps for creating a new SQL data source. Change the data source ID to sdsStudent, use your project's existing data connection, use the UniversityStudent table as the data source's data table, and select the StudentFirstName, StudentLastName, StudentMI, and StudentImageFile data fields. Order the records by StudentLastName and then by StudentFirstName.
4. Save the project.

Now you will format the control's fields. You will change the field labels, and specify not to display the image file name. (You will create the control to display the image later.)

To format the columns:

1. In Images.aspx in Design view, select dvStudent, open its Tasks list, and then click Edit Fields.
2. Select the StudentImageFile field, and change its Visible property to False.
3. Change the field HeaderText values as shown in Figure 8-26, and then click OK.
4. In the Tasks list, check the Enable Paging box to enable users to navigate through the control's records.
5. In the Tasks list, click Auto Format, select the Oceanica formatting scheme, and then click OK.
6. Save the project.

To display the image, you will create an Image control, which is a server control that displays an image from an image file. To reference the file name value to load the image, you will use the DetailsView control's DataKeyNames property. DataKeyNames creates a collection data structure that allows you to reference the values of individual bound fields in a control using the following syntax:

```
ControlName.DataKey.Values(IndexValue)
```

The *IndexValue* specifies the field's position in the collection. Because the StudentImageFilename is the only field in the record's collection, this value is zero when you assign the file name to the image.

Now you will create the Image control to display the student image. You will also create an event handler that you associate with the DetailsView control's DataBound event. (Recall that the DataBound event fires whenever the user navigates to a new record.) This event handler will set the Image control's URLLocation property using the DataKeyNames collection to specify the image file name.

To create the control and event handler to display the image:

1. With the Images.aspx Web form displayed in Design view, open the Toolbox, select the Image control, and drag it from the Toolbox and drop it onto the form's content area.

2. Change the image's ID property to imgStudent, and resize and reposition it as shown in Figure 8-26.

3. To create the DataKeyNames collection, select dvStudents, select DataKeyNames in the Properties window, and then click the Elipsis (. . .) button. The DataFieldsCollection Editor dialog box opens.

4. To add the StudentImageFile bound field to the collection, select StudentImageFile from the Available data fields list, and then click the Add button, which appears as a right-pointing arrow, to move it to the Selected data fields list. Then click OK.

5. To create the event handler declaration, select Images.aspx in the Solution Explorer and then click View Code to open the form's code file. Open the Objects list and select dvStudent, then open the Declarations list and select DataBound. The event handler declaration appears in the Code editor.

6. Add the following command to load the image file into the image control:

```
imgStudent.ImageUrl  =  "images\"  &  _
                        dvStudent.DataKey.Values(0).ToString
```

7. Run the project, and then click Student Images in the site map. Click the page numbers to scroll through students view the associated images.

8. Close the browser window, and then close the IDE.

IN CONCLUSION . . .

This chapter provides an overview of how to create Web-based database applications using ASP.NET. ASP.NET provides an excellent environment for creating and testing these applications, making them seem more similar to Windows applications than other Web-based applications. The main difference between creating Windows database applications and Web-based ASP.NET applications lies in the differences in data-bound controls and how data appears to the user. In a production environment, you need to be concerned with system response time and how the pages appear in browsers other than Internet Explorer. Factors that affect response times include the frequency of posting back to the Web server for event handling, the speed of the network, the speeds of the Web and database servers, and other advanced tuning options that are beyond the scope of a single chapter.

SUMMARY

- A Web-based database application runs on a Web browser on the client's workstation and accesses Web pages and/or database data from a remote server.
- In a Web-database architecture, the database server process usually runs on a separate server from the Web server because distributing the database and Web server processes across multiple servers improves system performance.
- ASP.NET is the .NET technology that supports development of Web-based applications. ASP.NET Web pages, called Web forms, contain server controls such as buttons and text boxes that allow the user to interact with the application.
- In ASP.NET Web page processing, users interact with Web forms by entering values or performing actions that cause event handlers to execute. Certain events cause the browser to post the Web form back to the server for processing, whereby the server processes all the accumulated event handlers along with the user inputs and then renders a new HTML document based on the event handler results.
- ASP.NET stores a Web page's HTML code and server controls in the Web form file, which has an .aspx extension, and its event handler code in the Web form's code file, which has an .aspx.vb extension.
- An ASP.NET Web site consists of multiple Web forms with similar security requirements. A Web site has a root folder containing all the site's files and an App_Data folder, which stores its database file.

- A Web site's master page contains items that appear on all the site's Web pages and that link to the pages, along with a site map displaying nodes that allow users to navigate to different pages.
- ASP.NET data-bound controls support complex data binding using SQL data sources or object data sources. You must create a new SQL data source for every data-bound control.
- You create single-record data displays using DetailsView controls and tabular data displays using GridView controls. Individual fields in a data-bound control are called bound fields.
- To create a pick list or validation control for a bound field, you must convert the bound field to a template field, which has associated HTML tags to enhance its appearance.
- A validation control validates user inputs for its associated template field and displays an appropriate error message when an input is invalid. You can create validation controls to check if users enter values for required fields, if the values fall within a specific range of values, or if the value matches one or more legal values.
- To create a master-detail data display, you configure the detail control's SELECT query so that it uses the master value as a search condition.
- To insert new detail values in a master-detail display, you must display a new form that uses program commands to insert the value.

KEY TERMS

Absolute positioning   Specifying a Web form item's position by dragging it to an exact location

Attribute   Value that modifies an HTML tag

Bound field   Field in a data-bound control

Client-side script   Program commands that the browser executes to perform calculations or data validation

Code file   File that stores the VB commands for a Web form's event handlers

Communication protocol   Agreement between a sender and a receiver that specifies how they will format, send, and receive data

Content page   Page that links to a master page and displays specific Web form content

Default document   Web page that a Web server returns when a browser request does not specify a Web page filename

Domain name   Human-friendly name that references a numeric IP address

Dynamic Web page   Web page that the server creates based on user inputs

Heading section   HTML document section containing the Web page title and special tags that instruct the browser how to display the document

HTML document   Text file with an .htm or .html extension that contains text and embedded HTML tags

HTML form   Enhanced HTML document containing controls such as text boxes and buttons that allow users to enter inputs and interact with the Web page

HyperText Markup Language (HTML)   Standardized notation for specifying the appearance and content of Web pages

HyperText Transfer Protocol (HTTP)   Communication protocol that works with and on top of IP, coordinates the messages between a browser and Web server, and determines how the Web server sends text and images to browsers

Input   Control on an HTML form

Internet Protocol (IP)   Primary communication protocol used on the Internet

IP port table   Table that a server maintains to associate port numbers and server process memory locations

Local loopback address   IP address 127.0.0.1, which references the local workstation

Master page   Template containing items that appear on forms in a Web site

Network   Communication path between a sender and a receiver

Object data source   ASP.NET data source that is defined in a custom class

Persistent cookie   Variable that a browser stores in a file

Port   Value that references a server process using a number between zero and 65,535

Post   Action that occurs when a browser sends an ASP.NET Web form back to the Web server for processing

Postback processing   ASP.NET processing approach whereby the user repeatedly interacts with a Web form and posts it back to the Web server

Relative positioning   Specifying a Web form item's position by placing it in a container object

Root folder   Folder that contains all the files for an ASP.NET Web site

Server control   ASP.NET control that allows a user to interact with a Web form

Server-side program   Program that runs on the Web server and processes HTML form inputs

Session variable   Variable that a browser stores for a specific time interval

SQL data source   Control that specifies a data connection and SQL queries to retrieve, insert, update, and delete data items

Static Web page   Web page whose content is fixed at design time

Tag   Formatting code that encloses a Web page element and instructs the browser how to process or display the element

Template field   Field that has associated HTML tags and elements to specify the field's appearance and behavior

Temporary cookie   Variable that a browser stores as long as a user is connected to a Web site

Uniform Resource Locator (URL)   Address that specifies a communication protocol, Web server IP address or domain name, and optional folder path and Web page filename

Validation control   ASP.NET server control that you associate with a template field to restrict input values

ViewState input   HTML form input that stores all the current values for form's controls

Virtual directory   Name that references a folder that can be located anywhere in a Web server's file system

Web browser   Client application that requests Web pages

Web form   ASP.NET Web page that consists of server controls and HTML tags and text

Web server   Computer running special Web server software that services client requests for Web pages

Web site   ASP.NET application that contains one or more Web forms with similar security requirements

Web site map   Tree structure that shows the layout of the Web site's forms and that allows users to navigate to different forms

World Wide Web (WWW)   Network of server and client computers that share information

STUDY QUESTIONS

Multiple-Choice Questions

1. When you place items in an area on the Template Editor, you use _____ positioning.
   a. Absolute
   b. Relative
   c. Fixed
   d. Static

2. _____ is a page layout language that specifies the contents and format of Web pages.
   a. HTML
   b. HTTP
   c. URL
   d. IP

3. To create a tabular data display, you use an ASP.NET _____ control.
   a. DetailsGrid
   b. DataGridView
   c. GridView
   d. DataGrid

4. A(n) _____ associates IP addresses and human-friendly Web site names.
   a. Port table
   b. ISP
   c. Local loopback address
   d. Domain name server

5. A Web form code file contains:
   a. HTML tags
   b. Server control tags
   c. VB event handler commands
   d. All of the above

6. In an ASP.NET Web site, you usually place the site map on the:
   a. Master page
   b. Detail page
   c. Site Map page
   d. Default document

7. You associate validation controls with:
   a. Template fields
   b. Bound fields
   c. HTML inputs
   d. Data-bound controls

8. A(n) _____ is an agreement between a sender and a receiver regarding how data will be formatted, sent, and received.
   a. URL
   b. Port
   c. Protocol
   d. Network

True/False Questions

1. You should always place the site map TreeView control on the master page's content placeholder.
2. Whenever a browser initially connects to a Web server, the server always returns its default document.
3. As ASP.NET Web site automatically creates an Images subfolder to store Web site images.
4. You cannot use an ASP.NET GridView control to insert new data records.
5. An ASP.NET Web form that uses postback processing is an example of a dynamic Web page.

Short Answer Questions

1. Describe the relationship between IP and HTTP.
2. List the three components of a URL.
3. When do you need to specify a port number in a URL?
4. List and describe the sections of an HTML document.
5. Discuss why ASP.NET Web forms do not post back to the Web server for every form event.
6. Why should you place a SQL Server database file in a Web site's App_Data folder?
7. Describe two situations in which you need to convert a bound field to a template field.
8. Describe the differences between a SQL data source and an object data source, and explain when you would use each data source type.
9. How do you create a master-detail relationship between data-bound controls on a Web form?

Guided Exercises

All the following exercises use the Sport Motors database, which Figures 3-2 and 3-4 illustrate.

1. **Creating a Web Site with a Master Page and Site Map**
   This exercise creates a Web site that stores the solutions for all the chapter's guided exercises. Figure 8-27 illustrates the Web site's home page.
   a. Create a new Web site, and specify its root folder as \SQLServer\Solutions\Chapter8\WebExercises.
   b. Create a master page that displays the site map shown in Figure 8-27. Specify the Web form .aspx filenames to be the same as the site map titles. (For example, the filename for the Employees node will be Employees.aspx.)
   c. Create a TreeView control on the master page that displays the site map.
   d. Delete the current Default.aspx Web page.
   e. Copy the Images folder and its contents from the \SQLServer\Datafiles\Chapter8 folder to your Web site root folder.
   f. Create a new Web form as a content page that links to the master page, then add the items to the home page, as shown in Figure 8-27. Specify the new Web form as the site's Start page. Use motox1.jpg as the image source.

2. **Creating a Read-Write Tabular Display**

   NOTE: This exercise assumes that you have completed Exercise 8-1.

   This exercise creates the Web form in Figure 8-28, which is a read-write tabular display that shows the values in the Sport Motors Suppliers table.
   a. Create a new Web form named Suppliers.aspx. Link the form to the master page you created in Exercise 8-1, and change the form's Title to Sport Suppliers.

FIGURE 8-27   Web site home page (Exercise 8-1)

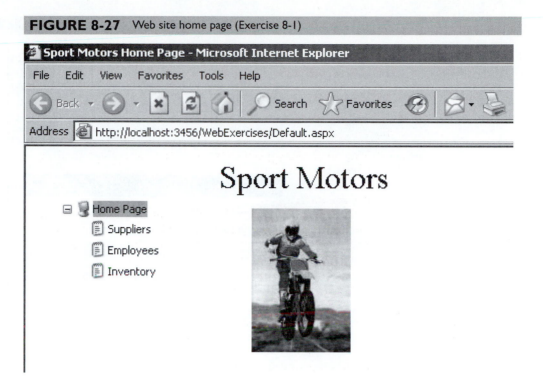

b. Create a GridView control to display the data records. Format the control using the Oceanica formatting scheme.

c. Create a SQL data source for the control that displays all the SportSupplier fields and that orders the fields by SupplierName.

d. Format the columns and column headings as shown in Figures 8-28 and 8-29, and change the column order as shown.

e. Create a pick list for the State field that displays the StateAbbreviation values from the StateAbbreviation table. Order the values by state abbreviation.

f. Create a validation control for the SupplierName field, which has a NOT NULL constraint. Format the GridView so that it appears as shown in Figure 8-30 when the user opens it for editing.

FIGURE 8-28   Left Side of Sport Motors Suppliers Web form (Exercise 8-2)

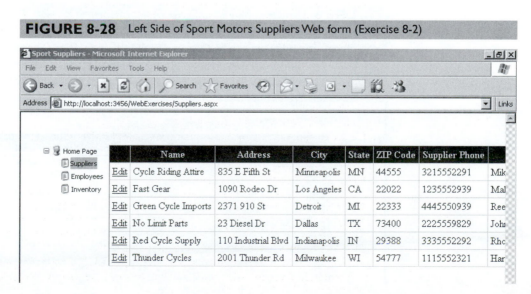

FIGURE 8-29   Right Side of Sport Motors Suppliers Web form (Exercise 8-2)

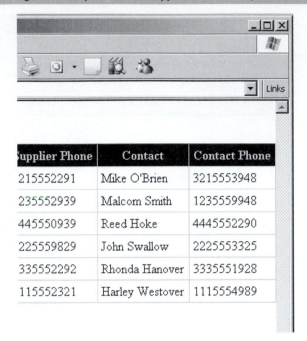

3. **Creating a Read-Write Single-Record Display with an Image**

NOTE: This exercise assumes that you have completed Exercise 8-1.

This exercise creates the Web form in Figure 8-31, which is a read-write single-record display that shows the values in the Sport Motors Employees table and displays employee images.
a. Create a new Web form named Employees.aspx. Link the form to the master page you created in Exercise 8-1, and change the form's Title to Sport Employees.
b. Create a DetailsView control to display the data records. Format the control using the Oceanica formatting scheme.

FIGURE 8-30   Sport Motors Suppliers Web form opened for editing (Exercise 8-2)

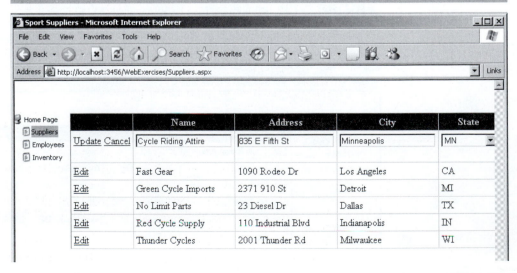

FIGURE 8-31   Sport Motors Employees Web form (Exercise 8-3)

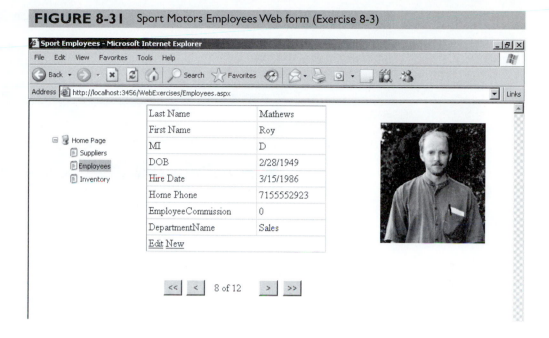

c. Create a SQL data source for the control that displays all the SportEmployee fields and orders the fields by EmployeeLastName.

d. Create a pick list for the DepartmentID field that allows the user to select from the DepartmentName values when inserting or updating records. (Be sure to modify the DetailsView control's SQL data source accordingly.)

e. Format the columns and column headings as shown in Figure 8-31, and change the column order as shown. To format the dates as shown, set the bound fields' DataFormatString property value to {0:d}. [Hint: To format a date column, convert the field to a template field, select Edit Templates, select ItemTemplate (and later repeat the following for AlternatingItemTemplate), select the label in the template, open its Tasks Dialog, select Edit DataBindings, and then add the following type of custom formatting expression: Bind("EmployeeDOB", "{0:d}").]

f. Create navigation buttons and a position locator label on the form as shown.

g. Create an Image control that displays the employee's image, based on the value of the EmployeeImageFilename field. (All the employees do not have associated image files.)

h. Create validation controls for EmployeeLastName and EmployeeCommission fields that have NOT NULL constraints.

i. Create a range validation control for the EmployeeCommission field to ensure that the input value is not greater than 0.05, and not less than 0. (Hint: Set the Type property of the validation control to Double.)

4. **Creating a Read-Write Master-Detail Display**

NOTE: This exercise assumes that you have completed Exercise 8-1.

This exercise creates the Web form in Figure 8-32, which is a read-write master-detail display that shows the different merchandise categories in a list, then displays the category's associated inventory items.

When the user clicks Add New Inventory Item, the Web form in Figure 8-33 appears, which shows a DetailsView control that is bound to the SportInventory table, and allows the user to insert new inventory items.

a. Create a new Web form named Inventory.aspx. Link the form to the master page you created in Exercise 8-1, and change the form's Title to Sport Inventory.

FIGURE 8-32 Merchandise categories master-detail form (Exercise 8-4)

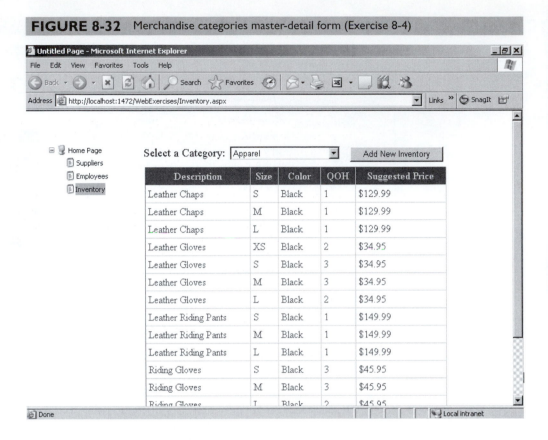

FIGURE 8-33 Add New Inventory form (Exercise 8-4)

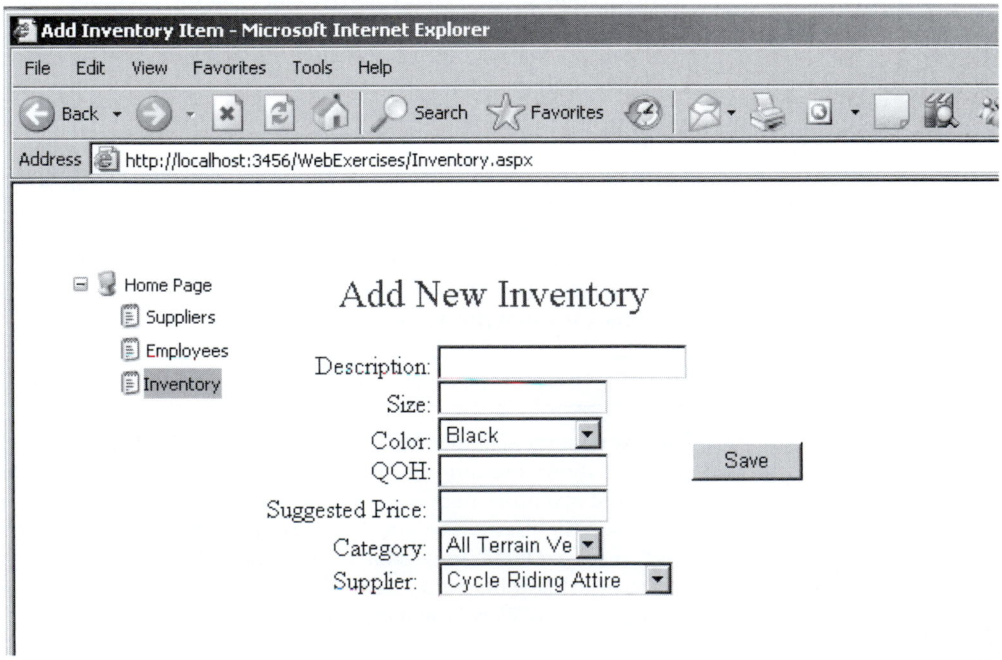

b. Create the label and DropDownList control to display the CategoryDescription values. (Be sure to include the CategoryID value in the control's SQL data source.) Configure the list so that the detail records refresh as soon as the user selects a list item.

c. Create a GridView control to display SportInventory items in the selected category. Configure the GridView control as read-only, and Autoformat the control using the Oceanica formatting scheme. Format the column headings as shown. [Hint: To format the Suggested Price column, convert the field to a template field, and then edit the template field label's DataBindings using the following custom formatting expression: Bind("InventorySuggestedPrice", "{0:c}"). If needed, review the hint in guided exercise 3's step e for more detail on how to do this.]

d. Create a new Web form named AddInventory.aspx. Link the form to the site's master page, and change its Title property value to Add New Inventory.

e. Create the text boxes, labels, drop-down list, and button controls shown in Figure 8-33. Configure the Color list to display all the fields from the SportColor table, the Category list to display all the CategoryDescription values, and the Supplier list to display supplier names. Sort all list values alphabetically. (The Category list does not need to display the current category selection on the master-detail form.)

f. Create an event handler for the Save button that contains VB program commands to insert the new inventory record into the SportInventory table, and an event handler for the Return button to redisplay the Sport Inventory form.

g. Create a label on the Add Inventory form that displays a confirmation message if the record is successfully inserted or the system error message if the insert operation fails.

h. Create the Add New Inventory Item button on the Sport Inventory form, and add the event handler commands to display the Add Inventory form.

CHAPTER 9

Using XML in Database Applications

Learning Objectives

At the conclusion of this chapter, you will be able to:

■ describe what XML is and how it assists database developers;

■ understand the logical and physical structure of an XML document and create an XML document;

■ write SQL queries that return XML-formatted data;

■ use XSLTs to transform XML documents into different formats;

■ use schema definitions to validate XML files;

■ process XML files using schema definition files;

■ create XML Web services and programs that access them.

eXtensible Markup Language (XML) is a markup language that uses tags and attributes to structure data. XML allows developers to create custom tags that define data items and their relationships. The original intent of XML was to "mark up" text data using these custom tags. It was quickly realized, however, that *XML documents,* which are XML-formatted text files, provide a standard way to share data across applications and hardware and software platforms. In addition, XML documents are often used to store configuration settings for programs and development environments like Visual Studio 2005.

This chapter introduces XML and explains how to create XML documents manually. It then shows how to retrieve XML-formatted data using SQL queries, as well as how to generate and use XML in .NET database applications. It also describes how to create Web services, which are processes that run on Web servers and use standard protocols to return XML-formatted information to applications.

NOTE: This chapter uses Management Studio to execute SQL queries, and Visual Studio 2005 (VS 2005) or Visual Web Developer (VWD) to create XML programs. You can write equivalent XML programs using VB Express, but it does not work as well because VB Express does not include the XML Editor, which provides color encoding and automatic tag completion.

NOTE: You can use either VWD or VS 2005 to create Web services; however, it is easier to write and test programs that connect to Web services using VS 2005. If you use VWD, you need to use VB Express to create the program, and you need to have the Internet Information Services (IIS) Web server installed and running on your local computer to test the program. IIS is included with the Windows XP Professional installation disk but is not automatically installed.

INTRODUCTION TO XML

A *markup language* is a language that uses tags or other symbols that are embedded in a document and define how the document content appears or acts. HTML is a markup language that uses embedded tags to control the appearance and behavior of Web pages.

The *Standard Generalized Markup Language (SGML)* is a high-level language for defining markup languages that was developed several decades ago. Early developers used SGML's *document type definitions (DTDs)* to define standard formatting notations. For example, the DTD for HTML specifies that characters enclosed in <b> tags appear in a boldface font and that <form> tags enclose HTML form input elements. XML is a subset of SGML that defines structured data using markup language notation. *Structured data* is data that is defined in a specific and unambiguous format, such as the data that a relational database table stores. As with HTML, XML uses tags and attributes. However, while the HTML standard specifies the exact meaning of each tag and attribute, XML allows developers to create custom tags that define data items and relationships.

You can use SGML to create DTDs to define custom tags that specify data formats and rules. So why do we need XML? SGML is complicated and requires a lot of training to use. XML contains the SGML features needed to define structured data and provides these features in a more straightforward way than SGML.

You can use XML documents to store relational database data in text files. You can then share the files with other systems that do not know anything about your relational database, but do understand XML. This is useful for creating database applications that share data either across multiple organizations or across different hardware and/or software platforms.

The following subsections illustrate the structure of XML documents, describe the XML Path language, and show how to use Visual Web Developer to create an XML document.

XML Document Structure

NOTE: In 1998, the World Wide Web Consortium (W3C) defined the XHTML 1.0 standard, which governs standards for the structure and tag syntax of XML documents. XHTML extends HTML using XML elements and guidelines. A major difference between the XHTML and HTML standards are that XHTML requires every opening tag to have a corresponding closing tag, and requires the use of specific tags to define document protocols and sections. In addition, all XHTML attributes must be enclosed by quotation marks while HTML allows omitting these, and XHTML is case-sensitive (like XML). In this book, our code examples follow the XHTML 1.0 standard.

The first tag in an XML document defines the *prolog,* which specifies that the document is an XML document, and provides information about the document. According to the official W3C XML specification, every XML document must have a prolog. However, if the document omits the prolog, most current XML processors assume default prolog values and process the document correctly. So for the time being, the prolog is really an optional element.

The prolog has the following requirements:

- It can be omitted.
- If present, it must be the very first tag in the document.

- It can contain a version declaration, a document type declaration, and comments and processing instructions.

The general format of the default prolog tag that Visual Studio 2005 adds to new XML documents is:

```
<?xml version="VersionNumber"encoding="EncodingScheme" ?>
```

The prolog tag specification is enclosed in question marks (?), and begins with the *xml* keyword. The *VersionNumber* attribute specifies that the document was created using XML Version 1.0, and the *EncodingScheme* attribute specifies the character set encoding scheme that the document uses. The default encoding scheme value is "utf-8," which defines the ASCII character set.

TIP: The ASCII character set is a table of numeric values that correspond to the letters of the alphabet, numbers, tabs, and other values used in text files.

An example prolog specification is:

```
<?xml version="1.0" encoding="utf-8" ?>
```

The tags that follow the prolog define the XML document's data structure and actual data values. Data in an XML document has a hierarchical structure, with a root node, branches, and leaf nodes. Individual data items in an XML document are called *elements*. Most elements have hierarchical relationships in which one parent element has multiple related child elements. XML documents must be *well-formed documents,* which specify that every opening tag must have an associated closing tag, the tags must be in the correct position, and every tag must appear in angle brackets. XML tags are case sensitive, so every instance of a tag must be identical throughout an XML document, and opening and closing tags must use identical formats in terms of upper- and lowercase letters.

NOTE: The latest XHTML standard specifies that all element and attribute names in an XML document appear in lowercase letters.

Figure 9-1 shows a hierarchical representation of some of the data in the Ironwood University database. The top element is universitystudents. The individual student data elements, which are named universitystudent, appear next and contain each student's first and last name. Recall that each student may enroll in many class sections. For example, student Clifford Wall has associated coursesection data, with associated sectionid elements with values of 1 and 10. (For the sake of simplicity, this diagram omits the rest of the student and enrollment data.)

How do you translate this structure into an XML document? The first step is to define the *root element,* which is a custom tag that defines the top or parent data element in the data tree. The root element is also called the *document element*. Every XML document must have a single root element, and the root element tags must enclose all other elements.

FIGURE 9-1   Hierarchical data structure

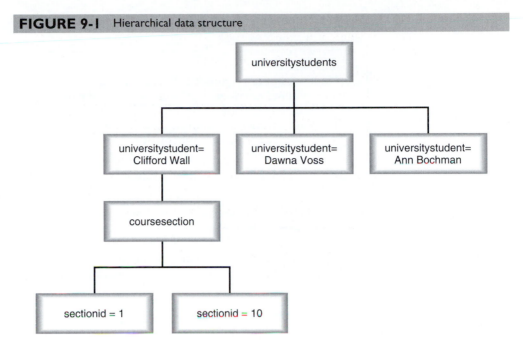

Elements under the root element are called *child elements*. Child elements can contain additional child elements, character data values, or a combination of child elements and character data values, or they can be empty.

For the data in Figure 9-1, the root element is universitystudents. The root element contains three child elements, one for each node in the tree in Figure 9-1. Each child element is named universitystudent (singular, not plural). The universitystudent child elements for students Dawna Voss and Ann Bochman contain only character data, which consists of the student's first and last names. The universitystudent child element for Clifford Wall contains both character data and a child element named coursesection. This child element contains two data elements that represent the sections in which Clifford has enrolled, and contain character data representing the sectionid values. These child elements, like any other child elements, can contain further child elements, additional character data, or a combination of both, or they can be empty.

You can use XML to represent the data relationships in Figure 9-1 by creating custom tags. An XML document encloses all the data in the root element tag, which we will name `<universitystudents>`. The student child elements are enclosed in custom tags named `<universitystudent>`, and the sectionid child elements are enclosed in custom tags named `<coursesection>`. To provide more structure to the data, you would probably enclose individual character data elements such as student names in tags that correspond to field name descriptors, such as `<studentfirstname>` and `<studentlastname>`.

Figure 9-2 shows the XML tags and values that represent this data. Note that the nesting order of elements defines the structure of the document data. The root element (`<universitystudents>`) tag is the highest-level element. The `<universitystudent>` tag defines the next level, and the `<coursesection>` tag defines the lowest level.

XML Path Language

The *XML Path Language (XPATH)* is a W3C standard that provides a way to identify components and locate nodes in an XML document. XPATH is also a programming

FIGURE 9-2 XML tags and values

```
<universitystudents>                                    ─── Root element
  <universitystudent>
    <studentfirstname>Clifford</studentfirstname>
    <studentlastname>Wall</studentlastname>
    <coursesection>
      <sectionid>1</sectionid>
      <sectionid>10</sectionid>
    </coursesection>
  </universitystudent>
  <universitystudent>                                   ─── Child elements
    <studentfirstname>Dawna</studentfirstname>
    <studentlastname>Voss</studentlastname>
  </universitystudent>
  <universitystudent>
    <studentfirstname>Ann</studentfirstname>
    <studentlastname>Bochman</studentlastname>
  </universitystudent>
</universitystudents>
```

language that provides functions for working with number, string, and Boolean data values. XPATH views an XML document as a logical tree that contains a series of nodes. The following XML document illustrates different types of XML nodes:

```
<?xml version="1.0" encoding="utf-8" ?>
<inventory xlmns=
  "http://www.sportmotors.biz/inventory">
  <!-- Define clothing element -->
  <item category="clothing">
    <inventorydescription>Leather Gloves</inventorydescription>
    <inventorysize>L</inventorysize>
    <color>Black</color>
    <?getSupplier SELECT * FROM Supplier
                 WHERE SupplierID=3?>
  </item>
</inventory>
```

XPATH defines the following node categories. (Note that a single node might fall into multiple categories.)

- **Root.** The root node is the topmost node and the parent of all other nodes. In this document, `<inventory>` specifies the root node.
- **Element.** Element nodes define data elements using opening and closing tags. The root node is also considered an element node.
- **Attribute.** An attribute node defines a name/value data pair in an element node. Attribute nodes provide an alternate way to specify data values in an element node. The `<item category="clothing">` node includes an element node (`<item>`), as well as an attribute node (`category="clothing"`).
- **Text.** Text nodes define character data contained within opening and closing element tags. Example text nodes include `<inventorydescription>`, `<inventorysize>`, and `<color>`. Note that you can also use attribute nodes to specify data values.

- **Namespace.** A namespace node distinguishes XML elements with the same name but different meanings. The example namespace node, specified by `xlmns="http://www.sportmotors.biz/inventory"` identifies the element's source location. In this example, a uniform resource identifier (URI) specifies the namespace. You can use any text as a URI, but most organizations use their registered domain name and a specific path. The path does not have to actually exist on the organization's Web server, but it must provide a unique identifier for the XML element. It may be necessary to specify a namespace when different organizations develop XML documents and define custom tags with the same name. For example, one company might create an XML element called `<customerid>` that stores customer ID values in the format `<customerid> 137-42-3499</customerid>`, and a second company might develop an element with the same name but store the values in the format `<customerid> 137423499</customerid>`. A developer working to link these systems has to be able to distinguish between the two elements to process them correctly. Aside from formatting, the first company might be storing totally different values, such as customer social security numbers, while the second company might be storing randomly assigned ID values. This could make a difference in how the data is processed because social security numbers must have higher security standards than a randomly generated ID values.

- **Processing instruction.** A processing instruction node contains processing instructions. For example, the processing instruction node (`<?getSupplier SELECT * FROM Supplier WHERE SupplierID=3?>`) specifies a SQL query for retrieving the document data. Processing instructions are uncommon but allow developers to enter instructions that are passed to the application processing the document.

- **Comment.** A comment node provides internal documentation in the file. In the example file, `<!--Define clothing element-->` specifies a comment node.

Creating XML Documents

You can create XML documents using any text editor. This book uses the Visual Studio XML Editor, which automatically inserts the prolog when a new XML document is created, uses color encoding to make errors easier to find and correct, and automatically inserts closing tags.

NOTE: The XML Editor is included in VS 2005 and in Visual Web Developer Express but is not included in VB Express.

The following steps show how to create a new XML document and how to add the tags and data to specify the XML data in Figure 9-2.

To create a new XML document:

1. Start VS 2005 or VWD Express. Click File on the menu bar, and then click New File. The New File dialog box opens.
2. Select General in the left window pane and the XML File template in the right window pane, and then click Open. A new XML file appears in the Document window in the XML Editor and displays the default prolog tag.
3. Place the insertion point on the line below the prolog tag, and add the commands in Figure 9-2 to create the universitystudents data structure. Notice that after you type an opening tag, the XML Editor automatically inserts the corresponding closing tag.

4. To save the file, click the Save XMLFile1.xml button on the toolbar, navigate to your \SQLServer\Solutions\Chapter9 folder, change the file name to Students.xml, and then click Save.

When you view an XML file in the Internet Explorer Web browser, it displays the elements as data nodes, as shown in Figure 9-3. The browser provides a hierarchical view of the data. If you enable blocked content, you can close data nodes to hide data and open a node to view its underlying elements. The following steps show how to open Students.xml in Internet Explorer and display its data structure.

To display the XML file in Internet Explorer:

1. Start Internet Explorer, click File on the menu bar, click Open, click Browse, and then navigate to the \SQLServer\Solutions\Chapter9 folder.
2. Open the Files of type list, select All Files, select Students.xml, click Open, and then click OK. The XML file appears as shown in Figure 9-3.
3. Open and close different nodes to view the data's structure.

HELP: Your browser's security settings might not allow you to open and close XML data nodes. If a security warning message appears, click the message, and then click Allow Blocked Content.

---

4. Close the browser window.
5. Close all open pages in the IDE Document window.

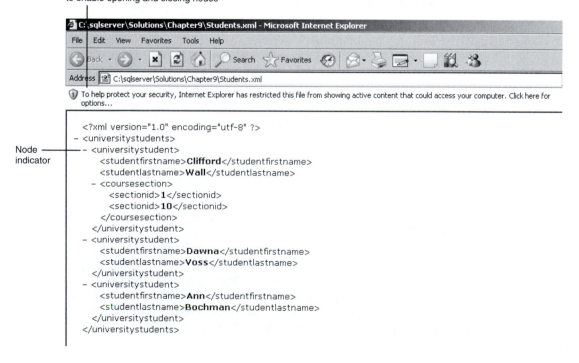

FIGURE 9-3   Browser display of XML file

CREATING SQL SERVER QUERIES TO RETRIEVE XML-FORMATTED DATA

You can create SQL Server 2005 SELECT queries to instruct the DBMS to return retrieved data values in XML format. SQL Server then encloses, or "wraps," each returned row in an element node and wraps each data value in a subnode. If needed, this XML-formatted data can then be shared across different applications and hardware and software platforms.

> **NOTE:** SQL Server does not add a prolog or enclose the element nodes in a root node, so the returned values do not represent a complete XML document.

To create a SELECT query that retrieves data values in XML format, use the following general syntax:

```
SELECT Query
FOR XML Mode[, ELEMENTS]
```

In this syntax, *SELECT Query* represents any SQL SELECT query, including joins, nested queries, set operations, and so forth. The ending FOR XML clause tells SQL Server to wrap the returned data in XML tags. *Mode* specifies how the DBMS wraps the data and can have the following values: *RAW,* which returns each row as a single XML element node, with the data stored as attribute node values in each row's element node; *AUTO,* which wraps each returned row in an element node and hierarchically nests child nodes under parent element node as text nodes based on a multitable query's JOIN condition; and *EXPLICIT,* which allows the data to be retrieved in a combination of attribute and text nodes. The ELEMENTS option formats data as text nodes rather than attribute values. The following subsections describe the XML outputs using different modes and options.

FOR XML RAW

The FOR XML RAW mode returns data in a single XML element and stores the data as attribute node values. The following query retrieves Ironwood University departments and their associated courses using FOR XML RAW:

```
SELECT DepartmentName, CourseName
FROM UniversityDepartment
INNER JOIN UniversityCourse
ON UniversityDepartment.DepartmentID = UniversityCourse.DepartmentID
ORDER BY DepartmentName, CourseName
FOR XML RAW

<row DepartmentName="Accounting" CourseName="ACCT 201" />
<row DepartmentName="Accounting" CourseName="ACCT 312" />
<row DepartmentName="Chemistry" CourseName="CHEM 205" />
. . .
```

Note that the DBMS wraps each row in a <row> tag and specifies the field names as attributes and the associated data values as attribute values enclosed in quotation marks. The front slashes (/) at the end of the <row> tags close the tags. This designates them as *self-terminating tags,* which are tags that do not require a matching closing tag.

TIP: In XML documents, all tags must have both opening and closing tags, or they must appear as self-terminating tags. Some HTML tags, such as `<br>` or `<hr>`, do not have closing tags. You can use these tags if you make them self-terminating tags such as `<br/>` or `<hr/>`.

The ELEMENTS option instructs the DBMS to place the data values in text nodes. The first three retrieved records appear as follows using the FOR XML RAW, ELEMENTS option:

```
SELECT DepartmentName, CourseName
FROM UniversityDepartment
INNER JOIN UniversityCourse
ON UniversityDepartment.DepartmentID = UniversityCourse.DepartmentID
ORDER BY DepartmentName, CourseName
FOR XML RAW, ELEMENTS

<row>
  <DepartmentName>Accounting</DepartmentName>
  <CourseName>ACCT 201</CourseName>
</row>
<row>
  <DepartmentName>Accounting</DepartmentName>
  <CourseName>ACCT 312</CourseName>
</row>
<row>
  <DepartmentName>Chemistry</DepartmentName>
  <CourseName>CHEM 205</CourseName>
</row>

. . .
```

FOR XML AUTO

The FOR XML AUTO mode retrieves data as attribute values and nests element values when queries join multiple tables. This mode retrieves the following values for the department/course query:

```
SELECT DepartmentName, CourseName
FROM UniversityDepartment
INNER JOIN UniversityCourse
ON UniversityDepartment.DepartmentID = UniversityCourse.DepartmentID
ORDER BY DepartmentName, CourseName
FOR XML AUTO

<UniversityDepartment DepartmentName="Accounting">
  <UniversityCourse CourseName="ACCT 201" />
  <UniversityCourse CourseName="ACCT 312" />
</UniversityDepartment>
<UniversityDepartment DepartmentName="Chemistry">
  <UniversityCourse CourseName="CHEM 205" />
</UniversityDepartment>
. . .
```

Note that the DBMS wraps each value in a tag that describes the table (such as `<UniversityDepartment>` and `<UniversityCourse>`), specifies the field names as attributes, and shows the associated data values as attribute values enclosed in quotation marks. The child table (<UniversityCourse>) values are enclosed in the parent table (<UniversityDepartment>) tags.

The FOR XML AUTO, ELEMENTS option stores the data from the previous query as text nodes rather than as attribute node values, as follows:

```
SELECT DepartmentName, CourseName
FROM UniversityDepartment
INNER JOIN UniversityCourse
ON UniversityDepartment.DepartmentID = UniversityCourse.DepartmentID
ORDER BY DepartmentName, CourseName
FOR XML AUTO, ELEMENTS

<UniversityDepartment>
  <DepartmentName>Accounting</DepartmentName>
  <UniversityCourse>
    <CourseName>ACCT 201</CourseName>
  </UniversityCourse>
  <UniversityCourse>
    <CourseName>ACCT 312</CourseName>
  </UniversityCourse>
</UniversityDepartment>
```

An alias provides an alternate name for a retrieved column in a SELECT query. You can create aliases for both columns and tables to change the names of the associated XML output nodes. For example, the following query assigns aliases (shown as shaded) to both retrieved tables and columns to shorten the names and to follow the XHTML standard requiring all lowercase letters for element and attribute names. The XML-formatted output for the first record that this query retrieves appears as follows, with nodes names changed to match the alias names.

```
SELECT DepartmentName AS dname,
CourseName AS cname
FROM UniversityDepartment department
INNER JOIN UniversityCourse course
ON department.DepartmentID = course.DepartmentID
ORDER BY dname, cname
FOR XML AUTO, ELEMENTS

<department>
  <dname>Accounting</dname>
  <course>
    <cname>ACCT 201</cname>
  </course>
  <course>
    <cname>ACCT 312</cname>
  </course>
</department>
. . .
```

FOR XML EXPLICIT

The FOR XML EXPLICIT option allows developers to control how the XML output is formatted in terms of hierarchical relationships and whether data appears as attribute node values, text node values, or a combination of both. It also provides an alternate way to allow developers to specify node names. This option makes queries much more difficult to configure but provides a higher degree of control over the query output.

With the EXPLICIT option, each SELECT query includes a *tag field* as the first field in the SELECT clause and a *parent field* as the second field in the SELECT clause. The query assigns numeric values, such as 1 or 2, to the tag and parent fields. These levels identify a corresponding level in the resulting XML tree. The following subsections describe how to use the FOR XML EXPLICIT option to create single-level and multiple-level XML outputs.

Single-Level Outputs

The simplest case for using the EXPLICIT option involves a SELECT query that retrieves data values from a single table, displays the values as an XML tree with a single level of output, and displays the data values as attribute values. In this situation, the tag field is 1, because this query defines the top level, and the parent field is NULL, because the top node has no parent. Consider the following query and its associated output:

```
SELECT 1 as tag,
  NULL as parent,
  DepartmentName AS [department!1!name]
FROM    UniversityDepartment
ORDER BY DepartmentName
FOR XML EXPLICIT

<department name="Accounting" />
<department name="Chemistry" />
<department name="Computer Science" />
```

In this query, the first and second fields in the SELECT clause assign the tag field value as 1 and the parent field value as NULL. The third field in the SELECT clause, which is highlighted in the preceding query, has the following general syntax:

```
DatabaseFieldName AS [XMLNodeName!XMLNodeLevel!DataName]
```

In this syntax, *DatabaseFieldName* specifies the name of the database field that the query retrieves, which is DepartmentName. The exclamation point (!) serves as a delimiter. *XMLNodeName* specifies the name of the node that wraps the retrieved data. *XMLNodeLevel* specifies the level of the corresponding XML node, which in this case is 1. *DataName* specifies the name of the attribute associated with each data value.

If you want to wrap data values in tags rather than express them as attributes, modify the third field in the SELECT clause so that it includes the !element option as follows:

```
SELECT 1 as tag,
  NULL as parent,
  DepartmentName AS [department!1!name!element]
FROM    UniversityDepartment
ORDER BY DepartmentName
FOR XML EXPLICIT

<department>
  <name>Accounting</name>
</department>
<department>
  <name>Chemistry</name>
```

```
</department>
<department>
  <name>Computer Science</name>
</department>
```

Sometimes you need to join multiple tables to create single-level XML outputs. For example, suppose you want to include department chair names (which are stored in the UniversityInstructor table) along with department names in the previous query. The next example joins two tables and shows the output in a single XML level:

```
SELECT 1 as tag,
  NULL as parent,
  DepartmentName As [department!1!departmentname!element],
  InstructorLastName As [department!1!chairname!element]
FROM UniversityDepartment
INNER JOIN UniversityInstructor
ON UniversityDepartment.DepartmentChairID =
  UniversityInstructor.InstructorID
ORDER BY DepartmentName
FOR XML EXPLICIT

<department>
  <departmentname>Accounting</departmentname>
  <chairname>Dutton</chairname>
</department>
<department>
  <departmentname>Chemistry</departmentname>
  <chairname>Harrison</chairname>
</department>
. . .
```

An important feature of the EXPLICIT option is that it allows you to format data using a combination of attribute values and text node values. If you delete the `!element` option in the third line of the preceding query, the output appears as follows:

```
<department departmentname="Accounting">
  <chairname>Dutton</chairname>
</department>
<department departmentname="Chemistry">
  <chairname>Harrison</chairname>
</department>
. . .
```

Multiple-Level Outputs

To create multiple XML output levels using the EXPLICIT option, create a separate SELECT query for each level, and join the levels using the UNION operator. The UNION operator joins the output of two unrelated SELECT queries into a single output. Every SELECT query in a UNION operation must return exactly the same number of fields, and they must be of the same corresponding data types. Therefore, the initial query must specify all fields that the query ultimately retrieves, and fields that appear in lower-level queries are designated as NULL values.

Consider the following query, which retrieves two levels of XML output consisting of department names and the associated courses for each department:

```
SELECT 1 As tag,
       NULL As parent,
       DepartmentName As [department!1!dname],
       NULL As [course!2!cname!element],
       NULL As [course!2!ctitle!element]
FROM   UniversityDepartment
UNION
SELECT 2 As tag,
       1 As parent,
       DepartmentName,CourseName, CourseTitle
FROM   UniversityDepartment
INNER JOIN UniversityCourse
ON UniversityDepartment.DepartmentID = UniversityCourse.DepartmentID
ORDER BY [department!1!dname], [course!2!cname!element]
FOR XML EXPLICIT

<department dname="Accounting">
  <course>
    <cname>ACCT 201</cname>
    <ctitle>Principles of Accounting</ctitle>
  </course>
  <course>
    <cname>ACCT 312</cname>
    <ctitle>Managerial Accounting</ctitle>
  </course>
</department>
<department dname="Chemistry">
  <course>
    <cname>CHEM 205</cname>
    <ctitle>Applied Physical Chemistry</ctitle>
  </course>
</department>
```

The query joins two SELECT queries using the UNION operator. The first query retrieves the data for the parent nodes, and the second query retrieves the data for both the parent and child nodes using an INNER JOIN operation. The first query includes NULL placeholders for the child data fields (CourseName and CourseCredits). These placeholders do not retrieve data but are responsible for formatting the XML output. The second query has a tag field value of 2 and a parent field value of 1, which indicates that it is hierarchically subordinate to the first query.

The ORDER BY clause is very important, because it specifies how the XML output structures the data hierarchy. If you omit the ORDER BY clause, the output appears as follows:

```
<department dname="Accounting" />
<department dname="Chemistry" />
<department dname="Computer Science" />
<department dname="Foreign Languages" />
<department dname="Geology" />
<department dname="Management Information Systems" />
<department dname="Physics">
  <course>
    <cname>ACCT 201</cname>
    <ctitle>Principles of Accounting</ctitle>
```

```
  </course>
  <course>
    <cname>ACCT 312</cname>
    <ctitle>Managerial Accounting</ctitle>
  </course>
```

To create lower hierarchical levels, create additional SELECT queries and join them using the UNION operator. The following query shows how to create three levels of XML output to show that the departments offer courses and that courses have associated course sections:

```
SELECT 1 As tag,
       NULL As parent,
       DepartmentName As [department!1!dname],
       NULL As [course!2!cname!element],
       NULL As [course!2!ctitle!element],
       NULL AS [section!3!sectionid!element]
FROM   UniversityDepartment
UNION
SELECT 2 As tag,
       1 As parent,
       DepartmentName,CourseName, CourseTitle,
       NULL AS [Section!3!SectionID!element]
FROM   UniversityDepartment
INNER JOIN UniversityCourse
ON UniversityDepartment.DepartmentID = UniversityCourse.DepartmentID
UNION
SELECT 3 As tag,
       2 As parent,
       DepartmentName,CourseName, CourseTitle, SectionID
FROM   UniversityDepartment
INNER JOIN UniversityCourse
ON UniversityDepartment.DepartmentID = UniversityCourse.DepartmentID
INNER JOIN UniversitySection
ON UniversitySection.CourseID = UniversityCourse.CourseID
ORDER BY [department!1!dname],
         [course!2!cname!element],
         [section!3!sectionid!element]
FOR XML EXPLICIT

<department dname="Accounting">
  <course>
    <cname>ACCT 201</cname>
    <ctitle>Principles of Accounting</ctitle>
    <section>
      <sectionid>2</sectionid>
    </section>
    <section>
      <sectionid>8</sectionid>
    </section>
    <section>
      <sectionid>20</sectionid>
    </section>
  </course>
```

Creating and Debugging FOR XML EXPLICIT Queries

As you write complex SQL SELECT queries that use the EXPLICIT option, it is a good practice to develop and debug the query incrementally. Create and debug the first SELECT query, then add the next query. Continue this process until the query retrieves all the required data.

The following exercise uses Management Studio to write and test a query to retrieve XML data that has three levels which show departments, their associated instructors, and the courses that each instructor teaches.

To create the XML query:

1. Start Management Studio, connect to your SQL Server database, and create a new query.
2. Type the following commands in the Query Editor to retrieve the department name. (Do not forget to replace *yourDatabaseName* with the name of your database.)

```
USE yourDatabaseName
SELECT 1 as tag, NULL as parent,
       DepartmentName As [department!1!dname],
       NULL As [instructor!2!ilname],
       NULL As [instructor!2!ifname],
       NULL As [course!3!cname!element]
FROM   UniversityDepartment
WHERE UniversityDepartment.DepartmentName =
       'Management Information Systems'
ORDER BY [department!1!dname]
FOR XML EXPLICIT
```

3. Execute the query, and debug it if necessary.
4. Click the link in the Results pane to display the output, which should appear as follows.

```
<department dname="Management Information Systems" />
```

5. Save the query as XMLQuery.sql in the \SQLServer\Solutions\Chapter9 folder.
6. To add the second SELECT query, which retrieves the instructor information, add the following highlighted commands:

```
USE yourDatabaseName
SELECT 1 as tag, NULL as parent,
       DepartmentName As [department!1!dname],
       NULL As [instructor!2!ilname],
       NULL As [instructor!2!ifname],
       NULL As [course!3!cname!element]
FROM   UniversityDepartment
WHERE UniversityDepartment.DepartmentName =
       'Management Information Systems'
UNION
SELECT 2 as tag, 1 as parent,
       DepartmentName,
       InstructorLastName,
       InstructorFirstName,
       NULL
FROM UniversityDepartment
INNER JOIN UniversityInstructor
ON UniversityDepartment.DepartmentID = UniversityInstructor.DepartmentID
WHERE UniversityDepartment.DepartmentName =
       'Management Information Systems'
ORDER BY [department!1!dname],
         [instructor!2!ilname]
FOR XML EXPLICIT
```

7. Save the query, and then execute and debug it as before. View the results, which should look like this:

```
<department dname="Management Information Systems">
  <instructor ilname="Buck" ifname="Ted" />
  <instructor ilname="Hogstad" ifname="Lillian" />
  <instructor ilname="Morrison" ifname="Lauren" />
  <instructor ilname="Sanchez" ifname="Roberta" />
</department>
```

8. To add the third SELECT query, which retrieves the course information, add the following highlighted commands to the end of the existing query:

```
. . .
WHERE UniversityDepartment.DepartmentName =
'Management Information Systems'
UNION
SELECT 3 as tag, 2 as parent,
       DepartmentName,
       InstructorLastName,
       InstructorFirstName,
       CourseName
FROM    UniversityDepartment INNER JOIN
UniversityInstructor
ON UniversityDepartment.DepartmentID =
    UniversityInstructor.DepartmentID
INNER JOIN UniversitySection
ON UniversityInstructor.InstructorID =
    UniversitySection.InstructorID
INNER JOIN UniversityCourse
ON UniversitySection.CourseID =
    UniversityCourse.CourseID
WHERE UniversityDepartment.DepartmentName =
       'Management Information Systems'
ORDER BY [department!1!dname],
         [instructor!2!ilname],
         [course!3!cname!element]
FOR XML EXPLICIT
```

9. Save, test, and debug the query as before. The final result for the first instructor should look like this. (Your data will include values for three additional instructors).

```
<department dname="Management Information Systems">
  <instructor ilname="Buck" ifname="Ted">
    <course>
      <cname>MIS 240</cname>
    </course>
    <course>
      <cname>MIS 345</cname>
    </course>
  </instructor>
```

10. Close all open document windows in the IDE.

FIGURE 9-4   VB program to write a FOR XML query output to an XML document

```
ForXML - Microsoft Visual Basic 2005 Express Edition                              _ |8| X|
File  Edit  View  Project  Build  Debug  Data  Tools  Window  Community  Help

frmForXML.vb   frmForXML.vb [Design]                                          ▼ ×
(frmForXML Events)                              ▼    Load                      ▼

Public Class frmForXML
Private Sub frmForXML_Load(ByVal sender As System.Object, ByVal e As System.EventArgs) Handles
    Dim cn As New Data.SqlClient.SqlConnection
    Dim da As New Data.SqlClient.SqlDataAdapter
    Dim sqlCommand As New Data.SqlClient.SqlCommand
    Dim ds As New Data.DataSet
    cn.ConnectionString = "Data Source=.\sqlexpress;" & _
                          "AttachDbFilename=|DataDirectory|\yourDatabaseName.mdf;" & _
                          "Integrated Security=True;User Instance=True"
    sqlCommand.CommandText = "SELECT DepartmentName, CourseName " & _
            "FROM UniversityDepartment INNER JOIN UniversityCourse " & _
            "ON UniversityDepartment.DepartmentID = UniversityCourse.DepartmentID " & _
            "ORDER BY DepartmentName, CourseName " & _
            "FOR XML AUTO"
    da.SelectCommand = sqlCommand
    da.SelectCommand.Connection = cn
    da.Fill(ds, "DeptCourse")
    Dim sw As New System.IO.StreamWriter("DeptCourse.xml")
        sw.Write("<?xml version=""1.0"" encoding=""utf-8""?>")
        sw.Write("<rootnode>")
            sw.Write(ds.Tables("DeptCourse").Rows(0).Item(0).ToString)
        sw.Write("</rootnode>")
    sw.Close()
    MessageBox.Show("Created the DeptCourse XML file")
End Sub
End Class

Item(s) Saved                                      Ln 6      Col 31    Ch 31    INS
```

Using XML Query Data

Recall that SELECT queries to retrieve data in XML format return the data as a stream of text. What can you do with this text? Well, you can copy and paste it from the Management Studio Results pane to where you need to use it. You can also write a program that retrieves XML-formatted database data and writes it to an XML document. Figure 9-4 displays a simple VB program that does this.

The program in Figure 9-4 contains commands to create and process a SQL query. The commands then write the output to a file named DeptCourse.xml. This file contains commands to define an XML prolog and the root node, along with the XML-formatted data values that the query retrieves.

EXTENSIBLE STYLESHEET LANGUAGE TRANSFORMATIONS (XSLTS)

So far, you have learned how to create an XML document manually and how to create a SQL query to retrieve XML data that you can insert into an XML document. In this section, you will learn how to transform the contents of an XML file using an *eXtensible Stylesheet Language* (*XSL*) program. XSL provides programming commands and structures to process and format XML data and provides far more flexibility for formatting XML than FOR XML EXPLICIT queries provide.

An XSL program is called an *XSL stylesheet* or an *eXtensible Stylesheet Language Transformation* (*XSLT*). XSLTs enable programmers to process, sort, filter, modify,

FIGURE 9-5   XSLT structure

```
<?xml version="1.0" encoding="UTF-8"?>              ———— Prolog
<!-- Root node definition -->
<xsl:stylesheet version="1.0"
    xmlns:xsl="http://www.w3.org/1999/XSL/Transform">   ———— Root node
                                                             definition
    <!-- Template definition -->
    <xsl:template match="XML Path">                    ———— Template
        <!-- Processing commands -->                        definition
        <XSL processing commands>                      ———— Processing
    </xsl:template>                                         commands
</xsl:stylesheet>
```

and format XML data, as well as transform its data structure. The following subsections describe the structure of an XSLT and show how to create an XSLT to process an XML document.

XSLT Structure

XSLTs use a template-oriented syntax, which specifies commands as tags that must appear in a certain position and order. An XSLT contains XPATH commands and can contain HTML formatting tags. XPATH commands retrieve and manipulate XML data and HTML formatting tags can be added if the data is going to be displayed in a browser.

Figure 9-5 illustrates the general structure of an XSLT. Because an XSLT is an XML document, its first tag is an XML prolog. The following subsections describe the other sections in an XSLT.

Root Node Definition

The second tag in an XSLT defines the root node, which specifies the XSLT's properties. The *xsl:stylesheet* element indicates that the document is an XSL style sheet. The *version* attribute indicates 1.0 as the current version, and the *xmlns:xsl* attribute defines an XML namespace. The *xsl* element prefixes the stylesheet tag, and is appended to the *xmlns* attribute, which defines xsl as the identifier for tags that contain XPATH commands.

XML namespaces distinguish XML elements with the same name but different meanings. This phenomenon occurs when elements are developed by different organizations or by different people in an organization. If you do not wish to specify a namespace value to define tags that belong to different entities, specify the value of the xmlns:xsl attribute as `http://www.w3.org/1999/XSL/Transform`, as shown in Figure 9-5. This instructs the processing program to recognize that the document uses the current XSLT standard.

Template Definitions

The next XSLT section includes one or more template definitions. A *template definition* specifies the *current context,* which defines the XML document elements that the associated XSLT commands process. For example, if you are creating an XSLT to process the Students.xml file that you created earlier, you might decide to process only the `<coursesection>` elements, so those elements would be the current context.

The current context is specified using an *XML path,* which specifies a location in an XML document. It is similar to a folder path: it starts at the root element and moves down the element structure, with the names of the individual elements in the structure separated by front slashes (/). An XML path value of "/" specifies the root node of the XML document.

XPATH supports two kinds of XML path specifications. An XML *absolute path* begins with a forward slash (/) and can contain one or more element names to move down the XML hierarchy. An absolute path always begins at the root node of the XML document and moves downward. In the Students.xml document in Figure 9-3, the absolute path to the beginning of the `<coursesection>` elements is `/universitystudents/universitystudent/`.

An XML *relative path* does not begin with a forward slash and is specified by moving upward or downward from the current context, which is the current position in the XML document. XML relative path navigation is similar to relative file path navigation: `../` specifies to move up one node from the current context. If the path begins with an element name that is a child element of the current element, navigation moves down the tree from the current context to the child element. For example, if the current context is `universitystudent`, then the XML relative path `coursesection` moves down the tree to that context.

An XSLT must contain at least one template definition and can contain several template definitions to define instructions for different types of processing as needed. If a document has only one template, then the XML path value must be "/".

NOTE: Defining and using multiple templates is an advanced topic that becomes complex to understand and apply. In short, templates behave much like loops. The XSLTs that you create in this book use a single template that defines the root of the XML document as the current context.

XSLT Processing Commands

An XSLT uses tags to create processing commands for loops, decision control structures, and other programming tasks. It can also use ordinary HTML tags to format the output of these operations. XSLTs often use loops to process all the elements in an XML document, with the loop's exit condition occurring when no more elements remain to be processed. An example of an XSLT loop is as follows:

```
<xsl:for-each
  select="universitystudents/universitystudent">
   <xsl:value-of select="studentfirstname"/>
   <xsl:value-of select="studentlastname"/>
</xsl:for-each>
```

In this syntax, the `<xsl:for-each . . .>` tag specifies an XSL loop. The *select* attribute specifies the XML path to the loop's starting element. In the example, specifying the select attribute value as "universitystudents/universitystudent" indicates that the path moves from the `<universitystudents>` element to each individual `<universitystudent>` element.

In the loop, the `<xsl:value-of . . .>` tag returns the value of the specified XML element. In the example code, these tags return the current character data values in the `<studentfirstname>` and `<studentlastname>` elements. The last character in these tags is a front slash (/), which designates them as self-terminating tags that do not require a matching closing tag.

Creating and Processing an XSLT

To use an XSLT to process an XML document, first write the XSLT that contains the processing code. Then create a program that runs an *XSLT processor,* which is a program that compiles and executes the XSLT. In this section, you will create and execute

FIGURE 9-6 Student data with a flat structure

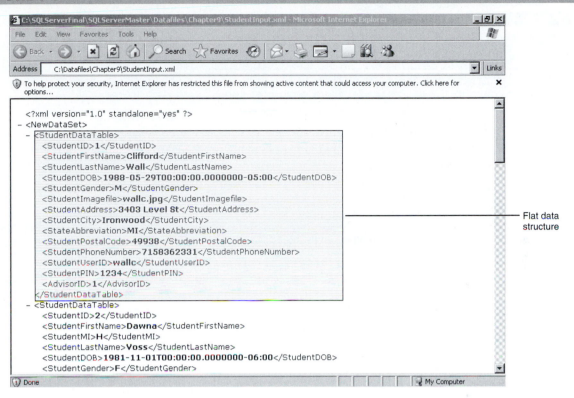

Flat data structure

an XSLT that transforms the structure of an XML document named StudentInput.xml, which contains data from the UniversityStudent table in the Ironwood University database. Figure 9-6 shows the file contents in a browser window.

> **NOTE:** We generated the StudentInput.xml file from the UniversityStudent table employing a .NET program that used a .NET method to retrieve and format the data. Although the XML standard specifies the use of all lowercase letters for element names, the .NET method that creates the XML file uses whatever case letters are derived from the SQL query retrieving the data. Although we could have, we did not alias the field names using lowercase letters when we generated this XML document.

Currently, the data has a flat data structure: Each <StudentDataTable> node contains all the data for a single student. An XSLT will transform the data so that it uses lowercase names and has a more hierarchical structure, as shown in Figure 9-7.

This structure adds a new element named studentname containing the student name components. The structure also omits some of the data and displays a subset of the original data elements.

The following steps enable you to create a new Web site, copy the StudentInput.xml file to the Web site, and then create the XSLT. The XSLT will use a loop to read each <StudentDataTable> element and restructure its child elements.

To create the Web site, copy the file, and create the XSLT:

1. In the VWD or VS 2005 IDE, create a new Web Site by clicking File on the menu bar, and then clicking New Web Site. The New Web Site dialog box opens.

FIGURE 9-7   Student data with a hierarchical structure

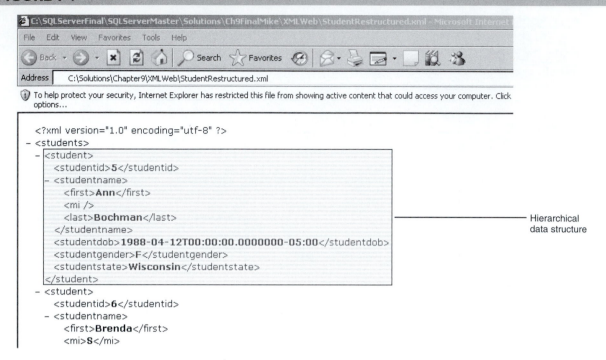

2. Select the ASP.NET Web Site template, and then click Browse. Navigate to your \SQLServer\Solutions\Chapter9 folder, and then type \XMLWeb at the end of the folder path to create the Web site root folder. If you are saving your solutions to your C:\ drive, the complete folder path appears as C:\SQLServer\Solutions\Chapter9\XMLWeb. Click OK.

3. In Windows Explorer, copy StudentInput.xml from \SQLServer\Datafiles\Chapter9 to your \SQLServer\Solutions\Chapter9\XMLWeb folder.

4. Switch back to the IDE. To create the XSLT file, right-click the Web site root folder in the Solution Explorer, click Add New Item, select the XSLT File template, change the Name field to StudentTransform.xsl, and then click Add. An XSLT template file appears in the Document window.

5. Place the insertion point just before the opening <html> tag, and delete all the commands through the closing </html> tag.

TIP: Sometimes the IDE XML Editor refuses to recognize the enter key, backspace key, arrow keys, and other keys. If your editor develops this problem, you can remove and then reinstall VS 2005 or VWD to try to get it working correctly (this is a bug in the current environment). Another option is to right-click the file in the Solution Explorer, select Open With, and select HTML Editor. This editor has been reliable and provides some color coding to the XML. You lose the code completion support the XML Editor supplies, however.

---

6. In place of the deleted commands, add the following commands to create the XSLT:

```
<students>
  <xsl:for-each
  select="NewDataSet/StudentDataTable">
    <student>
      <studentid>
        <xsl:value-of select="StudentID"/>
      </studentid>
        <studentname>
          <first>
            <xsl:value-of
              select="StudentFirstName"/>
          </first>
          <mi>
            <xsl:value-of select="StudentMI"/>
          </mi>
          <last>
            <xsl:value-of select="StudentLastName"/>
          </last>
        </studentname>
        <studentdob>
          <xsl:value-of select="StudentDOB"/>
        </studentdob>
        <studentgender><xsl:value-of
          select="StudentGender"/></studentgender>
    </student>
  </xsl:for-each>
</students>
```

7. Save the StudentTransform.xsl file.

TIP: If you are not sure where to put the preceding code, we provide the complete program listing at the end of this section.

The next step is to configure the Web form that processes the XSLT. Figure 9-8 shows the Web form's controls.

This Web form contains a label control that displays a message to confirm the success of the transformation or the resulting error message. It also displays three buttons: the first button executes the transformation, the second button displays the restructured

FIGURE 9-8   Web form to process the XSLT

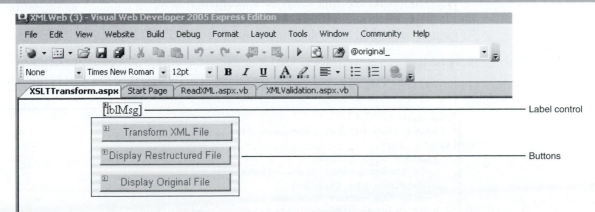

XML file, and the third button displays the original XML file. When the Web form first opens, only the first button is visible. After the user successfully transforms the XML file, the second and third buttons become visible.

To create the Web form controls:

1. In the Solution Explorer, right-click Default.aspx, click Rename, and change its name to XSLTTransform.aspx.
2. Double-click XSLTTransform.aspx in the Solution Explorer to open it in Design view. Change its Title property to XSLT Transform.
3. Open the Toolbox, and create a Label control and three Button controls. Resize and reposition the controls as shown in Figure 9-8.
4. Change the label control's ID property to lblMsg, and delete its Text property value.
5. Change the top button's ID property to btnTransform and its Text property value to Transform XML File.
6. Change the middle button's ID property to btnRestructured, its Text property value to Display Restructured File, and its Visible property value to False.
7. Change the bottom button's ID property value to btnOriginal, its Text property value to Display Original File, and its Visible property value to False.
8. Save the project.

The final task is to write the button event handlers. The event handler for the Transform File button uses an object of the `System.Xml.Xsl.XslCompiledTransform` class. This class provides the .NET framework's XSLT processor. Its `Load()` method compiles the XSLT, and its `Transform()` method executes the compiled transform on a specified input document and outputs the results to a specified output document.

The event handler uses the `Server.MapPath()` method, which retrieves the path to an existing file and applies the path to another file. We will use this method to retrieve the path of the XML source file and to write the transformed file to the same location as the source file. The event handler uses a Try/Catch block to perform the transformation. If the transformation succeeds, the event handler displays a confirmation message, and the other form buttons become visible. If the transformation fails, the resulting error message appears on the form.

Chapter 8 described the `Response.Redirect` command, which displays a new Web page in the browser window. The event handlers for the second and third buttons use `Response.Redirect` to display the transformed XML file and the original XML file.

The following steps show how to create the button event handlers, run the project, transform the XML file, and view the restructured and original files.

To create the button event handlers and run the project:

1. Double-click the Transform XML File button to create a Click event handler declaration, and then add the following commands to create the event handler:

```
Dim xslt As _
  New System.Xml.Xsl.XslCompiledTransform
Try
  'Load the XSLT file
  xslt.Load(MapPath("StudentTransform.xsl"))
  'Transform the file and
  'write the output to a new file
  xslt.Transform(MapPath("StudentInput.xml"), _
    MapPath("StudentRestructured.xml"))
```

```
      lblMsg.Text = "Success!"
      btnRestructured.Visible = True
      btnOriginal.Visible = True
      btnTransform.Visible = False
   Catch ex As Exception
      lblMsg.Text = ex.Message
   End Try
```

2. To create a new Click event handler for the Display Restructured File button, open the Objects list and select btnRestructured, then open the Declarations list and select Click. Add the following command to the event handler declaration to display the restructured XML file:

```
Response.Redirect("StudentRestructured.xml")
```

3. Create a Click event handler declaration for btnOriginal, and add the following command to display the original XML file:

```
Response.Redirect("StudentInput.xml")
```

4. Run the project. When the Debugging Not Enabled dialog box opens, click OK.
5. Click the Transform XML File button to transform the XML file using the XSLT. The "Success!" message appears in the form label, and the Transform XML File button no longer appears.
6. Click Display Restructured File. The restructured XML file should appear in the browser window, as shown in Figure 9-7.
7. Click Display Original File. The original XML file should appear, as shown in Figure 9-6.
8. Close the browser window.

Sorting Outputs

To process XML records so that they appear in a different order, add an *xsl:sort* tag immediately after the *xsl:for-each* tag that creates the loop to process the elements. The xsl:sort tag has the following general syntax:

```
<xsl:sort select="SortKeyElement" order="{ascending|descending}" />
```

In this tag, the *SortKeyElement* specifies the name of the element on which the XSLT sorts the values. For example, if you specify *SortKeyElement* to be StudentLastName, then the records appear sorted by the StudentLastName XML element. The *order* attribute specifies the sort order and can be either ascending or descending. The front slash (/) as the last tag character terminates the tag. The following steps add the xsl:sort tag to the StudentTransformation.xsl XSLT and sort the student data elements by StudentLastName values.

To change the sort order of the data elements:

1. Click the StudentTransform.xsl tab in the Document window. Place the insertion point after the closing angle bracket of the opening <xsl:for-each> tag, just before the first <student> node. Press Enter to add a new blank line, and then type the following command:

```
<xsl:sort select="StudentLastName" order="ascending" />
```

2. Select the XSLTTransform.aspx tab to select the Web form, then run the project and click the Transform XML File button. The "Success!" message should appear.
3. Click Display Restructured File, and note that the student names now appear sorted by last names.
4. Close the browser window.

Filtering Outputs

At this point, the XSLT processes every element in the XML file. To create an XSLT that processes selected elements in an XML file, you can filter the data by specifying a search condition. The search condition is added directly to the *select* attribute of the xsl:for-each tag, using the following syntax:

```
<xsl:for-each select="XMLPath[SearchCondition]">
```

In this syntax, XMLPath appears as before. The *SearchCondition* specifies a search condition using the following format:

```
element Operator value
```

In this syntax, *element* is a data element in the XML file. *Operator* specifies one of the standard comparison operators (=, <, >, etc.) and *value* specifies the target value. For example, the following <xsl:for-each> tag limits the processed elements in the StudentInput.xml file to <StudentGender> values that are equal to 'F':

```
<xsl:for-each select="NewDataSet/StudentDataTable[StudentGender='F']">
```

NOTE: Because XML files contain only character data values, *value* is always character data and always appears in single quotation marks.

The following steps modify the Students.xsl style sheet to process data elements only for students whose StudentGender value is 'F'.
To filter the data elements:

1. In the StudentTransform.xsl file in the Document window, modify the xsl:for-each tag by adding the highlighted text so that the tag appears as follows:

```
<xsl:for-each select="NewDataSet/StudentDataTable[StudentGender='F']">
```

2. Select and run the Web form, then click the Transform XML File button. When the "Success!" message appears, click Display Restructured File and confirm that the file displays data values for female students only.
3. Close the browser window.

Creating a Decision Structure

A decision structure allows a program to selectively execute or skip program commands based on the values of one or more variables. In an XSLT, you create a decision structure using the *xsl:if* tag, which has the following general syntax:

```
<xsl:if test="Condition">
    <tags that execute if Condition is TRUE>
</xsl:if>
```

If *Condition* is true, then the XSLT executes the tags in the xsl:if opening and closing tags. Note that the xsl:if tag does not support an ELSE structure to specify alternate instructions to apply if the condition is false. To handle this situation, add an additional xsl:if tag to test for the opposite of the first condition and process the resulting elements accordingly.

The following steps modify the XSLT so that it uses an xsl:if tag to test the value of the <StateAbbreviation> element for each student. If the <StateAbbreviation> value is WI, then the XSLT adds a new element named <StudentState> that has the value Wisconsin. If the <StateAbbreviation> value is MI, then the XSLT adds a <StudentState> element that has the value Michigan.

To add the xsl:if tag to the XSLT:

1. In the StudentTransform.xsl file, place the insertion point just before the closing </student> tag (and after the closing </studentgender> tag), and then press Enter to add a new blank line.
2. Add the following commands to create the xsl:if tag:

```
<xsl:if test="StateAbbreviation = 'WI'">
  <studentstate>Wisconsin</studentstate>
</xsl:if>
<xsl:if test="StateAbbreviation = 'MI'">
  <studentstate>Michigan</studentstate>
</xsl:if>
```

3. Select and run the Web form, and then click Transform XML File. The "Success!" message appears.
4. Click Display Restructured File. The new file should now display the <studentstate> elements and the corresponding state names.
5. Close the browser window, and then close all open documents in the IDE Document window. The following provides a complete code listing for StudentTransform.xsl:

```
<?xml version="1.0" encoding="utf-8"?>
<xsl:stylesheet version="1.0"
xmlns:xsl="http://www.w3.org/1999/XSL/Transform">
<xsl:template match="/">
<students>
  <xsl:for-each
    select="NewDataSet/StudentDataTable
    [StudentGender='F']">
  <xsl:sort select="StudentLastName" order="ascending" />
    <student>
      <studentid><xsl:value-of select="StudentID"/></studentid>
      <studentname>
        <first><xsl:value-of select="StudentFirstName"/></first>
        <mi><xsl:value-of select="StudentMI"/></mi>
        <last><xsl:value-of select="StudentLastName"/></last>
      </studentname>
      <studentdob><xsl:value-of select="StudentDOB"/></studentdob>
      <studentgender><xsl:value-of
        select="StudentGender"/></studentgender>
```

```
    <xsl:if test="StateAbbreviation = 'WI'">
      <studentstate>Wisconsin</studentstate>
    </xsl:if>
    <xsl:if test="StateAbbreviation = 'MI'">
      <studentstate>Michigan</studentstate>
    </xsl:if>
  </student>
 </xsl:for-each>
</students>
</xsl:template>
</xsl:stylesheet>
```

VALIDATING XML DOCUMENTS

Computer system files, including XML files, can become damaged and contain corrupted data. For XML documents to provide a viable alternative to relational databases for data storage, they need mechanisms to ensure data integrity. When you define a SQL Server database table, you specify field data types, integrity constraints for primary and foreign keys, and value constraints that specify allowable field values. XML documents need a similar way to define their content. A *valid XML document* is an XML document that contains all the elements that it is supposed to contain and all elements contain the correct type of data. Furthermore, the document correctly specifies the data relationships through nested element tags.

TIP: Recall that XML documents must be well formed, which means that the document follows the syntactic rules of XML. However, although a document may be well formed, it still might not be valid and have the expected elements, types of data, and relationships.

To validate XML documents, developers create XML Schema Definitions. An *XML Schema Definition (XSD)* defines the data structure of an XML document in terms of data types, relationships, order and grouping mechanisms, and constraints. To validate an XML document, developers write programs to compare an XML file to its corresponding XSD. Developers also use XSDs to describe an existing relational database structure, then *migrate,* or move, the database data to an XML document. The XSD stores all the database structure information from the original database while the XML document stores the actual data.

This section shows how to create an XSD and write a program to read an XML document and validate it against its XSD. The following subsections describe the structure of an XSD and describe how to create an XSD, then use it to validate an existing XML file.

XSD Structure

XSDs are written in XML, so the first line of an XSD is an XML prolog. The second line contains the *xs:schema* tag, which defines the file as an XSD. The schema tag has the following format:

```
<xs:schema xmlns:xs="http://www.w3.org/1999/XMLSchema" >
```

In this tag, the *xmlns:xs* attribute defines the XSD namespace that specifies the current XSD standard. This enables .NET to apply syntax checking, help, and validation that conform to this standard. The *xs* that follows the colon specifies that elements and data types come from this XSD standard. (You can change xs: to any other letters you might prefer, however.)

NOTE: The schema tag can also contain a number of other optional attributes, which we do not address.

To define an XML element in an XSD, use the *xs:element* tag, which has the following syntax:

```
<xs:element name="ElementName"
            minOccurs="LowerBound"
            maxOccurs="UpperBound"
            type="DataType" >
```

TIP: An element tag can contain additional attribute values to describe its structure and content, but these are the most common ones.

In this syntax, *ElementName* corresponds to the name of the element tag in the XML file. The *minOccurs* attribute defines the minimum number of occurrences of the element, and *maxOccurs* defines the maximum number of occurrences. The legal values for minOccurs are zero or one, and the default value is one. Specifying the minOccurs value as one defines the element as a required value. The legal values for maxOccurs can be any value greater than zero or the text string "unbounded," which specifies that there is no maximum value. The default value for maxOccurs is one. The type attribute defines the element's data type and appears only when the element contains a data value.

You can use the following xs:element tags to define the data value elements for the studentid, studentname, and studentdob elements in the XML document in Figure 9-7:

```
<xs:element name="studentid" maxOccurs="1" type="xs:long" />
<xs:element name="studentname" maxOccurs="1" type="xs:string" />
<xs:element name="studentdob" maxOccurs="1" type="xs:dateTime" />
```

A maxOccurs attribute value of one specifies that the data value occurs exactly once in a specific element. The type attribute value specifies an element's data type.

TIP: The XSD format for dateTime data values is yyyy-mm-ddThh:mm:ss.00000.

In an XSD, a *container element* is an element that contains other elements. In the XML file in Figure 9-7, <students> and <studentname> are container elements. To specify that an element is a container element in an XML structure, place the *xs:complexType* tag immediately after the element's xs:element tag. After defining a container element, you must immediately define a *compositor element,* which defines the type of child elements that the container element contains.

Compositor elements are defined using the xs:sequence, xs:choice, and xs:all tags. The *xs:sequence* tag indicates that multiple elements exist in the container and that the elements must appear in a specific sequence. The *xs:choice* tag indicates that one and only one of the elements that follow can appear in the related XML document. The *xs:all* tag specifies that the container's elements can appear in any order in the related XML document.

The following tags define the <students> container element and specify that the child elements must appear in a certain order. (These tags would all have corresponding closing tags that are not shown here.)

```
<xs:element name="students" minOccurs="1" maxOccurs="unbounded">
    <xs:complexType>
    <xs:sequence>
```

The following steps create an XSD to define the structure of the StudentRestructured.xml file in Figure 9-7. They create a new XML Schema file in the IDE, open it in the XML Editor, and then add the xs:element tags to define the data elements.

NOTE: VS 2005 provides a visual environment to create XSDs and automatically generate element definitions. We do not use it in this book.

To create an XSD:

1. Right-click the Web site root folder in the Solution Explorer, click Add New Item, select the XML File template, change the Name field to StudentRestructured.xsd, and then click Add.
2. Add the following schema tag command under the XML prolog tag:

```
<xs:schema xmlns:xs="http://www.w3.org/2001/XMLSchema">

</xs:schema>
```

3. Place the insertion point in the blank line between the opening and closing tags, and then add the following commands to specify the XSD elements.

CAUTION: Remember that XML commands are case sensitive.

```
<xs:element name="students">
  <xs:complexType>
  <xs:sequence>
    <xs:element name="student" maxOccurs="unbounded">
    <xs:complexType>
    <xs:sequence>
      <xs:element name="studentid" maxOccurs="1"
        type="xs:long" />
      <xs:element name="studentname" maxOccurs="1">
      <xs:complexType>
      <xs:sequence>
        <xs:element name="first"
          maxOccurs="1" type="xs:string" />
        <xs:element name="mi" minOccurs="0"
          maxOccurs="1" type="xs:string" />
        <xs:element name="last" maxOccurs="1"
          type="xs:string" />
```

```
      </xs:sequence>
      </xs:complexType>
      </xs:element>
      <xs:element name="studentdob" maxOccurs="1"
        type="xs:dateTime" />
      <xs:element name="studentgender" maxOccurs="1"
        type="xs:string" />
      <xs:element name="studentstate" maxOccurs="1"
        type="xs:string" />
    </xs:sequence>
    </xs:complexType>
  </xs:element>
  </xs:sequence>
  </xs:complexType>
</xs:element>
```

4. Save the file.

Using an XSD to Validate an XML Document

XSDs do not automatically validate XML documents. As with XSLTs, you must write a program that processes the XSD and compares its rules against a target XML file. The .NET framework provides a class named `System.Xml.XmlReader` to read the XML document and a class named `System.Xml.XmlReaderSettings` to configure the XmlReader object to validate the XML document against a specific XSD.

The following set of steps shows how to create the form in Figure 9-9, which uses the XSD to validate the StudentRestructured.xml file. This form has a Load event handler that contains commands to validate an XML file based on the schema in an XSD file. As it validates the nodes, the validated nodes appear in the form list. If a node cannot be validated, a message label displays the name of the invalid node.

The following steps create this Web form, its list, and its label controls. They add references to the System and System.XML classes so that the Web site can use the

FIGURE 9-9   Web form to validate XML file

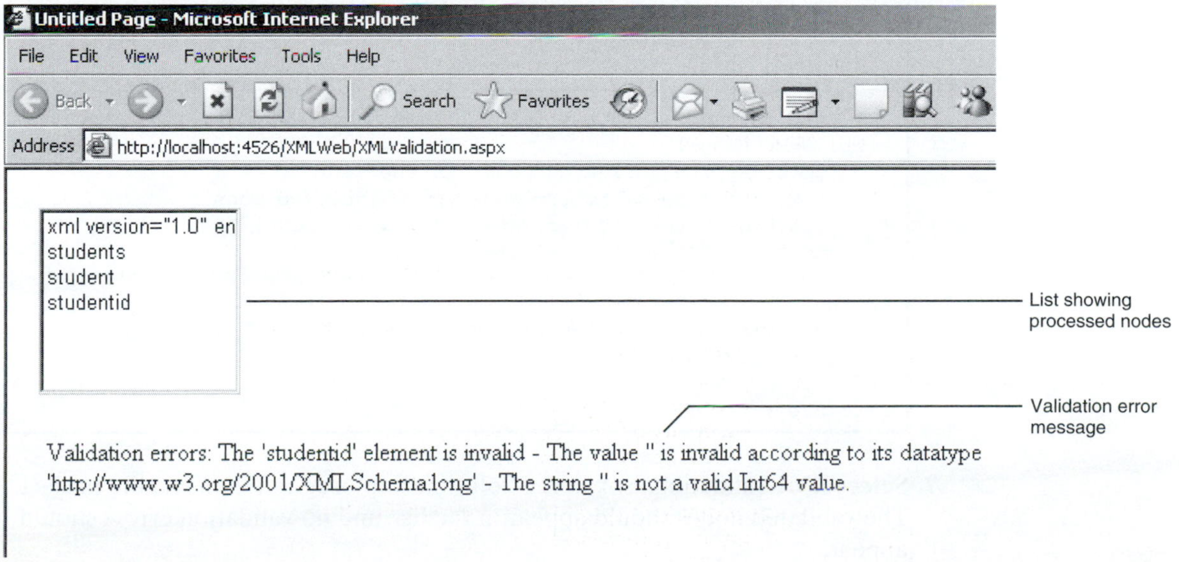

List showing processed nodes

Validation error message

Validation errors: The 'studentid' element is invalid - The value '' is invalid according to its datatype 'http://www.w3.org/2001/XMLSchema:long' - The string '' is not a valid Int64 value.

classes to create the objects to process the XSD. Then they create the Load event handler to validate the XML file.

To create the Web form to validate an XML document:

1. Create a new Web form named XMLValidation.aspx. (Be sure to check the Place code in a separate file check box.) Change the form's Title property value to XML Validation.

2. Open the form in Design view, open the Toolbox, select the ListBox control, and drag and drop it onto the Web form, as shown in Figure 9-9. Change the list box's ID property value to lstNodes.

3. Create the Label control shown in Figure 9-9 to display the validation error message. Change the label's ID property to lblMsg, and delete its Text property value.

4. Right-click any open area on the Web form, and then click View Code to open the form's code file.

5. To enable the form to use the System and System.XML classes, type the following commands as the first commands in the code file, before the `Partial Class XMLValidation` command:

```
Imports System
Imports System.Xml
```

6. To create the Load event handler declaration for the Web form, open the Objects list and select (Page Events), then open the Events list and select Load. Add the following commands to event handler:

```
Dim rs As New System.Xml.XmlReaderSettings
Dim xr As XmlReader
Try
  'specify XSD file location
  rs.Schemas.Add _
    ("", MapPath("StudentRestructured.xsd"))
  rs.ValidationType = ValidationType.Schema
Catch ex As Exception
  lblMsg.Text = "xsd file error: " & ex.Message
End Try
'specify XML file to be validated
xr = XmlReader.Create _
  (MapPath("StudentRestructured.xml"), rs)
Try
  ' loop through all the nodes in the file to validate
  While xr.Read()
    ' Display the validated nodes in the list
    If xr.NodeType <> Xml.XmlNodeType.Whitespace Then
      lstNodes.Items.Add(xr.Name & " " & xr.Value)
    End If
  End While
Catch ex As Exception
  lblMsg.Text += vbCr & vbCr & "Validation errors:" & _
  vbCr & ex.Message
End Try
xr.Close()
```

7. Select XMLValidation.aspx in the Solution Explorer and then run the project. The validated nodes should appear in the list, and no validation errors should appear.

HELP: If an error message appears, see if the error message begins with "xsd file error." If so, make sure that you specified your XSD exactly as shown in the previous set of steps. If the error message begins with "Validation errors," note the error message, then look at the nodes displayed in the list box. The error occurred when the node *after* the last displayed node was read. Check your XML file to see where the inconsistency occurs.

---

8. Close the browser window.

If everything went well, the list displays all the XML file nodes, and an error message does not appear. Since it is important to verify that the XSD will actually catch validation errors, the next set of steps will introduce an error into the XML document, then rerun the project and view the error message.

To introduce an error and verify that the XSD validates the XML file:

1. Double-click StudentRestructured.xml in the Solution Explorer to open it in the XML editor. The file data appears on one long line at the top of the editor.

HELP: If the file does not appear in the project, right-click the Web site root folder, and then click Refresh Folder.

---

2. Scroll to the `<studentid>5</studentid>` element, delete the 5, and then save the file.
3. Select the XMLValidation.aspx tab, and then run the project. An error message appears stating that the studentid value is invalid.
4. Close the browser window.
5. Restore the StudentRestructured.xml file by replacing the 5 and save the file.
6. Close all open documents in the Document window.

CREATING AND PROCESSING XML DOCUMENTS USING DATA SETS

The previous chapters showed how to create data-bound controls to process database data in Windows applications, Crystal Reports, and Web applications. In many cases, a data set was used to store the database data for these applications, which stores data internally in XML format. This section explains how to write an XML file from a .NET data set and how to read data from an XML file into a data set that is then bound to a data control.

Creating XML and XSD Files Using VB Commands

In Chapter 6, you learned how to use program commands to retrieve data from a relational database and store it in a data set. (If necessary, review the section titled "Creating Data Components Using Program Commands" in Chapter 6.) To write the contents of a data set to an XML file, use the data set's `WriteXml()` method. To create the associated XSD file, use the data set's `WriteXmlSchema()` method. The syntax to call these methods is:

```
DataSetName.Tables("DataTableName").WriteXml("XmlFilename.xml")
DataSetName.Tables("DataTableName").WriteXmlSchema("XsdFilename.xsd")
```

The following steps create a new Web form that uses program commands to retrieve all the records from the UniversitySection table, then place them in a data set.

They then use the `WriteXml()` and `WriteXmlSchema()` methods to create associated XML and XSD files. They use the MapPath method to refer to the Web site's root folder and write the files there.

To create XML and XSD files using data sets:

1. *If you are connecting to a local SQL Server database,* use Windows Explorer to copy *yourDatabaseName*.mdf from the SQLServer\Databases folder to your \SQLServer\Solutions\Chapter9\XMLWeb\App_Data folder.

2. In the IDE, create a new Web form named XMLWrite.aspx. Change the form's Title property value to XML Write.

3. Open XMLWrite.aspx in Design view, and create a Label control in the top left corner of the Web form. Change the label's ID property to lblMsg, and delete its Text property value.

4. Double-click any open area on the form to create the event handler declaration for the form's Load event. Add the following commands to the event handler:

```
'Declare the data objects
Dim cnSection As New Data.SqlClient.SqlConnection
Dim daSection As New Data.SqlClient.SqlDataAdapter
Dim sqlCmd As New Data.SqlClient.SqlCommand
Dim dsSection As New Data.DataSet

'Specify the connection string
'Change if you are connecting to a remote DB
cnSection.ConnectionString = "Data Source=.\SQLEXPRESS;" & _
  "AttachDbFilename=|DataDirectory|\yourDatabaseName.mdf;" & _
  "Integrated Security=True;"

'Specify the SQL query
sqlCmd.CommandText = "SELECT * FROM UniversitySection"

'Configure the data adapter
daSection.SelectCommand = sqlCmd
daSection.SelectCommand.Connection = cnSection
Try
  'Fill the data set
  daSection.Fill(dsSection, "SectionDataTable")

  'Write the data set contents to the XML and XSD files
  dsSection.Tables("SectionDataTable").WriteXml _
  (MapPath("Section.xml"))

  dsSection.Tables("SectionDataTable").WriteXmlSchema _
  (MapPath("Section.xsd"))

  lblMsg.Text = "Created the Section XML and XSD files"
Catch ex As Exception
  lblMsg.Text = ex.Message
End Try
```

5. Select XMLWrite in the Solution Explorer and then run the project. After the form loads, the form label should display "Created the Section XML and XSD files."

6. Close the browser window.

7. To view the files, right-click the Web site root folder, and then click Refresh Folder. The Section.xml and Section.xsd files should appear.

8. To view the XML file, right-click Section.xml in the Solution Explorer, then click View in Browser. The XML file appears in the browser and displays each record as a separate node. Close the browser window.

9. To view the XSD file commands, right-click Section.xsd in the Solution Explorer, click Open With, select XML Editor, and then click OK. The XSD element definitions appear.

10. If you are using VS 2005, to view the XSD in the Data Set Designer, double-click Section.xsd in the Solution Explorer. The Data Set Designer window opens and shows the SectionDataTable.

11. Close all open documents in the IDE Document window.

The VS 2005 IDE allows you to view XSD files generated in .NET using the Data Set Designer and to reconfigure the XSD in the Data Set Designer. When you generate an XSD in .NET, it adds extra attributes to the schema tag to configure the Data Set Designer display. The Data Set Designer will not display manually created XSD files.

Retrieving XML Data into a .NET Data Set

You can create a .NET program that accesses data in an XML file and places it into a data set for further processing. To do this, use the DataSet class's `ReadXml` method, which has the following syntax:

```
DatasetName.ReadXml("XMLFilename.xml")
```

This command assumes that the data set contains a single data table and always places the data into the data set's first data table, which it references using index value 0. After you place the XML data into a data set, access it using the following syntax:

```
DatasetName.Tables(0)
```

The following steps show how to insert the contents of the Sections.xml XML file into a data set and create a GridView control to display its contents. The commands use program commands to bind the GridView to a data set.

To insert XML data into a data set and then display the data in a GridView control:

1. Create a new Web form named XMLRead.aspx. Change the form's Title property value to Read XML.

2. Add a GridView control to the form, and set its ID property to gvSections.

3. Create a Load event handler for the form, and add to it the following commands to create the data set, load in it the XML data, and bind the data to the GridView control:

```
Dim dsSections As New Data.DataSet
'Read the XML file into the data set
dsSections.ReadXml(MapPath("Section.xml"))
If dsSections.Tables(0).Rows.Count > 0 Then
    'Set and bind the control's data source
    gvSections.DataSource = dsSections.Tables(0)
    gvSections.DataBind()
End If
```

4. Select XMLRead.aspx in the Solution Explorer and then run the project. The GridView control should display the student data.

5. Close the browser window, and then close all open documents in the IDE Document window.

USING .NET PROGRAM COMMANDS TO CREATE XML FILES AND ADD XML ELEMENTS

Sometimes developers use XML documents rather than relational databases to manage application data. This might be appropriate when an application runs in a remote location with slow network access and insufficient computing power to access or run a database. Alternatively, the application may have simple data management needs that do not warrant the complexity and overhead of a database, or perhaps the application in need of the data runs on a different operating system platform than the organization's database. If an XML-based application uses the same data that an organization's database stores, the application retrieves the data from the database, stores it in the XML file, modifies it as necessary, and then migrates the XML data back to the organizational database at a later time.

This section shows how to use .NET object classes and methods to write programs to create and add data to an XML document. We create a Web form that allows users to enter data values in form controls and writes the values to an XML file.

NOTE: We have provided an example VB Express project named VBExpressXML (stored in Datafiles\Chapter9\VBExpressXML) that demonstrates how to work with XML in a Windows application rather than in a Web application.

Overview of .NET Classes and Methods That Create and Update XML Documents

The `System.Xml.XmlDocument` class defines an XML document object in a program and provides methods for adding elements to an existing XML document. The `System.Xml.XmlNode` class creates an object to represent the XML document's root element. You create these object instances using the following syntax:

```
Dim DocumentObjectName As New XmlDocument
Dim xmlRootObjectName As XmlNode
```

NOTE: In this book, we place an xml prefix before the names of XML objects.

After defining an XML document and root node, the next step is to use the XmlDocument class's Load method to load the XML file into the document, then assign the root element to the document object. These commands use the following syntax:

```
DocumentObjectName.Load("xmlFilename.xml")
xmlRootObjectName = DocumentObjectName.DocumentElement
```

Finally, use the `System.Xml.XmlElement` class to create new element objects and add them to the root node, using the following commands:

```
Dim xmlChildObjectName As XmlElement = _
   DocumentObjectName.CreateElement("childelementname")
xmlRootObjectName.AppendChild(xmlChildObjectName)
```

The text that appears as "*childelementname*" is the actual node name that appears in the XML document, such as "studentid" or "studentgender." To adhere to the XML standard, this should appear in all lowercase letters.

The following commands show how to add elements to the StudentRestructured. xml file. It creates an object to represent the `<students>` root element, then adds an instance of the `<student>` child node.

```
'Create the document and root node objects
Dim StudentRestructured As New XmlDocument
Dim xmlRoot As XmlNode

'Load the file and associate
'the root to the document object
StudentRestructured.Load("StudentRestructured.xml")
xmlRoot = StudentRestructured.DocumentElement

'create a new student node and append it to the root
Dim xmlStudents As XmlElement = _
  StudentRestructured.CreateElement("student")
xmlRoot.AppendChild(xmlstudent)
```

NOTE: These commands assume that the StudentRestructured.xml file already exists and already contains a root element named `<students>`.

These commands create a child node in the root element. However, most XML documents have a hierarchical structure in which the root node contains one or more child nodes that contain associated child nodes and/or other elements. For example, the XML document in Figure 9-7 has a node named `<students>` that contains child nodes named `<student>`. The child nodes in turn contain nodes named `<studentid>`, `<studentname>`, and so forth. To create a child node in an existing child node, create a new XmlElement object, then append it to the existing child node. If the child node contains a data value, assign its value using the node element's InnerText method. Then append the new child element to its parent element.

Use the following commands to create the `<student>` node in Figure 9-7, along with its child `<studentid>` node. The InnerText method assigns the `<studentid>` node's value as 1.

```
'Create a student node and append it to the root node
Dim xmlStudent As XmlElement = _
StudentRestructured.CreateElement("student")
xmlRoot.AppendChild(xmlStudent)

'Create the studentid node and append it to the student node
Dim xmlStudentID As XmlElement = _
  RestructuredStudent.CreateElement("studentid")
xmlStudentID.InnerText = "1"
xmlStudent.AppendChild(xmlStudentID)
```

After defining all the XML elements, the final task is to save the changes to the XML file. This command uses the document class's Save method, as follows:

```
DocumentObjectName.Save("xmlFilename.xml")
```

There is one final issue to deal with: The current commands assume that the XML file already exists. What if the XML file does not exist? Use a Try/Catch block to try to load the XML file. If the file does not exist, add Catch block commands that use methods of the `System.Xml.XmlTextWriter` class to create the file. This Try/Catch block uses the following commands:

```
Try
  DocumentObjectName.Load("xmlFilename.xml")
Catch ex As Exception
  'If file isn't found, create it and write its starting element
  Dim TextWriterObjectName As New System.Xml.XmlTextWriter _
     ("xmlFilename.xml", System.Text.Encoding.UTF8)
  TextWriterObjectName.WriteStartElement("RootElementName")
  TextWriterObjectName.Close()
  DocumentObjectName.Load("xmlFilename.xml")
End Try
xmlRootObjectName = DocumentObjectName.DocumentElement
```

Creating a Web Form to Insert XML File Data

This section describes how to create a Web form using XML commands to allow users to insert data into an XML file. We create the Web form in Figure 9-10, which allows users to input CourseID and CourseName values, and then click a Submit button, which saves the data values to an XML file.

To create the XML data entry form and controls:

1. Create a new Web form named XMLInsert.aspx, and change the form's Title property value to XML Insert. Set the Web form as the Web site's Start Page.
2. In XMLInsert.aspx in Design view, open the Toolbox and create the three Label controls, two Textbox controls, and the Button control, as shown in Figure 9-10.
3. Change the Text properties of the Label controls as shown in Figure 9-10.
4. Change the first text box's ID property value to txtCourseID and the second text box's ID property value to txtCourseName.

FIGURE 9-10 XML data entry form

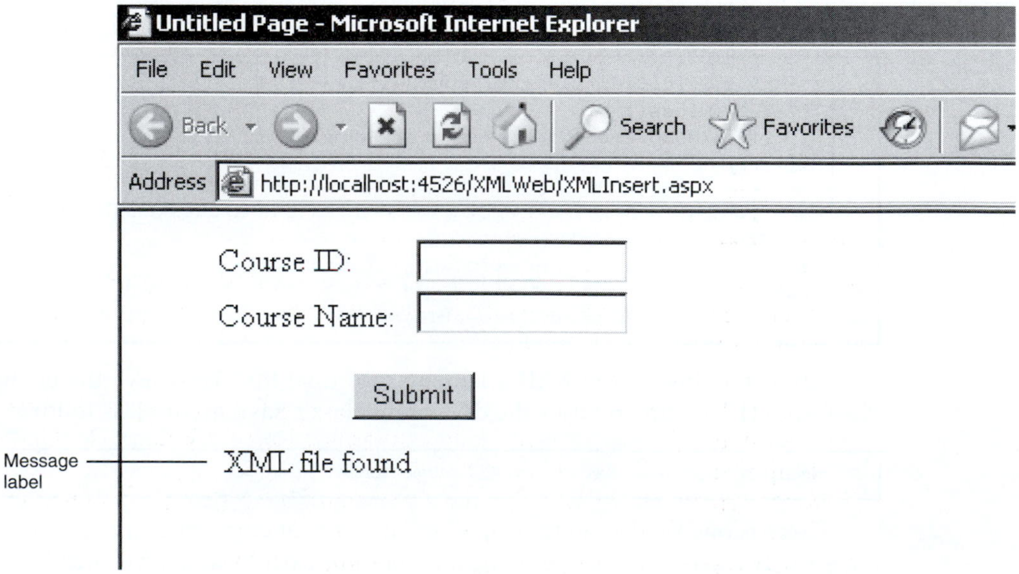

5. Change the message label's ID property value to lblMsg, and delete its Text property value.
6. Change the button's ID property value to btnSubmit and its Text property value to Submit.
7. Save the project.

The next task is to add the program commands to process the data inputs. The following steps add commands to the form's code file to import the System.Xml object class to the form and to define the XML document and root node objects. Then they create a Load event handler to determine if the XML file exists and, if it does not, create the file.

To create the commands to import the object class, define the XML objects, and create the Load event handler:

1. Double-click any open area on the form to create a Load event handler declaration for the form.
2. Add the following command as the very first command in the code file. (This command enables the form to use the System class.)

```
Imports System.Xml
```

3. To define the XML document object and root node, add the following highlighted commands to the form's class declaration:

```
Partial Class XMLInsert
    Inherits System.Web.UI.Page
    Private CourseXMLDocument As New XmlDocument
    Private xmlRoot As XmlNode
```

4. Add the following commands to the Load event handler to determine if the XML file exists, and create a new file if it does not:

```
Try
    CourseXMLDocument.Load(MapPath("Courses.xml"))
Catch ex As Exception
    'If file isn't found, create it
    Dim xmlTw As New System.Xml.XmlTextWriter(MapPath("Courses.xml"), _
        System.Text.Encoding.UTF8)
    xmlTw.WriteStartElement("courses")
    xmlTw.Close()
    CourseXMLDocument.Load(MapPath("Courses.xml"))
End Try
xmlRoot = CourseXMLDocument.DocumentElement
lblMsg.Text = "XML file found"
```

5. Select XMLInsert in the Solution Explorer and run the project. The form should appear as shown in Figure 9-10, and the message confirming that the XML document has been found should appear.
6. Close the browser window.
7. To view the XML file that the event handler created, right-click the Web site root folder in the Solution Explorer, and then click Refresh Folder. The Courses.xml file appears.
8. Double-click Courses.xml to view its contents. It consists of a single node named <courses>, which is the document's root node.
9. Close Courses.xml in the Document window.

FIGURE 9-11   XML data entry XML file

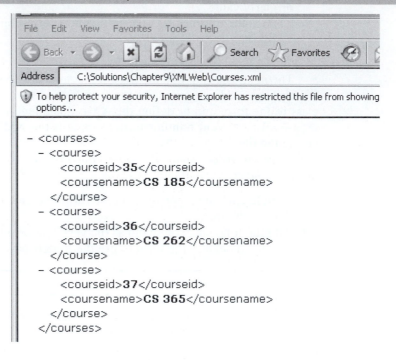

The final task is to create the Submit button's Click event handler to insert the user's inputs into the XML file. Figure 9-11 shows the structure of the underlying XML file. Its root node is named <courses> and already exists in the XML file. It has a child node named <course>, which contains two text nodes named <courseid> and <coursename>. The text nodes store the actual data values.

To create the button event handler that writes the inputs to the XML file:

1. Click the XMLInsert.aspx tab to open the Web form in Design view. Double-click the Submit button to create a new Click event handler, and then add the following commands to create the child nodes and specify their text values:

```
'Create a new course element
Dim xmlCourse As XmlElement = _
CourseXMLDocument.CreateElement("course")
xmlRoot.AppendChild(xmlCourse)

'Create a new courseid element and set its value
Dim xmlCourseID As XmlElement = _
  CourseXMLDocument.CreateElement("courseid")
xmlCourseID.InnerText = txtCourseID.Text
xmlCourse.AppendChild(xmlCourseID)

'Create a new coursename element and set its value
Dim xmlCourseName As XmlElement = _
  CourseXMLDocument.CreateElement("coursename")
xmlCourseName.InnerText = txtCourseName.Text
xmlCourse.AppendChild(xmlCourseName)

'Save the file and display confirmation message
CourseXMLDocument.Save(MapPath("Courses.xml"))
lblMsg.Text = "Course " & txtCourseName.Text & " Added"
```

```
'Reset the form text boxes
txtCourseID.Text = ""
txtCourseName.Text = ""
```

2. Open the form in Design view, and then run the project. The form opens in the browser window, and displays the message confirming that it successfully found the XML file.

3. Type 35 in the Course ID field and CS 185 in the Course Name field, and then click Submit. The confirmation message appears, stating that the course was added to the XML file, and the form text boxes are cleared.

4. Type 36 in the Course ID field and CS 262 in the Course Name field, and then click Submit. Then type 37 in the Course ID field and CS 365 in the Course Name field, and click Submit.

5. Close the browser window.

6. To view your entries in the XML file, right-click Courses.xml in the Solution Explorer, and then click View in Browser. The file appears as shown in Figure 9-11 and shows the new data values.

7. Close all documents in the IDE Document window, and then close the IDE.

This example illustrates how you can use a Web-based application to create a new XML file and add new element, or write elements to an existing XML file. In the Web environment, the Web form does not retain the element objects in memory each time the user submits the form to the Web server. This is why we saved the element values to the XML file every time the user entered a new value. You could improve performance of this application by not saving the data each time you add a new course. To do this, add commands to save the XmlDocument object as a session variable and restore the contents of the session variable to the XmlDocument object (CourseXMLDocument) each time the Web form is posted back to the Web server.

SHARING XML DATA USING XML WEB SERVICES

A *Web service* is a Web server process that uses standard Web-based protocols to service client application information requests. Web services are *loosely coupled,* which means that the applications requesting the data do not need to know how the Web service goes about retrieving the data. All they need to know is how to request the data. An *XML Web service* is a Web service that communicates with client applications using XML-formatted messages. The majority of Web services in use today are XML Web services, so from this point forward we refer to XML Web services simply as Web services. The following sections describe .NET Web service standards and how to use .NET to create Web services and client applications.

.NET Web Service Standards

Table 9-1 summarizes the primary industry standards that .NET uses for Web services.

Simple Object Access Protocol (SOAP)

In the past, developers struggled with creating distributed applications that communicated with one another. Different applications used incompatible technologies, usually due to differences in hardware and software platforms. This communication also posed security problems to the point that most network firewalls blocked interapplication communication. To address this problem, Web services use the HTTP protocol, which

TABLE 9-1   .NET Web service standards

Standard	Description
XML	Text format used to communicate with a Web service
SOAP (Simple Object Access Protocol)	XML- and HTTP-based message protocol that enables communication between Web services and clients
WSDL (Web Services Description Language)	XML document that describes what a Web service can do, where to locate it, and how to invoke it

is supported by most hardware platforms, all Internet browsers, and all Internet servers. In addition, network firewalls generally allow HTTP messages to pass through. The *Simple Object Access Protocol (SOAP)* uses the HTTP protocol to enable applications running on different platforms to communicate with each other using XML documents.

A SOAP message, formatted using XML, contains the following element nodes:

- **Envelope** identifies the document as a SOAP message.
- **Header** is an optional node that contains application-specific information and must be the first child element under the Element element node.
- **Body** contains call and response information.
- **Fault** is an optional element containing information about errors that might have occurred when the message was processed.

NOTE: You do not need to understand internal SOAP XML formats because the .NET framework and tools handle this formatting automatically.

Web Services Description Language (WSDL)

The *Web Services Description Language (WSDL)* stores XML-formatted information that allows applications to connect to Web services. .NET client applications use Web references that access WSDL files to retrieve information to connect to a Web service. You will learn how to create and use Web references later in this section.

TIP: Another Web service standard is UDDI. UDDI (Universal Description, Discovery, and Integration) services are similar to a telephone book in that they enable organizations to find one another's Web services. Internally, UDDI uses WSDL to describe Web service interfaces. If you know the location (URL) of a Web service, you do not need to use UDDI.

Creating a Web Service

The .NET framework provides an infrastructure and VS 2005 and VB Express provide tools to create Web services and Web service client applications that can interact with Web services using the standard protocols just described. A .NET Web service consists of two files: *serviceName*.asmx and *serviceName*.vb. The *serviceName*.asmx file contains the *WebService directive,* which is the addressable entry point for the Web service. (This is similar to how an .aspx file provides the entry point to the compiled code behind the file in an ASP.NET Web page.) The *serviceName*.vb file contains the *Web service class,* which defines the Web service class and its functionality. The following subsections describe these files in more detail.

Web Service Directive (.asmx) File

The Web service directive file is generated by the IDE and contains a single directive that specifies the location of the Web service class file, along with the name of the service class and its underlying programming language. This directive appears as follows:

```
<%@ WebService Language="vb"
    CodeBehind="~/App_Code/Service.vb" Class="Service" %>
```

> **TIP:** By default, the IDE places the Web Service directive and class in separate files, but some Web services combine both into a single .asmx file.

Web Service Class (.vb) File

The Web service class file, which has the default name Service.vb, defines and implements the Web service's functionality. Each Web service requires a unique namespace to differentiate it from other Web services that might use the same method names. By default, the IDE adds the default namespace using the following command: `Namespace:=http://tempuri.org/`. If you create a new Web service that will be deployed in a production environment, you must change tempuri.org to a unique URI.

The Web service class file contains the Web service's class definition, as well as public methods, called *WebMethods,* from which client applications request information. WebMethods are defined by prefacing the Public keyword with the `<System.Web.Services.WebMethod()>` attribute. However, because the IDE automatically adds an `Import` statement for `System.Web.Services` to the class, you can shorten this to `<WebMethod()>`. Use the following general syntax to define a WebMethod that is a public function:

```
<WebMethod()> _
  Public Function FunctionName As ReturnDataType
. . .
  End Function
```

ASP.NET Web services use the App_Data folder in the same way as Web forms: For enhanced security, any files stored in this folder can be accessed by commands in the Web service class but cannot be directly accessed by other browsers or programs.

The following steps show how to create a Web service.

> **NOTE:** Steps in a later section show how to create a Web service client application to test the Web service. If you are using VB Express, you have to deploy the Web service to a locally installed IIS Web server to test your client application against the Web service. VS 2005 users can test their client applications against their Web services without installing a Web server or deploying their Web service. This book addresses testing client applications against a Web service using VS 2005 only.

To create a Web service:

1. In VS 2005 or VWD, click File on the menu bar, click New Web Site, and select the ASP.NET Web Service template. Change the Location value to SqlServer\ Solutions\Chapter9\IronwoodService, and then click OK.

2. *If you are using a local database file connection,* use Windows Explorer to copy *yourDatabaseName*.mdf and *yourDatabaseName*.ldf to the Web service's App_Data folder.

3. In the Solution Explorer, open the App_Code folder, and then double-click Service.vb to open it in Code view.

4. Modify the default HelloWorld WebMethod by adding/modifying the highlighted text so that it appears as follows:

```
Public Class Service
  Inherits System.Web.Services.WebService
    <WebMethod()>Public Function _
   AllStudentsInformation() As Data.DataSet
     Dim cnStudent As New Data.SqlClient.SqlConnection
     Dim daStudent As New Data.SqlClient.SqlDataAdapter
     Dim sqlCommand As New Data.SqlClient.SqlCommand
     Dim dsStudent As New Data.DataSet

      ' Change your connection string as necessary
     cnStudent.ConnectionString = _
        "Data Source=.\sqlexpress;" & _
        "AttachDbFilename=|DataDirectory|\" & _
        "yourDatabaseName.mdf;" & _
        "Integrated Security=True;User Instance=True"

     sqlCommand.CommandText = _
        "SELECT StudentID, StudentLastName, " & _
          "StudentFirstName, StudentMI, StudentDOB, " & _
          "StudentGender, StudentAddress, " & _
          "StudentCity, StateAbbreviation, " & _
          "StudentPostalCode, StudentPhoneNumber " & _
        "FROM UniversityStudent " & _
        "ORDER BY StudentLastName, StudentFirstName, " & _
          "StudentMI"

     daStudent.SelectCommand = sqlCommand
     daStudent.SelectCommand.Connection = cnStudent
     daStudent.Fill(dsStudent, "Student")
     Return dsStudent
    End Function
```

5. Save the project.

In the next set of steps, you make a copy of this WebMethod function and change it slightly to add a search filter. You will also modify the query to use a parameter query that accepts a user input to find a particular student's data.
To copy the function and modify it to create a new function:

1. Copy *all* the AllStudentsInformation() WebMethod, starting with the the the `<WebMethod()>_` command and ending with the `End Function` command, and paste it just below the current AllStudentsInformation function's `End Function` line of code.

2. Modify the copied function's declaration so that it appears as follows:

```
<WebMethod()> _
Public Function StudentUserIDandPIN(ByVal _
StudentID As Long) As Data.DataSet
```

3. Add the following highlighted command to create a SQL parameter query, and then modify the query as follows to accept the parameter value:

```
sqlCommand.Parameters.Add(New _
  Data.SqlClient.SqlParameter("@StudentID", CStr(StudentID)))
sqlCommand.CommandText = _
  "SELECT StudentUserID, StudentPIN " & _
  "FROM UniversityStudent " & _
  "WHERE StudentID = @StudentID"
```

4. Run the project to test your Web service's WebMethods. A Web Service page that contains links to the service's AllStudentsInformation and StudentUserIDandPIN WebMethods appears, as shown in Figure 9-12. (Note that the default namespace value appears. To deploy this Web service to a production environment, you have to change this to a unique URI.)

5. Click the AllStudentsInformation link. The Web Service test page in Figure 9-13 appears, which allows you to test the Web service.

6. Click Invoke on the test page. If all goes well, the XML file that the Web service generates appears. Notice that the file begins with XSD elements that define the data attributes, followed by the actual data values.

HELP: If error messages appear, close the browser window, fix the errors, and then test the project again.

FIGURE 9-12   Web Service link page

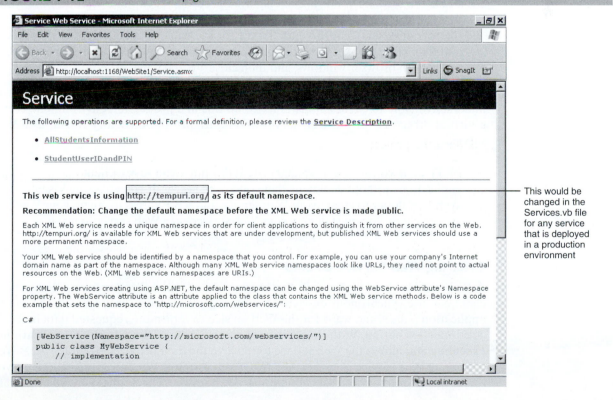

This would be changed in the Services.vb file for any service that is deployed in a production environment

FIGURE 9-13 Web Service test page

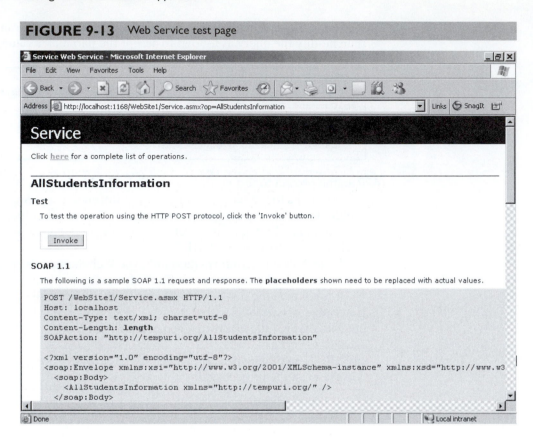

7. Close the browser window that displays the results, click the Back button on your browser toolbar to return to the AllStudentsInformation test page, and then click the StudentUserIDandPIN link. Type 1 for the value of the StudentID parameter and then click Invoke. The data for Student ID 1 (Clifford Wall) should appear. Close both browser windows, and then close VS 2005 or VWD.

After you create a Web service, the next step is to deploy it to a Web server to make it available to client applications. To do this in a production environment, create a virtual directory on the Web server and configure the directory to run as a Web service.

NOTE: If you are using VS 2005, the IDE allows you to test client applications without deploying them on a Web server. If you are using Visual Web Developer to create your Web service and VB Express to create your Web service client, you must deploy your Web service on a Web server to test it.

Creating Web Service Clients

A Web service client makes calls that request data from a Web service. A Web service client can use synchronous or asynchronous calls. With a *synchronous call,* the calling application pauses and waits for the Web service to return the requested data before it continues executing. With an *asynchronous call*, the calling application continues executing and allows the Web service to retrieve the data in a background process. You can create Web service clients in ASP.NET Web forms or Windows applications, or you can create a Web service that calls another Web service. The application type that calls the Web service affects whether you implement the Web service call as synchronous or asynchronous.

In a Windows application, you should use an asynchronous call to avoid "freezing" the user interface while waiting for a response. In a Web application this is less important, because the user can always click the browser's Back button if the Web service call takes too long. A call from one Web service to another Web service can be either synchronous or asynchronous based on performance criteria because freezing the user interface is not an issue.

This section describes how to use VS 2005 or VB Express to create a Windows application that makes asynchronous calls to a Web service. To do this, create a Windows application project, then a Web reference to access the Web service. A *Web reference* is a project component that defines an existing Web service in terms of its Web server location, service name, and other information about the service. When you add a Web reference to a VB project, the IDE generates the following four files in the project:

- **Service.wsdl** contains an XSD formatted schema of supported data types, methods provided by the Web service, and the message protocols accepted by the service.
- **Service.disco** is a discovery file that publishes links to the Web service and the service's .wsdl file.
- **Reference.map** is an XML document that contains the name of the .wsdl and .disco files.
- **Reference.vb** is a class that the IDE automatically generates based on the description in the WSDL and is used by the client application to access the public Web service methods.

TIP: All these files are based on industry standards, and all but the Reference.vb files are XML documents.

To add a Web reference to a project, open the Solution Explorer, right-click the client project name, and then select *Add Web Reference*. Figure 9-14 shows the Add Web Reference page that appears.

VS 2005 (non-Express) users can include the Web service project in the same solution as the client project, and then enter the reference to the Web service directly. To do this, click the *Web services in this solution* link. This action opens a dialog box that displays a list of the Web service projects contained in the solution. Click the link to the service, and the service's link page appears, as shown in Figure 9-12. If you click one of these links, the WebMethods test page appears (see Figure 9-13).

NOTE: VB Express does not allow developers to create solutions that contain multiple projects. The Web services in this solution link will be displayed but will not be functional.

Creating a Web reference also adds to the project a new class that contains public methods for accessing the Web service. To access the Web service, declare an object variable of this service class. For example, suppose you select one of the Web service methods in Figure 9-14 and click Add Reference. To create an object variable of this service class, add the following command to the client form's class definition:

```
Private objService As New localhost.Service
```

FIGURE 9-14 Adding a Web Reference

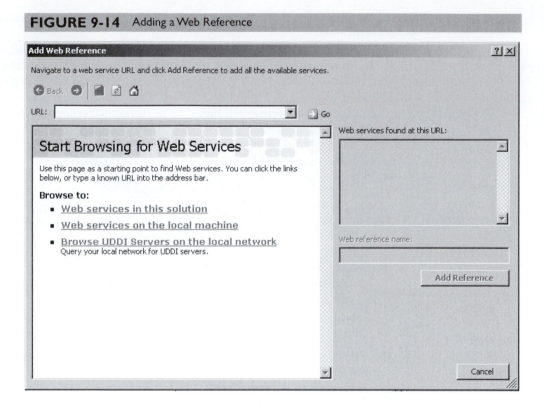

The Web reference class contains public methods for both synchronous and asynchronous access to the service's WebMethods.

> **NOTE:** To create an asynchronous call, you could create a BackgroundWorker component for asynchronous processing and call the Web service in the BackgroundWorker's DoWork event. (These components are described in Chapter 6 in the section titled "Retrieving Data Asynchronously.") However, a Web reference provides an asynchronous method for doing this in the Reference.vb class so there is no need to use a BackgoundWorker.

For example, you can use the following command to call the AllStudentsInformation WebMethod:

```
objService.AllStudentsInformation()
```

You also need to create an event handler that executes after the Web server data is retrieved. The IDE does not generate an event handler declaration for an object so you have to manually enter the code for the event handler's declaration, using the following syntax:

```
Private Sub handlerName(ByVal sender As Object, _
  ByVal e As ServiceName.MethodNameCompletedEventArgs)
End Sub
```

Wiring the event handler so that it executes at the proper time requires another line of code before the *serviceObjectName.WebMethodName*Async()

command. The general form for this code is:

```
AddHandler serviceObjectName.handlerName, AddressOf handlerName
```

When a Web service call is completed, the results from the call are accessed in the event handler using `e.Result`.

You can bind form controls to a data set that a Web service returns. However, the data source or connection that retrieves the data is in the Web service, not in the client application. This means you do not bind the control using the IDE. Therefore, to configure the control, which in this case is a DataGridView, you open its Tasks dialog box and use the Add Columns or Edit Columns button to specify columns. There will not be any columns listed initially. After putting an entry in each column, individually select each column using the Edit Columns dialog box and set its DataPropertyName to the name of the desired field being retrieved from the Web service. This means you must know the names of the fields that the Web service returns.

TIP: Suppose you do not know the names of the fields. Perhaps someone else created the Web service, you do not have access to the code, and no one told you the names of the fields being retrieved. These can be determined at the time a project's Web reference is added to the project by clicking on links similar to those shown in Figure 9-14 and invoking the WebMethods.

The following exercise creates the client application shown in Figure 9-15 that connects to the Web service. When the form loads, it connects to the AllStudentsInformation Web service, which returns the data for all students. The form then shows these values in a data grid view control. When the user selects a specific student, the form connects to the StudentUserIDAndPIN Web service, which returns the ID and PIN for the selected student. The form then shows these values in a message box.

NOTE: If you are using VB Express, you cannot create the client application's Web reference to the Web service unless you have already deployed the service to a Web server.

To create the Web service client application:

1. Start VS 2005 or VB Express, and create a new Windows Application project named IronwoodClient. Save the project in your SqlServer\Solutions\Chapter9 folder, and do not create a directory for the solution.

FIGURE 9-15   Web service client application

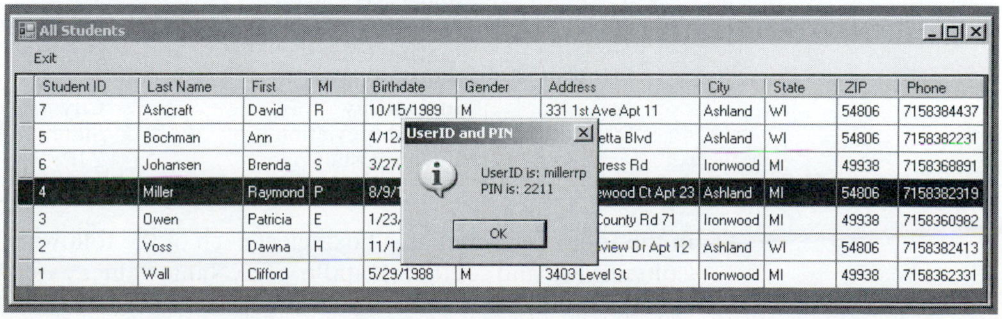

2. *If you are using VB Express, skip this step.*

   If you are using VS 2005 and not accessing the Web service from a local Web server, add the IronwoodService to your solution by clicking File on the menu bar, pointing to Add, and then clicking on Existing Web Site. In the Add Existing Web site window, make sure File System is selected in the left pane, then browse to your IronwoodService folder and click Open. At this point, two projects appear in the Solution Explorer.

3. Right click IronwoodClient in the Solution Explorer, and then click Add Web Reference. The window in Figure 9-14 opens.

4. *If you are using VS 2005 and not connecting to the Web service from a local Web server,* click the Web services in this solution link.

   If you are using VB Express, or if you are using VS 2005 and connecting to a local Web server, click the Web services on the local machine link.

5. Click the Service link corresponding to the IronwoodService. A Web service page similar to the one in Figure 9-12 opens.

6. Change the Web reference name field to IronwoodStudents and click Add Reference.

7. Rename Form1.vb to frmAllStudents.vb. Open the form in Design view, and change its Name property value to frmAllStudents, StartPosition to Center Screen, and Text property to Ironwood Students.

8. Add a DataGridView control to the form, and change its properties as follows:

Property	*New Value*
Name	dgStudents
AllowUserToAddRows	False
AllowUserToDeleteRows	False
AutoSizeColumnsMode	DisplayedCells
Dock	Fill
ReadOnly	True
RowHeadersWidth	15
SelectionMode	FullRowSelect

9. Click the dgStudent control's Properties tab to open its Tasks list, and clear the Enable Adding, Editing, and Deleting boxes.

10. In the Tasks list, click the Edit Column button, and then click the Add button. Add the following unbound columns by entering the Name and HeaderText properties for each column and then clicking on Add:

Name	*HeaderText*
StudentID	Student ID
StudentLastName	Last Name
StudentFirstName	First Name
StudentMI	MI
StudentDOB	Birthdate
StudentGender	Gender
StudentAddress	Address
StudentCity	City
StateAbbreviation	State
StudentPostalCode	ZIP
StudentPhoneNumber	Phone

11. In the Edit Columns dialog box, select each of the following columns in the Edit Columns list, and set their DataPropertyName values as shown. (You will need to enter the values manually because the control is not bound to a data source.)

Selected Column	*DataPropertyName*
Student ID	StudentID
Last Name	StudentLastName
First Name	StudentFirstName
Birthdate	StudentDOB
Gender	StudentGender
Address	StudentAddress
City	StudentCity
State	StateAbbreviation
ZIP	StudentPostalCode
Phone	StudentPhoneNumber

12. Click OK to close the Edit Columns dialog box.
13. Open the Toolbox and add a MenuStrip control to the form. Create a single top-level item that has the text "&Cancel Data Retrieval?".
14. Open the form in Code view, and add the following commands to the form's class declaration.

```
Public Class frmAllStudents
    Public service As New IronwoodStudents.Service
    Private Sub Students_Completed( _
      ByVal sender As Object, _
      ByVal e As IronwoodStudents. _
      AllStudentsInformationCompletedEventArgs)
      Try
          'commands to suppress extra columns
          dgStudents.AutoGenerateColumns = False
          dgStudents.DataSource = e.Result
          dgStudents.DataMember = "Student"
          CancelDataRetrievalToolStripMenuItem.Text = "&Exit"
      Catch ex As Exception
          MessageBox.Show(ex.Message)
      End Try
    End Sub
End Class
```

15. Create a form Load event handler and add to it the following commands:

```
Private Sub frmAllStudents_Load(. . .
    AddHandler service.AllStudentsInformationCompleted, _
            AddressOf Students_Completed
    Service.AllStudentsInformationAsync()
End Sub
```

16. Create an event handler for the Cancel Data Retrieval menu item that has the following command:

```
Me.Close()
```

17. Run the project, confirm that it displays the data shown in the data grid control in Figure 9-16, and then close the application.

The next exercise shows how to call a Web service and pass to it a parameter. When the user selects a row in the form's data grid view control, the form calls the

StudentUserIDandPIN Web service method. When the Web service returns the data, the form displays it in a message box.

To pass a parameter to a Web service:

1. To create the event handler that executes when the user selects a row, open the form in Code view, and add the following commands:

```
Private Sub StudentUserIDandPIN_Completed( _
  ByVal sender As Object, _
  ByVal e As IronwoodStudents. _
  StudentUserIDandPINCompletedEventArgs)
Dim ds As New Data.DataSet
ds = e.Result
MessageBox.Show("UserID is: " & _
  ds.Tables("Student").Rows(0).Item(0).ToString & _
  vbCr & "PIN is: " & _
  ds.Tables("Student").Rows(0).Item(1).ToString, _
  "UserID and PIN", MessageBoxButtons.OK, _
  MessageBoxIcon.Information)
End Sub
```

2. To link this event handler to the service's StudentUserIDandPINCompleted event, add the following command as the last line in the form's Load event handler:

```
AddHandler service.StudentUserIDandPINCompleted, _
          AddressOf StudentUserIDandPIN_Completed
```

3. To add a Click event handler to the dgStudents DataGridView control, select dgStudents in the Objects list, select Click in the Events list, and then add the following commands to the event handler:

```
Try
  service.StudentUserIDandPINAsync( _
  CLng(dgStudents.CurrentRow.Cells("StudentID").Value))
Catch
  MessageBox.Show("Please wait until the data from " & _
    "the previous student selection is returned " & _
    "before selecting another")
End Try
```

4. Run the application. Select different rows, and confirm that the UserID and PIN values appear in the message box, as shown in Figure 9-15.

IN CONCLUSION. . .

XML is an important technology to enable platform-independent data sharing. Its use is increasing, primarily due to the availability of improved tools and programming environments for creating and processing XML data. This chapter provides an overview describing XML and has shown how you can use different programming approaches to create, transform, and process XML documents. Using XML documents in database applications is likely to increase as more database applications require information sharing across different hardware and software platforms and across organizations.

SUMMARY

- XML defines a standard way to structure and store data in text files by allowing developers to create custom tags that define XML elements. XML elements are containers that can store character data and additional XML elements. The nested order of XML elements defines a hierarchical data structure.

- An XML document consists of a prolog that defines the XML version and encoding scheme, a root element that represents the first node in the data hierarchy, and nested element tags that define the XML document structure and contents. XML document files are saved as text files with an .xml extension.

- XML documents must be well formed documents: every opening tag must have a corresponding closing tag. XML tags are case sensitive, so every instance of a tag must be identical throughout the document.

- XPATH is a W3C standard that provides a way to identify XML components and locate nodes in an XML document. XPATH identifies seven distinct XML node types: root, element, attribute, text, namespace, processing instruction, and comment.

- XML namespaces distinguish XML elements having the same name but different meanings. This happens when different organizations or different groups in the same organization develop XML specifications for similar types of data.

- You can create SELECT queries in SQL Server that instruct the DBMS to format output in XML format by wrapping data values in nodes or structuring them as node attributes.

- In an XML-formatted SELECT query, RAW mode retrieves each data row as a single element, with data values stored as row attributes. AUTO mode retrieves data as attribute values and creates nested elements when queries join multiple tables. You can modify both RAW and AUTO mode with the ELEMENTS option to wrap data values outputs in text nodes rather than store them as attributes.

- The FOR XML EXPLICIT option allows developers to control how the DBMS formats XML output in terms of hierarchical relationships and whether it appears as attribute values, text nodes, or a combination of both.

- You can use XSLTs to format and transform elements in XML files. XSLTs contain XPATH program commands and HTML tags to format the output data. You can use XSLTs to perform looping and decision structure operations, as well as data sorting and filtering operations.

- A valid XML document contains all the elements that it is supposed to contain. In addition, the elements are of the correct data types, and the element relationships are correctly specified through nested tags. You can create XML Schema Definitions (XSDs) to define the required structure of an XML document. You can then validate the XML file against its XSD to confirm that the XML document is correct and complete.

- .NET provides classes and methods to create XML and XSD files from relational database data by retrieving the data into a data set, and then moving the data set contents into the XML file. .NET also provides classes to move XML document data into a data set for further processing.

- You can write a .NET application that uses program commands to create an XML file and add data elements to it.

- A Web service is a Web server process that uses standard Web-based protocols to service application information requests. You can use .NET to create Web services and Web service client applications.

- A .NET Web service consists of a directive file, which specifies the location of the Web service class file, the name of the service class, and its underlying programming language. It also has a class file, which defines the Web service class and its underlying methods.

- To create a .NET Windows application Web service client, you create the project, and add to it a Web reference to the target Web service.

KEY TERMS

Asynchronous call   Web service client call in which the calling application continues to execute while waiting for the Web service reply

Child element   Element under the root element in the XML document that can contain other elements, data, a combination of both, or can be empty

Compositor element   XSD element defining the type of child elements that a container element contains

Container element   XSD element that contains other elements

Current context   XML document elements that an XSLT processes

Document type definition (DTD)   Definition of a standard formatting notation in a markup language

Element   Individual data item in an XML document

eXtensible Markup Language (XML) Markup language that defines a standard way to structure and store data in text files using element tags and data values

eXtensible Stylesheet Language Transformation (XSLT) Program that uses XPATH commands and HTML tags to process, sort, filter, modify, and form XML data

Loosely coupled Processes that do not need to understand anything about one another except in the way they have to interact

Migrate Move data from one location to another

Parent field Second field in an XML SELECT query that uses the EXPLICIT OPTION and that specifies the hierarchical level of the parent field of the output

Root element Top or parent element in an XML document

SOAP (Simple Object Access Protocol) XML- and HTTP-based message protocol that enables communication between Web services and clients

Self-terminating tag Tag that ends with a forward slash (/) and does not require an associated closing tag

Standard Generalized Markup Language (SGML) High-level language for defining markup languages

Structured data Data defined in a specific and unambiguous format

Synchronous call Web service client call in which the calling application pauses while waiting for the Web service reply

Tag field First field in an XML SELECT query that uses the EXPLICIT OPTION; specifies the hierarchical level of the output

Template definition XSLT section that specifies the portion of the XML document to be processed

Valid XML document XML document that is complete and that contains the correct data types and relationships

WSDL (Web Services Description Language) XML document that describes what a Web service can do, where to locate it, and how to invoke it

Web reference Project application component in a .NET Windows application Web client that defines a target Web service

Web service Web server process that uses standard Web-based protocols to service application information requests

Web service class File with a .vb extension that defines the Web service class and its underlying functionality

Web service directive File with an .asmx extension that provides the addressable entry point for a .NET-generated Web service

Well formed document Markup language document in which every opening tag has a corresponding closing tag, and every tag appears in angle brackets

XML absolute path XML path specified by moving down from the root element

XML file or document XML-formatted text file

XML path Node location in an XML document

XML Path Language (XPATH) W3C standard that provides a way to identify components and locate nodes in an XML document

XML relative path XML path specified by moving forward or backward from the current context

XML Schema Definition (XSD) Definition of an XML file's data structure in terms of data types, relationships, order and grouping mechanisms, and constraints

XML Web service Web service that communicates with client applications using XML-formatted messages

XSLT processor Program that compiles and runs an XSLT

STUDY QUESTIONS

Multiple-Choice Questions

1. A well-formed XML document:
   a. Contains data that is the correct data type
   b. Has a prolog
   c. Has an associated XSD
   d. Has a closing tag for every opening tag
2. A(n) _____ is a program that contains commands to process XML elements.
   a. XSLT   c. DTD
   b. XSD   d. XML document
3. In .NET, you can create an XML document based on a database query by first placing the data in a .NET _____.
   a. Data set   c. Table adapter
   b. Data adapter   d. Data table
4. In an XSLT, a template definition specifies the document's:
   a. Namespace   c. Encoding scheme
   b. Current context   d. Version

5. You use an XSD to:
   a. Validate an existing XML document
   b. Specify the data types of comment elements in an XML document
   c. Create a valid XML document
   d. Both a and b
6. In the XPATH node categories, _____ and _____ nodes represent data values.
   a. Root, Element
   b. Element, Attribute
   c. Element, Text
   d. Attribute, Text
   e. Text, Namespace
7. An XSLT contains:
   a. XPATH commands
   b. A root node
   c. HTML formatting tags
   d. All of the above
   e. Both a and c
8. In a SQL query that retrieves XML-formatted output, you use _____ mode to retrieve data that is formatted using a combination of attribute values and text nodes.
   a. RAW
   b. AUTO
   c. EXPLICIT
   d. ELEMENTS
9. To specify alternate names for XML output nodes in an XML-formatted SELECT query, you:
   a. Use the FOR XML EXPLICIT option
   b. Use the ELEMENTS option
   c. Create column and table aliases
   d. Either a or c
10. A .NET Web service's _____ file contains the commands for the functions that service client application requests.
    a. Directive
    b. Class
    c. Namespace
    d. .asmx

True/False Questions

1. XML is a subset of SGML.
2. In an XML document, the prolog is optional.
3. An XSLT allows you to create a new XML document.
4. In an XSD, you always specify a compositor element immediate after a container element.
5. Every XML document must have a root element.
6. An XML document contains structured data.
7. An XML-formatted SELECT query that uses the RAW option always retrieves data as attribute values.
8. All Web services share data using XML-formatted messages.
9. Web service clients that are Web applications should always use asynchronous calls.

Short Answer Questions

1. Describe two instances when you might use XML in a database application.
2. When do you need to specify a namespace in an XML document?
3. List the four things that an XML element can contain.
4. Describe what happens when you add the ELEMENTS option to an XML-formatted SELECT query.
5. Assume an XML document contains the following elements:

```
<students/>
  <student/>
    <studentID/>
    <name/>
      <last/>
      <first/>
    <address/>
      <street/>
      <city/>
      <postalcode/>
```

a. If the current context is <students/>, what is the relative path to <city/>?

b. If the current context is <students/>, what is the absolute path to <city/>?

6. Why do you need to validate XML documents?

7. List and describe the two files that .NET generates when you create a Web service.

8. Describe when you should create a Web service client that uses a synchronous call, and when you should create a client that uses a synchronous call.

Guided Exercises

1. **Creating a Web Site with a Master Page and Site Map**

   This exercise creates a Web site that stores the solutions for all the chapter's guided exercises. Figure 9-16 illustrates the Web site's home page.

   a. Create a new Web site and specify its root folder as \SQLServer\Solutions\Chapter9\XMLWebExercises.

   b. Create a master page that displays the site map in Figure 9-16. Specify the following site map titles, file names, and descriptions:

Site Map Title	File Name	Description
XML Customer Orders	XMLCustomerOrders.xml	Customer Orders XML File
XSLT Categories	XSLTCategories.aspx	XSLT Category Transformation
XSD Customer Orders	XSDOrders.aspx	Customer Order Validation
XML Employees	XMLEmployees.aspx	Employees XML File
XML Departments	XMLDepartments.aspx	XML Department Insertions

   c. Create a TreeView control on the master page that displays the site map.

   d. Delete the current Default.aspx Web page.

   e. Copy the Images folder and its contents from the \SQLServer\Datafiles\Chapter9 folder to your Web site root folder.

FIGURE 9-16 Web site home page (Exercise 9-1)

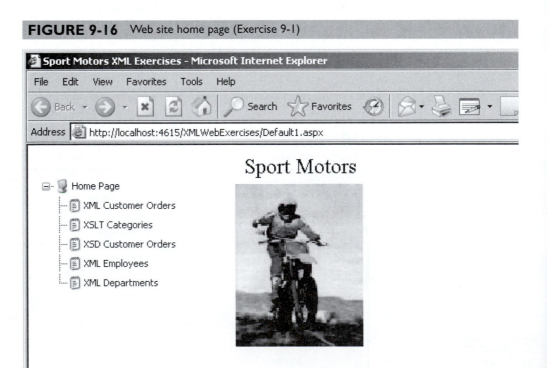

TABLE 9-2 Customer Order data (Exercise 9-2)

Customer FirstName	Customer LastName	OrderID	OrderDate	InventoryID	DetailQuantity	DetailUnitPrice
Allison	Scholten	1	3/11/2007	3	1	8595.00
				18	1	45.95
Robin	O'Conner	2	3/11/2007	27	1	95.99
				29	1	15.39
				32	4	8.99

f. Create a new Web form as a content page that links to the master page, then add the items to the home page, as shown in Figure 9-16. Specify the new Web form as the site's Start Page. Change the Web form's Title property value to Sport Motors XML Exercises, and use motox1.jpg as the image source.

2. **Creating an XML File To Display Customer Order Data**

NOTE: To complete this exercise, you must have already completed Exercise 9-1.

This exercise creates an XML file that displays the Customer Order data in Table 9-2, which displays data from the Sport Motors SportCustomer, SportOrders, and SportOrderDetails database tables in Figure 3-2:

a. In the Web site you created in Exercise 9-1, create a new XML file named XMLCustomerOrders.xml.

b. Use the XML Editor to add the XML elements and data values as shown. Create container nodes so that the order and order detail data appear as nested values, and do not repeat when you display the XML file in a browser window.

3. **Retrieving XML-Formatted Data Using SQL SELECT Queries**

This exercise uses Management Studio to write queries to retrieve XML-formatted data from the Sport Motors database in Figures 3-3 and 3-4. Create a new query file named 9Exercise3.sql that contains the following queries:

a. Retrieve the following data about departments and their associated employees. (Your results will show each row element on a single line and a total of 12 records.)

```
<row DepartmentName="Sales" EmployeeLastName="Mathews"
    EmployeeFirstName="Roy" EmployeeMI="D" />
<row DepartmentName="Sales" EmployeeLastName="Kaiser"
    EmployeeFirstName="Greg" EmployeeMI="M" />
. . .
```

b. Retrieve the same data, but formatted as follows:

```
<SportDepartment>
  <DepartmentName>Sales</DepartmentName>
  <SportEmployee>
    <EmployeeLastName>Mathews</EmployeeLastName>
    <EmployeeFirstName>Roy</EmployeeFirstName>
  </SportEmployee>
  <SportEmployee>
    <EmployeeLastName>Kaiser</EmployeeLastName>
    <EmployeeFirstName>Greg</EmployeeFirstName>
  </SportEmployee>
</SportDepartment>
. . .
```

c. Retrieve the following formatted data about categories, subcategories, and inventory items:

```
<SportCategory>
  <CategoryDescription>All Terrain Vehicles</CategoryDescription>
  <SportSubCategory>
    <SubCategoryDescription>Sport</SubCategoryDescription>
    <SportInventory>
      <InventoryID>9</InventoryID>
      <InventoryDescription>Sahara 600</InventoryDescription>
    </SportInventory>
  </SportSubCategory>
  <SportSubCategory>
    <SubCategoryDescription>Utility</SubCategoryDescription>
    <SportInventory>
      <InventoryID>10</InventoryID>
      <InventoryDescription>Mojave 400</InventoryDescription>
    </SportInventory>
  </SportSubCategory>
</SportCategory>
. . .
```

d. Retrieve the following XML-formatted data, sorted by CategoryDescription and InventoryID.

```
<SportCategory CategoryDescription="All Terrain Vehicles">
  <InvID>
    <InventoryID>9</InventoryID>
    <InventoryDescription>Sahara 600</InventoryDescription>
  </InvID>
  <InvID>
    <InventoryID>10</InventoryID>
    <InventoryDescription>Mojave 400</InventoryDescription>
  </InvID>
</SportCategory>
```

4. **Creating an XSLT to Transform Category and Subcategory Data**

NOTE: To complete this exercise, you must have already completed Exercise 9-1.

In this exercise, use an XSLT to transform the XML file shown in Figure 9-17, which displays data from the Sport Motors SportCategory and SportSubCategory tables. Currently, the data displays the category and subcategory ID and description values. Write an XSLT to transform the data so that it omits the ID values and sorts the data values by category description. After the transformation, the new XML file data will appear as shown in Figure 9-18.

a. Copy InputCategories.xml from the \SQLServer\Chapter9\Datafiles folder to your Web site's root folder.

b. Create a new XSLT file named CategoriesTransform.xsl, then delete the existing HTML tags in the template file.

c. Add XPATH commands to display the data in a hierarchical structure as shown in Figure 9-18. Show each category as a parent node and the category's subcategories as child nodes.

d. Create a new Web form named XSLTCategories.aspx. Link the form to the master page you created in Exercise 9-1, and change the form's title to XML Category File Transformation. Add a label and three button controls to the Web form so that it looks like the XSLTTransform.aspx Web form in Figure 9-8.

FIGURE 9-17   InputCategories.xml source file (Exercise 9-4)

```xml
<?xml version="1.0" standalone="yes" ?>
- <NewDataSet>
  - <CategoryDataTable>
      <CategoryID>1</CategoryID>
      <CategoryDescription>Apparel</CategoryDescription>
      <SubcategoryID>1</SubcategoryID>
      <SubCategoryDescription>Women's</SubCategoryDescription>
    </CategoryDataTable>
  - <CategoryDataTable>
      <CategoryID>1</CategoryID>
      <CategoryDescription>Apparel</CategoryDescription>
      <SubcategoryID>2</SubcategoryID>
      <SubCategoryDescription>Men's</SubCategoryDescription>
    </CategoryDataTable>
  - <CategoryDataTable>
      <CategoryID>1</CategoryID>
      <CategoryDescription>Apparel</CategoryDescription>
      <SubcategoryID>3</SubcategoryID>
      <SubCategoryDescription>Children's</SubCategoryDescription>
    </CategoryDataTable>
  - <CategoryDataTable>
      <CategoryID>2</CategoryID>
      <CategoryDescription>Motorcycles</CategoryDescription>
      <SubcategoryID>4</SubcategoryID>
      <SubCategoryDescription>Off Road</SubCategoryDescription>
    </CategoryDataTable>
  - <CategoryDataTable>
```

e. Create a Click event handler for the Transform XML File button that runs the XSLT and transforms the InputCategories.xml file and that writes the new data to a file named OutputCategories.xml in the Web site's root folder.

f. Create a Click event handler for the second button so that it displays the original InputCategories.xml file.

g. Create a Click event handler for the third button so that it displays the modified OutputCategories.xml file.

5. **Creating an XSD to Validate XML Customer Order Data**

NOTE: To complete this exercise, you must have already completed Exercise 9-1.

In this exercise, you create an XSD to validate the XMLValidateOrders.xml file shown in Figure 9-19, which contains data about Sport Motors customer orders. After you create the XSD, create a Web form to process the XSD and validate the XML file and confirm that its data elements are correct.

a. Copy XMLValidateOrders.xml from the \SQLServer\Chapter9\Datafiles folder to your Web site's root folder, and then refresh the root folder's contents.

b. Create a new XSD file named ValidateOrders.xsd, and then add the commands to specify the XSD schema. Specify that the file can contain an unlimited number of orders and that each order can have only one associated order ID, order date, customer, employee, and payment type. Specify appropriate data type values for each text element.

FIGURE 9-18   OutputCategories.xml output file (Exercise 9-4)

```
<?xml version="1.0" encoding="utf-8" ?>
- <categories>
  - <category>
      <categorydescription>All Terrain Vehicles</categorydescription>
    - <subcategories>
      - <subcategory>
          <subcategorydescription>Utility</subcategorydescription>
        </subcategory>
      </subcategories>
    </category>
  - <category>
      <categorydescription>All Terrain Vehicles</categorydescription>
    - <subcategories>
      - <subcategory>
          <subcategorydescription>Sport</subcategorydescription>
        </subcategory>
      </subcategories>
    </category>
  - <category>
      <categorydescription>Apparel</categorydescription>
    - <subcategories>
      - <subcategory>
          <subcategorydescription>Women's</subcategorydescription>
        </subcategory>
      </subcategories>
    </category>
  - <category>
      <categorydescription>Apparel</categorydescription>
    - <subcategories>
      - <subcategory>
          <subcategorydescription>Men's</subcategorydescription>
        </subcategory>
      </subcategories>
```

c. Create a new Web form named XSDOrders.aspx. Link the form to the master page you created in Exercise 9-1, and change the form's title to Validate Customer Orders. Add a list and label control to the Web form so that it looks like the Web form in Figure 9-9.

d. Create a Load event handler for a Web form that validates XMLValidateOrders.xml using ValidateOrders.xsl XSD. Display the validated nodes in the form list. If a node cannot be validated, display the name of the invalid node in the form's message label.

e. Modify the XML file as necessary until it is valid.

6. **Creating and Displaying XML Data Using a Relational Database Query**

NOTE: To complete this exercise, you must have already completed Exercise 9-1.

In this exercise, you create a Web form that generates an XML document that stores information about Sport Motors employees and then displays the information in a GridView control, as shown in Figure 9-20.

a. Create a new Web form named XMLEmployees.aspx. Link the form to the master page you created in Exercise 9-1, and change the form's title to Sport Motors Employees.

b. Create the form label and button controls as shown in Figure 9-20.

c. Add commands to the form's Load event to generate an Employees.xml file that contains the elements in Figure 9-21. Include commands to generate an associated Employees.xsd file. Order the query output by EmployeeLastName, and use the SQL CONVERT function to format the date values.

d. Add button Click event handlers to display the associated XML or XSD file in the browser window.

e. Create a GridView control on the form, and configure it to display the Employees.xml data when the form loads.

FIGURE 9-19   XMLValidateOrders.xml file (Exercise 9-5)

XMLValidateOrders.xml

```xml
<?xml version="1.0" encoding="utf-8" ?>
<orders>
  <order>
     <orderid>1</orderid>
     <orderdate>2007-03-11T00:00:00.00000</orderdate>
     <customer>
        <customerfirstname>Alison</customerfirstname>
        <customerlastname>Scholten</customerlastname>
     </customer>
     <employee>
       <employeefirstname>Greg</employeefirstname>
       <employeelastname>Kaiser</employeelastname>
     </employee>
     <paymenttype>Loan</paymenttype>
  </order>
  <order>
     <orderid>2</orderid>
     <orderdate>2007-03-11T00:00:00.00000</orderdate>
     <customer>
        <customerfirstname>Robin</customerfirstname>
        <customerlastname>O'Connor</customerlastname>
     </customer>
     <employee>
       <employeefirstname>Stacey</employeefirstname>
       <employeelastname>Knutson</employeelastname>
     </employee>
     <paymenttype>Check</paymenttype>
  </order>
```

7. **Creating an Application That Inserts Elements into an XML File**

NOTE: To complete this exercise, you must have already completed Exercise 9-1.

In this exercise, you create the Web form in Figure 9-22, which allows users to input data about Sport Motors departments into an XML document named Departments.xml.

a. Create a new Web form named XMLDepartments.aspx. Link the form to the master page you created in Exercise 9-1, and change the form's title to Add Sport Motors Departments.

b. Create the label and button controls on the form as shown in Figure 9-22.

c. Create a form Load event handler to determine if Departments.xml exists and, if it does not, create the file.

d. Create a Click event handler for the Submit button that inserts the user's inputs into the XML file. Figure 9-23 shows the XML file's structure. Add commands to clear the form text boxes after the insert and to display a confirmation message stating that the insertion was successful.

e. Insert the data values shown in Figure 9-23 to test your Web form.

FIGURE 9-20 Sport Motors Employees Web form (Exercise 9-6)

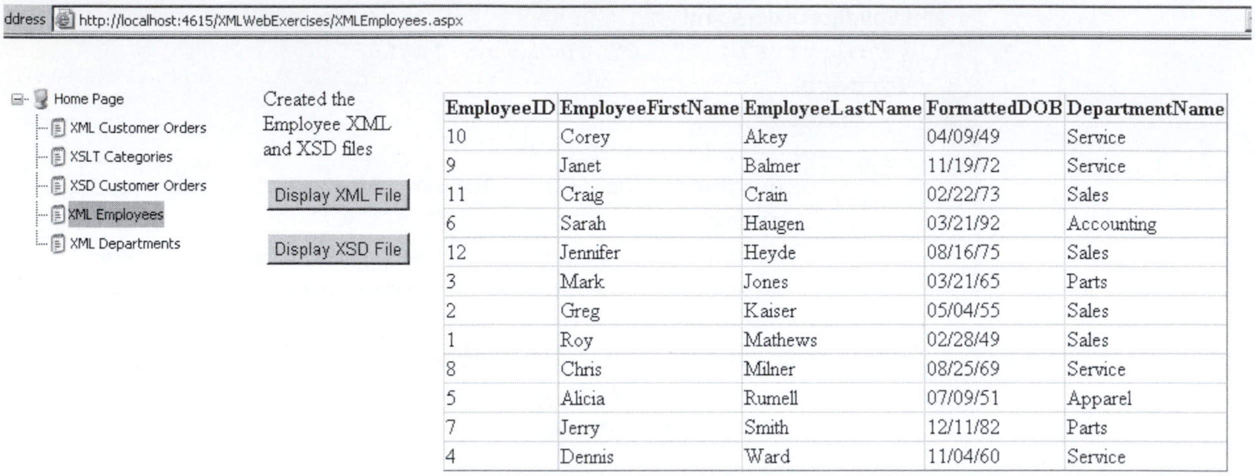

ddress  http://localhost:4615/XMLWebExercises/XMLEmployees.aspx

Home Page
- XML Customer Orders
- XSLT Categories
- XSD Customer Orders
- XML Employees
- XML Departments

Created the Employee XML and XSD files

Display XML File

Display XSD File

EmployeeID	EmployeeFirstName	EmployeeLastName	FormattedDOB	DepartmentName
10	Corey	Akey	04/09/49	Service
9	Janet	Balmer	11/19/72	Service
11	Craig	Crain	02/22/73	Sales
6	Sarah	Haugen	03/21/92	Accounting
12	Jennifer	Heyde	08/16/75	Sales
3	Mark	Jones	03/21/65	Parts
2	Greg	Kaiser	05/04/55	Sales
1	Roy	Mathews	02/28/49	Sales
8	Chris	Milner	08/25/69	Service
5	Alicia	Rumell	07/09/51	Apparel
7	Jerry	Smith	12/11/82	Parts
4	Dennis	Ward	11/04/60	Service

FIGURE 9-21 XML file from retrieved database data (Exercise 9-6)

```
<?xml version="1.0" standalone="yes" ?>
- <NewDataSet>
  - <EmployeeDataTable>
      <EmployeeID>10</EmployeeID>
      <EmployeeFirstName>Corey</EmployeeFirstName>
      <EmployeeLastName>Akey</EmployeeLastName>
      <FormattedDOB>04/09/49</FormattedDOB>
      <DepartmentName>Service</DepartmentName>
    </EmployeeDataTable>
  - <EmployeeDataTable>
      <EmployeeID>9</EmployeeID>
      <EmployeeFirstName>Janet</EmployeeFirstName>
      <EmployeeLastName>Balmer</EmployeeLastName>
      <FormattedDOB>11/19/72</FormattedDOB>
      <DepartmentName>Service</DepartmentName>
    </EmployeeDataTable>
  + <EmployeeDataTable>
  + <EmployeeDataTable>
  + <EmployeeDataTable>
  + <EmployeeDataTable>
  + <EmployeeDataTable>
  + <EmployeeDataTable>
  + <EmployeeDataTable>
  + <EmployeeDataTable>
  + <EmployeeDataTable>
  + <EmployeeDataTable>
</NewDataSet>
```

FIGURE 9-22   Add Sport Motors Departments Web form (Exercise 9-7)

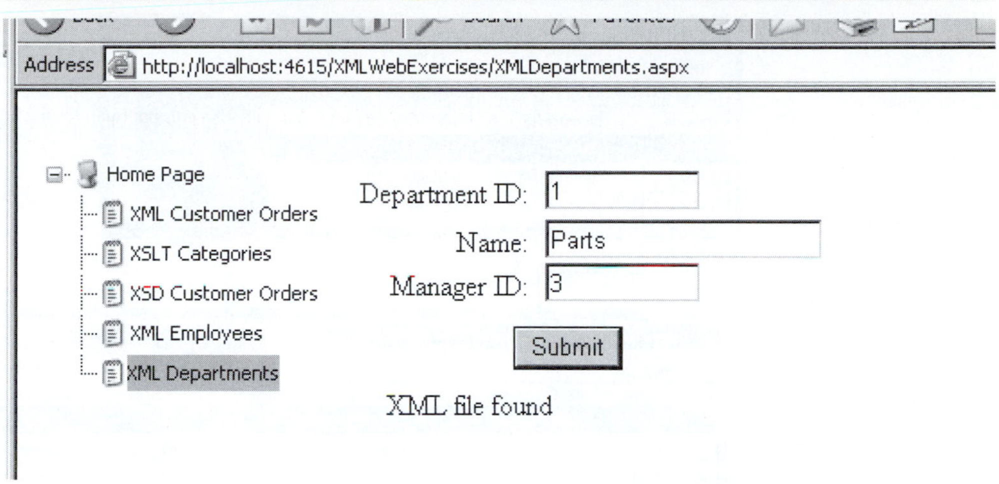

8. **Creating a Web Service and Client Application**

In this exercise, you create a Web service and associated client application. The client application will display the read-only Windows forms in Figure 9-24, which allow Sport Motors employees to select an employee and then display the orders taken by that employee.

a. Create a new Web service named SportMotorsService.

b. Create a WebMethod in your service that returns the data values appearing in the top data grid view in Figure 9-24, along with the EmployeeID, which is not displayed in the grid.

FIGURE 9-23   Departments.xml file contents (Exercise 9-7)

```
Departments.xml
  <Departments>
    <department>
      <departmentid>1</departmentid>
      <departmentname>Parts</departmentname>
      <managerid>2</managerid>
    </department>
    <department>
      <departmentid>2</departmentid>
      <departmentname>Service</departmentname>
      <managerid>3</managerid>
    </department>
    <department>
      <departmentid>3</departmentid>
      <departmentname>Sales</departmentname>
      <managerid>1</managerid>
    </department>
  </Departments>
```

FIGURE 9-24   Sport Motors Web service client application forms (Exercise 9-8)

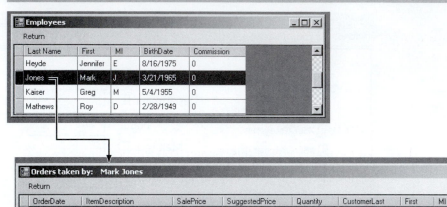

c. Create a second WebMethod that returns the data appearing in the lower data grid view in Figure 9-24. This WebMethod will have an EmployeeID parameter and use it as a filter to return orders taken by the selected employee.

d. Create a VB Windows application project named SportMotorsClient.

e. Create the application forms shown in Figure 9-24. Name the forms appropriately for the information they will be displaying.

f. Create DataGridView controls on the forms, and configure them to display the data as shown.

g. Link the DataGridView controls to the associated WebMethods. Configure the forms so that users can cancel data retrieval operations.

h. Configure the second form to display the name of the selected employee in the form's Title bar.

i. When testing your application, note that only three employees have taken orders: Jones, Kaiser, and Ward.

CHAPTER 10

Database Administration

Learning Objectives

At the conclusion of this chapter, you will be able to:

■ describe common database administration tasks;

■ use some of SQL Server 2005's primary data management tools;

■ create indexes to enhance database performance;

■ understand SQL Server user authentication approaches and security issues;

■ perform backup and recovery operations;

■ deploy Windows- and Web-based database applications.

A database system consists of the DBMS and the database applications that allow users to interact with the database data. This chapter addresses *database administration*, which involves installing, configuring, updating, and trouble-shooting database systems. Database administration also involves helping developers create database applications that use sound data design and implementation practices and that successfully coexist with other organizational systems. A *database administrator (DBA)* is a person who performs database administration tasks.

OVERVIEW OF DATABASE ADMINISTRATION

Database administration has two roles: a *service role,* which involves supporting users who interact with the database, and a *development role,* which involves supporting developers who create database applications. In the service role, DBAs and users interact daily as users use database applications. Database administration service tasks include:

- installing and upgrading the DBMS software;
- configuring how the DBMS stores data;
- developing, implementing, and updating database-related policies and procedures;
- creating regular backups;
- performing recovery operations as needed.

DBAs perform a development role when developers create new applications or roll out new versions of existing applications. Development database administration tasks include:

- assisting developers in designing and creating database tables;
- assisting with developing application architectures and selecting hardware and software platforms;
- designing applications that interact with systems outside the organization;
- migrating data between different storage platforms;
- tuning applications to ensure adequate performance;
- testing and debugging new applications;
- deploying database applications onto client workstations or through Web servers;
- training developers and users.

Additionally, DBAs have a *management liaison* role, which provides a link between developers, users, and organizational managers. DBAs assist in developing and implementing organizational policies in areas such as database security and application development practices, which affect both users and developers.

SQL SERVER DATABASE MANAGEMENT TOOLS

To perform database administration tasks, you use Management Studio or Management Studio Express. (Management Studio Express has fewer functions than Management Studio, but it has most of the functions you need to learn how to work with and administer a SQL Server 2005 DBMS.) This section reviews the capabilities of Management Studio, which you already used in earlier chapters, and describes important database administration utilities.

Management Studio

Figure 10-1 shows the Management Studio Object Explorer and Query Editor windows, as well as the database objects that appear in the Object Explorer. The top-level Object Explorer node is the database instance. Its child nodes are *Databases,* which shows all the existing databases in the SQL Server instance, and *Security,* which shows all the existing logins (username/password combinations that allow users to access the database). Note that in the Logins node, the sa (system administrator) login appears, which is the login for the default administration account that the installation process creates when *SQL Server and Windows Authentication* mode is selected. If *Windows Authentication* mode was selected when SQL Server was installed, this will not be present, and the default administration account will be the one used when the server was installed.

Object Explorer also displays the objects in a specific database, as shown in Figure 10-2. A database's node contains a *Database Diagrams* subnode, which allows creating visual depictions of a database's tables and relationships, as shown in Figures 3-1 and 3-3 for the case study databases. (This feature is not enabled in the Express version.) Other database subnodes are as follows:

- **Tables** contains all the database tables.
- **Views** contains the database's views.

FIGURE 10-1   Management Studio windows and database components

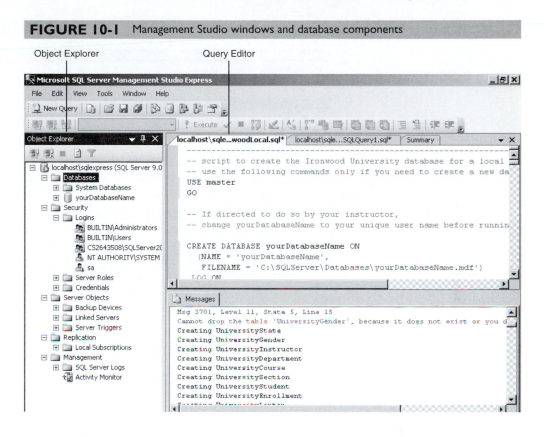

- **Synonyms** are alternate names for database tables that can be used to perform complex join operations.
- **Programmability** lists the database's system- and user-created stored procedures and functions.
- **Security** lists the database's SQL Server-authenticated logins.

A specific table's node contains the following subnodes:

- **Columns** contains subnodes representing all the table's columns. The Columns node displays each column's name and data type specification as a subnode. Primary keys appear as solid-colored keys, and foreign keys appear as grayed-out keys.
- **Keys, Constraints, Triggers, Indexes,** and **Statistics** are subnodes describing these table properties.

Management Studio also displays the following top-level nodes to enable DBAs to perform a variety of administrative tasks:

- **Security** allows DBAs to manage SQL Server-authenticated user accounts.
- **Server Objects** allows DBAs to link and back up servers.
- **Replication** allows DBAs to set up "Subscriptions" to allow users to replicate databases.
- **Management** allows DBAs to set up and enforce backup and recovery operations.

Management Studio enables DBAs and developers to create, view, and modify database components using visual windows.

FIGURE 10-2 Database objects

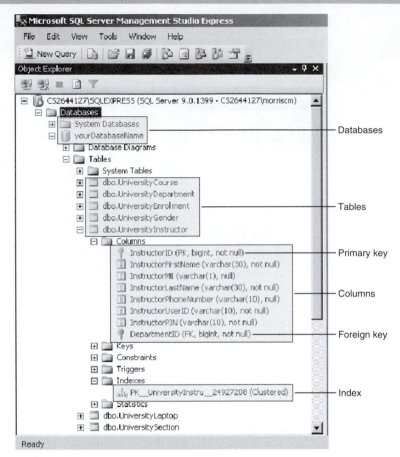

If you right-click a top-level node and then click New *ObjectType,* a window is opened to create a new object. You can right-click an existing object and then click Modify to modify an object's properties. For example, to create a new database table, right-click the Tables node in a database and then click New Table. Figure 10-3 shows the interface for creating a new database table.

When you create a new database table, a grid appears allowing you to specify column names, select data types from lists, and specify NOT NULL constraints using check boxes. You can configure additional table properties using the Table properties box in the lower window. Additionally, you can right-click anywhere in the window and click Generate Change Script, and the associated SQL or T-SQL command appears in the Query Editor.

SQL Server Configuration and Performance Tools

The SQL Server Configuration tools are a set of utilities that enable DBAs to monitor and modify the configuration of a SQL Server DBMS. They consist of two primary applications, Configuration Manager and Surface Area Configuration, and are included in both the full and Express versions of the SQL Server 2005 DBMS. The full (non-Express) SQL Server 2005 DBMS also includes a set of Performance tools, which include SQL Profiler and Database Tuning Advisor. The following subsections describe these applications.

FIGURE 10-3   Creating a new database table in Management Studio

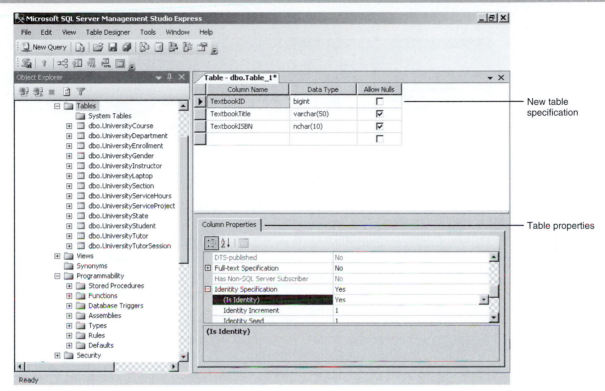

NOTE: To start these applications, click Start on the server taskbar, point to All Programs, point to Microsoft SQL Server 2005, point to Configuration Tools or Performance Tools, and then select the application.

Configuration Manager

Configuration Manager enables DBAs to manage services related to SQL Server 2005, such as server protocols, client protocols, and client aliases. With Configuration Manager you can:

- start, stop, and pause SQL Server–related services;
- configure services to start automatically or manually, disable services, and change other service properties;
- change the accounts and passwords that you use to run SQL Server services;
- view and modify service properties;
- configure, enable, or disable a SQL Server network protocol;
- on a client computer, configure how the client connects to SQL Server DBMS.

TIP: Some of the tasks that you perform in Configuration Manager can be accomplished using the Windows Services utility on the Control Panel; however, Configuration Manager performs additional tasks such as applying the correct permissions when the service account is changed. You should not use the Windows Services utility to directly configure SQL Server 2005 because it could cause the DBMS to crash.

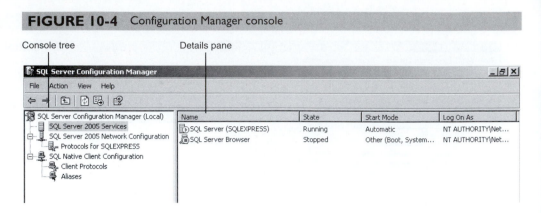

FIGURE 10-4 Configuration Manager console

Figure 10-4 shows the Configuration Manager console for a SQL Server Express DBMS. Configuration Manager runs in the *Microsoft Management Console (MMC)*, which is an environment for administering computer resources. The *Console tree*, which appears in the left pane, displays the resource to be managed. The *Details pane* displays details about the selected resource, including its name, state (Running or Stopped), start mode (Automatic or Manual), and log on authority name. When a service's start mode is Automatic, it automatically starts when the computer boots. When its start mode is Manual, it must be manually started each time the computer boots.

Figure 10-4 shows that the SQL Server (SQLEXPRESS) service is currently running and its Start Mode is Automatic, while the SQL Browser process, which is a service that identifies the ports on which named instances listen, is Stopped, and its start mode is Other. If you start the SQL Browser process, it makes the database visible on the network, which allows remote VS 2005 developers to see the database in the Add Connection dialog box's Server name combo box.

If you right-click the service in the Console tree and select Properties, the dialog box shown in Figure 10-5 is opened. In the Server Properties window, the *Service* tab dialog allows you to set the service to start automatically when the computer boots. The *Advanced* tab allows you to perform tasks such as enabling or disabling error reporting and assigning startup parameters.

Surface Area Configuration

The *Surface Area Configuration* utility allows DBAs to reduce the *surface area,* or visibility, of the database instance. By default, many SQL Server features are disabled to make the installation more secure. Surface Area Configuration makes it easy for you to find and enable these features when they are needed.

Surface Area Configuration reduces the system's attackable surface area by selectively installing and activating key services and features. For example, SQL Server 2005 Express is initially configured to respond only to local connections, which are connections from programs running on the same computer as the SQL Server Express DBMS. If you need to enable remote connections to SQL Server Express, it is done here.

> **NOTE:** SQL Server 2005 (full, not Express) defaults to allowing both local and remote connections.

When Surface Area Configuration is started, a screen appears that allows you to select from two options: Surface Area Configuration for Services and Connections, or Surface Area Configuration for Features. If you select the first option, the *Surface Area Configuration for Services and Connections* window appears, as shown in Figure 10-6.

FIGURE 10-5 Server Properties window

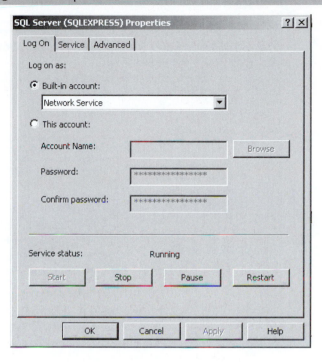

FIGURE 10-6 Surface Area Configuration for Services and Connections window

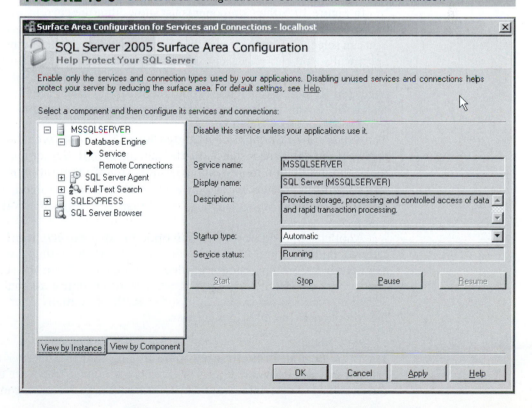

FIGURE 10-7 Using Surface Area Configuration to enable remote database connections

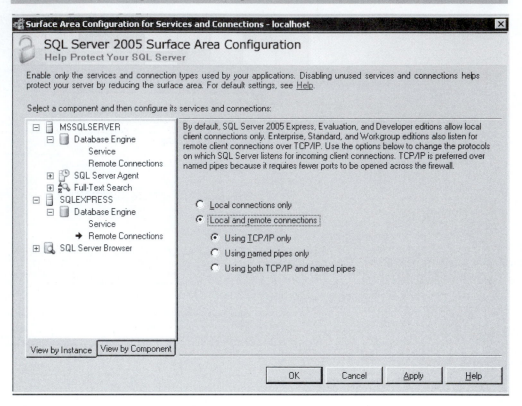

In Figure 10-6, the Components list shows that the current workstation is running both a SQL Server 2005 DBMS instance and a SQL Server Express DBMS instance. You can select a component and then configure its properties in the right Details pane. Specifically, you can select an existing service and change its startup mode. You can also enable remote database connections, as shown in Figure 10-7. For this example, select the Remote Connections component for the SQLEXPRESS service, and then select the Local and remote connections option to configure it to allow remote connections.

If you select the *Surface Area Configuration for Features* option, the choices in Figure 10-8 appear. The *Common Language Runtime (CLR) integration* node allows you to configure the server to allow creating stored procedures, triggers, and functions using any .NET framework language. By default, this is disabled; if you want to write stored procedures using a language other than T-SQL (such as VB or C#), it must be enabled.

Another important configuration option is *xp_cmdshell,* which allows stored procedures, functions, and triggers to directly execute operating system commands. For example, if a stored procedure needed to write to a file on the server, this has to be enabled. By default, it is disabled. It is a hazardous option to enable, because if SQL Server is compromised by malicious software, this essentially gives complete control of the computer to the malicious software.

SQL Profiler

The *SQL Profiler* utility is a real-time tracing tool that creates a *trace,* which is a process that monitors and reports on database activities. Traces are useful during application testing to determine whether performance improvements can be made. They are

FIGURE 10-8   Surface Area Configuration for Features window

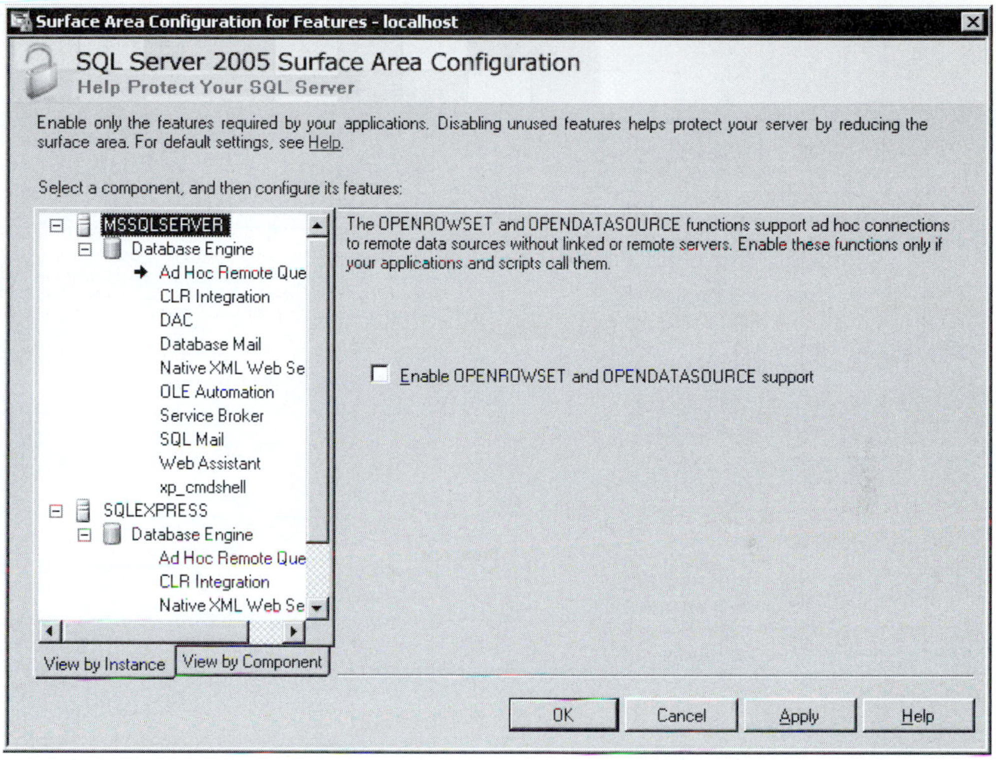

also useful for monitoring user activities and identifying unauthorized connections. A *trace file* is used to record the monitored information.

The steps for running SQL Profiler begin with creating a new trace file. This is done by selecting File on the menu bar, then clicking New Trace. If you have not yet logged onto the server, you are prompted to do so. The login account has to have system administrator privileges to create a trace. Figure 10-9 shows the Trace Properties window, which allows you to configure a trace.

In the Trace Properties window, the General tab specifies general properties for the trace. The *Trace provider name* specifies the name of the SQL Server database instance. The *Use the template* combo box allows you to select a *trace template*, which is a set of defined events, fields, and filters that specify what will appear in the trace.

NOTE: Template files have .trd file extensions and are stored in the C:\Program Files\Microsoft SQL Server\90\Tools\Profiler\Templates\ Microsoft SQL Server\90 folder. To use a custom trace template, you must copy it into this folder so that it appears in the *Use the template combo* box.

After you specify the trace provider and template, you can check the *Save to file* check box to specify the trace filename, which stores the trace results. You can also check *Save to table* and select a database table to which to save the trace results, which creates a *trace table*. If you do not check either box, you can view the trace but not save it. The Enable trace stop time check box enables you to set a time for the trace to stop. This lets you leave the trace running and come back later to check the results.

FIGURE 10-9 Trace Properties window (General tab)

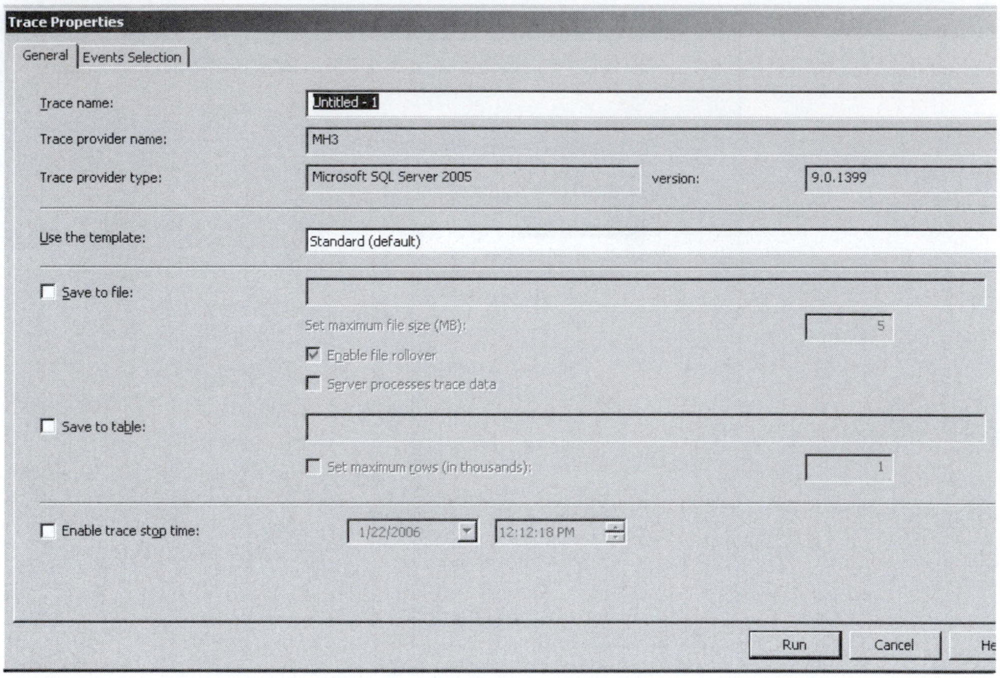

TIP: You should not allow traces to run indefinitely because this slows down the server.

The Events Selection tab, which Figure 10-10 illustrates, allows you to edit the trace template and specify the events and data values that the trace records. The *Events Selection tab* lists the events that the trace tracks, as well as the data items that the trace records for each event. Figure 10-10 shows the events and data values records by the Standard (Default) template. The default set of events and data items is small; however, if you check the Show all events and Show all columns check boxes, many additional events and columns appear.

This tab has a dynamic help feature: When you place the mouse pointer on a specific row heading, a description of the selection appears in the *Row description* area. Similarly, when you place the mouse pointer on a specific column heading, the *Column description* area describes the column selection.

To modify the data that appears, click the column heading for a data item to open the Edit Filter window, as shown in Figure 10-11. The *Edit Filter window* allows you to fine-tune the data that the trace captures. For example, you might want to limit what is displayed in the NTUserName column to a specific account name, as shown in Figure 10-11.

Database Tuning Advisor

The *Database Tuning Advisor* analyzes the performance of T-SQL scripts, trace files, and trace tables. It then provides recommendations for improving the item's performance such as creating indexes, partitioning the database into multiple files, and/or storing the files on different hard drives.

Figure 10-12 illustrates the Database Tuning Advisor window. The Database Tuning Advisor has the following pages:

FIGURE 10-10   Trace Properties window (Events Selection tab)

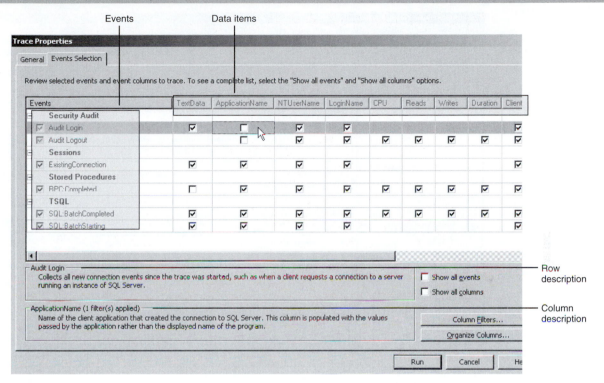

- **General** allows you to specify the tuning session name, server name, and item being tuned (file, table, or query) and to select the database or database tables for the tuning operation.
- **Tuning Options** allows you to limit how long the tuning session runs and set advanced options.

FIGURE 10-11   Edit Filter window

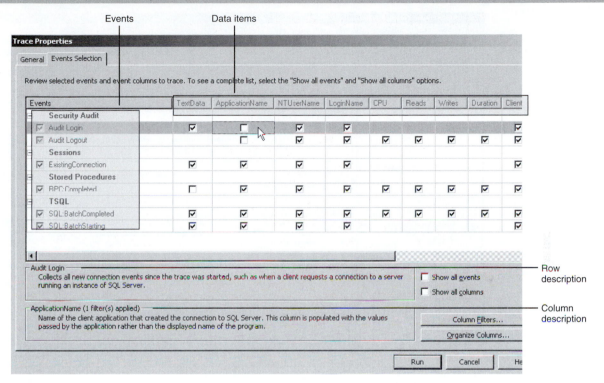

FIGURE 10-12   Database Tuning Advisor window

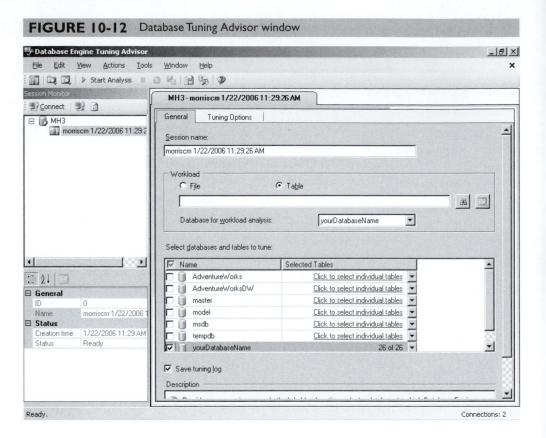

DATABASE INDEXING

An index provides a way to find information quickly. For example, a book's index provides keywords along with associated page numbers that contain information about the keyword. Similarly, a database field index enables the DBMS to quickly find a record that contains a specific field value.

Consider the following query on the UniversitySection table in the Ironwood University database, which retrieves records for all course sections whose enrollment falls between 10 and 20 students:

```
SELECT SectionID, SectionTerm, SectionCurrentEnrollment
FROM UniversitySection
WHERE SectionCurrentEnrollment >= 10 AND
      SectionCurrentEnrollment <= 20
```

Table 10-1 shows the records that the query retrieves.

TABLE 10-1   UniversitySection query data

SectionID	SectionTerm	SectionCurrentEnrollment
2	SUMM08	19
20	SPR09	17
24	SPR09	12
28	SUMM08	19
46	SPR09	17
50	SPR09	12

FIGURE 10-13   Index B-tree structure

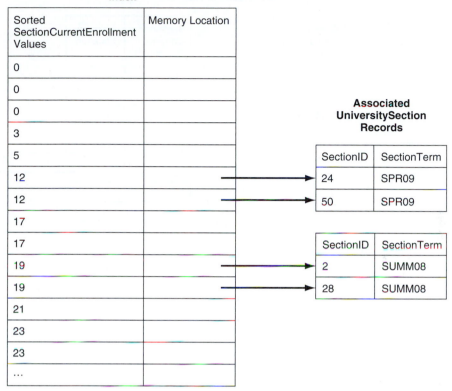

The DBMS must examine all 26 records in the UniversitySection table to find the correct records. If the table is large, containing thousands or millions of records, performance will be unacceptably slow. An index created on the Section-CurrentEnrollment field would considerably improve the performance.

An *index* is a database object that stores field values in a data structure called a *B-tree,* which supports fast searches with minimum disk reads. This enables the DBMS to find the records that satisfy query search conditions on the indexed field quickly. Indexes also improve performance in join queries and in queries that include an ORDER BY clause.

You can envision an index as having the structure shown in Figure 10-13. The indexed field values are sorted and stored in the index. The index maintains a reference to the memory location that stores the actual data value of the corresponding row. When the DBMS executes the query, it scans the index, finds the rows that match the search condition, and quickly retrieves them. In this example, the index stores the sorted SectionCurrentEnrollment values and memory locations of the associated records, and the memory location reference for sections with a current enrollment of 12 students points to Section IDs 24 and 50.

You can create a *composite index,* which is an index that contains multiple sorted fields in its B-tree data structure. For example, suppose you want to modify the query that retrieves UniversitySection records so that it searches by SectionTerm along

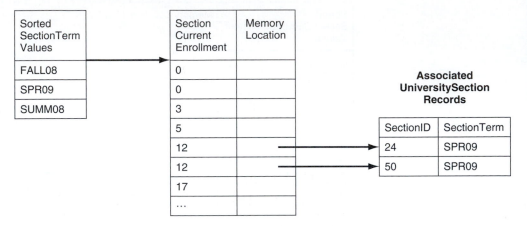

FIGURE 10-14   Composite index B-tree structure

with the Section CurrentEnrollment:

```
SELECT SectionID, SectionTerm, SectionCurrentEnrollment
FROM UniversitySection
WHERE SectionCurrentEnrollment >= 10 AND
      SectionCurrentEnrollment <= 20 AND
      SectionTerm = 'SPR09'
```

If the application that uses this query always searches by SectionTerm, then it makes sense to create the index in Figure 10-14, which sorts the records first by SectionTerm and then by SectionCurrentEnrollment. When you create a composite index, you must specify a sort order that decreases the *search space,* or the number of records that the DBMS needs to examine, as quickly as possible.

You can create a *unique index,* which is an index specifying that the indexed field value must be unique and cannot repeat. The indexes in Figures 10-13 and 10-14 are not unique because the SectionCurrentEnrollment values repeat for different records. If you attempt to create a unique index on values that repeat, an error occurs.

An index can be clustered or nonclustered. With a *clustered index,* the DBMS physically stores the indexed records in the order in which they appear in the index. As a result, a table can have only one clustered index. With a *nonclustered index,* the index order does not necessarily match the physical order in which the data file stores the records. As a result, a table can have multiple nonclustered indexes on different fields.

A clustered index provides the most benefit for queries that require very fast processing; however, you should create clustered indexes with caution. Whenever a user inserts, updates, or deletes a record in the clustered index table, the DBMS must place the values in the correct memory location, and this may involve moving existing data. The slower performance for action queries must be weighed against the faster performance for select queries.

By default, SQL Server creates unique clustered indexes on primary key fields and on fields that have UNIQUE constraints. The following subsections describe how to create, drop, and view indexes, and discuss when you should create indexes.

TABLE 10-2	Index prefix values	
Index Type		*Prefix*
Clustered, no constraints		c
Foreign key, clustered		fkc
Foreign key, nonclustered		fknc
Nonclustered, no constraints		nc
Primary key, clustered		pkc
Primary key, nonclustered		pknc
Unique, clustered		uc
Unique nonclustered		unc

Creating and Dropping Indexes

To create an index, you specify the table and field being indexed, the sort order, and the index name. Every index in a database must have a unique name. We recommend using the following format for index names:

```
IndexPrefix_TableName_FieldName
```

IndexPrefix specifies whether the index is clustered or nonclustered, whether it is a unique index, and whether it is on a primary key or foreign key field. Table 10-2 illustrates index prefix values for the different index types.

Suppose you create a nonclustered index on the SectionCurrentEnrollment field in the UniversitySection table. You would specify the index name as follows:

```
nc_UniversitySection_SectionCurrentEnrollment
```

When you create composite indexes, list the index columns in the order in which you want to sort the columns in the index. For example, use the following name for the composite index in Figure 10-14:

```
nc_UniversitySection_SectionTerm_SectionCurrentEnrollment
```

You can create and drop indexes using SQL commands, or through dialog boxes in Management Studio. The following sections describe both approaches.

Using SQL Commands to Create and Drop Indexes

To create an index using a SQL command, use the following general syntax:

```
CREATE [UNIQUE] [CLUSTERED|NONCLUSTERED]
INDEX IndexName ON [TableName|ViewName]
(Column1[ASC|DESC], Column2[ASC|DESC], ...)
```

In this syntax, `UNIQUE` specifies whether the index is unique, and `CLUSTERED|NONCLUSTERED` specifies whether it is clustered or nonclustered. Next comes *IndexName,* followed by the name of the table or view on which you base the index. Finally, insert the column name, and specify whether the column values are sorted in ascending (ASC) or descending (DESC) order. If you omit the sort order, the index defaults to ascending. To create a composite index, list the second indexed column after the first.

The following command creates the index on the CurrentSectionEnrollment field shown in Figure 10-13. The index defaults to an ascending sort order.

```
CREATE NONCLUSTERED INDEX nc_UniversitySection_SectionCurrentEnrollment
ON UniversitySection(SectionCurrentEnrollment)
```

The following command creates the composite index in Figure 10-14, which indexes the values first on SectionTerm values and then on SectionCurrentEnrollment values and which defaults to an ascending sort order.

```
CREATE NONCLUSTERED INDEX
nc_UniversitySection_SectionTerm_SectionCurrentEnrollment
ON UniversitySection(SectionTerm, SectionCurrentEnrollment)
```

When the CREATE INDEX command is executed, the DBMS allocates memory space to store the index structure; it also creates the index and the references to the associated memory locations. Depending on the number of records that the index involves, this may take minutes, hours, or even days. As users insert, update, and delete records in the indexed table, the DBMS continually updates the index, which adds processing overhead to the system.

To remove an index, use the following general syntax:

```
DROP INDEX TableName.IndexName
```

For example, the following command removes the noncomposite index on the SectionCurrentEnrollment table:

```
DROP INDEX
UniversitySection.nc_UniversitySection_SectionCurrentEnrollment
```

After this command executes, the DBMS makes all the memory space that the index occupied available for other database objects. You cannot drop an index on a system table or a field that is a primary key or that has a UNIQUE constraint unless you first drop the constraint.

Using Management Studio to Create, Modify, and Drop Indexes

To work with indexes in Management Studio, open the table that contains the index, then select the Indexes node. Figure 10-15 shows the UniversitySection's Indexes node in Management Studio.

The UniversitySection table's Indexes node displays the index for the table's primary key, as well as a user-defined composite index on the SectionTerm and SectionCurrentEnrollment fields. To create a new index, right-click the table's Indexes node, then click New Index. The New Index dialog box opens, as shown in Figure 10-16.

The primary pages you use on the New Index dialog box are the *General page,* which allows you to select the index field and specify whether the index is clustered or nonclustered or unique, and the *Included Columns page,* which allows you to create a composite index by specifying the secondary sort key. The Options, Storage, and Extended Properties pages allow you to specify advanced index properties. When you click the Script tab at the top of the New Index dialog box, the utility writes the SQL command to create the index to the Query Editor window.

You can use Management Studio to modify and delete existing indexes. When you right-click a specific index node, a menu opens that enables you to perform operations such as rebuilding, disabling, renaming, or deleting the index. If you right-click an index and then click Properties, the index's Properties window opens, as shown in Figure 10-17.

FIGURE 10-15 Indexes node in Management Studio

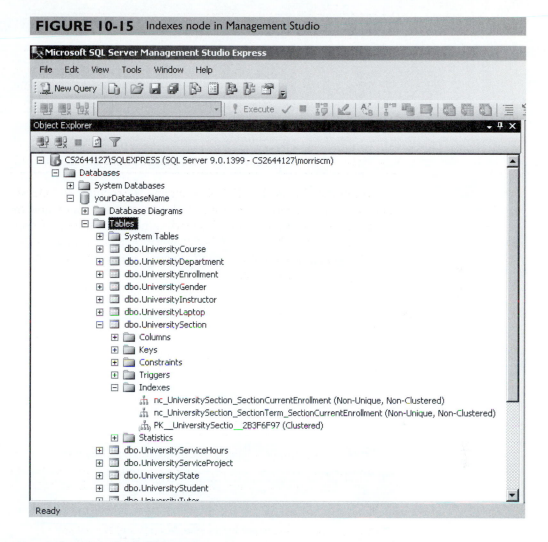

The Index Properties window has similar pages to the New Index dialog box and allows you to reconfigure certain index properties such as the indexed field(s) and the clustering option. Note that you cannot modify the index's name.

When to Create an Index

The need to create an index depends on factors such as the database load, network speed, database size, and the nature of the database operations. Often you are not aware of performance bottlenecks until you test applications under realistic user and load conditions. Because indexes add processing overhead for insert, update, and delete operations, you should be cautious about creating new indexes.

An index will probably improve application data retrieval when:

- the table contains a large number of records (generally more than 100,000);
- the indexed field contains a large number of different data values and/or a large number of NULL values;
- queries retrieve a small number (less than 5%) of the total table records.

You often create indexes on foreign key fields, search condition fields, and the first field in an ORDER BY clause. The decision to create indexes is usually based on experience and benchmark testing.

FIGURE 10-16 New Index dialog box

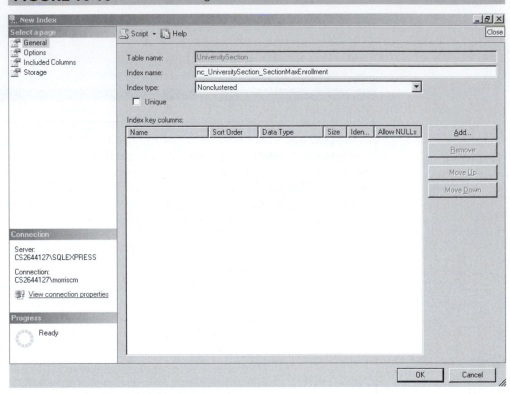

FIGURE 10-17 Index Properties window

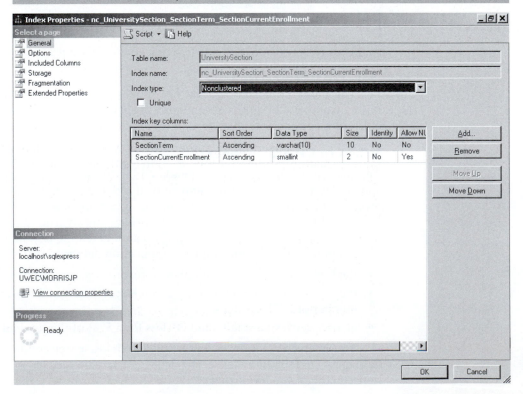

SECURITY AND USER AUTHENTICATION

The goal of security in a SQL Server database system is to enable legitimate users to connect to the system and to keep unwanted intruders out. Recall that a SQL Server database supports two modes of user authentication: Windows authentication, which authenticates users based on their operating system connection, and mixed-mode authentication, which authenticates users based on either Windows authentication or SQL Server user accounts and passwords.

Windows authentication is a more secure option because it does not send login names and passwords over the network. Additionally, users do not need to remember multiple user names and passwords and perform multiple login operations to access the database. (Do you know people who write passwords on sticky notes and attach them to their monitors?) Windows authentication is also easier for DBAs: User authentication is administered in the operating system, and mundane administrative tasks such as creating and maintaining accounts can be delegated to the networking support staff.

There are reasons, however, for using mixed-mode authentication and allowing users to log in using separate SQL Server accounts. The main reason is to maintain backward-compatibility: applications made with older SQL Server versions accept only SQL Server authentication. Another reason is to enable users who are in different network domains to access the database, and DBAs can configure user permissions for certain database objects more precisely using SQL Server authentication.

So which approach should you use? It depends on your system setup and user needs. Windows authentication creates a more secure installation and for mission-critical systems, that is usually Goal Number One. However, mixed-mode authentication provides more options for authenticating users.

TIP: This book's authors prefer to use SQL Server accounts for students rather than Windows authentication. We have used both successfully; however, SQL Server accounts are sometimes easier to connect to from off-campus locations. Also, we create a separate database for each student when we create the account and make that his or her default database. We then have students include their SQL Server user name and password in connection strings. This guarantees connecting to that student's database when assessing a student's work.

To enable mixed-mode authentication, you need to understand the SQL Server authentication model and how it controls database access. The following sections describe this model and show how DBAs use permissions and roles to control access to specific database objects. The final section presents ideas for creating secure SQL Server installations.

SQL Server Authentication Model

In a SQL Server database, authentication has two stages. The first stage authenticates the user at the level of the SQL Server DBMS instance.

NOTE: A DBMS instance is a specific DBMS process running on a server. There can be more than one DBMS instance on a single server, each controlling a different group of databases.

The second stage authenticates the user at the level of an individual database.

NOTE: A single DBMS instance can control many individual databases.

To connect to a DBMS instance, the user must have a valid *login,* which is a name that can access the DBMS instance. This may be a Windows domain login to which the DBA grants access to the DBMS, or it may be a SQL Server login. To access the objects in a specific database, the login must have access to the database and permission to use its objects.

TIP: SQL Server maintains its logins in the master system database, so if you use SQL Server authentication, you need to maintain regular backups of the master database.

Administering logins is a three-step process: first the DBA creates a SQL Server login for the user or configures the user's Windows login so that it can connect to the database instance. Then the DBA grants the login permission to access one or more databases. Finally, the DBA grants the login permission to perform specific actions on the database's objects.

When configuring a login, a DBA can assign to the login a *default database,* which is the primary database that the login is expected to use. Assigning a default database to a login does not automatically grant the login the right to access it; this must be done in a separate step. If a login does not have an assigned default database, then the default database is the master system database—which is usually a bad idea.

The following subsections describe how to create logins and database access rights and how to grant database permissions.

Creating Logins

For a system that uses Windows authentication, the DBA must specify which Windows users can access the DBMS. For a system that uses mixed-mode authentication, the DBA can create SQL Server logins, which by default can connect to the database instance. With mixed-mode authentication, the user can specify whether to use Windows authentication or SQL Server authentication when connecting to the database.

SQL Server provides a set of T-SQL system stored procedures to create and manage logins. Table 10-3 summarizes these stored procedures. You can execute these commands in Management Studio. Figure 10-18 illustrates executing the sp_addlogin stored procedure to create a new login named morrisjp.

After you enter and execute the command, the confirmation message appears in the Results pane and the new login appears in the database instance's Security node. You can right-click the login and click Properties to view a Properties window that allows you to modify properties of the login, such as the password and default database.

Granting Database Access to a Login

The login in Figure 10-18 allows the user to connect to the database but does not yet allow the user to access the yourDatabaseName database or any of its objects. SQL Server provides stored procedures to grant and revoke database access to logins and to view information about the current login's database access rights. Table 10-4 summarizes these procedures.

When you execute the commands in Table 10-4, you must be using the target database. To use a database, select the database from the database list or execute the USE command. Note that the `sp_grantdbaccess` command allows you to specify an alternate username for a user in a database.

TABLE 10-3   T-SQL system stored procedures to create and manage logins

Stored Procedure Name	Description	Basic Syntax/Example
sp_addlogin	Creates a new login that allows users to connect to SQL Server using SQL Server authentication.	sp_addlogin 'Username', 'Password', 'DefaultDB' sp_addlogin 'morrisjp', 'secret', 'yourDatabaseName'
sp_grantlogin	Allows a Windows user account or group to connect to SQL Server using Windows authentication.	sp_grantlogin 'WindowsDomainName/WindowsUsername' sp_grantlogin 'UWEC/morrisjp'
sp_droplogin	Drops a SQL Server login.	sp_droplogin 'Username' sp_droplogin 'morrisjp'
sp_revokelogin	Drops a Windows login/group from SQL Server.	sp_revokelogin 'WindowsDomainName/WindowsUsername' sp_revokelogin 'UWEC/morrisjp'
sp_password	Adds or changes the password for a SQL Server login.	sp_password 'OldPassword', 'NewPassword', 'Username' sp_password 'secret', 'inigomontoya', 'morrisjp'
sp_defaultdb	Changes the default database for a login.	sp_defaultdb 'Username', 'NewDefaultDB' sp_defaultdb 'morrisjp', 'master'
sp_helplogins	Provides information about logins and their associated users in each database; if you omit the Username parameter, then returns information about all system logins.	sp_helplogins ['Username'] sp_helplogins sp_helplogins 'morrisjp'

Figure 10-19 illustrates executing sp_grantdbaccess and shows that the new username appears in the database's Security node. It also shows the information that the sp_helpuser procedure retrieves. (Each command is followed by the GO command because each command must execute before the one that follows it.)

Permissions

The next step in managing SQL Server authentication is to grant permissions to the login. In a SQL Server database system, a *permission* grants the right to perform a specific task. You can grant permissions at the server level, such as the permission to create a new login or a new database or to shut down the database instance. Server-level permissions are called *server permissions*. You can also grant permissions at the database level, such as the permission to create a new table or stored procedure in the database or to view records in a specific table. Database-level permissions are called *object permissions*.

To grant permissions, DBAs use the GRANT command, which has the following syntax:

```
GRANT {ALL| Permission1, Permission2, ... }
[ON ObjectName]TO Username WITH GRANT OPTION
```

FIGURE 10-18 Creating a new SQL Server login

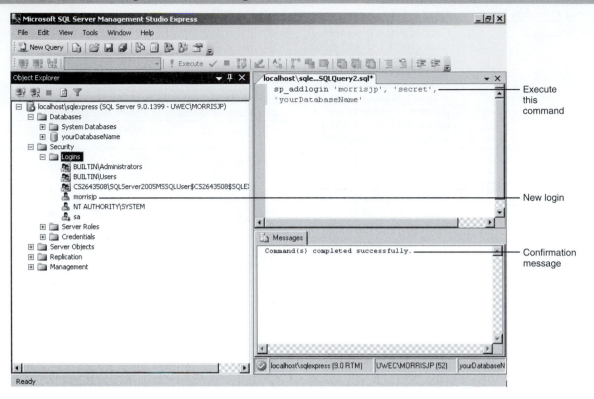

In this syntax, the GRANT clause specifies the permissions you want to grant. You can specify these permissions using the keyword ALL, which grants all available permissions to the user, or in a permissions list in which you list each permission separately. The TO clause specifies the user to which you grant the privilege, and the WITH GRANT OPTION clause specifies that the user can grant the permission(s) to other users.

Grants for server permissions omit the ON clause, because these permissions are not being assigned to database objects. SQL Server has many available server permissions; examples include SHUTDOWN, which allows the user to shut down the DBMS

TABLE 10-4 T-SQL system stored procedures to grant and manage database access

Stored Procedure Name	Description	Basic Syntax/Example
sp_grantdbaccess	Adds an associated user account in the current database for a SQL Server login or Windows login.	sp_grantdbaccess 'Username' [,'DBUserName'] sp_grantdbaccess 'morrisjp', 'WonderWoman'
sp_revokedbaccess	Drops a user account from the current database.	sp_revokedbaccess 'Username' sp_revokedbaccess 'morrisjp'
sp_helpuser	Reports information about the users and roles in the current database.	sp_helpuser 'Username' sp_helpuser 'WonderWoman'

FIGURE 10-19   Granting access to a database and viewing user information

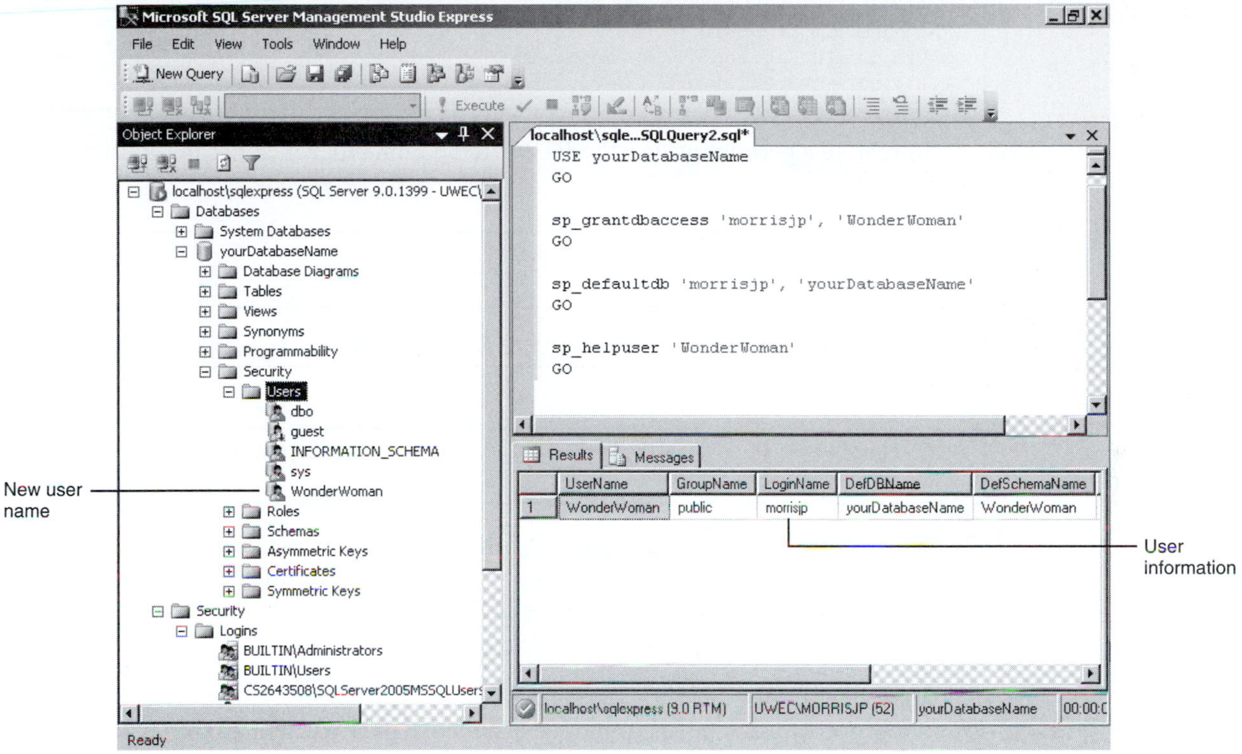

New user
name

User
information

instance, and CREATE ANY DATABASE, which allows the user to create new databases. The following command grants these permissions to user morrisjp:

```
GRANT SHUTDOWN, CREATE ANY DATABASE TO morrisjp
```

User morrisjp would need to be a very trustworthy employee to be granted these permissions. Normally you do not grant server permissions individually, but instead as groups of permissions to a role, which we will discuss shortly.

Object permission values are typically SELECT, INSERT, UPDATE, or DELETE. These permissions allow the user to run the associated query type on the object. REFERENCES is another object permission. This allows the owner of another table to use columns from the table for which he or she has been granted the REFERENCES permission to as the target for a foreign key constraint. Finally, the EXECUTE permission allows a user to execute a stored procedure.

TIP: The SELECT permission would also allow referring to a column in a foreign key constraint, but REFERENCES does this without allowing the user to retrieve data from the table.

When you grant an object permission, the ON clause identifies the object to which you are granting the permission, which can be a table, view, stored procedure, or a number of other database objects. The following command grants user WonderWoman the SELECT, INSERT, and UPDATE permissions on the UniversitySection table in the Ironwood University database, with the grant option:

```
GRANT SELECT, INSERT, UPDATE
ON UniversitySection TO WonderWoman
WITH GRANT OPTION
```

To revoke a permission, use the REVOKE command, which has the following general syntax:

```
REVOKE {ALL | Permission1, Permission2, ... }
[ON ObjectName] TO Username
```

To deny a permission, use the DENY command, which has the following general syntax:

```
DENY {ALL | Permission1, Permission2, ... }
[ON ObjectName] TO Username
```

What is the difference between REVOKE and DENY? REVOKE takes back permissions that the user has been granted. Use REVOKE to reverse a GRANT operation. Alternatively, DENY explicitly denies permissions that users may have gotten through a role. The next section describes roles.

Roles

Often a group of users needs to have the same permissions. For example, DBAs need to perform similar tasks, such as creating new databases and logins. DBAs associated with developing new Ironwood University database applications need to be able to create new tables in the database. Conversely, Ironwood University data entry personnel need to be able to add and update table records, but they do not need to create new tables. Rather than explicitly granting individual permissions to each user, DBAs create roles. A *role* is a set of permissions you can grant to one or more users.

SQL Server has several predefined, or *fixed,* roles. It categorizes these as *fixed server roles,* which define system and database administration tasks, and *fixed database roles,* which define common tasks that database users need to perform. Table 10-5 summarizes the fixed server roles and describes the types of tasks that the roles enable their users to perform.

Table 10-6 summarizes the fixed database roles. These roles contain all the object privileges that the user needs to perform the described tasks.

TABLE 10-5 SQL Server fixed server roles	
Fixed Server Role	*Role Tasks*
sysadmin	Perform any SQL Server activity
serveradmin	Set server-wide configuration options and shut down the server
setupadmin	Manage linked servers and startup procedures
securityadmin	Manage logins and CREATE DATABASE permissions, read error logs, and change passwords
processadmin	Manage processes running in SQL Server
dbcreator	Create, alter, and drop databases
diskadmin	Manage disk files

TABLE 10-6   SQL Server fixed database roles

Fixed Database Role	Role Tasks
db_owner	All database tasks
db_accessadmin	Add or remove user logins
db_securityadmin	Manage all permissions, object ownerships, roles, and role memberships
db_ddladmin	Execute any action query, but cannot execute GRANT, REVOKE, or DENY statements
db_backupoperator	Execute DBCC, CHECKPOINT, and BACKUP statements
db_datareader	Select all data from any database table
db_datawriter	Modify any data in any database table
db_denydatareader	Cannot select any data from any database table
db_denydatawriter	Cannot modify any data in any database table

You can create *user-defined roles,* which define a specific set of permissions that you want to grant to a group of users, using the following command:

```
CREATE ROLE RoleName
```

In this syntax, *RoleName* is a text string that describes the role. After creating a role, use the GRANT command to grant to it specific permissions. For example, the following commands create a role named IronwoodStudent and grant to the role permissions to view and update the UniversitySection table:

```
CREATE ROLE IronwoodStudent
GO
GRANT SELECT, UPDATE
ON UniversitySection TO IronwoodStudent
```

To add a login to a role, use the following general syntax:

```
sp_addrolemember 'RoleName', 'LoginName'
```

For example, the following command adds login morrisjp to the db_datawriter role:

```
sp_addrolemember 'db_datawriter', 'morrisjp'
```

Managing Permissions in Management Studio

You can use the Properties window in Management Studio to manage server and object permissions and to create and manage roles. To manage login server permissions, right-click the Login name in the server's Security node, then click Properties to open the login's Properties window, as shown in Figure 10-20.

The Logins Properties window has the following pages:

- **General** allows you to modify general properties about the login, such as the password and default database.
- **Server Roles** allows you to assign server roles to the login.
- **User Mapping** allows you to view associations between user names and logins.

FIGURE 10-20 Logins Properties window in Management Studio

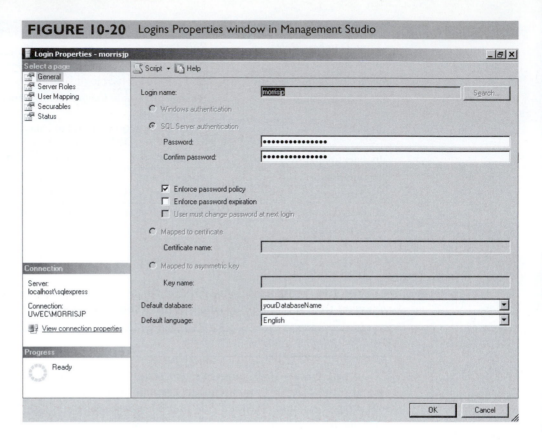

- **Securables** allows you to assign object permissions to the login.
- **Status** allows you to disable the login or not allow it to connect to the database.

To manage object permissions for a specific database user, right-click the user under the database's Security node, then open the Database User Properties window, as shown in Figure 10-21. The Database User Properties window has the following pages:

- **General** specifies the schemas that the user owns and the roles the user has been granted.

TIP: A schema is a database object that contains related database tables, views, stored procedures, and so forth. A schema can have only one owner.

- **Securables** allows you to grant, revoke, and deny specific permissions on specific database objects.
- **Extended Properties** allows the user to access extended properties in the database. Extended Properties are user-defined properties that enhance the definition of a data object such as a field.

You can also use Management Studio to create and manage roles. To create a user-defined role, right-click the Database Roles node in a specific database, then click New Database Role. This Properties window has the same pages as the Database Users window and allows you to specify properties in a similar way.

FIGURE 10-21   Database User Properties window in Management Studio

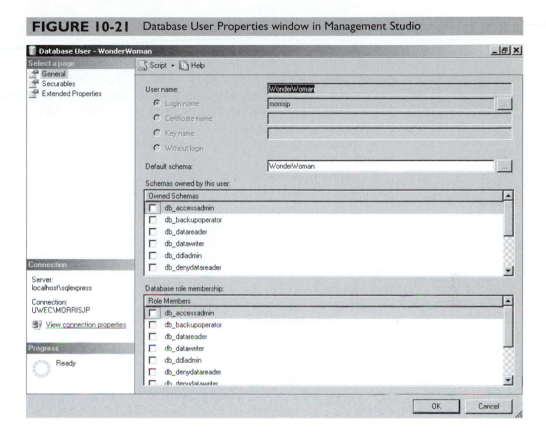

SQL Server Security Strategies

A strong SQL Server security setup in a Windows environment starts with configuring SQL Server to use Windows authentication, then grouping users into different global domain groups based on their data access needs. You then consolidate the global groups into local groups and grant the local groups access to log onto the SQL Server database instance. Assign fixed server and database roles as necessary, and create additional database roles as needed to fine-tune permissions.

If you choose to use mixed-mode authentication, make sure to use complex passwords for the sa account and all other SQL Server logins. These passwords should use mixed-case letters and require numbers and/or special characters. Promptly remove the SQL Server logins of employees who have left your organization, especially in the case of employees who have been fired or laid off. If your system uses a Web server, place the Web server process on a different computer than the DBMS process.

You should physically restrict access to the computer that runs the server DBMS process and lock it when it is not in use. Ensure that all file and disk shares on the server are read only. If you must create read-write shares, limit access to these shares. Always install the latest service packs and security patches that Microsoft releases.

Whenever possible, let your users query views instead of giving them access to the underlying base tables. If your databases contain sensitive information such as credit card and social security numbers, consider encrypting these values.

BACKUP AND RECOVERY

In the course of everyday use, hardware fails, and files become corrupted. Moreover, natural disasters such as fires and floods can occur that take out database servers or entire systems. Also, do not forget about disgruntled employees and malicious hackers who seek to damage or destroy your system. As a result, every database system needs a backup and recovery plan. *Backup* involves creating copies of database files, and *recovery* involves restoring the database to its original state after a failure.

The first step in developing a backup and recovery plan is to establish an acceptable level of loss for your system. Can it survive the loss of an hour's worth of transactions? A day's worth? The answers to these questions depend on the type of business and the volume of transactions that the database processes. For an organization such as a stock exchange, losing an hour's worth of data is catastrophic. For a university registration system, it is not as serious—except during the time period when students register for courses. Organizations also need to evaluate the amount of database downtime that they can tolerate.

The following subsections describe SQL Server backup and recovery options, illustrating how to use Management Studio to perform backup and recovery operations. The final subsection discusses backup and recovery practices.

SQL Server Backup Options

SQL Server offers two backup options: full backups and differential backups. A *full backup* stores a complete copy of the database to media such as tape or disk. You can create a full backup without stopping the database; however, creating a full backup consumes a high volume of system resources so while the system is creating the backup, system response times are noticeably slower.

Most databases contain a large amount of information that does not change very often. A *differential backup* stores a copy of the data that has changed since the last full backup. As a result, a differential backup is much smaller and takes much less time and consumes significantly fewer resources than a full backup. Differential backups require an initial full backup, and it is a good idea to create full backups periodically to avoid having to piece together too many differential backups to an old full backup. For example, you might schedule a full system backup every Saturday night, then create a differential backup the remaining nights of the week.

If the system fails, you lose the transactions that have occurred since the last differential backup. You can recover these transactions using the *transaction log*. During normal operations, a SQL Server DBMS creates a transaction log, which is a file that records all database modifications. In the case of a failure, the DBA can use the transaction log to "redo" all committed transactions since the last differential backup.

TIP: A system failure does not necessary mean that a transaction log and all data on the DBMS server are lost, but this "can" happen. Therefore, protecting the transaction log requires mirroring transactions as they occur to a second server. Levels of mirroring vary from mirroring the transaction log to mirroring the entire DBMS.

Two other options exist to back up smaller portions of a single database. A *file/filegroup* backup backs up individual files and filegroups in a database.

(A *filegroup* is a collection of related database files.) A *file differential* backup combines differential backups and file/filegroup backups.

Recovery Options

Recovery options work in conjunction with the backup options. There are three basic recovery options:

- **Simple recovery** is used to recover to the point of the last full and/or differential backup. It does not use transaction logs to recover transactions committed since the last differential backup, so these transactions are lost.
- **Full recovery** is used for databases or files that you need to recover to their state at the time of failure. This recovery option logs all database operations and uses full, differential, and transaction log backups.
- **Bulk-logged recovery** is similar to full recovery, but it reduces the amount of log space required. With this option, the DBMS records minimal transaction log information for bulk operations. (A *bulk operation* is a data operation involving a large volume of data that the SQL Server DBMS provides special commands to process.) This backup strategy assumes that bulk operations can be repeated to recover their transactions.

By default, the master, msdb, and tempdb system databases use the simple recovery model, and the model database uses the full recovery model. All new databases use the simple recovery model. You can modify a database to use the full recovery model by executing the following command:

```
ALTER DATABASE [DatabaseName] SET RECOVERY FULL WITH NO_WAIT
```

You can also change a database's recovery model by opening its Properties window in Management Studio, moving to the Options page, then selecting the desired recovery model from the Recovery model list.

Creating a Backup

To create a backup, first create a *backup device,* which is an object that references the device where the DBMS writes the backup file. Then instruct the DBMS to back up the database. As with most database operations, you can back up a database using either T-SQL commands or Management Studio dialog boxes.

Creating the Backup Device

When you create a backup device, the system records the backup device's properties in the master database's sysdevices table. You then reference the device in subsequent backup and recovery operations. A backup device can be a path to a disk file or tape device.

To create a backup device using program commands, use the T-SQL sp_adddumpdevice stored procedure, which has the following general syntax:

```
sp_addumpdevice 'DeviceType', 'BackupName', 'PhysicalLocation'
```

In this syntax, *DeviceType* specifies the type of backup device; legal values are disk, tape, and pipe. *BackupName* specifies the logical name of the backup device that you are creating and that you will use to reference the device in backup and recovery operations. *PhysicalLocation* specifies the full path to the disk file, or the network

FIGURE 10-22 Creating a new backup device in Management Studio

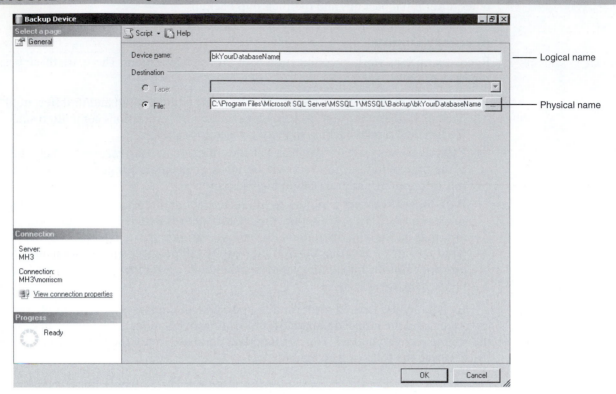

name of the tape device. You would use the following command to create a backup device named yourDatabaseNameBK that is stored in a file named DBBackup:

```
sp_addumpdevice 'disk', 'yourDatabaseNameBK',
'C:\SQLServer\Solutions\Chapter10\DBBackup'
```

Alternatively, you can create a backup device using a Management Studio dialog box. To do this, open the server instance's Server Objects node, right-click the Backup Devices node, and then click New Backup Device. (This is available only in the full (non-Express) SQL Server DBMS.) The Backup Device dialog box in Figure 10-22 opens.

You specify the device's type, backup name, and physical location. (The Tape option button is enabled only when the current server has a local tape device.) When you click OK, the system creates the backup device, and it appears under the Backup Devices node in the Object Explorer.

Backing Up the Database

To back up a database, transaction log, or file/filegroup, use the T-SQL BACKUP command. Table 10-7 summarizes the syntax for this command for different types of backups.

Figure 10-23 illustrates the commands to create a backup device and back up a database. Management Studio displays the results message as shown when you successfully create a full database backup.

Alternatively, to back up a database in Management Studio, right-click the node of the new backup device that you created, and then click Back Up a Database. The Back Up Database dialog box opens, as shown in Figure 10-24.

TABLE 10-7   T-SQL backup commands

Backup Type	General Syntax	Example
Full database	BACKUP DATABASE *DatabaseName* TO *DeviceName*	BACKUP DATABASE yourDatabaseName TO yourDatabaseNameBK
Differential database	BACKUP DATABASE *DatabaseName* TO *DeviceName* WITH DIFFERENTIAL	BACKUP DATABASE yourDatabaseName TO yourDatabaseNameBK WITH DIFFERENTIAL
File or Filegroup	BACKUP DATABASE *DatabaseName* FILE = FileName[, FILEGROUP = FileGroupName] TO *DeviceName*	BACKUP DATABASE your*DatabaseName* FILE = yourDatabaseName.mdf TO yourDatabaseNameBK
Transaction Log	BACKUP LOG *DatabaseName* TO *DeviceName*	BACKUP LOG *yourDatabaseName* TO yourDatabaseNameBK

The Back Up Database dialog box allows you to select the target database and the backup type (Full, Differential, or Transaction Log). The *Backup set* defines the specific backup using a name, description, and date, and the *Destination* specifies the backup device.

Recovering a Database

You can restore a database to either the same server or a different server. Table 10-8 summarizes the T-SQL RESTORE commands to restore a database.

FIGURE 10-23   Commands to create a backup device and back up a database

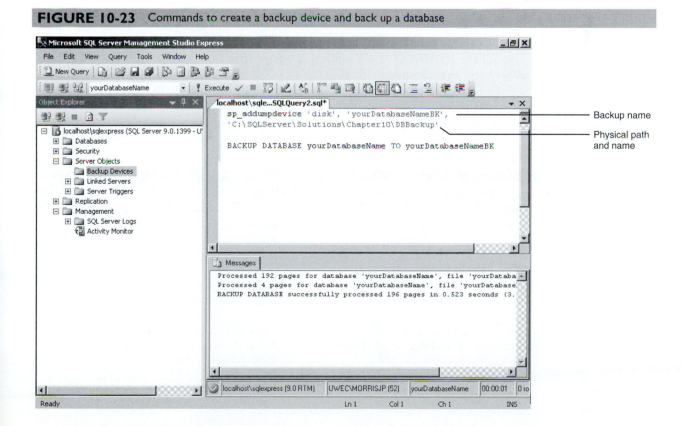

FIGURE 10-24   Backing up a database in Management Studio

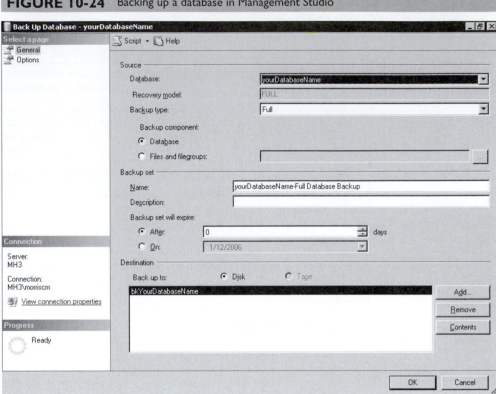

In these commands *DatabaseName* references the database in which you restore the backup. By default, a recovery operation overwrites the existing database contents. The WITH NORECOVERY option specifies that the backup does not restore the contents of the transaction log files.

To recover a database in Management Studio, right-click the Databases node in the Object Explorer, then click Restore Database. The Restore Database dialog box in Figure 10-25 opens.

TABLE 10-8   T-SQL recovery commands

Backup Type	*General Syntax*	*Example*
Simple database	`RESTORE DATABASE DatabaseName FROM DeviceName`	`RESTORE DATABASE yourDatabaseName FROM yourDatabaseNameBK WITH REPLACE`
Full database	`RESTORE DATABASE DatabaseName FROM DeviceName`	`RESTORE DATABASE yourDatabaseName FROM yourDatabaseNameBK`
Differential database	`RESTORE DATABASE DatabaseName FROM DeviceName WITH NORECOVERY`	`RESTORE DATABASE yourDatabaseName FROM yourDatabaseNameBK WITH NORECOVERY`
File or Filegroup	`RESTORE DATABASE DatabaseName FILE = FileName[, FILEGROUP = FileGroupName] FROM DeviceName WITH NORECOVERY`	`RESTORE DATABASE yourDatabaseName FILE = yourDatabaseName.mdf FROM yourDatabaseNameBK WITH NORECOVERY`
Transaction Log	`RESTORE LOG DatabaseName FROM DeviceName LOG`	`RESTORE LOG yourDatabaseName FROM yourDatabaseNameBK`

FIGURE 10-25   Restoring a database in Management Studio

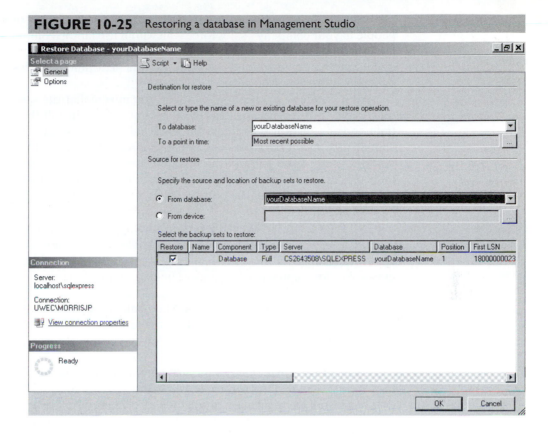

This dialog box allows you to select the database to restore, the restore source, and the backup sets. When you click OK, Management Studio performs the recovery operation.

Backup and Recovery Practices

Backup and recovery are the most important functions that a database administrator oversees. DBAs should design and implement disaster recovery plans for every database system the organization uses. Backups for mission-critical systems should reside on a *warm backup server,* which is a server that can be put into production with minimal downtime. DBAs should test backups regularly and confirm that recovery operations are successful. Backup files should be kept at off-site storage sites to protect them from natural disasters such as fires and floods. DBAs also need to document the backup and recovery plan, in addition to training personnel and users in disaster recovery procedures.

DEPLOYING DATABASE APPLICATIONS

An important database administration task involves deploying database applications to client workstations. When you *deploy* an application, you make it available to users. In this section, we describe how to deploy Windows and Web applications.

Windows Applications

In recent years, organizations have moved to Web-based applications over Windows-based applications due to the difficulty of distributing and updating Windows applications. Just imagine rolling out an upgrade to a program used by thousands of people in your company's sales force—all whom use laptop computers and all of whom are usually working out in the field. For a Web application, this is no problem: place the update on the organization's Web site, and the next time the salesperson connects, he or she uses the new Web pages.

For a Windows application, however, you must collar the salespeople if and when they come to the office, confiscate their laptops, and install the software. This takes time and can disrupt schedules and work habits. Also, what if the updated program contains the new prices for the company's products and has to get to the sales force ASAP? Even if you roll out the updated program to employees who are usually in their offices, you must gain access to their computers and ensure that the computers are online and available. The bottom line is the process of installing new programs can be slow and difficult.

.NET 2005 has introduced a new technology for deploying Windows applications called *ClickOnce*. This Web publishing technology allows users to download Windows applications and run them on their local workstations. It makes distributing and running a Windows application as easy as linking to a Web page.

TIP: Microsoft also supplies the Microsoft Installer (MSI) with Visual Studio 2005 (but not with their Express products). This is a utility that creates traditional installation programs for VS 2005 applications.

You can use ClickOnce to publish completed or updated Windows applications to a Web server, FTP server, or network drive. When connecting to the network, the user can install an application or upgrade by clicking a link in a Web page. Each time a user runs an application, the system checks to see if updates are available and installs them as necessary. The intent is to make published applications as easy to deploy as Web applications.

The following subsections describe security issues with Windows-based programs and show how to use ClickOnce to deploy Windows applications.

Windows Security Issues

There is a dark side to running Windows applications rather than Web-based applications. Typically, Windows-based applications can access all the files and system commands on their host computer, which allows malicious or poorly written code to damage the computer. Conversely, Web applications cannot access host system files (except cookies) and cannot access system commands. They can access remote databases, but this does not endanger the user's local computer.

To address the dangers of running Windows applications, the .NET Framework provides a security mechanism named *Code Access Security (CAS)*, which allows code from unknown origins to run with protection in a host operating system. This keeps code from trusted origins from accidentally (or intentionally) compromising security. To implement CAS, developers specify the permissions that a program requires, as well as the permissions that their program does not need. When the program runs, the application passes these permissions to the .NET runtime engine as a request that the run-time engine evaluates. A program never receives more permissions than the local computer's current system security policies allow and receives less if its permission request asks for less.

Managers, DBAs, and network administrators set and administer system security policies. When an application attempts to run a program, the .NET run-time engine uses the system's security policy to determine which permissions to grant to it. .NET looks at the application's publisher, its site, and its zone when determining the permissions the code will be allowed. (In a system security model, a *zone* specifies a network location that has a specific security setting. Examples of zones are the Internet and the computer's local intranet.)

Administrators can configure security policies to allow individual sites and publishers more or fewer permissions than the defaults. For example, an administrator might give one set of permissions to programs that employees download from the company's internal Web site and other more restrictive permissions to programs that employees download from external sites.

Network administrators use the .NET Framework Configuration Code Access Security (CAS) tool to manage security policies for the enterprise or for individual machines or users. You start the CAS utility on computers on which the .NET framework has been installed by clicking Start, clicking Control Panel, clicking Administrative Tools, and then double-clicking Microsoft .NET Framework 2.0 Configuration. Figure 10-26 shows the Runtime Security Policy page for this tool, which appears when you open the My Computer node in the left window pane, and then select Runtime Security Policy.

The CAS utility allows administrators to:

- view policy, code groups, and permission sets;
- create, modify, and removed named permission sets;
- add, modify, and delete code groups;
- assign permissions and attributes to code groups;
- analyze security settings on assemblies;
- undo policy changes.

FIGURE 10-26   .NET Code Access Security (CAS) utility

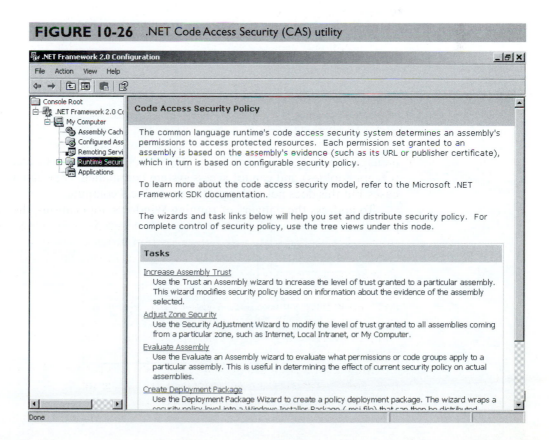

> **NOTE:** Administrators can alternatively use the Code Access Security Policy (caspol.exe) tool, which is located at `C:\WINDOWS\Microsoft.NET\Framework\v2.xxxxx`, to write batch scripts to configure security policy. Batch scripts make it easier to set policies for multiple users on a network.

To change the security level for a specific application's assembly, click the Increase Assembly Trust link shown in Figure 10-26. A dialog box opens asking if you want to make changes for this computer, which affects everyone logging in to the computer, or make changes for the current user only. The next dialog box allows you to select the target assembly file, and the next allows you to change the trust level for the specific assembly or for all assemblies from the same publisher. The next dialog box allows you to choose among four security levels, as shown in Figure 10-27.

You can adjust the assembly's security, ranging from None (not allowing any of the assembly's programs to execute) to Full (allowing all of them to execute).

To adjust the security level for *all* assemblies that run on the computer, click the Adjust Zone Security link shown in Figure 10-26. This again allows you to select whether to adjust the security level for the computer or the current user only, but specifies security levels for all assemblies instead of a selected assembly.

Publishing a Windows Application

After you create a Windows application, such as the DBExamples project created in Chapter 6, you can deploy, or publish, the application to other computers. Once you publish an application, users can install it onto their computers by opening the application's Publish.htm Web page and clicking the Launch link. VS 2005 creates this Web page when you publish the application. If the user has not yet installed the .NET framework or SQL Server Express, this must be done first by clicking Setup on the

---

FIGURE 10-27   Assembly security levels

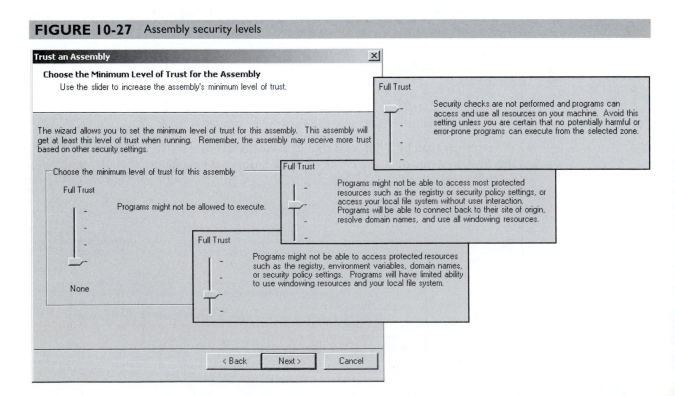

application's Web page to install these components. This has to be done only once and is not needed for subsequent applications.

When you publish a Windows application with ClickOnce, .NET automatically generates a Software Publisher Certificate (SPC) if you have not specified a certificate and used it to sign the published application. A *Software Publisher Certificate* (*SPC*) is a certificate that certifies who you are and that contains a legally binding pledge that your software does not knowingly contain viruses or other malicious items.

SPCs can be self-generated, generated through a third party such as Verisign, or generated through an administrator in your company. With a self-generated certificate, you become both the certificate authority and the publisher that the certificate represents. Self-generated certificates are used only for development purposes. When you are ready to roll out an application to production users, you should obtain a third-party certificate.

The naming convention for a self-generated SPC is *ProjectName*_TemporaryKey. pfx. The signing process uses a public key/private key encryption method to apply a digital signature to all the files being published (and later deployed). This guarantees the files have not been altered in any way and that they are from who they say they are from.

The following steps show how to modify a project's properties to publish it. First we will modify the properties of the project's self-generated SPC.

NOTE: You can alternatively use the .NET Publish Wizard to publish applications, which provides default access security settings and other settings. Setting a project's properties first and then publishing the project manually provides greater control over how the project is published.

To open the project and modify its SPC properties:

1. In Windows Explorer, copy the PublishExample folder and all its contents from \SQLServer\ DataFiles\Chapter10 to your \SQLServer\Solutions\Chapter10 folder.
2. Start VB Express or VS 2005, and open the project.
3. In the Solution Explorer, right click the PublishExample project folder, and then click Properties.
4. Select the Signing tab. Check the Sign the ClickOnce manifests check box, and check the Sign the assembly check box.
5. Click the Create Test Certificate button, type secret in the Password and Confirm Password fields, and then click OK.

A project can be a *full-trust* application, which means it can perform any actions in the host system, or a *partial-trust* application, which means that its actions are restricted. For a partial-trust application, you must specify whether to include or exclude 20 different permissions. Ideally, every published application should use the partial trust option and contain the minimum number of permissions that allow it to run. This requires some experimenting to find the right combination of permissions. When you deploy the project, it can still run into difficulties if the local computer's CAS settings are more restrictive than the minimum set of permissions that the application requires.

The following steps show how to specify the project's security properties using the project's Security page in Figure 10-28. We will make it a full-trust application.

To specify the project's security settings:

1. Select the Security tab, check the Enable ClickOnce Security Settings check box, and accept the default full trust application setting
2. Save the project.

FIGURE 10-28 Project Security page

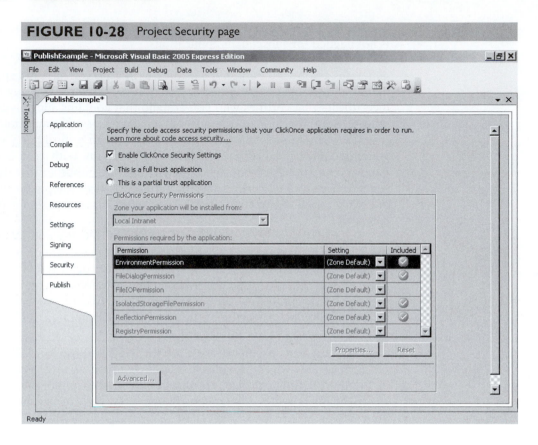

Now you will publish the project by configuring the properties on the Publish properties page, as shown in Figure 10-29. On the Publish properties page, you specify where you want to publish the project, which can be a Web site, FTP server, or shared server drive. You also specify whether the application will be available both online and offline, or available only online. *Online applications* require a network connection and are run from a Web page link. When the link is clicked, the local computer's cache is checked; if the cached version is the same as the online version, the cached version runs on the local computer. If the cached version is older than the online version, it is downloaded and executed on the local computer. When the application is closed, if the application is not yet in the cache, it is stored in the cache. If a newer version was downloaded, it replaces the older version in the cache. The default size for this cache is 250 megabytes. Applications that run *offline* as well as online are installed locally on the client computer and are accessible from the user's Start menu.

TIP: The ClickOnce application cache is a file located in \Documents & Settings*yourUserAccount*\Local Settings\Apps. Caching an online only application results in faster startup times because the system does not need to download the application each time the user starts it.

On the Publish properties page, the Application Files button displays a dialog box that shows all available project files. You cannot add additional files, but you can choose to exclude some of the project files if the project does not need them. The

FIGURE 10-29 Publish properties page

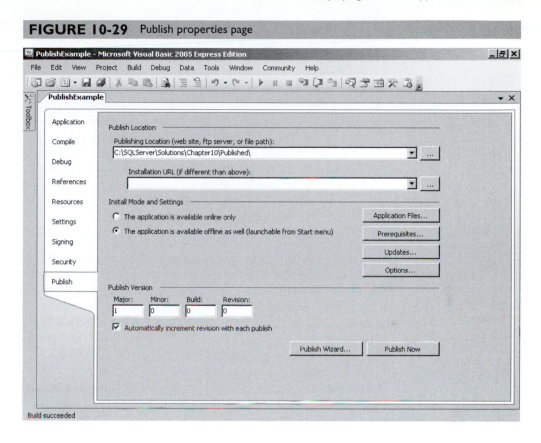

Prerequisites button lets you choose how to distribute .NET Framework and other support programs and files to client computers. You can choose to distribute them from the vendor, from your published application's location, or from any other location you specify. The Updates button lets you choose whether the application should always check for updates and, if so, whether it should check when it starts or when it closes.

The Options button displays a dialog box that allows you to specify the publisher's name, the product name, and other project information. You should always specify the publisher and product name. It also provides an option for automatically starting a CD when the user inserts it. Publishing a project creates setup files that can be copied to a CD and later installed from the CD rather than over a network connection.

The following steps show how to configure the publishing properties by specifying where we will publish the project, which will be a folder named Published in the Chapter10 folder on your disk. We also specify that the project will be available offline. We then specify the publisher and product name. Before we publish the project, we build (compile) the project to ensure that the published product contains the final software version.

To specify the project location and properties, and publish the project:

1. Select the Publish tab, and type C:\SQLServer\Solutions\Chapter10\Published\ in the Publishing Location field. The system automatically creates the Published folder.
2. Type *YourComputerName*\c$\SQLServer\Solutions\Chapter10\Published\ in the Installation URL field. (Your computer name should appear on your Windows desktop.)

3. Make sure that the *The application is available offline as well (launchable from the Start menu)* option button is selected.

4. Click the Options button. In the Publish Options dialog box, type your name in the Publisher name field, and type Publish Example as the product name.

5. Type Published.htm in the Deployment web page field.

6. Check the boxes labeled *Open deployment web page after publish* and *For CD installations, automatically start Setup when CD is inserted*.

7. Accept the other default settings, then click OK.

8. To ensure that the project includes the latest changes to all project files, click Build on the IDE menu bar, and then click Build PublishExample.

9. Click Publish Now. The Publish Now and Publish Wizard buttons will be disabled until the publishing process finishes. You can track the progress by looking in the lower left corner of the status bar for messages.

10. After publishing the project, a Web page similar to the one in Figure 10-30 opens.

This is the Web page that users will access to install the application. The security warning appears on the page, because Internet Explorer blocks all Web pages that have *active content*, which is a program that attempts to install something on your computer. Users must first click this warning, then select the option that allows them to unblock the content. Users can then click the Install link to install the required prerequisite programs. The user who already has the prerequisite programs can click the Launch link and run the application.

When you install a published application on your computer, .NET installs the application files in the C:\Documents and Settings*loginName*\Local Settings\Apps folder. It also creates required entries in the system registry to run the program. If you want to remove the application, use the Control Panel's Add or Remove Programs utility to remove it from your computer.

FIGURE 10-30   Publish Example Web page

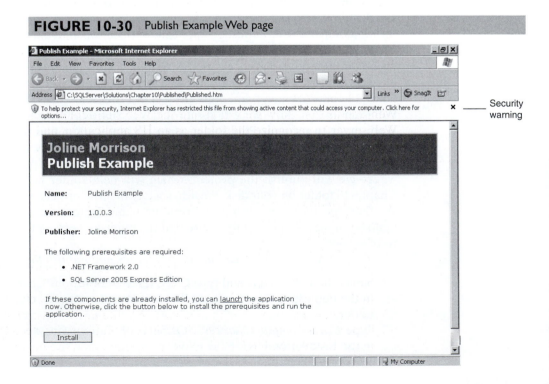

Web Applications

NOTE: This section describes the steps for deploying a Web database application that you create in Visual Web Developer. To perform the steps in this section, you must be a local administrator on your computer.

After you create a Web site in Visual Web Developer, there are two approaches for deploying it to users. You can create an *uncompiled Web application,* which copies the site's components directly to the Web server as source code files. You can also deploy it as a *precompiled Web application,* which precompiles the Web site's .aspx and .aspx.vb files into assemblies and strips the program code out of the source files. It then publishes the Web site as compiled Web pages. You use the .NET *Copy Web* utility to create uncompiled Web applications, and the .NET *Publish Web* utility to create precompiled Web applications.

NOTE: Copy Web is included with Visual Web Developer and VS 2005, while Publish Web is provided only with VS 2005.

The advantage of using Publish Web and deploying the application as compiled pages is that it protects your intellectual property by making it harder for others to access your source code. This is especially important when you create Web applications that you sell to other organizations. Another advantage is that compiled Web pages provide faster initial response times. (Recall that with ASP.NET, the first time a user requests a Web form, .NET compiles the form and stores it as a compiled Web page.)

A major disadvantage of using the precompiling approach is that it is harder to change the Web site's contents. Making even a minor change in a single page requires recompiling the entire site before sending the changes to the production Web server.

The following subsections describe how to create an uncompiled Web site using Copy Web and how to create a precompiled Web site using Publish Web. The first step in deploying a Web site using either approach is to configure your Web server so that its target folder is an Internet Information Services (IIS) application that will store your Web site. *Internet Information Services (IIS)* is Microsoft's Web server application. An *IIS application* is a Web server virtual directory, which is a directory referencing a folder in a Web server's file system that is configured to allow running a Web application. Now we will create the Web site deployment folder, configure the Web server to recognize the folder as an IIS application, and then configure the IIS application to use ASP.NET Version 2 instead of earlier versions. We use the IIS administration utility to perform these tasks.

To create and configure the Web site IIS application:

1. Use Windows Explorer to create a folder named IronwoodUniversity in the target Web server's root folder.
2. To start IIS, click Start on the taskbar, point to Control Panel, point to Administrative Tools, and then click Internet Information Services. The IIS window has a console tree, which represents the Web site contents, and a Details pane, which displays details about the selected object.
3. In the console tree, open the node that represents your Web server, open the Web Sites node, and then open the Default Web Site node. Its contents display the folders in the wwwroot folder, which is your Web server's default folder.
4. Right-click the IronwoodUniversity folder, and then click Properties to open the folder's Properties window.

5. Click the Create button in the Properties window to convert IronwoodUniversity into an IIS Application. Notice that the glyph representing this folder in the console tree changes from a yellow folder to a gray opening box with a green starburst inside, indicating that it is an IIS application.
6. To configure the application to use ASP.NET Version 2, click the ASP.NET tab on the Properties window, open the ASP.NET version list, and select 2.xxx. (Your version number may vary.)
7. Repeat steps 1 through 6 to create a second IIS application named IronwoodPrecompiled.
8. Close IIS.

Deploying an Uncompiled Web Site

The following steps show how to deploy an uncompiled Web site. To do this, we will use the Copy Web utility and copy the WebExamples project that we created in Chapter 8 to the target Web server.

To deploy an uncompiled Web site:

1. Start Visual Web Developer, and open the \SQLServer\Solutions\Chapter8\ WebExamples Web site.

HELP: If you did not create this Web site in Chapter 8, you can use any ASP.NET Web site that you have created.

---

2. Click Web Site on the menu bar, and then click Copy Web Site. The Copy Web page opens in the Document window.
3. To connect to your Web site, click Connect on the Connections toolbar. The Open Web Site dialog box opens.

This dialog box allows you to select the target location where you want to copy the Web site. Select the location type (File System, Local IIS, FTP Site, or Remote Site) in the left pane, and then select a specific location in the right pane. Since you are copying your Web site to a Web site virtual directory that is on your local computer, you can select either the File System or Local IIS location. You will use the Local IIS location because you created an IIS application for your Web site in the previous steps. Then you will copy all the Web site contents to the target location. Finally, you will test the Web site.

To select the target location, copy the Web site files, and test the Web site:

1. In the Open Web Site dialog box, select Local IIS in the left pane. In the right pane, open the Default Web Site node, select IronwoodUniversity, and then click Open.
2. To copy all the Web site contents to the target location, select the first item in the Source Web site list, press and hold Shift, and then select the last list item. Click the Copy button, which appears as a right-pointing arrow.
3. To test the Web site, open Internet Explorer, type http://localhost/ ironwooduniversity in the Address field, and then press Enter. The Ironwood University Web site should open and display its home page.
4. Close the browser window.

If you connected to a remote SQL Server database when you created this Web site, then the Web site works correctly. However, if you connected to a local database .mdf file, the Web site does not allow you to insert, update, or delete data. This is because the Web server has sufficient Windows NTFS file permissions to open and select data from the .mdf file, but does not have permissions to modify the file.

To solve this problem, you must configure your NTFS permissions for the Web site's App_data folder. Do this using the Windows Explorer.

To reconfigure the folder permissions:

1. In Windows Explorer, navigate to the C:\Inetpub\wwwroot\IronwoodUniversity\App_Data folder, right-click, and then click Properties. The IronwoodUniversity Properties window opens.
2. Select the Security tab, and then click Advanced.

HELP: If the Security tab does not appear at the top of the Properties window, close it. Then select Tools from the menu bar, click Folder Options, select the View tab, scroll to the bottom, uncheck the *Use Simple File Sharing (Recommended)* check box, and then click OK. Exit Windows Explorer and restart it. Then repeat steps 1 and 2.

---

3. If necessary, clear the *Inherit from parent* check box. Click Copy, and then click OK.
4. Remove all but the Administrators groups and/or specific user names from the top pane. (To do this, select the name, and then click Remove.)
5. Click Add, type ASPNET in the *Enter object names to select* field, and then click OK.
6. On the Security tab, confirm that ASP.NET Machine Account is selected in the User names list, check Modify in the Permissions window, and then click OK to apply the changes and exit the Security dialog box.
7. Test the deployed site again, and confirm that you can change the site's data.
8. Close the browser window.
9. Close the VWD IDE.

If you are connecting to a remote server the file permissions problem does not occur, which makes deployment easier. The code access security concerns and certificates used when deploying Windows applications do not apply in a Web environment. The ASP.NET programs run on the server, not on the client, so client security is not an issue.

Deploying a Precompiled Web Site

This section describes how to publish a precompiled Web site using the VS 2005 Publish Web utility. Recall that earlier we created an IIS application named IronwoodPrecompiled to store the precompiled Web site.

To deploy a compiled Web site:

1. Start VS 2005, and open the \SQLServer\Solutions\Chapter8\WebExamples Web site.
2. Click Build on the menu bar, and then click Publish C:\...\WebExamples\. The Publish Web Site dialog box opens.
3. Click the ellipsis (. . .)button beside the Target Location field, navigate to the C:\Inetpub\wwwroot\IronwoodPrecompiled folder, and then click Open.
4. Accept the default Build properties, and then click OK.
5. Modify the Web site's App_Data folder permissions using the instructions in the previous set of steps.
6. To test the Web site, start Internet Explorer; in the address field, type: http://localhost/IronwoodPrecompiled. Then press Enter. The Ironwood home page appears, and the Web site should be fully functional.
7. Close the browser window, and then close the IDE.

If you view the files in the IronwoodPrecompiled folder, you find that the \bin folder no longer contains .aspx and .aspx.vb files, but instead contains .dll files that contain the compiled code for the Web forms. If you open the deployed project in VS 2005, you find that you can add controls and change the appearance of the existing Web forms, but you cannot open their code windows and add code or modify existing code. This approach protects the Web site's existing code while allowing developers to modify existing forms and add new ones. This could be useful for a Web site that is sold commercially to other companies who might need to modify it for their needs.

IN CONCLUSION . . .

Database administration is a large and complex topic. This chapter shows how SQL Server DBAs perform administration tasks and describes the Management Studio utilities and SQL commands for performing the tasks. It also describes strategies for creating and managing indexes, setting up user authentication, and creating backup and recovery plans. And, it describes deployment tools provided with .NET applications. To be a DBA, you must have excellent technical abilities along with organizational management and policy-making skills. This is an excellent career path for technology students with managerial aspirations.

SUMMARY

- Database administration involves installing, configuring, updating, and troubleshooting database systems, and a database administrator (DBA) is a person who performs database administration tasks.
- Database administration has a service role, which involves supporting users who interact with the database; a development role, which involves supporting developers who create database applications; and a management liaison role, for providing a link between developers, users, and organizational managers in developing and implementing organizational database-related policies.
- You can perform database administration tasks using either SQL commands or Management Studio dialog boxes.
- Management Studio has an Object Explorer that displays the database instance, databases, and database objects as nodes. These nodes allow you to create and manage database objects.
- The SQL Server Configuration Manager allows you to start and stop database services, as well as configure service properties. The SQL Server Surface Area Configuration utility allows you to minimize the visibility of the database instance by disabling unused services.
- Management Studio's SQL Profiler utility allows you to create a trace to monitor and report on database activities. The Database Tuning Advisor utility analyzes the performance of T-SQL scripts, trace files, and trace tables, and it provides suggestions for improving performance.
- An index is a database object that stores field values in a data structure supporting fast searches with minimum disk reads. This enables the DBMS to quickly retrieve records in which the indexed field is involved in a search condition, join condition, or ORDER BY clause.
- A composite index contains multiple sorted fields in its searchable data structure, and a unique index specifies that the indexed field must be unique and cannot repeat. A clustered index stores its underlying data records in the same order in which the index is sorted, while the order of a nonclustered index's data records does not correspond to the sorted index values.
- A SQL Server database system can use Windows authentication, which grants users access based on their operating system accounts, and mixed-mode authentication, which grants access based either on user operating system accounts or on SQL Server user logins, which are user name/password combinations. Windows authentication provides a more secure system, while SQL Server accounts provide more flexibility for configuring user permissions.
- To create a SQL Server login, the DBA creates the login, configures it so that it can connect to the

database instance, and then grants it permission to access one or more databases. Finally, the DBA must grant the login permissions to access database objects.

- SQL Server permissions can be server permissions, which allow users to perform actions on the overall server, or object permissions, which allow users to perform actions on specific database objects.
- A role is a set of permissions that you can grant to multiple users. SQL Server provides fixed roles that define sets of permissions that DBAs commonly grant to users. You can also create user-defined roles to meet the needs of specific applications.
- In a database system, backup involves creating copies of database files, and recovery involves restoring the database to its original state after a failure.
- In SQL Server, a full backup stores a complete copy of the database to a backup medium, and a differential backup stores a copy of only the data that has changed since the last full backup. A file/filegroup backup backs up individual files and filegroups in a database, and a file differential backup combines differential backups and file or filegroup backups. A transaction log records transactions that have occurred since the last differential backup.
- A simple recovery recovers the database to the point of the last backup, using full and differential backups. A full recovery recovers the database to its state at the time of failure, using full and differential backups and transaction log backups.
- To make a backup, you create the backup device, which is a database object that references the backup device and/or location. Then you back up the database to the backup device. You can recover a database back to the same database or to a different database.
- Deploying an application makes it available to users. Web-based applications are easier to deploy than Windows-based applications because users can easily link to the Web server and download the new

application. Windows-based applications usually must be physically installed on the computer, which can be inconvenient and time-consuming.
- Microsoft's ClickOnce technology attempts to make deploying Windows-based applications similar to deploying Web-based applications. When you use ClickOnce to deploy a Windows application, .NET generates a Software Publisher Certificate to verify that the application does not contain any malicious items.
- When you deploy a Windows application in .NET, you should configure the application's deployment properties in its project Property pages because this provides maximum flexibility in specifying configuration settings.
- A Windows application can be a full-trust application, which means it can perform any actions in the host system, or a partial-trust application, which means that its actions are restricted.
- You can deploy a Windows application as an online application, which you run from a Web page link, and as both an online and an offline application, which distributes processing between the local computer and the online source.
- You can deploy Web applications as uncompiled applications, which copy the site's source code file to your Web server, or as precompiled applications, which precompiles the Web form files, strips out the form code, and stores it in DLL files.
- You use the Copy Web utility to create uncompiled Web applications and the Publish Web utility to create precompiled applications.
- To deploy a Web application, you must create an IIS application to store the Web application files. Then you deploy the application using the Copy Web or Publish Web utility. For applications that use local database files, you must reconfigure folder permissions to allow users to modify the database files.

KEY TERMS

Authentication mode SQL Server user verification approach that controls user access and specifies user privileges

Backup Copy of database files used to recover the database in the case of a system failure

Backup device Object that references the device to which the DBMS writes a backup file

Both online and offline application Application that can run with or without a network connection.

B-tree Data structure that supports fast searches with minimum disk reads and stores database index values

Bulk operation Special data operation that involves a large volume of data

Bulk-logged recovery Similar to full recovery but does not recover bulk operations

Clustered index Index in which the DBMS physically stores the indexed records in the order in which they appear in the index

Common Language Runtime (CLR) integration
.NET feature that allows you to create stored procedures, triggers, and functions using any .NET framework language

Composite index   Index that contains multiple sorted fields in its B-tree data structure

Database administration   Tasks that involve installing, configuring, updating, and troubleshooting database systems

Database administration development role
Supporting developers who create database applications

Database administration management liaison role
Role providing a link between developers, users, and organizational managers to develop and implement database policy

Database administration service role   Supporting users who interact with the database

Database administrator (DBA)   Person who performs database administration tasks

Default database   The main database that a login uses

Default instance   Database instance on a server to which users automatically connect

Deploy   To make an application available to users

Differential backup   Stores a copy of only the data that has changed since the last full backup

File differential backup   Combination of a differential and file/filegroup backup

File/filegroup backup   Backup of individual files and filegroups

Fixed database roles   Predefined SQL server roles that define common database tasks

Fixed server roles   Predefined SQL server roles that define common server tasks

Full backup   Stores a complete copy of the database to a backup media

Full recovery   Recovery to the state at the time of failure

Full-trust application   Application that can perform any actions in the host system

IIS application   Web server virtual directory that is configured to run a Web application

Index   Database object that stores field values in a data structure that supports fast searches with minimum disk reads

Internet Information Services (IIS)   Microsoft's Web server application

Local Service account   Built-in operating system account designed to run services with a reduced set of permissions

Login   Name that can access a SQL Server database

Mixed-mode authentication   SQL Server authentication mode that can use either Windows authentication or SQL Server authentication, which authenticates

users based on separate SQL Server logins that the DBA creates and maintains

Named instance   Database instance on a server that has a unique name

Nonclustered index   Index in which the physical order of the stored records does not necessarily match the index sort order

Object permission   Right to perform a task on a database object

Online application   Application that you run from a Web page link and that runs on the Web server

Partial-trust application   Application whose actions are restricted in the host system

Permission   Right to perform a specific task on a database object

Precompiled Web application   Web application in which the Web site's .aspx and .aspx.vb files are compiled into assemblies and source code files are not placed on the Web server

Recovery   Restoration of a database to its original state

Role   Set of permissions that you can grant to multiple users

Server permission   Right to perform a server-level task

Service   Server process that runs in the background and performs some sort of task

Simple recovery   Recovers a databases to the point of its last full or differential backup

Software Publisher Certificate (SPC)   Certificate that certifies who you are and contains a legally binding pledge that your software does not knowingly contain viruses or other malicious items

Surface area   Visibility of a database instance

System administrator (sa) account   Master SQL Server account that has all database permissions

Trace   Process that monitors and reports on database activities

Trace file   File that records trace properties

Trace table   Database table that records trace properties

Trace template   Set of defined events, fields, and filters that specify what appears in a trace

Transaction log   Log file that records all transactions since the last differential backup

Uncompiled Web application   Web application that places the Web site's source files on the Web server

Unique index   Index specifying that the indexed field value must be unique and cannot repeat

Warm backup server   Server that can be put into production with minimal downtime

Windows authentication   SQL Server authentication mode that authenticates users based on their operating system account logins

Zone   Network location that has specific security settings

STUDY QUESTIONS

Multiple-Choice Questions

1. A _____ recovery recovers the system to its state at the time of the failure.
   - a. Simple
   - b. Complete
   - c. Full
   - d. System

2. Before you can install a SQL Server 2005 database, you must first install:
   - a. SQL Express
   - b. Visual Studio 2005
   - c. Windows Service Pack 2.0
   - d. The .NET Framework 2.0
   - e. All of the above

3. To improve query performance, you might create an index on a query field that appears:
   - a. In a join condition
   - b. In a SELECT clause
   - c. In an ORDER BY clause
   - d. Both a and c

4. A(n) _____ Web site contains source code files for dynamic Web pages.
   - a. Deployed
   - b. Production
   - c. Uncompiled
   - d. Precompiled

5. Designing database applications is a task in the database administration _____ role.
   - a. Service
   - b. Development
   - c. Management liaison
   - d. Systems analysis

6. You should use Windows authentication when:
   - a. You want the system to be extremely secure
   - b. The system does not need to be backward-compatible with older SQL Server versions
   - c. Most of your users are Windows domain users
   - d. All of the above

7. The SQL Server DBMS automatically creates indexes on:
   - a. Primary keys
   - b. Foreign keys
   - c. Fields with NOT NULL constraints
   - d. All of the above

8. The permissions necessary to manage user logins would probably be granted through:
   - a. A fixed server role
   - b. A fixed database role
   - c. A fixed object role
   - d. A user-defined role

9. You must use transaction logs to enable a _____ recovery.
   - a. Simple
   - b. Full
   - c. Bulk-logged
   - d. File differential
   - e. Both b and c

10. You use SQL Server Configuration Manager to:
    - a. Start and stop the database instance
    - b. Create traces
    - c. Create new logins
    - d. Install and activate key database services

True/False Questions

1. When you deploy a Windows application in Visual Studio/VB Express, you create a third-party Software Publisher Certificate.
2. When you create a new SQL Server login and assign to it a default database, the user can immediately connect to the system and access the default database tables.
3. You can use SQL Express to create database objects only by executing SQL commands.
4. After you create a trace, the Database Tuning Advisor utility provides suggestions regarding how to improve the trace's underlying processes.
5. Mixed-mode authentication can use Windows authentication.
6. An index improves query performance most when the query retrieves only a few of the table's records.

7. A simple recovery uses both full and differential backups to recover the system.
8. The SQL Server Surface Area Configuration utility is available with both Management Studio and SQL Express.

Short Answer Questions

1. Describe the differences between Windows authentication and mixed-mode authentication in a SQL Server database system and discuss the advantages of each approach.
2. Briefly describe the purpose of each of the five database administration utilities: SQL Express/Management Studio, Configuration Manager, Surface Area Configuration, SQL Profiler, and Database Tuning Advisor.
3. Describe the difference between a clustered and a nonclustered index.
4. Write the SQL command to create a composite clustered index that indexes the values in the CategoryID and SupplierID fields in the SportInventory table (see Figure 3-2). Sort the index by CategoryID, then by SupplierID. Use the naming convention that the chapter describes to name the index.
5. As a DBA, when should you REVOKE a permission and when should you DENY?
6. Describe a role and when you should create one.
7. Discuss when you should use a simple recovery approach and when you should use a full recovery approach.
8. Describe the differences between a full-trust and a partial-trust application.
9. When should you deploy a Web site as an uncompiled site, and when should you deploy it as a precompiled site?

Guided Exercises

Save the solution files for all exercises in your \SQLServer\Solutions\Chapter10 folder.

1. **Creating Database Indexes**
   In this exercise, you will create a script file named 10Exercise1.sql that will contain SQL commands to create a series of indexes for the SportMotors database shown in Figures 3-2 and 3-4. (If you are connecting to a remote SQL Server database, you will not be able to execute the SQL commands.)
   a. Write the SQL command to create an index on the EmployeeUsername field in the Sport Employee table. Specify that the index is nonclustered and unique.
   b. Write the SQL command to create an index on the OrderDate field in the SportOrder table. Specify that the index is nonclustered, and sort the indexed values in descending order.
   c. Write the SQL command to create a composite index on the OrderID and InventoryID fields in the SportOrderDetail table. Specify that the index is nonclustered and unique. Sort the OrderID field values in descending order and the InventoryID values in ascending order. Add commands to drop all the indexes you created.

2. **Creating and Managing SQL Server Logins**
   In this exercise, you will create a script file named 10Exercise2.sql that contains system stored procedures and SQL commands to create and manage SQL Server logins. (If you are connecting to a remote SQL Server database, you will not be able to execute these commands to test them.)
   a. Create a new login named 10Exercise2Login, with the password *secret* that defaults to the *yourDatabaseName* database.
   b. Change the 10Exercise2Login password to *TamaracK*.
   c. Grant the 10Exercise2Login login access to the *yourDatabaseName* database under the user name *Frodo*.
   d. Configure the Frodo login so that it can run SELECT queries on the SportInventory table in the Sport Motors database without the grant option.
   e. Grant the db_datareader role to the Frodo login.
   f. Create a user-defined role named SportEmployeeRole.

g. Allow SportEmployeeRole members to insert, update, and delete records in the SportOrder and SportOrderDetail tables.

h. Make the Frodo login a member of the SportEmployeeRole.

i. Modify the Frodo login so that it cannot SELECT any data from the SportEmployee table.

3. **Creating Backup and Recovery Scripts**

In this exercise, you will create a script file named 10Exercise3.sql that contains system stored procedures and SQL commands to create and manage SQL Server backup and recovery operations. (If you are connecting to a remote SQL Server database, you will not be able to execute these commands to test them.)

a. Create a backup device named BKFULL that stores the backup to a disk file named 10Exercise3BKFULL that you store in your \SQLServer\Solutions\Chapter10 folder.

b. Create a backup device named BKDIFF that stores the backup to a disk file named 10Exercise3BKDIFF that you store in your \SQLServer\Solutions\Chapter10 folder.

c. Create a full database backup of the yourDatabaseName database to the BKFULL device.

d. Create a differential database backup of the yourDatabaseName database to the BKDIFF device.

e. Perform a simple recovery to the yourDatabaseName database from the BKFULL device.

APPENDIX A

Installing the SQL Server Database

Chapters 2–10 require users to be able to connect to either a SQL Server 2005 or SQL Express database. This appendix describes how to install these applications (as of the time this book is going to press—Microsoft occasionally changes their web site and these instructions might need revising by the time you read them). The following subsections describe the minimum system requirements for either installation, discuss DBMS configuration options, and illustrate how to install the .NET framework, SQL Server 2005 DBMS, and SQL Server Express DBMS.

Minimum System Requirements

To install either SQL Server 2005 or SQL Server Express, your system should have at least 512 megabytes of main memory. Microsoft states that the required hard drive space varies based on the database size and the tools you install. (For this book, 50–100 MB of free disk space should be adequate.) Your system must have a Pentium III-compatible or higher processor that runs at 500 megahertz, although 1 gigahertz is recommended.

If your system has one of the following operating systems, you can install SQL Server Express: Windows XP Professional (Service Pack 1 or later); Windows 2000 Professional (Service Pack 4 or later). If your system has one of these operating systems, you can install either SQL Server 2005 or SQL Server Express: Windows Server 2003 Standard, Enterprise, or Datacenter Edition; or Windows 2000 Server, Advanced Server, or Datacenter Server (Service Pack 4 or later). Regardless of the operating system selected, It must also run Internet Explorer Version 6.0 (Service Pack 1 or later) and have the Microsoft .NET Framework 2.0 installed.

DBMS Configuration Options

To install a SQL Server 2005 or SQL Server Express DBMS, you must specify some options during the installation process, including the SQL Server 2005 components you want to install and the name of the database instance (SQL Server 2005 DBMS only).

You must also configure the server account that manages the database instance service and select the database instance's authentication mode. The following subsections describe these options.

Installation Components

SQL Server 2005 has the following available components.

- **Database Services** includes the database engine (DBMS).
- **Analysis Services** is a tool for analyzing and optimizing complex queries.
- **Notification Services** enables you to develop applications that notify users when certain conditions occur in the database.
- **Workstation components, Books Online, and development tools** provide the SQL Server database administration tools, an online help system, and components for developing database applications.

NOTE: SQL Express provides a subset of these components.

To install a DBMS to support the operations in this book, you will install the Database Services and Workstation components. These options are available in both SQL Server 2005 and SQL Express DBMS versions.

Database Instance Name (SQL Server 2005 Only)

A database instance is a specific database server process that runs on a specific server workstation. A single server can run multiple instances. If your server runs only one database instance, then you can designate the instance as the *default instance,* and users who connect to your server always connect to this instance. If your server runs multiple database instances, then you must create a *named instance* and designate each instance using a unique name. When users connect to a DBMS that uses a named instance, they must specify the instance name in their connect string.

Service Account (SQL Server 2005 Only)

In a Windows operating system installation, a *service* is a server process that runs in the background and performs some sort of task. When you install a SQL Server 2005 DBMS, it runs as a service and listens for and services user requests. Services are protected using a security management model that restricts the users who can manage the service and perform tasks such as changing its configuration options or starting or stopping it. To restrict access to the DBMS service, we recommend that you use the *Local Service account,* which is a built-in operating system account designed to run services with a reduced set of permissions.

DBMS Authentication Mode

The DBMS *authentication mode* controls user access and specifies user privileges. SQL Server 2005 supports two authentication modes:

- **Windows authentication** authenticates users based on their operating system logon account.
- **Mixed-mode authentication,** in which the system can use either Windows authentication or *SQL Server authentication,* which authenticates users based on separate SQL Server accounts and passwords that the DBA creates and maintains.

When you connect to a SQL Server database instance using Management Studio or .NET, you select whether you use Windows or SQL Server authentication. We discuss the advantages and disadvantages of both approaches in the section titled "Security and User Authentication" in Chapter 10.

When you install a SQL Server database, you specify the sa account password. The *sa (system administrator)* account, the master account for the database instance, has all available rights and privileges. From the sa account, you can create new accounts with more restrictive privileges. You should safeguard the sa account password carefully.

Installing the SQL Server Express DBMS

You can download the .NET Framework 2.0 and SQL Server Express from Microsoft's MSDN Web site for no charge. The following steps describe the installation process.

To install the .NET Framework:

1. Start your Web browser and, in the Address field, type: http://msdn.microsoft.com/vstudio/express. The Microsoft Express Editions page opens.

2. Point to the SQL Server Express link, and then click Download.

3. If the .NET Framework is installed, the download page will display "You have the .NET Framework 2.0 installed" under step one of the installation instructions. If this isn't displayed, follow the instructions in step 1 for installing it.

4. Next, install the SQL Server Express DBMS by following Step 3 and downloading and running the SQL Server 2005 Express Edition versions for SQL Server 2005 and Management Studio Express. (The Advanced Services versions aren't needed for the exercises in this book.)

Installing the SQL Server 2005 DBMS

You can obtain the SQL Server 2005 DBMS directly from Microsoft, and it is available at a reduced cost to academic institutions through the Microsoft Developers Network Academic Alliance (http://msdn.microsoft.com/academic). SQL Server 2005 provides the complete SQL Server DBMS for large-scale database installations, as well as Management Studio, which provides a comprehensive set of database administration tools.

To install the SQL Server 2005 DBMS:

1. If necessary, download and install the .NET framework.

2. Place the CD in your CD-ROM drive. The CD automatically runs and displays the SQL Server 2005 Installation Start Page.

3. When the End User License Agreement dialog box opens, check the *I accept the licensing terms and conditions* check box, and then click Next.

4. When the SQL Server Component Update page appears, click Install. Depending on your system hardware and configurations, this may take several minutes.

5. The Microsoft SQL Server Installation Wizard Welcome page opens. Click Next.

6. The System Configuration Check page appears and (presumably) confirms that your system configuration is compatible for installing SQL Server 2005. Click Next.

7. The Microsoft Server Installation page appears and configures the setup operation. When it finishes, click Next.

8. When the Registration Information page appears, type your name in the Name field, your company name in the Company field, and your 25-digit product key in the Product Key fields. Then click Next. The Components to Install page appears.

9. On the Components to Install page, check the Database Services and Workstation components, Books Online and development tools check boxes, and then click Next.

10. On the Feature Selection page, make sure that the Database Services and Workstation Components nodes are designated to be installed, accept the default installation path, and then click Next.

11. On the Instance Name page, accept the Default instance option, and then click Next.

12. On the Service Account page, select the *Use the built-in system account* option button, and check the Auto-start service check box.

13. On the Authentication Mode page, select the Mixed Mode option button, type a password value in the Password and Confirm Password fields, and then click Next.

14. On the Collation Settings page, select the SQL collations option button, and click Next.

15. On the Error and Usage Report Settings page, check the Automatically send Error reports and Automatically send Feature Usage data check boxes if you want to send these reports. (Sending these reports may slow down your system response times.) Click Next.

16. On the Ready to Install page, confirm that SQL Server Database Services and Client Components appear as the components to install, and then click Install.

17. The Setup Progress page appears, and monitors the progress of the installation. When the setup of all components finishes, click Next.

18. On the Completing Microsoft SQL Server 2005 Setup page, click Finish.

APPENDIX B

Installing Application Development Tools

This book requires users to have access to several application development tools. Table B-1 summarizes the application tools required for each book chapter. Appendix A describes how to install Management Studio. This Appendix describes how to install the remaining applications.

TABLE B-1	Application tools required for different book chapters

Chapter	Application Tool
1	No software needed
2, 3, 4, 10	Management Studio or Management Studio Express
5, 6	VB Express or Visual Studio 2005
7	Visual Studio 2005 with Crystal Reports installed
8, 9	Visual Studio 2005 or Visual Web Developer

Installing the .NET Applications

To perform the tutorials and exercises in this book, you can use either Visual Studio 2005, or VB Express and Visual Web Developer. VB Express and Visual Web Developer contain a subset of Visual Studio 2005's features and functions, and provide all you need to create VB and Web database applications. Projects that you create in VS 2005 can be opened, edited, and executed in VB Express and Visual Web Developer, and vice versa.

Installing Visual Studio 2005

Visual Studio 2005 provides options to perform a *Default, Full,* or *Custom* installation. Either the Default or the Full option installs all that is needed for working with this book. The Default installation requires 2.7 gigabytes of disk space, and the Full installation requires 3.2 gigabytes. Both options install additional languages and features that the book does not require. You can perform a Custom installation, which reduces the required disk space to 1.3 gigabytes, by installing everything *except* the following:

- Under Language Tools, omit Visual C#, Visual J#, and Visual C++.
- Under Optional, omit Microsoft SQL Server 2005 Express Edition if you are using a remote SQL Server DBMS.

To install Visual Studio 2005:

1. Insert the Visual Studio 2005 installation disk. If the initial Setup dialog box does not appear, start Windows Explorer, open the vs subfolder on the installation disk, and then double-click setup.exe.
2. Click the Install Visual Studio 2005 link. After a short pause (while some files are copied to your computer), click Next.
3. Accept the license agreement, and enter the Product Key value.
4. The next page displays the choices of Default, Full, or Custom.
5. Select your installation option. When installation is complete, click Finish. You will be returned to the original install dialog box.
6. Install the Product Documentation.

Installing VB Express

To install VB Express:

1. Start your Web browser, and go to http://msdn.microsoft.com/vstudio/express/. Point to the Visual Basic link, click Download, and then click Download on the Download Now! page.
2. When the File Download—Security Warning dialog box opens, click run and follow Microsoft's directions.
3. Follow the instructions provided by Microsoft during the installation. When asked, check the box for installing the Microsoft MSDN 2005

Express Edition library. This is large and takes awhile to install, but is necessary if you want help enabled with VB Express.

Installing Visual Web Developer

To install Visual Web Developer:

1. Start your Web browser and go to http://msdn.microsoft.com/vstudio/express/.

Point to the Visual Web Developer link, click Download, and then click Download on the Download Now! page.

2. When the File Download—Security Warning dialog box opens click run and follow Microsoft's directions.

Index